*Naglieri Nonverbal Ability Test
Oral and Written Language Scales (OWLS)
Otis–Lennon School Ability Test, Seventh Edition (OLSAT 7)
*Peabody Individual Achievement Test–Revised–Normative Update (PIAT-R-NU)
Peabody Picture Vocabulary Test–III (PPVT-III)
Preschool Evaluation Scale (PES)
Responsibility and Independence Scale for Adolescents (RISA)
Riverside 2000 Assessment Series: ITBS, TAP, ITED
Scales of Independent Behavior–Revised (SIB-R)
Standardized Reading Inventory (SRI)
*Standardized Test for the Assessment of Reading (S.T.A.R.)
*STAR Math
Stanford Achievement Test Series (SESAT, SAT, TASK)
Stanford–Binet Intelligence Scale, Fourth Edition (SB)
Stanford Diagnostic Mathematics Test 4 (SDMT4)
Stanford Diagnostic Reading Test 4 (SDRT4)
Systematic Screening for Behavior Disorders (SSBD)
Teacher's Report Form and 1991 Profile for Ages 5–18 (TRF)
*Terra Nova
Test of Adolescent Language–3 (TOAL-3)
Test of Auditory Comprehension of Language–Revised (TACL-R)
Test of Early Mathematics Ability, Second Edition (TEMA-2)
Test of Early Reading Ability, Revised (TERA-2)
*Test of Language Development, Intermediate: 3 (TOLD-I:3)
*Test of Language Development, Primary: Third Edition (TOLD-P:3)
Test of Mathematical Abilities–2 (TOMA-2)
*Test of Nonverbal Intelligence–3 (TONI-3)
Test of Reading Comprehension–3 (TORC-3)
Test of Visual–Motor Integration (TVMI)
Test of Written Language–3 (TOWL-3)
*Test of Written Spelling–4 (TWS-4)
Tests of Achievement and Proficiency (TAP)
*Universal Nonverbal Intelligence Test
Vineland Adaptive Behavior Scale (VABS)
Walker–McConnell Scale of Social Competence and School Adjustment
Wechsler Individual Achievement Test (WIAT)
The Wechsler Scales (WAIS-III, WISC-III, WPPSI-R, WASI*)
Wide Range Achievement Test 3 (WRAT3)
Woodcock Diagnostic Reading Battery (WDRB)
Woodcock–Johnson Psychoeducational Battery–III (WJ-III)
*Woodcock Reading Mastery Test–Revised, Normative Update (WRMT-R-NU)
*Work Sampling System (WSS)
Youth Self-Report and 1991 Profile for Ages 11–18 (YSR)

Assessment

Eighth Edition

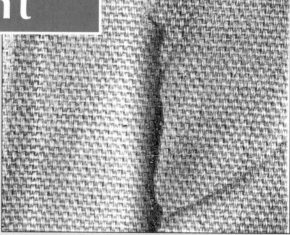

John Salvia
The Pennsylvania State University

James E. Ysseldyke
University of Minnesota

HOUGHTON MIFFLIN COMPANY   Boston   New York

Editor-in-Chief: Patricia Coryell
Senior Sponsoring Editor: Loretta Wolozin
Development Editor: Lisa Mafrici
Senior Project Editor: Aileen Mason
Senior Production/Design Coordinator: Jill Haber
Senior Manufacturing Coordinator: Priscilla Bailey
Marketing Associate: Caroline Guy

Cover design: Ann Schroeder
Cover image: *Reunion,* 1999. By Ann Schroeder

Printed in the U.S.A.

Library of Congress Catalog Card Number: 00-103673

ISBN: 0-618-04281-4

456789-DOC-04 03 02 01

Brief Contents

Contents

Preface

The eighth edition of *Assessment* is being published at a time when different philosophies have resulted in varied approaches to educational and psychological assessment. We see profound differences in the value placed on standardized and unstandardized test administration, objective and subjective scoring, generalizable and ungeneralizable measurement, interpersonal and intrapersonal comparisons, and so forth.

After carefully considering the various approaches to assessment, we remain committed to approaches that facilitate data-based decision making. Thus we believe students and society are best served by the objective, reliable, and valid assessment of student abilities and meaningful educational outcomes. Our position is based on several conclusions. First, objective assessment usually leads to better decision making. Second, we are encouraged by the substantial improvement in assessment devices and practices over the past twenty plus years. Third, although some alternatives are merely unproven, other innovative approaches to assessment—especially those that celebrate subjectivity—have severe shortcomings that have been understood since early last century. Fourth, we believe it is unwise to abandon effective procedures without substantial evidence that the proposed alternatives are really better. Too often, we learned that an educational innovation was ineffective at high human cost. Finally, objective assessment is mandated in federal legislation.

However, our commitment is not the same as unqualified acceptance. From the first edition of *Assessment* we have criticized poor assessment procedures and practices that fall short of accepted standards. Although we recognize that objective assessment has improved, there is still much room for improvement. Some tests are still published with poor technical characteristics. Many achievement tests need to become even more authentic, more contextualized, and less disconnected with learning and instruction. We welcome the renewed interest in assessment. We hope that better theory and practice will emerge from the heated debates. These are indeed exciting times.

● ●

Audience for This Book

Assessment, Eighth Edition, is intended for a first course in assessment taken by those whose careers require understanding and informed use of assessment data. The primary audience is made up of those who are or will be teachers in special education at the elementary or secondary level. The secondary audience is the large support system for special educators: school psychologists, child development specialists, counselors, educational administrators, nurses, preschool educators, reading specialists, social workers, speech and language specialists, and specialists in therapeutic recreation. Additionally, in today's reform climate, many classroom teachers enroll in the assessment course as part of their own professional development. In writing for those who are taking their first course in assessment, we have assumed no prior knowledge of measurement and statistical concepts.

● ●

Purpose

Students have the right to an appropriate education in the least restrictive educational environment. Decisions regarding the most appropriate environment and the most appropriate program for an individual should be data-based decisions. Assessment is one part of the process of collecting the data necessary for educational decision making, and the administration of tests is one part of assessment. Unfortunately, tests have sometimes been used to restrict educational opportunities; many assessment practices have not been in the best interests of students. Those who assess have a tremendous responsibility; assessment results are used to make decisions that directly and significantly affect students' lives. Those who assess are responsible for knowing the devices they use and for understanding the limitations of those devices and the procedures they require.

Teachers are confronted with the results of tests, checklists, scales, and batteries almost daily. This information is intended to be useful to them in understanding and making educational plans for their students. But the intended use and actual use of assessment information have often differed. However good the intentions of test designers, misuse and misunderstanding of tests may well occur unless teachers are informed consumers and users of tests. To be an informed consumer and user of tests, a teacher must bring to the task certain domains of knowledge, including knowledge of the basic uses of tests, the important attributes of good tests, and the kinds of behaviors sampled by particular tests. This text aims at helping education professionals acquire that knowledge.

• •

The New Edition

Coverage

The eighth edition retains the style, content, and organization of the first seven editions. It continues to offer evenhanded, documented evaluations of standardized tests in each domain; straightforward and clear coverage of basic assessment concepts; and illustrations of applications to the decision-making process. Most chapters have been updated, and several have been revised substantially. Our updates reflect changes brought about by the reauthorizationof the Individuals with Disabilities Education Act; for example, Chapter 3 "Legal and Ethical Considerations in Assessment" has been generally rewritten and extended as a result of new legislation and court decisions. The chapters on the assessment of oral language and the assessment of written language have been combined into a single chapter (Chapter 23, "Assessment of Oral and Written Language"). Chapter 17 ("Assessment of Intelligence: Individual Tests"), Chapter 21 ("Assessment of Reading"), and Chapter 28 ("Developmental Appraisal") have been revised substantially. Finally, Chapter 29 ("Outcomes-Based Accountability Assessment") provides new coverage of how state assessments are now used to measure progress toward meeting standards.

Test information has been updated and new reviews have been added. These new tests are indicated by an asterisk in the list of all tests reviewed in this edition, which appears on the inside front cover and first page of this book. Several tests have also been dropped because they have become outdated or because their use has decreased.

End-of-chapter materials have been substantially revised. New web sites have been added for students to visit in order to find additional information related to each chapter. We selected web sites that we believed were relevant to the materials presented in the chapter and that were likely to endure—that is, sites maintained by publishers, professional or scientific organizations, or university research centers with a record of longevity. The web sites were active at the time we prepared the text, but we are, of course, not responsible for their continued presence. In addition, new readings have been added to most chapters.

Organization

Part 1, "Assessment: An Overview," places testing in the broader context of assessment: Assessment is described as a multifaceted process, the kinds of decisions made using assessment data are delineated, and basic terminology and concepts are introduced. In Chapter 3, "Legal and Ethical Considerations in Assessment," we describe the ways assessment practices are regulated and mandated by legislation and litigation. In Part 2, "Basic Concepts of Measurement," we give readers an understanding of the measurement principles needed not only to comprehend the content in Parts 3 and 4 but also to apply and use information obtained from tests they may administer.

In Parts 3 and 4, we review the most commonly used assessment instruments and approaches. In Part 3, "Assessment in Classrooms," we address the kinds of assessments that typically take place in classroom settings. The focus of these chapters is on observations, interviews, non-test-based approaches, and those test-based approaches designed specifically to provide information on effective instruction. In Part 4, "Assessment Using Formal Measures," we review formal (usually standardized) testing that occurs for the most part outside of classrooms.

Test evaluations follow a similar format. Initially we describe the kinds of behaviors sampled by tests in the domain; then we describe specific tests. For each test, we examine the kinds of behaviors it samples, the adequacy of its norms, the kinds of scores provided, and evidence for technical adequacy (reliability and validity). Consistent with our earlier editions, we evaluate the technical adequacy of tests in light of the standards set by three professional associations (the American Psychological Association, the American Educational Research Association, and the National Council on Measurement in Education) in their document entitled *Standards for Educational and Psychological Testing*. Test evaluations are virtually a handbook for assessment practitioners.

A summary of chapter content, a list of additional reading, several sites on the World Wide Web, and several questions for review and thought appear at the end of each chapter to help readers expand their knowledge and apply the fundamental concepts developed. Appendixes at the end of the text include a table of statistical data, a list of equations used in the text, suggestions for how to review a test, and a description of item-response theory. Complete references for in-text citations follow the appendixes.

Assessment is a controversial topic; we have attempted to be objective and evenhanded in our review and portrayal of current assessment practices.

Acknowledgments

Over the years, many people have assisted in our efforts. In the preparation of this edition, we wish to express our sincere appreciation to Tom Frank for his continuing contributions to the section dealing with hearing assessment. We also appreciate the assistance of Heather Briggs Niermans for her help with the web site material and Ruth Nelson for her work on the Instructor's Resource Manual with Test Items, which accompanies this text. We also wish to thank Elisa Adams for her assistance throughout the development of this edition. We remain indebted to Houghton Mifflin and especially Loretta Wolozin, Senior Sponsoring Editor for Education, and Lisa Mafrici, Development Editor, for their ongoing support and commitment to *Assessment*.

Each edition of this text has been a collaborative effort. We believe we have produced an integrated text that speaks for both of us.

John Salvia
Jim Ysseldyke

Assessment

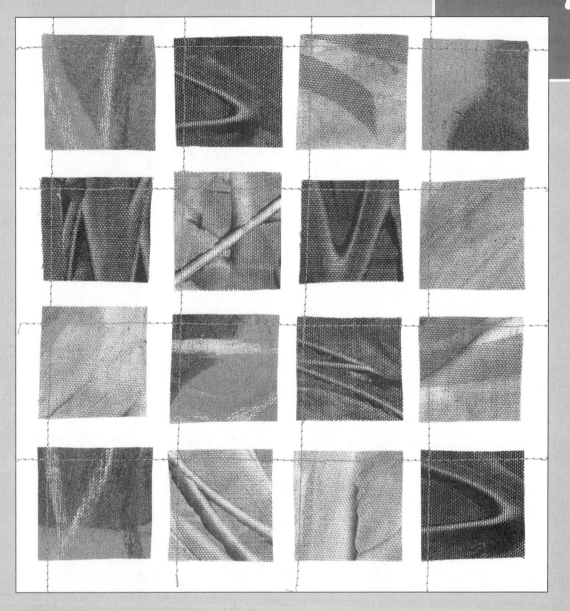

part 1

Assessment: An Overview

School personnel regularly use assessment information to make important decisions about students. Part 1 of this text is a description of basic considerations in psychological and educational assessment of students.

Chapter 1 is a description of assessment and includes a delineation of the factors that must be considered in assessment, the various kinds of assessment information that school personnel collect, and the steps in the assessment process. In Chapter 2, assessment is more specifically defined, the purposes of assessing students are described, and fundamental assumptions underlying assessment are discussed. Chapter 3 is a description of fundamental legal and ethical considerations in assessment.

The concepts and principles introduced in Part 1 constitute a foundation for informed and critical use of terms and the information they provide.

Assessment of Students

Assessment touches everyone's life. It especially affects the lives of people who work with children and who work in schools. As you begin this course on assessment of students, consider the following:

- You apply for a part-time job to work your way through school. You learn that as part of the application process, you must take a test of word-processing speed and a personality test.
- Mr. and Mrs. Johnson receive a call from their child's third-grade teacher, who says he is concerned about Morgan's performance on a reading test. He would like to refer Morgan for further testing to see whether Morgan has a learning disability.
- Mr. and Mrs. Esquirol tell you that their son is not eligible for special-education services because he scored "too high" on an intelligence test.
- The U.S. Secretary of Education issues a call for higher educational standards for all students, in response to publication of test results showing that U.S. students rank low in comparison to students in other nations.
- Departments of education in most states are developing tests to assess the extent to which students are meeting the educational standards specified by the states.
- The superintendent of schools in a large urban district learns that only 40 percent of the students in her school district who took the state graduation test passed it.
- Your local school district asks for volunteers to serve on a task force to design a measure of technological literacy to use as a test with students.

Assessment is a process of collecting data for the purpose of making decisions about individuals and groups, and this decision-making role is the reason that assessment touches so many people's lives. A quick perusal of newspaper headlines shows that assessment is one of the most hotly debated issues among not only educators but also the general public. People react strongly when test scores are used to make interpersonal comparisons in which they or those they love look inferior. Entire communities are keenly interested when test scores from their schools are reported and compared with scores from schools in other communities. We expect that you would have strong positive or negative reactions to the use of test scores to make decisions about whether you or your child could enter college, be promoted to the next grade, receive special education, or graduate. You would probably question the kinds of tests used, the skills or behaviors they measured, and their technical adequacy. Probably no other activity that takes place in education brings with it so many challenges. In this text, you will learn about assessment practices, the kinds of decisions made, the types of tests used, and the technical adequacy of these tests.

Assessment takes place on a large stage, and there are many players. School personnel have always used test information to make decisions about what students have learned, as well as what and where they should be taught. Throughout their professional careers, teachers, guidance counselors, school social workers, school psychologists, and school administrators are required to give, score, and interpret a wide variety of tests. Because professional school personnel routinely receive test information from their colleagues within the schools and from community agencies outside the schools, they need a working knowledge of important aspects of testing.

School districts today are increasingly being held accountable for the performance of their pupils. Parents, the general public, legislators, and bureaucrats want to know the extent to which students are profiting from their schooling experiences. Educators estimate that students attending U.S. public schools take more than 250 million standardized tests each year. School-district personnel use these tests to document the achievement of a population of students that gets more diverse every year. Some states (such as Kentucky) have put plans into place to make the size of teachers' pay increases and the resources individual schools receive dependent on (among very few other things) the magnitude of student gains on achievement tests. New kinds of assessments, such as performance assessments and portfolio assessments, are being used and refined. (Educators refer to these new forms of assessment as "alternative assessments" and sometimes as "authentic assessments.") Goals 2000, the Educate America Act, signed into law in 1994, contains specific provisions for states to develop high educational standards and to use tests to measure the extent to which students meet the standards. The Improving America's Schools Act, signed into law in 1996, calls for schools to assess and report on the progress of all students. The 1997 Individuals with Disabilities Education Act requires that schools and states report on the performance and progress of all students with disabilities. Clearly, assessment is in the forefront of activities in education.

In this text, we address primarily the use of tests to make educational decisions about individuals and groups. We also describe the use of tests in making accountability decisions for schools and school systems. We examine norm-referenced or standardized tests, reporting on each measure's suitability for particular types of decisions. We include chapters on performance assessment and the use of portfolios, teacher-made tests, assessment of instructional environments, and outcomes-based accountability, recognizing shifts and tension points in assessment practices today. Our coverage of assessments thus is broad, including both formal and informal assessments, multiple methods for collecting information, and the many purposes for which the collected information is used.

● ●

Testing Is One Part of Assessment

Testing consists of administering a particular set of questions to an individual or group of individuals to obtain a score. That score is the end product of testing. Testing may be part of the larger process known as assessment; however, testing and assessment are not synonymous. Assessment in educational settings is a multifaceted process that involves far more than just administering a test. When we assess students, we consider the way they perform a variety of tasks in a variety of settings or contexts, the meaning of their performance in terms of the total functioning of each individual, and the likely explanations for those performances. High-quality assessment procedures take into consideration the fact that anyone's performance on any task is influenced by (1) the demands of the task itself, (2) the history and characteristics the individual brings to the task, and (3) the factors inherent in the context in which the assessment is carried out.

We have defined assessment as the process of collecting data for the purpose of making decisions about students. When we assess students, we measure their *competence*. Specifically, we measure their progress toward attaining those competencies their schools or parents want them to master. In schools, we are concerned about competence in three domains in which teachers provide interventions: academic, behavioral (including social), and physical.

Historically in special and remedial education, and now increasingly in regular education settings, the focus of assessment has been on measuring student progress toward instructional goals or outcomes and on diagnosing the need for special programs and related services. For example, we may want to know whether Antoine needs special services to assist him in developing reading skills (need for service in an academic domain) or the extent to which Ellen is developing physically at a normal rate (progress decision in the physical domain). Figure 1.1 shows the 13 kinds of decisions that use assessment information and the three domains in which these decisions are made. Throughout this book we try always to be very specific in our discussions of assessment activities, and to differentiate assessment practices on the basis of the domain and the kind of decisions being made. We try never to talk about assessment by itself, but instead about assessment for a spe-

● ● ● **FIGURE 1.1**   The Assessment Decision–Problem Area Matrix

	Problem Area		
Prereferral Classroom Decisions	**Academic**	**Behavioral**	**Physical**
Provision of Special Help or Enrichment			
Referral to an Intervention Assistance Team			
Provision of Intervention Assistance			

Entitlement Decisions			
Screening			
Referral			
Exceptionality			
Documentation of Special Learning Needs			
Eligibility			

Postentitlement Classroom Decisions			
Instructional Planning			
Setting			
Progress Evaluation			

Accountability/Outcome Decisions			
Program Evaluation			
Accountability			

cific purpose. Note that we have organized the 13 kinds of decisions into four major types: (1) prereferral classroom decisions, (2) entitlement decisions, (3) postentitlement classroom decisions, and (4) accountability/outcomes decisions.

● ● ● ● ● ● ● ● ● ● ● ● ● ● ● ● ● ● ● ●

Types of Decisions

The decisions that use assessment information are varied and complex, and they occur in and out of classrooms. Some are decisions about who is eligible for the benefits of special-education services, some are about planning instructional

TABLE 1.1 ● Decisions Made Using Assessment Information

	Decision Area	Question to Be Answered
Prereferral Classroom Decisions	Provision of Special Help or Enrichment	Should the student be provided with remediation, compensation, or enrichment so that difficulty in learning can be overcome?
	Referral to an Intervention Assistance Team	Should the teacher seek the assistance of an intervention assistance team (composed of other teachers) in planning instructional interventions for an individual student?
	Provision of Intervention Assistance	Should the intervention assistance team provide the student with intensified remediation, compensation, or enrichment?
Entitlement Decisions	Screening	Is more intensive assessment necessary?
	Referral to a Child Study Team	Should the student be referred for formal psychoeducational evaluation, to be conducted by members of a child study team?
	Exceptionality	Does the child meet state criteria for assigning a disability label or a label of gifted and talented?
	Special or Unique Learning Needs	Does the student have special learning needs that require special-education assistance so that the outcomes of schooling can be achieved?
	Eligibility	Is the student eligible for special-education services?
Postentitlement Classroom Decisions	Instructional Planning	What should a teacher teach, and how should he or she teach?
	Setting	Where should students be taught?
	Progress Evaluation	To what extent are students making progress toward specific instructional goals?
Accountability Decisions	Program Evaluation	Are specific instructional programs working as school personnel want them to work?
	Accountability	To what extent is education working for students? (Accountability decisions usually are made at the national, state, or school district level.)

interventions for students, and others are about the extent to which students are benefiting from services they receive. In Table 1.1, we list and briefly define the 13 kinds of decisions. The table and the following discussion are organized around the four types just identified.

Prereferral Classroom Decisions

When students show academic, behavioral, or physical difficulties, their classroom teacher typically tries out a number of teaching alternatives. Most states now require that teachers implement and document the effectiveness of several alternative instructional approaches before they are allowed to refer students for formal assessment. These prereferral classroom decisions center on whether to provide special help or enrichment, to refer the student to an intervention assistance team, or to provide intervention assistance.

Provision of Special Help or Enrichment

Teachers use classroom tests, daily observations, and interviews to decide whether a student is in need of special assistance. Generally, when a student's rate of progress is 20 to 50 percent of that of other students, the teacher has reason to provide special help. When a student's progress is significantly better than that of other students, there is reason to provide enrichment. The process of collecting and using data to decide to provide special help or enrichment is an assessment process. The assessment decision is a judgment by the teacher that the student is not as competent as other students (or is working above the level of other students) and needs special assistance (or enrichment). Special assistance does not mean special-education services. Rather, the help may be in the form of tutoring, Title I assistance, assignment of a study buddy, or adaptation of classroom materials and instruction. It may be designed to remediate a deficiency, compensate for a disability, or provide enrichment. The special assistance might also be provided at home. Parents might assist the student with homework or hire a tutor.

Referral to an Intervention Assistance Team

The teacher uses both assessment information obtained as a part of routine instruction/assessment and information derived from monitoring the success of efforts to provide special help. The assessment is the teacher's judgment or observation that the student is having difficulty acquiring or retaining behavioral or academic skills. Skill acquisition may require simultaneous elimination of undesirable skills or behaviors.

When the student does not make satisfactory progress even with special help, the teacher may seek assistance from an intervention assistance team (IAT), usually composed of regular education teachers whose role is to help one another come up with ways to teach difficult-to-teach students. The IAT (sometimes called a prereferral team, teacher assistance team [TAT], mainstream assistance team [MAT], or schoolwide assistance team [SWAT]) works as a problem-solving team. Sometimes the members of the IAT gather data through observation, interview, or testing. When they do so, they are engaging in assessment. The interventions that are developed and put in place by IATs often are called "prereferral interventions" because they occur prior to formal referral for child study.

Whom do teachers refer to IATs? Although that question can be answered simply—they refer students who bother them—it is not easy to predict whether a student will be referred. Different teachers are bothered by different behaviors, although some behaviors and characteristics will probably bother most, if not all, teachers.

Provision of Intervention Assistance

In 1980, very few states required prereferral interventions. Currently about three fourths of the states do. The prereferral intervention (or intervention assistance) process has been put in place in states and local school districts in an effort to reduce referral for testing and overidentification of students as needing special-education services. The process is based on the notion that many of the difficulties for which students are formally referred can be alleviated by adjusting classroom interventions. The purpose of prereferral intervention in fact is twofold: (1) to try to alleviate difficulties, and (2) to document the kinds of techniques that do and do not improve student outcomes.

One of the best examples of prereferral intervention is found in Iowa, where a mandatory problem-solving process is used to systematically examine the nature and severity of an education-related problem. The focus is on developing effective educational interventions. Steps in the Iowa problem-solving process are shown in Figure 1.2.

Each local education agency, in conjunction with a regional area education agency, attempts to resolve problems or behaviors of concern directly in the general education environment, prior to conducting a full and individual evaluation. General education interventions include teacher consultation with special educators and collaboration among general educators in attempts to improve student performance. Activities are documented and include (1) measurable and goal-directed attempts to resolve problems and behaviors of concern, (2) communication with parents, (3) collection of related data, (4) intervention design and implementation, and (5) systematic monitoring of student progress and of the effects of the intervention. If these general education interventions do not alleviate the academic or behavior problem, a full and individual intervention is conducted.

Entitlement Decisions

Screening Decisions

Screening is the process of collecting data to decide whether more intensive assessment is necessary. Implicit in screening is the notion that students' difficulties may go unnoticed if teachers do not test for them. It is assumed, for example, that a student might have a hearing difficulty or cognitive deficit that would go unrecognized without screening. Because there is some variability in teachers' tolerances for and awareness of various problems, there may be students in classrooms who are exceptional but are not having their needs met. School districts want to find these students and provide special services to them, so screening programs are started.

Screening decisions are essentially administrative in nature. All students in particular schools or school districts are given preliminary tests to identify those who differ significantly from their classmates (in either a positive or a negative sense) and therefore may be eligible for special-education services. Just as vision and hearing tests are routinely given to identify pupils with vision or hearing problems, intelligence tests may be administered to identify students who need special attention, either because of limited intellectual capacity or because of highly su-

● ● ● ● **FIGURE 1.2**   *Steps in the Iowa Problem-Solving Process*

Description of the problem.   The problem or behavior of concern is described in objective, measurable terms that focus on alterable characteristics of the individual and the environment, and describe the degree of discrepancy between the demands of the educational setting and the individual's performance.

Data collection and problem analysis.   A systematic data-based process for examining all that is known about the problem is used to identify interventions that have a high likelihood of success. Relevant data are collected in multiple settings using multiple sources and methods. The data collection procedures are individually tailored, valid, and reliable and allow for frequent and repeated measurement of the effectiveness of proposed interventions.

Intervention design and implementation.   Interventions are chosen and designed based on the preceding analysis, the defined problem, parent input, and professional judgments about their potential effectiveness. They are described in an intervention plan that includes goals and strategies, a progress monitoring plan, a decision-making plan for summarizing student progress and analyzing the extent to which it is appropriate, and the names of the responsible parties. Interventions are implemented as developed and can be modified on the basis of objective data and with the agreement of the responsible parties.

Progress monitoring.   Systematic monitoring of student progress includes regular and frequent data collection and analysis of individual performance across time. Interventions are modified as frequently as necessary based on this monitoring.

Evaluation of intervention effects.   The effectiveness of interventions is evaluated through a systematic procedure in which patterns of individual performance are analyzed, summarized, and compared to initial levels of performance.

SOURCE: Adapted from Special Education Rules, Iowa Department of Education, 1998.

perior intellectual ability. *Achievement tests,* measures of what has been taught to and learned by students, are routinely given to identify students who are experiencing academic difficulty and for whom further assessment may be appropriate.

Screening is an initial stage during which students who may evidence a particular problem, disorder, disability, or disease are sorted out from the general population. Screening has its origins in medicine and uses terminology from medical screening practices. We speak of individuals who perform poorly on screening measures as being "at risk"; we describe individuals as "false positives" when they perform poorly on screening measures but do well on later follow-up assessments, which show that they do not have the condition for which they were screened. Sometimes students show no problems at the time of screening and are

TABLE 1.2 ● Hits and Misses in Making Screening Decisions

	Reality	
Result of Screening	**Student has a certain characteristic**	**Student doesn't have the characteristic**
Student has a certain characteristic	Hit	False positive
Student doesn't have the characteristic	False negative	Normal

considered "normal," but later they evidence the very problems for which screening was conducted. These students are said to be "false negatives." Finally, when we talk about the accuracy of screening decisions, we often speak of the "hit rate" (proportion of accurate positive decisions) for screening. Table 1.2 shows the relationship between screening decisions and accurately diagnosed conditions.

Screening takes place at all levels of education. Children are screened before they enter kindergarten or first grade to determine their academic readiness in terms of language, cognitive, and motor development and social and emotional functioning. We want to know the competencies they do and do not have. They may also be given vision and hearing screening tests. After they are tested, their performance is compared with standards established by those who make the screening tests. For example, if two thirds of the children who took the test when it was being developed scored 300 points or better, children who score below 300 could be considered at risk. Test developers usually provide cutoff scores to help educators make decisions. Sometimes students are denied school entrance if they score low on a screening test (parents are asked to delay school entry until the child is deemed ready to enter school),[1] and sometimes low performance results in the child's being marked for observation and monitoring.

Screening also is used throughout the school years to identify students who need extra attention because their performance is markedly different from normal or average performance. When this screening is done, student performance is judged *relative to that of others*. Cutoff scores are based on the average performance of students at various ages or grade levels. The scores of this norm group are used in deciding whether more testing is necessary. Decisions about performance usually are based on single snapshots of student performance or behavior. Decisions about progress usually are made by looking at student performance over time, often using the same test. Judgments about student competence or progress over time may also be made *relative to an absolute standard*. Absolute standards typically are statements about the competencies schools want students to have at specific points in time (such as graduation or completion of grade 9).

1. School administrators vary greatly in their views on which skills, abilities, and behaviors students need in order to enter school. Many view all children as ready for school and focus their efforts on getting the schools ready for students.

At some point, educators may come to believe that a student's academic or behavioral needs are so different that they cannot be met using the current approaches, and that the child needs special education to achieve desired outcomes. When students' scores indicate a special need, students may be referred for psychoeducational assessment and given individually administered psychological and educational tests. These tests help to determine the specific reasons for a student's performance on a screening measure.

Referral Decisions

When a student fails to make satisfactory progress, even with the help of an IAT, the student may be referred for formal psychoeducational evaluation. *Referral* usually is a formal process involving the completion of a referral form and a request for a team of professionals to decide whether a student's academic, behavioral, or physical development warrants the provision of special-education services. The team of professionals is usually called a "child study team," though in some states and districts within states, these teams go by other names: In Colorado and Massachusetts, they are called "IEP teams"; in Texas, "admission, review, and dismissal (ARD) teams." Child study teams make two kinds of decisions: decisions about exceptionality (whether the child is disabled or gifted) and decisions about special learning needs. These teams are composed of regular education teachers, special-education teachers, one or more administrators, the student's parent(s), and related services personnel, such as the school psychologist, nurse, social worker, counselor, and so forth, depending on the nature of the case. Recent surveys show that each year, 3 to 5 percent of the students in public schools are referred for psychological and educational assessment. About 92 percent of those students who are referred are tested, and about 73 percent of those who are tested are declared eligible for special-education services (Algozzine, Christenson, & Ysseldyke, 1982; Ysseldyke, Vanderwood, & Shriner, 1997).

Exceptionality Decisions

In making exceptionality decisions, the child study team decides whether a student meets the eligibility criteria for special education, as specified by the state in which the student lives. If, for example, the student must be shown to have both an IQ below 70 and deficits in adaptive behavior in order to be called "mentally retarded," one or more team members will administer tests to see whether the child scores below the required levels. The team does the official assigning of an exceptionality name, and the criteria used to make the decision are state-established criteria. For example, teams identify, according to state criteria, categorical conditions such as blind, deaf, mentally retarded, emotionally disturbed, learning disabled, and so forth. They also decide whether youngsters are gifted or talented. Given that some students are multiply disabled, teams must identify the category under which services will be provided. Teams are required to gather assessment information, and it is illegal to base exceptionality decisions on a single test.

Documentation of Special Learning Needs

Child study teams also make decisions about whether students have special learning needs that require provision of special-education services. For example, they may document that a student who is blind or visually impaired experiences academic difficulties without instruction in Braille or the use of large-print books. They make a formal statement that the student has special learning needs that require special-education assistance, and they link these learning needs to statements about the kinds of assistance required. Increasingly, child study teams rely on the data they receive from those who have conducted prereferral interventions with individual children.

Eligibility Decisions

Before the Education for All Handicapped Children Act was passed in 1975, eligibility, labeling, and placement decisions typically were made by administrators or school psychologists. Members of the U.S. Congress, acting on the belief that individual decision making was capricious and too often wrong, decided that these decisions should be made by teams using multiple sources of information.

Before a student may be declared eligible for special-education services, he or she must be shown to have an exceptionality (a disability or a gift or talent) *and* to have special learning needs. It is not enough to be disabled *or* to have special learning needs. Students can be disabled and not require special education. Students can have special learning needs but not meet the state criteria for being declared disabled. Students who receive special education (a) have diagnosed disabilities (or special gifts or talents), (b) have special learning needs, and (c) need special-education services to achieve educational outcomes.

In addition to the classification system employed by the federal government, every state has an education code that specifies the kinds of students considered disabled. States have different names for the same disability. For example, in California, some students are called "deaf" or "hard of hearing"; in other states, such as Colorado, the same kinds of students are called "hearing impaired." Different states have different standards for classification of the same disability. In Pennsylvania, the maximum IQ for mentally retarded individuals is 80; in Minnesota, the maximum IQ is 70; in California, an African American student cannot be classified as mentally retarded on the basis of an individual intelligence test. Some states consider gifted students to be exceptional and entitled to special-education services; other states do not.

Postentitlement Classroom Decisions

Instructional Planning Decisions

Regular education teachers are able to take a standard curriculum and plan instruction around it. Although curricula vary from district to district—largely as a function of the values of community and school—they are appropriate for most students at a given age or grade level. However, what should teachers do for those students who differ significantly from their peers or from district standards in their academic and behavioral competencies? These students need special help to benefit from classroom curriculum and instruction, and school personnel must gather data to plan special programs for these students.

Three kinds of decisions are made in instructional planning: (1) what to teach, (2) how to teach it, and (3) what expectations are realistic. Deciding what to teach is a content decision, usually made on the basis of a systematic analysis of the skills that students do and do not have. Scores on tests and other information help teachers decide whether students have specific competencies. Test information might be used to determine placement in reading groups or assignment to specific compensatory or remedial programs. Teachers also use information gathered from observations and interviews to decide what to teach. They obtain information about how to teach by trying different methods of teaching and monitoring students' progress toward instructional goals. Finally, decisions about realistic expectations are always inferences, based largely on observations of performance in school settings and performance on tests.

With the increased attention given to learning disabilities and with federal and state requirements for individualized education programs for exceptional students, we have seen an expansion in the use of curriculum-based assessment procedures in planning instructional efforts. The merits and limitations of tests in planning specific education programs are discussed in several chapters in Parts 3 and 4 of this text. Instructional planning for students with disabilities involves development of an individualized educational plan (IEP). The IEP and the components required to be included in it are described in Chapter 14.

Setting Decisions

Setting decisions are often called "placement decisions." Educators determine where to put students so that they may receive the most appropriate services. Students with disabilities are educated in different kinds of settings, and the settings vary in their location, the kinds of other students enrolled, and the kind of curriculum taught. Federal law and regulations allow for a "continuum of alternative placements," and educators must decide which setting is least restrictive to the student. The law says that each public agency must ensure

1. that to the maximum extent appropriate, children with disabilities, including children in public or private institutions or other care facilities, are educated with children who are nondisabled; and

2. that special classes, separate schooling or other removal of children with disabilities from the regular educational environment occurs only if the nature or severity or the disability is such that education in regular classes with the use of supplementary aids and services cannot be achieved satisfactorily. (§300.550)

The continuum of alternative placements must include these placements: instruction in regular classes, special classes, special schools, home instruction, and instruction in hospitals and institutions. In addition, provision must be made for supplementary services (such as resource rooms or itinerant instruction) to be provided in conjunction with regular class placement.

Setting decisions must be made by an IEP team that includes the parents and other persons knowledgeable about the student. Student placements must be determined at least annually, based on the child's IEP, and must be as close as possible to the child's home. Unless their IEPs indicate otherwise, children are to be educated in the school they would attend if they were nondisabled. Federal law also requires that in selecting educational placements, school personnel give consideration to any potential harmful effect on the child or on the quality of services that he or she needs. Students with disabilities are not to be removed from regular classrooms solely because of needed modifications in the general curriculum (§300.552).

It is incumbent on school personnel to demonstrate that students are educated in the least restrictive setting that is *appropriate*, not simply a setting in which they can physically be put.

Progress Evaluation Decisions

Parents, teachers, and students themselves have a right and a need to know how students are progressing in school. How do we know whether students are learning and developing competence? One way to know, of course, is to rely on our observations of a student's behavior and our own feelings about and impressions of the student's work. Just as a parent evaluates a child's development on the basis of general impressions or observations, so teachers evaluate students' progress on the basis of subjective general impressions.

Teachers also collect assessment information to decide whether their students are making progress. They may give unit tests, or they may evaluate portfolios of the students' work (sometimes called "portfolio assessment"). The data that are collected as part of the process of evaluating pupil progress are used to fine-tune education programs or to make changes in teaching strategies. Some of the data collected in progress evaluations tell teachers and parents whether specific instructional objectives have been achieved.

When tests are used to make progress evaluation decisions, it is critical that there be good correspondence between the test and the curriculum. When discussing tests, we must distinguish between attainment and achievement. *Attainment* is what an individual has learned, regardless of where it has been learned. *Achievement* is what has been learned as a result of instruction in the schools. Any test of factual information measures attainment; however, a test of factual information is an achievement test only if it measures what has been directly taught. Only achievement tests can be used to monitor pupil progress. It would be pointless to use a test that did not assess what a teacher had taught.

The best way to collect data for the purpose of evaluating individual students' progress is to sample the skills that are being taught. This method allows teachers to measure the extent to which students have mastered content and to chart their progress toward meeting instructional objectives.

Accountability/Outcomes Decisions

Assessment information is used to make decisions about the extent to which educational programs in school systems are working. It is also used to make decisions about the extent to which education is working for students, including students with disabilities.

Program-Evaluation Decisions

Assessment data are collected to evaluate specific programs. Here the emphasis is on gauging the effectiveness of the curriculum in meeting the goals and objectives of the school. School personnel typically use this information for schoolwide curriculum planning. For example, schools can compare two approaches to teaching in a content area by (1) giving tests at the beginning of the year, (2) teaching two comparable groups two different ways, and (3) giving tests at the end of the year. By comparing students' performances before and after, the schools are able to evaluate the effectiveness of the two competing approaches.

The process of assessing educational programs can be complex if numerous students are involved and if the criteria for making decisions are written in statistical terms. For example, an evaluation of two instructional programs might involve gathering data from hundreds of students and comparing their performances using many statistical tests. Program costs, teacher and student opinions, and the nature of each program's goals and objectives might be compared to determine which program is more effective. This kind of large-scale evaluation probably would be undertaken by a group of administrators working for a school district.

Of course, program evaluations can be much less formal. Martha, a friend of ours, is a third-grade teacher. When Martha wants to know the effectiveness of an instructional method she is using, she does her own evaluation. For example, recently she wanted to know whether having students complete activities in their basal readers was as effective as having them use language-experience activities. She compared students' written products using both methods and concluded that the use of language-experience activities was a better way to help them achieve competence.

Accountability Decisions

Public schools in the United States have come under increasing criticism over the past 15 to 20 years. In 1983, a special study panel commissioned by the U.S. Department of Education issued a report called "A Nation at Risk," which raised concerns about education in the United States and about the accomplishments of U.S. students. Increasingly, parents want reports on how students are doing in their schools, legislators want to know how the schools are doing, and policy makers want data on the educational performance of the nation's youth. School personnel regularly administer tests to students, engage in portfolio assessment or performance assessment, and issue reports on the achievement of the students in their schools. Such practices are sometimes called "outcomes-based accountability practices."

Making Assessment Decisions

We have described *assessment* as the process of collecting data for the purpose of making decisions about students. However, assessment and decision making are seldom straightforward. Students are not uniformly referred, tested, declared eligible, placed in special education, and then taught. Rather, the assessment process proceeds differently in different places for different students. Decisions made about students are neither sequential nor mutually exclusive. For example, a teacher may be providing Dominic with special assistance in reading, during which time the speech–language pathologist may administer a language screening test to him.

Sometimes it takes a long while to go through the sequence of decisions; at other times, the interval from screening or referral to provision of services is very short. Some students perform poorly on a screening measure and are referred immediately to an IAT or child study team. Other students come to the attention of the IAT only after the teacher has provided considerable assistance and the student has not profited to the extent desired.[2] IATs may try a number of interventions, and then students who fail to perform as expected will be referred to the child study team. Assessment is dynamic and ongoing. After the declaration of eligibility for services and specification of learning needs for a student, teachers continue to observe how the student performs under differing circumstances and to modify instruction accordingly (Algozzine, Ysseldyke, & Elliott, 1997).

When is assessment started? Timing is largely a function of the severity of a disability. The assessment and decision-making process may be shortened in some instances, such as when a parent of a child with severe disabilities initiates a referral. Parents know very early in a child's life that severe disabilities are present. They may contact their family physician, who may need very little time to decide that a child has a disability—it may be readily apparent. On the other hand, sometimes it is necessary for assessment personnel to engage in extensive assessment to ascertain whether a child has a developmental disorder. In general, it takes longer to decide to declare students with mild disabilities eligible for special-education services than it does to make the same decision for students with severe disabilities. Some disabilities do not show up until students are in school and experience difficulty with schoolwork.

Assessment Domains

Assessment relies on the specification and verification of problems for the purpose of making different kinds of decisions. We just described the kinds of decisions

---

2. Referral may result from a teacher's observations, a parent's request, or the student's own request. Context can affect assessment practices. Some students are not referred to an intervention assistance team because their regular class teacher has special expertise in dealing with their disability. Students with some disabilities are most likely to receive assistance in a particular district or state than if they live elsewhere.

that are made in educational settings. We now describe three kinds of problems with which assessment is usually concerned: academic problems, behavior problems, and physical problems.

Academic Problems

The most common reason students are referred for psychological or educational assessment is that a teacher or parent believes that they are not performing as well academically as could be expected. Teachers usually make that decision on the basis of their observations of pupil performance in core content areas: reading, mathematics, and written language and communication. When referring students to IATs or child study teams for assessment, teachers must specify their concerns. Teachers who refer students for assessment because of vague "reading problems" provide diagnostic personnel with limited information. To the extent that teachers describe and specify the nature of a student's problems (for example, "Rachel is the poorest reader in the class and consistently has difficulty associating letters with sounds"), they help diagnostic personnel. Some very effective teachers regularly gather information about pupil progress in academic content areas and use those data to make decisions about special assistance or to refer students.

Academic competence is nearly always assessed in making exceptionality and eligibility decisions. For example, a student referred for reading problems might be given a reading test to provide a comparison of his or her reading skills with those of other students in the school or even the nation. The results of the test would be used to verify or disconfirm the existence of a problem. Academic performance is also usually assessed in making instructional-planning decisions. In deciding what to teach a student, the teacher or team must specify which academic competencies the student already has.

Behavior Problems

Students are often referred for psychological or educational assessment because they demonstrate behavior problems. Students for whom severe behavior problems can be specified and verified are often declared eligible for special-education services. *Behavior problems* include failure to get along with peers, delinquent activities, and excessive withdrawal, as well as disruptive and noncompliant behavior. For example, Ms. Swanson may be troubled because Larry is so quiet and withdrawn. She might begin to verify that this is actually the problem by counting the frequency of Larry's interactions with his peers. A low count would not, by itself, indicate a problem. Therefore, Ms. Swanson might select another boy whose behavior she judged to be appropriate and count the frequency of his interactions with his peers. She could then verify that Larry interacted much less frequently than a boy who had no problem interacting. Ms. Swanson might plan a social-skills training program for Larry to increase the number of positive interactions that he has with his classmates. She could systematically collect data on the effectiveness of this new program and reach some decisions about Larry's progress.

Physical Problems

Physical problems include sensory disabilities (such as in vision or hearing), problems of physical structure (for example, spina bifida or cerebral palsy), and chronic health problems (such as diabetes or asthma). Severe physical problems are often brought to the attention of parents by physicians before a child enters school. When a child with a severe physical problem enters school, the parents may supply the school with specific information from physicians, confirming and specifying the physical nature of the child's problem.

Milder, but nonetheless important, problems that have not been noticed by the parents are often discovered during routine screening. For example, suppose White Haven Area School District requires that the school nurse, Mr. Slique, regularly conduct hearing tests (such as a pure-tone audiometric test for hearing within the specific range). When he screens the first-grade students, Mr. Slique notes that Jane has a 65-decibel loss in her more-sensitive ear. A hearing loss of such magnitude, if confirmed, would have serious educational implications and would necessitate substantial educational modifications so that Jane could profit from her education. However, the screening assessment was conducted in the nurse's room, which was not soundproofed, and with equipment that had not been checked recently for accuracy. Therefore, Mr. Slique decides that it would be best to have an audiologist see Jane and diagnose her hearing problem. He works with the child study team to refer Jane to the audiologist for more extensive testing of her hearing.

● ●

Assessment and Society

The students we teach in assessment classes often come with questions about the role that testing plays in social decision making. They ask such questions as, "Is it fair to place students in special education on the basis of their performance on a test?" "What do tests say about a person?" and "Should an employer decide whether to hire a person on the basis of how that person does on a test?" Our students also question the use of tests in making decisions about college entrance or admission to graduate school. Throughout this text, when appropriate, we address these and other issues surrounding the use of tests in schools. Testing does play a critical role in schools and in the wider society. Many times, tests are used to make high-stakes decisions that may have a direct and significant effect on individuals' life opportunities or on the continued funding of schools and school systems. The joint committee of three professional associations that developed a set of standards for test construction and use has addressed the kinds of issues our students often raise:

> Educational and psychological testing represents one of the most important contributions of behavioral science to our society. It has provided fundamental and significant improvements over previous practices in industry, government, and education. It has

provided a tool for broader and more equitable access to education and employment. Although not all tests are well-developed, nor are all testing practices wise and beneficial, available evidence supports the judgment that the proper use of well-constructed and validated tests provides a better basis for making some important decisions about individuals and programs than would otherwise be available.

Educational and psychological testing has also been the target of extensive scrutiny, criticism, and debate both outside and within the professional testing community. The most frequent criticisms are that tests play too great a role in the lives of students and employees and that tests are biased and exclusionary. Individuals and institutions benefit when testing helps them achieve their goals. Society, in turn, benefits when the achievement of individual and institutional goals contributes to the general good. (American Educational Research Association, American Psychological Association, & National Council on Measurement in Education, 1997, p. 1)

Summary

Testing is part of a larger concept: assessment. Assessment data are used to document the competencies that students do or do not have, and to clarify and verify the existence of educational problems in the areas of academic functioning, behavioral and social adaptation, and physical development. Assessment provides data to facilitate decision making. Thirteen kinds of decisions are made using assessment information: decisions about provision of special assistance, referral to an intervention assistance team, provision of intervention assistance, screening, referral to a child study team, exceptionality, documentation of a special learning need, eligibility, instructional planning, setting, progress evaluation, program evaluation, and accountability. Many complex social, political, and ethical issues arise when tests are used to make important decisions about individuals. Assessment is an important activity, and it is critical that it be done right.

Questions for Chapter Review and Thought

1. What is the difference between testing and assessment?

2. Attack or defend the generalization: Different kinds of data are needed for the purpose of making different kinds of educational decisions.

3. What five kinds of decisions are made in determining whether students are entitled to special-education services?

4. Imagine that, as a member of a debate team, you are required to take the position that educational and psychological tests are either detrimental or beneficial to society. Select the position that you wish to take, and provide an argument for your position.

Resources for Further Investigation

Project

Three types of problems—academic, behavioral, and physical—which could be highly related, are specified and verified through assessment procedures. Create a case in which these three problems are interrelated, and identify the implications that this complexity has for assessment procedures after the student has been referred for behavior problems.

Print Resources

Algozzine, B. A., Ysseldyke, J. E., & Elliott, J. (1997). *Strategies and tactics for effective instruction* (2nd ed.). Longmont, CO: Sopris West.

Ysseldyke, J. E., Vanderwood, M., & Shriner, J. (1997). Changes over the past decade in special education referral to placement probability. *Diagnostique, 23*(1), 193–201.

Technology Resources

American Educational Research Association

http://www.aera.net/

This website provides information to professionals interested in educational research and its practical application. The organization is divided into 12 divisions, and information on assessment is located in the following areas: Teaching and Teacher Education, School Evaluation & Program Development, and Measurement & Research Methodology.

American Psychological Association

http://www.apa.org/

This connects to APA's PsychNET, where it is possible to search for information about psychology, education, and employment opportunities. There is also information on APA membership and publications.

National Education Association

http://www.nea.org/

This is the home page for this national organization of teachers and educators. There is an information center about public education and a resource room containing tips for teachers to help students learn.

U.S. Department of Education

http://www.ed.gov/index.html

This page provides news and information about the government's educational initiatives. There is a listing of programs, services, publications, and products.

Council for Exceptional Children

http://www.cec.sped.org

The Council for Exceptional Children (CEC) home page disseminates information on special-education issues and legislation, scholarships and awards for students with special needs, and CEC services. It often contains information on assessment.

ERIC Clearinghouse on Assessment and Evaluation

http://www.ericae.net

This web site provides balanced information concerning educational assessment and resources to encourage responsible use of tests.

Regional Resource and Federal Center (RRFC) Network

http:/www.dssc.org/frc/rrfc.htm

This is a network of seven technical assistance agencies (six Regional Resource Centers and one Federal Resource Center) funded by the U.S. Department of Education, Office of Special Education Programs. The RRFC Network delivers technical assistance to state education agencies, helping them improve special-education policies, programs, and practices. The RRCs regularly track assessment legislation.

American Federation of Teachers

http://www.aft.org/

This is the home page for this national organization of teachers and educators. Featured are the Education Issues Department, Research Department, Where We Stand, selected Web Resources, and many others.

Council of Chief State School Officers (CCSSO)

http://www.ccsso.org/

CCSSO is a nationwide nonprofit organization composed of public officials who lead the departments responsible for elementary and secondary education in the 50 states, the U.S. extrastate jurisdictions, the District of Columbia, and the Department of Defense Dependents Schools.

Education Week

http://www.edweek.org

This is the web site of the weekly publication of current local, state, national, and international education news. The On Assignment and Commentary sections highlight specific education issues.

Assessment Processes and Concerns

*I*n the context of education, assessment is performed to gain an understanding of an individual learner's strengths and weaknesses in order to make appropriate educational decisions. Any textbook description of this interactive, individualized, and complex process is necessarily general and linear; thus, to some extent, descriptions of data collection and decision making can distort and oversimplify these processes. This chapter begins with a description of the process of collecting data to gain an understanding of a student's strengths and weaknesses. It ends with a description of frequently voiced concerns about assessment and subsequent decision making.

Underlying this chapter is the belief that the best educational decisions are based on information; usually, better decisions are based on more information. Although good decisions can be based on a flash of insight, more often they are the result of generating hypotheses, carefully amassing information, carefully analyzing that information for consistencies and inconsistencies, and then deciding whether there is sufficient evidence to support or reject the hypotheses.

● ●

The Process of Assessment

When a student is experiencing difficulty in school, two related and complementary types of assessment should be performed. First, the instruction a student has received is assessed to ascertain whether the student's difficulties stem from inappropriate curriculum or inadequate teaching. When instruction is found to be inadequate, the student should be given appropriate instruction to see whether it alleviates the difficulty. When appropriate instruction fails to remediate the difficulty, further assessment of the student is carried out. Each approach is described in this section.

● ●

Assessing Instruction

Until the early 1980s, most assessment activities in school settings consisted of efforts to assess the learner. Yet school personnel often have difficulty developing instructional recommendations solely on the basis of information about the characteristics of students. Englemann, Granzin, and Severson (1979) recommended that assessment begin with instructional diagnosis "to determine aspects of instruction that are inadequate, to find out precisely how they are inadequate, and to imply what must be done to correct their inadequacy" (p. 361). In this approach, assessment consists of systematic analysis of instruction in terms of its appropriateness for the learner. Two dimensions are usually considered when instruction is assessed: instructional challenge and instructional environment.

Instructional Challenge

For instruction to be effective, it must be possible for the learner, with a reasonable effort, to master the information (the facts, skills, behaviors, or processes) being taught. If the degree to which information challenges a learner is thought of as a continuum, we can think of material as ranging from too easy (unchallenging), through about right in degree of difficulty (appropriately challenging), to too difficult (overly challenging).

Unchallenging Content

Instruction that is too easy for a student teaches information that requires no additional practice for acquisition or retention; the student understands the information and can use it. Usually, unchallenging instruction occurs for two reasons. First, a teacher may hold previously mastered goals as the current goals of instruction. Thus, the teacher teaches what the student already knows. Obviously, if a student already has met the goal, additional instruction or practice wastes time and bores the student. Second, the pace of challenge may be too slow. In this case, a teacher initially provides instruction on new information but fails to recognize when the student has mastered it. Here, too, time is wasted, and the student is bored. Needed levels of mastery vary with the capabilities of individual students and the design of the curriculum. However, as a rule of thumb, educators frequently use a criterion of a 95 percent correct response rate as the point beyond which students no longer need even independent practice.

Appropriately Challenging Content

Instruction that is appropriately challenging is, of course, neither too easy nor too difficult. Moreover, such instruction is usually motivating because students can see that, with some effort, they will succeed. Depending on the student and the task, challenging material usually produces rates of correct student response of between 85 and 95 percent.

Overly Challenging Content

Instruction that is too difficult for a student attempts to teach information for which the student lacks significant prerequisites. This problem occurs for two related reasons. First, instruction can be too challenging if a student lacks facts, concepts, behaviors, or strategies on which the new instruction is based. Two examples illustrate: (1) If students do not understand addition, they will probably be unsuccessful in learning multiplication beyond some rote memorization; (2) if students do not understand that deciduous trees go dormant in the winter, they may not grasp the difference between dead trees and healthy but dormant ones.

Second, instruction can be too difficult when its pace is too fast. In this case, the student has been exposed to prerequisite information but has not yet mastered it. For example, a youngster may still be learning to control writing movement when the teacher moves on to printing letters. As a result, the student may still be concentrating on pencil grip instead of learning how specific letters are formed.

Like information that is too easy, what is too difficult for a student varies with the capabilities of the student and the design of the curriculum. However, educators generally believe that when average students cannot respond with about 85 percent accuracy, the material is too difficult; for students with severe cognitive handicaps, rates of correct response of less than 90 percent may indicate that the material is too challenging for guided practice. When instruction is too challenging, students do not learn efficiently and often experience frustration; such students are occasionally termed *curriculum casualties.*

Instructional Environment

Instruction involves more than appropriate curriculum. It is a complex activity, the outcomes of which depend on the interaction of many factors. Recognition of this fact has led to efforts to assess the qualitative nature of students' instructional environments (Ysseldyke & Christenson, 1993).

Assessment of the instructional environment consists of systematically analyzing the extent to which those factors that are known to make a difference in pupils' learning are present in the instruction that students receive. Since the early 1970s, psychologists and educators have learned much about the attributes of instruction that result in efficient and motivated learning. Yet in many classrooms, instruction is not particularly effective. Too often, teachers use a strategy of "cover and pray"; they talk about the content and pray that the students learn it. In these classrooms, students are exposed to information, not taught; teachers hope that students somehow learn the information, but they do not assess to make sure that their students have learned it. In these classrooms, some students master the curriculum because they are sufficiently capable of learning from exposure or are taught by their parents. Others do not master the curriculum and become teaching disabled. Through no fault of their own, their learning is not commensurate with their abilities. Thus, when students experience difficulty learning, a necessary component of assessment is evaluating the quality of the instruction that students have received. Although Chapter 13 deals in greater detail with the ecology of instruction, two dimensions of instruction (classroom management and learning management) are worth describing here.

Classroom Management

Classroom management refers to a collection of organizational goals centered on using time wisely in order to maximize learning and on maintaining a safe classroom environment that is conducive to student learning. In classrooms that are poorly organized, students lose learning opportunities because of disruptions by other students, ineffective grouping, poor transitions between activities, and so forth. In contrast, well-organized classrooms have clearly stated and well-understood procedures, consistent consequences for student behavior, and student freedom within a structured environment.

Learning Management

The organization and management of the classroom to ensure learning require careful attention to detail. Essentially, teachers must oversee the learning situation. Effective teachers do the following:

- Demonstrate what is to be learned and then provide adequate opportunities for meaningful rehearsal and guided and independent practice with appropriate materials until skills become automatic
- Give students immediate, specific, and corrective feedback about their performances and provide opportunities to correct mistakes
- Reinforce desired outcomes
- Stress understanding, application, and transfer of information

• •

Assessing Learners

When students have received appropriate instruction but are still experiencing academic or behavioral problems, school personnel usually begin to assemble existing information to document the nature of the problem (that is, to identify specific learning strengths and weaknesses) and to generate hypotheses about the problem's likely cause.

Kinds of Information

A test is only one of several assessment techniques or procedures available for gathering information. During the process of assessment, data from observations, recollections, tests, and professional judgments all come into play.

Observations

Observations can provide highly accurate, detailed, verifiable information, not only about the person being assessed, but also about the surrounding contexts. Observations can be categorized as either nonsystematic or systematic.

Nonsystematic Observation   In *nonsystematic* or informal *observation,* the observer simply watches an individual in his or her environment and notes the behaviors, characteristics, and personal interactions that seem significant. Nonsystematic observation tends to be anecdotal and can be subjective and unreplicable. However, nonsystematic observations can provide the basis for determining what to observe systematically.

Systematic Observation   In *systematic observation,* the observer sets out to observe one or more precisely defined behaviors. The observer specifies observable events that define the behavior and then counts the frequency or measures the frequency, duration, amplitude, or latency of the behaviors. The observer must be careful to observe the important behaviors and characteristics—not just those that are convenient to measure.

Disadvantages of Observations   There are three potential disadvantages in using observations to collect information: imperfect observation, time demands, and distortion of the context of observation.

A substantial body of research indicates that humans often imperfectly observe, interpret observations, and reach decisions based on their observations. Two types of imperfect observation are particularly noteworthy: the halo effect and expectancy.

The *halo effect* is the tendency to make subjective judgments on the basis of general attributes. Thus, one characteristic of a subject, such as race, may alter the way in which the subject's peer interactions are seen. Salvia and Meisel (1980) have documented the impact on observation of several student characteristics: social class, given names, surnames, race, facial attractiveness, and labels of exceptionality. The halo effect is most likely to influence observations when the behavior or attributes under consideration are not easily observed, are not clearly defined, involve reactions of other people, or are of high moral importance (Guilford, 1936, p. 275). Conversely, providing observers with systematic training in observation, specific observation procedures, and highly objective situations can substantially reduce or eliminate biased observations (Salvia & Meisel, 1980).

Expectancy is the tendency to see behaviors that are consistent with one's beliefs about what should happen; the observers never would have seen these behaviors with their own eyes unless they already believed in them. For example, teachers are more likely to observe improved behavior on the part of their classes when they believe that their interventions are effective. Expectancy is most likely to influence observations when teachers have beliefs about instructional and behavior interventions and when the behavior is difficult to observe or not clearly defined. The most effective way to prevent expectancies from influencing observations is to keep observers blind—that is, uninformed about who is receiving intervention or about the nature of the intervention. However, this technique is very difficult to implement in schools.

The second disadvantage of observation is that it can be very time-consuming. The more precisely and carefully they are made, the more time-consuming observations become. Thus, an assessor pays for accurate information by not being able to collect other information. The third disadvantage is that the very presence of an observer may distort or otherwise alter the situation to such a degree that the behavior of the individual being observed also is altered. For example, students may be hesitant to misbehave when an outsider is observing in the classroom.

Recollections

Recalled observations and *interpretations* of behavior and events are frequently used as an additional source of information. People who are familiar with the student can be very useful in providing information through interviews and rating scales.

Interviews   Interviews can range in structure from casual conversations to highly structured processes in which the interviewer has a predetermined set of questions that are asked in a specified sequence. Generally, the more structured the interview, the more accurate the comparisons of the results of several different interviews.

Rating Scales   Rating scales can be considered the most formal type of interview. Rating scales allow questions to be asked in a standardized way and to be accompanied by the same stimulus materials, and they provide a standardized and limited set of response options. The two most commonly used types of response options are Likert-like scaling and frequency estimates. With *Likert-like formats,* a person is usually required to agree or disagree with a statement by indicating whether he or she strongly agrees, agrees, disagrees, or strongly disagrees. Occasionally, this type of scale has a neutral midpoint (neither agree nor disagree). With *frequency estimates,* a person responds by indicating how often a behavior or situation occurs. The estimate may be verbal (always, frequently, seldom, or never) or numerical (more than 95% of the time, between 50% and 95% of the time, and so on).

Disadvantages of Recollections   In addition to having some of the same disadvantages associated with direct observation, recollections suffer from two other disadvantages. First, the longer the time between observation and recollection, the greater the chance that some memory distortion will occur. For example, important details may be forgotten, and some things that are generally consistent with the remembrance may be invented. Second, individuals may not be truthful. People may be unwilling to divulge painful or embarrassing details. They may filter what they tell an interviewer according to what they believe the interviewer hopes to hear. They may provide information selectively or over- or understate problems to further their own agendas. For example, parents who do not want their child placed in special education may assert that a child's school avoidance is infrequent, even though it is a daily problem.

Tests

A *test* is a predetermined set of questions or tasks for which predetermined types of behavioral responses are sought. Tests are particularly useful because they permit tasks and questions to be presented in exactly the same way to each person tested. Because a tester elicits and scores behavior in a predetermined and consistent manner, the performances of several different test takers can be compared, no matter who does the testing. Hence, tests tend to make many contextual factors in assessment consistent for all those tested. The price of this consistency is that the predetermined questions, tasks, and responses may not be equally relevant to all students.

Basically, two types of information—quantitative and qualitative—result from the administration of a test. *Quantitative data* are the actual scores achieved on the test. An example of quantitative data is Lee's score of 80 on her math test. *Qualitative data* consist of other observations made while a student is tested; they tell us how Lee achieved her score. For example, in earning a score of 80 on her math test, Lee may have solved all of the addition and subtraction problems, with the exception of those that required regrouping. On a language test, Henry may have performed best on measures of his ability to define words, while demonstrating a weakness in comprehending verbal statements. When tests are used in assessment, it is not enough simply to know the scores a student earned on a given test; it is important to know how the student earned those scores.

Interpreting Quantitative Test Performance   Once gathered, quantitative data must be interpreted: What do the numbers mean? Interpretation occurs along two dimensions: performance standards and informational context. Thus, the meaning of a student's performance on a test depends on the standard against which the performance is compared. For example, if Juan got 75 percent correct on his weekly spelling test, his teacher might want to know how other students did on that test (that is, a comparative standard), or the teacher might evaluate Juan's performance on an absolute basis (for example, he did not get 90 percent correct, but he improved his score over that on his previous test). Second, the meaning of a specific performance depends on the other information that has been amassed; in other words, the performance must be contextualized to show how it relates to the other information that has been collected. These two dimensions are often related. Depending on the purpose of assessment and the context, assessors may select test procedures that will provide a particular kind of interpretive information.

All tests should be *objective,* in the sense that there are predetermined answers or standards for scoring a response. Legally, assessments must be objective, in the sense that the attitudes, opinions, and idiosyncrasies of the examiner do not affect scoring; any two examiners should score a response in the same way. *Objective scoring,* per se, does not imply fair scoring; it implies only predetermined criteria and standardized scoring procedures. A *subjective* test, by contrast, lacks a predetermined correct answer. Therefore, the examiner's subjective judgments, attitudes, and opinions can affect the scoring. Many people erroneously define an essay test as a subjective test. Such a test can be objective if there are predetermined, explicit criteria for correct responses, so that the same response would be assigned the same score by two or more examiners.

Normative Standards   Most assessments that occur outside of the classroom are *norm-referenced*—that is, an individual's performance is compared with the performance of many peers. In norm-referenced assessment, although the learning of particular content or skills is important, the resulting score is used primarily to ascertain the extent of differential learning, which allows the tester to rank individuals from those who have learned many skills to those who have learned few.

Commercially prepared norm-referenced devices typically are designed primarily to do one thing: to yield a distribution of scores that distinguish the performances of individuals. They allow the tester to discriminate among the performances of a number of individuals and to interpret how one person's performance compares with those of other individuals with similar characteristics. Thus, a person's performance on a test is measured in reference to the performances of others who are presumably like that person in other respects.

Commercially prepared norm-referenced tests are standardized on groups of individuals representative of all children, and typical performances for students of certain ages or in certain grades are obtained. The *raw score* that an individual student earns on a test, which is the number of questions answered correctly, is compared with the raw scores earned by other students. A *transformed score,* such as a percentile rank, is used to express the given student's standing in the group of all children of that age or grade.

Classroom teachers, counselors, psychologists, speech and language therapists, and others may create their own assessment devices for their own purposes. The primary differences between commercially prepared and custom-made tests are the representatives of the comparison group (see Chapter 6) and the specificity of the content (see the discussion of content validity in Chapter 8). Teacher-made tests are illustrative of the class of custom-made tests. Teachers usually limit the group with whom an individual's performance is compared. Thus, as one example, a teacher may compare Juan's performance only with that of his classmates—not with that of all students in the same grade. Moreover, what Juan is asked to do (the content of the test) usually reflects the classroom curriculum directly. Thus, Juan's teacher learns how Juan compares with other students in the classroom who have received the same instruction on the same content. As a second example, Jim's special-education teacher might want to know whether Jim can be integrated into a regular fourth-grade class for reading instruction. This teacher could ask the regular class teacher to nominate two or three other students who are reading at an acceptable level. The special-education teacher could assess Jim's reading and the reading of these nominated students to ascertain whether Jim is reading as well as his peers. If he is, his reading skills are sufficient for integration.

Absolute Standards   In contrast to norm-referenced tests, *criterion-referenced tests* do not indicate a person's relative standing in skill development; they measure a person's mastery of particular information and skills in terms of absolute standards. Thus, criterion-referenced tests provide answers to specific questions, such as "Does Maureen spell the word *dog* correctly?" "Does Geraldo read beginning fourth-grade material with 90 percent accuracy?" "Has Jennifer passed 75 percent of the questions on the driver's test?" In criterion-referenced assessment, the emphasis is on passing one or a series of questions. The test giver is interested in what the particular individual can and cannot do, rather than in how that individual's performance compares with those of other people.

When teachers use criterion-referenced tests, the items are often linked directly to specific instructional objectives and therefore facilitate the writing of such objectives. Test items frequently sample sequential skills, enabling a teacher not only to know the specific point at which to begin instruction, but also to plan those instructional aspects that follow directly in the curricular sequence.

School personnel use different terms to refer to assessment activities that are parts or derivatives of criterion-referenced assessment, including, for example, *curriculum-based assessment, objective-referenced assessment, performance* or *direct assessment,* and *formative evaluation* of student progress. *Curriculum-based assessment* is defined as "a procedure for determining the instructional needs of a student based on the student's ongoing performance with existing course content" (Tucker, 1985, p. 200). In *objective-referenced assessment,* tests are referenced to specific instructional objectives rather than to the performance of a peer group or norm group. Pupil performance is evaluated by measuring whether the student has met specific objectives. In *performance assessment,* a student is required to perform specific skills, the teacher does not make inferences about the student's ability to perform the skill. For example, rather than inferring writing skill from tests of writing mechanics and spelling, a teacher would ask a student to write a story. Finally, *formative evaluation* refers to the assessment of progress toward a long-term or major objective (see Bloom, Hastings, & Madaus, 1971).

Comparing Normative and Absolute Standards   Interpretation of a student's performance in both normative and absolute terms is useful in special education. No single form of interpretive information is preferred in all situations.

Obviously, when normative comparisons are required, norm-referenced assessments should be made. Norm-referenced interpretations are usually required in screening decisions. For example, if Suang has 20/100 vision, she sees things at 20 feet that normal individuals see at 100 feet. Suang's poor vision, as compared with other people's, warrants further assessment and treatment. Norm-referenced interpretations are usually required for decisions about exceptionality when a cognitive handicap is suspected; tests of intelligence are always norm-referenced.

When tests are administered to help the classroom teacher plan and evaluate instructional programs for children, criterion-referenced interpretations are recommended. For example, when planning a program for an individual student, a teacher obviously should be more concerned with identifying the specific skills that the student does or does not have than with knowing how the student compares with others.

Professional Judgments

Assessment requires judgment, and the judgments and assessments made by others can play an important role in assessment. When a *diagnostician* (the person responsible for performing an assessment) lacks competence to render a judgment, the judgments of those who possess the necessary competence are essential. Diagnosticians seek out other professionals to complement their own skills and background. Thus, referring a student to various specialists (hearing specialists, vision specialists, reading teachers, and so on) is a common and desirable practice in assessment. Judgments by teachers, counselors, psychologists, and practically any other professional school employee may be useful in particular circumstances.

Expertise in making judgments is often a function of familiarity with the student being assessed. Teachers regularly express professional judgments; for example, report-card grades represent the teacher's judgment of a student's academic progress during the marking period; referrals for psychological evaluation represent a different type of judgment, based on experience with many students and observations of the particular student. Judgments represent both the best and the worst of assessment data. Judgments made by conscientious, capable, and objective individuals can be invaluable aids in the assessment process. Inaccurate, biased, and subjective judgments can be misleading at best and harmful at worst.

The Gathering of Information

Information can be categorized as describing either how a person is functioning now or how a person has functioned in the past. Obviously, the distinction between current and historical information blurs, and the point at which current information becomes historical information depends in part on the particular fact or bit of information. For example, if Johnny had his appendix removed three years ago, we know he currently has no appendix. However, if Johnny was a poor reader two years ago while in the first grade, he may or may not be a poor reader today.

Using Extant Information

There are three general sources of information available to school personnel: cumulative records, student products, and anedoctal records.

Cumulative Records   State law requires schools to maintain files on each student. Thus, schools maintain extensive records about students, and sometimes about their families. Although there is some variability from state to state and district to district, these files are likely to contain basic identifying information (such as name, address, and birthdate), current educational status (such as grade and school), and basic educational history. This history may contain previous report cards, results of standardized tests, and attendance records. The cumulative records of exceptional students will also probably contain the results of individually administered tests, reports from other professionals (such as language or occupational therapists), multidisciplinary team evaluations, individualized education plans, assorted state-required paperwork, and perhaps medical information. Thus, a student's cumulative record contains a potential wealth of information about that student's development. This information may be useful in deciding whether a problem is chronic or recent, what has been tried with the student, who are the important persons in the student's educational life, and so forth.

Although these records are not *public*, in the sense that anyone can read them, access to them can be gained legally in two ways. First, anyone in the school with a legitimate need for the information can obtain access. Thus, for example, a school psychologist, teacher, or counselor may inspect the permanent files of students with whom he or she is working. Second, parents may authorize professionals working with their children to exchange information with professionals outside the schools. Thus, for example, parents can authorize their family physician to provide information to a school psychologist about their child's medications or health; parents can authorize teachers or school psychologists to provide information to the family physician about the effect of medication on the student's activity level and attention.

Student Products   Students generate volumes of permanent products: essays, drawings, completed worksheets and tests, and so forth. Although some of these products invariably find their way home, a number of products may remain in the teacher's possession. Some teachers assemble portfolios of student work, keep their own files of student work, and display student work in the classroom. Teachers also maintain summaries of student work. These summaries can take the form of charts of student progress or evaluations recorded in a grade book. Permanent products and grades are useful sources of information about a student's current level of performance and accomplishment. A student's work can be compared with the permanent products created by other students of similar age and expected outcomes.

Anecdotal Records   Some teachers keep personal notes about unusual occurrences during the school year. These notes may be prepared for several reasons, two of which are especially noteworthy. First, anecdotal records may be useful in documenting the characteristics of problem behaviors and the conditions under which they occur. For example, a teacher might note the antecedents and consequences of a problem behavior in order to form hypotheses about effective interventions. Second, anecdotal records may be useful in providing a fuller record to justify or document a teacher's actions. For example, a teacher might document a parent's concerns mentioned during a telephone conversation in order to establish a record of parent contacts.

Limitations of Extant Information   Extant information has three limitations of which diagnosticians must be aware. First, someone must cull currently important information from other recorded information. Second, a diagnostician cannot control what information was collected in the past; crucial bits of information may never have been collected. Third, the conditions under which the information was collected are unknown or often difficult to evaluate.

Gathering New Data

There are three advantages to having and using current information. The first is the most obvious: Current information describes a person's current behavior and characteristics. Information about current status is required for most educational decisions. Second, the diagnostician can select the specific information needed to make the desired decisions. This advantage is particularly relevant because assessment is dynamic. Frequently, information leads to further questions that require additional information to answer. Third, current information can be verified.

Putting It Together

As shown in Table 2.1, there are eight general classes of diagnostic information sources (four historical types and four current ones). The classification depends on the source of information, the currency of the information (current or historical), and the kinds of information collected (tests, observations, and so forth).

No single diagnostician has the time, competence, or opportunity to collect all possible types of information. In cases where specialized information is needed, diagnosticians must rely on the observations, tests, and judgments of others. If a behavior occurs infrequently or is demonstrated only outside of school, the diagnostician may have to rely on the observations and judgments of others who have more opportunity to collect the information—parents, or perhaps ward attendants in institutional settings. For example, throwing a tantrum at bedtime obviously does not occur at school; however, without specific reasons to distrust parental reports, most diagnosticians would accept these reports of such behavior as accurate. Moreover, if the problem were intermittent, a diagnostician would have to spend several evenings at the child's home to get a first hand estimate of the frequency and severity of the tantrums.

Finally, it is usually the responsibility of a team to integrate the information and make decisions. Teams and the types of decisions they make are discussed in Chapters 14 and 15.

Educational Prognosis

Assessment and educational decision making involve explicit or implicit predictions. A prognosis may be offered for students in their current environment and life circumstances or in some therapeutic or remedial environment. For example,

TABLE 2.1 ● Examples of Different Types of Historical and Current
Diagnostic Information

Type of Information	Time at Which Information Is Gathered	
	Historical	*Current*
Observations	Previous individualized education plans prepared by teachers or psychologists	Anecdotal records placed in personal files by teacher
	Disciplinary notes in permanent file	Momentary time sampling of on-task behavior
Recollections	Student's developmental history previously given by parent	Interviews with former teachers of target student
	Rating scale completed the previous year by parent or teacher	Rating scale completed this year by parent or teacher
Tests	Scores from first-grade screening test	Scores on an individual intelligence test
	Scores from third-grade group-achievement tests	Results of criterion-referenced tests given by teacher
Judgments	Physician's diagnosis of attention-deficit disorder	Teacher's decision to refer student for evaluation
	Grades from previous teachers	Multidisciplinary team's classification of student as learning disabled (LD)

knowing that Harry is mentally retarded and has not profited from instruction leads to the predictions that (a) he probably will not profit from the same types of instruction in the future; (b) he may fall farther behind the other children and perhaps even develop problem behaviors; and (c) if he is placed in an environment where he can receive more individual attention and specially designed instruction, he should make more progress academically and socially.

In education, as in most other human-service ventures, predictions are not often sufficiently sophisticated to allow mathematical specification. Rather, diagnosticians rely on developmental theory and intervention research to make hypotheses about the variables that should influence outcomes or that should intensify or attenuate a given variable's impact. In reaching decisions and making predictions, they then weigh a child's current life circumstances and developmental history in light of various contextual factors.

Current Life Circumstances

Any interpretation of an individual's performance and predictions about future success must include an understanding of that individual's current circumstances. Current life circumstances include the student's family, community and friends, and physical abilities and health.

Family   A student's family life contributes enormously to that student's ability to profit educationally. Yet, too frequently, there are significant challenges at home: families headed by a single parent, families in which both parents work or neither parent works, and families that are homeless. Some families are simply dysfunctional. Because of either increasing awareness and reporting of problems or increasing family stress, educators seem to be seeing more students from families with histories of physical, sexual, psychological, and substance abuse. For students who experience difficulties in both school and home, the prognosis frequently is not good. No matter how well intentioned they are, school personnel seldom can assume the family's nurturing role to overcome the effects of a dysfunctional milieu that affects a student's life for 18 or more hours each day.

A student's acculturation also is of great importance. Attitudes and values, especially in the early years, are shaped by the family. These attitudes and values have an important relationship to success in school and later life. Beliefs about the worth of schooling, the relationship between effort and outcome, and the ability to overcome adversity are all important to school success. Culturally determined attitudes about gender roles can have negative effects when they limit a girl's or a young woman's educational options, when they dampen the respect of a boy or young man for a female teacher, and so forth. Willingness to take risks, to trust and cooperate with a relatively unfamiliar adult, and to give substantial effort to tasks similarly influences school performance. Finally, a student's working knowledge of the public culture (that is, societal mores and values, standard American English, and the fund of general and specific cultural information) influences performance on school-related tasks.

Community and Friends   As a child grows older, community and friends play increasingly important roles. To the extent that they are dysfunctional, the student is at risk of failing in school and in life. Two concerns are especially noteworthy. The first is the safety of the community. For some students, the trip to school is literally a matter of life and death; murder is the leading cause of death in some age groups of children, and the risks are especially great for children of color. Some students must daily pass by crack houses, roving gangs of thugs ready to steal or extort everything from clothing to lunch money, and metal detectors at the school entrance. The second concern relates to the values instilled by community and friends. When a student's community and friends value education, the student has an enhanced prognosis for success in school and in the rest of life.

Physical Abilities and Health   Sensory and physical limitations have serious implications for assessment and schooling. Vision, hearing, and physical handicaps have long-term implications for instruction and assessment; different instructional and assessment procedures may be used with such students. Acute health conditions can produce short-term sensory or physical limitations; for example, otitis media may result in temporary hearing loss.

A student's health and nutritional status can play an important role in the student's performances on a wide variety of tasks and on academic development in general. Sick or malnourished children are apt to be lethargic, inattentive, and perhaps irritable. A temporary illness, such as the flu, can result in lost or reduced opportunities for learning. Moreover, children from economically impoverished backgrounds tend to be at greater risk of physical or health limitations for two reasons: (1) Their physical environments may be more hazardous, and (2) their parents may lack the funds to secure medical treatment.

Developmental History

A person's current life circumstances are shaped by the events that make up his or her history of development. Deleterious events may have profound effects on physical and psychological development. Physical and sensory limitations may restrict a student's opportunity to acquire various skills and abilities. A history of poor health or poor nutrition may result in missed opportunities to acquire various skills and abilities. An individual's history of reward and punishment can shape what that person will achieve and how that person will react to others. In short, it is not enough to assess a student's current level of performance; those who assess must also understand what has shaped that current performance.

Contextual Factors

In addition to the skills, characteristics, and abilities a pupil brings to any task, other factors affect the assessment process. How another person interprets or reacts to various behaviors or characteristics can determine whether an individual will even be assessed. For example, some teachers do not understand that a certain amount of physical aggression is typical of young children or that verbal aggression is typical of older students. Such teachers may refer normally aggressive children for assessment because they have interpreted aggression as a symptom of some underlying problem.

The theoretical orientation of the diagnostician also plays an important part in the assessment process. Diagnosticians' backgrounds and training may predispose them to look for certain types of pathologies. Just as Freudians may look for unresolved conflicts and behaviorists may look for antecedents and consequences of particular behaviors, diagnosticians may let their own theoretical orientation color their interpretation of particular information.

Finally, the conditions under which a student is observed or the conditions under which particular behaviors are elicited can influence that student's performance. For example, the level of language used in a question or the presence of competing stimuli in the immediate environment can affect a pupil's responses.

Decision Making

Diagnosticians reach an understanding of a student by integrating information about current performance with information about current life circumstances and developmental history. They try to make sure that their understanding is not tainted by subjectivity or personal values and beliefs. Combined with their knowledge of appropriate practices and legal requirements, their understanding guides decision making and predictions about future performance. For example, a decision to classify a student as exceptional is reached when the assessor makes a judgment that, when all things are considered, the student fits a particular diagnostic category. Obviously, such a decision requires thorough knowledge of the criteria that define a category, in addition to detailed knowledge of the student and his or her current life circumstances.

● ● ● ● ● ● ● ● ● ● ● ● ● ● ● ● ● ● ● ●

Assessment Concerns

Decisions in school frequently have important, and occasionally lifelong, consequences. The procedures for gathering data and conducting assessments are matters that are rightfully of great concern to the general public—both individuals who are directly affected by the assessments (such as parents, students, and classroom teachers) and individuals who are indirectly affected (for example, taxpayers and elected officials). These matters are also of great concern to individuals and agencies that license or certify assessors to work in the schools. Finally, these matters are of great concern to the assessment community itself. For convenience, the concerns of these groups are discussed separately; however, the reader should recognize that many of the concerns overlap and are not the exclusive domain of one group or another. Thus, the final portion of this section discusses the social validity of an assessment in relationship to various groups.

Concerns of the General Public

The individuals who are affected by educational decisions are rightly concerned about assessment procedures. They want, and deserve, good decisions. However, any decision can have undesired consequences. Decision making creates "haves" and "have nots." Most people who take a test for a driver's license pass the test; some people fail the test and are denied driving privileges. College-entrance tests determine admission for some students and exclusion for others. In the same way, decisions about special and remedial education have consequences. Some consequences are desired, such as extra services for students who are entitled to special education. Other consequences are unwanted, such as denial of special-education services or diminished self-esteem resulting from a disability label.

Moreover, the desirability of some decisions varies, depending on the student. For example, a decision that a child is eligible for special education as a mentally retarded student may be greeted enthusiastically by some parents but roundly rejected by other parents. Concerns of laypeople generally surface when the educational decisions have undesired consequences and are viewed as undemocratic, elitist, or just unfair.

Fairness

Fairness is an imprecise concept both psychometrically and legally. It is probably best viewed as a marker for a class of conditions and situations in which the outcomes are thought to be disadvantageous, inaccurate, or wrong. Thus, issues of fairness usually imply dissatisfaction with an outcome. Allegations of unfair procedures might focus on any of the following complaints.

Lack of Opportunity   Equal opportunity to learn is a complex and often highly charged issue. The issue is not whether a student lacks a particular skill or whether an assessment fairly ascertains what skills a student does and does not possess. The issue is the meaning of absent skills and information. When a student lacks information and skill because of restricted or different opportunities to learn, inferences about what that lack of information or skill means must be made with the greatest of care. For example, tests of intelligence assume that test takers have had comparable opportunity to acquire the information and concepts elicited. When a student has not had that opportunity, inferences about intelligence are dubious. Lack of opportunity probably has as many causes as any social malady. The following list is intended to be not exhaustive, but illustrative.

- *Inadequate District Resources.* In most states, the costs of education are borne largely by local school districts, which rely on property taxes. Because the assessed value of property located within district boundaries varies from district to district, some districts have larger tax bases than others. Thus, the same rate of taxation produces less revenue in poor districts than in richer districts. Moreover, poorer districts usually tax at much higher rates while generating less revenue than wealthier districts. Limited district resources translate directly into lost opportunities for students: teachers with emergency certificates, rather than complete qualifications; curriculum narrowing, resulting in a lack of enrichment or advanced courses; old materials; lack of equipment such as computers, laboratory equipment, or equipment for vocational shop classes; and so forth.
- *Inadequate Instruction.* A teacher or a district's curriculum may not cover essential content, leading students to be tested on material and concepts that were never taught or were inadequately taught.
- *Student Deficiencies.* Through no fault of their own, students may be unable to take advantage of adequate resources. For example, acute or chronic illness may restrict a student's opportunity to learn material.
- *Inadequate Home Supervision.* Parents may not (a) ensure that children get enough sleep, (b) limit television viewing time, (c) encourage completion of homework, or (d) stress the value of education.

Ethnic and Gender Bias   Related to questions of opportunity are issues of ethnic, racial, and gender bias. Although we struggle to achieve a society in which the accomplishments of all individuals are valued, not all groups are treated equally. The issue of ensuring unbiased assessment for an individual from a minority group has a long history in the law, philosophy, and education. Three aspects of the issue are particularly relevant to this section of this book.

1. *Representation of Individuals from Diverse Backgrounds in Assessment Materials.* Test materials should present people of color and women in both nonstereotypic

and traditional roles and situations. It is widely believed that failure to do this has a chilling effect on students of color and young women and girls.

2. *Experiential Opportunities of Individuals from Diverse Backgrounds.* To the extent that students of color, girls, and young women undergo different acculturation, test materials should account for differences in experiential background for acquiring the tested skills, information, and values. For example, tests should have an equal number of questions that are more advantageous for males and questions that are more advantageous for females.[1] Alternatively, test makers could delete questions that elicit pronounced differences in results between males and females or among members of culturally diverse groups.

3. *Language and Concepts.* The language and concepts describing students of color and women and girls should not be racist or sexist.

Subjective Scoring   It is frequently thought to be inappropriate to assess student performance when the criteria for scoring student responses are subjective. Although students who receive the benefit of subjective scoring may not complain, assessors should be prepared to defend an indefensible position when questioned by students who are penalized by subjective scoring procedures. Most people would have trouble accepting scoring criteria that cannot be explicated; for example, a teacher might say to a student that this is a "B" paper without being able to explain how the paper differed from an "A" paper. A subjective criterion of "I know one when I see one" is seldom acceptable to people who have not produced "one."

Similarly, when instructors with the same background and qualifications as the assessor reach different judgments about a student's work, that judgment is seldom satisfactory to students who receive lower grades. For example, almost all the professors in the education department use one definition of a behavioral objective, but Professor Smith uses a different definition. When students are accustomed to producing objectives that meet the wider definition of all previous instructors, they may argue with Professor Smith's judgment in considering their objectives to be wrong.

Finally, if criteria for scoring are not explicit and objective, marking student answers wrong can lead to accusations of gender, racial, or ethnic discrimination.

Unequal Treatment   Students and parents expect marking standards to be applied consistently. Perhaps no situation is more troubling than when two students receive different scores for essentially the same product. When no cheating is suspected, one would expect student work to be marked uniformly.

Unfair Comparisons   People are frequently sensitive about the people with whom they (or their children) are compared. Thus, comparison groups should be appropriate. It would be inappropriate to compare an 8-year-old's elapsed time in a 100-meter dash with that of a 16-year-old. Moreover, comparative evaluations

---

1. This is usually determined empirically by identifying items on which either boys or girls score higher.

should make logical sense. For example, high school and college students frequently complain when examinations are graded on a curve because this practice requires that some students get lower grades. In the worst case, even students who knew the material well could receive a poor grade.

Finally, comparisons should take into account issues of diversity. Years ago, test publishers frequently excluded people of color from comparison groups used to establish norms; European American people were apparently thought to be the only people of interest. Such comparisons failed to take into account the potential impact of cultural differences associated with ethnic or racial differences. Today, most test authors and publishers have moved beyond such simplistic conceptualizations of comparison groups and have included individuals from all of the larger minority groups in the United States. Nonetheless, even these more broadly representative norms may be unsuitable for use with students who are members of smaller minority groups (those that make up 1 percent of the population or less). When testing students from numerically small minorities that differ substantially in acculturation, there is no simple answer to the question of whether to make normative comparisons. In some cases, where no inferences are made about underlying ability (for example, oral reading), normative comparison might be legitimate. In other cases (for example, in the assessment of intelligence or adaptive behavior), such comparisons are probably unwise.

Face Validity

An evaluation procedure should bear a logical relationship to the decision that is to be made. Although there is much more to valid assessment than the mere appearance of the test (see Chapter 8), what is being asked should make intuitive sense to the test taker or his or her parents. For example, an employment test should obviously have something to do with work to be done by the prospective employee. In the same way, school tests should be authentic, in that they should measure outcomes sought by the school.

Concerns of Certification Boards

Certification and licensure boards establish standards to ensure that assessors are appropriately qualified to conduct assessments, and these boards also sanction professionals for practicing beyond their competence. Test administration, scoring, and interpretation require different degrees of training and expertise, depending on the kind of test being administered and the degree of interpretation required to obtain meaning from the test taker's performance. Although most teachers can readily administer or learn to administer group intelligence and achievement tests, as well as classroom assessments of achievement, a person must have considerable training to score and interpret most individual intelligence and personality tests. Therefore, all states certify teachers and psychologists who work in the schools on the basis of formal training and sometimes the demonstration of competence.

When pupils are tested, we should be able to assume that the person doing the testing has adequate training to administer the test correctly. We also should be able to assume that the tester can establish rapport with pupils because students generally perform best in an atmosphere of trust and security. We further assume that the tester knows how to administer the test correctly. Testing consists of standardized presentation of stimuli. To the extent that the person giving the test does not correctly present the questions or materials, the obtained scores lose interpretability. We also assume that the person who administers a test knows how to score the test. Correct scoring is a prerequisite to attaining a meaningful picture of a student. Finally, we assume that accurate interpretations can and will be made.

Obviously, professionals should administer only those tests that they are qualified to administer. Too often, unfortunately, we hear of people with no training in individual intelligence testing who nonetheless administer individual intelligence tests, or we see people with no formal training in personality assessment administering or interpreting personality tests. Such tests may look easy enough to give; however, the correct administration, scoring, and interpretation are complex. Because tests are so often used to make decisions that will affect a child's future, having a skilled observer or tester is especially important.

Concerns of Assessors

Although those responsible for making educational decisions are also concerned with fair and valid testing, their concerns are generally more precise and detailed. There are four generally held areas of concern: accuracy, generalizability, meaning, and utility.

Accuracy

Accuracy is rightly considered a property of the diagnostician. Observations should not distort or incorrectly represent reality—diagnosticians must see what is there. No matter what form assessment takes, the diagnostician must always categorize a student's behavior or products. For example, in classifying behavior, an observer might ask the question, "Did Bob hit Harry?" In this case, the diagnostician uses explicit or implicit criteria to make a judgment about Bob's behavior; that is, the diagnostician has a definition of "hit" and decides whether Bob's behavior matches that definition. Similarly, when a diagnostician tests Bob, Bob's responses are classified as correct, partially correct, or incorrect; that is, the diagnostician has a definition of "correct" and decides whether Bob's response matches that definition.

Inaccuracies occur in assessment because a diagnostician has applied criteria incorrectly or inconsistently and therefore has made decisions that are in error. Errors occur when a diagnostician either allows a definition to drift or change over time or loses focus or objectivity. The situation in which observations are made has a substantial impact on the accuracy of the observations. For example, accuracy can be jeopardized when the behavior is difficult to observe, when there are too many behaviors to observe, when the decision rules are too complex, or when the definition of behavior is unclear or insufficiently detailed. As Chapter 7 shows, it is possible to estimate the accuracy of observations.

Generalizability

Seldom are educators and psychologists interested in a single behavior or response at one specific time in one context. Usually, diagnosticians want to generalize a student's performance along three dimensions: domain, times, and settings.

Generalization to a Larger Domain   Usually, diagnosticians want to generalize from a student's performance on a few questions to that student's performance on all other similar items. For example, when a student is given a math quiz containing ten multiplication facts, the teacher would like to infer that student's knowledge of all 100 multiplication facts. To allow generalization to other related performances, the sample of behavior must be sufficiently large. Moreover, the behavior sample must be representative of the domain. Thus, a teacher might be willing to generalize answering ten multiplication facts to general knowledge of multiplication facts but should be unwilling to infer skill in all facets of multiplication (such as solving problems with two multiplicands) because the sample is not representative of the entire domain.

Generalization to Other Times   In most cases, a diagnostician would like to assume that behavior observed on one occasion will be observed on similar future occasions. For example, if Kim knows ten multiplication facts today, we would like to assume that she will know those same facts tomorrow and next week. In this sense, every observation is a prediction.

Although assessments are usually stable, they are not invariably stable. Luck is not stable; a student who makes a lot of lucky guesses today may not be so lucky tomorrow. Behaviors and skills that are emerging are unlikely to be stable. For example, a student who is learning consonant sounds will not consistently give the correct sound for a consonant until the information is mastered.

Unusual conditions in the student being examined often produce unstable results. If Abdul has a cold or otitis media, he may not do what he is capable of doing otherwise on a test. Similarly, unusual conditions in the assessment setting may produce unstable results. For example, if Abdul is distracted during a test, his performance may not indicate what he usually can do.

Generalization to Other Settings   Just as assessors are concerned with generalization to larger domains and other times, they are also concerned with generalization to other settings. For example, if Jill reads accurately in school, we would like to assume that she can read materials of similar difficulty at home. When behavior and skills fail to generalize to other settings, teachers and psychologists frequently look for differences across the settings, in an attempt to ascertain what conditions or stimuli functionally control the behavior.

Meaning

Implicit in the preceding discussion is the idea that accurately observed and generalizable behavior may have meaning beyond what is directly observed. For example, a child's completion of a human-figure drawing may represent artistic ability, intellectual ability, various personality traits, or perceptual-motor skill. None of these constructs are observable; they are inferred from behavior and products that are observable, and the inferences to be made vary, depending on the student's opportunity to learn.

Students all come to school with unique background experiences in educational, social, and cultural environments—background experiences that are inextricably intertwined with their school experiences. Diagnosticians often must try to unravel these relationships. One of the most common examples is when psychologists assess a student's intellectual ability. To some extent, all tests of intelligence measure cultural learning in some form (for example, language, general information, and social values). Moreover, the inference drawn from the results of intellectual testing is that students who have learned more than other students from comparable backgrounds have more ability to learn.

However, when cultural backgrounds vary, differences in what has been learned cannot be attributed to the ability to learn. A simple example illustrates the problem. A child may be asked to name the four seasons of the year, and the correct (keyed) answer is "summer, fall, winter, and spring." However, in some parts of the country, many boys and girls associate seasons with hunting; thus, they might respond, "buck, doe, rabbit, and turkey." Their response, although not the keyed response, is not wrong; it represents different acculturation.

A similar problem occurs when commercially prepared achievement tests are used. When a student's curriculum does not address tested information (or does not address it comprehensively), the student has not had comparable opportunity to learn that information. Inferences about the student's ability to profit from instruction are, at best, tenuous.

Finally, acculturation is a matter of experiential background rather than of gender, skin color, race, or ethnic background (although one's acculturation may be associated with any of these). When we say that a child's acculturation differs from that of the majority, we are saying that the child's *experiential background* differs. It is that different experience, and not the child's ethnic origin, for example, that leads the child to respond differently from the children on whom the test was standardized.

Another way in which opportunity affects the meaning of a student's performance is the presence of a disability. Not only do students with disabilities frequently undergo different acculturation, but their sensory and physical limitations can have significant impact on tested performance. A test or an individual test item invariably measures an individual's ability to receive a stimulus and then express a response. Skill in the content area measured by a test cannot be measured accurately if meeting the stimulus and response demands of a question is beyond the capabilities of the student.

Common sense tells us that if a student cannot read directions or write responses, a test requiring these abilities is inappropriate. In such cases, the test measures inability in reading directions or writing answers, rather than skill or ability in the content being assessed. A student with a severe visual disability may know the content of a written test but earn a low score because of visual impairment. A student without arms may know the content of the test but may not answer any questions correctly because of an inability to write. Similarly, students with communication disorders may know the answers to the questions a tester asks but may be unable (or unwilling) to respond to even the most sensitively administered individual test that requires oral answers. Children with physical or sensory handicaps may also perform more slowly than nonhandicapped children; a test that awards points for the speed, as well as the accuracy, of response would not be a valid test of such a child's mastery of content.

A major clue to the meaningfulness of a test is the presence of individuals of different backgrounds and abilities in the standardization sample. When students from diverse backgrounds and with diverse physical abilities are included, test authors have the possibility of discovering whether their test materials are meaningful (as well as unbiased) for children from a variety of backgrounds. When students from diverse backgrounds and with diverse physical abilities are included in the norms in the same proportions in which they are found in the general population, the derived scores are potentially meaningful.

Utility

Finally, diagnosticians are concerned about the usefulness of their assessment procedures. Several topics could be considered in a discussion of utility, but two—efficiency and sensitivity—are particularly relevant for our purposes.

Efficiency   *Efficiency* refers to the speed and economy of data collection. Diagnosticians try to gather a wide variety of general information, sacrificing some accuracy to delineate the problem, and then focus their efforts with more accurate and sensitive, but time-consuming, assessments. Usually, highly accurate and specific information takes longer to accumulate than less accurate and less specific information.

For example, group-administered tests are far more efficient than individually administered tests. However, a group test often provides substantially less information than an individual test does. Most group tests survey content rather than provide detailed information about a student's abilities and weaknesses. In addition, valuable qualitative information cannot be collected because of the format of group tests. The examiner may provide oral directions for younger children, but for children beyond the fourth grade, the directions usually are written. The examiner typically cannot rephrase, probe, clarify, or prompt to elicit a student's best performance or control the tempo and pace of the testing or interrupt or terminate the test when a student becomes fatigued.

The scoring of group-administered tests is also more efficient because students usually write or mark answers rather than make extended responses that take more time to score; indeed, because most group tests are machine scored, examiners seldom see a student's responses to individual questions. Similarly, teacher judgments or ratings of behavior are more efficient to collect than systematic behavioral observations; however, behavioral observations tend to be more accurate and are usually less subject to various biases.

Sensitivity   *Sensitivity* refers to the ability of an assessment procedure to detect small differences across groups of students and within individual students. Sensitivity is especially important when assessments are made to ascertain whether students have made relatively small changes as a result of instruction or when diagnosticians want to make fine discriminations among test takers. For instruction to be both sensitive and efficient, the narrow range of development in which the student is functioning is assessed with sufficient items to discriminate. Thus, the teacher or psychologist must have an accurate idea of where a student currently functions.

Social Validity of Assessment

Social validity refers to consumers' access to and satisfaction with the assessment procedures. Three classes of consumers are relevant in this discussion: (1) parents and students, (2) diagnosticians, and (3) school administrators.

Parents and Students

For parents and students, social validity generally translates into issues of access and disposition. *Access* refers to the availability of the assessment. For example, can parents and students get to the physical location where the assessment will be conducted? Is the assessment scheduled at a convenient time? Because of the large number of families with a single parent or with two parents who work, finding a convenient time and location often means that teachers and psychologists must work outside of normal school hours. *Disposition* refers to the willingness of students or parents to complete the assessment. For students, this means giving their best efforts during assessment; for parents, this means cooperating during interviews, completing questionnaires, and participating in decision making.

Diagnosticians

For diagnosticians, social validity translates into issues of ease of administration and utility. If diagnosticians find a particular test or approach undesirable, it is less likely that they will use that approach. Many relatively worthwhile tests stay on the shelf because they are very difficult to administer or score. Others are not used because school personnel do not like the test items, format, or some other aspect of the test. Still others are not used because school personnel believe the measures provide meaningless or useless information.

School Administrators

For administrators, the acceptability of an assessment procedure often becomes an issue of money and risk management. A key responsibility of administrators is to manage money. Thus, when two assessment procedures produce comparable information, the less expensive one (in terms of both personnel time and direct cost) is preferred. Thus, procedures that result in fewer completed assessments or assessments that require overtime pay for diagnosticians are typically not used if there are comparable procedures that do not make such demands on resources. Similarly, if an assessment procedure increases the risk of litigation or due-process proceedings, it is less likely to be used than procedures with minimal risk.

. . . .

Summary

When a student is experiencing difficulty in school, the instruction the student has received is assessed to ascertain the probable cause of that student's difficulties. A curriculum is inappropriate when it is too easy or too hard; instruction can be ineffective because of poor classroom management (lack of organization, disruptive behavior, poor transitions, and so forth) or poor learning management (lack of opportunity for student practice, lack of feedback, failure to teach for higher-level thinking skills, and so forth). Students who experience difficulties and have had inadequate instruction should be given appropriate instruction before it is assumed that the students themselves are the root of the problem.

When instruction is deemed appropriate, the learners are assessed. A variety of information from multiple sources is usually collected or pulled together from existing data. This information may take the form of systematic or nonsystematic observations, interviews, rating scales, judgments of other professionals, and tests. Student performances may be evaluated by comparing them with the performances of other students or with an absolute standard (such as a criterion of 90% correct). This information is used to make predictions about students, either in their current situation or in some alternative (such as therapeutic) situation. A variety of factors are considered in reaching a prognosis: the student's family situation, community ties and friendships, physical ability and health, and developmental history.

Because the process of assessment is quite complex and educational decisions frequently have lifelong consequences, people are rightfully concerned about the entire process. Parents and the general public are frequently concerned about fairness, equal opportunity, ethnic and gender bias, and the appearance of proper assessment procedures. Individuals charged with overseeing the qualifications of persons conducting assessments are rightfully concerned about diagnostician qualifications and training. Also, diagnosticians themselves are concerned about the accuracy, generalizability, and meaning of the information they collect to facilitate decision making.

Questions for Chapter Review and Thought

1. Identify three different ways to begin an assessment. Describe an optimal sequence of activities for assessing a student.

2. What are two factors that may have a significant effect on a student's performance during assessment?

3. When and why might you want to administer a group test individually?

4. What is the difference between a norm-referenced and a criterion-referenced test? Cite an advantage of each.

5. How might you evaluate the extent to which students you assess are acculturated in a manner that is comparable to those in a test's norm group?

6. Lupe's parents have just moved into the area. Lupe is enrolled in second grade a few weeks before the annual standardized achievement tests are administered. The decision is made to let her take the tests in Mr. Peño's room, although he is not her teacher, because he speaks Spanish (the language that Lupe speaks at home). Is this sufficient to ensure test validity for Lupe? Why or why not?

7. In this text we identified several concerns about the fairness of assessments. Create a scenario for

each of at least two of the concerns, showing specifically the ways in which each is important to testing students with disabilities.

Resources for Further Investigation

Project

Interview a school principal or a person who tests students about the standardized achievement tests administered in a local school or school district. Specifically ask about how children with disabilities are involved in the standardized assessments. How do the policies and practices compare with those recommended in this textbook?

Print Resources

Boehm, A., & Weinberg, R. A. (1997). *The classroom observer: A guide for developing observation skills*. New York: Teachers College Press.

Christenson, S. L., & Ysseldyke, J. E. (1989). Assessing student performance: An important change is needed. *Journal of School Psychology, 27,* 409–426.

Deno, S. L. (1985). Curriculum-based assessment: The emerging alternative. *Exceptional Children, 52,* 219–232.

Deno, S. L. (1986). Formative evaluation of individual school programs: A new role for school psychologists. *School Psychology Review, 15,* 358–374.

Fuchs, L. S., & Fuchs, D. (Eds.). (1986). Linking assessment to instructional interventions: An overview. *School Psychology Review, 15.*

Howell, K. W. (1986). Direct assessment of academic performance. *School Psychology Review, 15,* 324–335.

Lentz, F. E., & Shapiro, E. S. (1986). Functional assessment of the academic environment. *School Psychology Review, 15,* 346–357.

Shapiro, E. S. (1996). *Academic skills problems: Direct assessment and intervention* (2nd ed.). New York: Guilford Press.

Shapiro, E. S., & Kratochwill, T. R. (Eds.) (1988). *Behavioral assessment in schools: Conceptual foundations and practical applications*. New York: Guilford Press.

Ysseldyke, J. E., & Christenson, S. L. (1987). Evaluating students' instructional environments. *Remedial and Special Education, 8,* 17–24.

Ysseldyke, J., & Christenson, S. (1993). *The Instructional Environmental System–II*. Longmont, CO: Sopris West.

Technology Resources

Pathways to School Improvement

http://www.ncrel.org/sdrs/pathwayg.htm

Click on the *Assessment* topic button to find information about critical issues in assessment and links to other assessment pages. Also, click on the search button to do a keyword search for articles about critical issues in assessment.

CRESST Home Page

http://crest96.cse.ucla.edu/index.htm

The National Center for Research on Evaluation, Standards, and Student Testing home page provides access to a large amount of assessment information, including newsletters, technical reports, videos, CD-ROMs, papers, and resources.

National Institute on Student Achievement, Curriculum & Assessment

http://www.ed.gov/offices/OERI/SAI

The National Institute on Student Achievement, Curriculum & Assessment home page has links to several sites that describe projects that are ongoing in areas such as assessment, content standards, and other research projects designed to improve student achievement.

Shippensburg University Institutional Research & Planning

http://www.ship.edu/~irp/irlinks.htm

Office of Educational Research and Improvement

http://www.ed.gov/offices/OERI/index.html

Psychwatch.com: Assessment & Evaluation Info for School Psychologists

http://www.psychwatch.com/school_assess.htm

Legal and Ethical Considerations in Assessment

Much of the practice of assessing students is the direct result of legislation, guidelines, and court cases. If you were to interview directors of special education in your area and ask them why students are assessed, they might initially tell you that students are assessed in order to provide information about how best to teach them. Pressed harder, these directors would probably tell you that students are assessed because assessment is required by law. They might also tell you that specific kinds of students (for example, some minority students) are not assessed because in some instances, such assessments have been forbidden by the court. Federal laws mandate that students be assessed before they are entitled to special-education services. Such laws also mandate that there be an individualized education program for every student with a disability and that instructional objectives for each of these students be derived from a comprehensive individualized assessment.

In this chapter, we first examine legislation that has affected assessment. We then talk about some of the ethical standards for assessment that have been developed by professional associations. We close the chapter by reviewing guidelines for the collection, maintenance, and dissemination of pupil records.

Laws

Six laws have had important effects on assessment practices: Section 504 of the Rehabilitation Act of 1973 (Public Law 93-112); the Education for All Handicapped Children Act of 1975 (Public Law 94-142); the 1986 Amendments to the

TABLE 3.1 ● *Major Federal Laws and Their Key Provisions*

Act	Provisions
Section 504 of the Rehabilitation Act of 1973 (Public Law 93-112)	It is illegal to deny participation in activities or benefits of programs, or to in any way discriminate against a person with a disability solely because of the disability. Individuals with disabilities must have equal access to programs and services. Auxiliary aids must be provided to individuals with impaired speaking, manual, or sensory skills.
Education for All Handicapped Children Act of 1975 (Public Law 94-142)	Students with disabilities have the right to a free, appropriate public education. Schools must have on file an individualized education program for each student determined to be eligible for services under the act. Parents have the right to inspect school records on their children. When changes are made in a student's educational placement or program, parents must be informed. Parents have the right to challenge what is in records or to challenge changes in placement. Students with disabilities have the right to be educated in the least restrictive educational environment. Students with disabilities must be assessed in ways that are considered fair and nondiscriminatory. They have specific protections.
1986 Amendments to the Education for All Handicapped Children Act (Public Law 99-457)	All rights of the Education for All Handicapped Children Act are extended to preschoolers with disabilities. Each school district must conduct a multidisciplinary assessment and develop an individualized family service plan (IFSP) for each preschool child with a disability.
Individuals with Disabilities Education Act of 1990 (IDEA; Public Law 101-476)	This act reauthorizes the Education for All Handicapped Children Act. Two new disability categories (traumatic brain injury and autism) are added to the definition of students with disabilities. A comprehensive definition of transition services is added.
Americans with Disabilities Act of 1992 (Public Law 101-336)	Discrimination on the basis of disability is prohibited in employment, services rendered by state and local governments, places of public accommodation, transportation, and telecommunication services.
1997 Amendments to the Individuals with Disabilities Education Act (Public Law 105-17).	These amendments added a number of significant provisions to IDEA and restructured the law. A number of changes in the IEP and participation of students with disabilities in state- and districtwide assessments are mandated. Significant provisions on mediation of disputes and discipline of students with disabilities are added. Funding of special education is restructured.

Education for All Handicapped Children Act (Public Law 99-457); the Individuals with Disabilities Education Act of 1990 (IDEA; Public Law 101-476); the Americans with Disabilities Act of 1992 (Public Law 101-336); and the 1997 Amendments to the Individuals with Disabilities Education Act (Public Law 105-17). Table 3.1 lists the major provisions of these six laws.

Section 504 of the Rehabilitation Act of 1973

Section 504 of the Rehabilitation Act of 1973 (Public Law 93-112) prohibits discrimination against persons with disabilities. The act states,

> No otherwise qualified handicapped individual shall, solely by reason of his handicap, be excluded from the participation in, be denied the benefits of, or be subjected to discrimination in any program or activity receiving federal financial assistance.

If the Office of Civil Rights (OCR) of the U.S. Department of Education finds that a state education agency (SEA) or local education agency (LEA) is not in compliance with Section 504, and that district chooses not to act to correct the noncompliance, OCR may withhold federal funds from that SEA or LEA.

Most of the provisions of Section 504 were incorporated into and expanded in the Education for All Handicapped Children Act of 1975 (Public Law 94-142) and the Americans with Disabilities Act of 1992 (Public Law 101-336). Section 504 and the Americans with Disabilities Act are broader than the Education for All Handicapped Children Act because their provisions are not restricted to a specific age group or to education. Section 504 is the law most often cited in court cases involving either employment of people with disabilities or appropriate education in colleges and universities for students with disabilities. Section 504 has been used to secure services for students with conditions not formally listed in the disabilities education legislation. For example, since the 1980s, Section 504 has been used to get services for students who have attention deficit disorders (ADD/ADHD), which are not classified as disabilities within the Individuals with Disabilities Education Act.

The Education for All Handicapped Children Act of 1975

Education is a responsibility of the state rather than the federal government. No provision of the U.S. Constitution mandates education. Yet every state has compulsory education laws, which require students to attend school. In 1975, the U.S. Congress passed a compulsory special-education law, the Education for All Handicapped Children Act (often known by its congressional number, Public Law 94-142). That law was designed to serve four major purposes:

1. To guarantee that special-education services are available to children who need them

2. To ensure that decisions about providing services to students with disabilities are made in fair and appropriate ways

3. To set clear management and auditing requirements and procedures for special education at all levels of government

4. To provide federal funds to help states educate students with disabilities

Much of what happens in assessment is directly mandated by one of the four provisions of Public Law 94-142. These provisions are described in the section on the 1997 Amendments to IDEA.

The 1986 Amendments to the Education for All Handicapped Children Act

In 1986, Congress passed a major set of amendments to the Education for All Handicapped Children Act, extending all rights and protections of the law to preschoolers with disabilities. The provisions of this set of amendments, Public Law 99-457, required states to provide a free appropriate public education to children ages 3 through 5 years with disabilities by school year 1990–1991. In addition, these amendments provided grants to states so they could offer interdisciplinary educational services both to infants and toddlers with disabilities and to their families. Thus, states now have a significant incentive to serve children with disabilities from birth through age 2 years. This bill also expanded Public Law 94-142 by requiring that noneducational federal, state, and local resources and services be made available to all children with disabilities. Federal or state-funded agencies other than schools can no longer argue that they cannot provide services to children if the services can be provided by schools.

Public Law 99-457 specified that each school district use a multidisciplinary assessment to develop an individualized family service plan (IFSP) for each child. The IFSP must include the following:

* A statement of the child's present level of cognitive, social, speech and language, and self-help development
* A statement of the family's strengths and needs related to enhancing the child's development
* A statement of the major outcomes expected for the child and family
* Criteria, procedures, and timelines for measuring progress
* A statement of the specific early intervention services necessary to meet the unique needs of the child and family, including methods, frequency, and intensity of service
* Projected dates for initiation and expected duration of services
* The name of the person who will manage the case
* Procedures for transition from early intervention into a preschool program.

The Individuals with Disabilities Education Act (IDEA)

The Individuals with Disabilities Education Act of 1990 (IDEA; Public Law 101-476) is a reauthorization of Public Law 94-142. Congress renamed the Education for All Handicapped Children Act and reaffirmed a national intention to support alternative education for students with special learning needs. To reflect contemporary practices, Congress replaced references to "handicapped children" with "children with disabilities." Two new disability categories (autism and traumatic brain injury) were added, and a comprehensive definition of *transition services* (services to ensure smooth movement from school to postschool activities) was added. The law also specified that schools must develop individualized transition plans for students who are 16 years of age or older.

The Americans with Disabilities Act (ADA)

The purpose of the Americans with Disabilities Act of 1992 (ADA; Public Law 101-336) is to extend to people with disabilities civil rights equal to those guaranteed without regard to race, color, national origin, gender, and religion through the Civil Rights Act of 1964. ADA prohibited discrimination on the basis of disability in employment, in the provision of services by state and local governments, in places of public accommodation, in the provision of transportation, and in the provision of telecommunication services, such as phones. It said that employers cannot discriminate against individuals with disabilities. Employers must use employment application procedures (including assessments) that enable individuals with disabilities to apply for jobs. In making decisions about whom to hire, promote, or discharge, employers are not allowed to take into account a person's disability. Individuals with disabilities should not be paid differently from others, they have the same rights to job training, and they are to have the same privileges of employment as others.

1997 Amendments to the Individuals with Disabilities Education Act (1997 IDEA)

The IDEA amendments of 1997 clarified and added to the 1990 IDEA. In the following sections we describe those parts of the law that are directly applicable to assessment of students with disabilities.

The Individualized Education Program (IEP) Provisions

Public Law 94-142 specified that all students with disabilities have the right to a free, appropriate public education and that schools must have an individualized education plan (IEP) for each student with a disability. In the IEP, school personnel must specify the long-term and short-term goals of the instructional program. IEPs must be based on a comprehensive assessment by a multidisciplinary team. We stress that assessment data are collected for the purpose of helping team members specify the components of the IEP. The team must specify not only goals and objectives but also plans for implementing the instructional program. They must specify how and when progress toward accomplishment of objectives will be evaluated. Figure 3.1 illustrates an IEP for a student in a Minnesota school district. Note that specific assessment activities that form the basis for the program are

FIGURE 3.1   An Individualized Education Program

INDIVIDUALIZED EDUCATION PROGRAM   11/11/00

       Date

Thompson   *J.*

STUDENT: Last Name   First   Middle

                        5.3   8/4/90

School of Attendance   Home School   Grade Level   Birthdate/Age

School Address   School Telephone Number

Child Study Team Members   *LD Teacher*

                        Case Manager

       Homeroom   *Parents*

Name   Title   Name   Title

       Facilitator

Name   Title   Name   Title

       Speech

Name   Title   Name   Title

Summary of Assessment Results

IDENTIFIED STUDENT NEEDS: *Reading from last half of DISTAR II – present performance level*

LONG-TERM GOALS: *To improve reading achievement level by at least one year's gain. To improve math achievement to grade level. To improve language skills by one year's gain.*

SHORT-TERM GOALS: *Master Level 4 vocabulary and reading skills. Master math skills in basic curriculum. Master spelling words from Level 3 list. Complete units 1-9 from Level 3 curriculum.*

MAINSTREAM MODIFICATIONS:

(continued)

Description of Services to Be Provided

Type of service	Teacher	Starting date	Amt. of time per day	OBJECTIVES AND CRITERIA FOR ATTAINMENT
SLD Level III	LD Teacher	11/11/00	2½ hrs	*Reading:* Will know all vocabulary through the "Honeycomb" level. Will master skills as presented through DISTAR II. Will know 123 sound-symbols presented in "Sound Way to Reading." *Math:* Will pass all tests at basic 4 level. *Spelling:* 5 words each week from Level 3 list. *Language:* Will complete units 1-9 of the grade 4 language program. Will also complete supplemental units from "Language Step by Step."

Mainstream classes	Teacher	Amt. of time per day	OBJECTIVES AND CRITERIA FOR ATTAINMENT
		3½ hrs	*Out-of-seat behavior:* Sit attentively and listen during mainstream class discussions. A simple management plan will be implemented if he does not meet this expectation. *Mainstream modifications of social studies:* Will keep a folder in which he expresses through drawing the topics his class will cover. Modified district social studies curriculum. No formal testing will be done. An oral reader will read text to him, and oral questions will be asked.

The following equipment, and other changes in personnel, transportation, curriculum, methods, and educational services will be made:

DISTAR II reading program spelling Level 3; "Sound Way to Reading" program; vocabulary tapes

Substantiation of least restrictive alternatives: *The planning team has determined the student's academic needs are best met with direct SLD support in reading, math, language, and spelling.*

Anticipated Length of Plan: __1 yr__   The next periodic review will be held: __May 2001__

☐ I do approve this program placement and the above IEP

☐ I do not approve this placement and/or the IEP

☐ I request a conciliation conference

_____
PARENT/GUARDIAN

_____
PRINCIPAL or Designee

listed, as are specific instructional goals or objectives. IEPs are to be formulated by a multidisciplinary child study team that meets with the parents. Parents have the right to agree or disagree with the contents of the program.

In 1997 amendments, Congress mandated a number of changes to the IEP. The core IEP team was expanded to include both a special-education teacher and a general-education teacher. The new law also specified that students with disabilities are to be included in state- and districtwide assessments and that states must report on the performance and progress of all students, including students with disabilities. The IEP team must decide whether the student will take the test with or without accommodations or take an alternative assessment.

Protection in Evaluation Procedures (PEP) Provisions

Congress included a number of specific requirements in Public Law 94-142. These requirements were designed to protect students and help ensure that assessment procedures and activities would be fair, equitable, and nondiscriminatory. Specifically, Congress mandated eight provisions:

1. Tests are to be selected and administered so as to be racially and culturally nondiscriminatory.

2. To the extent feasible, students are to be assessed in their native language or primary mode of communication (such as American Sign Language and communication board).

3. Tests must have been validated for the specific purpose for which they are used.

4. Tests must be administered by trained personnel in conformance with the instructions provided by the test producer.

5. Tests used with students must include those designed to provide information about specific educational needs, not just a general intelligence quotient.

6. Decisions about students are to be based on more than their performance on a single test.

7. Evaluations are to be made by a multidisciplinary team that includes at least one teacher or other specialist with knowledge in the area of suspected disability.

8. Children must be assessed in all areas related to a specific disability, including— where appropriate—health, vision, hearing, social and emotional status, general intelligence, academic performance, communicative skills, and motor skills.

Least Restrictive Environment (LRE) Provisions

In writing the Education for All Handicapped Children Act, Congress wanted to ensure that, to the greatest extent appropriate, students with disabilities would be placed in settings that would maximize their opportunities to interact with students without disabilities. Section 612(S)(B) states,

> To the maximum extent appropriate, handicapped children . . . are educated with children who are not handicapped, and that special classes, separate schooling, or other re-

moval of handicapped children from the regular educational environment occurs only when the nature or the severity of the handicap is such that education in regular classes with the use of supplementary aids and services cannot be achieved satisfactorily.

The LRE provisions arose out of court cases in which state and federal courts had ruled that when two equally appropriate placements were available for a student with a disability, the most normal (that is, least restrictive) placement was preferred.

Due-Process Provisions

In Section 615 of Public Law 94-142, Congress specified the procedures that schools and school personnel would have to follow to ensure due process in decision making. Specifically, when a decision affecting identification, evaluation, or placement of a student with disabilities is to be made, the student's parents or guardians must be given both the opportunity to be heard and the right to have an impartial due-process hearing to resolve conflicting opinions.

Schools must provide opportunities for parents to inspect the records that are kept on their children and to challenge material that they believe should not be included in those records. Parents have the right to have their child evaluated by an independent party and to have the results of that evaluation considered when psychoeducational decisions are made. In addition, parents must receive written notification before any education agency can begin an evaluation that might result in changes in the placement of a student.

In the 1997 amendments to IDEA, Congress specified that states must offer mediation as a voluntary option to parents and educators as an initial part of dispute resolution. If mediation is not successful, either party may request a due-process hearing.

● ●

Ethical Considerations

Professionals who assess students have the responsibility to engage in ethical behavior. Many professional associations have put together sets of ethical standards to guide the practice of their members; many of these standards relate directly to assessment practices. Here we cite a number of important ethical considerations, borrowing heavily from the American Psychological Association's *Ethical Principles of Psychologists and Code of Conduct* (APA, 1992) and the National Association of School Psychologists' *Principles for Professional Ethics* (NASP, 1997). We have not cited the standards explicitly, but we have distilled from them a number of specific ethical considerations.

Responsibility for the Consequences of Professional Work

The assessment of students is a social act that has specific social and educational consequences. Those who assess students use assessment data to make decisions about the students, and these decisions can significantly affect an individual's life opportunities. Those who assess students must accept responsibility for the consequences of their work, and they must make every effort to be certain that their services are used appropriately. In short, they are committed to the application of professional expertise to promote improvement in the quality of life available to the student, family, school, and community. For the individual who assesses students, this ethical standard may mean refusing to engage in assessment activities that are desired by a school system but that are clearly inappropriate.

Recognizing the Boundaries of Professional Competence

Those who are entrusted with the responsibility for assessing and making decisions about students have differing degrees of competence. Not only must professionals regularly engage in self-assessment to be aware of their own limitations, but they should also recognize the limitations of the techniques they use. For individuals, this sometimes means refusing to engage in activities in areas in which they lack competence. It also means using techniques that meet recognized standards and engaging in the continuing education necessary to maintain high standards of competence.

As schools become increasingly diverse, professionals must demonstrate sensitivity in working with people from different cultural and linguistic backgrounds and with children who have different types of disabling conditions. Assessors should have experience working with students of diverse backgrounds and should demonstrate competence in doing so, or they should refrain from assessing and making decisions about such students.

Confidentiality of Information

Those who assess students regularly obtain a considerable amount of very personal information about those students. Such information must be held in strict confidence. A general ethical principle held by most professional organizations is that confidentiality may be broken only when there is clear and imminent danger to an individual or to society. Results of pupil performance on tests must not be discussed informally with school staff members. Formal reports of pupil performance on tests must be released only with the permission of the persons tested or their parents or guardians.

Those who assess students are to make provisions for maintaining confidentiality in the storage and disposal of records. When working with minors or other persons who are unable to give voluntary informed consent, assessors are to take special care to protect these persons' best interests.

Adherence to Professional Standards on Assessment

A joint committee of the American Educational Research Association, the American Psychological Association, and the National Council on Measurement in

Education publishes a document entitled *Standards for Educational and Psychological Testing*. These standards specify a set of requirements for test development and use. It is imperative that those who develop tests behave in accordance with the standards and that those who assess students use instruments and techniques that meet the standards.

In Parts 3 and 4 of this text, we review commonly used tests and talk about the extent to which those tests meet the standards. We provide information to help test users make informed judgments about the technical adequacy of specific tests. There is no federal or state agency that acts to limit the publication or use of technically inadequate tests. Only by refusing to use technically inadequate tests will users force developers to improve them. After all, if you were a test developer, would you continue to publish a test that few people purchased and used? Would you invest your company's resources to make changes in a technically inadequate test that yielded a large annual profit to your firm if people continued to buy and use it the way it was?

Test Security

Those who assess students are expected to maintain test security. It is expected that assessors will not reveal to others the content of specific tests or test items. At the same time, assessors must be willing and able to back up with test data decisions that may adversely affect individuals.

● ● ● ● ● ● ● ● ● ● ● ● ● ● ● ● ● ● ● ●

Pupil Records: Collection, Maintenance, and Dissemination

Policies and standards for the collection, maintenance, and dissemination of information about children must balance two sometimes conflicting needs. Parents and children have a basic right to privacy; schools need to collect and use information about children (and sometimes parents) in order to plan appropriate educational programs. Schools and parents have a common goal: to promote the welfare of children. In theory, schools and parents should agree on what constitutes and promotes a child's welfare, and in practice, schools and parents generally do work cooperatively.

Yet there have been situations in which there has been no cooperation, or in which schools have operated against the best interests and basic rights of children and parents. School personnel have often flagrantly disregarded the rights to privacy of parents and children. Educationally irrelevant information about the personal lives of parents, as well as subjective, impressionistic, unverified information about parents and children, has been amassed by some schools. Parents and children have been denied access to pupil records, and therefore they have effectively been denied the opportunity to challenge, correct, or supplement those records. On the other hand, schools have on occasion irresponsibly released pupil information to public and private agencies that had no legitimate need for or right to the information. Worse yet, parents and children were often not even informed that the information had been accumulated or released.

Abuses in the collection, maintenance, and dissemination of pupil information were of sufficient magnitude that the Russell Sage Foundation convened a conference in 1969 to deal with the problem. The voluntary guidelines that were developed at the Russell Sage Foundation conference (Goslin, 1969) have been widely accepted, implemented, and incorporated into federal laws.

In 1974, many of these recommended guidelines became federal law when the Family Educational Rights and Privacy Act (Public Law 93-380, commonly called the Buckley amendment) was enacted. The basic provisions of the act are quite simple. All educational agencies that accept federal money (preschools, elementary and secondary schools, community colleges, and colleges and universities) must grant parents the opportunity to inspect and challenge student records; if records are found to be inaccurate, parents have the right to correct them. The only records to which parental access may be denied are the personal notes of teachers, supervisors, administrators, and other educational personnel that are kept in the sole possession of the maker of the records. (Students age 18 years or older are given the same rights as parents in regard to their own records.) Also, educational agencies must not release identifiable data without the parents' written consent. Violators of the provisions of the Family Educational Rights and Privacy Act are subject to sanctions; federal funds may be withheld from agencies found to be in violation of the law.

The remainder of this chapter deals with specific issues and principles in the collection, maintenance, and dissemination of pupil information.

Collection of Pupil Information

Schools collect massive amounts of information about individual pupils and their parents. As we said in Chapter 1, information can be used for a number of legitimate educational decisions: special assistance, referral, screening, exceptionality, eligibility, instructional planning, pupil-evaluation, setting, and program-evaluation decisions. Considerable data must be collected if a school system is to function effectively, both in delivering educational services to children and in reporting the results of its educational programs to the various community, state, and federal agencies to which it may be responsible.

Consent

In its section on procedural safeguards, the Individuals with Disabilities Education Act mandates that prior written notice be given to the parents or guardians of a child whenever an educational agency proposes to initiate or change (or refuses to initiate or change) either the identification, evaluation, or educational placement of the child or the provision of a free and appropriate education to the child. It further requires that the notice fully inform the parent, in the parent's native language, regarding all appeal procedures available. Thus, schools must inform parents of their right to present any and all complaints regarding the identification, evaluation, or placement of their child, their right to an impartial due-process hearing, and their right to appeal decisions reached at a due-process hearing, if necessary, by bringing civil action against a school district.

The collection of research data requires the individual informed consent of parents. Various professional groups, such as the American Psychological Association and the National Association of School Psychologists, consider the collection of data without informed consent to be unethical; according to the Buckley amendment, it is *illegal* to experiment with children without prior informed consent. Typically, informed consent for research-related data collection requires that the pupil or parents understand (a) the purpose of and procedures involved in the investigations, (b) any risks inherent in participation in the research, (c) the fact that all participants will remain anonymous, and (d) the participants' option to withdraw from the research at any time.

Verification

Verifying information means ascertaining or confirming the information's truth, accuracy, or correctness. Depending on the type of information, verification may take several forms. For observations or ratings, verification means confirmation by another individual. For standardized test data, verification means conducting a reliable and valid assessment.[1]

Unverified information can be collected, but every attempt should be made to verify such information before it is retained in a student's records. For example, serious misconduct or extremely withdrawn behavior is of direct concern to the schools. Initial reports of such behavior by a teacher or counselor are typically based on unverified observations. The unverified information provides hints, hypotheses, and starting points for diagnosis. However, if the data are not confirmable, they should not be collected and must not be retained. Similarly, data from unreliable tests should, we believe, be considered unverified information unless other data are presented to confirm the results.

Maintenance of Pupil Information

The decision to keep test results and other information should be governed by three principles: (1) retention of pupil information for limited periods of time, (2) parental rights of inspection and amendment, and (3) assurance of protection against inappropriate snooping. First, the information should be retained only as long as there is a continuing need for it. Only verified data of clear educational value should be retained. A pupil's school records should be periodically examined, and information that is no longer educationally relevant or no longer accurate should be removed. Natural transition points (for example, promotion from

1. The concepts of reliability and validity are defined and discussed in detail in Chapters 7 and 8.

elementary school to junior high) should always be used to remove material from students' files.

The second major principle in the maintenance of pupil information is that parents have the right to inspect, challenge, and supplement student records. Parents of children with disabilities or with special gifts and talents have had the right to inspect, challenge, and supplement their children's school records for some time. Parents or guardians must be given the opportunity to examine all relevant records with respect to the identification, evaluation, and educational placement of the child and the free and appropriate public education of the child, and the opportunity to obtain an independent evaluation of the child. Again, if parents have complaints, they may request an impartial due-process hearing to challenge either the records or the school's decision regarding their child. The 1997 reauthorization of IDEA specifies further that parents have the right to (a) be accompanied and advised by counsel and by individuals with special knowledge or training with respect to the problems of children with disabilities, (b) present evidence and confront, cross-examine, and compel the attendance of witnesses, (c) have a written or electronic verbatim record of such a hearing, and (d) have written findings of facts and decisions.

The third major principle in the maintenance of pupil records is that the records should be protected from snoopers, both inside and outside the school system. In the past, secretaries, custodians, and even other students have had access, at least potentially, to pupil records. Curious teachers and administrators who had no legitimate educational interest had access. Individuals outside the schools, such as credit bureaus, have often found it easy to obtain information about former or current students. To make sure that only individuals with a legitimate need have access to the information contained in a pupil's records, it is recommended that pupil records be kept under lock and key. Adequate security mechanisms are necessary to ensure that the information in a pupil's records is not available to unauthorized personnel.

Dissemination of Pupil Information

Educators need to consider both access to information by officials and dissemination of information to individuals and agencies outside the school. In both cases, the guiding principles are (a) the protection of pupils' and parents' rights to privacy and (b) the legitimate need to know particular information, as demonstrated by the person or agency to whom the information is disseminated.

Access Within the Schools

Those desiring access to pupil records should sign a form stating why they need to inspect the records; a list of people who have had access to their child's files and the reasons why access was sought should be available to parents. The provisions of the Buckley amendment state that

> All persons, agencies, or organizations desiring access to the records of a student shall be required to sign a written form which shall be kept permanently with the file of the

student, but only for inspection by the parents or student, indicating specifically the legitimate educational or other interest that each person, agency, or organization has in seeking this information. (§ 438, 4A)

When a pupil transfers from one school district to another, that pupil's records are also transferred. The Buckley amendment is very specific as to the conditions of transfer. When a pupil's file is transferred to another school or school system in which the pupil plans to enroll, the school must (1) notify the pupil's parents that the records have been transferred, (2) send the parents a copy of the transferred records if the parents so desire, and (3) provide the parents with an opportunity to challenge the content of the transferred data.

Access for Individuals and Agencies Outside the Schools

School personnel collect information about pupils enrolled in the school system for educationally relevant purposes. There is an implicit agreement between the schools and the parents that the only justification for collecting and keeping any pupil data is educational relevance. However, because the schools have so much information about pupils, they are often asked for pupil data by potential employers, credit agencies, insurance companies, police, the armed services, the courts, and various social agencies. To divulge information to any of these sources is a violation of this implicit trust, unless the pupil (if over age 18) or the parents request that the information be released. Note that the courts and various administrative agencies have the power to subpoena pupil records from schools. In such cases, the Buckley amendment requires that the parents be notified that the records will be turned over in compliance with the subpoena.

Except in the case of the subpoena of records or the transfer of records to another school district, no school personnel should release any pupil information without the written consent of the parents. The Buckley amendment states that no educational agency may release pupil information unless "there is written consent from the student's parents specifying records to be released, the reasons for such release, and to whom, and with a copy of the records to be released to the student's parents and the student if desired by the parents" (§ 438, b2A).

Communicating in Language the General Public Can Understand

Those who assess students have a responsibility to make certain that the information they disseminate is put in the hands of authorized persons and is used to help the individual assessed. Assessment findings are to be communicated in language readily understood by the school staff members. In communicating written information, those who assess students must be certain that their interpretations of test results are clear and in language that is easily understood so that the information may be used for the betterment of the student assessed.

Summary

The practice of assessing students takes place in a social, political, and legal context. Much assessment takes place because it is mandated by law. School personnel are required to assess students before declaring them eligible for special-education services. The major piece of legislation that currently serves as a guide for assessment activities is the 1997 Amendments to the Individuals with Disabilities Education Act (Public Law 105-17). The law reauthorized the Individuals with Disabilities Education Act (Public Law 101-476), which included provisions specifying that (a) schools must have individualized education programs for students, (b) students must be educated in least restrictive environments, and (c) students who are assessed have due-process rights. The law also specified a number of ways in which students who are evaluated are to be protected.

Public Law 99-457, a set of amendments to the Education for All Handicapped Children Act, was enacted in 1986 (a) to extend the right to an education to include preschoolers with disabilities and (b) to extend the right to noneducational federal, state, and local resources and services to all children with disabilities.

Those who assess students have certain ethical responsibilities. They are responsible for the consequences of their actions and for recognizing the limits of their competence. There are specific requirements for confidentiality of information obtained in assessment and for keeping the content of tests secure. Those who assess students should adhere to the professional standards outlined in *Standards for Educational and Psychological Testing*.

Schools are entrusted with the lives of children. Each day, decisions are made that are intended to be in the children's best interests. These decisions are based on both objective information and professional interpretation of that information. The schools must exercise their power over the lives of children very carefully. When school personnel collect data, they must make sure that the data are educationally relevant; their authority does not include the power to snoop and pry needlessly. The schools need latitude in deciding what information is educationally relevant, but the parents must have the right to check and halt the school's attempts to collect some types of information. Parents' informed consent to the collection of information about their children is basic to the family's right to privacy.

The schools should periodically examine all pupil records and destroy all information that is not of immediate or long-term utility or that has not been verified. The information that is retained must be guarded. Parents and students over age 18 years must be given the opportunity to examine records, to correct or delete information, and to supplement the data contained in files. Sometimes the release of information that has been gathered could be damaging or embarrassing to children and their families. Schools must not release data to outside agencies except under subpoena or with the written consent of parents or a pupil who is over age 18. As in all areas of testing and data maintenance, common sense and common decency are required.

Questions for Chapter Review and Thought

1. What were the major purposes of Public Law 94-142, the Education for All Handicapped Children Act of 1975? How did the 1997 Amendments to the Individuals with Disabilities Education Act update Public Law 94-142? What new provisions were added?

2. What four things must be specified in an individualized education plan (IEP)?

3. Identify and explain the importance of three ethical considerations that are relevant to assessment practices.

4. Assume that you are a researcher who is about to conduct a study on reading comprehension in the schools. Write a letter to the parent of a potential subject that would meet the requirements of the law regarding informed consent about research participation. Make up information about the study if you need to do so, but be as brief as you can, remembering that parents will differ in research sophistication and reading ability.

Resources for Further Investigation

Project

Visit various special-education settings (regular classrooms, resource rooms, self-contained classrooms, special schools). Write or discuss how each can be described as a least restrictive appropriate environment for an individual student.

Print Resources

American Educational Research Association, American Psychological Association, and National Council on Measurement in Education. (1997). *Standards for educational and psychological testing.* Washington, DC: American Psychological Association.

Rothstein, L. F. (1995). *Special education law.* White Plains, NY: Longman.

Sage, D. D., & Burrello, L. C. (1988). *Public policy and management in special education.* Englewood Cliffs, NJ: Prentice-Hall.

Yell, M. (1998). *The law and special education.* Upper Saddle River, NJ: Prentice-Hall.

Ysseldyke, J. E., Algozzine, B., & Thurlow, M. L. (1999). *Critical issues in special education* (3rd ed.). Boston: Houghton Mifflin. (Chapter 8: Legal issues in special education)

Zerkel, P., & Richardson, S. N. (1988). *A digest of Supreme Court decisions affecting education* (2nd ed.). Bloomington, IN: Phi Delta Kappa Educational Foundation.

Technology Resources

EDLAW, Inc.

http://www.edlaw.net/

EDLAW, Inc., provides access to legal documents associated with the Individuals with Disabilities Education ACT (IDEA), selected IDEA regulations, Section 504 of the Rehabilitation Act, and related education resources. There is also a link to a home page of legal briefs concerning education.

The Individuals with Disabilities Education Act (IDEA) Amendments of 1997

http://www.ed.gov/offices/Osers/IDEA/index.html

This web site explains the IDEA amendments that were proposed in 1997 to improve the law.

The Resource Center

http://www.educ.drake.edu/rc/rc.html

The mission of the Resource Center is to create, promote, and facilitate positive changes in the systems serving individuals with disabilities, those with other diverse needs, and the families of these individuals. This web site contains links to several resources, including the federal government.

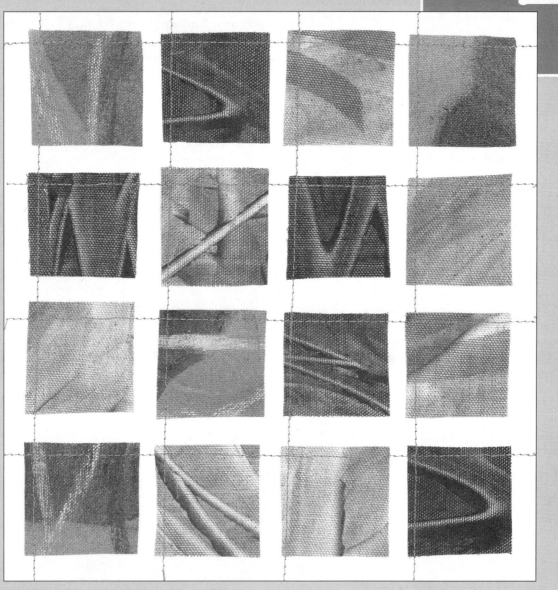

part 2

Basic Concepts of Measurement

Part 2 deals with basic statistical and measurement concepts. Chapter 4 is intended for the person with little or no background in descriptive statistics; it contains a discussion of the major concepts necessary for understanding most of the remaining chapters in this part and later parts of the book. Chapter 5 discusses the scores typically used in norm-referenced and criterion-referenced assessment. The most frequently used scores in norm-referenced assessment compare a student with other students who make up the test norms. Criterion-referenced scores are most often used in classrooms. The two most useful types of criterion-referenced scores are percentage correct (accuracy) and rate of correct responses (fluency). Chapter 6 discusses how normative samples are usually obtained and the important characteristics of individuals in these samples. Chapter 7 provides an introduction to reliability and is often the most difficult chapter for students. This chapter deals with (a) the important concept that scores are fallible and (b) the amount of error associated with scores. Chapter 8, the last chapter in this part of the text, introduces the concept of test validity. *Validity,* the extent to which a test or other procedure leads to valid inferences about tested performance, is *the* most important and inclusive aspect of a test's technical adequacy.

Basic statistics and psychometric theory are the foundation of test development and use. Neither subject is easy to master, but both are important. The development and use of tests by people who lack understanding of either statistics or theory have resulted in many abuses in educational evaluation and decision making. This is the rationale for including Part 2. We realize that numbers and formulas often scare both beginning students and seasoned veterans. Yet, they sit at the heart of testing. Everyone who uses tests and test results must understand both in order to evaluate students fairly and intelligently.

The reader should bear in mind that many nuances and subtleties of basic statistics and measurement are not discussed, and no derivations or proofs are presented. We explain psychometric theory from a classical perspective and provide equations and computational examples to show how particular numbers are obtained, as well as to provide material for a logical understanding of critical measurement concepts. However, some widely used tests are constructed using item-response (or latent trait) theory; we provide a brief overview of this procedure in Appendix 4 but do not discuss this theory in the body of the text. Finally, we alert the reader that this text has many audiences, some of whom may have advanced understanding of other theories and statistical procedures that are clearly beyond the scope of this book. For these readers, we identify advanced multivariate statistical procedures used to validate specific hypotheses, but we provide no explanations of the procedures. Thus, Part 2 and the remaining sections of this book emphasize the basic technical information that a consumer needs to understand in order to interpret most tests.

Descriptive Statistics

W e use *descriptive statistics* to describe or summarize data. In testing, the data are scores: several scores on one individual, one score on several individuals, or several scores on several individuals. Descriptive statistics are calculated using the basic mathematical operations of addition, subtraction, multiplication, and division, as well as simple exponential operations (squares and square roots); advanced knowledge of mathematics is not required. Although many calculations are repetitive and tedious, calculators and computers facilitate these calculations, and for many applications, test authors provide tables of all the pertinent descriptive statistics. This chapter deals with the basic concepts needed for an understanding of descriptive statistics. Specifically, it discusses scales of measurement, distributions, measures of central tendency, measures of dispersion, and measures of relationship (correlation).

● ●

Scales of Measurement

The ways in which data can be summarized depend on some characteristics of the scores that are to be described. With some types of scores, we can use all the basic mathematical operations; with other types of scores, none of the basic mathematical operations can be used. The scale on which performances are measured determines how we can describe those performances. There are four types of measurement scales: nominal, ordinal, ratio, and equal interval.[1]

1. See S. S. Stevens (1951), "Mathematics, Measurement, and Psychophysics," in S. S. Stevens (Ed.), *Handbook of Experimental Psychology*, p. 23 (New York: Wiley).

● ● ● **FIGURE 4.1**   Adjacent and Nonadjacent Values

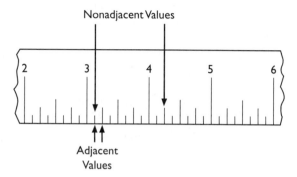

    Ordinal and equal-interval scales are the most frequently used scales in norm-referenced measurement. Nominal and ratio scales are seldom used. The four scales are distinguished primarily on the basis of the relationship between adjacent, or consecutive, values on the measurement continuum. An *adjacent value* in this case means a potential or possible value, rather than an obtained or measured value. In Figure 4.1, which depicts a portion of a yardstick, the possible values are any points between 2 inches and 6 inches, measured in intervals of eighths of an inch. Any two consecutive points (for instance, $3\frac{1}{8}$ inches and $3\frac{1}{4}$ inches) are adjacent values. Any two points on the scale that have values intervening between them (for instance $3\frac{1}{8}$ inches and $4\frac{1}{4}$ inches) are *not* adjacent points. We could, of course, think of adjacent intervals larger than $\frac{1}{8}$ of an inch. For example, adjacent 1-inch intervals could be considered, and the adjacent points would then be 1 inch, 2 inches, and so on.

Nominal Scales

On *nominal scales,* adjacent values have no inherent relationship. Nominal scales name values on the scale. For example, at the local ice cream shop, ice cream flavor is a variable. The specific values that this variable can take are names: chocolate, strawberry, tutti-frutti, mocha almond fudge, and others. The first flavor listed is not better than the second flavor listed. Banana sherbet is not better than orange sherbet (although many people may prefer one or the other). In education and psychology, we occasionally use nominal scales to describe attributes (for example, sex or eye color), geographic region in which a person resides (for example, the Pacific Northwest), educational classification (for example, learning disabled or emotionally disturbed), and so forth. However, few, if any, test scores are nominal.

    Because values on a nominal scale represent names, the various mathematical operations cannot be performed with these values. For example, we cannot average banana and orange sherbet. Mathematically, all we can do with nominal scales is determine the frequency of each value (for example, how many times orange sherbet is chosen).

An occasionally confusing aspect of nominal scales is that numbers may be used as names. For example, numbers on athletic shirts identify players, in the same way that social security numbers identify people. When numbers are used only to name people or objects, with these numbers having no inherent relationship to one another in terms of their adjacent values, the scale of measurement is a nominal scale. An obvious illustration of a nominal scale is the assignment of numbers to football players. A number is used simply to refer to an individual player. The player who wears number 80 is not necessarily a better player than the player who wears number 70 or number 77; 80 is just a different player. Numbers 68 and 69, which are typically thought of as adjacent values, have no relationship to each other on a nominal scale; there is no implied rank ordering in the numbers worn on the shirts. It would not make any sense to add up shirt numbers or to compute the players' average social security number to determine which athletic team is the best.

Ordinal Scales

Ordinal scales order things from better to worse or from worse to better. A scale may be ordinal whether or not numbers are used to designate locations on the scale. For example, locations on ordinal scales are sometimes designated by names. All adjectival comparisons are ordinal: good, better, best; tall, taller, tallest; poor, worse, worst; and so forth. Classroom teachers may use other adjectives (for example, novice, intermediate, and expert) to name the values of a variable. Thus, an ordinal scale may have as few as two or three adjectives as values, one of which is assigned to each individual being ranked. Such names always imply the quantitative relationship of higher or lower. More frequently, ordinal scales use numbers to designate locations of the variable. Ordinal numbers (that is, first, second, third, and so on) designate locations; for example, ordinal numbers are used to indicate standing in the graduating class, a ranking of the top 20 football or basketball teams, the winner and finalists in the Miss America Contest, and so forth. Thus, ordinal values can be assigned all along the continuum (for example, class standing) or only in some parts of the continuum (for example, the top 20 teams); in the latter case, there are implicit losers, those not in the top 20.

A simple example of an ordinal scale is a ranking of persons from first to last on some trait or characteristic, such as weight or test scores. Suppose Ms. Smith administers a test to her arithmetic class, in which 25 students are enrolled. The test results are reported in Table 4.1. Column 1 gives the name of each student, and Column 2 contains each child's raw score. Column 3 contains the ranking of the 25 students; the children are listed in decreasing rank order, from the student with the best performance to the student with the poorest performance. It is important to note that the difference between each student's raw score and the raw score of the immediately preceding student is not the same as the difference in rank for the two. Differences in adjacent *ranks* do not reflect the magnitude of differences in raw scores. The difficult concept to keep in mind is that although the

TABLE 4.1 ● Ranking of Students in Ms. Smith's Arithmetic Class

Student	Raw-Score Total	Rank	Difference Between Score and Next Higher Score
Bob	27	1	0
Lucy	26	2	1
Sam	22	3	4
Mary	20	4	2
Luis	18	5	2
Barbara	17	6	1
Carmen	16		
Jane	16	8	1
Charles J.	16		
Hector	14		
Virginia	14		
Frankie	14		
Sean	14	13	2
Joanne	14		
Jim	14		
John	14		
Charles B.	12		
Jing-Jen	12	18	2
Ron	12		
Carole	11	20	1
Bernice	10	21	1
Hugh	8	22	2
Lance	6	23	2
Ludwig	2	24	4
Harpo	1	25	1

difference between *rank scores* (first, second, third, and so on) is 1 everywhere on the scale, the differences between the raw scores that correspond to the ranks are not necessarily equal.

Educators often use ordinal scales. As Chapter 5 shows, many test scores are ordinal: age equivalents, grade equivalents, and percentiles. Thus, ordinal scales have some interpretive value; however, they are not suitable for more complex interpretations that require some mathematical comparison (for example, calculating averages or differences between achievement in mathematics and achievement in reading).

Ratio Scales

Ratio scales have all the characteristics of ordinal scales and two additional ones. First, the magnitude of the difference between any two adjacent points on the scale is the same. For example, weight in pounds is measured on a ratio scale; the 1-pound difference between 15 and 16 pounds is the same as the 1-pound difference between 124 and 125 pounds. In Table 4.1, if we assume that each raw-score point in the student's total score is of the same value, then the total test score is on a ratio scale. This assumption requires that we accept the notion that the difference between 18 and 17 items correct is the same as the difference between 11 and 10 items correct (or between any other pair of adjacent scores).

The second additional characteristic is that ratio scales have an absolute and logical zero. For instance, temperature on the Kelvin scale is a ratio scale. Absolute zero on that scale indicates the complete cessation of molecular action, or the absence of heat. The absolute zero of a ratio scale allows scores to be compared as ratios. For example, if John weighs 200 pounds and Shawn weighs 100 pounds, John weighs twice as much as Shawn. Few, if any, educational or psychological tests give this type of score.

When ratio scales are used, all mathematical operations can be performed. We can add scores, square scores, create ratios of and differences between scores, and so forth. Thus, ratio scales are potentially very useful. In education and psychology, ratio scales are associated almost exclusively with the measurement of physical characteristics (for example, height and weight) and some time-based measures (for example, times in a 100-meter dash).

Equal-Interval Scales

Equal-interval scales are ratio scales without an absolute and logical zero. Fahrenheit and Celsius temperature scales are equal-interval, not ratio, scales—neither zero Fahrenheit nor zero Celsius indicates an absolute absence of heat. Because equal-interval scales lack an absolute zero, we cannot construct ratios with data measured on these scales. For example, 64 degrees Fahrenheit is not considered "twice as hot" as 32 degrees Fahrenheit.

Consider the information in Figure 4.2. The differences among lines A, B, C, and D are readily measured. We can start measuring from any point, such as from the point where Line S intersects Lines A, B, C, and D. The portion of Line A to the right of S is $\frac{1}{2}$ inch long; that of Line B to the right of S is 1 inch long; that of Line C to the right of S is $1\frac{1}{4}$ inches long; and that of Line D to the right of S is $1\frac{3}{4}$ inches long. The lines are measured on an equal-interval scale, and the differences among the lines would be the same no matter where the starting point S was located. However, because S is not a logical and absolute zero, we cannot make ratio comparisons among the lines. Although when we began measuring from S, we found Line A to measure $\frac{1}{2}$ inch from S and Line B to measure 1 inch from S, the whole of Line B is obviously not twice as long as the whole of line A. In the same way that Line B is not twice as long as Line A, an IQ of 100 is not twice as large as an IQ of 50; IQ is not measured on a ratio scale.

● ● ● **FIGURE 4.2**   The Measurement of Lines as a Function of the Starting Point

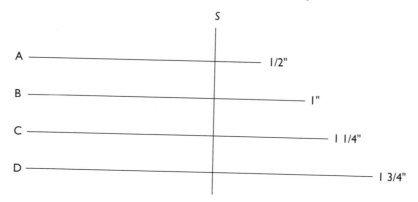

In education and psychology, we often use equal-interval scales. As Chapter 5 shows, all standard scores use equal-interval scales. Because we can add, subtract, multiply, and divide data measured on an equal-interval scale, these scales can be very useful when test givers make complex interpretations of test scores.

Distributions

Distributions of scores may be graphed to demonstrate visually the relations among the scores in the group or set. In such graphs, the horizontal axis (*abscissa*) is the continuum on which the individuals are measured; the vertical axis (*ordinate*) is the frequency (that is, the number) or percentage of individuals earning any given score shown on the abscissa. Three types of graphs of distributions are common in education and psychology: histograms, polygrams, and curves. To illustrate these, we graph the examination scores already presented in Table 4.1. The scores earned on Ms. Smith's arithmetic examination can be grouped in three-point intervals (that is, 1 to 3, 4 to 6, . . . , 25 to 27). The grouped scores are presented as a *histogram* in the upper part of Figure 4.3. In the middle part of that figure, the same data are presented as a *polygram*; note that the midpoints of the intervals used in the histogram are connected in constructing the polygram. The lower part of Figure 4.3 shows a *smoothed curve*.

Distributions are defined by four characteristics: mean, variance, skew, and kurtosis. The *mean* is the arithmetic average of the scores and is the balance point of the distribution. The *variance* describes the spread, or clustering, of scores in a distribution. Both of these characteristics are discussed in greater detail in later sections.

Skew refers to the symmetry of a distribution. The distribution of scores from Ms. Smith's exam is not skewed; the distribution is *symmetrical*. However, if Ms.

● ● ● **FIGURE 4.3**   Distribution of Ms. Smith's Pupils on a Histogram, a Polygram, and a Curve

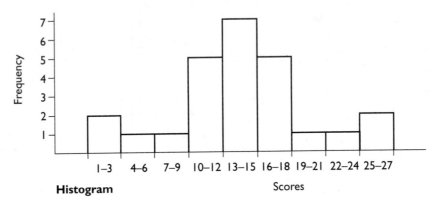

Histogram

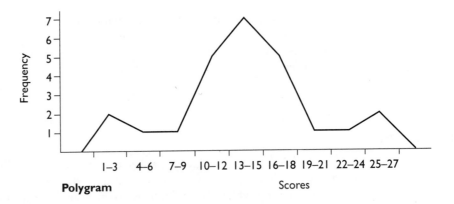

Polygram

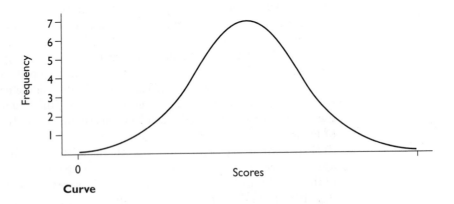

Curve

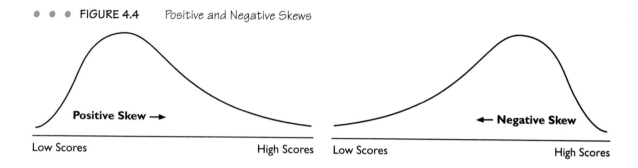

● ● ● **FIGURE 4.4**   *Positive and Negative Skews*

Smith had given a very easy test, on which many students earned very high scores while only a few students earned low scores, the distribution would have been skewed. In such a case, the distribution would have "tailed off" to the low end and would be termed a *negatively skewed* distribution. On the other hand, if she had given a very hard test, on which most of her students earned low scores and relatively few earned high scores, the distribution of scores would have tailed off to the higher end of the continuum. Such a distribution is termed a *positively skewed* distribution. Figure 4.4 shows an example of a positively skewed curve and a negatively skewed curve. The label assigned to a skewed distribution is determined by the direction of the tail of the distribution. Skewed distributions in which the tail is in the upper (higher-score) end are positively skewed, whereas those in which the tail slopes toward the lower end are negatively skewed.

Kurtosis, the fourth characteristic of curves, describes the peakedness of a curve, or the rate at which a curve rises. Distributions that are flat and rise slowly are termed *platykurtic curves*. (Platykurtic curves are flat, just as a plate or a plateau is flat.) Fast-rising curves are termed *leptokurtic curves*. Tests that do not "spread out" (or discriminate among) the scores of those taking the test are typically graphed as leptokurtic. Figure 4.5 illustrates a platykurtic and a leptokurtic curve.

● ● ● **FIGURE 4.5**   *A Platykurtic and a Leptokurtic Curve*

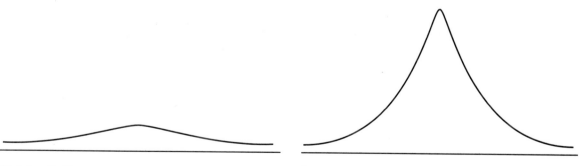

Platykurtic Curve   **Leptokurtic Curve**

The *normal curve* is a particular symmetrical curve. Many variables are distributed normally in nature; many are not. The *only* value of the normal curve lies in the fact that for this curve, the proportion of cases that fall between any two points on the horizontal axis of the curve is known exactly.

● ●

Basic Notation

A number of symbols are used in statistics, and different authors use different symbols. Table 4.2 lists the symbols that we use in this book. The summation sign Σ means "add the following"; X denotes any score. The number of scores in a distribution is symbolized by N; f is used to denote the frequency of occurrence of a particular score. The arithmetic average (mean) of a distribution is denoted by $\overline{X}$. The variance of a distribution is symbolized by S^2, and the standard deviation, by S.

● ●

Measures of Central Tendency

A set of scores can be described by its average (for example, the average score on this week's spelling test was 92 percent correct). This information gives us a general description of how the group as a whole performed. Actually, three different averages are used: mode, median, and mean. The *mode* is defined as the score most frequently obtained. A mode (if there is one) can be found for data on a nominal, ordinal, ratio, or equal-interval scale. Distributions may have two modes (if they do, they are called "bimodal distributions"), or they may have more than two. The mode of the distribution of raw scores obtained by Ms. Smith's class on the arithmetic test is readily apparent from an inspection of the data in Table 4.1 and the graphs in Figure 4.3. The mode of this distribution is 14; seven children earned this score.

TABLE 4.2   ●   *Commonly Used Statistical Symbols*

Symbol	Meaning
Σ	Summation sign
X	Any score
N	Number of cases
f	Frequency
$\overline{X}$	Mean
S^2	Variance
S	Standard deviation

The *median* is the score that divides the top 50 percent of test takers from the bottom 50 percent. It is that point on a scale above which 50 percent of the cases (people, *not* scores) occur and below which 50 percent of the cases occur. Medians can be found for data on ordinal, equal-interval, and ratio scales; they should not be used with nominal scales. The median score may or may not actually be earned by a student. For the set of scores 4, 5, 7, and 8, the median is 6, although no one earned a score of 6. For the set of scores 4, 5, 6, 7, and 8, the median is 6, and someone earned that score.

The *mean* is the arithmetic average of the scores in a distribution. It is the sum of the scores divided by the number of scores. The mean, like the median, may or may not be earned by any child in the distribution. Means should be computed only for data on ratio and equal-interval scales. The formula for computing the mean, using statistical notation, is given in Equation 4.1:

$$X = \frac{\Sigma X}{N}$$

(4.1)

Using the scores obtained from Ms. Smith's arithmetic examination (Table 4.1), we find that the sum of the scores is 350 and that the number of scores is 25. The mean (arithmetic average), then, is 14. The mean was earned by seven children in the class.

The mode, median, and mean have particular relationships, depending on the symmetry (skew) of a distribution. As Figure 4.6 shows, in symmetrical *unimodal*

● ● ● ● **FIGURE 4.6**   Relationships Among Mode, Median, and Mean for Symmetrical and Asymmetrical Distributions

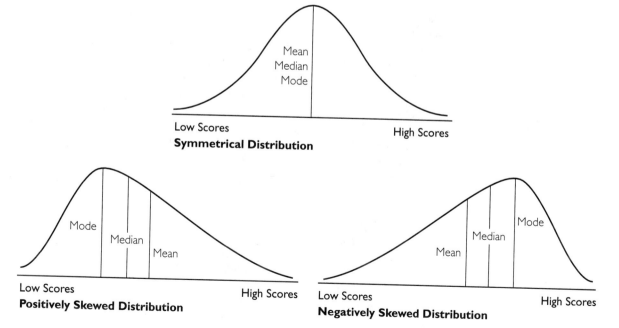

(that is, having just one mode) distributions, the mode, median, and mean are at the same point. In positively skewed distributions, the median and mean are displaced toward the positive tail of the curve; the mode is a lower value than the median, and the median is a lower value than the mean. In negatively skewed distributions, the median and mean are displaced toward the negative tail of the curve; the mode is a higher value than the median, and the median is a higher value than the mean.

Measures of Dispersion

Although a mean tells us about a group's average performance, it does not tell us how close to the average people scored. For example, did everyone earn 92 percent correct on the weekly spelling test, or were the scores spread out from 0 to 100 percent? To describe how scores spread out, we use three indexes of dispersion: range, variance, and standard deviation. All three measures can be computed when the scale of measurement is ratio or equal-interval, and none of the three can be computed when the scale of measurement is nominal. Range can be calculated with ordinal data.

The *range* is the distance between the extremes of a distribution, including those extremes; it is the highest score less the lowest score plus 1. On Ms. Smith's test (Table 4.1), it is 27 (27 = 27 − 1 + 1). The range is a relatively crude measure of dispersion because it is based on only two bits of information. The variance and the standard deviation are the most important indexes of dispersion. The *variance* is a numerical index describing the dispersion of a set of scores around the mean of the distribution. Specifically, the *variance* (S^2) is the average squared distance of the scores from the mean. Because the variance is an average, it is not affected by the number of cases in the set or the distribution. Large sets of scores may have large or small variances; small sets of scores may have large or small variances. Also, because the variance is measured in terms of distance from the mean, it is not related to the actual value of the mean. Distributions with large means may have large or small variances; distributions with small means may have large or small variances. The variance of a distribution may be computed with Equation 4.2. The variance (S^2) equals the sum (Σ) of the square of each score less the mean [$(X − \overline{X})^2$] divided by the number of scores (N).

$$S^2 = \frac{\Sigma(X-\overline{X})^2}{N} \tag{4.2}$$

As an example, we use the scores from Ms. Smith's arithmetic test again to compute variance (see Table 4.3). Column 2 in Table 4.3 contains the score earned by each student. The first step in computing the variance is to find the mean. Therefore, the scores are added, and the sum (350) is divided by the number of scores (25). The mean in this example is 14. The next step is to subtract the mean from each score; this is done in Column 3 of Table 4.3, which is labeled $X −$ $\overline{X}$. Note that scores above the mean are positive, scores at the mean are zero, and

TABLE 4.3 ● *Computation of the Variance of Ms. Smith's Arithmetic Test*

Student	Test Score	$X - \bar{X}$	$(X - \bar{X})^2$
Bob	27	13	169
Lucy	26	12	144
Sam	22	8	64
Mary	20	6	36
Luis	18	4	16
Barbara	17	3	9
Carmen	16	2	4
Jane	16	2	4
Charles J.	16	2	4
Hector	14	0	0
Virginia	14	0	0
Frankie	14	0	0
Sean	14	0	0
Joanne	14	0	0
Jim	14	0	0
John	14	0	0
Charles B.	12	−2	4
Jing-Jen	12	−2	4
Ron	12	−2	4
Carole	11	−3	9
Bernice	10	−4	16
Hugh	8	−6	36
Lance	6	−8	64
Ludwig	2	−12	144
Harpo	1	−13	169
SUM	350	0	900

scores below the mean are negative. The differences (Column 3) are then squared (multiplied by themselves); the squared differences are in Column 4, labeled $(X - \bar{X})^2$. Note that all numbers in this column are positive. The squared differences are then summed; in this example, the sum of all the squared distances of scores from the mean is 900. The variance equals the sum of all the squared distances of scores from the mean divided by the number of scores; in this case, the variance equals 900/25, or 36.

The variance is very important in psychometric theory but has very limited application in score interpretation. However, its calculation is necessary for the computation of the standard deviation (*S*), which is very important in the interpretation of test scores. The *standard deviation* is the positive square root ($\sqrt{}$) of the variance.[2] Thus, in our example, because the variance is 36, the standard

2. The square root of a particular number is the number that, when multiplied by itself, produces the particular number. For example: $\sqrt{144} = 12$, $\sqrt{25} = 5$, $\sqrt{4} = 2$.

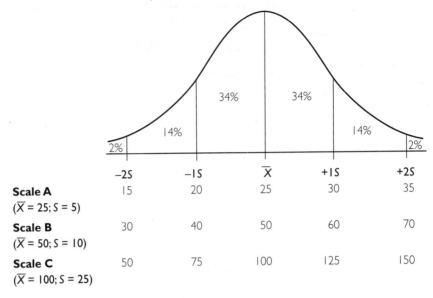

	−2S	−1S	$\overline{X}$	+1S	+2S
Scale A	15	20	25	30	35
($\overline{X}$ = 25; S = 5)					
Scale B	30	40	50	60	70
($\overline{X}$ = 50; S = 10)					
Scale C	50	75	100	125	150
($\overline{X}$ = 100; S = 25)					

deviation is 6. In later chapters, the standard deviation will be used in other computations, such as standard scores and the standard error of measurement.

The standard deviation is used as a *unit of measurement* in much the same way that an inch or a ton is used as a unit of measurement. When scores are equal-interval, they can be measured in terms of standard-deviation units from the mean. The advantage of measuring in standard deviations is that when the distribution is normal, we know exactly what proportion of cases occurs between the mean and the particular standard deviation. As shown in Figure 4.7, approximately 34 percent of the cases in a normal distribution always occur between the mean and one standard deviation (S) either above or below the mean. Thus, approximately 68 percent of all cases occur between one standard deviation below and one standard deviation above the mean (34% + 34% = 68%). Approximately 14 percent of the cases occur between one and two standard deviations below the mean or between one and two standard deviations above the mean. Thus, about 48 percent of all cases occur between the mean and two standard deviations either above or below the mean (34% + 14% = 48%). About 96 percent of all cases occur between two standard deviations above and two standard deviations below the mean.

Appendix 1 lists the proportion of cases in a normal distribution occurring between the mean and any standard deviation above or below the mean. As an example, if we enter Appendix 1 at 0.44 (that is 0.4 plus 0.04), we find the number .1700. This number means that 1,700/10,000 (17%) of the cases in the normal curve occur between the mean and 0.44 standard deviation from the mean, either below or above the mean. Thus 33 percent of the cases fall below 0.44 standard deviation below the mean. (Half the cases, 50%, fall below the mean; 17% fall between -0.44 S and the mean; 50% minus 17% equals 33%.)

As shown by the positions and values for Scales A, B, and C in Figure 4.7, it does not matter what the values of the mean and the standard deviation are. The relationship holds for various obtained values of the mean and the standard deviation. For Scale A, where the mean is 25 and the standard deviation is 5, 34 percent of the scores occur between the mean (25) and one standard deviation below the mean (20) or between the mean and one standard deviation above the mean (30). Similarly, for Scale B, where the mean is 50 and the standard deviation is 10, 34 percent of the cases occur between the mean (50) and one standard deviation below the mean (40) or between the mean and one standard deviation above the mean (60).

It is extremely important that those who use tests to make decisions about students be aware of the means and standard deviations of the tests they use. Some intelligence tests, for example, have a mean of 100 and a standard deviation of 16. If scores on those tests are normally distributed, we would expect approximately 68 percent of the school population to have IQs between 84 and 116. Another intelligence test may have a mean of 100 and a standard deviation of 24. We would expect approximately 68 percent of the school population to have IQs between 76 and 124 if scores on that test are normally distributed. The meaning of a score in a distribution depends on the mean, the standard deviation, and the shape of that distribution. This is an obvious point, yet it is often overlooked.

For example, some states use an absolute score in the school code for the placement and retention of mentally retarded children in special-education programs; Pennsylvania uses a score of 79 for maintaining eligibility for placement. On the Stanford–Binet Intelligence Scale (fourth edition) or the third edition of the Wechsler Intelligence Scale for Children (WISC-III), which have a standard deviation of 15, a score of 79 is 1.4 standard deviations below the mean $[(79 - 100)/15]$. On some older tests that have a standard deviation of 16 (such as the McCarthy Scales of Children's Abilities), an IQ of 79 is 1.3 standard deviations below the mean $[(79 - 100)/16]$. If a single absolute score is specified, different levels of eligibility for special-education classes may be inadvertently written into the school code.

● ●

Correlation

Correlations quantify relationships between variables. *Correlation coefficients* are numerical indexes of these relationships. They tell us the extent to which any two variables go together, the extent to which changes in one variable are reflected by changes in the second variable. These coefficients are used in measurement to estimate both the reliability and the validity of a test. Correlation coefficients can range in value from .00 to *either* +1.00 or −1.00. The sign (+ or −) indicates the direction of the relationship; the number indicates the magnitude of the relationship. A correlation coefficient of .00 between two variables means that there is no

TABLE 4.4   ● Scores Earned on Two Tests Administered by Ms. Smith to Her Arithmetic Class

Student	Raw Score, Test 1	Raw Score, Test 2
Bob	27	26
Lucy	26	22
Sam	23	20
Mary	20	27
Luis	18	14
Barbara	17	18
Carmen	16	16
Jane	16	17
Charles J.	16	16
Hector	14	14
Virginia	14	14
Frankie	14	16
Sean	14	14
Joanne	14	12
Jim	14	14
John	14	12
Charles B.	12	14
Jing-Jen	12	11
Ron	12	12
Carole	11	10
Bernice	10	14
Hugh	8	6
Lance	6	1
Ludwig	2	2
Harpo	1	8

relationship between the variables. The variables are independent; changes in one variable are not related to changes in the second variable. A correlation coefficient of either +1.00 or −1.00 indicates a perfect relationship between two variables. Thus, if you know a person's score on one variable, you can predict that person's score on the second variable without error. Correlation coefficients between .00 and 1.00 (or −1.00) allow some prediction, and the greater the coefficient, the greater its predictive power.

Correlation coefficients are very important in assessment. Chapter 7 shows how correlations are used to estimate the amount of error associated with measurement. Chapter 8 shows how correlation coefficients are also used to estimate a test's validity.

The Pearson Product–Moment Correlation Coefficient

The most commonly used correlation coefficient is the *Pearson product–moment correlation coefficient* (*r*). This is an index of the straight-line (linear) relationship

● ● ● **FIGURE 4.8**   *Scatterplot of the Two Tests Administered by Ms. Smith*

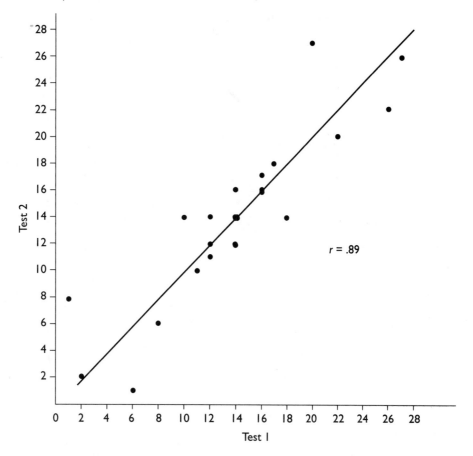

r = .89

between two variables measured on an equal-interval scale. Suppose Ms. Smith administered a second exam to her arithmetic class. The results of the first exam (the data from Table 4.1) are reproduced in Column 2 of Table 4.4; the results of the second exam are presented in Column 3. (For the sake of simplicity, the example has been constructed so that the second test has the same mean and the same standard deviation as the first test—that is, 14 and 6, respectively). The two scores for each student are plotted on a graph (termed a *scattergram,* or *scatterplot*) in Figure 4.8. The scatterplot contains 25 points, one for each child. The figure indicates that there is a pronounced tendency for high scores on the first test to be associated with high scores on the second test. There is a *positive* relationship (correlation) between the first and second tests. The line drawn through the scatterplot in Figure 4.8 is termed a *regression line.* When the points corresponding to each pair of scores cluster closely around the regression line, there is a high degree of relationship. The points from Table 4.4 do cluster closely around the regression line; there is a high correlation (specifically, .89) between the first and

● ● ● **FIGURE 4.9**   Six Scatterplots of Different Degrees and Directions of Relationship

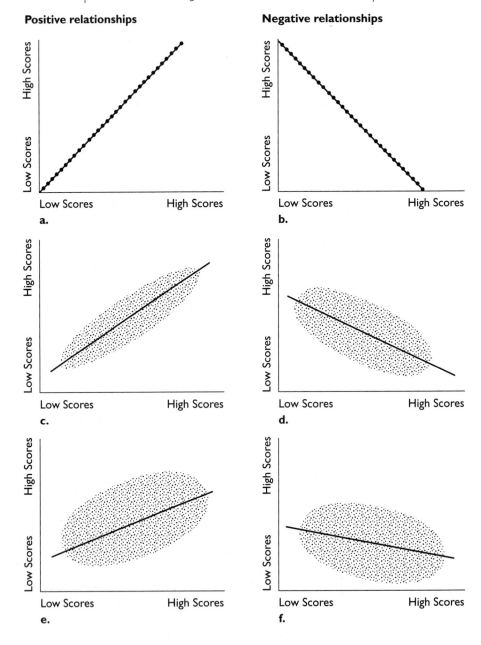

second tests.[3] If all the points fell directly on the regression line, there would be a perfect correlation (1.00).

Figure 4.9 shows six scatterplots of different degrees of relationship. In parts a and b, all points fall on the regression line, and so the correlation between the variables is perfect. Part a has a correlation coefficient of +1.00; high scores on one test are associated with high scores on the other test. Part b has a correlation of −1.00; high scores on one test are associated with low scores on the other test (this negative correlation is sometimes termed an *inverse* relationship). Parts c and d show a high degree of positive and negative relationship, respectively. Note that the departures from the regression lines are associated with lower degrees of relationship. Parts e and f show scatterplots with a low degree of relationship. Note the wide departures from the regression lines.

Zero correlation can occur in three ways, as shown in Figure 4.10. First, if the scatterplot is essentially circular (part a), the correlation is .00. In such a case, there is no relationship between the two variables; each value of the first variable can be associated with any (and perhaps all) values of the second variable. Second, if either variable is constant (part b), the correlation is .00. For example, if a researcher tried to correlate sex and reading achievement with a sample made up entirely of boys, the correlation would be zero because sex would have only one value (male); sex would be a constant, not a variable. Third, two variables can be related in a nonlinear way (part c). For example, willingness to take risks is related to age. Younger children and adults are less willing to take risks than are teenagers. Although there is a strong curvilinear relationship, the *linear* regression line would parallel one of the axes. Thus, there is a curvilinear relationship, but the coefficient of linear correlation is approximately .00.

Pearson Family Correlation Coefficients

Test authors may report correlation coefficients by different names to indicate a variable's scale of measurement and whether one or both variables in the relationship are dichotomous (have only two values) or continuous (have many values). The most commonly reported coefficients are members of the Pearson family of correlation coefficients, meaning that they are all computed by computationally equivalent formulas. When both variables to be correlated are measured on an equal-interval or ratio scale (such as IQ and SAT verbal score), the correlation coefficient is called a *Pearson product–moment correlation coefficient*. The symbol for this statistic is *r*. When both variables to be correlated are measured on an ordinal scale (such as class standing and rank on the school's competency examination for seniors), the correlation coefficient is called a *Spearman rho*; the sym-

---

3. The correlation coefficient can be computed with the following formula, where X is a raw score on one measure, and Y is a raw score on a second measure.

$$r = \frac{N\Sigma XY - (\Sigma X)(\Sigma Y)}{\sqrt{N\Sigma X^2 - (\Sigma X)^2}\ \sqrt{N\Sigma Y^2 - (\Sigma Y)^2}}$$

● ● ● **FIGURE 4.10**   Three Zero-Order, Linear Correlations

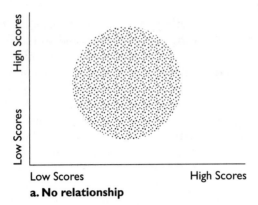

a. No relationship

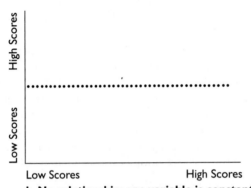

b. No relationship; one variable is constant

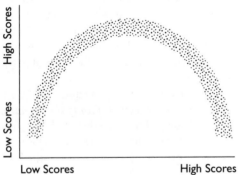

c. No linear relationship; relationship is curvilinear

bol for rho is ρ. Sometimes the variables to be correlated are dichotomous (for instance, male/female). When two dichotomous variables are correlated, the correlation coefficient is called a *phi coefficient*; the symbol for phi is ϕ. When one of the variables is dichotomous (right or wrong on a test question) and the other variable is continuous (total number correct on the test), the correlation coefficient is called a *point biserial* correlation coefficient; its symbol is r_{ptbis}. While there are other kinds of Pearson family coefficients (such as *biserial rho*) and computationally different coefficients[4] (such as *tetrachoric* and *biserial*), they are seldom reported in test manuals.

Causality

No discussion of correlation is complete without a mention of causality. Correlation is a necessary but not a sufficient condition for causality. Two variables cannot be causally related unless they are correlated. However, the mere presence of a correlation does not establish causality. For any correlation coefficient between variables (A and B), there are four possible interpretations.

First, the variables may be correlated by chance. For example, the incidence of chickenpox in Egypt (A) may be highly correlated with the sale of Purina Puppy Chow in the state of Arizona (B). There is simply no logical or reasonable explanation for the correlation other than serendipity.[5] There can be three nonchance reasons for A and B to be correlated. A can cause B; for example, burning buildings (A) cause firefighters to be present (B). B can cause A; for example, Bradbury (1953) reports that firefighters (B) cause fires (A). Finally, a third variable (C) can cause both A and B. For example, there actually is a positive relationship between shoe size and mental age. Clearly, big feet do not cause mental development (A does not cause B). Moreover, mental development does not cause big feet (B does not cause A). The most satisfactory explanation of the correlation is that maturation, a third variable (C), causes both A and B: As children grow older, they develop both mentally and physically.

Although the preceding examples illustrate obvious instances of inappropriate reasoning, in testing situations the errors or potential errors are not so clear. For example, IQ scores and scores on achievement tests are correlated. Some argue that intelligence causes achievement; others argue that achievement causes intelligence. Because there are at least four possible interpretations of correlational data—and because correlational data do not tell us which interpretation is true—we must never draw causal conclusions from such data alone.

4. Explanation of these correlation coefficients may be found in previous editions.
5. The probability of a correlation coefficient of a specific value occurring by chance can be determined; when a correlation coefficient is found to be "statistically significant" at the .05 level, a correlation of that magnitude occurs by chance only 5 times in 100.

Summary

Descriptive statistics provide summary information about groups of individuals. Data can be obtained on one of four types of measurement scales: *nominal, ordinal, ratio,* and *equal-interval* scales. Collections of scores are termed *distributions*. Distributions are defined by four characteristics: *mean, variance, skew,* and *kurtosis*. Depending on the scale of measurement, three indexes may be used to indicate a distribution's central tendency: the *mode* (the most frequent score), the *median* (the score that separates the top 50 percent from the bottom 50 percent), and the *mean* (the arithmetic average). Depending on the scale of measurement, the dispersion of a distribution can be described by three indexes: the *range* of scores, the *variance,* and the *standard deviation.*

The quantification of the relationship between two variables is termed *correlation*. When there is no relationship between variables, the correlation is zero. When there is a perfect relationship between variables, the correlation is one. A plus or a minus sign indicates the type of relationship, not the magnitude of the relationship. A *positive correlation* indicates that high scores on one variable are associated with high scores on the second variable. A *negative correlation* indicates an inverse relationship: High scores on one variable are associated with low scores on the other variable. There are several types of correlations that are often used in describing tests.

Questions for Chapter Review and Thought

1. After all third-grade students in the state took an achievement test, statewide norms were developed. The superintendent of public instruction reviewed the test results and in a news conference voiced concern for the quality of education in the state. The superintendent reported, "Half the third-grade children in this state performed below the state average." What is foolish about that statement?

2. What is the relationship among the mode, the median, and the mean in a normal distribution?

3. The following statements about Test A and Test B are true: Tests A and B measure the same behavior; Tests A and B have means of 100; Test A has a standard deviation of 15; and Test B has a standard deviation of 5.

   a. Following classroom instruction, the pupils in Mr. Radley's room earn an average score of 130 on Test A. Pupils in Ms. Purple's room earn an average score of 110 on Test B. On this basis, the local principal concludes that Mr. Radley's students learn more than Ms. Purple's. What is fallacious about this conclusion?

   b. Assuming that the pupils were equal prior to instruction, what conclusions could the principal legitimately make?

4. On the Stanford–Binet Intelligence Scale, Harry earns an IQ of 52, and Ralph earns an IQ of 104. Their teacher concludes that Ralph is twice as smart as Harry. Why is this conclusion wrong?

5. Discuss the relationship between correlation and causality.

6. In one state, the criteria for identifying a student as being mentally retarded include, among other things, the requirement that the student have an IQ of 79 or less. The use of this criterion for IQ means that several different levels of eligibility are written into the state's rules. Explain why this is so.

Problems

1. Ms. Robbins administers a test to ten children in her class. The children earn the following scores: 14, 28, 49, 49, 49, 77, 84, 84, 91, and 105. For this distribution of scores, find the following:

   a. Mode

   b. Mean

   c. Range

   d. Variance and standard deviation

2. Mr. García administers a test to six children in his class. The children earn the following scores: 21, 27, 30, 54, 39, and 63. For these scores, find the following:

   a. Mean

   b. Range

   c. Variance and standard deviation

3. Ms. Shumway administers a test to six children in her nursery-school program. The children earn the following scores: 23, 33, 38, 53, 78, and 93. Find the mean and standard deviation of these six scores.

4. Using Appendix 2, find the proportion of cases that occur

   a. Between the mean and the following standard-deviation units: -1.5, $+.37$, $+.08$, $+2.75$.

   b. Between $+$ and $-1.7S$, between $+$ and $-0.55S$, and between $+$ and $-2.1S$.

   c. Above $-0.7S$, above $+1.3S$, and above $+1.9S$.

   d. Below $-0.7S$, below $+1.3S$, and below $+1.9S$.

Answers

1. (a) 49; (b) 63; (c) 92; (d) 784 and 28
2. (a) 39; (b) 43; (c) 225 and 15
3. Mean = 53; standard deviation = 25
4. (a) .4332, .1443, .0319, .4970; (b) .9108, .4176, .9642; (c) .7580, .0968, .0287; (d) .2420, .9032, .9713

Resources for Further Investigation

Technology Resources

The Data and Story Library (DASL)

http://lib.stat.cmu.edu/DASL/

DASL is a library on the web that contains data files and stories to illustrate basic statistical concepts.

Under *List All Methods,* the searcher can find stories about keywords, such as *distribution, mean, median,* and *scatterplots.*

Welcome to HyperStat

http://www.ruf.rice.edu/~lane/hyperstat/index.html

Look here for further explanations about distributions and data.

Statistical Home Page

http://www.uvm.edu/~dhowell/StatPages/StatHomePage.html

This is David Howell's home page, designed for faculty and students interested in statistics. There are a number of data files and tutorials available for practice, including subjects such as correlation and analyses of variance (ANOVAs).

Measurement, Statistics, and Methodological Studies Program

http://research.ed.asu.edu

Contains research methods resources from the College of Education at Arizona State University with links to other sites including the Statistical Instruction Internet Palette (SIIP).

Web Pages That Perform Statistical Calculations:

http://members.aol.com/johnp71/javastat.html

This page links to over 300 other pages that perform statistical calculations and contain other statistical resources.

Surfstat Australia: An Online Text in Introductory Statistics

http://surfstat.newcastle.edu.au/surfstat/main/surfstat.html

This page contains information on summarizing and presenting data, producing data, variation and probability, and statistical inference.

Introduction to Descriptive Statistics

http://www.mste.uiuc.edu/hill/dstat/dstat.hmtl

Contains great examples of such statistics as central tendency, variance, and standard deviation.

chapter

5

Quantification
of Test Performance

Most behaviors occur without being systematically observed, quantified, and evaluated, and the vast majority occur in situations that are not specifically structured to quantify and evaluate the behaviors. Assessment is an exception. Tests and systematic observations occur in structured, standardized situations. Tests require the presentation of standardized materials to an individual in a predetermined manner in order to evaluate that individual's responses, using predetermined criteria. Systematic observations require the use of predetermined definitions of behavior to be observed at predetermined times and settings.

How the individual's responses are quantified depends on the materials used, the intent of the test author, and the diagnostician's intention in choosing the procedure. If we were interested only in determining whether a student had learned a specific fact or concept (for example, "What is 3 + 5?"), we would make explicit the criteria for what constitutes a correct response and would classify the student's response as right or wrong, without quantifying the result. If we were interested in determining whether a student had learned a finite set of facts (for example, the sums of all combinations of single-digit numbers), we could readily quantify a student's performance as the number or percentage of facts known. However, the assessment of every element (that is, every fact, concept, and skill) would require not only that all elements be specified but also that each student's progress be monitored. Therefore, this approach is generally reserved for the most essential information that a student must master.

More often, the information we wish to assess is not finite, and it is impractical or impossible to assess all the facts and relationships that might be tested. For example, it seems unlikely that anyone could make up a test to assess a student's knowledge of every aspect of all Shakespeare's plays; however, even if that were possible, administering all the possible questions to a student in one or even several sittings would be virtually impossible. Even when we cannot test much of the information on a topic, we still may want to estimate the amount of information students have learned. To do this, testers are forced to ask a few questions and to base their inferences about all the information, termed the *domain*, on student responses to the sample of questions.

When we sample a student's knowledge of an entire domain by assessing a smaller number of items, we assume that a student's performance on all the items in the domain can be accurately inferred from the performance on the sample of items. Particular items are important only as representatives of the domain; they have little individual importance. Moreover, we generally cannot infer the percentage correct on the entire domain directly from a test unless the items are representative of the domain, a condition that is never known on an a priori basis.

● ●

Scores Used in Norm-Referenced Assessment

When a large domain is assessed, a student's performance is typically interpreted by comparing it with the performances of a group of subjects of known demographic characteristics (age, sex, grade in school, and so on). This group is called a *normative sample* or *norm group*. The comparison scores are called *derived scores* and are of two types: developmental scores and scores of relative standing.

Developmental Scores

Developmental Equivalents

Developmental equivalents are one type of derived (or transformed) score. The most common types of developmental equivalents are age equivalents (mental ages, for example) and grade equivalents. Suppose the average performance of 10-year-old children on an intelligence test was 27 correct answers. Further, suppose that Horace answered 27 questions correctly. Horace answered as many questions correctly as the average of 10-year-old children. He earns a mental age of 10 years. An *age equivalent* means that a child's raw score is the average (the median or mean) performance for that age group. Age equivalents are expressed in years and months; a hyphen is used in age scores (for example, 7-1 for 7 years, 1 month old). A *grade equivalent* means that a child's raw score is the average (the median or mean) performance for a particular grade. Grade equivalents are expressed in grades and tenths of grades; a decimal point is used in grade scores (for example, 7.1 for grade 7$\frac{1}{10}$). Age-equivalent and grade-equivalent scores are interpreted as a performance equal to the average of X-year-olds and the average of Xth-graders' performance, respectively.

Suppose we gave a test to 1,000 children, 100 of each age (within two weeks of their birthday) from 5 to 14 years. For each 100 children at each age, there is a distribution with a mean. These hypothetical means are shown in Figure 5.1,

Mean Number Correct for Ten Age Groups: An Example of Arriving at Age-Equivalent Scores

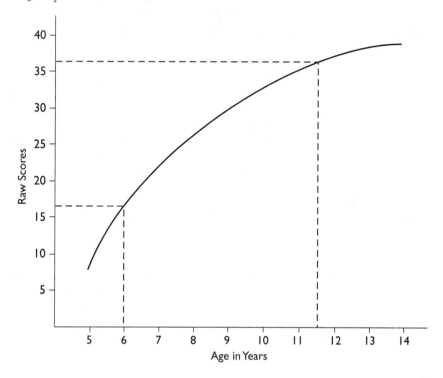

connected by a curved line. As the figure shows, a raw score of 16 corresponds exactly to the average score earned by children in the 6-year-old distribution. Thus, the child who earns a score of 16 has an age equivalent of 6 years, 0 months, or 6-0. A score of 36, by contrast, falls between the average of the 11-year-old distribution and the average of the 12-year-old distribution. A raw score of 36 would be estimated (*interpolated*) as an age score of 11-6; it would be awarded a score between 11 and 12, despite the fact that no children between 11 and 12 years of age were tested. A score of 4 would fall below the average of the lowest age group, the 5-year-olds. If a child earned a raw score of 4, that child's age equivalent would be estimated (*extrapolated*) by continuing the curve in Figure 5.1. A raw score of 4 could be extrapolated to be the equivalent of an age score of 3-6, although no children that young were included in the sample. Similarly, a score greater than the average performance of the oldest children could also be extrapolated.

The interpretation of age and grade equivalents requires great care. Five problems occur in the use of developmental scores:

1. *Systematic Misinterpretation.* Students who earn an age equivalent of 12-0 have merely answered as many questions correctly as the average for children 12

years of age. They have not necessarily performed as a 12-year-old child would; they may well have attacked the problems in a different way or demonstrated a different performance pattern from many 12-year-old students. Similarly, a second-grader and a ninth-grader may both earn grade equivalents of 4.0, but they probably have not performed identically. Thorndike and Hagen (1978) have suggested that it is more likely that the younger child has performed lower-level work with greater accuracy (for instance, successfully answered 38 of the 45 problems attempted), whereas the older child has attempted more problems with less accuracy (for instance, successfully answered 38 of the 78 problems attempted).

2. *Need for Interpolation and Extrapolation.* Average age and grade scores are estimated for groups of children who are never tested. Consequently, a child can earn a grade equivalent of 3.2, although no children at grade 3.2 were in the norm group (for example, only children in the beginning and at the middle of third grade were in the norm group that was tested); or a child can earn a grade equivalent of 8.0, even though no children above the sixth grade were in the norm group that was tested.

3. *The Promotion of Typological Thinking.* The average 12-0 pupil is a statistical abstraction surrounded by a family with 1.2 other children, 0.8 of a dog, and 2.3 automobiles; in other words, the average child does not exist. Average 12-0 children more accurately represent a range of performances, typically the middle 50 percent.

4. *Implication of a False Standard of Performance.* Educators expect a third-grader to perform at a third-grade level and a 9-year-old to perform at a 9-year-old level. However, the way equivalent scores are constructed ensures that 50 percent of any age or grade group will perform below age or grade level because half of the test takers earn scores below the median.

5. *Tendency for Scales to Be Ordinal, Not Equal Interval.* The line relating the number correct to the various ages is typically curved, with a flattening of the curve at higher ages or grades. Figure 5.1 is a typical developmental curve. Because the scales are ordinal and not based on equal-interval units, scores on these scales should not be added or multiplied in any computation.

Developmental Quotients

Before we try to interpret a developmental score (for example, a mental age), we must know the age of the person whose score is being calculated. Knowing developmental age as well as chronological age (CA) allows us to judge an individual's relative performance. Suppose that Ana earns a mental age (MA) of 120 months. If Ana is 8 years (96 months) old, her performance is above average. If she is 35 years old, however, it is below average. The relationship between developmental age and chronological age is often quantified as a developmental quotient. For example, a *ratio* IQ is

$$IQ = MA \text{ (in months)} \times 100 \div CA \text{ (in months)}$$

The *developmental age* is often interpreted as the level of functioning, whereas the *developmental quotient* is interpreted as the rate of development. In any such scheme, a third variable, chronological age, is always involved. Of the three variables, only chronological age and the developmental quotient are independent of each other (that is, uncorrelated). The developmental age is related to both of the other two variables. In the case of intelligence, the developmental age is far more closely associated with chronological age than it is with the developmental quotient (Kappauf, 1973). Developmental levels do not provide independent information. They only summarize data for age (or grade) and relative standing.

All the problems that apply to developmental levels also apply to developmental quotients. There is one additional problem that is particularly bothersome: The variance of developmental scores within different chronological age or grade groups may not be the same. This can cause two related problems. First, the same quotient may mean different things at different ages. For example, a developmental quotient of 120 at age 5 may mean that Billy performs better than 55 percent of 5-year-olds. However, a developmental quotient of 120 at age 11 may mean that Billy performs better than 53 or 58 percent (or some other percentage) of the 11-year-olds. Second, different quotients at different ages can mean the same thing. For example, whereas a developmental quotient of 120 at age 5 may mean that Sally performs better than 55 percent of other 5-year-olds, a developmental quotient of 110 at age 10 could mean that Sally performs better than 55 percent of 10-year-olds. Thus, different variances at different ages and grades render it impossible to interpret scores without knowing the variances.

Scores of Relative Standing

Unlike developmental scores, scores of relative standing use more information than the mean or median to interpret a person's test score. Moreover, when the same type of relative-standing score is used, the units of measurement are exactly the same. Thus, we can compare the performances of different people even when they differ in age, and we can compare one person's scores on several different tests. This specificity of meaning is very useful. For example, it is not particularly helpful to know that George is 70 inches tall, Bridget is 6 feet 3 inches tall, Bruce is 1.93 meters tall, and Alexandra is 177.8 centimeters tall. To compare their heights, it is necessary to transform the heights into comparable units. In feet and inches, their heights are as follows: George, 5 feet 10 inches; Bridget, 6 feet 3 inches; Bruce, 6 feet 4 inches; and Alexandra, 5 feet 10 inches. Scores of relative standing put raw scores into comparable units, such as percentiles or standard scores.

Percentile Family

Percentile ranks (percentiles) can be used when the scale of measurement is ordinal or equal interval. They are derived scores indicating the percentage of people whose scores are *at or below* a given raw score. The percentage correct is *not* the same as the percentage of people scoring at or below a given score. Percentiles corresponding to particular scores can be computed by the following four-step sequence:

1. Arrange the scores from the highest to the lowest (that is, best to worst).

2. Compute the percentage of people with scores *below* the score to which you wish to assign a percentile rank.

3. Compute the percentage of people with scores *at* the score to which you wish to assign a percentile rank.

4. Add the percentage of people with scores below the score to one half the percentage of people with scores at the score to obtain the percentile rank.

Table 5.1 gives a numerical example. Mr. Greenberg gave a test to his developmental reading class, which has an enrollment of 25 children. The scores are presented in Column 1, and the number of children obtaining each score (the *frequency*) is shown in Column 2. Column 3 gives the percentage of all 25 scores that each obtained score represents. Column 4 contains the percentage of all 25 scores that were below that particular score. In the last group of columns, the percentile rank is computed. Only one child scored 24; the one score is $\frac{1}{25}$ of the class,

TABLE 5.1 ● Computing Percentile Ranks for a Hypothetical Class of Twenty-Five

			Percentile Rank				
Score	Frequency	Percentage at the Score	Percentage Below the Score	+	Half of Percentage at the Score	=	Percentile
50	2	8	92	+	(1/2)(8)	=	96
49	0						
48	4	16	76	+	(1/2)(16)	=	84
47	0						
46	5	20	56	+	(1/2)(20)	=	66
45	5	20	36	+	(1/2)(20)	=	46
44	3	12	24	+	(1/2)(12)	=	30
43	2	8	16	+	(1/2)(8)	=	20
42	0	—					
41	0	—					
40	2	8	8	+	(1/2)(8)	=	12
39	0	—					
38	1	4	4	+	(1/2)(4)	=	6
.							
.							
.							
24	1	4	0	+	(1/2)(4)	=	2

or 4 percent. No one scored lower than 24; so 0 percent ($\frac{0}{25}$) of the scores is below 24. The child who scored 24 received a percentile rank of 2—that is, 0 plus one half of 4. The next score obtained is 38, and again only one child received this score. Thus, 4 percent of the total ($\frac{1}{25}$) scored at 38, and 4 percent of the total scored below 38. Therefore, the percentile rank corresponding to a score of 38 is 6—that is, $4 + (\frac{1}{2})(4)$. Two children earned a score of 40, and two children scored below 40. Therefore, the percentile rank for a score of 40 is 12—that is, $8 + (\frac{1}{2})(8)$. The same procedure is followed for every score obtained. The best score in the class, 50, was obtained by two students. The percentile rank corresponding to the highest score in the class is 96.

The interpretation of percentile ranks is based on the percentage of *people*. The data from Table 5.1 provide a specific example. All students who score 48 on the test have a percentile rank of 84. These four students have *scored as well as or better than* 84 percent of their classmates on the test. Similarly, an individual who obtains a percentile rank of 21 on an intelligence test has scored as well as or better than 21 percent of the people in the norm sample.

Because the percentile rank is computed using one half the percentage of those obtaining a particular score, it is not possible to have a percentile rank of either 0 or 100. Generally, percentile ranks contain decimals, so it is possible for a score to receive a percentile rank of 99.9 or 0.1. The fiftieth percentile rank is the median.

Deciles are bands of percentiles that are ten percentile ranks in width; each decile contains 10 percent of the norm group. The first decile contains percentile ranks from 0.1 to 9.9; the second decile contains percentile ranks from 10 to 19.9; the tenth decile contains percentile ranks from 90 to 99.9.

Quartiles are bands of percentiles that are 25 percentile ranks in width; each quartile contains 25 percent of the norm group. The first quartile contains percentile ranks from 0.1 to 24.9; the fourth quartile contains the ranks 75 to 99.9.

Standard Scores

A *standardized distribution* is a set of scores that have been transformed so that the mean and standard deviation of the set take predetermined (standard) values. The most basic standardized distribution is the z distribution. A z distribution has a predetermined mean of zero and a predetermined standard deviation of one. To transform raw scores (for example, the number correct on a test) to z-scores, the mean of the distribution is subtracted from each raw score; this operation sets the mean at zero. Next, the difference between the raw score and the mean is divided by the standard deviation; this operation sets the standard deviation at one.

Standard score is the general name for any derived score that has been standardized. Although a distribution of scores can be standardized to produce any predetermined mean and standard deviation, there are four commonly used standard-score distributions: z-scores, T-scores, deviation IQs, and normal-curve equivalents.

z-Scores   As just indicated, *z-scores* are standard scores, the distribution of which has a mean of zero and a standard deviation of one. Any raw score can be converted to a *z*-score by using Equation 5.1:

$$z = (X - \overline{X}) \div S \qquad (5.1)$$

A *z*-score equals the raw score less the mean of the distribution, divided by the standard deviation of the distribution. The *z*-scores are interpreted as standard-deviation units. Thus, a *z*-score of +1.5 means that the score is 1.5 standard deviations *above* the mean of the group. A *z*-score of −0.6 means that the score is 0.6 standard deviation *below* the mean. A *z*-score of 0 is the mean performance.

Because + and − signs have a tendency to get lost and decimals may be awkward in practical situations, *z*-scores often are transformed to other standard scores. The general formula for changing a *z*-score into a different standard score is given by Equation 5.2. In the equation, SS stands for any standard score, as does the subscript *ss*. Thus, any standard score equals the mean of the distribution of standard scores ($\overline{X}_{ss}$) plus the product of the standard deviation of the distribution of standard scores (S_{ss}) multiplied by the *z*-score.

$$SS = \overline{X}_{ss} + (S_{ss})(z) \qquad (5.2)$$

T-Scores   A *T-score* is a standard score with a mean of 50 and a standard deviation of 10. In Table 5.2, five *z*-scores are converted to *T*-scores. A *T*-score of 60 is 10 points above the mean (50). Because the standard deviation is 10, a *T*-score of 60 is always one standard deviation above the mean.

Deviation IQs   When it was first introduced, the IQ was defined as the ratio of mental age (MA) to chronological age (CA), multiplied by 100. Statisticians soon found that MA has different variances and standard deviations at different chronological ages. Consequently, the same ratio IQ has different meanings at different ages—the same ratio IQ corresponds to different *z*-scores at different ages. To remedy that situation, MAs are converted to *z*-scores for each age group, and *z*-scores are converted to deviation IQs. *Deviation IQs* are standard scores with a mean of 100 and a standard deviation that is usually 15 but is occasionally 16. A

TABLE 5.2 ● *Converting z-Scores to T-Scores*

z-Score	T-Score = 50 + (10)(z)
z = +1.0	60 = 50 + (10)(+1.0)
z = −1.5	35 = 50 + (10)(−1.5)
z = −2.1	29 = 50 + (10)(−2.1)
z = +3.6	86 = 50 + (10)(+3.6)
z = 0.0	50 = 50 + (10)(0.0)

TABLE 5.3   ●   *Converting z-Scores to Deviation IQs* ($\overline{X} = 100$)

z-Score	IQ($S = 15$)	IQ ($S = 16$)
−2.00	70	68
−1.00	85	84
.00	100	100
+1.00	115	116
+2.00	130	132

z-score can be converted to a deviation IQ by using Equation 5.2. In Table 5.3, five z-scores are converted to deviation IQs with standard deviations of 15 (Column 2) and 16 (Column 3).

Normal-Curve Equivalents   *Normal-curve equivalents* are standard scores with a mean equal to 50 and a standard deviation equal to 21.06. Although the standard deviation may at first appear a bit strange, this scale divides the normal curve into 100 equal intervals.

Stanines   *Stanines* (short for *standard nines*) are standard-score bands that divide a distribution into nine parts. The first stanine includes all scores that are 1.75 standard deviations or more below the mean, and the ninth stanine includes all scores 1.75 or more standard deviations above the mean. The second through eighth stanines are each 0.5 standard deviation in width, with the fifth stanine ranging from 0.25 standard deviation below the mean to 0.25 standard deviation above the mean.

Advantages and Disadvantages of Standard Scores   Standard scores are frequently more difficult to interpret than percentile scores because the concepts of means and standard deviations are not widely understood by people without some statistical knowledge. Thus, standard scores may be more difficult for students and their parents to understand. Aside from this disadvantage, standard scores offer all the advantages of percentiles plus an additional advantage: Because standard scores are equal interval, they can be combined (for example, added or averaged).[1]

1. Standard scores also solve another subtle problem. When scores are combined in a total or composite, the elements of that composite (for example, 18 scores from weekly spelling tests that are combined to obtain a semester average) do not count the same (that is, they do not carry the same weight) *unless they have equal variances.* Tests that have larger variances contribute more to the composite than tests with smaller variances. When each of the elements has been standardized into the same standard scores (for example, when each of the weekly spelling tests has been standardized as z-scores), the elements (that is, the weekly scores) will carry exactly the same weight when they are combined. Moreover, the only way a teacher can weight tests differentially is to standardize all the tests and then multiply by the weight. For example, if a teacher wished to count the second test as three times the first test, the scores on both tests would have to be standardized, and the scores on the second test would then be multiplied by three before the scores were combined.

Concluding Comments on Derived Scores

Test authors provide tables to convert raw scores into derived scores. Thus, test users do not have to calculate derived scores. However, test users may wish to convert raw scores to other standard scores for which no conversion tables are provided. Because all standard scores are based on z-scores, standard scores have the same relationship to each other, regardless of a distribution's shape. Therefore, standard scores can be transformed into other standard scores readily, using the formulas provided earlier in this chapter. Standard scores can be converted to percentiles without conversion tables only when the distribution of scores is normal. In normal distributions, the relationship between percentiles and standard scores is known. Figure 5.2 compares various standard scores and percentiles for normal distributions. When the distribution of scores is not normal, conversion tables are necessary in order to convert percentiles to standard scores (or vice versa). These conversion tables are test-specific, so they can be provided only by a test author. Moreover, conversion tables are always required in order to convert developmental scores to scores of relative standing, even when the distribution of test scores is normal. If the only derived score available for a test is an age equivalent, then there is no way for a test user to convert raw scores to percentiles. However, age or grade equivalents can be converted back to raw scores, which can be converted to standard scores *if* the raw-score mean and standard deviation are provided.

The selection of the particular type of score to use and to report depends on the purpose of testing and the sophistication of the consumer. In our opinion,

● ● ● **FIGURE 5.2**   Relationship Among Selected Standard Scores, Percentiles, and the Normal Curve

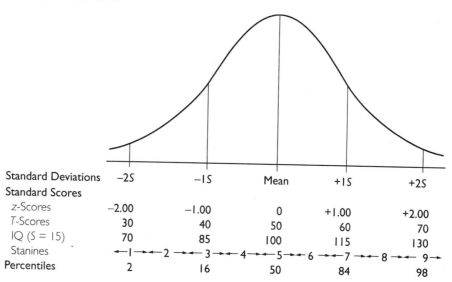

Standard Deviations	−2S	−1S	Mean	+1S	+2S
Standard Scores					
z-Scores	−2.00	−1.00	0	+1.00	+2.00
T-Scores	30	40	50	60	70
IQ (S = 15)	70	85	100	115	130
Stanines	←1→←2→←3→←4→←5→←6→←7→←8→←9→				
Percentiles	2	16	50	84	98

developmental scores should never be used. These scores are readily misinterpreted by both laypeople and professionals. In order to understand the precise meaning of developmental scores, the interpreter must generally know both the mean and the standard deviation and then convert the developmental score to a more meaningful score, a score of relative standing. Various professional organizations (for example, the International Reading Association, the American Psychological Association, the National Council on Measurement in Education, and the Council for Exceptional Children) also hold very negative official opinions about developmental scores and quotients.

Standard scores are convenient for test authors. Their use allows an author to give equal weight to various test components or subtests. Their utility for the consumer is twofold. First, *if* the score distribution is normal, the consumer can readily convert standard scores to percentile ranks. Second, because standard scores are equal-interval scores, they are useful in analyzing strengths and weaknesses of individual students and in research.

We favor the use of percentiles. These unpretentious scores require the fewest assumptions for accurate interpretation. The scale of measurement need only be ordinal, although it is very appropriate to compute percentiles on equal-interval or ratio data. The distribution of scores need not be normal; percentiles can be computed for any shape of distribution. They are readily understood by professionals, parents, and students. Most important, however, is the fact that percentiles tell us nothing more than what any norm-referenced derived score can tell us—namely, an individual's relative standing in a group. Reporting scores in percentiles may remove some of the aura surrounding test scores, and it permits test results to be presented in terms users can understand.

● ●

Scores Used in Criterion-Referenced Assessment

Unlike norm-referenced scores, which compare a student's performance to the performances of other students, criterion-referenced scores compare a student's performance against an objective and absolute standard (criterion) of performance. Criterion-referenced measures are of two types: scores on single skills and scores on multiple skills.

Single-Skill Scores

The most basic score used in criterion-referenced assessment is pass–fail, right–wrong, or some variation on this theme. Usually, one option in this dichotomous scoring scheme is defined precisely, and the other option is scored by default. For example, a correct response to "1 + 2 = ?" might be defined as "3, written intelligibly and in the correct orientation"; a wrong response would be one that fails to meet one or more of the criteria for a correct response.

Single-skill scores may also be scored along a continuum that ranges from completely correct to completely incorrect. For example, a teacher might give partial credit for a response because the student used the correct algorithm to solve a mathematics problem, even though the student's answer was incorrect. Frequently, continuum scoring of single skills is used to show progress toward mastery of a skill. For example, in a daily-living or life-skills curriculum, a teacher might scale drinking from a cup without assistance in several ways. For instance, the teacher might observe frequency of proper drinking and scale it as usually, frequently, seldom, or never drinks from a cup without assistance. Alternatively, that teacher might scale drinking on the basis of assistance needed by a student (drinks from a cup without assistance, drinks from a cup with verbal prompts, drinks from a cup with physical guidance, or does not drink from a cup). Of course, each point on the continuum requires careful definition. However, having multiple points along a continuum can be useful when trying to document slow progress toward a goal.

Some newer types of assessment (for example, portfolio assessment and authentic assessment) appear to be similar to single-dimension, criterion-referenced assessment. These newer forms of assessment frequently scale performance from "novice" to "expert" on some dimension. However, the points along the continuum are frequently so subjective that they are virtually impossible to define or assess consistently. We view these types of assessments as scaled opinions about student performance, rather than meaningful assessments of student performance; therefore, we are reluctant to consider them within the category of criterion-referenced assessment.

Multiple-Skill Scores

When multiple skills (for example, addition facts), complex skills (for example, oral reading), or multiple observations of single skills are assessed, it is common to express the number of correct or incorrect responses as a function of the total number of responses (for example, percentage correct) or as a function of time (for example, the number of correct responses per minute). In this section, we refer to these two types of scores as *percentages* and *rates*. We realize that percentages are, indeed, rates, but the professional literature frequently refers to scores expressed in time units as rates and distinguishes these scores from percentages based on the number of opportunities. We use the professional jargon with the understanding that it is at odds with the usual meanings.

Percentage

Percentages are widely used in a variety of assessment contexts. For example, *percentage correct* is probably the score most frequently used by teachers in the assessment of academic skills; *prevalence* (the percentage of time a behavior occurs) is frequently used in systematic observation. Percentages are often the basis of other criterion-referenced scores. Three of the most commonly used derivative scores are accuracy, retention, and verbal labels for percentages (such as instructional level).

Accuracy   *Accuracy* refers to one of two different scores that define percentage correct. The first is based on the number of possible correct responses and is calculated by multiplying 100 times the ratio of the number of correct responses to the number of possible responses. For example, if Ben gets 25 correct answers on a 50-item test, he earns a score of 50 percent correct. The second type of percentage score is based on the number of *attempted* responses and is calculated by multiplying 100 times the ratio of the number of correct responses to the number of attempted responses. This form of percentage correct is most commonly used when a teacher intentionally uses an assessment procedure that precludes a student from responding to all items.[2] For example, a teacher may ask a student to read orally for two minutes, but it may not be possible for that student (or any other student) to read the entire passage in the time allotted. Thus, Benny may attempt 175 words in a 350-word passage in two minutes; if he reads 150 words correctly, his percentage correct would be about 86 percent—that is, 100 × (150/175).

Retention   *Retention* refers to the percentage of learned information that is recalled. Retention may also be termed *recall, maintenance,* or *memory* of what has been learned. Regardless of the label, it is calculated in the same way: Divide the number recalled by the number originally learned, and multiply that ratio by 100. For example, if Helen learned 40 sight vocabulary words and recalled 30 of them two weeks later, her retention would be 75 percent; that is, 100 × (30/40). Because forgetting becomes more likely as the interval between the learning and the retention assessment increases, retention is usually qualified by the period of time between attainment of mastery and assessment of recall. Thus, Helen's retention would be stated as 75 percent over a two-week period.

Verbal Labels for Percentages   Frequently, percentages are given verbal labels that are intended to facilitate instruction. The two most commonly used labels are "mastery" and "instructional level." *Mastery* divides the percentage continuum in two: *Mastery* is generally set at 90 percent correct, and *nonmastery* is less than 90 percent. The criterion of 90 percent for mastery is arbitrary, and in real life we sometimes set the skill level for mastery considerably higher. For example, we would probably want to define mastery of looking both ways before crossing a street as 100 percent correct.

   Instructional level divides the percentage range into three segments: frustration, instructional, and independent levels. By convention, *frustration level* is usually defined as less than 85 percent correct, *instructional level* is defined as between 85 and 95 percent correct, and *independent level* is defined as above 95 percent correct. For example, in reading, students who decode more than 95 percent of the words should be able to read a passage without assistance;[3] students

2. A situation in which there are more opportunities to respond than time to respond is termed a *free operant.* Free-operant situations arise in assessments that are timed to allow the opportunity for unlimited increases in rate.
3. Students should not be given homework (independent practice) unless they are at the independent level.

who decode between 85 and 95 percent of the words in a passage should be able to read and comprehend that passage with assistance; students who cannot decode 85 percent of the words in a passage will probably have difficulty comprehending the material, even with assistance.

Rate

Teachers often want their students to have a supply of information at their fingertips, so that they can respond fluently (or automatically) without thinking. For example, teachers may want their students to recognize sight words without having to sound them out, recall addition facts without having to think about them, or supply Spanish words for their English equivalents. When fluency or automaticity is the desired level of performance, teachers may calculate the rate of correct response. *Rate* is defined as the number of correct responses within a specific time frame (for example, the number of words read correctly per minute). Criterion rates for successful performance are usually determined empirically. For example, readers with satisfactory comprehension usually read connected prose at rates of 100 or more words per minute (Mercer & Mercer, 1985). Readers interested in desired rates for a variety of academic skills are referred to Salvia and Hughes (1990).

A Word About Global Ratings

Teachers and psychologists sometimes use global ratings of pupil performance. These ratings may be used to judge performance as a whole (*holistic ratings*); for example, an essay may be judged to be excellent, average, or poor. These ratings may also be used to judge specific elements of a performance; for example, *scoring rubrics* may be used to rate the spelling, capitalization, word choice, and cohesiveness of an essay. Unlike the types of scores previously discussed in this chapter, however, global ratings usually are not based on systematic analysis and quantification of behavior in structured situations. Rather, *global ratings* are judgments of performance in which the criteria for awarding a score tend to be incompletely explicated and in which the elements of performance may vary from time to time.

At times, global ratings may appear to be norm-referenced scores. The global rating may look like a score of relative standing; for example, a teacher may rate a student as relatively advanced, comparable to other students, or behind other students in the same grade or in terms of writing mechanics. The global rating may look like a developmental score; for example, a teacher may rate a student's performance as best exemplifying the performance of a novice, an average student, or an expert. However, the criteria for placing a student in one of these categories are seldom explicated or objective. At other times, global ratings may appear to be criterion-referenced scores; for example, a teacher may rate a student's performance as demonstrating mastery of the use of commas. However, objective and absolute standards (criteria for evaluating performance) are not used.

Therefore, one cannot be sure either that all uses of the comma are included in the rating or what criteria were used to establish mastery (for example, 90% correct usage).

Once made, global ratings can be quantified, just as any other score can be quantified. Means and standard deviations can be calculated for ratings, and an individual rating can be compared with the ratings for other students. For example, adaptive-behavior and child-behavior scales frequently require parents to rate their child's behavior, and these ratings are compared with the ratings of other children by their parents. Although the psychometric properties may appear to be excellent, the basis of the scores remains subjective.

● ●

Summary

One method of interpreting student scores is to compare them with the scores of a group of students of known characteristics, called a *norm group*. Scores interpreted this way are called *norm-referenced scores*. Two types of norm-referenced comparisons can be made—across ages and within ages. *Developmental scores* (that is, age and grade equivalents) compare students' performances across age or grade groups. Within a group, comparisons can be made using several different types of scores that have different characteristics. A *developmental quotient* (an age or grade equivalent divided by chronological age or actual grade placement, respectively) is the least desirable within-age comparison. Of greater value are *standard scores* (for example, *z*-scores, *T*-scores, and deviation IQs). Such scores have a predetermined mean and standard deviation that define them. In our view, the best derived scores for general use are percentile ranks.

A second method of interpreting student scores is to compare scores with an absolute standard of performance. Two types of criterion-referenced scores are commonly used: single-skill scores and multiple-skill scores. Single-skill scores are usually scored dichotomously (for example, pass–fail) but may be scaled on a continuum (for example, usually, frequently, never). Whether an instrument is scored dichotomously or along a continuum, the scoring criteria always should be expressed in precise and observable terms. Multiple skills (for example, weekly writing of spelling words) are scored as the percentage correct or as the number

of correct responses in a specific period of time (for example, number of words read correctly per minute).

Finally, global ratings are occasionally used as scores. Although these scores may appear to be either norm-referenced or criterion-referenced scores, the bases for developing them are judgments that are seldom objective or precise.

Questions for Chapter Review and Thought

1. Eleanore and Ahmad take an intelligence test. Eleanore obtains an MA (mental age) of 3-5, and Ahmad obtains an MA of 12-2. The test had been standardized on 50 boys and girls at each of the following ages: 3-0 to 3-1, 4-0 to 4-1, 5-0 to 5-1, 6-0 to 6-1, and 7-0 to 7-1. The psychologist reports that Eleanore functions like a child age 3 years and 5 months, whereas Ahmad has the MA of a child 12 years and 2 months old. Identify five problems inherent in these interpretations.

2. Differentiate between a ratio IQ (developmental quotient) and a deviation IQ. Why is a deviation IQ preferable?

3. Shu-Yu earned a percentile rank of 83 on a kindergarten admission test. What is the statistical meaning of her score? To what decile does the score correspond? To what quartile does the score correspond?

4. Marvina takes a battery of standardized tests. The results are as follows:

Test A: Mental age = 8-6
Test B: Reading grade equivalent = 3.1
Test C: Developmental age = 8-4
Test D: Developmental quotient = 103
Test E: Percentile rank = 56

What must the teacher do in order to interpret Marvina's performances on these five scales and compare the performances with one another?

5. Andrew earns a stanine of 1 on an intelligence test. To what z-scores, percentile ranks, and T-scores does his stanine score correspond?

6. Distinguish among frustration level, instructional level, and independent level. Why are these distinctions important?

7. Although scores are frequently reported as developmental scores, a number of problems are inherent in the use of these scores. Discuss three of these problems.

Problems

Turn back to Table 4.4, which shows the results of the two tests Ms. Smith gave to her arithmetic class. For Test 1, make the following computations:

1. Compute the percentile rank for each student.

2. Compute each student's z-score.

3. Convert Bob's, Sam's, Sean's, and Carole's z-scores to T-scores.

4. Convert Lucy's, Carmen's, John's, and Ludwig's z-scores to deviation IQs with a mean of 100 and a standard deviation of 15.

Answers

1. 98, 94, 90, 86, 82, 78, 70, 70, 70, 50, 50, 50, 50, 50, 50, 50, 30, 30, 30, 22, 18, 14, 10, 6, 2

2. 2.17, 2.00, 1.33, 1.00, .67, .5, .33, .33, .33, 0, 0, 0, 0, 0, 0, 0, −.33, −.33, −.33, −.5, −.67, −1.00, −1.33, −2.00, −2.17

3. 72, 63, 50, 45

4. 130, 105, 100, 70

Resources for Further Investigation

Technology Resources

Stafsoft Electronic Textbook

http://www.statsoft.com/textbook/stathome.html

This is essentially a textbook online that, by typing in keywords, one can search for information on terms and general statistical concepts. It is very well organized and extremely comprehensive.

Introductory Statistics: Concepts, Models, and Applications

http://psychstat.smsu.edu/sbk00.htm

A broad range of statistical topics is covered here, including t-tests and critical values. It also includes a section on how to use a statistical calculator and a section with practice exercises.

The Royal Windsor Society for Nursing Research

http://www.windsor.igs.net/~nhodgins/design_and_analysis.html

This web site covers topics such as study methods and designs, instrument reliability and validity, and analysis of study data and statistical tests.

Norms

As discussed in Chapter 5, derived scores (such as percentiles, standard scores, and developmental scores) compare a person's test performance with the performances of others on the same test. For example, if Kareem scored at the sixty-fifth percentile, we know he did equal to or better than 65 percent of the people with whom he is compared. The percentile rank tells us nothing, however, about the people with whom we compare Kareem's performance.

To understand a student's performance, we must also know the characteristics and abilities of the people with whom we compare a test taker, such as Kareem. In norm-referenced testing, we compare a test taker with a group of students tested by the test author; this group is usually called the *norm* or *standardization sample*.[1] Obviously, the meaning of a derived score is inextricably tied to the characteristics of the norm sample. For example, suppose Kareem earned a percentile rank of 50 on an intelligence test. If the norm group comprised only students enrolled in programs for the mentally retarded, a score at the fiftieth percentile would indicate limited intellectual ability. However, if the norm group consisted of individuals enrolled in programs for the gifted, Kareem's score would indicate superior intellectual ability. Unless otherwise stated, the *implicit reference* is that test norms are representative of the population of persons living in the United States.[2]

---

1. Test authors may also defer the final selection of test items until they see how the individual test items perform when administered to large numbers of students.
2. In practice, it is impossible to test the entire population because the membership of the population is constantly changing. Fortunately, the characteristics of a population can be accurately estimated from the characteristics of a representative sample.

● ● ● ● ● ● ● ● ● ● ● ● ● ● ● ● ● ● ● ●

Representativeness

Representativeness hinges on two questions: (1) Does the norm sample contain individuals with relevant characteristics and experiences? and (2) Are the characteristics and experiences present in the sample in the same proportion as they are in the population of reference?[3]

General Characteristics and Experiences

What makes a characteristic or experience relevant depends on the construct being measured. Characteristics are relevant when they have a logical and empirical relationship to the construct being measured. For example, the time needed to run 100 meters is related to a person's age and sex. For instance, 10-year-olds are usually faster than 4-year-olds; after puberty, males are usually faster than females. Experiences are also relevant when they have a logical and empirical relationship to the construct. For example, reading achievement is related to pupil grade placement because grade in school is a fairly good measure of the amount of reading experience and instruction.

Some characteristics lack a direct theoretical relationship to a construct but are nonetheless relevant because they have an empirical relationship to that construct. For example, parental income is associated with school achievement. Income, per se, has no direct theoretical bearing on achievement. However, income is an intervening variable for many other variables that do have a theoretical relationship to achievement (access to nutritious foods and medical care, parenting styles, high-quality schools, and so on).

Several characteristics are important for any psychoeducational construct. Following is a brief discussion of and rationale for the most commonly considered factors: age, school grade, gender, acculturation of parents, geography, race and culture, and intelligence.

Age

We typically think of the range of ages for the norm groups as being one year. However, because we have known for more than 30 years that different psychological abilities develop at different rates (see Guilford, 1967, pp. 417–426), a one-year range may be inappropriate. When an ability or skill is developing rapidly (for example, locomotion in infants and toddlers), the age range of the norm group must be much less than one year. It would make no sense to conclude that a 3-month-old infant is motorically delayed when compared with a 1-year-old. Thus, on scales used to assess infants and young children, we often see norms in three-month ranges. Similarly, after an ability has matured, a one-year

---

3. Characteristics expressed by less than 1 or 2 percent of the population may not be represented accurately.

interval is unnecessary. If there are no meaningful differences in the distribution of 40-, 41-, 42-, and 43-year-olds, separate age norms for these groups are unnecessary. As a result, we often see norms in ten-year ranges on adult scales. Therefore, while one-year norms are most common, developmental theory and research can suggest norms of lesser or greater age ranges.

Grade in School

All achievement tests and some intelligence tests measure learned fact, concepts, and behavior. Students of different ages are present in most grades, and grade in school bears a more direct relationship to what is taught in school than does age. Some 7-year-old children may not be enrolled in school; some may be in kindergarten, some in first grade, some in second, and some even in third. The academic proficiency of 7-year-olds can be expected to be more closely related to what they have been taught than to their age. Consequently, grade norms are more appropriate than are age norms for achievement tests used with students of school age.

Gender

Males and females sometimes differ on their tested performances. Some of these differences can be appropriately attributed to biological differences, especially physical differences after puberty. For example, men tend to be larger, stronger, and more aggressive than women. Some sex differences can also be appropriately attributed to differences in cultural expectations and experiences. Although gender-role expectations are changing, gender still may systematically limit the types of activities a child participates in because of modeling, peer pressure, or the responses of significant adults. Finally, we are still speculating about the causes of sex differences in yet other areas. For example, why do women tend to perform better on essay examinations while men tend to do better on multiple-choice tests? Although the causes of sex differences are interesting both scientifically and politically, trying to unravel biological and cultural causes is beyond the scope of this text.

On most psychological and educational tests, sex differences are small, and the distributions of scores of males and females tend to overlap considerably. When sex differences are minor, norm groups clearly should contain the appropriate proportions of males (about 48%) and females (about 52%)—the proportion found in the general U.S. population. However, when sex differences are substantial, the correct course of action is unclear. Some favor separate norms for males and females. (Separate norms remove any differences in derived scores.[4]) Others favor norms containing proportional representation of both sexes, which leaves one sex, on average, scoring lower than the other.

---

4. The raw scores associated with particular derived scores (such as the fiftieth percentile) will be different, of course.

Acculturation of Parents

Acculturation is an imprecise concept that refers to an understanding of the language (including conventions and pragmatics), history, values, and social conventions of society at large. Nowhere are the complexities of acculturation more readily illustrated than in the area of language. Acculturation requires people to know more than standard American English; they must also know the appropriate contexts for various words and idioms, appropriate volume and distance between speaker and listener, appropriate posture to indicate respect, and so forth.

Because acculturation is a broad and somewhat diffuse construct, it is difficult to define or measure precisely. Typically, test authors use the educational or occupational attainment (socioeconomic status) of the parents as a general indication of the level of acculturation of the home. As it turns out, the socioeconomic status of a student's parents is strongly related to that student's scores on all sorts of tests—intelligence, achievement, adaptive behavior, social functioning, and so forth. The children of middle- and upper-class parents tend to score higher on such tests. The causes of these consistent social-class differences have been debated for decades (see Gottesman, 1968; Herrnstein & Murray, 1994), with some scholars favoring genetic interpretations of differences, others favoring environmental interpretations, and still others favoring interpretations based on the interaction of genetics and environment. Whatever the reasons for class differences in child development, clearly, norm samples must include all segments of society (in the same proportion as in the general population) in order to be representative.

Geography

As is readily apparent from any current test manual, there are differences in the attainment of individuals living in different geographic regions of the United States, and various psychoeducational tests reflect these regional differences. Most consistently, the average scores of individuals living in the southeastern part of the United States (excluding Florida) are often lower than the average scores of individuals living in other regions of the country. Moreover, community size, population density, and changes in population have also been related to academic and intellectual development. There are several seemingly logical explanations for many of these relationships. For example, educational attainment is related to educational expenditures, and there are regional differences in the financial support of public education. Well-educated young adults tend to move away from communities with limited employment and cultural opportunities. When brighter and better-educated individuals leave a community, the average intellectual ability and educational attainment in that community go down, and the average ability and attainment of the communities to which the brighter individuals move go up. Regardless of the reasons for geographical differences, test norms should include individuals from all geographic regions, as well as from urban, suburban, and rural communities.

Race and Cultural Identity

Race and cultural identity continue to be emotionally charged issues for U.S. society. The scientific and educational communities have been often insensitive and occasionally blatantly racist (for example, Down, 1866/1969). As recently as 1972, a widely used test of intelligence, the Stanford–Binet, excluded nonwhite individuals from the standardization sample. Today, individuals of color are still too often faced with limited opportunities and discrimination on a daily basis in public education, as well as in the broader society.

Race and culture are particularly relevant to our discussion of norms. First, we note that there are persistent differences in *tested* achievement and intelligence among races and cultural groups, although these differences continue to narrow.[5] As a result of these differences, students of color are placed in special-education programs at rates higher than would be expected based on their proportions in the general population. As we saw in Chapter 3, some of this overrepresentation can be attributed to the inappropriate use of tests. However, some of the differences in achievement, intelligence, or behavior are believed to be real. A discussion of the causes of these differences is well beyond the scope of this book. Suffice it to say that, as in the case of social-class differences, differences are attributed to genetic causes, environmental causes, or the interaction of genetics and environment.

It is important to include individuals of all racial and cultural groups, both in field tests of items and in the standardization of a test, for two reasons. First, to the extent that individuals of different races undergo cultural experiences that differ even within a given social class and geographic region, norm samples that exclude (or underrepresent) one race are unrepresentative of the total population. Second, if individuals from different cultures are excluded from field tests of test items, item-difficulty estimates (p-values) and point-biserial (item–total) correlations may be inaccurate, and the test's scaling may be in error. Thus, even if test designers could justify culturally homogeneous norms (and we are not saying that they could), the exclusion or underrepresentation of individuals of color in norm samples gives the appearance of bias.

Intelligence

A representative sample of individuals, in terms of their level of intellectual functioning, is essential for standardizing an intelligence test—or any other kind of test. Intelligence is related to a number of variables that are considered in psychoeducational assessment. It is certainly related to achievement because most intelligence tests were actually developed to predict school success. Correlations of achievement and intelligence ranging between .60 and .80 are typical (for example, Hieronymus, Hoover, & Lindquist, 1986). Because language develop-

---

5. We also note that perhaps as much as 90 percent of observed racial and cultural differences can be attributed to socioeconomic differences.

ment and facility are often considered an indication of intellectual development, intelligence tests are often verbally oriented. Consequently, we would also expect to find substantial correlations between scores on tests of intelligence and scores on tests of linguistic or psycholinguistic ability. In addition, items thought to reflect perceptual ability appear on intelligence tests, and as early as 1944, Thurstone found various perceptual tasks to be a factor in intelligence. Thus, intelligence must be considered in the development of norms for perceptual and perceptual–motor tests.

In the development of norms, it is essential to test the full range of intellectual ability. Limiting the sample to students enrolled in and attending school (usually regular classes) restricts the norms. Failure to consider individuals classified as mentally retarded in standardization procedures introduces systematic bias into test norms by underestimating the population mean and standard deviation.[6]

Relevant Special Characteristics

Some characteristics of the sample and the population are important only for particular types of tests. For example, test authors often caution test users to make sure that the content of achievement tests reflects the content of the test user's classroom curriculum. However, the test author must also make sure that the content is appropriate for the norm sample. Thus, authors of diagnostic reading tests (which often measure specific skills such as syllabication and sound blending) should specify the curriculum followed by the students in the norm samples. For example, suppose that a whole-language, sight-vocabulary orientation is used by students in the norm sample. The derived scores of students taught by a phonics method may be inflated; that is, the student taught by the phonics methods may earn relatively high scores when compared with the less-skilled students in the norm group.

. . . .

Technical Considerations

Finding People

Finding a broadly representative sample of people requires careful planning. Therefore, test authors or publishers usually develop sampling plans to try to locate potential participants with the needed characteristics. Sampling plans involve finding communities of specific sizes within geographic regions. Cluster sampling and selection of representative communities (or some combination of the two) are two common methods of choosing these communities. In *cluster sampling,* urban

---

6. In Chapter 29, we discuss the inclusion of students with disabilities in the assessment of educational outcomes.

areas and the surrounding suburban and rural communities are selected. Such sampling plans have the advantage of requiring fewer testers and less travel. When a sampling plan calls for the selection of representative communities, a *representative* community is usually defined as one in which the mean demographic characteristics (such as educational level and income) of residents are approximately the same as the national or regional average. For example, in the 1990 U.S. census, about 52 percent of the population was female; 19 percent had attended college for at least four years; about 30 percent had not completed high school; and so forth. A representative community would thus be one in which about 52 percent of the population was female, about 19 percent had attended college for four years, and so on.

Proportional Representation

Explicit in the preceding discussion of characteristics of people in a representative normative sample is the idea that various kinds of people should be included in the sample in the same proportion as they occur in the general population. However, neither cluster sampling nor selection of representative communities guarantees that the participants, as a group, are representative of the population. Consequently, test authors may adjust norms to make them representative. One method of adjusting norms is to systematically oversample subjects (that is, to select many more subjects than are needed) and then to drop subjects until a representative sample has been achieved. Another method is to weight subjects within the normative sample differentially. Subjects with underrepresented characteristics may be counted as more than one subject, and subjects with overrepresented characteristics may be counted as fractions of persons. Both methods may be used. In such ways, norm samples can be manipulated to conform with population characteristics.

No matter how test norms are constructed, test authors should systematically compare the relevant characteristics of the population and their standardization samples. Although we frequently use the singular (that is, norm sample or group) when discussing norms, it is important to understand that tests have multiple normative samples. For example, an achievement test intended for use with students in kindergarten through twelfth grade has 13 norm groups (1 for each grade). If that achievement test has separate norms for males and females at each grade, then there are 26 norm groups. When we test a second-grade boy, we do not compare his performance with the performances of all students in the total norm sample. Rather, we compare the boy's performance with that of other second-graders (or of other second-grade boys if there are separate norms for boys and girls). Thus, the preceding discussions of representatives and the number of subjects apply to each specific comparison group within the norms—not to the aggregated or combined samples. Representativeness should be demonstrated for each comparison group. For example, Table 6.1 shows such a comparison for RISA (Salvia, Neisworth, & Schmidt, 1990), a norm-referenced adaptive behavior scale for use

TABLE 6.1 • *Percentage of the 1980 U.S. Population and RISA Weighted Norms by Selected Demographic Characteristics*

	1980 U.S.	Age Groups							
		12	13	14	15	16	17	18	19
n		231	272	260	291	254	281	187	124
Sex									
Male	47.2	47.2	47.2	47.2	47.2	47.0	47.2	47.2	47.2
Female	52.8	52.8	52.8	52.8	52.8	53.0	52.8	52.8	52.8
Community									
Urban	73.7	73.6	73.5	73.7	73.7	73.7	73.7	73.7	73.7
Rural	26.3	26.4	26.5	26.3	26.3	26.3	26.3	26.3	26.3
Education									
Less than high school	29.2	29.3	29.2	29.3	29.3	29.1	29.2	29.2	29.3
High school graduate	36.5	36.6	36.4	36.5	36.4	36.3	36.6	36.3	36.2
Some college	15.3	15.2	15.6	15.2	15.3	15.7	15.3	15.5	15.3
College graduate or more		18.9	18.9	18.9	19.0	18.9	19.0	19.0	19.2
Region									
Northeast	21.7	21.4	21.5	21.9	21.8	21.5	21.8	20.7	21.5
North Central	26.0	26.5	25.6	25.9	25.8	26.0	26.1	26.0	26.0
South	33.3	33.2	33.9	33.3	33.4	33.0	33.3	33.1	33.5
West	19.0	18.8	18.9	18.9	19.0	19.5	18.9	20.2	19.0
Caucasian	79.6	79.8	75.9	65.1	78.1	78.4	66.8	73.0	66.7

SOURCE: Salvia, J., Neisworth, J., & Schmidt, M. (1990). *Examiner's manual: Responsibility and Independence Scale for Adolescents.* Allen, TX: DLM.

with adolescents between the ages of 12 and 19 years. Tables such as these allow a test user to judge the representativeness of a test's norms.

Finally, the systematic development of representative norms is time-consuming and expensive. Samples that are convenient, such as volunteers from all the parochial schools in a big city, reduce the time needed to locate subjects and are less expensive; however, they are unlikely to be representative, even when the number of subjects is impressively large.

Number of Subjects

The number of participants in a norm sample is important for several reasons. First, the number of subjects should be large enough to guarantee stability. If a sample is very small, another group of participants might have a different mean and standard deviation. Second, the number of participants should be large enough to represent infrequent characteristics. For example, if about 1 percent of the population is Native American, a sample of 25 or 50 people will be unlikely to contain even 1 Native American. Third, there should be enough subjects so that there can be a full range of derived scores. In practice, 100 participants in each age or grade is considered the minimum.

Smoothing Norms

After the norm sample has been finalized, norm tables are prepared. Because of minor sampling fluctuations, even well-selected norm groups will show minor variations in distribution shape. Minor smoothing is believed to result in better estimates of derived scores, means, and standard deviations. For example, there might be a few outliers—scores at the extremes of a distribution that are not contiguous to the distribution of scores but are several points beyond what would be considered the highest or lowest score in a distribution. A test author might drop these outliers. Similarly, the progression of group means from age to age may not be consistent, or group variances may differ slightly from age to age for no apparent reason. As a result, test developers will often smooth these values to conform to a theoretical or empirically generated model of performance (for example, using predicted means rather than obtained means).

Smoothing is also done to remove unwanted fluctuations in the shapes of age or grade distributions by adjusting the relationship between standard scores and percentiles. Even when normal test distributions are expected on the basis of theory, the obtained distributions of scores are never completely normal. For example, several models of intelligence posit a normal distribution of scores; in practice, the distribution of test scores is skewed because of an excess of low-scoring individuals. Thus, standard scores do not correspond to the percentile ranks that are expected in a normal distribution. In such cases, a test author may force standard scores into a normal distribution by assigning them to percentile ranks on the basis of the relationship between standard scores and percentiles found in normal distributions.

For example, a raw score corresponding to the eighty-fourth percentile will be assigned a *T*-score of 60, regardless of the calculated value. The process, called *area transformation* or *normalizing a distribution,* is discussed in detail in advanced measurement texts. When normal distributions are not expected, a test developer may remove minor inconsistencies in distribution shapes from age to age or grade to grade. To smooth out minor inconsistencies, test authors may average the percentile ranks associated with specific standard scores. For example, a *T*-score of 60 might be associated with percentile ranks of 72, 74, and 73 in 6-, 7-, and 8-year-old groups, respectively. These percentiles could be averaged, and *T*-scores of 60 in each of the age groups could be assigned a percentile rank of 73.

Age of Norms

For a norm sample to be representative, it must represent the current population. Levels of skill and ability change over time. Skilled athletes of today run faster, jump higher, and are stronger than the best athletes of a generation ago. Some of the improvement can be attributed to better training, but some can also be attributed to better nutrition and societal changes. Similarly, intellectual and educational performances have increased from generation to generation, although these increases are neither steady nor linear.

For example, on norm-referenced achievement tests, considerably more than half the students score above the average after the test has been in use from five to seven years. In such cases, the test norms are clearly dated, because only half the population can ever be above the median (Linn, Graue, & Sanders, 1990). While some increase in tested achievement can be attributed to teacher familiarity with test content (Linn et al., 1990), there is little doubt that some of the changes represent real improvement in achievement.

There are probably multiple causes for these increases. For example, during the late 1960s and 1970s, the social fabric of the United States changed substantially. The civil-rights, women's, and right-to-education movements brought much-needed reform to the U.S. education system. The computer revolution forever changed the availability of information. Never before has there been so much knowledge accessible to so many people. Students of today know more than did the students of the 1970s or the 1980s. Students of today also probably know less than will the students of tomorrow.

The important point is that old norms tend to estimate a student's relative standing in the population erroneously because the old norms are too easy. The point at which norms become outdated will depend in part on the ability or skill being assessed. With this caution, it seems to us that 15 years is about the maximum useful life for norm samples used in ability testing; 7 years appears to be the maximum for norm life for achievement tests.

Normative Updates

Because the development of systematically standardized tests is so expensive, test publishers may update a test's norms more frequently than they revise the test. Normative updating can be done in two ways. First, a completely different set of norms may be systematically developed. Procedurally, this kind of update is identical to the development of any set of norms. Second, statistics based on a small representative sample can be used to adjust (or recalibrate) the old norms. The necessary statistics (for example, mean and standard deviation in classical test theory or difficulty, discrimination, and guessing parameters in item-response theory) can be accurately estimated from a small sample of individuals. The old norms are linearly transformed using the new statistics, and new tables are prepared to convert raw scores to standard scores. Moreover, if the distribution of scores is normal, new percentiles can be calculated based on their relationship with standard scores.

The difficulty with normative updates is that the content is unchanged. This is not a problem when content is timeless. However, if the content becomes easier (as is frequently the case with achievement tests), the new norms may not discriminate among high scorers. In addition, normative updates probably will not fix problems associated with reliability or validity (apart from normative considerations).

Relevance of Norms

Norms must provide comparisons that are relevant in terms of the purpose of assessment. National norms are the most appropriate if we are interested in knowing how a particular student is developing intellectually, perceptually, linguistically, or physically. In other circumstances, norms developed on a particular portion of the population may be meaningful. For example, if we wish to ascertain the degree to which Ramona has profited from her 12 years of schooling, norms developed for the particular school districts she attended are appropriate.

Local norms are usually more useful in retrospective interpretations of a student's performance than in predictive interpretations. In some cases, norms based on particular groups may be more relevant than those based on the population as a whole. Some devices are standardized on special populations (for example, the AAMR Adaptive Behavior Scale was standardized on individuals with mental retardation). Aptitude tests are often standardized on individuals in specific trades or professions. The utility of special population norms is similar to the utility of local norms: They are likely to be more useful in retrospective comparisons then in future predictions. Unless we know how the special population corresponds to the general population, predictions may not be appropriate.

There are specific instances in which special population norms have been misused. Just because a person's performance is similar to that of a special population, that does not mean that the person belongs to or should belong to that population. When Mary earns the same score as a typical lawyer on a test of legal aptitude, her score does not mean that Mary is or should become a lawyer. The argument that she should contains a logical fallacy, an undistributed middle term. (According to this logic, if dogs eat meat and university professors eat meat, then dogs are or should be university professors—clearly not the case.)

Reasoning of this sort is often inferred when criterion groups are used in test standardization. Such inferences are valid if it can be demonstrated that only members of a particular group score in a particular manner. If some people who are not members of the particular group earn the same scores as members of that group, the relationship between group membership and scores should be quantified. For example, let us assume that 90 percent of youngsters with brain damage make unusual (perhaps rotated, distorted, or simplified) reproductions of geometric designs. Let us also assume that 3 percent of the total population is brain injured. If individuals without brain damage were the only ones who made normal drawings, we could say with certainty that anyone who makes normal drawings is not brain injured. However, because 10 percent of individuals with brain injuries make normal reproductions, we cannot be sure: 0.31 percent of the individuals who make normal drawings are brain injured. Moreover, in some instances, the normal population makes deviant responses. Assume that 20 percent of the normal population and all brain-injured children make unusual drawings.

If 3 percent of the population is brain injured, then 22.4 percent of the population will perform as brain-injured test takers do ([100% of 3%] + 20% of 97%] = 22.4%). A deviant performance on the test would mean only a 13 percent (0.03/0.224) chance that the person was brain injured.

Using Norms Correctly

The manuals accompanying commercially prepared tests usually contain a table that allows a tester to convert raw scores to various derived scores, such as percentile ranks, without tedious calculations. Occasionally, the tester is even confronted with several tables for converting raw scores. For example, it is not uncommon for the same manual to contain one set of tables for converting raw scores to percentile ranks on the basis of the age of the person tested and another set of tables for converting raw scores to percentile ranks on the basis of the school grade of the person tested. To select the appropriate table, the tester must determine the population to which the performance of the sample is inferred. This can be learned by examining how the norm group was selected. If the test author sampled by grades in school, then the population of reference is students in a particular grade; consequently, the grade tables should be used for converting raw scores to derived scores. Conversely, if the test author sampled by age, the age tables should be used because the population of reference is a particular age group.

Tests often lose their power to discriminate near the extremes of the distribution, and it may not be possible for a student to earn a score more than about 2.5 standard deviations from the mean. For example, a student might not be able to earn an IQ less than 50 even if no test items were passed. Because complete failure on a test provides little or no information about what a person can do, testers often administer tests based on a norm sample of people younger than the test taker. Although such a procedure may provide useful qualitative information, it cannot provide norm-referenced interpretations because the ages of the individuals in the norm group and the age of the person being tested are not the same.

Another serious error is committed when the tester uses a person's mental age to obtain derived scores from conversion tables set up on the basis of chronological age. We suppose the reasoning behind such practices is that if the person functions as an 8-year-old child intellectually, the use of conversion tables based on the performance of 8-year-old children can be justified. However, such practices are incorrect because the norms were not established by sampling persons by mental age. When assessing the reading skill of an adolescent or adult who performs below the first percentile, a tester has little need for further or more precise norm-referenced comparisons. The tester already knows that the person is not a good reader. If the examiner wants to ascertain which reading skills a person has or lacks, a criterion-referenced (norm-free) device will be more suitable. Sometimes the most appropriate use of norms is no use at all.

● ● ● ● ● ● ● ● ● ● ● ● ● ● ● ● ● ● ● ●

Concluding Comment: Caveat Emptor

If the test author recognizes that the test norms are inadequate, the test user should be explicitly cautioned (AERA et al., 1997). The inadequacies do not, however, disappear with the inclusion of a cautionary note; the test is still inadequate. Some may argue, incorrectly, that inadequate norms are better than no norms at all. However, inadequate norms do not allow meaningful and accurate inferences about performance. If poor norms are used, misinterpretations follow.

A joint committee of the American Educational Research Association (AERA), the American Psychological Association, and the National Council on Measurement in Education (1997) prepared a pamphlet, *Standards for Educational and Psychological Testing,* that outlines the standards to which test authors should adhere: "Norms that are presented should refer to clearly described groups. These groups should be the ones with whom users of the test will ordinarily wish to compare the people who are tested" (p. 33). The pamphlet states that the test author should report how the sample was selected and whether any bias was present in the sample. The author should also describe the sampling techniques and the resultant sample in sufficient detail for the test user to judge the utility of the norms. "Reports of norming studies should include the year in which normative data were collected, provide descriptive statistics, and describe the sampling design and participation rates in sufficient detail so that the study can be evaluated for appropriateness" (p. 33).

In the marketplace of testing, let the buyer beware.

● ●

Summary

The primary purpose of norms is to compare a student's tested performance with the performance of other students. The group with which the student is compared is called a *norm group.* Norm groups must be representative of the target population on all relevant characteristics. Although special characteristics may be relevant for some specialized tests, many characteristics are relevant for most tests: student's age, school grade, gender, place of residence (geography), racial and cultural background, and general intellectual functioning, and also the acculturation of the student's parents. These factors are important because most skills and abilities depend on (or are strongly related to) these factors. However, it is not enough simply to have the right kinds of people in the norms. The relevant characteristics must be represented in proportions that correspond to those in the target population.

To develop representative norms, test authors and publishers develop sampling plans to obtain enough individuals to prepare normative groups large enough to allow the use of derived scores. After a large number of individuals are tested, authors may adjust the norms to make them more representative. Thus, they may drop subjects, differentially weight subjects, or smooth norms.

However, in evaluating a test's norms, users should consider not only whether the norms are generally representative, but also the age of the norms (that is, Are the norms current?), the relevance of the norms (that is, Is it appropriate to compare the performance of a specific test taker with the performances represented by the norm sample?), and the appropriate use of the norms (that is, Are the inferences derived from the comparisons appropriate?).

Questions for Chapter Review and Thought

1. Although the gap is decreasing, why might nonwhite children still score lower than white children on intellectual and achievement tests?

2. How might the author of a test demonstrate that its normative sample is representative of the population of children attending school in the United States?

3. Read the manual of any achievement test. How were the individuals in the normative sample selected? Is the normative sample representative in terms of gender, ethnicity, and parental educational attainment? Were students with disabilities included in the norms? (If so, how did the test authors ensure that they would be included in the correct proportions?)

4. Discuss three approaches to tinkering with norms that you might use as a test developer to produce better norms.

Resources for Further Investigation

Project

Obtain a copy of the latest U.S. census. Determine how well you and your classmates currently represent the general population. If you and your classmates were now 8 years old and attending the third grade in your local school system, how representative would you be of the general population?

Print Resources

American Educational Research Association, American Psychological Association, and National Council on Measurement in Education. (1997). *Standards for educational and psychological testing.* Washington, DC: American Psychological Association.

Cannell, J. J. (1988). Nationally normed elementary achievement testing in America's public schools: How all 50 states are above the national average. *Educational Measurement: Issues and Practice, 7*(2), 5–9.

Herrnstein, R., & Murray, C. (1996). *The bell curve: Intelligence and class structure in American life.* New York: The Free Press.

Linn, R., Graue, E., & Sanders, N. (1990). Comparing state and district test results to national norms: The validity of claims that "everyone is above average." *Educational Measurement: Issues and Practice, 9*(3), 5–14.

Salvia, J., Neisworth, J., & Schmidt, M. (1990). *Examiner's manual: Responsibility and Independence Scale for Adolescents.* Allen, TX: DLM.

Technology Resources

About the NCME

http://www.assessment.iupui.edu/NCME/

The home page for the National Council on Measurement in Education (NCME) provides information on the organization and links to other relevant measurement-related web sites.

Criterion- versus Norm-Related Testing

http://www.valdosta.peachnet.edu/~whuitt/psy702/measeval/crnmref.html

This page provides a table that outlines the difference between criterion- and norm-related testing on the basis of dimensions including purpose, content, and score interpretation.

Guide to Norm-Referenced Testing

http://www.sccoe.k12.ca.us/standards/second_page.html

This is a document adopted from an essay by W. James Popham that describes standardized tests, norms, and what goes into the testing process.

Reliability

W hen we assess, we are interested in generalizing what we see today, under one set of conditions, to other occasions and conditions. For example, if we cannot generalize from Linda's reading skills that are observed during testing to her skills in the classroom situation, then the test data are of little or no value. To the extent that we can generalize from a particular set of observations (a test, for example), those observations are *reliable*.

Reliability is a major consideration in evaluating an assessment procedure. For example, when we give a person an individually administered test, we would like to be able to generalize the results in three different ways. First, we would like to assume that similar, but different, test questions would give us the same results—we would like to be able to generalize to other test items in the same domain. Suppose Ms. Amig wanted to assess her kindergartners' recognition of upper- and lowercase letters of the English alphabet. She could assess the domain—all 52 upper- and lowercase letters—or she could sample from the domain. For example, she could ask each of her students to name the following letters: A, h, j, L, q, r, u, V, w. She would like to assume that her students would earn about the same score (say, percent correct or percentile rank) whether they were tested on this sample, on the entire domain of letters, or on any other sample of letters (say, b, E, k, m, s, T, U, x, Y, z); she would like to be able to generalize from one sample of items to any and all other samples from the domain.

Second, we would like to assume that the behavior we see today would be seen tomorrow (or next week) if we were to test again—we would like to be able to generalize to similar times. Suppose Ms. Amig tests her pupils on Monday at 9:30 A.M. She would like to assume that the students would earn the same scores if they were tested Tuesday at 1:45 P.M.—or at any other time during the day or evening.

There is a domain of times, as well as a domain of items. A test on any one occasion is a sample from the domain of all times. Ms. Amig would like to generalize the results found at one sample of time to the total domain (all times).

Third, we would like to assume that if any other comparably qualified examiner were to give the test, the results would be the same—we would like to be able to generalize to similar testers. Suppose Ms. Amig listened to her students say the letters of the alphabet. It would not be very useful if she assigned Barney a score of 70 percent correct, while another teacher (or parent) who listened to Barney awarded a score of 50 percent correct or 90 percent correct for the same performance. Ms. Amig would like to assume that any other teacher (or parent) would score her students' responses in just the same way. Thus, there are three kinds of reliability: (1) Reliability for generalizing to other test items is termed *alternate-form reliability* or *internal consistency*; reliability for generalizing to different times is called *stability* or *test–retest reliability*; and reliability for generalizing to different scorers is termed *interrater* or *interscore reliability.*

An easy way to think of reliability is to think of any obtained score as consisting of two parts: true score and error. By definition, error is uncorrelated with true score and is essentially random. *Error* is best thought of as lack of generalizability that results from the failure to get a representative sample from the domain. For example, a sample of alphabet letters that consisted of A, B, C, D, and E would probably provide a much easier test than other samples of letters. A systematically easier sample would inflate the scores earned by Ms. Amig's students. Similarly, a sample made up of the most difficult letters would probably deflate the scores earned by her students. Thus, error—failure to select a representative sample of items—can raise or lower scores. The average (mean) error in the long run is equal to zero. In the long run, across a large number of samples, the samples that raise scores are balanced by samples that lower scores. If Ms. Amig made up and administered all the possible four-letter tests, a student's mean performance would be that student's true score. There would be no error associated with that score. However, there would be a distribution of test scores around that mean; it would be a distribution of obtained test scores centered on the true score.

Another way to think of a *true score* is to view it as the score that a student would earn if the entire domain of items were assessed. On achievement tests dealing with beginning material and with certain types of behavioral observations, it is occasionally possible to assess an entire domain (for example, reading and writing the letters of the alphabet or knowing all the addition, subtraction, multiplication, and division facts). In such cases, the obtained score is a student's true score, and there is no need to estimate the test's item reliability. Opportunities to assess an entire domain are very limited, however, even in the primary grades. In more advanced curricula, it is often impossible to assess an entire achievement domain. Moreover, it is never possible to assess the entire domain when a hypothetical construct (such as intelligence or visual perception) is being assessed. Therefore, in these cases, item reliability should always be estimated.

The same argument can be made for reliability (generalization) over times and scores. If one time makes up the entire domain, then the student's performance at that time is the student's true score, although such a situation is difficult to imagine. Similarly, if evaluation by only one person makes up the entire domain, then the performance as assessed by that one person constitutes the entire domain, and the student's scores are true scores. Although such a situation is also difficult to imagine in the schools, outside of school, personal evaluations are frequently all that matters. For example, your evaluation of the food at a restaurant is probably the only evaluation that is important in determining whether the food was good.

As you may recall from the discussion in Chapter 2, people should always be concerned about error during assessment. Although there is always some degree of error, the important question is, How much error is attached to a particular score? Unfortunately, a direct answer to this question is not readily available. To estimate both the amount of error attached to a score and the amount of error in general, two statistics are needed: (1) a reliability coefficient for the particular generalization, and (2) the standard error of measurement.

● ●

The Reliability Coefficient

The symbol used to denote a reliability coefficient is r with two identical subscripts (for example, r_{xx} or r_{aa}). The reliability coefficient is generally defined as the square of the correlation between obtained scores and true scores on a measure (r_{xt}^2), where x is the obtained score and t is the hypothetical true score. This quantity is identical to the ratio of the variance of true scores to the variance of obtained scores for a distribution. (The variance of obtained scores equals the variance of true scores plus the variance of error.) Accordingly, a *reliability coefficient* indicates the proportion of variability in a set of scores that reflects true differences among individuals. In the special case where two equivalent forms of a test exist, the Pearson product–moment correlation coefficient between scores from the two forms is equal to the reliability coefficient for either form. These relationships are summarized in Equation 7.1, where x and x' are parallel measures, and S^2 is, of course, the variance.

$$r_{xx'} = r_{xt}^2 = \frac{S^2_{\text{true scores}}}{S^2_{\text{obtained scores}}} \tag{7.1}$$

If there is relatively little error, the ratio of true-score variance to obtained-score variance approaches a reliability index of 1.00 (perfect reliability); if there is a relatively large amount of error, the ratio of true-score variance to obtained-score variance approaches .00 (total unreliability).[1] Thus, a test with a reliability coefficient of .90 has relatively less error of measurement and is more reliable than a test with a reliability coefficient of .50.

---

1. Although it is mathematically possible to obtain a negative reliability estimate, such an obtained estimate is theoretically meaningless.

Different methods of estimating a reliability coefficient are used, depending on what generalization the test giver wishes to make. Test authors should always report the extent to which test givers can generalize to different times and the degree to which they can generalize to different samples of questions or items. If a test is difficult to score, the test author should also report the extent to which test givers can generalize to different scorers.

Generalizing to Different Times

Test–retest reliability is an index of stability. Educators are interested in many human traits and characteristics that, theoretically, change very little over time. For example, children diagnosed as colorblind at age 5 are expected to be diagnosed as colorblind at any time in their lives. Colorblindness is an inherited trait that cannot be corrected. Consequently, the trait should be perfectly stable. When an assessment identifies a student as colorblind on one occasion and not colorblind on a later occasion, the assessment is unreliable.

Other traits are less stable than color vision over a long period of time; they are developmental. For example, people's heights will increase from birth through adulthood. The increases are relatively slow and predictable. Consequently, measurement with a reliable ruler should indicate few changes in height over a one-month period. Radical changes in people's heights (especially decreases) over short periods of time would cause us to question the reliability of the measurement device. Most educational and psychological characteristics are conceptualized much as height is. For example, we expect reading achievement to increase with length of schooling but to be relatively stable over short periods of time, such as two weeks. Devices used to assess traits and characteristics must produce sufficiently consistent and stable results if those results are to have practical meaning for making educational decisions.

The procedure for obtaining a stability coefficient is fairly simple. A large number of students are tested. A short time later (preferably two weeks, but in practice, the time interval can vary from one day to several months), they are retested with the same device. The students' scores from the two administrations are then correlated. The obtained correlation coefficient is the stability coefficient.

Estimates of the amount of error derived from stability coefficients tend to be inflated. Any change in a student's true score that is attributable to maturation or learning is added to the error variance unless every student in the sample changes in the same way. Thus, if there is a "maturational spurt" between the two test administrations for only a few students, the change in the true score is incorporated into the error term. Similarly, if some of the students cannot answer some of the questions on the first administration of the test but learn the answers by the second administration, the learning (change in true score) is interpreted as error. The experience of taking the test once may also make answering the same questions the second time easier; the first test may sensitize the student to the second administration of the test. Generally, however, the closer together in time the test and retest are, the higher the reliability is, because within a shorter time span there is less chance of true scores changing.

Generalizing to Different Item Samples

There are two main approaches to estimating the extent to which we can generalize to different samples of items. The first approach requires that test authors develop two (or more) similar tests, called "alternate forms"; the second approach does not.

Alternate forms of a test are defined as two tests that (a) measure the same trait or skill to the same extent and (b) are standardized on the same population. Alternate forms offer essentially equivalent tests; sometimes, in fact, they're called equivalent forms. A nonpsychometric example illustrates this equivalence. Each 12-inch ruler sold at a local variety store is thought to be the equivalent (or alternate form) of any other ruler. If you purchased a red ruler and a green ruler and measured several objects with both, you would expect a high correlation between the green measurements and the red measurements. This example is analogous to alternate-form reliability. There is one important difference, however: Alternate forms of tests do not contain the same items. Still, although the items are different, the means and variances for the two tests are assumed to be (or should be) the same. In the absence of error of measurement, any subject would be expected to earn the same score on both forms.

To estimate the reliability coefficient for two alternate forms (A and B) of a test, a large sample of students is tested with both forms. Half the subjects receive form A, then form B; the other half receive form B, then form A. Scores from the two forms are correlated. The resulting correlation coefficient is a reliability coefficient.

Estimates of reliability based on alternate forms are subject to one of the same constraints as stability coefficients: The more time that passes between the administration of the two (or more) forms, the greater the likelihood of change in true scores. Alternate-form reliability estimates are less subject to a sensitization effect than are stability coefficients, because the subjects are not tested with the same items twice.

The second approach to estimating the extent to which we can generalize to different test items does not require that the authors develop more than one form of the test. This method of estimating a test's reliability, called *internal consistency,* is a little different.

Suppose we wanted to use this second method to estimate the reliability of a ten-item test. After the test was constructed, we would administer it to a sample of students (for example, 20 students). The results of this hypothetical test are presented in Table 7.1. If the ten individual test items all measure the same skill or ability, we can divide the test into 2 five-item tests, each measuring that same skill or ability. Thus, after the test is administered, we can create two alternate forms of the test, each containing one half of the total number of test items, or five items. We can then correlate the two sets of scores and obtain an estimate of the relia-

TABLE 7.1 ● Hypothetical Performance of Twenty Children on a Ten-Item Test

	Items										Totals		
Child	1	2	3	4	5	6	7	8	9	10	Total Test	Evens Correct	Odds Correct
1	+	+	+	−	+	−	−	−	+	−	5	1	4
2	+	+	+	+	−	+	+	+	−	+	8	5	3
3	+	+	−	+	+	+	+	−	+	+	8	4	4
4	+	+	+	+	+	+	+	+	−	+	9	5	4
5	+	+	+	+	+	+	+	+	+	−	9	4	5
6	+	+	−	+	−	+	+	+	+	+	8	5	3
7	+	+	+	+	+	−	+	−	+	+	8	3	5
8	+	+	+	−	+	+	+	+	+	+	9	4	5
9	+	+	+	+	+	+	−	+	+	+	9	5	4
10	+	+	+	+	+	−	+	+	+	+	9	4	5
11	+	+	+	+	+	−	+	−	−	−	6	2	4
12	+	+	−	+	+	+	+	+	+	+	9	5	4
13	+	+	+	−	−	+	+	+	−	−	5	3	2
14	+	+	+	+	+	+	+	−	+	+	9	4	5
15	+	+	−	+	+	−	−	−	−	−	4	2	2
16	+	+	+	+	+	+	+	+	+	+	10	5	5
17	+	−	+	−	−	−	−	−	−	−	2	0	2
18	+	−	+	+	+	+	+	+	+	+	9	4	5
19	+	+	+	+	−	+	+	+	+	+	9	5	4
20	+	−	−	−	−	+	−	+	−	−	3	2	1

bility of each of the two halves in the same way we would estimate the reliability of two alternate forms of a test. This procedure for estimating a test's reliability is called a *split-half reliability estimate.*

It should be apparent that there are many ways to divide a test into two equal-length tests. The aforementioned ten-item test can be divided into more than 100 different pairs of five-item tests. If the ten items in our full test are arranged in order of increasing difficulty, both halves should contain items from the beginning of the test (that is, easier items) and items from the end of the test (harder items). There are many ways of dividing such a test (for example, grouping Items 1, 4, 5, 8, 9 and Items 2, 3, 6, 7, 10). The most common way to divide a test is by odd-numbered and even-numbered items (see the columns labeled "Evens Correct" and "Odds Correct" in Table 7.1).

Odd–even division and the subsequent correlation of the two halves of a test is a common method for estimating a test's internal-consistency reliability, but it is not necessarily the best method. A more generalizable method of estimating internal consistency has been developed by Cronbach (1951) and is called coefficient alpha. *Coefficient alpha* is the average split-half correlation based on all possible divisions of a test into two parts. In practice, there is no need to compute all possible correlation coefficients; coefficient alpha or r_{aa} can be computed from the variances of individual test items and the variance of the total test score, as shown in Equation 7.2, where k is the number of items in the test.

$$r_{aa} = \frac{k}{k-1} \left(1 - \frac{\Sigma S^2_{items}}{S^2_{test}} \right) \tag{7.2}$$

Coefficient alpha can be used when test items are scored pass–fail or when more than one point is awarded for a correct response. An earlier, more restricted method of estimating a test's reliability, based on the average correlation between all possible split halves, was developed by Kuder and Richardson. This procedure, called *KR-20*, is coefficient alpha for dichotomously scored test items (that is, items that can be scored only right or wrong). Equation 7.2 can be used with dichotomous data; however, in this case, the resulting estimate of reliability is usually called a "KR-20 estimate" rather than "coefficient alpha."[2]

There are two major considerations in the use of internal-consistency estimates. First, this method should not be used for timed tests or tests that are not completed by all those being tested. Second, it provides no estimate of stability over time.

Generalizing to Different Scorers

There are two very different approaches to estimating the extent to which we can generalize to different scorers: a correlational approach and a percentage of agreement approach. The correlational approach is similar to the ways of estimating generalizability that we have just discussed. Two testers score a set of tests independently. Scores obtained by each tester for the set are then correlated. The resulting correlation coefficient is a reliability coefficient for scorers. For example, suppose that a psychologist (Ms. Jimenez) were interested in the distortion of body image in emotionally disturbed schoolchildren. Further, suppose she decided to assess distortion by evaluating the human-figure drawings of such children. Even with explicit criteria for what constitutes a distorted image, scoring of human-figure drawings is difficult. Would another, equally trained, tester—Mr. Torrance—arrive at the same conclusions as Ms. Jimenez? Can Ms. Jimenez's judgments be generalized to other testers and scorers?

To quantify the extent to which this type of generalization is possible, the two testers could evaluate the human-figure drawings made by a class of emotionally disturbed pupils. As shown in Table 7.2, there would be two ratings of distortion of body image for each drawing, and these two scores could be correlated. The resulting correlation coefficient (phi = .41) would be an estimate of interscorer reliability or agreement.

---

2. Sometimes a test author will estimate KR-20 with a formula called KR-21.

TABLE 7.2 • *Judgment of Distorted Body Image in a Class of Emotionally Disturbed Children*

Child Number	Ms. Jimenez	Mr. Torrance
1	normal	normal
2	distorted	distorted
3	distorted	normal
4	normal	normal
5	normal	normal
6	distorted	distorted
7	distorted	distorted
8	distorted	normal
9	normal	normal
10	normal	distorted
11	distorted	distorted
12	normal	normal
13	normal	normal
14	normal	normal
15	distorted	distorted
16	normal	distorted
17	normal	normal
18	distorted	distorted
19	normal	distorted
20	normal	distorted

The second approach to estimating generalizability to different scorers is prevalent in applied behavioral analysis. Instead of correlating the two scorers' ratings, the percentage of agreement between raters is computed. Four indexes of percentage of agreement are used: simple agreement, point-to-point agreement, agreement on the occurrence of target behavior, and the kappa index of agreement. *Simple agreement* is calculated by dividing the smaller number of occurrences by the larger number of occurrences and multiplying the quotient by 100. As Table 7.2 shows, Ms. Jimenez observed eight distorted drawings and Mr. Torrance observed ten distorted drawings. Their simple agreement is 80 percent; that is, (8/10)(100). This index may be quite misleading, however, because agreement for each observation is not considered. Thus, it is possible (although not very likely) for two scorers to observe the same number of distorted drawings but to disagree with each other on which drawings are distorted. Therefore, the use of simple agreement should be restricted to those circumstances in which it is the only index that can be computed (for example, in assessing the latency of a response or the frequency of behavior under continuous observation).

A more precise way of computing percentage of agreement is to consider agreement for each data point. The computation of *point-to-point agreement* takes each data point into consideration (see Equation 7.3).

TABLE 7.3   ●   Summary of Agreements and Disagreements from Table 7.2

	Ms. Jimenez Distorted Drawings	Ms. Jimenez Normal Drawings	
Mr. Torrance normal drawings	2	8	$\Sigma = 10$
Mr. Torrance distorted drawings	6	4	$\Sigma = 10$
	$\Sigma = 8$	$\Sigma = 12$	$N = 20$

Percentage of point-to-point agreement =

$$\frac{(100)\text{number of agreements on occurrence and nonoccurrence}}{\text{number of observations}} \qquad (7.3)$$

The data from Table 7.2 are summarized in Table 7.3. The point-to-point agreement is computed by adding the frequency of agreement for occurrence (in this example, the occurrence of distorted drawings, $n = 6$) and the frequency of agreement for nonoccurrence (in this example, nonoccurrence is represented by normal drawings, $n = 8$), dividing this sum by the total number of observations, and multiplying the quotient by 100. Point-to-point agreement for the data in Table 7.3 is .70 [that is, $(14/20)(100)$].

When the occurrences and nonoccurrences of a behavior differ substantially, point-to-point agreement overestimates the accuracy of the set of observations. In such cases, a more precise way of computing the percentage of agreement is to compute the *percentage of agreement for the occurrence of the target behavior* (see Equation 7.4).

Percentage of agreement for occurrence =

$$\frac{(100)\text{number of agreements on occurrence}}{\text{number of observations} - \text{number of agreements on nonoccurrence}} \qquad (7.4)$$

In this example, because Ms. Jimenez is interested in the occurrences of distorted body image, it might make better sense to look only at how well the two raters agree on the occurrence. The eight nonoccurrences (normal drawings) on which Ms. Jimenez and Mr. Torrance agree are not of interest and are ignored. Using the data in Table 7.3, the percentage of agreement for occurrence is 50 percent [that is, $(100)(6)/(20 - 8)$].

Both the point-to-point agreement and the agreement of occurrence indexes can be affected systematically by chance agreement. Thus, both indexes tend to overestimate agreement. Cohen (1960) developed a coefficient of agreement, called *kappa,* that adjusts the proportion of agreement by removing the propor-

TABLE 7.4 ● Proportions of Agreements and Disagreements from Table 7.2

	Ms. Jimenez Distorted Drawings	Ms. Jimenez Normal Drawings	Row Proportions
Mr. Torrance normal drawings	.10 (i.e., 2/10)	.40 (i.e., 8/20)	(.50)
Mr. Torrance distorted drawings	.30 (i.e., 6/20)	.20 (i.e., 4/20)	(.50)
Column proportions	(.40)	(.60)	

tion of agreement that would occur by chance. Kappa values range from −1.00 (total disagreement) to +1.00 (total agreement); a value of 0 indicates chance agreement. Thus, a positive index of agreement indicates agreement above what test givers would expect to find by chance. The computation of kappa is more complicated than the computation of other agreement indexes (see Equation 7.5, where P equals proportion).

$$\text{Kappa} = \frac{P_{\text{occurrence}} - P_{\text{expected}}}{1 - P_{\text{expected}}} \tag{7.5}$$

Because kappa is more readily calculated using proportions rather than frequencies, the frequencies from Table 7.3 are displayed in Table 7.4 as proportions (that is, the frequency divided by the 20 total observations); the marginal frequencies (that is, Ms. Jimenez's and Mr. Torrance's proportions of normal and distorted drawings) are in parentheses.

The expected proportion of occurrence (that is, of distorted drawings) equals the product of the proportions of occurrence for each observer (in this example, .50 and .40); the expected proportion of nonoccurrence (that is, of normal drawings) equals the product of the proportions of nonoccurrence for each observer (in this example, .50 and .60). The expected proportion of agreement equals the sum of the expected proportion of agreement for occurrence and the expected proportion of agreement for nonoccurrence—in this example, .50 = (.50 × .40) + (.50 × .60). Substituting these values into Equation 7.5, we find that kappa equals .40; that is, (.40 + .30 − .20 − .30) / (1 − .20 − .30). Thus, the ratings of drawings by Ms. Jimenez and Mr. Torrance demonstrate some agreement beyond what would be expected by chance; however, we should not have great confidence in their scoring.

Given the increased interest in subjective forms of assessment such as portfolio assessment (see Chapter 12), holistic scoring, and holistic observation, interscorer agreement takes on added importance. Unfortunately, we find that subjective assessments usually lack interscorer agreement.

● ●

Factors Affecting Reliability

Several factors affect a test's reliability and can inflate or deflate reliability estimates: test length, test–retest interval, constriction or extension of range, guessing, and variation within the testing situation.

Test Length

As a general rule, the more items there are in a test, the more reliable the test. Thus, long tests tend to be more reliable than short tests. This fact is especially important in an internal-consistency estimate of reliability because in this kind of estimate, the number of test items is reduced by 50 percent. Split-half estimates of reliability actually estimate the reliability of half the test. Therefore, such estimates are appropriately corrected by a formula developed by Spearman and Brown. As shown in Equation 7.6, the reliability of the total test is equal to twice the reliability as estimated by internal consistency divided by the sum of 1 plus the reliability estimate.

$$r_{xx} = \frac{2r_{(\frac{1}{2})(\frac{1}{2})}}{1 + r_{(\frac{1}{2})(\frac{1}{2})}} \tag{7.6}$$

For example, if a split-half estimate of internal consistency were computed for a test and found to be .80, the corrected estimated reliability would be .89:

$$\frac{(2)(.80)}{1 + .80} = \frac{1.60}{1.80} = .89$$

A related issue is the number of effective items for each test taker. Tests are generally more reliable in the middle ranges of scores (for example, within $\pm 1.5S$). For a test to be effective at the extremes of a distribution, there must be both enough difficult items for very superior pupils and enough easy items for deficient pupils. Often, there are not enough very easy and very hard items on a test. Therefore, extremely high or extremely low scores tend to be less reliable than scores in the middle of a distribution.

Test–Retest Interval

As previously noted, a person's true abilities can and do change between two administrations of a test. The greater the amount of time between the two administrations, the more likely the possibility that true scores will change. Thus, when employing stability or alternate-form estimates of reliability, test evaluators must pay close attention to the interval between tests. Generally, the shorter the interval, the higher the estimated reliability.

Constriction or Extension of Range

Constriction or *extension of range* refers to narrowing (constriction) or widening (extension) the range of ability of the people whose performances are used to estimate a test's reliability. When the range of ability of these people is less than the range of ability in the population, a test's reliability will be underestimated. The more constricted the range of ability, the more biased (underestimated) the reliability coefficient will be.

As Figure 7.1 shows, alternative forms of a test produce a strong positive correlation when the entire range of the test is used. However, within any restricted range of the test, as illustrated by the dark rectangular outline, the correlation may be very low. (Although it is possible to correct a correlation coefficient for restriction in range, it is generally unwise to do so.)

A related problem is that extension of range overestimates a test's reliability. Figure 7.2 illustrates correlations of scores on alternate-form tests given to students in the first, third, and fifth grades. The scatterplot for each grade, considered separately, indicates poor reliability. However, spelling-test scores increase as a function of schooling; students in higher grades earn higher scores. When test authors combine the scores for several grades (or from several ages), poor correlations may be combined to produce a spuriously high correlation.

● ● ● **FIGURE 7.1**   Constricting the Range of Test Scores and the Resulting Reduction of the Estimate of a Test's Reliability

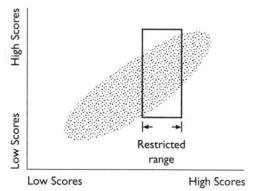

SOURCE: *Psychological Testing,* 6e by A. Anastasi, © 1988. Reprinted by permission of Prentice-Hall, Inc., Upper Saddle River, NJ.

● ● ● **FIGURE 7.2**   Extending the Range of Test Scores and the Possible Spurious Increase in the Estimate of a Test's Reliability

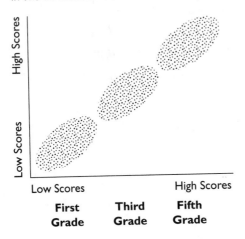

Guessing

Guessing is responding randomly to items. Even if a guess results in a correct response, it introduces error into a test score and into our interpretation of that score.

Variation Within the Testing Situation

The amount of error that the testing situation introduces into the results of testing can vary considerably. Children can misread or misunderstand the directions for a test, get a headache halfway through testing, lose their place on the answer sheet, break the point of their pencil, or choose to watch a squirrel eat nuts on the windowsill of the classroom rather than take the test. All such situational variations introduce an indeterminate amount of error in testing and, in doing so, lower reliability.

● ●

Determining Which Reliability Method to Use

The first consideration in choosing a method of determining a test's reliability is the type of generalization we wish to make. We must select the method that goes with the type of generalization. For example, if we were interested in generalizing about the stability of a score or observation, the appropriate method would be test–retest correlations. It would be inappropriate to use interscorer agreement as an estimate of the extent to which we can generalize to different times. Additional considerations in selecting the reliability method to be used include the following:

1. When estimating stability, the convention is to retest after two weeks. There is nothing special about the two-week period, but if all test authors used the same interval, it would be easier to compare the relative stability of tests.

2. When estimating the extent to which we can generalize to similar test items, we subscribe to Nunnally's (1967, p. 217) hierarchy for estimating reliability. The first choice is to use alternate-form reliability with a two-week interval. (Again, there is nothing special about two weeks; it is just a convention.) If alternate forms are not available, divide the test into equivalent halves and administer the halves with a two-week interval, correcting the correlation by the Spearman–Brown formula given in Equation 7.6. When alternate forms are not available and subjects cannot be tested more than once, use coefficient alpha.

3. When estimating the extent to which we can generalize among different scorers, we prefer computing correlation coefficients rather than percentages of agreement. Correlation coefficients bear a direct relationship to other indicators of reliability and other uses of reliability coefficients; percentages of agreement do not. We also realize that current practice is to report percentages of agreement and not to bother with the other uses of the reliability coefficient. If percentage of agreement is to be used to estimate interscorer reliability, we feel that kappa should be used when possible.

Standard Error of Measurement

The standard error of measurement (SEM) is another index of test error. The SEM allows us to estimate the amount of each type of error associated with true scores. We can compute standard errors of measurement for scorers, times, and item samples. However, SEMs are usually computed only for stability and item samples.

Earlier, we discussed the generalization of performance on one sample of items to the domain. This process provides a convenient example for the interpretation of the SEM. Consider the alphabet-recognition task again. There are many samples of ten-letter tests that could be developed. If we constructed 100 of these tests and tested just one kindergartner, we would probably find that the distribution of scores for that kindergartner was approximately normal. The mean of that distribution would be the student's true score. The distribution around the true score would be the result of imperfect samples of letters; some letter samples would overestimate the pupil's ability, and others would underestimate it. Thus, the variance around the mean would be the result of error. The standard deviation of that distribution is the standard deviation of errors attributable to sampling and is called the "standard error of measurement."

● ● ● ● **FIGURE 7.3**   The Standard Error of Measurement: The Standard Deviation of the
Error Distribution Around a True Score for One Subject

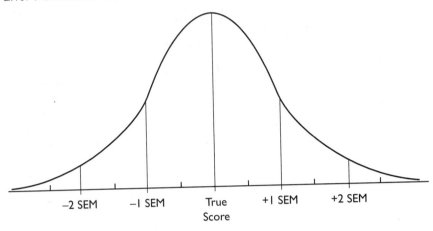

-2 SEM   -1 SEM   True   +1 SEM   +2 SEM
                            Score

When students are assessed with norm-referenced tests, they are typically
tested only once. Therefore, we cannot generate a distribution similar to the one
shown in Figure 7.3. Consequently, we do not know the test taker's true score or
the variance of the measurement error that forms the distribution around that
person's true score. By using what we know about the test's standard deviation
and its reliability for items, we can estimate what that error distribution would
be. However, when estimating the error distribution for one student, test users
should understand that the SEM is an average; some standard errors will be
greater than that average, and some will be less.

Equation 7.7 is the general formula for finding the SEM. The SEM equals the
standard deviation of the obtained scores (S) multiplied by the square root of 1
minus the reliability coefficient ($\sqrt{1 - r_{xx}}$). The type of unit (IQ, raw score, and so
forth) in which the standard deviation is expressed is the unit in which the SEM
is expressed. Thus, if the test scores have been converted to T-scores, the standard
deviation is in T-score units and is 10; the SEM is also in T-score units. Similarly,
if the reliability coefficient is based on stability, then the SEM is for times of testing. If the reliability coefficient is based on different scorers, then the SEM is for
testers or scorers.

$$SEM = S\sqrt{1 - r_{xx}} \tag{7.7}$$

From Equation 7.7, it is apparent that as the standard deviation increases, the
SEM increases; and as the reliability coefficient decreases, the SEM increases. In
Part A of Table 7.5, the same standard deviation (10) is used with different reliability coefficients. As reliability coefficients decrease, SEMs increase. When the reliability coefficient is .96, the SEM is 2; when the reliability coefficient is 64, the

TABLE 7.5 ● Relationship (Part A) Between Reliability Coefficient (r_{xx}) and SEM and (Part B) Between Standard Deviation (S) and SEM

Part A			Part B		
S	r_{xx}	*SEM*	*S*	r_{xx}	*SEM*
10	.96	2	5	.91	1.5
10	.84	4	10	.91	3.0
10	.75	5	15	.91	4.5
10	.64	6	20	.91	6.0
10	.36	8	25	.91	7.5

SEM is 6. In Part B of Table 7.5, different standard deviations are used with the same reliability coefficient (r_{xx} = .91). As standard deviations increase, SEMs increase.

Because measurement error is unavoidable, there is always some uncertainty about an individual's true score. The SEM provides information about the certainty or confidence with which a test score can be interpreted. When the SEM is relatively large, the uncertainty is large; we cannot be very sure of the individual's score. When the SEM is relatively small, the uncertainty is small; we can be more certain of the score.

● ●

Estimated True Scores

Unfortunately, we never know a subject's true score. Moreover, the obtained score on a test is not the best estimate of the true score. As mentioned in the previous discussion, true scores and errors are uncorrelated. However, obtained scores and errors are correlated. Scores above the test mean have more "lucky" error (error that raises the obtained score above the true score), whereas scores below the mean have more "unlucky" error (error that lowers the obtained score below the true score). An easy way to understand this effect is to think of a test on which a student guesses on half the test items. If all the guesses are correct, the student has been very lucky and earns a high grade. However, if all the guesses are incorrect, the student has been unlucky and earns a low grade. Thus, obtained scores above or below the mean are often more discrepant from the true scores than obtained scores closer to the mean. As Figure 7.4 illustrates, the less reliable the test, the greater the discrepancy between obtained scores and true scores. Nunnally (1967, p. 220) has provided an equation (Equation 7.8) for determining the estimated true score (X'). The estimated true score equals the test mean plus the product of the reliability coefficient and the difference between the obtained score and the group mean.

The Discrepancy Between Obtained Scores and True Scores for Reliable and Unreliable Tests

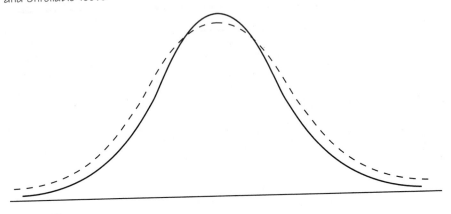

Reliable Test

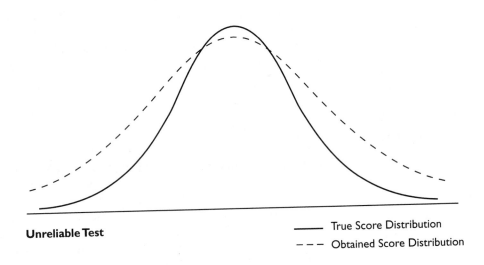

Unreliable Test

—— True Score Distribution

– – – Obtained Score Distribution

$$X' = \overline{X} + (r_{xx})(X - \overline{X}) \tag{7.8}$$

The particular mean that is used has been the subject of some controversy. We believe that the preferred mean is the mean of the demographic group that best represents the particular child. Thus, if the student is Asian and resides in a middle-class urban area, the most appropriate mean would be the mean of same-age Asian students from middle socioeconomic backgrounds who live in urban areas. In the absence of means for particular students of particular backgrounds, we are

TABLE 7.6 ● Estimated True Scores for Different Obtained Scores on Tests with Different Reliability Coefficients

Test Mean $(\overline{X})$	Reliability Coefficient (r_{xx})	Obtained Score (X)	Estimated True Score (X')	Difference Between Estimated True Score and Observed Score
100	.90	90	91.0	+1.0
100	.90	75	77.5	+2.5
100	.90	50	55.0	+5.0
100	.70	90	93.0	+3.0
100	.70	75	82.5	+7.5
100	.70	50	65.0	+15.0
100	.50	90	95.0	+5.0
100	.50	75	87.5	+12.5
100	.50	50	75.0	+25.0

forced to use the overall mean for the student's age. As mentioned earlier in this chapter, the choice of reliability coefficient depends on the type of generalization to be made.

The discrepancy between obtained scores and estimated true scores is a function of both the reliability of the obtained scores and the difference between the obtained score and the mean. Table 7.6 illustrates a general case in which the mean in each example is 100 and the obtained scores are 90, 75, and 50. The reliability coefficients are .90, .70, and .50.

When the reliability coefficient is constant, the further an obtained score is from the mean, the greater the discrepancy between the obtained score and the estimated true score. For example, when the obtained score is 90 and the estimated reliability is .90, the estimated true score is 91 [that is, $91 = 100 + (.90)(90 - 100)$]. Thus, the difference between the estimated true score and the obtained score is 1. However, when the obtained score is 50 and the reliability coefficient is .90, the estimated true score is 55 [that is, $100 + (.90)(50 - 100)$]. Thus, the difference between the estimated true score and the obtained score is 5.

When the reliability coefficient changes, less reliable measures produce larger differences between obtained and estimated true scores. For example, when the obtained score is 75 and the reliability coefficient is .90, the estimated true score is 77.5 [that is, $100 + (.90)(75 - 100)$]. Thus, the difference between the estimated true score and the obtained score is 2.5. However, when the reliability coefficient is .50, the estimated true score rises to 87.5 [that is, $100 + (.50)(75 - 100)$]. Thus, the difference between the estimated true score and the obtained score is 12.5.

When the obtained score is below the test mean and the reliability coefficient is less than 1.00, the estimated true score is always higher than the obtained score.

Conversely, when the obtained score is above the test mean and the reliability co-efficient is less than 1.00, the estimated true score is always lower than the obtained score. Note that Equation 7.8 does not give the true score, only the estimated true score.

Confidence Intervals

Although we can never know a person's true score, we can estimate the likelihood that a person's true score will be found within a specified range of scores. This range is called a "confidence interval." A *50 percent confidence interval* is a range of values within which the true score will be found about 50 percent of the time. Of course, about 50 percent of the time, the true score will be outside the interval. A larger range—a wider confidence interval—could make us feel more certain that we have included the true score within the range. For example, 90 percent, 95 percent, and 99 percent confidence intervals can be constructed; with confidence intervals as certain as these, the chances of the true score's falling outside of the confidence interval are about 10 percent, 5 percent, and 1 percent, respectively.

There is some disagreement over how to construct confidence intervals (see Kubiszyn & Borich, 1984) or even whether to construct them at all (see Sabers, Feldt, & Reschly, 1988). In the following sections, we use the statistics recommended by Nunnally (1978): estimated true score and SEM. Others (for example, Kubiszyn & Borich, 1984) prefer to use the estimated true score and the *standard error of estimation*[3] (which is the average standard deviation of true scores around an obtained score) rather than the SEM. When test reliability is high, the difference between the two procedures is negligible.

Establishing Confidence Intervals for True Scores

The characteristics of a normal curve have already been discussed. We can apply the relationship between *z*-scores and areas under the normal curve to the normal distribution of error around a true score. We can use Equation 7.8 to estimate the mean of the distribution (the true score) and Equation 7.7 to estimate the standard deviation of the distribution (the SEM). With these two estimates, we can construct a confidence interval for the true score. Because 68 percent of all elements in a normal distribution fall within one standard deviation of the mean, there is about a 68 percent chance that the true score is within one SEM of the estimated true score. We can construct an interval with almost any degree of confidence except 100 percent confidence.

3. The *standard error of estimation* (SEE) equals the product of the standard deviation and the square root of the product of the reliability coefficient and 1 minus the reliability coefficient:

$$\text{SEE} = S\sqrt{r_{xx}\,(1 - r_{xx})}$$

TABLE 7.7 ● Commonly Used z-Scores, Extreme Areas, and
Area Included Between + and – z-Score Values

z-Score	Extreme Area	Area Between + and –
.67	25.0%	50%
1.00	16.0%	68%
1.64	5.0%	90%
1.96	2.5%	95%
2.33	1.0%	98%
2.57	.5%	99%

Table 7.7 shows the extreme area for the z-scores most commonly used in constructing confidence intervals. The extreme area is the proportion of cases in the tail of the curve—that is, the area from plus or minus two standard deviations to the end of the curve. The general formula for a confidence interval (c.i.) is given in Equation 7.9. The lower limit of the confidence interval equals the estimated true score less the product of the z-score associated with that level of confidence and the SEM. The upper limit of the confidence interval is the estimated true score plus the product of the z-score and the SEM.

$$\text{Lower limit of c.i.} = X' - (z\text{-score})(\text{SEM})$$
$$\text{Upper limit of c.i.} = X' + (z\text{-score})(\text{SEM}) \tag{7.9}$$

1. Select the degree of confidence—for example, 95 percent.

2. Find the z-score associated with that degree of confidence (for example, a 95% confidence interval is between z-scores of −1.96 and +1.96).

3. Multiply each z-score associated with the confidence interval (for example, 1.96 for 95% confidence) by the SEM.

4. Find the estimated true score.

5. Add the product of the z-score and the SEM to the estimated true score to obtain the upper limit of the confidence interval; subtract the product of the z-score and the SEM from the estimated true score to obtain the lower limit of the confidence interval.

For example, assume that a person's estimated true score is 75 and the SEM is 5. Further assume that you wish to be about 68 percent sure of constructing an interval that will contain the true score. Table 7.7 shows that a 68 percent degree of confidence is associated with a z-score of 1. Thus, about 68 percent of the time, the true score will be contained in the interval of 70 to 80 [that is, 75 − (1)(5) to 75 + (1)(5)]; there is about a 16 percent chance that the true score is less than 70 and about a 16 percent chance that the true score is greater than 80. If you are unwilling to be wrong about 32 percent of the time, you must increase the width of the confidence interval. Thus, with the same true score (75) and SEM (5), if you wish 95 percent confidence, the size of the interval must be increased; it would have to range from 65 to 85 [that is, 75 −(1.96)(5) to 75 + (1.96)(5)]. About 95 percent of the time, the true score will be contained within that interval; there is about a 2.5 percent chance that the true score is less than 65, and there is about a 2.5 percent chance that it is greater than 85.

● ● ● ● ● ● ● ● ● ● ● ● ● ● ● ● ● ● ● ●

Difference Scores

In many applied settings, we are interested in differences between two scores. For example, we might wish to know whether a student's reading achievement is commensurate with her intellectual ability, or we might want to know whether the achievement score obtained after instruction (that is, on a posttest) is greater than the achievement score obtained prior to instruction (that is, on a pretest). In many definitions of educational disorders (for example, learning disabilities), a "significant" discrepancy is a defining characteristic of the disorder. In other disorders (for example, mental retardation), significant discrepancies are not expected.

Because significant differences are used so frequently in special and remedial education, it is important for users of test information to understand the meaning of a "significant discrepancy." Salvia and Good (1982) have discussed three different meanings of the term *significant difference*: (1) reliable difference, (2) rare discrepancy or difference, and (3) educationally meaningful difference. The first meaning, a reliable difference, is the most pertinent to our discussion of reliability, although it is not the most important consideration in general. A difference is considered reliable when it is unlikely to have occurred by chance. Because every test score has some error associated with it, two test scores could appear discrepant by chance or because of the measurement error associated with each test score. However, Salvia and Good point out that the fact that a difference is real does not mean that it is rare. A large proportion of students may show reliable discrepancies. Moreover, even if a difference is reliable and rare, it may not have educational implications.

Educators and psychologists are interested in meaningful differences. We can be sure that unreliable differences are not meaningful. (These differences are the result of chance.) Probably because only reliable differences can be meaningful and because too little emphasis has been placed on the rarity and meaningfulness of a difference, diagnosticians have relied heavily on a difference's reliability for interpretation.

Difference scores are usually less reliable than the scores on which the differences are based. The reliability of a difference between two scores (A and B) is a function of three things: (1) the reliability of test A, (2) the reliability of test B, and (3) the correlation between tests A and B. In addition, differences in norm groups can produce differences in obtained scores. For example, suppose that June was absolutely average in reading and intellectual ability. Further suppose that she was tested with an intelligence test normed on a sample of students somewhat lower in ability than the general population. June would earn an IQ above the mean. Suppose the test to measure reading was normed on a sample of students whose achievement was somewhat higher than that of the general population. June would earn a reading score somewhat lower than the mean. If the disparity in norms were sufficiently large, June might appear to have a significant discrepancy between her intellectual ability and her reading achievement. However, that discrepancy would be an artifact of inaccurate norms.

There are several approaches to evaluating the reliability of a difference. The following two methods are particularly useful but rest on different assumptions and combine the data in different ways (that is, use different formulas). One method uses a regression model and was originally described by Thorndike (1963). In this model, one score is presumed to cause the second score. For example, intelligence is believed to determine achievement. Therefore, intelligence is identified as an independent (or predictor) variable, and achievement is identified as the dependent (or predicted) variable. When the predicted score (for example, the predicted achievement score) differs from the achievement score that is actually obtained, a deficit exists. The reliability of a predicted difference is given by Equation 7.10.

$$\hat{D} = \frac{r_{bb} + (r_{aa})(r^2_{ab}) - 2r^2_{ab}}{1 - r^2_{ab}} \tag{7.10}$$

The reliability of a predicted difference ($\hat{D}$) is equal to the reliability of the dependent variable (r_{bb}) plus the product of the reliability of the independent variable and the square of the correlation between the independent variable and the dependent variable ($r_{aa}r^2_{ab}$) less twice the squared correlation between the independent and dependent variable ($2r^2_{ab}$). This value is divided by 1 minus the squared correlation between the independent and dependent variables ($1 - r^2_{ab}$). The standard deviation of predicted differences ($S_{\hat{D}}$) also called "standard error of the estimate" (SE_{est}), is given in Equation 7.11. The standard deviation of predicted differences ($S_{\hat{D}}$) is equal to the standard deviation of the dependent variable (S_b) multiplied by the square root of 1 minus the squared correlation between the independent and dependent variables ($\sqrt{1 - r^2_{ab}}$).

$$S_{\hat{D}} = S_b\sqrt{1 - r^2_{ab}} \tag{7.11}$$

The second method of evaluating the reliability of a difference was proposed by Stake and Wardrop (1971). In this method, one variable is not assumed to be the cause of the other; neither variable is identified as the independent variable. However, this method does require that both measures be in the same unit of measurement (for example, T-scores or IQs). The reliability of a difference in obtained scores is given in Equation 7.12. The reliability of an obtained difference (r_{dif}) equals the average reliability of the two tests [$\frac{1}{2}(r_{aa} + r_{bb})$] less the correlation between the two tests (r_{ab}); this difference is divided by 1 minus the correlation between the two tests ($1 - r_{ab}$).

$$r_{dif} = \frac{\frac{1}{2}(r_{aa} + r_{bb}) - r_{ab}}{1 - r_{ab}} \tag{7.12}$$

The standard deviation for obtained differences is given in Equation 7.13.

$$S_{dif} = \sqrt{S^2_a + S^2_b - 2r_{ab}S_aS_b} \qquad (7.13)$$

The standard deviation of an obtained difference (S_{dif}) is equal to the square root of the sum of the variances of tests A and B ($S_a^2 + S_b^2$) less twice the product of the correlation of A and B multiplied by the standard deviations of A and B ($2r_{ab}S_aS_b$).

The reliability and standard deviation of an obtained difference can be combined to estimate the SEM of the obtained difference (SEM_{dif}) using Equation 7.7. The standard deviation of the difference (S_{dif}; see Equation 7.13) is substituted for the test's standard deviation (S) in that equation; the reliability of the difference (r_{dif}; see Equation 7.12) is substituted for the test's reliability (r_{xx}) in the equation. These substitutions generate Equation 7.14.

$$SEM_{dif} = \sqrt{S^2_a + S^2_b - 2r_{ab}S_aS_b} \ \sqrt{1 - \frac{\frac{1}{2}(r_{aa} + r_{bb}) - r_{ab}}{1 - r_{ab}}} \qquad (7.14)$$

The standard error of measurement of a difference (SEM_{dif}) describes the distribution of differences between obtained scores. To evaluate difference scores, the simplest method is to establish a level of confidence (for example, 95%) and find the z-score associated with that level of confidence (1.96). We then divide the obtained difference by the SEM of the difference. If the quotient exceeds the z-score associated with the level of confidence selected (1.96), the obtained difference is reliable. We can also estimate the true difference in the same manner as we estimate a true score on one test. In general, we assume that the group mean difference is 0.00. Thus, the formula for estimating the true difference for a particular student simplifies to Equation 7.15.

$$\text{Estimated true difference} = (\text{obtained difference})(r_{dif}) \qquad (7.15)$$

● ● ● ● ● ● ● ● ● ● ● ● ● ● ● ● ● ● ● ●

Desirable Standards

It is important for test authors to present sufficient information in test manuals for the test user to be able to interpret test results accurately. For a test to be valid (that is, to measure what its authors claim it measures), it must be reliable. Although reliability is not the only condition that must be met, it is a necessary condition for validity. No test can measure what it purports to measure unless it is reliable. No score is interpretable unless it is reliable.

Therefore, test authors and publishers must present sufficient reliability data to allow the user to evaluate the reliability of the test scores that are to be interpreted. Thus, reliability estimates should be presented for intermediate (for example, subtest) scores when they are to be interpreted. Moreover, reliability estimates should be reported for each age and grade. Furthermore, these indexes should be presented clearly in tabular form in one place. Test authors should not play hide-and-seek with reliability data. Test authors who recommend computing difference scores should provide, whenever possible, the reliability of the difference (r_{dif}) and the SEM of the difference (SEM_{dif}). Once test users have access to reliability data, they must judge the adequacy of the test.

How high must a test's reliability be before it can be used in applied settings? The answer depends on the use to which test data are put. A simple answer is to use the most reliable test available. However, that response may be misleading, for the "best" test may be too unreliable for any application (for example, its reliability may only be .45). We recommend that the following two standards of reliability be used in applied settings:

1. *Group Data.* If test scores are to be used for administrative purposes and are reported for groups of individuals, a reliability of .60 should probably be the minimum.

2. *Individual Data.* If a test score is to be used to make a decision concerning an individual student, a much higher standard of reliability is demanded. When important educational decisions are to be made for a student, such as decisions about tracking and placement in a special class, the minimum standard should be .90. When the decision being made is a screening decision, such as a recommendation that a child receive further assessment, there is still a need for high reliability. For screening devices, we recommend an .80 standard.

Finally, we strongly recommend that confidence intervals be used when reporting test performance.

· ·

Summary

The term *reliability* refers to the ability to generalize from a sample to a domain. The domains to which we usually want to generalize are other times (stability or test–retest reliability), other scorers (interrater or interscorer reliability), and other items (alternate-form or internal-consistency reliability). Reliability coefficients may range from .00 (total lack of reliability) to 1.00 (total reliability); .90 is recommended as the minimum standard for tests used to make important educational decisions for students. Several factors affect reliability: the method used for calculating the reliability coefficient, the test length, the test–retest interval, constriction or extension of range, guessing, and variation within the testing situation.

In diagnostic work, the reliability coefficient has four major uses: It allows the user to estimate (1) the test's relative freedom from measurement error, (2) an individual subject's true score, (3) the standard error of measurement, and (4) confidence intervals for a subject's true score.

The discussion of estimated true scores, standard error of measurement, and confidence intervals can be extended to difference or discrepancy scores. The reliability of a difference score is affected by the reliability of the tests and by the correlation between the tests on which the difference is based. Differences in norm samples also affect difference scores, but this effect cannot be evaluated. Provided that the two tests are correlated, difference scores are less reliable than the average of the reliabilities of the tests on which the difference is based.

Although we have devoted an entire chapter to reliability, readers must bear in mind that reliability is important only insofar as it affects the validity of an assessment.

Questions for Chapter Review and Thought

1. Why is it necessary for a test to be reliable?

2. Test A and test B have identical means and standard deviations. Test A has a SEM of 4.8; test B has a SEM of 16.3. Which test is more reliable, and why?

3. What is the greatest limitation of reliability estimates based on test–retest correlation?

4. List and explain five factors that affect the estimated reliability of a test.

5. The SEM is the standard deviation of what? Illustrate your answer with a drawing.

6. Compare and contrast the two major approaches to estimating the extent to which we can generalize from different samples of items.

Problems

1. Mr. Treacher administers an intelligence test to his class. For this test, $\overline{X} = 100$, $S = 16$, and $r_{rx} = .75$. Five children earn the following scores: 68, 124, 84, 100, and 148. What are the estimated true scores for these children?

2. What is the SEM for the intelligence test in Problem 1?

3. What are the upper and lower boundaries of a symmetrical confidence interval of 95 percent for the first child in Problem 1?

4. What are the upper and lower boundaries of a symmetrical confidence interval of 50 percent for the child in Problem 1 who earns a score of 100?

5. Test A and test B have reliabilities of .90 and .80; the correlation between tests A and B is .50. What is the reliability of a difference between scores on test A and test B?

Answers

1. 76, 118, 88, 100, 136

2. 8

3. 92, 60

4. 105, 95

5. .70

Resources for Further Investigation

Project

Obtain the test manual for any standardized test. Remembering that it is the author's responsibility to prove reliability, check for a section on reliability. Check for evidence of each appropriate type of reliability. Are there reliability estimates for each subtest at each grade or age? Is the SEM provided? Which scores are stressed? Evaluate the adequacy of the test's reliability.

Print Resource

Crocker, L., & Algina, J. (1986). *Introduction to classical and modern test theory* (Chapter 7, Procedures for estimating reliability). New York: Holt, Rinehart, and Winston.

Technology Resources

Welcome to HyperStat

http://www.ruf.rice.edu/~lane/hyperstat/contents.html

Look here for further explanations about confidence intervals and hypothesis testing with standard errors.

Surfstat.australia: An Online Text in Introductory Statistics

http://surfstat.newcastle.edu.au/surfstat/main/surfstat.html

This page contains information on summarizing and presenting data, producing data, variation and probability, and statistical inference.

Reliability

http://coenp.idbsu.edu/mbarrer/te330/reliability/index.htm

This web site contains information of different types of reliability and standards for reliability.

Validity

*V*alidity refers to "the appropriateness, meaningfulness, and usefulness of the specific inferences" (AERA et al., 1997, p. 9) that can be made on the basis of observations or test results. Some inferences may be valid; others may not be. Thus, validity is a property of test-based inferences and not a property of the test itself.[1] In a real sense, all questions of validity are local, asking whether the testing process leads to correct inferences about a specific person in a specific situation for a specific purpose.

Clearly, local inferences are a function of the purpose of testing and the type of test being used. For example, when using a test of reading achievement, the test giver is interested in drawing inferences about a student's skill in reading; for a test of intelligence, the inferences of interest center on a student's level of intellectual ability. Thus, the type and the quality of a test generally relate to the validity of the inferences that can be drawn from it.

However, a test that leads to valid inferences about most students may not yield valid inferences about a specific student. Two circumstances illustrate this. First, unless a student has been systematically acculturated in the values, behavior, and knowledge found in the public culture of the United States, a test that assumes such cultural information is unlikely to lead to appropriate inferences about that student. Consider, for example, the inappropriateness of administering a verbally loaded intelligence test to a recent U.S. immigrant. Correct inferences about this person's intellectual ability cannot be drawn from the testing because

1. Validity is a property of any type of assessment procedure (not just tests), although systematic validation is most highly developed for commercially available tests and rating scales.

the intelligence test requires not only proficiency in English but also proficiency in U.S. culture and mores.

Second, unless a student has been systematically instructed in the content of an achievement test, a test assuming such academic instruction is unlikely to lead to appropriate inferences about that student's ability to profit from instruction. It would be inappropriate to administer a standardized test of written language (which counts misspelled words as errors) to a student who has been encouraged to use inventive spelling and reinforced for doing so. It is unlikely that the test results would lead to correct inferences about that student's ability to profit from systematic instruction in spelling.

Because it is impossible to validate all inferences that might be drawn from a test performance, test authors typically validate just the most common inferences. In so doing, they should consider each inference separately. Thus, test users should expect some information about the degree to which each commonly encouraged inference has (or lacks) validity. While the validity of each inference is based on all the information that accumulates over time, test authors are expected to provide some evidence of a test's validity for specific inferences at the time the test is offered for use.

Because it is impossible to validate each inference within the context of every possible set of life circumstances, test authors should validate the inferences for *typical* groups of students (that is, groups of students who are represented in the norm samples). Thus, it is incumbent on the test author to demonstrate that the test leads to valid inferences for the kinds of individuals in the normative sample. Obviously, we would expect some variability (error) for individuals within groups.

● ● ● ● ● ● ● ● ● ● ● ● ● ● ● ● ● ● ●

Methods of Validating Test Inferences

The process of gathering information about the appropriateness of inferences is termed *validation*. The evidence of an inference's validity can be categorized to facilitate explanation. Yet, the reader should keep in mind that categorization is an artificial device to explain the possibilities; there are not separate kinds of validity.

We have already discussed some evidence of a test's validity in preceding chapters (that is, the meaning of test scores, reliability, and the adequacy of the test's standardization and, when applicable, the test's norms). In this chapter, three additional sources of evidence are considered: content validity, criterion-related validity, and construct validity.

Content Validity

To judge a test's validity, those who assess students must have a clear understanding of the traits, abilities, or skills that are to be measured. Test authors must define what is to be measured before deciding how the measuring is to be done. The specific definition will depend on a test author's own definition of and assumptions about the domain to be measured, as well as scientific consensus.

Content validity is the extent to which a test's items actually represent the domain or universe to be measured. It is a major source of evidence in the validation process for any educational or psychological test and many other forms of assessment (such as observations and ratings). Evidence of valid content is especially important in the measurement of achievement and adaptive behavior, and it is most easily understood in this context. A careful examination of a test's content is necessary; frequently, test developers rely on panels of experts for judgments about the appropriateness of test content. Whether test content is examined by experts or by those who use the tests, the examination is judgmental in nature and requires a clear definition of the domain or universe represented.

The test author should describe both the relevance of the test universe to the proposed test use and the way in which procedures for generating test content were designed to represent that test universe (AERA et al., 1997, p. 14). Thus, in developing a test, a test developer must consider the purposes for which a test is going to be used and then specify adequately the universe of content that the test is intended to represent. If a test is to be used for making instructional decisions, it is important that there be agreement between the test and the specific instructional or curricular areas that the test is meant to cover. Assessors must also make sure that the format and the response properties of the items or tasks that make up a test represent the universe of possible item and response types for the particular area being assessed.

Evidence of content validity is associated with three factors: the appropriateness of the types of items included in a test, the completeness of the item sample in relation to the item universe, and the way in which the items assess the content.

Appropriateness of Included Items

In examining the appropriateness of the items included in a test, we must ask, Is this an appropriate test question? and, Does this test item really measure the domain or construct? Consider the four test items from a hypothetical primary (kindergarten through grade 2) arithmetic achievement test presented in Figure 8.1. The first item requires the student to read and add two single-digit numbers, the sum of which is less than 10. This seems to be an appropriate item for an elementary arithmetic achievement test. The second item requires the student to complete a geometric progression. Although this item is mathematical, the skills and knowledge required to complete the question correctly are not taught in any elementary school curriculum by the second grade. Therefore, the question should be rejected as an invalid item for an arithmetic achievement test to be used with children from kindergarten through the second grade. The third item also requires the student to read and add two single-digit numbers, the sum of which is less than 10. However, the question is written in Spanish. Although the content of the question is suitable (this is an elementary addition problem), the method of presentation requires language skills that most U.S. students do not have. Failure to

● ● ● **FIGURE 8.1**   *Sample Multiple-Choice Questions for a Primary-Grade (K–2) Arithmetic Achievement Test*

---

1. Three and six are _____.

   a. 4
   b. 7
   c. 8
   d. 9

2. What number follows in this series?
   1, 2.5, 6.25, _____

   a. 10
   b. 12.5
   c. 15.625
   d. 18.50

3. ¿Cuántos son tres y dos?

   a. 3
   b. 4
   c. 5
   d. 6

4. Ille puer puellas _____.

   a. amo
   b. amat
   c. amamus
   d. amant

---

complete the item correctly could be attributed either to the fact that the child does not know Spanish or to the fact that the child does not know that $3 + 2 = 5$. Test givers should conclude that the item is not valid for an arithmetic test for children who do not read Spanish. The fourth item requires that the student select the correct form of the Latin verb *amare* ("to love"). Clearly, this is an inappropriate item for an arithmetic test and should be rejected as invalid.

In addition to making judgments about how appropriately an item fits within a domain, test developers often rely on point-biserial correlations between individual test items and the total score to make decisions about item appropriateness (see Chapter 4). Items that do not correlate positively and at least moderately (that is, .25 or .30 or more) with the total score are dropped. Retaining only items that have positive correlations with the total score ensures homogeneous test items and internally consistent (reliable) tests. Moreover, when test items are homogeneous, they are likely to be measuring the same skill or trait. Therefore, to obtain reliable tests, test developers are likely to drop items that do not statistically fit the domain.

When domains are not homogeneous, test authors can jeopardize validity by selecting items on the basis of point-biserial correlations to produce an internally consistent test. Therefore, it is generally a good idea to analyze the structure of a domain, either logically or statistically.[2] When a domain comprises two or more homogeneous classes of test items, homogeneous subtests (representing each factor) can be developed using point-biserial correlations. In this way, the validity of the test can be heightened.

---

2. Advanced statistical techniques such as factor analysis are appropriately used in this sort of analysis. These statistical procedures are well beyond the discussion of descriptive statistics provided in Chapter 4. The interested reader should consult a text on multivariate statistical analysis.

Completeness of Content

Test content must be examined to ascertain the completeness of the item sample. The validity of any elementary arithmetic test would be questioned if it included only problems requiring the addition of single-digit numbers with a sum less than 10. Educators would reasonably expect an arithmetic test to include a far broader sample of tasks (for example, addition of two- and three-digit numbers, subtraction, understanding of the process of addition, and so forth). Incomplete assessment of a domain usually results in an invalid appraisal.

How Content Is Measured

Content must be examined to ascertain how the test items assess content. The *how* of measurement is multifaceted. In one question in Figure 8.1, the student was expected to add two single-digit numbers, the sum of which was less than 10. However, test givers could evaluate a child's arithmetic skills in a variety of ways. The child might be required to recognize the correct answer in a multiple-choice array, supply the correct answer, demonstrate the addition process with manipulatives, apply the proper addition facts in a word problem, or analyze the condition under which the mathematical relationship obtains. The method of measurement may affect the outcome.[3]

Ensuring Content Validity

To ensure that a test has appropriate content, we can conceptualize its content precisely. One way to do this is by developing a table of specifications that maps the major areas of content and the desired ways of measuring that content. Although there are several approaches to content mapping, the procedures described by Bloom, Hastings, and Madaus (1971) in their classic text *Handbook of Formative and Summative Evaluation of Student Learning* are illustrative. They recommended that authors of achievement tests use a table of specifications to map the content to be tested. Such a table can be readily generalized to other types of tests. A table of specifications formally enumerates the particular contents of a test and the processes (or behaviors) it assesses.

   Content refers to the particular domains or subdomains the test author wishes to assess. The task of test authors is to specify the content as precisely as possible in order to convey clearly what is being measured. The next step is to specify how the particular content objectives will be measured (the process by which the measurement will occur). Several types of measurement are possible; they range from knowledge objectives to evaluation objectives. The definitions used by Bloom (1956) and colleagues (Bloom et al., 1971) follow.

---

3. This aspect of validity is currently being hotly debated by those favoring constructed responses such as extended answers, performances, or demonstrations. Current theory and research methods as they apply to trait or ability congruence under different methods of measurement are still emerging. Much of the current methodology grew out of Campbell and Fiske's (1959) early work and is beyond the scope of this text. There is, however, an emerging consensus that the methods used to assess student knowledge or ability should closely parallel those used in instruction.

1. *Knowledge* is the "recall or recognition of specific elements in a subject area" (Bloom et al., 1971, p. 41).

2. *Comprehension* is evaluated with three types of measurement: translation, interpretation, and extrapolation. *Translation* refers to rewording information or putting it into the learner's own words. *Interpretation* is evidenced "when a student can go beyond recognizing the separate parts of a communication and can see the interrelationships among the parts" (Bloom et al., 1971, p. 149). Interpretation also is evidenced when a student can differentiate the essentials of a message from unimportant elements. *Extrapolation* refers to the student's ability to go beyond literal comprehension and to make inferences about what the anticipated outcome of an action is or what will happen next.

3. *Application* is "the use of abstractions in particular and concrete situations. The abstractions may be in the form of general ideas, rules or procedures, or generalized methods. The abstractions may also be technical principles, ideas, and theories which must be remembered and applied" (Bloom, 1956, p. 205).

4. *Analysis* is "the breakdown of a communication into its constituent elements or parts such that the relative hierarchy of ideas is made clear and/or the relations between ideas expressed are made explicit. Such analyses are intended to clarify the communication, to indicate how the communication is organized, and the way in which it manages to convey its effects, as well as its basis and arrangements" (Bloom, 1956, p. 205).

5. *Synthesis* refers to "the putting together of elements and parts so as to form a whole. This involves the process of working with pieces, parts, elements, etc., and arranging and combining them in such a way as to constitute a pattern or structure not clearly there before" (Bloom, 1956, p. 206).

6. *Evaluation* means "the making of judgments about the value, for some purpose, of ideas, works, solutions, methods, material, etc. It involves the use of criteria as well as standards for appraising the extent to which particulars are accurate, effective, economical, or satisfying. The judgments may be quantitative or qualitative, and the criteria may be either those determined by the student or those which are given to him" (Bloom, 1956, p. 185).

To illustrate how a table of specifications can be used, let us assume that we wish to develop a test to assess the understanding of reliability demonstrated by beginning students. The first step is to enumerate *the content areas* of the domain. Using Chapter 7 as a guide, we could assess the following areas: the reliability coefficient (its meaning, methods of estimating it, and factors affecting it), standard error of measurement (its meaning and computation), estimated true scores, confidence intervals (their meaning and computation), and difference scores. We might reasonably expect a test user to have a better understanding of the meaning of the reliability coefficient and the construction and interpretation of confidence intervals. Therefore, these content areas could be stressed.

The next step is to specify the *processes* by which the content areas are to be measured. We might expect beginning students to demonstrate understanding at

TABLE 8.1 ● Specifications for a Hypothetical Reliability Test

Processes	Contents				
	Reliability Coefficient	*Standard Error of Measurement*	*Estimated True Scores*	*Confidence Intervals*	*Difference Scores*
Knowledge	3 questions	2 questions	1 question	1 question	1 question
Comprehension	5 questions	2 questions	1 question	3 questions	1 question
Application	Not tested	2 questions	1 question	5 questions	Not tested
Analysis	Not tested	Not tested	Not tested	Not tested	Not tested
Synthesis	Not tested	Not tested	Not tested	Not tested	Not tested
Evaluation	Not tested	Not tested	Not tested	Not tested	Not tested

the *knowledge, comprehension,* and *application* levels only. Therefore, the test might not contain items assessing analysis, synthesis, or evaluation. A table of specifications for this hypothetical test would resemble Table 8.1.

The number of questions used to assess each cell also is given in the table. The table of specifications shows that, of the 28 questions in the test, 8 deal with the reliability coefficient and 9 deal with confidence intervals; 8 questions assess knowledge, 12 questions assess comprehension, and 8 assess application. Thus, the hypothetical test assesses a student's understanding of reliability by emphasizing comprehension of the reliability coefficient and applications of confidence intervals.

Extension to Other Forms of Assessment

The preceding discussion of content validity also applies to other forms of assessment. In systematic observation, the content of the observation protocol takes two forms. First, the contexts in which observation takes place can be considered an issue of content validity. For example, a behavior can occur in several contexts; thus, a teacher might observe Harry to see the frequency of his hitting in class, at recess, during lunch, and so forth. Second, when states or traits are observed (for example, cooperation), the specific behaviors chosen to represent the state or trait are clearly issues of content validity. For example, taking turns, sharing toys, and using polite language (such as saying "please") could be considered exemplars of cooperation.

In unstandardized assessment procedures such as portfolio assessment, content validity is an especially critical issue. The contents of the portfolio—what is included and what is excluded—should accurately portray the student's work in the domain. The student's work should represent all important dimensions within the domain, and work not pertinent to the domain should be excluded from the assessment process (although such work may be kept in the student's portfolio).

Criterion-Related Validity

Criterion-related validity refers to the extent to which a person's performance on a criterion measure can be estimated from that person's performance on the assessment procedure being validated. This prediction is usually expressed as a correlation between the assessment procedure (for example, a test) and the criterion. The correlation coefficient is termed a *validity coefficient.*

Two types of criterion-related validity are commonly described: concurrent validity and predictive validity. These terms denote the time at which a person's performance on the criterion measure is obtained. *Concurrent* criterion-related validity refers to how accurately a person's current performance (for example, test score) estimates that person's performance on the criterion measure *at the same time.* *Predictive* criterion-related validity refers to how accurately a person's current performance (for example, test score) estimates that person's performance on the criterion measure *at a later time.* Thus, concurrent and predictive criterion-related validity refer to the temporal sequence by which a person's performance on some criterion measure is estimated on the basis of that person's current assessment; concurrent and predictive validity differ in the time at which scores on the criterion measure are obtained.

The nature of the criterion measure is extremely important. The criterion itself must be valid if it is to be used to establish the validity of another measure. Let's investigate this point by looking briefly at two examples of criterion-related validation, the first concurrent and the second predictive.

An Example of Concurrent Criterion-Related Validity

A basic concurrent criterion-related validity question is, Does a person's performance measured with a new or experimental test allow the accurate estimation of that person's performance on a criterion measure that has been widely accepted as valid? For example, if the Acme Ruler Company manufactures yardsticks, how do we know that a person's height, as measured by an Acme yardstick, is that person's true height? How do we know that the "Acme foot" is really a foot? The first step is to find a valid criterion measure.

The National Bureau of Standards maintains "the" foot (0.3048 meter), and this foot is the logical choice for a criterion measure. We can take several things to the bureau and measure them with both the Acme foot and the standard foot. If the two sets of measurements correspond closely (that is, are highly correlated and have very similar means and standard deviations), we can conclude that the Acme foot is a valid measure of length.

Similarly, if we are developing a test of achievement, we can ask, How does knowledge of a person's score on our achievement test allow the estimation of that person's score on a criterion measure? How do we know that our new test really measures achievement? Again, the first step is to find a valid criterion measure. However, there is no National Bureau of Standards for educational tests. Therefore, we must turn to a less-than-perfect criterion. There are two basic choices: (1)

other achievement tests that are presumed to be valid; and (2) judgments of achievement by teachers, parents, and the students themselves. We can, of course, use both tests and judgments. If our new test presents evidence of content validity and elicits test scores corresponding closely (correlating significantly) to judgments and scores from other achievement tests that are presumed to be valid, we can conclude that there is evidence for our new test's criterion-related validity.

An Example of Predictive Criterion-Related Validity

The basic predictive criterion-related validity question is, Does knowledge of a person's score allow an accurate estimation of that person's score on a criterion measure administered some time in the future? For example, if Acme Ruler Company decides to diversify and manufacture tests of color vision, how do we know that a diagnosis of colorblindness made on the basis of the Acme test is accurate? How do we know that an Acme-based diagnosis will correspond to next month's diagnosis made by an ophthalmologist? We can test several children with the Acme test, schedule appointments with an ophthalmologist, and compare the Acme-based diagnoses with the ophthalmologist's diagnoses. If the Acme test accurately predicts the ophthalmologist's diagnoses, we can conclude that the Acme test is a valid measure of color vision.

Similarly, if we are developing a test to assess reading readiness, we can ask, Does knowledge of a student's score on our reading readiness test allow an accurate estimation of the student's actual readiness for subsequent instruction? How do we know that our test really assesses reading readiness? Again, the first step is to find a valid criterion measure. In this case, the student's initial progress in reading can be used. Reading progress can be assessed by a reading achievement test (presumed to be valid) or by teacher judgments of reading ability or reading readiness at the time reading instruction is actually begun. If our reading readiness test has content validity and corresponds closely with either later teacher judgments of readiness or validly assessed reading skill, we can conclude that ours is a valid test of reading readiness.

Three aspects of criterion-related validity are extremely important. First, "All criterion measures should be described accurately, and the rationale for choosing them as relevant criteria should be made explicit" (AERA et al., 1997, p. 16). Obviously, because the validity of the assessment procedure (for example, a test) is established by its relationship to a criterion, the criterion itself must be valid. Thus, test authors need to present sufficient information to allow test users to judge the adequacy of the criterion.

Second, "A report of a criterion-related validity study should provide a description of the sample and the statistical analysis used to determine the degree of predictive accuracy. Basic statistics should include numbers of cases (and the reasons for eliminating any cases), measures of central tendency and variability, relationships, and a description of any marked tendency toward non-normality of distribution" (AERA et al., 1997, p. 16). You will see in later sections of this book that many of the validity studies for tests we review are based on small samples, samples of convenience, or very restrictive samples (taken, for example, from one location or one private school). It is important that test authors show that their test is valid not only for the recommended purposes of the test but also for the kinds of people who will be tested.

Third, test authors must provide information on the limits of generalizability of validity information.

Extension to Other Forms of Assessment

The preceding discussion of criterion-related validity also applies to other forms of assessment. For example, in systematic observation, some form of time sampling is often used. An observer might use momentary time sampling (see Chapter 10) and record what a target pupil is doing every 10 seconds. An appropriate question is, Does the sampling procedure affect the record of the student's performance? To investigate this question, assessors usually compare the data obtained when using continuous observation of target students with data from observations when using momentary time sampling. Similarly, if assessors wished to evaluate the criterion validity of portfolio assessment, an appropriate criterion would have to be selected (for example, all of a student's work—tests, work not included in the portfolio, and so forth). The score or scores assigned to the portfolio could then be compared with the score or scores based on the totality of student work during the marking period.

Construct Validity

Construct validity refers to the extent to which a procedure or test measures a theoretical trait or characteristic. Construct validity is especially important for measures of process, such as intelligence or scientific inquiry. To provide evidence of construct validity, a test author must rely on indirect evidence and inference. The definition of the construct and the theory from which the construct is derived allow us to make certain predictions that can be confirmed or disconfirmed. In a real sense, we do not validate inferences from tests or other assessment procedures; rather, we conduct experiments to demonstrate that the inferences are not valid. The continued inability to disconfirm the inferences, in effect, validates the inferences.

For example, intellectual ability is generally believed to be developmental. We could hypothesize that if we were to conduct an investigation, intelligence test scores would be correlated with chronological age. If we found that a test of intelligence did not correlate with chronological age, this finding would cast serious doubt on the test as a measure of intelligence. (The experiment would disconfirm the test as a measure of intelligence.) However, the presence of a substantial correlation between chronological age and scores on the test does not confirm that the test is a measure of intelligence.[4] Gradually, the test developer accumulates evidence that the test continues to act in the way that it would if it were a valid measure of the construct. As the research evidence accumulates, the developer can make some claim to construct validity.

Several types of evidence are generally brought to bear in research on construct validity. For example, we often expect differences in the behavior of individuals with different levels of a trait or characteristic. Thus, a test to assess learning ability should be able to differentiate between fast and slow learners. We can predict, therefore, that the individuals who learn more in a given amount of time have more learning ability; that is, they will have higher scores on a measure of learning ability. If children with IQs of 125 on test X learn more material in one week than do children with IQs of 100 on test X, there will be a failure to disconfirm the test as a valid measure of learning ability. This failure to disconfirm its validity offers some evidence for inferring that the test measures intelligence. Other examples of this type of research are numerous. We would expect tests of intelligence to predict school achievement, readiness tests to predict school achievement, and so forth.

● ●

Factors Affecting General Validity

Whenever an assessment procedure fails to measure what it purports to measure, validity is threatened. Consequently, any factor that results in measuring "something else" affects validity. Both unsystematic error (unreliability) and systematic error (bias) threaten validity.

Reliability

Reliability sets the upper limit of a test's validity, so reliability is a necessary but not a sufficient condition for valid measurement. Thus, all valid tests are reliable; unreliable tests are not valid; and reliable tests may or may not be valid. The validity of a particular procedure can never exceed the reliability of that procedure because unreliable procedures measure error; valid procedures measure the traits they are designed to measure. The relationship between the reliability and the validity of any procedure is expressed in Equation 8.1. The empirically determined validity coefficient (r_{xy}) equals the correlation between true scores on the two

---

4. Many test authors systematically ensure that their tests will be correlated with age. Authors may use a positive correlation between age or grade and passing an item as a criterion for item inclusion. Some psychometricians advocate even more sophisticated methods—for example, item-characteristic curves (Thorndike, 1982)—to ensure that test scores are correlated with chronological age. Many other abilities besides intelligence correlate with chronological age—for example, achievement, perceptual abilities, and language skills.

variables ($r_{x(t)y(t)}$) multiplied by the square root of the product of the reliability co-efficients of test X and test Y ($r_{xx}r_{yy}$).

$$r_{xy} = r_{x(t)y(t)} \sqrt{r_{xx}r_{yy}} \tag{8.1}$$

Systematic Bias

Method of Measurement

The method used to measure a skill or trait is often believed to affect what score a child will receive. A true score can be considered a composite of trait variance and method-of-measurement variance (Campbell & Fiske, 1959). To take a classic example, Werner and Strauss (1941) conducted a series of experiments to ascertain the effect of brain injury on figure–background perception; all of their subjects were individuals with mental retardation. They presented stimulus items for a fraction of a second and asked their subjects to name what they saw. They found that individuals with brain injury responded to the background stimuli more often than did the individuals without brain injury. They concluded that brain injury results in a dysfunction in figure–ground perception. However, the method of testing and the trait to be tested (figure–ground perception) were confounded by the testing procedure. Rubin (1969) later demonstrated that under different testing procedures, there were no differences between individuals with and those without brain injury in figure–background perceptual responses. The differences between the findings of Werner and Strauss and those of Rubin are attributable to how figure–background perception was measured. It seems likely that Werner and Strauss were measuring perceptual speed because of their method of measurement. To the extent that trait or skill scores include variance attributable to the method of measurement, these scores may lack validity.

Enabling Behaviors

Enabling behaviors and knowledge are *skills* and facts that a person must rely on to demonstrate a target behavior or knowledge. For example, to demonstrate knowledge of causes of the American Civil War on an essay examination, a student must additionally be able to write. The student cannot produce the targeted behavior (the written answer) without the enabling behavior (writing).

Several behaviors are assumed in any testing situation. We must assume that the subject is fluent in the language in which the test is prepared and administered if there are any verbal components to the test directions or test responses. Yet in many states with substantial Spanish-speaking populations, students whose primary language is not English are nonetheless tested in English. Intelligence testing in English of non–English-speaking children has been sufficiently commonplace that a group of parents brought suit against a school district (*Diana v. State Board of Education,* 1970). Deaf students are routinely given the Performance subtests of the Wechsler Adult Intelligence Scales (Baumgardner, 1993) even though they cannot hear the directions. Children with communication disorders often are required to respond orally to test questions. Such obvious limitations in or absences of enabling behaviors are frequently overlooked in testing situations, even though they invalidate the test's inferences for these students.

Differential Item Effectiveness

Test items should work the same way for various groups of students. Jensen (1980) has discussed several empirical ways to assess item effectiveness for different groups of test takers. First, we should expect that the relative difficulty of items is maintained across different groups. For example, the most difficult item for males should also be the most difficult item for females; the easiest item for whites should be the easiest item for nonwhites; and so forth. Second, the factor structure of a test should be identical for all groups of test takers. For example, if a test measures four independent factors for males, it should measure four factors for females, and so on. Third, the predictive validity should be the same for all groups of test takers. For example, if the correlation between an intelligence test and a reading achievement test is .80 for whites, the correlation between the two tests should also be .80 (+ or − sampling error) for nonwhites.

The most likely explanation for items having differential effectiveness for different groups of people is differential exposure to test content. Test items may not work in the same ways for students who experience different acculturation or academic instruction. For example, standardized achievement tests presume that the students who are taking the tests have been exposed to similar curricula. If teachers have not taught the content being tested, that content will be more difficult for their students (and inferences about the students' ability to profit from instruction will probably be incorrect).

Administration Errors

Unless a test is administered according to the standardized procedures, the inferences based on the test are invalid. Suppose Ms. Williams wishes to demonstrate how effective her teaching is by administering an intelligence test and an achievement test to her class. She allows the students five minutes less than the standardized time limits on the intelligence test and five minutes more on the standardized achievement test. The result is that the students earn higher achievement test scores (because they had too much time) and lower intelligence test scores (because they did not have enough time). The inference that less-intelligent students have learned more than anticipated is valid.

Norms

Scores based on the performance of unrepresentative norms lead to incorrect estimates of relative standing in the general population. To the extent that the normative sample is systematically unrepresentative of the general population in either central tendency or variability, the differences based on such scores are incorrect and invalid.

Responsibility for Valid Assessment

The valid use of assessment procedures is the responsibility of both the author and the user of the assessment procedure.

Evidence of validity should be presented for the major types of inferences for which the use of a test is recommended. A rationale should be provided to support the particular mix of evidence presented for the intended uses. . . . If validity for some common interpretation has not been investigated, that fact should be made clear, and potential users should be cautioned about making such interpretations. (AERA et al., 1997, p. 13)

Summary

Validity is the only technical characteristic of an assessment procedure in which we are interested. All other technical considerations, such as reliability, are subsumed under the concept of validity and are analyzed separately to simplify the discussion of validity. We must know whether inferences derived from an assessment are accurate. Adequate norms, reliability, and lack of bias are all necessary conditions for validity. None—separately or in total—is sufficient to guarantee validity for a particular test taker.

Systematic evaluation of validity is based on several types of information. The content may be inspected to see whether each item is valid and to ensure that all aspects of the domain are represented. If a standard or criterion of known validity is available, the test should be compared against that standard. The construct validity of all tests should be examined.

Several factors affect the validity of inferences derived from tests: reliability, systematic bias, enabling behaviors, item selection, administration errors, and test norms. Problems with these factors can invalidate test inferences.

Questions for Chapter Review and Thought

1. Why must test authors demonstrate validity for inferences based on their tests?

2. What is the relationship between reliability and validity?

3. How can a table of specifications assist in developing a valid test?

4. What is the difference between concurrent and predictive criterion-related validity?

5. Many test manuals contain no evidence of validity, but the tests are used in schools to make important educational decisions about children. Under what circumstances could such tests be used?

6. Kim Ngo, a recent arrival from a Vietnamese orphanage, speaks no English. When she enrolls in a U.S. school, her intelligence is assessed by a verbal test that has English directions and requires English responses. Kim performs poorly on the test, earning an IQ of 37. The tester concludes that Kim has severe mental retardation and recommends placement in a special class. What are two major errors in the interpretation of the test result?

7. Professor Johnson develops a test that he claims can be used to identify learning-disabled children who will profit from perceptual–motor training. What must he do to demonstrate that his test is valid?

Resources for Further Investigation

Project

Obtain the test manual for any standardized test. Remembering that it is the author's responsibility to prove validity, evaluate the validity data. How does the author recommend using the test? What domains are measured, and how does the test author prove that these domains are measured? How were items chosen for the test? What types of validity data are provided? What assertions are made about particular uses of the test or certain scores? What data are provided to support these assertions?

Print Resources

Crocker, L., & Algina, J. (1986). *Introduction to classical and modern test theory* (Chapter 10: Introduction to validity). New York: Holt, Rinehart, and Winston.

Gronlund, N. (1985). *Measurement and evaluation in teaching* (5th ed.). New York: Macmillan.

Jensen, A. R. (1980). *Bias in mental testing.* New York: Free Press.

Messick, S. (1980). Test validity and the ethics of assessment. *American Psychologist, 35,* 1012–1027.

Messick, S. (1989). Meaning and values in test validation: The science and ethics of assessment. *Educational Researcher, 18*(2), 5–11.

Messick, S. (1993). Validity. In R. L. Linn (Ed.), *Educational measurement* (4th ed., pp. 13–103). New York: ACE/Macmillan.

Technology Resources

National Center for Education Statistics

http://nces.ed.gov/

This web site offers an extensive set of statistical tables, charts, and studies produced by the National Center for Education Statistics (NCES) to report the condition and progress of education.

Validity

http://coehp.idbsu.edu/mbarrer/te330/validity/index.htm.

This site contains information on properties of validity and how the content is measured.

The Royal Windsor Society for Nursing Research

http://www.windsor.igs.net/~nhodgins/design_and_analysis.html

This web site covers topics such as study methods and design, instrument reliability and validity, and analysis of study data and statistical tests.

Adapting Tests to Accommodate Students with Disabilities

Not until the sixth edition of this text (1995) was there a separate chapter on testing accommodations, modifications, or adaptations. Up to that time, we talked about adapting measures for students with disabilities and about such matters as out-of-level testing as part of the discussions of domain-specific testing. So, for example, when we described intelligence tests, we devoted a portion of the chapter to tests that included modified stimulus or response properties, or that were normed on separate groups of students with disabilities, and that thus were designed for use with special populations of students. Why, then, do we now devote a separate chapter to this topic?

Why Be Concerned About Testing Adaptations?

Changes in Student Population

Since the mid-1970s, considerable attention has been focused on including all students in neighborhood schools, general education settings, and regular instructional programs. Clearly, the most attention has been focused on including students who are considered developmentally, physically, or behaviorally at the margins. Contemporary students need higher-level skills and considerably more formal schooling than did students in the past. As legislators and educational bureaucrats make educational policies, they are now compelled to make them for *all* children and youths, including those with severe disabilities. Also, as policymakers attempt to develop practices that will result in improved educational outcomes, they rely on data from district- and state-administered tests. However, relying on assessment data presents challenges. One set of challenges involves deciding whom to include in assessments and the kinds of modifications that can be made to include students with disabilities. Another set of challenges arises as states and school districts try to move to new forms of assessment, such as performance tests or portfolio assessments, and try to have all students participate in those assessments.

If students with disabilities are excluded from assessments, then the data on which policy decisions are made represent only part of the school population, the top 85 percent. If students with disabilities are excluded from accountability systems, they may also be removed from instructional systems. If data are going to be gathered on all students, then major decisions must be made regarding the kinds of data to be collected and how tests are to be modified or adapted to include students with disabilities. Historically, there has been widespread exclusion of students with disabilities from state and national testing and this continues today (McGrew, Thurlow, Shriner, & Spiegel, 1992).

Changes in Educational Standards

Part of major efforts to reform or restructure schools has been a push to specify high standards for student achievement and an accompanying push to measure the extent to which students meet those high standards. The school reform act, Goals 2000: The Educate America Act, is a major impetus for including students with disabilities in assessments, especially assessments completed for accountability purposes. The Goals 2000 act specifies that high content standards are to be developed in specific academic areas and that states should develop suitable standards and assessments. Both the Improving America's Schools Act (IASA; 1995) and the 1999 revised Individuals with Disabilities Education Act include language indicating that school districts are to report on the progress and performance of all students, including those with disabilities.

State education agencies (SEAs) in nearly every state are engaging in critical analyses of the standards, objectives, outcomes, results, skills, or behaviors that they want students to demonstrate upon completion of school. Content area professional agencies, such as the National Council of Teachers of Mathematics and the National Science Foundation, have developed sets of standards in specific content areas, such as math, geography, and science. As they do so, they must decide on the extent to which standards should be the same for students with and without disabilities. Also, of course, groups that develop standards must come up with ways of assessing the extent to which students are meeting the standards. They then must decide which kinds of assessments to use and the extent to which assessments ought to be the same for students with and without disabilities. In his second State of the Union Address, President Clinton specified that all fourth-grade students would be assessed in reading, and all eighth-graders in math. Educators must now decide how this will be accomplished, what tests will be used, and whether accommodations will be permitted.

The Need for Accurate Measurement

It is critical that the assessment practices used for gathering information on individual students provide accurate information. Unless modifications or accommodations are made in testing, testing practices run the risk of being unfair for students with disabilities. Students with disabilities have difficulty taking tests if the item format is such that, because of their disability, it is harder or impossible for them to understand what they are supposed to do or what the response requirements are. They also experience difficulty if they attempt to take a test but their disability makes it impossible for them to respond in a way that can be evaluated accurately.

In this chapter, we first review the two major issues of who should participate in assessment and how assessments should be adapted to accommodate diverse students. In doing so, we focus more on group measurement activities than on individual appraisal. We then describe some major legal considerations in participation and accommodation. We also identify things that impede getting an accurate picture of students. In the remainder of the chapter, we describe both current practice and best practice in (a) making decisions about who ought to participate in assessments, and (b) making accommodation decisions.

As you read this chapter, remember that the major objective of assessment is to benefit students. Assessment can do so either by enabling us to develop interventions that help a child achieve the objectives of schooling or by informing local, state, and national policy decisions that benefit all students, including individuals with disabilities.

● ●

The Twin Issues of Participation and Accommodation in Testing

Although many issues surround the assessment of students with disabilities, most of these can be grouped into two areas: participation and accommodation. In this section, we introduce these two issues. In later sections, we provide considerably more detail on them.

Participation

Educators use assessment information for many purposes. When screening, program evaluation, or accountability decisions are made, inclusion in testing is an issue. Too often, prior to testing, educators make assumptions that certain students should be excluded because "we already know how they would perform" or because "the student should not be subjected to the pain of participation" or because "they could not possibly respond correctly to the test items."

When data are collected for large-scale (district, state, or national) assessments, the outcomes have major implications for funding, real-estate values, and reputations of teachers and administrators. Because it is widely believed that the inclusion of students with disabilities will lower scores, these students are often excluded from participation.

Current legislation explicitly states that national educational goals and standards are to apply to all students. If students with disabilities are not included in assessment, then a biased picture of local, state, or national performance is presented. As demonstrated in Chapter 6, exclusion of low-scoring students does inflate the mean and reduce the variance of scores. This bias has a substantial effect when cutoff scores are used to identify individual students, although the effect on mean performance is not particularly large.

Accommodation

Accommodation means adapting tests to enable students with disabilities to participate in assessment. What legitimate changes can be made in assessment materials or procedures that still allow valid assessment results to be obtained? Reschly (1993, p. 37) put the issue well when he stated,

> My experience as a member of the state of Georgia Assessment Advisory Board (where state-wide educational assessment programs in Georgia and other states are reviewed) and the American Psychological Association Committee on Psychological Tests and Assessments (where various proposals for national literacy tests or assessment have been reviewed) indicates that assessment mechanics (e.g., item types), test content, and scaling typically dominate discussions at the expense of consideration of why the assessment is done, what will be assessed, what interpretation will result, how the results will be used, and what consequences will be established for good and poor performance.

Concern about accommodation applies to individual and large-scale group assessments. The concerns are both legal (such as, Do individuals have a right to take modified tests?) and technical (for example, To what extent can we modify measures and still have technically adequate tests?)

* * * * * * * * * * * * * * * * * * * *

Factors Affecting Accurate Assessment

Five factors can impede getting an accurate picture of students' abilities and skills: (1) the students' ability to understand assessment stimuli, (2) the students' ability to respond to assessment stimuli, (3) the nature of the norm group, (4) the appropriateness of the level of the items (sufficient basal and ceiling items), and (5) the students' exposure to the curriculum being tested.

Ability to Understand Assessment Stimuli

Assessments are considered unfair if the test stimuli are in a format that, because of a disability, the student does not understand. For example, tests in print are considered unfair for students with severe visual impairments such as blindness. Tests with oral directions are considered unfair for students with hearing impairments. In fact, because the law requires that students be assessed in their primary language, and because the primary language of many deaf students is not English, written assessments in English are considered unfair and invalid for many deaf students. When students cannot understand test stimuli because of a sensory or physical limitation, then performance on the test is more reflective of the sensory or physical limitation than of actual academic skill or ability. Such a test is invalid and is now also illegal.

A major issue arises when tests with directions or stimuli in English are administered to students who primarily speak other languages. It often is assumed that the test giver must simply translate a test into another language, and then it can be used with students who speak that language. However, simply translating a test usually also changes its psychometric properties, because we cannot assume that the words and the concepts they represent are of equal difficulty in both languages. Suppose that a test requiring a student to read the word *cat* were translated into Spanish. *Cat* translates to *gato*. In English, the word contains two of the first three letters of the alphabet; in Spanish, it contains one of the first three letters. In English, the word is one syllable; in Spanish, it is two syllables.

The cultural relevance of the word may differ as well. If the referent for the word is a four-legged feline, cats may not have the same cultural familiarity. For example, are cats as commonly kept as household pets in Bolivia or in U.S. barrios as in Anglo-American homes? If the referent for the word is not a four-legged feline, there may be conceptual confusion. For example, the slang term *cool cat* may be meaningless within certain Spanish-speaking cultures.

Although the literal translation of a test is relatively easy, inferences cannot be drawn from scores on translated tests without first establishing the validity of these tests in the new language and culture. Usually, a translated test should be renormed within the particular culture, and new evidence for reliability and validity must be established.

Ability to Respond to Assessment Stimuli

All assessment measures require students to produce a response. For example, intelligence tests require verbal or written (multiple-choice) responses, and perceptual–motor measures require a motor response. To the extent that physical or sensory limitations inhibit accurate responding, these test results are invalid and illegal.

The Nature of the Norm Group

Norm-referenced tests are standardized on groups of individuals, and the performance of the person assessed is compared with the performance of the norm group. To the extent that the test was administered to the student differently from the way it was administered to the norm group, the comparison is considered unfair and invalid. Modification of measures requires changing either stimulus presentation or response requirements. The modification may make the test items easier or harder, and it may change the construct being measured. Although qualitative or criterion-referenced interpretations of such test performances are acceptable, norm-referenced comparisons are flawed. The *Standards for Educational and Psychological Testing* (AERA et al., 1997), a joint publication of three professional associations, specifies that when tests are modified, they must be renormed or be considered invalid.

Appropriateness of the Level of the Items

In earlier chapters, we pointed out that tests are developed for students who are in specific age ranges or who have a particular range of skills. One issue to be decided regarding participation and accommodation is the extent to which a student can and should be given an *out-of-level test* (one intended for use with older or younger students). Assessors are tempted to give out-of-level tests when an age-appropriate test contains either an insufficient number of easy items or not enough hard items for the student being assessed. Of course, when out-of-level tests are given and norm-referenced interpretations are made, the student is being compared with a group of students who differ from him or her. We have no idea how same-age or same-grade students would perform on the given test. Out-of-level testing sometimes is appropriate for instructional planning. It is inappropriate for accountability purposes.

Exposure to the Curriculum Being Tested

One of the issues of fairness raised by the general public is the administration of tests that contain material that students have not had an opportunity to learn. This same issue applies to the making of accommodation decisions. Students with motor disabilities have not had an opportunity to learn the content of a test requiring motor responses. Students with sensory impairments have not had an opportunity to learn the content of test items that use verbal or auditory stimuli.

Addressing this issue is especially challenging when students have been raised and educated in cultures that differ quite markedly from the culture of the test developer. To the extent that students have not had an opportunity to learn the content of the test (that is, they were absent when the content was taught, the content is not taught in the schools in which they were present, or the content was taught in ways that were not effective for the student), they probably will not perform well on the test. Their performance will reflect more a lack of opportunity to learn than limited skill and ability.

• •

Legal Considerations

By law, students with disabilities have a right to be included in assessments, and accommodations in testing should be made in order to enable them to participate. This legal argument is derived largely from the Fourteenth Amendment to the U.S. Constitution (which guarantees the right to equal protection and to due process of law). The Individuals with Disabilities Education Act guarantees the right to education and to due process. Also, Section 504 of the Rehabilitation Act of 1973 indicates that it is illegal to exclude people from participation solely because of a disability.

The Americans with Disabilities Act of 1992 (ADA) mandates that all individuals must have access to exams used to provide credentials or licenses. Agencies administering tests must provide either auxiliary aids or modifications to enable individuals with disabilities to participate in assessment; and they may not charge the individual for costs incurred in making special provisions. Modifications that may be provided include an architecturally accessible testing site, a distraction-free space, or an alternative location; test schedule variation or extended time; the use of a scribe, sign language interpreter, reader, or adaptive equipment; and modifications of the test presentation or response format.

The 1999 Individuals with Disabilities Education Act mandates that states include students with disabilities in their statewide assessment systems. The necessary accommodations are to be provided to enable students to participate.

By July 2000, states were to have available alternative assessments. These are to be used by students who are unable to participate in the regular assessment even with accommodations. Alternative assessments are substitute ways of gathering data, often by means of portfolios or performance measures.

Recommendations for Making Participation Decisions

Students with disabilities routinely are included in testing to make screening and eligibility decisions. Our discussion of participation in testing is specific to participation in large-scale assessments. Elliott, Thurlow, and Ysseldyke (1996) indicate that states should have clear written guidelines for students' participation in assessments. They list the following as criteria for judging the adequacy of the guidelines:

- The guidelines should include the premise that all students, including those with disabilities, are to participate in state or district accountability systems.
- Decisions about participation should be made by a person or group who knows the student.
- Decisions about participation should be based on the student's current level of functioning and learning characteristics.
- There should be a form listing variables to consider in making participation decisions.
- The kind of tests a student is to take should be documented on his or her IEP.
- Students must participate in an assessment if they receive any instruction on the content assessed, regardless of where instruction occurs.
- Decisions about participation should not be based on program setting, category of disability, or percentage of time spent in general education classrooms.
- Decisions about participation should allow some students to participate either in an alternate assessment or in part of an assessment.

- The guidelines should specify that only a small percentage of students with disabilities are allowed to participate in an alternate assessment ($\frac{1}{2}$ to 2%).
- Parents should understand the participation options and the implications of their child's not being included in an assessment or accountability system.
- Decisions about participation should be documented on the student's IEP.

Current Practice in Testing Accommodations

Practice in making test accommodations runs the gamut from permitting no modifications and requiring that any students who are included in local, state, and national assessments take standard versions of tests being used, to allowing extensive alternative assessment procedures. Thurlow, Ysseldyke, and Silverstein (1993) investigated the kinds of testing accommodations, adaptations, and modifications allowed in state and national assessments. These are listed in Table 9.1. Note that some of the modifications involve changes in the way the test is presented, some are modifications in response format, others are setting adaptations, and still others involve relaxing time constraints. The American College Testing Program is the organization responsible for organizing and administering the American College Test (ACT). The following accommodations for students with disabilities are allowed on the ACT: extended time, large type, Braille, audio-cassette editions of the test, the use of a reader, assistance in filling out the answer folder, and signing of instructions. Individuals with disabilities may bring to the exam assistive devices such as a Brailler, template and stylus, magnifying glass, or tape recorder.

Educational Testing Service (ETS) is the organization responsible for administering the Scholastic Aptitude Test (SAT) and the Graduate Record Exam (GRE). It offers alternative test formats (Braille, cassette, large type), alternative ways to record answers (large-type answer sheets, typewriter), assistive personnel such as a reader or an *amanuensis* (a person who writes down the response for the student being tested), assistive devices such as an abacus or opticon, separate testing locations, and extra time. Neither ETS nor ACT will allow students who contend that they have dyscalculia to use calculators. This is an issue in court cases (Phillips, 1992).

Thurlow, Seyfarth, Scott, and Ysseldyke (1997) summarized information on testing accommodations obtained from 33 states. The accommodations permitted are shown as X's in Table 9.1. Accommodations that are expressly prohibited are shown as O's. When there are both X's and O's indicated, this means that the state permits the accommodation under certain circumstances and prohibits it under others. It may also mean, for example, that certain kinds of equipment are permitted while other kinds are prohibited. Note that kinds of accommodations that are permitted in one state may be expressly prohibited in another. Clearly, there is considerable variation among states in the kinds of accommodations that are permitted in assessments.

TABLE 9.1 ● Accommodations Allowed by States

State	Presentation						Response					Setting					Scheduling				Other	
	Read Aloud	Interpreter for Instruction	Braille	Clarify Direction	Large Print	Other	Comm. Device	Proctor/ Scribe	Calculator	Write in test booklet	Other	Individual	Small Group	Separate Room	Seat Location	Other	Extended Time	With Breaks	Time Beneficial to stud.	Other	IEP Determined	Used for Instruction
AL	XO	X	XO	X	X			XO		X	O	X	X		X		XO	X	X	X	X	X
AK	XO	X	X	X	X	XO	X	X	XO	X	X	X	X	X			X	X	X	X	X	X
AZ	XO	X	X	X		X		X	XO	X	X	X	X	X			X	XO	X	X	X	X
AR	O	X	X		X			X		X	X	X		X	X		O	XO	XO			X
CA			X	X	X		X	X	X	X	X	X	X	X		X	X	X	X	X	X	X
CO	XO	X	X	X	X		X	X	O	X	X	X					X	X	X		X	
CT	XO	X	X	X	X	X	X	XO		XO	XO	X		X			X	X	X	X	X	X
DE	XO	X	X	X	X	X	XO	XO	XO	X	X	X	X				X			X	X	X
FL	XO	X	X	X	XO	X	X	X		X	X	X									X	X
GA	X	X	X	X	X	X	X			X	X	X	X	X	X						X	X
HI	O			O	XO			O		X	O	X	X		X		O	O	O		X	X
ID	XO	X	X	X	X	X	X	X		X	X	X	X	X	X		XO		O		X	X
IL	XO		X	X	X	X		X		X	X	X	X	X	X		X	X	X	X	X	X
IN	XO	X	X	O	X		X	X		X	O	X	X	X	X		X	X		X	X	
IA	X		X	X	X			X	X	X	X	X	X	X	X		X			X	X	XO
KS	X	X	X	X	X			X	X	X	X	X	X	X	X		X	X	X	X	X	
KY	X	X	X	X	X		X	X	X	X	X	X	X	X	X						X	X
LA	XO	XO	X	X	X	XO	X	X	O	X	X	X	X	X	X		X	X	X	X	X	XO
MA	XO	X	X	X	X	X	XO	XO	XO	X	X	X	X	X	X		X	X	X	X	X	X
ME	XO	X	X	X	X	X	X	XO		X	X	X	X	X	X		X	X	X	X	X	
MD	XO	X	X	X	X	XO	X	X	X	X	XO	X	X	X	X		X	X	X	X	X	
MI	X	X	X	X	X	XO	X	X	X	X	X	X		X	X		X	X			X	XO
MN	X	X	X	XO	XO	XO	X	X	X	X	X	X	X	X	X		X	X	XO		X	X
MS	XO	O	X	X	X	X		X	O	X	XO	X	X	X			X	XO	XO		X	X
MO	XO		X	X	X	X	X	X	X	X	X	X	X	X	X		X	X			X	X
MT	X	X	X	X	X	X		X	X	X	X	X		X			X			X	X	X
NV	X	X	X	X	X	X		XO	X	X	X	X	X	X	X			X			X	X
NH	XO	X	X	X	X	X	X	XO	X	X	X	X	X	X	X	X		X		X	X	X
NJ	XO	X	XO	X	X	X	X	XO	XO	X	X	X	X	X	X	X		X	X	X	X	X
NM		X		X																	X	
NY	X		X	X	XO	XO	X	X	XO	X	X	X	X	X	X		X	X	X	X	X	
NC	XO	X	X	X	X	X	X	X		X	X	X	X	X	X	X	X	X	X	X	X	
ND	X		X	X	X	X	X	X	X	X	X	X	X	X	X	X	X	X	X	X	X	X
OH			X	X	X	X					X	X		X			X	X			X	
OK	XO	X	X	X	X	X	X	X	X	X	X	X	X	X	X	X	X	X	X	X	X	X
OR	XO	X	X	X	X	X	X	X	XO	X	X	X	X	X	X		X	X	X	X	X	
PA	XO	X	X	X	X	X	X	X		X	XO	X	X	X	X	XO	X	X	X	X	X	
RI	XO	X	X	X	X	X	X	X	O	X	XO	X	X	X	X		X	XO	XO		X	
SC	X	X	X	X	X	X	X	X		X	X	X	X	X			X	X			X	
SD	X		X	X	X	X		XO		X	X	X	X	X	X		X	X	X	X	X	X
TN	O	X	X	X	X	X	X	X	O	X	X	X	X	X	X		O				X	X
TX	XO	X	X	X	X	X	X	X		X	X	X	X	X	X		X	X		X	X	X
UT	X	X	X		X						X										X	X
VA	X		X	X	X	X	X	X	X	X	X	X	X	X	X		X	X		X	X	X
VT					X				X				X			X	X	X	X		X	
WA	X	X	X	X	X	X		X	X	X	X	X	X	X	X		X	X		X	X	X
WV	X	X	X	X	X	X	X	X	X	X	X	X	X	X	X	X	X	X	X	X	X	X
WI	X	X	X	X	X	X	X	X	X	X	X	X	X	X	X		X	X	X	X	X	X
WY	X	X	X	X	X	X	X	X	X	X	X	X	X	X	X		X	X	X	X	X	X

NOTE: X = allowed, O = prohibited, XO = allowed in some situations, prohibited in others. Information in table from Thurlow, House, Boys, Scott, & Ysseldyke (2000).

Recommendations on Making Accommodation Decisions

There are major debates about the kinds of accommodations that ought to be permitted in testing. There are also major arguments about the extent to which accommodations in testing destroy the technical adequacy of tests.

Making Decisions About Individuals

The issues in making accommodation decisions extend to more than screening and accountability. In fact, they play a major role in decisions about exceptionality, special need, eligibility, and instructional planning. We think there are some reasonable guidelines for best practice in making decisions about individuals.

- Conduct all assessments in the student's native language or mode of communication. In a recent ruling on this issue, Davilla (1989, p. 1), then assistant secretary of education, wrote, "If a person is deaf or blind, or has no written language, the mode of communication would be that normally used by the person (such as sign language, Braille, or oral communication)," and "under the Education of the Handicapped Act, testing or evaluation materials must be administered in a child's native language or other mode of communication appropriate to the child." Loeding and Crittenden (1993, p. 19) point out that for students who are deaf, the primary communication mode is either a visual–spatial, natural sign language used by members of the American Deaf Community called American Sign Language (ASL) or a manually coded form of English, such as Signed English, Pidgin Sign English (PSE), Seeing Essential English (SEE 1), Signing Exact English (SEE 2), or Sign-Supported Speech/English. Therefore, they argue, "traditional paper-and-pencil tests are inaccessible, invalid and inappropriate to the deaf student because the tests are written in English only."
- Make accommodations in format when the purpose of testing is not substantially impaired. It should be demonstrated that the accommodations assist the individual in responding but do not provide content assistance (for example, a scribe should record the response of the person being tested—not interpret what the person says, include his or her additional knowledge, and then record a response).
- Permit adaptations in assessment only for individuals with a disability documented by a licensed professional.
- With students who are deaf, use multimedia-based assessments that use videodisk, CD-ROM, CD-1, or digital video interactive technology. A videodisk-based assessment designed for individuals with hearing impairments is currently at the prototype stage and has been developed for a portion of the Scholastic Aptitude Test. The prototype makes both ASL and English-order signs available.

- Make normative comparisons only with groups whose membership includes students with background sets of experiences and opportunities like those of the students being tested.

Making Decisions About Groups

Many recommendations can be implemented when collecting assessment data to make decisions about groups of students. Among these are the following, suggested by Thurlow, Elliott, and Ysseldyke (1998):

- States and districts should have written guidelines for the use of accommodations in large-scale assessments used for accountability purposes.
- Decisions about accommodations should be made by one or more persons who know the student.
- Decisions about accommodations should be based on the student's current level of functioning and learning characteristics.
- A form should be used to document for each student the kinds of accommodations that were made and the reasons for them. The form should be kept in the student's file.
- Accommodation guidelines should require alignment of instructional accommodations and assessment accommodations.
- Decisions about accommodations permitted should not be based on program setting, category of disability, or percentage of time in general education classes.
- Decisions about accommodations should be documented on students' IEPs.
- Parents should be informed about accommodation options and about the implications of their child's not being included in assessment or accountability systems.

• •

Summary

Education legislation mandates high standards for all students. It also mandates that all students, including those with disabilities, participate in assessments to ascertain the extent to which those high standards are being met. Although the system of standards and assessments is voluntary, states cannot have them approved without specifying how students with disabilities will participate. This chapter outlined recommendations for making decisions about who should participate in assessments. We recommended that students with disabilities should be included in test development and should take tests, and that any reports of results of pupil performance should include reports on how students with disabilities performed.

To enable students with disabilities to participate in assessments, certain accommodations will be necessary. We outlined a set of recommendations for making accommodations in assessments.

Questions for Chapter Review and Thought

1. What major factors have served as impetus for increased participation of students with disabilities in large-scale state and national assessments?

2. We have recommended a set of practices for including students with disabilities in assessments. What things can teachers and other school personnel do to ensure that participation happens?

3. Describe what is meant by *out-of-level testing*. Explain why out-of-level testing is considered to be an appropriate accommodation. When might out-of-level testing be acceptable?

Resources for Further Investigation

Project

Obtain several of the reports that ETS has provided on testing accommodations for the SAT and the GRE. Identify the criteria that ETS uses to decide whether an accommodation is appropriate. Examine the instructions accompanying these assessments to determine what happens when accommodations are used during these assessments.

Print Resources

Elliott, J., Thurlow, M. L., & Ysseldyke, J. (1996). *Assessment guidelines that maximize the participation of students with disabilities in large-scale assessments.* Minneapolis, MN: University of Minnesota, National Center on Educational Outcomes.

Phillips, S. E. (1994). High-stakes testing accommodations: Validity versus disabled rights. *Applied Measurement in Education, 7,* 93–120.

Siskind, T. G. (1993). Modifications in statewide criterion-referenced testing programs to accommodate pupils with disabilities. *Diagnostique, 18,* 233–249.

Thurlow, M. L., Elliott, J., & Ysseldyke, J. E. (1998). *Testing students with disabilities: Practical strategies for complying with district and state requirements.* Thousand Oaks, CA: Corwin Press.

Thurlow, M. L., Olsen, K., Elliott, J., Ysseldyke, J., Erickson, R., & Ahearn, E. (1997). *Alternate Assessment,* Policy Directions Paper No. 2. Minneapolis, MN: University of Minnesota, National Center on Educational Outcomes.

Thurlow, M. L., Seyfarth, A., Scott, D., & Ysseldyke, J. (1997). *State policies on participation and accommodations in state assessments for students with disabilities.* Synthesis Report No. 31, Minneapolis, MN: University of Minnesota, National Center on Educational Outcomes.

Ysseldyke, J. E., Thurlow, M. L., McGrew, K. S., & Shriner, J. G. (1994). *Recommendations for making decisions about the participation of students with disabilities in statewide assessment programs* (Synthesis Report 15). Minneapolis, MN: University of Minnesota, National Center on Educational Outcomes. (Copies can be ordered for $10.00 by calling 612-626-1530.)

Technology Resources

Fairness in Performance Assessment

http://www.uncg.edu/~ericcas2/assessment/diga25.html

This home page contains an article by Tony C. M. Lam about bias and fairness in assessment. The author describes the extent to which using performance assessment helps to minimize bias in testing.

Special Education Resources

http://www.geocities.com/Wellesley/9641/sped.html

This home page offers suggestions for adapting tests to students with visual impairments or with severe disabilities.

ERIC Clearinghouse on Disabilities and Gifted Education

http://ericec.org/

From this web site, one can search the database for literature, information, and resources on education and development of individuals who are disabled and/or gifted. It includes links to the U.S. Department of Education and the federal regulations for IDEA amendments of 1997.

Students with Disabilities and Statewide Assessment

http://www.dpi.state.wi.us/dpi/disea/een/index.html

This is the web site for the Special Education Team of the Wisconsin Department of Public Instruction. It includes links to sites on students with disabilities and statewide assessment, and federal data collection, among others.

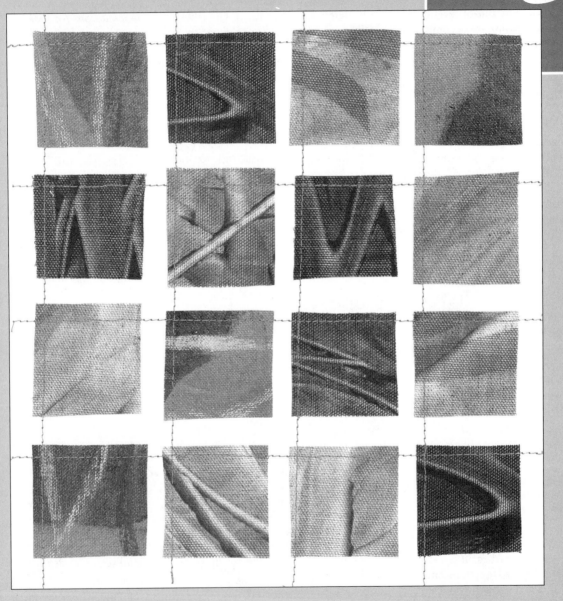

Assessment in Classrooms

The development of assessment has never been static, and its improvement has seldom been merely incremental. Scientific positivism was embraced by the mental-testing (such as intelligence tests) movement, and objective (scientific) tests gained widespread acceptance during the first half of the twentieth century. By the 1960s, however, experience with the use of norm-referenced, objectively scored tests suggested that they had a variety of technical shortcomings. A subsequent flurry of activity produced norm-referenced tests with greater reliability and substantially better norms. Nonetheless, educators frequently used these tests in inappropriate ways (for example, to plan and evaluate instruction).

As educators learned that these tests could not be used effectively to facilitate classroom decisions, other assessment procedures were developed. Thus, systematic observation procedures, so successful in experimental psychology, were adopted for classroom use. Similarly, there was renewed interest in the development of teacher-made tests. Although systematic observation and teacher-made tests were widely accepted and effectively used, many educators were still dissatisfied with the perceived limitations of these assessment techniques. During the late 1980s and early 1990s, interest grew in more subjective and qualitative approaches to assessment.

Educational assessment may appear to have come full circle, but educators have gotten off at different points. Thus, today there is no shortage of opinions about how classroom assessments ought to be conducted. Some educators still rely on norm-referenced achievement tests to plan and evaluate instruction; some rely on systematic observation; some rely on teacher-made tests and curriculum-based assessment; some rely on subjective and qualitative judgments to assess classroom learning; and some rely on a combination of approaches.

In Part 3 of this text, we discuss the approaches most likely to be used by classroom teachers. We do not consider these approaches to be informal or unstandardized. They are frequently formal: Students know that they are being assessed and that the assessments count for something. They are also frequently standardized: Students receive the same directions and tasks, and their responses are frequently scored using the same criteria. These approaches to assessment are used most frequently by classroom teachers, but we recognize that some specialists (such as school psychologists and speech and language therapists) may also use these approaches.

Part 3 begins with Chapter 10, on observation, which provides a general overview of basic considerations and good practice. The next chapter (11), deals with assessing the instructional ecology of classrooms. Chapter 12 provides an overview of objective and performance measures constructed by teachers. Chapter 13 provides an overview of an emerging, but controversial, approach to classroom assessment, using student portfolios. The last chapter (14) in this part discusses the decisions made by regular and special-education teachers.

Assessing Behavior Through Observation

In its ordinary meaning, the term *observation* refers to the process of gaining information through the senses—visual, auditory, and so forth. Observation can be used to assess behavior, states, physical characteristics, and permanent products of behavior (such as a child's poem). In this chapter, we use the term *behavioral observation* to refer to nontest behavior.

There are two basic approaches to observation: qualitative and quantitative. *Qualitative observation* is essentially descriptive. The observer begins without preconceived ideas about what will be observed and describes behavior that seems important. There are also two basic approaches to qualitative observation: ethnographic and participant–observer (see Suen & Ary, 1989). The difference between the two approaches lies in the behavior of the observer. In *ethnographic observation*, the observer only watches what is occurring. In the *participant–observer approach*, the observer joins the target social group and participates in its activities. In either case, observation occurs over prolonged periods, and the observer tries to note all the activities and contexts. Although qualitative approaches may have intuitive appeal, they suffer from four limitations: (1) Sophisticated and highly trained observers are required; (2) data collection requires a burdensome investment of time (sometimes years); (3) the observer's notes can be difficult to interpret and summarize; and (4) it is often difficult to maintain scientific objectivity (Suen & Ary, 1989).

Often, some qualitative observation precedes quantitative observation. For example, an observer might watch students in specific situations in order to get a general feel for what is going on. Then that observer might set out to measure specific behaviors that are thought to be particularly important. This form of qualitative observation is sometimes referred to as *nonsystematic observation* or *monitoring* (that is, paying attention and noting important events). Probably the most common way of conducting nonsystematic observations is to keep anecdotal records (descriptions and dates of behaviors that seem important to the observer). These records should, at the minimum, contain a complete description of the behavior and the context in which it occurred.

In this chapter, we stress quantitative approaches to observation. (Chapter 13 offers more coverage of qualitative approaches.) *Quantitative observation* is distinguished by five characteristics: (1) The goal of observation is to measure (for example, count) specific behaviors; (2) the behaviors being observed have been precisely defined previously; (3) before observation, procedures for gathering objective and replicable information about the behavior are developed; (4) the times and places for observation are carefully selected and specified; and (5) the ways in which behavior will be quantified are specified prior to observation.

The major criticism of quantitative approaches is that they may oversimplify the meaning and interpretation of behavior. Despite this criticism, quantitative analysis of behavior has proved to be very useful in developing theory and practice related to the modification of human behavior. Assessment based on quantitative behavioral observation is a topic suitable for an entire text, and only a general overview of good practices for those who develop and use behavioral observations can be provided in this chapter; interested readers are referred to texts by Boehm and Weinberg (1988), Alberto and Troutman (1990), and Salvia and Hughes (1990), among others. Readers interested in the statistical bases of measurement procedures used in systematic observation may consult the text by Suen and Ary (1989). Finally, the procedures and concepts discussed in detail in preceding chapters are not explained again here.

Why Do Teachers Observe Behavior?

Humans are always monitoring external events, and the behavior of others is a primary target of our attention. Teachers are constantly monitoring themselves and their students. Sometimes they are just keeping an eye on things to make sure that their classrooms are safe and goal oriented, to anticipate disruptive or dangerous situations, or just to keep track of how things are going in a general sense. Often, teachers notice behavior or situations that seem important and require their attention: The fire alarm has sounded, Harvey has a knife, Betty is asleep, Jo is wandering around the classroom, and so forth. In other situations, often as a result of their general monitoring, teachers look for very specific behavior to observe: social behavior that should be reinforced, attention to task, performance of particular skills, and so forth. Information gained from observation can be used to make academic and social instructional decisions—for example, planning or evaluating instructional programs for individuals or groups of students.

● ● ● ● ● ● ● ● ● ● ● ● ● ● ● ● ● ●

General Considerations

Behavior that is to be analyzed quantitatively can be observed as it occurs (in real time) or, by means of devices such as video or audio recorders that can replay, slow down, or speed up records of behavior displays, after it has occurred. Observation can be enhanced with equipment (for example, a telescope), or it can occur with only the observer's unaided senses.

Observational systems can be classified along two dimensions: (1) obtrusive versus unobtrusive and (2) contrived versus naturalistic. These two dimensions are relatively independent and yield four combinations (such as obtrusive contrived observation).

Obtrusive Versus Unobtrusive Observation

When antisocial, offensive, or highly personal or undesirable behaviors are targeted for assessment, observation often is conducted surreptitiously. Behaviors of these types tend not to occur if they are overtly monitored. For example, parents who hit their children privately may be very hesitant to do so publicly. To make observations of such behavior, observers can either use hidden cameras that require minimum light or use extrasensitive recorders, or a human observer can become a trusted person around whom the target individual will act naturally.

Behavior that is not antisocial, immoral, or highly personal may nonetheless be distorted by observation. For example, when a principal sits in the back of a probationary teacher's classroom for a periodic evaluation, both the teacher's and the students' behaviors may be affected by the principal's presence. Often, students are better behaved or respond more enthusiastically, in the mistaken belief that the principal is there to watch them. The teacher may write on the chalkboard more frequently, repeat directions more often, ask more questions of particular students, or give more positive reinforcement than usual, in the belief that the principal values those techniques. Moreover, a videocamera, an audio microphone, unusually bright light, or one-way mirrors can signal that someone is watching and thus can become stimuli for atypical behavior.

Unobtrusive observations do not affect the way people behave. It is fortunate that most people quickly become desensitized to observers or observation equipment when the observers or equipment are part of their daily environment. A number of things can be done to hasten desensitization. Observers can sit behind or to the side of a classroom, and they can avoid eye contact and verbal interactions with students. Recording equipment that cannot be hidden can be left in operating position at all times. Moreover, any indication that the equipment is operating can be avoided. For example, if a red light comes on when a videocamera is recording, students are likely to pay attention to the camera when the light is on; the red light should be disabled or hidden. Observation and recording can become part of the everyday classroom routine. In any event, assessment should not begin until the persons to be observed are desensitized and are acting in their usual ways.

Contrived Versus Naturalistic Observation

Contrived observations occur when a situation is set up before a student is introduced into it. For example, a playroom may be set up with toys that encourage aggressive play (such as guns or punching-bag dolls) or with items that promote other types of behavior. A child may be given a book and told to go into the room and read or may simply be told to wait in the room. Other adults or children in the situation may be confederates of the observer and may be instructed to behave in particular ways. For example, an older child may be told not to share toys with the child who is the target of the observation, or an adult may be told to initiate a conversation on a specific topic with the target child.

In contrast, *naturalistic settings* are not contrived. For example, specific toys are not added to or removed from a playroom; the furniture is arranged as it always is arranged.

Defining Behavior

Behavior is usually defined in terms of its topography, its function, and its characteristics. The function that a behavior serves in the environment is not observable, whereas the characteristics and topography of behavior can be measured with varying degrees of accuracy.

Topography of Behavior

Behavioral topography refers to the way a behavior is performed. For example, suppose the behavior of interest is holding a pencil to write and we are interested in Patty's topography for that behavior. The topography is readily observable: Patty holds the pencil at a 45-degree angle to the paper, grasped between her thumb and index finger; she supports the pencil with her middle finger; and so forth. Paul's topography for holding a pencil is quite different. Paul holds the pencil between his great toe and the second toe so that the point of the pencil is toward the sole of his foot, and so forth.

Function of Behavior

The *function of* a behavior is the reason a person behaves as he or she does or the purpose the behavior serves. Obviously, the reason for a behavior cannot be observed; it can only be inferred. Sometimes a person may offer an explanation of a behavior's function (for example, "I was holding the pencil to write a letter"), and we can accept or reject the reason given. Sometimes we can infer a behavior's function from its consequences. For example, Billy stands screaming at the rear door of his house until his mother opens the door, then Billy runs into the back yard and stops screaming. We can infer that the function of Billy's screaming is to have the door opened. Finally, sometimes we cannot infer a reason for behavior with much confidence (for example, the hand-flapping of a child with autism).

Currently, there is increased interest in functional analyses of behavior, especially behavior that is disruptive or dangerous. The hope is that individuals can be taught more acceptable behavior that serves the same function. When they have more acceptable ways to attain their goals, these individuals can participate more fully in a variety of activities.

Measurable Characteristics of Behavior

The measurement of behavior, whether individual behavior or a category of behavior, is based on four characteristics: duration, latency, frequency, and amplitude. These characteristics can be measured directly.

Duration

Behaviors that have discrete beginnings and endings may be assessed in terms of their *duration*—that is, the length of time a behavior lasts. The duration of a behavior is usually standardized in two ways: average duration and total duration. For example, in computing average duration, suppose that Janice is out of her seat four times during a 30-minute activity, and the durations of the episodes are 1 minute, 3 minutes, 7 minutes, and 5 minutes. In this example, the average duration is 4 minutes—that is, (1 + 3 + 7 + 5)/4. To compute Janice's total duration, we add 1 + 3 + 7 + 5 to conclude that she was out of her seat a total of 16 minutes. Often, total duration is expressed as a rate, by dividing the total occurrence by the length of an observation. This proportion of duration is often called the "prevalence of the behavior." In the preceding example, Janice's prevalence is .53 (that is, 16/30).

Latency

Latency refers to the length of time between a signal to perform and the beginning of the behavior. For example, a teacher might ask students to take out their books. Sam's latency for that task is the length of time between the teacher's request and Sam's placing his book on his desk. For latency to be assessed, the behavior must have a discrete beginning.

Frequency

For behaviors with discrete beginnings and endings, we often count *frequency*— that is, how often the behaviors occur. When the time periods during which the behavior is counted vary, frequencies are usually converted to rates. Using rate of behavior allows observers to compare the occurrence of behavior across different time periods and settings. For example, three episodes of out-of-seat behavior in 15 minutes may be converted to a rate of 12 per hour.

Alberto and Troutman (1990) suggest that frequency should not be used under two conditions: (1) when the behavior occurs at such a high rate that it cannot be counted accurately (for example, many stereotypic behaviors, such as foot tapping, can occur almost constantly), and (2) when the behavior occurs over a prolonged period of time (for example, cooperative play during a game of Monopoly).

Amplitude

Amplitude refers to the intensity of the behavior. In many settings, amplitude can be measured precisely (for example, with noise meters). However, in the classroom, it is usually measured with less precision. Often, amplitude is estimated by rating the behavior on a scale that crudely calibrates amplitude in terms of the behavior itself (for example, crying might be scaled as "whimpering," "sobbing," "crying," and "screaming." Amplitude may also be calibrated in terms of its objective or subjective impact on others. For example, the objective impact of hitting might be scaled as "without apparent physical damage," "resulting in bruising," and "causing bleeding." More subjective behavior ratings estimate the internal impact on others; for example, a student's humming could be scaled as "does not disturb others," "disturbs students seated nearby," or "disturbs students in the adjoining classroom."

Selecting the Characteristic to Measure

The behavioral characteristic to be assessed should make sense; we should assess the most relevant aspect of behavior in a particular situation. For example, if Burl is wandering around the classroom during the reading period, observing the duration of that behavior makes more sense than observing the frequency, latency, or amplitude of the behavior. If Camilla's teacher is concerned about her loud utterances, amplitude may be the most salient characteristic to observe. If Molly is always slow to follow directions, observing her latency makes more sense than assessing the frequency or amplitude of her behavior. For most behaviors, however, frequency and duration are the characteristics measured.

Sampling Behavior

As with any assessment procedure, we can assess the entire domain if it is finite and convenient. If it is not, we can sample from the domain. As previously discussed in Chapters 7 and 8, observation samples include the contexts in which the behaviors occur, the times in which the behaviors occur, and the behaviors themselves.

Contexts

When specific behaviors become the targets of intervention, it is useful to measure the behavior in a variety of contexts. Usually, the sampling of contexts is purposeful rather than random. We might want to know, for example, how Jesse's behavior in the resource room differs from his behavior in the regular classroom. Consistent or inconsistent performance across settings and contexts can provide useful information about what events might set the occasion for the behavior. Differences between the settings in which a behavior does and does not occur can provide potentially useful hypotheses about *setting events* (that is, environmental events that set the occasion for the performance of an action) and *discriminative stimuli* (that is, stimuli that are consistently present when a behavior is reinforced and that come to bring out behavior even in the absence of the original reinforcer).[1] Bringing behavior under the control of a discriminative stimulus is often an effective way of modifying it. For example, students might be taught to talk quietly (to use their "inside voice") when they are in the classroom or hallway.

Similarly, consistent or inconsistent performance across settings and contexts can provide useful information about how the consequences of a behavior are affecting that behavior. Some consequences of a behavior maintain, increase, or decrease behavior. Thus, manipulating the consequences of a behavior can increase or decrease its occurrence. For example, assume that Joey's friends usually laugh and congratulate him when he makes a sexist remark and that Joey is reinforced by his friends' behavior. If his friends could be made to stop laughing and congratulating him, Joey would probably make fewer sexist remarks.

Times

With the exception of some criminal acts, few behaviors are noteworthy unless they happen more than once. Behavioral recurrence over time is termed *stability* or *maintenance*. In a person's lifetime, there are almost an infinite number of times to exhibit a particular behavior. Moreover, it is probably impossible and certainly unnecessary to observe a person continuously during his or her entire life. Thus, temporal sampling is always performed, and any single observation is merely a sample from the person's behavioral domain.

Time sampling always requires the establishment of blocks of time, termed *observation sessions,* in which observations will be made. A session might consist of a continuous period of time (for example, one school day). More often, sessions are discontinuous blocks of time (for example, every Monday for a semester). Moreover, observers can record behavior continuously within sessions, or they can sample within a session (that is, record discontinuously). Continuous observation requires the expenditure of more resources than does discontinuous observation. When the observation session is long (for example, when it spans several days), continuous sampling can be very expensive and is often intrusive.

Two options are commonly used to estimate behavior in very long observation sessions: the use of rating scales to make estimates, and systematic observation to

---

1. *Discriminative stimuli* are not conditioned stimuli in the Pavlovian sense that they elicit reflexive behavior. Discriminative stimuli provide a signal to the individual to engage in a particular behavior because that behavior has been reinforced in the presence of that signal.

make more precise estimates. In the first option, rating scales can be used to obtain approximate estimates of the four characteristics of behavior. Following are some examples of such ratings:

- *Frequency.* A parent might be asked to rate the frequency of a behavior. How often does Patsy usually pick up her toys—always, frequently, seldom, never?
- *Duration.* A parent might be asked to rate how long Bernie typically watches TV each night—more than 3 hours, 2–3, 1–2, or less than 1 hour?
- *Latency.* A parent might be asked to rate how quickly Marisa usually responds to requests—immediately, quickly, slowly, or not at all (ignores requests)?
- *Amplitude.* A parent might be asked to rate how much of a fuss Jessica usually makes at bedtime—screams, cries, begs to stay up, or goes to bed without fuss?

In the second observation option, duration and frequency are sampled systematically during prolonged observation intervals. Three different sampling plans have been advocated: whole-interval recording, partial-interval recording, and momentary time sampling.

Whole-Interval Recording

In whole-interval recording, an observation session is subdivided into intervals. Usually, observation intervals of equal length are spaced equally through the session, although the recording and observation intervals need not be the same length. In whole-interval recording, a behavior is scored as having occurred only when it occurs throughout the entire interval. Thus, it is scored only if it is occurring when the interval begins and continues through the end of the interval.

Partial-Interval Recording

Partial-interval recording is quite similar to whole-interval recording. An observation session is subdivided into intervals, and the intervals in which the behavior occurs are noted. The difference between the whole-interval and the partial-interval procedures is that in partial-interval recording, an occurrence is scored if it occurs during any part of the interval. Thus, if a behavior begins before the interval begins and ends within the interval, an occurrence is scored; if a behavior starts after the beginning of the interval, an occurrence is scored; if two or more episodes of behavior begin and end within the interval, one occurrence is scored.

Momentary Time Sampling

Momentary time sampling is the most efficient sampling procedure. An observation session is subdivided into intervals. If a behavior is occurring at the last moment of the interval, an occurrence is recorded; if the behavior is not occurring at the last moment of the interval, a nonoccurrence is recorded.

Which Time-Sampling Procedure to Use

Salvia and Hughes (1990) have summarized a number of studies investigating the accuracy of these time-sampling procedures. Both whole-interval and partial-interval sampling procedures provide inaccurate estimates of duration and frequency.[2] Momentary time sampling provides an unbiased estimate of the proportion of time the behavior occurs but can underestimate the frequency of a behavior. The simplest and most accurate way to estimate frequency seems to be continuous recording with shorter observation sessions.

Behaviors

Teachers and psychologists may be interested in measurement of a particular behavior or a constellation of behaviors thought to represent a trait (for example, cooperation). When an observer views a target behavior as important in and of itself, only that specific behavior is observed. However, when a specific behavior is thought to be one element in a constellation of behaviors, other important behaviors within the constellation must also be observed in order to establish the content validity of the behavioral constellation. For example, if taking turns on a slide were viewed as one element of cooperation, we should also observe other behaviors indicative of cooperation (such as taking turns on other equipment, following the rules of games, working with others to attain a common goal, and so forth).[3]

Whether the behavior is important in and of itself or is representative of a larger constellation of behavior, it should be assessed in multiple contexts and at multiple times. For example, does Marc fail to take turns at the slide before school, during recess, and after school? Does the behavior manifest itself at home and at his neighborhood playground, as well as at school?

● ● ● ● ● ● ● ● ● ● ● ● ● ● ● ● ● ● ● ●

Targeting Behavior for Observation

Observations are usually conducted on two types of behavior. First, we regularly observe behavior that is desirable and that we are trying to increase. Behavior of this type includes all academic performances (for example, oral reading or science knowledge) and prosocial behavior (for example, cooperative behavior or polite language). Second, we regularly observe behavior that is undesirable or may indicate a disabling condition. These behaviors are harmful, stereotypic, inappropriately infrequent, or inappropriate at the times exhibited.

---

2. Suen and Ary (1989) have provided procedures whereby the sampled frequencies can be adjusted to provide accurate frequency estimates, and the error associated with estimates of prevalence can be readily determined for each sampling plan.
3. Each of the behaviors in a behavioral constellation can be treated separately or aggregated for the purposes of observation and reporting.

Harmful Behavior

Behavior that is self-injurious or physically dangerous to others is almost always targeted for intervention. Self-injurious behavior includes such actions as head banging, eye gouging, self-biting or self-hitting, smoking, drug abuse, and so forth. Potentially harmful behavior can include leaning back in a desk or being careless with reagents in a chemistry experiment. Behaviors harmful to others are those that directly inflict injury (for example, hitting or stabbing) or are likely to injure others (for example, pushing other students on stairs or subway platforms, bullying, or verbally instigating physical altercations). Unusually aggressive behavior may also be targeted for intervention. Although most students will display aggressive behavior, some children go far beyond what can be considered typical or acceptable. These students may be described as hot-tempered, quick-tempered, or volatile. Overly aggressive behavior may be physical or verbal. In addition to the possibility of causing physical harm, high rates of aggressive behavior may isolate the aggressor socially.

Stereotypic Behavior

Stereotypic behavior, or *stereotypies* (for example, hand flapping, rocking, and certain verbalizations such as inappropriate shrieks), are outside the realm of culturally normative behavior. Such behavior calls attention to students and marks them as abnormal to trained psychologists, or unusual to untrained observers. Stereotypic behaviors are often targeted for intervention.

Infrequent or Absent Desirable Behavior

Incompletely developed behavior, especially behavior related to physiological development (for example, walking), is often targeted for intervention. Intervention usually occurs when development of these behaviors will enable desirable functional skills or social acceptance. Shaping is usually used to develop absent behavior, whereas reinforcement is used to increase the frequency of behavior that is within a student's repertoire but exhibited at rates that are too low.

Normal Behavior Exhibited in Inappropriate Contexts

Many behaviors are appropriate in very specific contexts but are considered inappropriate or even abnormal when exhibited in other contexts. Usually, the problems caused by behavior in inappropriate contexts are attributed to lack of stimulus control. Behavior that is commonly termed *private* falls into this category; elimination and sexual activity are two examples. The goal of intervention should be not to get rid of these behaviors but to confine them to socially appropriate conditions. Behavior that is often called "disruptive" also falls into this category. For example, running and yelling are very acceptable and normal when exhibited on the playground; they are disruptive in a classroom.

A teacher may decide on the basis of logic and experience that a particular behavior should be modified. For example, harmful behavior should not be tolerated in a classroom or school, and behavior that is a prerequisite for learning academic material must be developed. In other cases, a teacher may seek the advice of a colleague, supervisor, or parent about the desirability of intervention. For example, a teacher might not know whether certain behavior is typical of a culturally different student. In yet other cases, a teacher might rely on the judgments of students or adults as to whether a particular behavior is troublesome or distracting for them. For example, are others bothered when Bob reads problems aloud during arithmetic tests? To ascertain whether a particular behavior bothers others, teachers can ask students directly, have them rate disturbing or distracting behavior, or perhaps use sociometric techniques to learn whether a student is being rejected or isolated because of his or her behavior.[4]

For infrequent prosocial behavior or frequent disturbing behavior, a teacher may well wish to get a better idea of the magnitude and pervasiveness of the problem before initiating a comprehensive observational analysis. Casual observation can provide information about the frequency and amplitude of the behavior; carefully noting the antecedents, consequences, and contexts may provide useful information about possible interventions, if an intervention is warranted. If casual observations are made, anecdotal records of these casual observations should be maintained.

● ● ● ● ● ● ● ● ● ● ● ● ● ● ● ● ● ● ●

Conducting Systematic Observations

Preparation

Careful preparation is essential to obtaining accurate and valid observational data. Five steps should guide the preparation for systematic observation:

1. *Define target behaviors.* Target behaviors should be defined precisely in observable terms. References to internal processes (for example, understanding or appreciating) are avoided. It is also useful to anticipate potentially difficult discriminations and to include examples of instances and noninstances of the behavior. Therefore, instances should include subtle exhibitions of the target behavior, and noninstances should include related behaviors and behavior with similar topographies. The definition of the target behavior should include the characteristic of the behavior that will be measured (for example, frequency or latency).

4. The *sociometric technique* is a method for evaluating the social acceptance of individual pupils and the social structure of a group: Students complete a form indicating their choice of companions for seating, work, or play. Teachers look at the number of times an individual student is chosen by others. They also look at who chooses whom.

2. *Select contexts.* The target behavior should be observed systematically in at least three contexts: the context in which the behavior was noted as troublesome (for example, in reading instruction), a similar context (for example, in math instruction), and a dissimilar context (for example, in physical education or recess).

3. *Select an observation schedule.* Two choices must be made, and these choices are related to the contexts for observation: session length and continuous versus discontinuous observation. In the schools, session length cannot exceed the period of time spanning a student's arrival and departure (including getting on and off the school bus, if appropriate). More often, session length is related to instructional periods or blocks of time within an instructional period (for example, 15 minutes in the middle of small-group reading instruction).

    The choice of continuous or discontinuous observation will depend on the resources available and the specific behaviors that are to be observed. When very-low-frequency behavior or behavior that must be stopped (for example, physical assaults) is observed, continuous recording is convenient and efficient. For other behavior, discontinuous observation is usually preferred, and momentary time sampling usually is the easiest and most accurate for teachers and psychologists to use.

    When a discontinuous observation schedule is used, the observer requires some equipment to signal exactly when observation is to occur. The most common equipment is a portable audiocassette player and a tape with pure tones, recorded at the desired intervals. One student or several students in sequence may be observed. For example, three students can be observed in a series of 5-second intervals. An audiotape would signal every 5 seconds. On the first signal, Henry would be observed; on the second signal, Joyce would be observed; on the third signal, Bruce would be observed; on the fourth signal, Henry would be observed again; and so forth.

4. *Develop recording procedures.* The recording of observations must also be planned. When a few students are observed for the occurrence of relatively infrequent behaviors, simple procedures can be used. The behaviors can be observed continuously and counted, using a tally sheet or a wrist counter. When time sampling is used, observations must be recorded for each time interval; thus, some type of recording form is required. In the simplest form, the recording sheet contains identifying information (for example, name of target student, name of observer, date and time of observation session, observation-interval length, and so forth) and two columns. The first column shows the time interval, and the second column contains places for the observer to indicate whether the behavior occurred during each interval. More complicated recording forms may be used for multiple behaviors and students. When multiple behaviors are observed, they are often given code numbers. For example, "out of seat" might be coded as 1; "in seat but off task" might be coded as 2; "in seat and on task" might be coded 3; and "no opportunity to observe" might be coded 4. Such codes should be included on the observation record form. Figure 10.1 shows a simple form on which to record multiple behaviors of students.

● ● ● **FIGURE 10.1**   A Simple Recording Form for Three Students and Two Behaviors

Observer: *Mr. Kowalski*

Date: *2/15/97*

Times of observation: *10:15 to 11:00*

Observation interval: *10 sec*

Instructional activity: *Oral reading*

Students observed: Codes:

S1 = *Henry J.*   1 = out of seat
                                   2 = in seat but off task
S2 = *Bruce H.*   3 = in seat, on task
                                   4 = no opportunity to observe
S3 = *Joyce W.*

	S1	S2	S3
1	___	___	___
2	___	___	___
3	___	___	___
4	___	___	___
5	___	___	___
.			
.			
.			
179	___	___	___
180	___	___	___

Complex observational systems tend to be less accurate than simple ones. Complexity increases as a function of the number of different behaviors that are assessed and the number of individuals who are observed. Moreover, both the proportion of target individuals to total individuals and the proportion of target behaviors observed to the number of target behaviors to be recorded also have an impact on accuracy. The surest way to reduce inaccuracies in observations attributable to complexity is to keep things relatively simple.

5. *Select the means of observation.* The choice of human observers or electronic recorders will depend on the availability of resources. If electronic recorders are available and can be used in the desired environments and contexts, they may be appropriate when continuous observation is warranted. If other personnel are

available, they can be trained to observe and record the target behaviors accurately. Training should include didactic instruction in defining the target behavior, the use of time sampling (if it is to be used), and the way in which to record behavior, as well as practice in using the observation system. Training is always continued until the desired level of accuracy is reached. Observers' accuracy is evaluated by comparing each observer's responses with those of the others or with a criterion rating (usually a previously scored videotape). Generally, very high agreement is required before anyone can assume that observers are ready to conduct observations independently. Ultimately, the decision of how to collect the data should also be based on efficiency. For example, if it takes longer to desensitize students to an obtrusive videorecorder than it takes to train observers, human observers are preferred.

Data Gathering

As with any type of assessment information, two general sources of error can reduce the accuracy of observation: First, random error can result in over- or underestimates of behavior; second, systematic error can bias the data in a consistent direction—for example, behavior may be systematically overcounted or undercounted. Careful preparation and systematic monitoring of the observation process can head off trouble. Before observation begins, human observers should make sure that they have an extra supply of recording forms, spare pens or pencils, and something to write on (for example, a clipboard or tabletop). When electronic recording is used, equipment should be checked before every observation session to make sure it is in good working condition. When portable equipment is employed, the observer should have extra batteries, signal tapes, or recording tapes available. Before beginning an observation, the observer can prepare a checklist of equipment and materials that will be used during the observation and can assemble everything that is needed for the observation session. Also, before the observation session, the observer should check out the setting to locate appropriate vantage points for equipment or furniture.

Random Error

Random errors in observation and recording usually affect observer agreement. Observers may change the criteria for the occurrence of a behavior, they may forget behavior codes, or they may use the recording forms incorrectly. Because changes in agreement can signal that something is wrong, the accuracy of observational data should be checked periodically. The usual procedure is to have two people observe and record on the same schedule in the same session. The two records are then compared, and an index of agreement (for example, kappa—see Chapter 7) is computed. Poor agreement suggests the need for retraining or for revision of the observation procedures. To alleviate some of these problems, provide periodic retraining, and allow observers to keep the definitions and codes for target behaviors with them. Finally, when observers know that their accuracy is being systematically checked, they are usually more accurate. Thus, observers might be led to believe that their observations are always being checked.

One of the most vexing factors affecting the accuracy of observations is the incorrect recording of correctly observed behavior. Even when observers have applied the criterion for the occurrence of a behavior correctly, they may record their decision incorrectly. For example, if 1 is used to indicate occurrence and 0 (zero) is used to indicate nonoccurrence, the observer might accidentally record 0 for a behavior that has occurred. Inaccuracy can be attributed to three related factors:

1. *Lack of familiarity with the recording system.* Observers definitely need practice in using a recording system when several behaviors or several students are to be observed. They also need practice when the target behaviors are difficult to define or when they are difficult to observe.

2. *Insufficient time to record.* Sufficient time must be allowed to record the occurrence of behavior. Problems can arise when using momentary time sampling if the observation intervals are spaced too closely (for example, 1- or 5-second intervals). Observers who are counting several different high-frequency behaviors may record inaccurately. Generally, inadequate opportunities for observers to record can be circumvented by electronic recording of the observation session; when observers can stop and replay segments of interest, they essentially have unlimited time to observe and record.

3. *Lack of concentration.* It may be hard for observers to remain alert for long periods of time (for example, one hour), especially if the target behavior occurs infrequently and is difficult to detect. Observers can reduce the time that they must maintain vigilance by either taking turns with several observers or recording observation sessions for later evaluation. Similarly, when it is difficult to maintain vigilance because the observational context is noisy, busy, or otherwise distracting, electronic recording may be useful in focusing on target subjects and eliminating ambient noise.

Unusual events and departures from the observation plan (for example, a missed observation interval) can be noted directly on the observation form. Finally, observation should begin and end at the planned times.

Systematic Error

Systematic errors are difficult to detect. To minimize error, four steps can be taken:

1. *Guard against unintended changes in the observation process.*[5] When assessment is carried out over extended periods of time, observers may talk to each other about the definitions that they are using or about how they cope with difficult discriminations. Consequently, one observer's departure from standardized pro-

---

5. Technically, general changes in the observation process over time are termed *instrumentation problems.*

cedures may spread to other observers. When the observers change together, modifications of the standard procedures and definitions will not be detected by examining interobserver agreement. Techniques for reducing changes in observers over time include keeping the scoring criteria available to observers, meeting with the observers on a regular basis to discuss difficulties encountered during observation, and providing periodic retraining.

Surprisingly, even recording equipment can change over time. Audio signal tapes (used to indicate the moment a student should be observed) may stretch after repeated uses; a 10-second interval may become an 11-second interval. Similarly, the batteries in playback units can lose power, and signal tapes may play more slowly). Therefore, equipment should be cleaned periodically, and signal tapes should be checked for accuracy.

2. *Desensitize students.* The introduction of equipment or new adults into a classroom, and also changes in teacher routines, can signal to students that observations are going on. Overt measurement can alter the target behavior or the topography of the behavior. Usually, the pupil change is temporary. For example, when Janey knows that she is being observed, she may be more accurate, deliberate, or compliant. However, as observation becomes a part of the daily routine, students' behavior usually returns to what is typical for them. This return to typical patterns of behavior functionally defines desensitization. The data generated from systematic observation should not be used until the students who are observed are no longer affected by the observation procedures and equipment or personnel. However, sometimes the change in behavior is permanent. For example, if a teacher were watching for the extortion of lunch money, Robbie might wait until no observers were present or might demand the money in more subtle ways. In such cases, valid data would not be obtained through overt observation, and either different procedures would have to be developed or the observation would have to be abandoned.

3. *Minimize observer expectancies.* Sometimes, what an observer believes will happen affects what is seen and recorded. For example, if an observer expects an intervention to increase a behavior, that observer might unconsciously alter the criteria for evaluating that behavior or might evaluate approximations of the target behavior as having occurred. The more subtle or complex the target behavior is, the more susceptible it may be to expectation effects. The easiest way to avoid expectations during observations is for the observer to be blind to the purpose of the assessment. When video- or audiotapes are used to record behavior, the order in which they are evaluated can be randomized so that observers do not know what portion of an observation is being scored. When it is impossible or impractical to keep observers blind to the purpose, the importance of accurate observation should be stressed and such observation rewarded.

4. *Motivate observers.* Inaccurate observation is sometimes attributed to lack of motivation on the part of an observer. Motivation can be increased by providing rewards and feedback, stressing the importance of the observations, reducing the length of observation sessions, and not allowing observation sessions to become routine.

Data Summarization

Depending on the particular characteristic of behavior being measured, observational data may be summarized in different ways. When duration or frequency is the characteristic of interest, observations are usually summarized as rates (that is, the prevalence or the number of occurrences per minute or other time interval). Latency and amplitude should be summarized statistically by the mean and the standard deviation or by the median and the range. All counts and calculations should be checked for accuracy.

Criteria for Evaluating Observed Performances

Once accurate observational data have been collected and summarized, they must be interpreted. Some behavior can be judged on an a priori basis—for example, unsafe and harmful behavior. Most behavior is not evaluated simply by its presence, however. For example, knowing that the prevalence of Marie's out-of-seat behavior is 10 percent during instruction in content areas does not provide much information about whether that behavior should be decreased.

Behavior rates can be evaluated in several ways. Normative data may be available for some behavior, or, in some cases, data from behavior rating scales and tests can provide general guidelines. In the absence of such data, social comparisons can be made. In social comparison, a peer whose behavior is considered appropriate is observed. The peer's rate of behavior is then used as the standard against which to evaluate the target student's rate of behavior. The social tolerance for a behavior can also be used as a criterion. For example, the degree to which different rates of out-of-seat behavior disturb a teacher or peers can be assessed. Teachers and peers could be asked to rate how disturbing is the out-of-seat behavior of students who exhibit different rates of behavior. In a somewhat different vein, the contagion of the behavior to others can be a crucial consideration in teacher judgments of unacceptable behavior. Thus, the effects of different rates of behavior can be assessed to see whether there is a threshold above which other students initiate undesirable behavior.

Summary

Behavioral observation is the process of gaining information visually, aurally, or through other senses. It can be used to assess any behavior or product of behavior; it cannot be used to assess events that are not observable (for example, thinking, feeling, or believing). Although behavior may be defined functionally or topographically, it is measured in terms of its duration, latency, frequency, and amplitude. Moreover, observers can assess the entire domain of behavior or can sample from the domain along three dimensions: contexts, behaviors, and times. Each dimension can provide important and useful information about the behavior and how it is maintained in the environment. Three different sampling plans have been advocated for measuring the duration and frequency of behavior: whole-interval recording, partial-interval recording, and momentary time sampling. Of these three methods, momentary time sampling is the most useful and in general is the most accurate.

Observations are usually conducted on behavior that may require modification or behavior that may indicate a disability condition: harmful behavior, stereotypic behavior, infrequent or absent desirable behavior, or normal behavior shown in inappropriate contexts.

Systematic observations require as much care and precision as testing does, in terms of preparation, data gathering, and data summarization. When observers are preparing to conduct systematic observations, they must (1) carefully define the target behaviors; (2) carefully select both the contexts in which observations will be conducted and the observation schedule itself; (3) thoughtfully develop the recording procedures; and (4) determine the means by which data will be collected (for example, using human observers).

When gathering data, the observer should minimize both random and systematic error. *Random error* is usually attributed to lack of familiarity with the recording system, to insufficient time to record, or to lack of concentration. *Systematic error* is usually attributed to unintended changes in the observation process, to failure to desensitize target students, to observer expectancies, or to unmotivated observers. Finally, like all other assessment procedures, observations of student performances must be evaluated. Some behavior can be judged on an a priori basis—for example, unsafe and harmful behavior. Other behavior is evaluated on the basis of normative data, social comparison, or social tolerance.

Questions for Chapter Review and Thought

1. Describe each of the four types of behavior that are frequently targeted for intervention.

2. Name four types of systematic errors that can occur during observation. What can an observer do to minimize these types of errors?

3. Name three types of random errors that can occur during observation. What can an observer do to minimize these types of errors?

4. Joey has been referred for assessment. His teacher reports that he seems to be lethargic all the time. A specific example provided by the teacher was that when Joey's hand is raised and he is called on, it takes him much longer than any other child to begin giving his answer or asking his question. What type of observational data would you want to collect to check the teacher's informal observation?

5. A frustrating problem in observations is the occurrence of inaccurate coding of behavior that was correctly observed. Give an example of this problem, and list three ways to reduce the likelihood of its occurrence.

Resources for Further Investigation

Project

Read an article in which an observational study is reported. Identify the kind of data collected and how the data are summarized.

Print Resources

Alberto, P., & Troutman, A. (1999). *Applied behavior analysis for teachers* (4th ed.). Columbus, OH: Merrill.

Greenwood, C. R., Peterson, P., & Sideridis, G. (1995). Conceptual, methodological, and technological advances in classroom observational assessment. *Diagnostique, 20,* 73–99.

Hartmann, D. P. (Ed.). (1988). *Using observers to study behavior: New directions for methodology of social and behavioral science series,* No. 14 (pp. 5–20, Observer effects: Reactivity of direct observation, and pp. 21–36, Developing a behavior code). San Francisco: Jossey-Bass.

Technology Resources

Observing and Recording Student Performance

http://para.unl.edu/ServedDocuments/observation/Intro.html

This web site discusses the issues and techniques involved in gathering information about student behavior through observation. The five lessons presented include examples and practice activities.

Assessnet

http://longman.awl.com/assessnet/links_5.htm

This page includes a connection to a chapter on observing and recording student performance. This site provides basic information about conducting observations as well as links to related information.

Fairness in Performance Assessment

http://ericae.net/db/edo/ED391982.htm

This ERIC document discusses the bias, unfairness, and equality in classroom assessment.

chapter

11

Assessing Instructional Ecology

$\mathcal{S}$ tudent assessment cannot be considered complete without an assessment of the student's instructional needs in the context of the classroom. This observation seems so obvious that few would disagree with it. Yet, in practice, most psychoeducational decisions for a student are made without careful, systematic analysis of the instructional ecology. In this chapter, we review systematic assessment of instructional environments. It is important to assess instructional environments because the quickest, most direct way to change student performance and outcomes is to modify or adapt the environment in which students are taught.

As early as 1964, Ogden Lindsley introduced the concept of *prosthetic environments*—environments for maximizing the behavioral efficiency of children with disabilities who show deficits when forced to behave in average environments. He described procedures for modifying the environment to improve student performance. Before teachers or assessors can modify instructional environments, however, they need to know a lot about the nature of the environments in which students are being taught.

In this chapter, we first consider instructional ecology and the kinds of factors that are related to instructional outcomes and then describe ways to gather data on (assess the presence or absence of) those factors.

What Is Instructional Ecology?

Ecology is the term we use to refer to mutual relations between organisms and their environments. When we talk about *instructional ecology*, we are referring to the relationships between students and their instructional environments. Students' behavior and academic performance are influenced by the environment in which they are taught. Each student brings to instructional settings a set of individual characteristics and a learning history. Each student also responds differently to teachers' instructional efforts. There is a reciprocal relationship between students and instructional environments, and those who assess the instructional ecology are interested in that relationship.

The product of schooling (what students learn, or *outcomes*) is a function of (a) the content goals of the school, as expressed in scheduling and implementation of instruction; and (b) the instructional procedures employed by teachers, as expressed in terms of their success in managing students' responses to academic tasks (Greenwood, Carta, Kamps, & Arreaga-Mayer, 1990). Those who engage in assessments of instructional environments evaluate, among other things, classroom structures, the amount of time allocated to instruction, the amount of time students are actively engaged in responding to instruction, the ways in which instructions are given for school tasks, the pacing of instruction, and the ways in which teachers use information about student performance to change or adapt instruction.

The Importance of Home Support for Learning

Instructional outcomes are a function of the interaction between individuals and instructional ecologies. However, the nature of this interaction is, in part, determined by the extent to which there is home support for the learning that occurs in school. Outcomes are better when there is a strong collaborative relationship between homes and schools. When parents support teachers, supplement instruction in classrooms, and provide their children with an educative environment—and when teachers in turn support parents—outcomes improve. Those who assess instructional ecologies have devised procedures for systematic assessment of home support for learning.

Factors That Contribute to Academic and Behavioral Problems in School

When educators are asked to indicate why students experience difficulty and fail in school, they give four categories of causes: students' deficits or disabilities, students' home and family problems, ineffective instruction, and unsuitable school organization. (Of course, educators also attribute success in school to these same four factors.) First, educators most often argue that school difficulties are caused by deficits, disorders, dysfunctions, or disabilities suffered by the student—for example, the child may be brain injured, mentally retarded, blind, emotionally disturbed, or learning disabled in some way. Second, educators contend that students who experience difficulty in school come from dysfunctional families, families in which there is little or no discipline, and home settings in which there is not an educative environment. Third, some educators argue that we know a great deal about the kinds of instructional practices that enhance student outcomes. When these factors are not present or are not present in ways that they should be, students experience academic and behavioral problems. Finally, some of the difficulties that students experience in school may be due to the ways schools are organized, ways that just do not make sense for some students. In this chapter, our focus is on the third and fourth factors for success or failure. We consider ways in which the effectiveness of instruction and the suitability of school organization contribute to school outcomes.

In the first part of this chapter, we review factors that are related to instructional results for students, and in the sections that follow, we review current practice in ecobehavioral assessment and assessment of instructional environments.

Carroll's Model of School Learning

More than 30 years ago, John Carroll (1963) proposed a model of school learning that is the basis for most models of learning applied in schools today. Carroll's model is shown in Figure 11.1. According to Carroll, how much a student learns is a function of the amount of time the student actually spends learning, divided by the amount of time the student needs in order to learn what is being taught. The amount of time spent learning is influenced by *opportunity,* which represents the time officially scheduled for learning and the time allocated by teachers and instructional programs, and by *perseverance,* which represents the amount of time the student is willing to engage actively in learning, particularly when the task becomes more difficult and the student may be facing failure.

Carroll posited that the time needed for learning depends on the student's aptitude and ability to understand instruction and on the quality of instruction. He defines *aptitude* as the amount of time needed to learn a task under optimal conditions. Carroll talks about aptitude as being task specific and speaks of students'

● ● ● **FIGURE 11.1**   Carroll's Model of School Learning

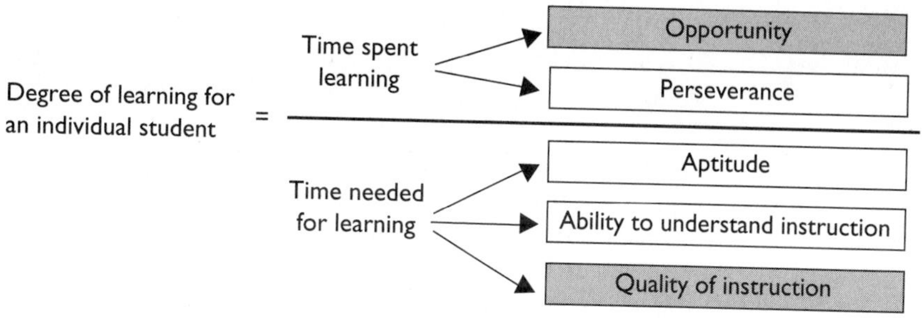

SOURCE: From J.B. Carroll, "A Model of School Learning", *Teaching College Record,* v. 64, pp. 723–733. Copyright © 1963. Reprinted by permission of the publisher.

"aptitude for learning this task" (Carroll, 1985, p. 63). *Ability to understand instruction* is seen as a function of the student's general intelligence and of how adequately tasks are explained. *Quality of instruction*, in Carroll's model, is a function of the nature, objectives, content, and hierarchical structure of teacher-provided instruction and instructional materials. Quality of instruction varies as a function of the clarity of the task requirements, the adequacy of task presentation and of sequencing and pacing, and the degree to which the learner's unique needs have been considered during the instructional presentation. In Figure 11.1, we have shaded "opportunity" and "quality of instruction," because these are the factors we consider in detail in this chapter.

Walberg's Meta-analytic Research

Walberg (1984) reported the results of a quantitative synthesis of the results of more than 3,000 studies of factors that influence student educational outcomes. He identified three causal influences:

1. *Aptitude* (ability, development, and motivation to learn)

2. *Instruction* (quality of the instructional experience and amount of student engagement in it)

3. *Environment* (home, classroom peers, and television)

Note that the factors that Walberg concluded are important to student learning outcomes parallel those that Carroll argued were important, with one exception: Walberg concluded that it is important to have home support for learning in school.

Algozzine and Ysseldyke's Model of Effective Instruction

Ysseldyke and Christenson (1987a) conducted a review of the literature on effective instruction. They identified student characteristics that were said or shown to be related to student outcomes. They also found environmental factors (school district conditions, within-school conditions, and general family characteristics) and instructional factors related to instructional outcomes.

The Ysseldyke and Christenson review served as the foundation for the development of the Algozzine–Ysseldyke Model of Effective Instruction (see Figure 11.2 on pp. 198–199). Algozzine and Ysseldyke (1992) identified four components of effective instruction (planning, managing, delivering, and evaluating), the major principles of effective instruction for each component, and several strategies for putting principles into practice in classrooms. Whether they are instructing students who are gifted, nondisabled, mildly disabled, or severely disabled, teachers must plan, manage, deliver, and evaluate instruction. The most recent version of the Algozzine–Ysseldyke model (Algozzine, Ysseldyke, & Elliott, 1997) is shown in Figure 11.2.

Instructional Planning

Effective instruction does not occur by chance. It must be planned. Instructional outcomes are enhanced by effective *instructional planning* for individual students. If all students in a class were at the same instructional level and if the goals and objectives of schooling were clearly defined and the same for all students, then instruction would consist of doing the same things with all students, being certain to do them in the right order and at the right time. However, students are not all alike, and the goals and objectives of instruction are not the same for all students. Schools are becoming increasingly diverse environments each year. This is why instructional planning is such an important part of teaching and assessment.

Outcomes are enhanced when teaching goals and teacher expectations for student performance and success are stated clearly and are understood by the student. Those who plan instruction must (1) decide what to teach, (2) decide how to teach, and (3) communicate realistic expectations to individual learners.

Deciding What to Teach Decisions about what to teach are enhanced by accurate assessment of student characteristics (e.g., skill levels, motivation), task characteristics (e.g., cognitive demands), and classroom characteristics (e.g., materials, instructional groupings). Using this information, effective teachers plan their instruction to produce logical lessons that best match student, task, and classroom characteristics to the instructional demands of the content they are teaching. The goal when deciding what to teach is to accurately determine the appropriate content to present, based on what is known about individual students and their learning needs/development. We can check on a school's performance in this area by looking at the extent to which school personnel have accurately diagnosed learner strengths and weaknesses, identified gaps between actual and expected levels of performance, considered the kinds of skills taught in the curriculum, sequenced the instruction in a logical way, and matched the student to the content of instruction at the right level.

Deciding How to Teach Decisions must also be made about how to teach. It is difficult to know ahead of time the kinds of instructional practices that will be effective with individual students. Rather, teachers experiment with alternative teaching approaches until they identify the combination of approaches that works best in moving their students toward instructional goals. Educators can assess the extent to which there are clear instructional goals for individual students, the grouping structures are used appropriately, the instruction is paced appropriately, and the students' performance is monitored and used to plan subsequent instruction.

Communicating Realistic Expectations The third principle of effective instructional planning is that results are enhanced when teachers communicate realistic expectations to students. Effective teachers set instructional goals and objectives that are realistic—neither too low nor too high. The goals and expectations must also be communicated clearly to the student. Outcomes are enhanced when students understand what they are expected to do. Note that failure to communicate goals and expectations can occur either because the teacher fails to communicate clearly or because the child does not understand what is communicated.

● ● ● **FIGURE 11.2**   The Algozzine–Ysseldyke Model of Effective Instruction

Component	Principle	Strategy
Planning Instruction	Decide What to Teach	Assess skill levels to identify gaps between actual and expected level of performance Establish logical sequences of instruction Consider contextual variables
	Decide How to Teach	Set instructional goals Establish performance standards Choose instructional methods and materials Establish grouping structures Pace instruction appropriately Monitor students' performance and use performance to plan instruction
	Communicate Realistic Expectations	Teach goals, objectives, and standards Teach students to be active, involved learners Teach students consequences of performance
Managing Instruction	Prepare for Instruction	Set classroom rules Communicate classroom rules Teach rule compliance Handle disruptions efficiently Communicate consequences of behavior Teach students to manage their own behavior
	Use Time Productively	Establish routines and procedures Organize physical space Give task directions Keep transitions short Allocate time to academic activities Maintain academic focus
	Establish Positive Classroom Environment	Make classrooms pleasant, friendly places Accept individual differences Keep interactions positive Establish supportive, cooperative environment Make students respond and participate
Delivering Instruction	Present Instruction	**For Presenting Content** Gain students' attention Review prior skills or lessons Provide organized, relevant lessons Maintain students' attention Interact positively with students **For Teaching Thinking Skills** Model thinking skills Teach fact-finding skills Teach divergent thinking Teach learning strategies

Component	Principle	Strategy
Delivering Instruction	Present Instruction	**For Motivating Students** Show enthusiasm and interest Help students value schoolwork Use rewards effectively Consider level and student interest **For Providing Relevant Practice** Develop automaticity Vary opportunities for practice Use seatwork effectively Provide students with help Use relevant tasks and varied materials Assign the right amount of work Vary methods during practice
	Monitor Instruction	**For Providing Feedback** Give immediate, frequent, explicit feedback Provide specific praise and encouragement Model correct performance Provide prompts and cues Check student understanding **For Keeping Students Actively Involved** Monitor performance regularly Monitor performance during practice Use peers to provide instruction Provide opportunities for success Limit opportunities for failure Monitor engagement rates
	Adjust Instruction	Adjust lessons to meet student needs Provide many instructional options Adjust pace
Evaluating Instruction	Monitor Student Understanding	Check understanding of directions Check process understanding Monitor success rate
	Monitor Engaged Time	Check student participation Teach students to monitor their own participation
	Maintain Records of Student Progress	Teach students to chart their own progress Regularly inform students of performance Maintain records of student performance
	Use Data to Make Decisions	Use data on student progress to decide when more services are warranted Use student progress to make teaching decisions Use student progress to make decisions about when to change service delivery

SOURCE: Reprinted with permission from Algozzine, B. and Ysseldyke, J. (1997). *Strategies and Tactics for Effective Instruction* (2nd ed.). Longmont, CO: Sopris West.

Managing Instruction

Discipline is consistently identified as a concern in public and professional opinion polls about education. Classroom discipline and desirable instructional outcomes are enhanced by efficient yet warm classroom management. Principles of effective classroom management include preparing for effective instruction, using time effectively, and establishing a positive classroom environment. Appropriate discipline practices emerge when these principles are put into practice.

Preparing for Effective Instruction   Effective teachers establish classroom rules and communicate them early in the school year. They teach individual students to comply with rules, show students the consequences of either following or not following their rules, and handle rule infractions and other disruptions as quickly as possible after these occur. When teachers fail to establish and communicate classroom rules, instructional outcomes are diminished. In evaluating the instructional ecology, assessors take into account the extent to which rules have been communicated to the individual student, whether the student knows and understands the rules, and whether rule infractions by the student are handled immediately. Not all the onus is on the teacher; rather, students can be taught to manage their own behavior.

Using Time Productively   Students achieve better instructional outcomes when they make effective use of their time. Teachers can modify the instructional environment to help students make good use of their time by establishing routines (for example, students know what to do when they are finished with their work), organizing physical space so that students are placed in settings that limit distractions, keeping students focused on academic work, allocating specific time to academic activities, and making sure that students understand task directions.

Establishing a Positive Classroom Environment   Students are more motivated to learn in environments in which they feel accepted. Assessors should take into account whether the classroom environment is both accepting of individual differences and supportive of students. Assessors should also look at the extent to which the student's teachers interact positively with him or her and encourage him or her to respond and participate in class.

Delivering Instruction

Instructional delivery is a complex process involving appropriate instructional matches, the clear presentation of lessons while following specific instructional procedures, the allocation of sufficient time for instructing individual learners, and sufficient opportunity for students to respond. Effective teachers use very specific strategies to present information, monitor presentations, and adjust presentations in light of student performance and progress. These strategies are listed in Figure 11.2.

Presenting Information   This requires decisions about content, how to motivate students, how to teach thinking skills, and how to provide relevant practice. When presenting content, effective teachers gain their students' attention, review previously covered material, provide organized lessons, introduce new material by relating it to known content whenever possible, and interact positively with their students. It is important to assess the extent to which these teaching actions are present in the instruction of individual students. When teaching thinking skills, effective teachers show students how to solve problems and give them alternative ways of finding answers. When motivating students, effective teachers focus on using internal sources of satisfaction as well as external sources of satisfaction. When providing relevant practice, effective teachers help students develop automatic responses. They also provide ample time and relevant, varied activities for guided and independent practice. The goal in presenting information is to teach students something they do not know.

Monitoring Presentations   This calls for decisions about how to provide feedback and how to keep students actively involved when delivering instruction. When providing feedback, effective teachers provide immediate, frequent, explicit information that supports correct responses and provides models for improvement of incorrect responses. When keeping students actively involved, effective teachers regularly monitor responses during instructional presentations, use peers to enhance engagement, and provide ample, varied opportunities for supporting success and correcting failure. The goal in monitoring presentations is to ensure that students are learning the content as it was presented.

Adjusting Presentations   This relies on decisions about how to change instruction by modifying lessons, using alternative instructional options, and using differing levels of pace to meet the individual needs of students. Effective teachers teach skills until students master them, and they use information gathered during instructional presentations and practice sessions to decide when and how to modify their teaching so that all students can be successful. The goal in adjusting presentations is to make any changes needed to ensure that all students benefit from instruction.

Evaluating Instruction

Evaluation, an important part of teaching, is the means by which teachers decide whether the approach they are using is effective with individual students. Assessors must take into account the extent to which teachers monitor student understanding, monitor engaged time, keep records of student progress, and use evaluation data to make decisions. In checking on the ways in which teachers monitor student understanding, it is important to examine the extent to which they check whether or not students understand directions and understand the procedures to be followed in solving problems. Effective teachers regularly do this, and they also monitor the success rate experienced by individual students.

In evaluating instruction, assessors must also look at how teachers go about teaching students to monitor their own behavior and chart their own progress. They check for evidence that students are informed of how they are doing and that teachers are keeping records of student performance. Effective teachers use evaluation data to make decisions about students. Assessors will want to know how teachers use data to make teaching decisions, to decide whether more services are warranted, to decide whether and when to refer, and to decide when to discontinue services.

● ●

Approaches to Gathering Data on Instructional Ecology

In this chapter, we consider two approaches to gathering data on students' instructional environments or ecologies: ecobehavioral assessment and the Instructional Environment System–II. *Ecobehavioral assessment* is used to gather data on how students spend their time in school, looking specifically at opportunity to learn and academic engaged time. *The Instructional Environment System–II*, a methodology developed by Ysseldyke and Christenson (1993), is used to systematically analyze the qualitative nature of the instruction that students receive in classroom and home environments.

Ecobehavioral Assessment

The term *ecobehavioral assessment* is used in educational assessment to describe observations of functional relationships (or interactions) between student behavior and its ecological contexts. The approach is used to identify interactions among student behavior, teacher behavior, time allocated to instruction, physical grouping structures, types of tasks being used, and instructional content. Ecobehavioral assessment thus enables educators to identify natural instructional conditions that are associated with academic success, behavioral competence, or challenging behaviors. Increasingly, ecobehavioral assessment is being used to develop and validate specific instructional procedures, develop a number of approaches to the reduction of challenging behaviors, improve understanding of the components of effective instruction (including the identification of instructional risk factors), and provide a better understanding of how the quality of instructional implementation affects student outcomes (Greenwood, Carta & Atwater, 1991). Ecobehavioral assessment is one way to gather data on the opportunity to learn, an important component of Carroll's Model of School Learning and the Algozzine–Ysseldyke Model of Effective Instruction.

Code for Instructional Structure and Student Academic Response (CISSAR)

Ecobehavioral-assessment approaches have been developed by Charles Greenwood, Judith Carta, Joe Delquadri, and their colleagues at the Juniper Gardens Children's Project in Kansas City, Kansas. The first version of the system was developed by Greenwood, Delquadri, and Hall (1978) and was called the Code for Instructional Structure and Student Academic Response (abbreviated as CISSAR). Using this system, assessors can categorize ecobehavioral events into student behaviors, teacher behaviors, and ecology. The original system defined 19 student-behavioral codes that could be combined into three composite variables. The current CISSAR taxonomy is shown in Figure 11.3.

CISSAR uses momentary time sampling (10-second intervals) over the entire school day. Observers record the ecology (specific activity, task used to control instruction, and class structure), teacher behavior (teacher position and actions), and student behavior (academic responses, competing responses, and task-management responses). After observational data have been recorded, the assessor can determine the frequency of occurrence of specific behaviors and the interactions among behaviors and environmental stimuli.

Two derivatives of CISSAR have been developed over the past 12 to 15 years. One of these, Ecobehavioral System for Complex Assessments of Preschool Environments (ESCAPE), was developed for use with preschool children. The other, the mainstream version of CISSAR (MS-CISSAR), was designed to be used in observations of students with disabilities in regular classes. The MS-CISSAR taxonomy is shown in Figure 11.4. The three derivative ecobehavioral-assessment

● ● ● ● **FIGURE 11.3**   CISSAR Taxonomy

BEHAVIOR

STUDENT BEHAVIORS   TEACHER BEHAVIORS

Academic Responses	Task Management	Competing Responses	Teacher Position	Teacher Behavior
1. Writing	1. AttndTask	1. Disrupt	1. InFront	1. NoResp
2. PlayAca	2. RaiseHnd	2. PlayInapp	2. AtDesk	2. Teaching
3. ReadAloud	3. LookMtrls	3. TaskInapp	3. AmongStud	3. OtherTalk
4. RdSilent	4. Moves	4. TalkInapp	4. Side	4. Approval
5. TalkAca	5. PlayApp	5. LocInapp	5. Back	5. Disapprov
6. AnsAcaQst		6. LookArnd	6. Out	
7. AskAcaQst		7. Self-Stim		

ECOLOGY

Activity	Task	Structure
1. Reading	1. Readers	1. EntirGrp
2. Math	2. Workbooks	2. SmallGrp
3. Spelling	3. Worksheet	3. Indiv
4. Hndwrtng	4. Paper&Pen	
5. Language	5. LstnLect	
6. Science	6. OthMedia	
7. SocStud	7. Tch/StDis	
8. Arts/Crft	8. Fetch/Put	
9. FreeTime		
10. BusMgmnt		
11. Transit		
12. Cn'tTell		

● ● ● **FIGURE 11.4** MS-CISSAR Taxonomy

BEHAVIOR

STUDENT BEHAVIORS

Academic Responses	Task Management	Competing Responses
1. Writing	1. RaiseHnd	1. Agression
2. TskPartic	2. PlayAppro	2. Disrupt
3. ReadAloud	3. ManipMtl	3. TalkInapp
4. RdSilent	4. Move	4. LookArnd
5. TalkAca	5. TalkMgmnt	5. NonComply
6. NoAcaRsp	6. Attention	6. Self-Stim
	7. NoMgmnt	7. SelfAbuse
		8. NoInappro

TEACHER BEHAVIORS

Teacher Definition	Teacher Behavior	Teacher Approval	Teacher Focus	Teacher Position
1. Regular	1. QuestAca	1. Approval	1. Target	1. InFront
2. SpecialEd	2. QuestMgmt	2. DisApprov	2. Targt+Oth	2. AtDesk
3. Aide/Para	3. QstDscpln	3. Neither	3. NoOne	3. OutOfRoom
4. StudntTch	4. CmndAca		4. Other	4. Side
5. Volunteer	5. CmndMgmnt			5. Back
6. RelatdSrv	6. CmdDscpln			
7. Substitut	7. TalkAca			
8. PeerTutor	8. TalkMgmnt			
9. NoStaff	9. TalkDscpln			
	10. TlkNonAca			
	11. NonVbPrmt			
	12. Attention			
	13. ReadAloud			
	14. Sing			
	15. NoRespons			

ECOLOGY

Setting	Activity	Task	Physical Arrangement	Instructional Grouping
1. ReglarCls	1. Reading	1. Readers	1. EntirGrp	1. WholeClss
2. SpecialEd	2. Math	2. Workbooks	2. DivideGrp	2. SmallGrp
3. ResrceRm	3. Spelling	3. Worksheet	3. Individual	3. OneOnOne
4. Chapt I Lab	4. Hndwrtng	4. Paper&Pen		4. Indepndnt
5. Library	5. Language	5. LstnLect		5. NoInstrct
6. MusicRm	6. Science	6. OthMedia		
7. ArtRoom	7. SocStud	7. Discussn		
8. TherapyRm	8. PreVocat	8. Fetch/Put		
9. Hall	9. GrssMotor	9. NoTask		
10. Auditori	10. DailyLiv			
11. Other	11. Self-Care			
	12. Arts/Crft			
	13. FreeTime			
	14. BusMgmnt			
	15. Transit			
	16. Music			
	17. TimeOut			
	18. NoActvty			
	19. Cn'tTell			
	20. Other			

systems (CISSAR, ESCAPE, and MS-CISSAR) have been combined in a new software program, EcoBehavioral Assessment System Software (EBASS).

EcoBehavioral Assessment System Software (EBASS)

EBASS (Greenwood, Carta, Kamps, & Delquadri, 1995) is an MS-DOS software system that enables school personnel to conduct systematic classroom observational assessments using laptop, notebook, or hand-held computers with at least one 720K floppy-disk drive. The EBASS package contains an assessment manual, a technical manual, computer software, and videotapes (to illustrate use of the system).

EBASS was designed specifically for school psychologists, but it may be used by other professionals responsible for assessment, teacher training, and program-evaluation activities, including instructional staff in regular and special education. Typical applications include assessments of individual students for the purpose of planning instructional interventions, evaluating individual pupil progress, and evaluating educational programs. Computerization allows computer-assisted training in instrument use, calibration of reliability checks, instrument modification (each of the three measures can be downsized into shorter measures), simple and complex data analyses, caseload management, and database capabilities.

Methodology   The classroom observer chooses whichever observational instrument is appropriate (ESCAPE, CISSAR, or MS-CISSAR) and goes into classrooms with a portable computer to gather data in 10-second intervals. The training package available with EBASS is used for teaching observers what to look for and how to code behaviors. The training system is self-instructional and includes short lessons, classroom video examples, computer exercises with feedback, and observational practice. It takes about eight to ten hours to learn any of the three instruments, and additional time is needed for practice in data collection.

Reports   Reports from an observation may be in one of two basic forms: (1) percentage occurrence for all events, or (2) probabilities of student behavior, given specific arrangements of the classroom ecology. These latter probabilities are called *conditional probabilities*. The computer can generate reports based on a single observation, on observations sequenced by time of observation, and on observations pooled over time. The professional who uses EBASS is able to give the teacher information on academic engaged time, the occurrence of inappropriate behavior, and the occurrence of task-management responses. The strength of EBASS is that it provides very precise information on the frequency of occurrence of specific kinds of behaviors (such as writing, playing inappropriately, waiting, and disruptive behavior) and on the kinds of contextual factors associated with the occurrence of each of the behaviors.

Examples of EBASS reports are shown in Figures 11.5 (p. 206) and 11.6 (p. 207). Figure 11.5 illustrates the academic-response profile for an individual student. The student was observed for an entire day. He spent 11.94 percent of the day writing, 20.65 percent of the day reading silently, and so forth. The profile also shows that this student was responding to academic content 53.65 percent of the school day and making no academic response 49.35 percent of the day.

● ● ● ● **FIGURE 11.5**   EBASS Academic Response Profile

```
--------------------------------------------------------------------
CODES          FREQ           PERCENTAGE OCCURRENCE
--------------------------------------------------------0--20--40--60--80--100
Writing         37           11.94%        |X
TskPartic       11            3.55%        |
ReadAloud       12            3.87%        |
RdSilent        64           20.65%        |XXX
TalkAca         29            9.35%        |X
--------------------------------------------------------------------
AcaRspComp     154           53.65%        |XXXXXXXX
NoAcaRsp       153           49.35%        |XXXXXXXX
Missing          4            1.29%        |
--------------------------------------------------------------------
TOTAL          310          100.00%
--------------------------------------------------------------------
Press ENTER to continue.
```

Figure 11.6 shows a probability analysis for writing behavior and illustrates that there are important relationships between students' writing behavior and environmental conditions. The probability of outcome behaviors (writing), given context variables, is shown in the bottom half of Figure 11.6. The probability of writing was .01 when readers were used, versus .27 when paper-and-pencil tasks were used, versus .04 during discussion; this was in comparison with an unconditional probability of .15. The assessor would be able to tell the teacher that the probability of writing behavior decreased significantly when readers were used and increased significantly when paper-and-pencil tasks were used during reading. Discussion also reduced the probability of a writing response.

EBASS may also be used in making *normative peer comparisons*—comparisons of the behaviors of an individual student with the average of a peer group. Figure 11.7 (p. 208) illustrates a normative peer comparison. It shows that the target student was looking around during 12 intervals (3.88% of the day) and talking inappropriately during eight intervals (2.59% of the day). The student's peers look around 3.29 percent of the time and talk inappropriately only 0.33 percent of the time. The difference in competing student and peer responses is also shown, and the magnitude of the differences has been computed. When D-STAT[1] = 0, the student's performance is exactly like that of his or her peers. The larger the D-STAT, the more different the student is from the peer group. Normative peer comparison data are very useful in making eligibility or exceptionality decisions.

---

1. D-STAT, or Difference Statistic, is an index of the discrepancy between the student's performance and that of his or her peers.

● ● ● **FIGURE 11.6**   *EBASS Probability Analysis of Ecobehavioral Relations*

```
--------<ECOLOGICAL MODEL>----------|----<OUTCOME Behavior>---

        ACTIVITY AND TASK                ACADEMIC RESPONDING


                                      OUTCOME BEHAVIORS:Writing
----------------------------------|-------------------------
--<ECOLOGICAL MODEL>---|---<VALUES>      COND          SIGNIFI-
(at least 10% of data)  FREQ PCT  FREQ PROB Z-SCORE CANCE
-----------------------  ---- ---  ---- ---- -------- ------
Writing+Readers          75   30    1  0.01 -2.664   .01
Writing+Paper/Pen        71   29   19  0.27  2.295   .05
Writing+Discussn         56   22    2  0.04 -1.980   .05
Spelling+Paper/Pen       47   19   15  0.32  2.782   .01
----------------------------------|-------------------------
                                      UNCONDITIONAL
                                      PROBABILITY

                                  |-------------------------
TOTAL SEQUENCES USED    249   80   37  0.15
TOTAL SEQUENCES RECORDED 310
----------------------------------|-------------------------
Press ENTER to continue.
```

```
                      Probability of Outcome Behaviors
ECOLOGICAL MODEL    0      0.1       0.2       0.3       0.4
      Values        |--------|---------|---------|---------|-

Writing+Readers   0.01XXXXXXXXXXXXX|
Writing+Paper/Pen                  |XXXXXXXXXXXXX0.27
Writing+Discussn    0.04XXXXXXXXXX|
Spelling+Paper/Pen                 |XXXXXXXXXXXXXXXXX0.32
                                   |
                            0.15
                   (base probability level)
Press ENTER to continue.
```

The Instructional Environment System–II (TIES-II)

We've said that according to Carroll, the degree of learning achieved by an individual student is a function of time spent learning divided by time needed to learn. An important aspect of time needed to learn is the quality of instruction. We noted earlier that quality of instruction varies according to several factors, including the clarity of task demands, adequacy of task presentation, adequacy of pacing, and the like. The Algozzine–Ysseldyke model of effective instruction includes

● ● ● **FIGURE 11.7**   EBASS Normative Peer Comparison

```
COMPETING RESPONSE: (Descriptive Comparison)
-------------------------------------------------------------
CODES     TARGET PROFILE   INDEX PROFILE  DISCREPANCY PROFILE
--------|---------------|---------------|--------------------
          Freq  Percent   Freq  Percent   Diff  DiffSq
          ----  -------   ----  -------    ----  ------
Agression   0    0.00      0     0.00      0.00   0.00
Disrupt     0    0.00      0     0.00      0.00   0.00
TalkInapp   8    2.59      1     0.33      2.26   5.11
LookArnd   12    3.88     10     3.29      0.59   0.35
NonComply   0    0.00      0     0.00      0.00   0.00
Self-Stim   0    0.00      7     2.30     -2.30   5.30
SelfAbuse   1    0.32      1     0.33     -0.01   0.00
NoInappro 285   92.23    274    90.13      2.10   4.42
Missing     3    0.97     11     3.62     -2.65   7.01
--------|---------------|---------------|--------------------
TOTAL     309             304              9.9   22.188 SUM
                                                  4.71  D-STAT
-------------------------------------------------------------
Press ENTER to continue.
```

```
COMPETING RESPONSE: (Graphic Display)
-------------------------------------------------------------
CODES      TARGET PROFILE   INDEX PROFILE  DISCREPANCY PROFILE
-----------|---------------|---------------|-------------------
Agression          |               |                  |
Disrupt            |               |                  |
TalkInapp   2.6%|_         0.3%|_        2.3%     |_
LookArnd    3.9%|_         3.3%|_        0.6%     |_
NonComply          |               |                  |
Self-Stim          |         2.3%|_       -2.3%     _|
SelfAbuse   0.3%|_         0.3%|_       -0.0%     _|
NoInappro  92.2%|____     90.1%|____     2.1%     |_
Missing     1.0%|_         3.6%|_       -2.6%     _|
-----------|---------------|---------------|-------------------
TOTAL     100.0% (n=309) 100.0% (n=304)
-------------------------------------------------------------
Press ENTER to continue.
```

a number of principles and strategies that, if present, will enhance the likelihood that students will achieve desired outcomes. The Instructional Environment System–II (TIES-II) is designed to be used to gather data on the extent to which components of effective instruction are present in a student's instructional environment (home, school, or a combination of both).

In 1987, Ysseldyke and Christenson published TIES (Ysseldyke & Christenson, 1987b), the first comprehensive methodology enabling education professionals to systematically gather data on the extent to which components of effective instruction are present in students' instructional environments at school. In 1993, TIES was updated and expanded as TIES-II. The focus of TIES-II is on the referred student, and the question for the important adults in the referred student's life is, "How can the classroom and home environments be manipulated to elicit more appropriate responses from the student?"

Based on the belief that student performance in school is a function of an interaction between the student and the learning (instructional) environment, TIES-II provides a set of observational and interview forms, administration procedures, and an organizational structure that allows educators to both identify and address the instructional needs of individual students. The system is used to help professionals gather essential information on 12 instructional-environment components and 5 home-support-for-learning components. The instructional and home components on which data are collected are listed and defined briefly in Table 11.1.

TIES-II is a flexible system that allows professionals to select the data-collection tools they will use. Among the tools available for use are an instructional-needs form, which is a checklist, and a free-response form to be completed by the teacher, indicating both the kinds of things that have been found effective and those that have proven ineffective with the referred student. The assessor uses an observation form to gather data in the classroom. The student is observed, and the observation form is completed; the student is interviewed, and the student-interview form is completed. Similarly, when the teacher is interviewed, the teacher-interview form is completed. The observer then uses the instructional-environment form to rate the extent to which each of the 12 classroom components is (1) present and (2) important in the student's instructional environment. A parent interview form is used to gather data on the extent to which each of the 5 home-learning components is present in the student's home environment. After the assessor interviews the parents or receives the completed form from them, he or she completes the home-support-for-learning form. All ratings are *qualitative judgments*—judgments by a professional regarding the extent to which the factors are present.

The assessor meets with a team of professionals, including the teacher, to plan an instructional intervention for the student. TIES-II outlines a detailed intervention-planning process. The TIES-II manual includes a very extensive review of the literature on effective instruction, which served as a basis for identification of the components of effective instruction and the home-support-for-learning components.

TABLE 11.1 ● *Components of the TIES-II*

	Component	Definition
Instructional-environment components	*Instructional match*	The student's needs are assessed accurately, and instruction is matched appropriately to the results of the instructional diagnosis.
	Teacher expectations	There are realistic, yet high expectations for both the amount and the accuracy of work to be completed by the student, and these are communicated clearly to the student.
	Classroom environment	The classroom-management techniques used are effective for this student; there is a positive, supportive classroom atmosphere, and time is used productively.
	Instructional presentation	Instruction is presented in a clear and effective manner; directions contain sufficient information for this student to understand what kinds of behaviors or skills are to be demonstrated, and the student's understanding is checked.
	Cognitive emphasis	Thinking skills and learning strategies for completing assignments are communicated explicitly to the student.
	Motivational strategies	Effective strategies for heightening student interest and student effort are used.
	Relevant practice	The student is given adequate opportunity to practice with appropriate materials and to achieve a high success rate. Classroom tasks are clearly important to achieving instructional goals.
	Informed feedback	The student receives relatively immediate and specific information on his or her performance or behavior; when the student makes mistakes, correction is provided.
	Academic engaged time	The student is actively engaged in responding to academic content; the teacher monitors the extent to which the student is actively engaged and redirects the student when the student is disengaged.
	Adaptive instruction	The curriculum is modified, within reason, to accommodate the student's unique and specific instructional needs.
	Progress evaluation	There is direct, frequent measurement of the student's progress toward completion of instructional objectives; data on the student's performance and progress are used to plan future instruction.
	Student understanding	The student demonstrates an accurate understanding of what is to be done in the classroom.
Home-support-for-learning components	*Expectations and attributions*	High, realistic expectations about schoolwork are communicated to the child; the value of working hard in school is emphasized.

TABLE 11.1 ● Components of the TIES-II (cont.)

	Component	Definition
Home-support-for-learning components (cont.)	*Discipline orientation*	There is an authoritative, not permissive or authoritarian, approach to discipline; the child is monitored and supervised by adults.
	Effective home environment	The parent–child relationship is generally positive and supportive.
	Parent participation	There is an educative home environment, and others participate in the child's schooling at home and/or at school.
	Structure for learning	Organization and daily routines facilitate the completion of schoolwork, and the child's academic learning is supported.

SOURCE: Components of the TIES-II from "Identifying Students' Instructional Needs in the Classroom and Home Environments" by J. Ysseldyke, S. L. Christenson, and J. F. Kovaleski, *Teaching Exceptional Children*, 26, (1994), 37–41. Copyright 1994 by The Council for Exceptional Children. Reprinted with permission.

Summary

Learning happens when the learning environment is modified to facilitate an appropriate response from the student. Education and psychology have rich traditions of assessing students in order to identify causes of academic and behavioral difficulties and to develop interventions. More recently, the focus has shifted to the belief that the quickest way to close the gap between actual and desired student performance is to apply principles of effective instruction. Doing so requires identification of the extent to which the learner is getting an opportunity to learn and is willing to engage actively in learning, particularly when tasks become very difficult. It also requires identification of the extent to which components of effective instruction are present in a student's instructional environment and components of effective home support for learning are present in the home environment. In this chapter, we reviewed two systems—the Eco-Behavioral Assessment System Software (EBASS) and the Instructional Environment System–II (TIES-II).

EBASS is a computerized observational system designed to be used to gather very specific information on student behavior in class. TIES-II is a qualitative observation-and-interview system designed to provide more global judgments of the extent to which a student is exposed to effective instruction. Both systems are new ways of taking into account the interactions among students, tasks, and instructional methodologies that determine the extent to which a student achieves desired outcomes. They provide a new way to look at complex interactions among individuals and contextual factors and enable us to identify naturally occurring effective procedures in classrooms.

Questions for Chapter Review and Thought

1. What is instructional ecology, and why is it important to take this into account in assessment?

2. Identify and describe the four components of effective instruction.

3. Select one component of the Algozzine–Ysseldyke Model of Effective Instruction, and then describe the component in detail.

4. Describe the advantages and disadvantages of using both EBASS and TIES-II for assessing instructional ecology.

Resources for Further Investigation

Project

Talk to a school psychologist about the need to assess the instructional ecology of a student referred for academic difficulties. Discuss both the need for this type of assessment and the extent to which the psychologist views it as relevant to his or her particular duties.

Print Resources

Algozzine, B., Ysseldyke, J., & Elliot, J. (1997). Strategies and tactics for effective instruction (2nd ed.). Longmont, CO: Sopris West.

Elliott, J., Algozzine, B. & Ysseldyke, J. E. (1998). *Timesavers for educators*. Longmont, CO: Sopris West.

Greenwood, C. R., Carta, J. J., Kamps, D., Terry, B., & Delquadri, J. (1994). Development and validation of standard classroom observation systems for school practitioners: Ecobehavioral assessment systems software (EBASS). *Exceptional Children, 61*, 197–210.

Greenwood, C., Carta, J., Kamps, D., & Delquadri, J. (1995). *Ecobehavioral Assessment System Software*. Kansas City, KS: Juniper Gardens Children's Center.

Ysseldyke, J. E., & Christenson, S. L. (1993). *The Instructional Environment System–II*. Longmont, CO: Sopris West.

Ysseldyke, J. E., Christenson, S. L., & Kovaleski, J. F. (1994). Identifying students' instructional needs in the context of classroom and home environments. *Teaching Exceptional Children, 26*(3), 37–41.

Technology Resources

The Juniper Gardens

http://www.lsi.ukans.edu/jg/jgcpindx.html

The home page for the Juniper Gardens Children's Project presents the background, purpose, and results of research on teaching and services for youth and children with disabilities in the Kansas City area.

Assessment

http://www.ncrel.org/ncrel/sdrs/areas/as0cont.htm.

This page provides links to pages that examine critical issues in assessment, including integrating assessment and instruction in ways that support learning.

ERIC Clearinghouse on Assessment and Evaluation

http://www.ericae.net

This web site provides balanced information concerning educational assessment and resources to encourage responsible use of tests.

Sopris West

http://www.sopriswest.com/

This is the web site for Sopris West, publisher of materials used to help meet the needs of students at risk. Descriptions of products are available, including the TIES-II.

chapter

12

Teacher-made Tests
of Achievement

Most evaluations of student achievement are conducted by teachers with materials that they have developed themselves. While the specific assessment practices that they actually use in their classrooms are not well documented, the professional literature suggests that assessment practices vary along a continuum from objective–analytic to subjective–holistic. When applied to assessment, the term *objective* carries two connotations. First, objective assessments are not influenced by emotion, conjecture, or personal prejudice; second, they are based on observable phenomena.[1] The term *analytic* suggests an examination of the individual elements in a performance, although it does not preclude examining the whole performance, as well. The term *subjective* suggests that evaluations are limited to personal perceptions and are essentially unverifiable using external criteria. The term *holistic* implies attention only to performance as a whole, not to discrete elements of a performance.

Within an *objective–analytic* approach, teachers systematically assess both the key components of performance and the key elements within each component. Suppose, for example, that a teacher required students to conduct and document a scientific experiment in a lab book. The key components and elements the teacher might look for could include the following:

1. Follow each step in the scientific method—

    a. Make observations.

    b. Generate hypotheses.

---

1. We recognize that complete objectivity may be difficult, if not impossible, to attain in some situations. However, greater objectivity is always better than lower objectivity.

    c. Develop procedures for collecting data.

    d. Collect data.

    e. Test hypotheses.

2. Follow each prescribed safety procedure—

    a. Wear safety glasses or goggles.

    b. Turn on hood fans.

    c. Keep caps on reagent bottles.

3. Write a description of the experiment—

    a. Use complete and grammatically correct sentences.

    b. Spell scientific terms correctly.

    c. Write in ink.

    d. Put the descriptions in lab notebooks.

After identifying the key elements in the task, the teacher then develops objective scoring standards to assess student performance. For example, the teacher can prepare a list of scientific terms that must be correctly spelled and deduct one point for each misspelled term (but not for each repeated misspelling of the same term). In this scenario, the scoring relies on both observable performance or products (the written spelling of scientific terms) and explicit criteria for a correct response applied to all students.

Within a *subjective–holistic* approach, the key components, key elements, and criteria for scoring need not be specified. At the extreme, this approach may be as simple as reading a product, getting an overall sense of correctness, and then awarding a grade based on that general impression. For example, a teacher might award an A to a report that contained no major errors or omissions. However, what constitutes a *major* error or omission could take into account any number of factors besides the student's actual performance. For example, a teacher might consider a student's performance history in awarding a grade. Thus, a minor error committed by a student with a history of excellent work could be viewed more negatively than the same error committed by a student who had a history of poor work.

Subjective–holistic approaches frequently use *scoring rubrics* to guide teachers in reaching summary evaluations. A scoring rubric contains the important components (often called *dimensions*) that should be considered in reaching an overall rating. For example, a teacher might rate the written description of a scientific experiment on three dimensions: following the scientific method, following safety procedures, and showing a high quality of written description. However, scoring rubrics do not enumerate the critical elements or provide objective criteria for rating performance on the dimensions. Rubrics can be as simple as a list of components that are awarded a summary grade (for example, following the scientific method = B, following safety procedures = A, and showing a high quality of written description = B–, overall grade = B). Dimensions within a rubric are sometimes scaled. For example, following the scientific method could be scaled from *emerging* to *mastery*. However, the scoring anchors (for example, *emerging*) are seldom objective.

We prefer an objective–analytic approach for three reasons. First, a student should earn the same score, no matter who does the scoring. An objective–analytic approach produces high interscorer reliability; a subjective–holistic approach does not.[2] Second, fairness and equity require that students be evaluated on the same dimensions with the same criteria. An objective–analytic approach applies the same criteria on the same dimensions to all students; a subjective–holistic approach celebrates different standards for different students. Third, students need to know what mistakes have been made or how to improve their performances. An objective–analytic approach provides this type of information; a subjective–holistic approach does not.

In addition, the use of objective–analytic methods is not merely a matter of personal preference. Federal regulations require that students with disabilities be evaluated using objective procedures. Thus, special educators are usually trained in objective–analytic procedures. However, because general educators are usually trained in subjective–holistic approaches, the difference in paradigms can cause all sorts of problems when general and special educators work together to provide an education for mainstreamed or included students.

This chapter provides a general overview of objective–analytic practices for teachers who develop their own tests for classroom assessment in the core areas of reading, mathematics, spelling, and written language. Classroom assessment is a topic suitable for an entire text, and this chapter provides only a general overview of the formats for testing and the criteria for evaluating pupil performance. For more specific information on test construction, educational decision making, and managing assessment within the classroom, refer to texts such as those by Gronlund (1985) and by Salvia and Hughes (1990). In addition, refer to other chapters in this text for discussion of various specific assessment procedures.

Why Do Teachers Assess Achievement?

Teachers regularly set aside time to assess their pupils for a variety of purposes. Most commonly, teachers make up tests to ascertain the extent to which their students have learned or are learning what has been taught or assigned. Knowledge about the extent to which students have mastered curricula allows teachers to make decisions on a variety of fronts—selection of current and future instructional objectives, placement of students in instructional groups, evaluation of the teachers' own instructional performances, and the necessity of referring students to other educational specialists for additional instructional services. Each of these decisions should be based on student achievement of instructional objectives.

2. The section on score reliability in Chapter 13, on using student portfolios, provides several references to the limited reliability of holistic scoring of writing samples.

When students have met their instructional objectives, it is time to move on to new or related objectives. Students who meet objectives so rapidly that they are being held back by slower peers can be grouped for enrichment activities or faster-paced instruction; slower students can be grouped so that they can learn necessary concepts to the point of mastery without impeding the progress of their faster-learning peers. When many students in a classroom fail to learn material, teachers should suspect that something is wrong with their materials, their techniques, or some other aspect of instruction. For example, the students may lack prerequisite concepts or skills, or the instruction may be too fast paced or poorly sequenced. Finally, when students lag far behind their peers in crucial curricular areas, teachers may seek outside help. For example, a student may be given *Chapter I assistance* (special remedial or compensatory instruction for students with difficulties who attend schools with large numbers of poor students), be tutored, be placed in a slower educational track, or be referred to a child-study team to determine entitlement to receive other special-educational services.

Advantages of Teacher-made Tests

Often teacher-made tests are not held in high regard. For example, some measurement specialists (such as Thorndike & Hagen, 1978) list carefully prepared test items as an advantage of norm-referenced achievement tests. By implication, careful preparation of questions may not be a characteristic of teacher-made tests. In addition, terms such as "informal" or "unstandardized" may be used to describe teacher-made tests. As a group, however, teacher-made tests cannot be considered informal, because they are not given haphazardly or casually. They also cannot be considered unstandardized, because students usually receive the same materials and directions, and the same criteria usually are used in correcting student answers. Perhaps a better characterization of teacher-made tests is that they are not usually subject to public scrutiny and may be more variable than commercial tests in terms of their technical adequacy (that is, reliability and validity). However, these characterizations are, themselves, speculative.

Teacher-made tests can be better suited to evaluation of student achievement than are commercially prepared, norm-referenced achievement tests. The disadvantages of commercially prepared tests readily illustrate the two potential advantages of teacher-made tests: curriculum match and sensitivity.

First, commercially prepared tests are rarely designed to assess achievement within specific curricula. Rather, these tests are intentionally constructed to have general applicability so that they can be used with students in almost any curriculum. This intentional generality is in sharp contrast to the development of distinctive curricula. It has become increasingly clear that various curriculum series differ from one another in the particular educational objectives covered, the performance level expected of students, and the sequence of objectives; for example, DISTAR mathematics differs from Scott, Foresman mathematics (Shriner &

Salvia, 1988). Even within the same curriculum series, teachers modify instruction to provide enrichment or remedial instruction. Thus, two teachers using the same curriculum series may offer different instruction. Although teachers may not construct tests that match the curriculum, they are in the best position to know precisely what has been taught and what level of performance is expected from students. Consequently, they are the only ones who *can* match testing to instruction.

Second, the overwhelming majority of commercially prepared, norm-referenced tests are intended, first and foremost, to discriminate among test takers efficiently. Developers of norm-referenced tests try to strike a balance between including the minimum number of test items to allow reliable discrimination and including enough items to ensure content validity. This practice results in relatively insensitive tests that are unable to discriminate small changes in pupil performance. For example, to produce a reliable, norm-referenced test, it may be unnecessary to discriminate students who know the single-digit addition facts with 2s, 4s, and 6s from those who also know them with 3s, 5s, and 7s. However, when instruction on all single-digit addends is provided, teachers probably will want to know, for example, which students have not yet mastered the 4s (and which of the 4s), so that they can provide further instruction as needed. Moreover, once students have mastered the 4s, the change in their skill level should be observable from changes in test performance.

In short, teachers need tests that are sensitive to small changes in knowledge. Norm-referenced tests are not well suited to this purpose, not only because they contain relatively few relevant items, but also because they seldom are published in multiple forms.[3] Teachers who are concerned with pupil mastery of specific concepts and skills are in a position to test a narrow range of objectives directly and frequently.

Testing Formats Used by Teachers

When a teacher wants either to compare the performance of several students on a skill or set of skills or to assess pupil performance over time, the assessment must be standardized. Otherwise, observed differences could be reasonably attributed to differences in testing procedures. To be standardized, tests must use consistent directions, criteria for scoring, and procedures (for example, time allowed to complete a test). Almost any test can be standardized if it results in observable behavior or a permanent product (for example, a student's written response).

When a teacher wants to use a test to assess the extent to which a pupil has mastered a skill or a set of skills, then it is important that the competencies to be

---

3. Teachers assess frequently to detect changes in student achievement. However, frequent testing with exactly the same test usually produces a practice effect. Unless there are multiple forms for a test, student learning may be confused with practice effect.

demonstrated are specified clearly. Teachers will need to know the objectives, standards, or outcomes that they expect students to work toward mastering, and they will need to specify the level of performance that is acceptable.

Test formats can be classified along two dimensions: (1) the modality through which the item is *presented*—test items usually require a student to look at or to listen to the question, although other modalities may be substituted, depending on the particulars of a situation or on characteristics of students—and (2) the modality through which a student *responds*—test items usually require an oral or written response, although pointing responses are frequently used with nonverbal students. Teachers may use the terms "see–write," "see–say," "hear–write," and "hear–say" to specify the testing-modality dimensions.

In addition, "write" formats can be of two types. *Select formats* require students to indicate their choice from an array of possible answers (usually termed *response options*). True–false, multiple-choice, and matching are the three common select formats. However, they are not the only ones possible; for example, students may be required to circle incorrectly spelled words or words that should be capitalized in text. Formats requiring students to select the correct answer can be used to assess much more than the recognition of information, although they are certainly useful for that purpose. They can also be used to assess students' understanding, their ability to draw inferences, and their correct application of principles. Select questions are not usually well suited for assessing achievement at the levels of analysis, synthesis, and evaluation. (See Chapter 8 for a discussion of these types of assessment.)

Supply formats require a student to produce a written or oral response. This response can be as restricted as the answer to a computation problem or a one-word response to the question, "When did the potato famine begin in Ireland?" Often, the response to supply questions is more involved and can require a student to produce a sentence, a paragraph, or several pages.

As a general rule, supply questions can be prepared fairly quickly, but scoring them may be very time-consuming. Even when one-word responses or numbers are requested, teachers may have difficulty finding the response on a student's test paper, deciphering the handwriting, or correctly applying criteria for awarding points. In contrast, select formats usually require a considerable amount of time to prepare, but once prepared, the tests can be scored quickly and by almost anyone.

The particular formats teachers choose are influenced by the purposes for testing and the characteristics of the test takers. Testing formats are essentially bottom up or top down. *Bottom-up* formats assess the mastery of specific objectives to allow generalizations about student competence in a particular domain. *Top-down* formats survey general competence in a domain and assess in greater depth those topics for which mastery is incomplete. For day-to-day monitoring of instruction and selecting short-term instructional objectives, we favor bottom-up assessment. With this type of assessment, a teacher can be relatively sure that specific objectives have been mastered and that he or she is not spending needless instructional time teaching students what they already know. For determining starting places for instruction with new students and for assessing maintenance and generalization of previously learned material, we favor top-down assessment. Generally, this approach should be more efficient in terms of teachers' and students' time because broader survey tests can cover a lot of material in a short period of time.

With students who are able to read and write independently, *see–write* formats are generally more efficient for both individual students and groups. When testing individual students, teachers or teacher aides can give the testing materials to the students and can proceed with other activities while the students are completing the test. Moreover, when students write their responses, a teacher can defer correcting the examinations until a convenient time.

See–say formats are also useful. Teacher aides or other students can listen to the test takers' responses and can correct them on the spot or record them for later evaluation. Moreover, many teachers have access to electronic equipment that can greatly facilitate the use of see–say formats (for example, tape recorders or videotape camcorders).

The *hear–write* format is especially useful with select formats for younger students and students who cannot read independently. This format can also be used for testing groups of students and is routinely used in the assessment of spelling when students are required to write words from dictation. With other content, teachers can give directions and read the test questions aloud, and students can mark their responses. The primary difficulty with a hear–write format with groups of students is the pacing of test items; teachers must allot sufficient time between items for slower-responding students to make their selections.

Hear–say formats are most suitable for assessing individual students who do not write independently or who write at such slow speeds that their written responses are unrepresentative of what they know. Even with this format, teachers need not preside over the assessment; other students or a teacher aide can administer, record, and perhaps evaluate the student's responses.

Considerations in Preparing Tests

Teachers need to build skills in developing tests that are fair, reliable, and valid. The following kinds of considerations are important in developing or preparing tests.

Selecting Specific Areas of the Curriculum

Tests are samples of behavior. When narrow skills are being assessed (for example, spelling words from dictation), either all the components of the domain should be tested (in this case, all the assigned spelling words), or a representative sample should be selected and assessed. The qualifier *representative* implies that an appropriate number of easy and difficult words—and of words from the beginning, middle, and end of the assignment—will be selected. When more complex domains are assessed, teachers should concentrate on the more important facts or relationships and avoid the trivial.

Writing Relevant Questions

Teachers must select and use enough questions to allow valid inferences about students' mastery of all the material taught in class. Nothing offends test takers quite as much as a test's failure to cover material they have studied and know, except perhaps their own failure to guess what content a teacher believes to be important enough to test. In addition, fairness demands that the way in which the question is asked be familiar and expected by the student. For example, if students were to take a test on the addition of single-digit integers, it would be a bad idea to test them using a missing-addend format (for example, "4 + ____ = 7") unless that format had been specifically taught and was expected by the students.

Organizing and Sequencing Items

The organization of a test is a function of many factors. When a teacher wants a student to complete all the items and to indicate mastery of content (a power test), then it is best to intersperse easy and difficult items. When the desire is to measure automaticity or the number of items that can be completed within a specific time period (a timed test), it is best to organize items from easy to difficult. Pages of test questions or problems to be solved should not be cluttered.

Developing Formats for Presentation and Response Modes

Different response formats can be used within the same test, although it is generally a good idea to group together questions with the same format. Regardless of the format used, the primary consideration is that the test questions be a fair sample of the material being assessed.

Writing Directions for Administration

Regardless of question format, the directions should indicate clearly what a student is to do—for example, "Circle the correct option," "Choose the best answer," "Match each item in column b to one item in column a," and so forth. Also, teachers should explain what, if any, materials may be used by students, any time limits, any unusual scoring procedures (for example, penalties for guessing), and point values when the students are mature enough to be given questions that have different point values.

Developing Systematic Procedures for Scoring Responses

As discussed in the opening paragraphs of this chapter, teachers must have predetermined and systematic criteria for scoring responses. However, if a teacher discovers an error or omission in criteria, the criteria should be modified. Obviously, previously scored responses must be rescored with the revised criteria.

Establishing Criteria to Interpret Student Performance

Teachers should specify in advance the criteria they will use for assigning grades or weighting assignments. For example, they may want to specify that students who earn a certain number of points on a test will earn a specific grade, or they may want to assign grades on the basis of the class distribution of performance. In either case, they must specify what it takes to earn certain grades or how assignments will be evaluated and weighted.

Response Formats

Select Formats

Three types of select formats are commonly used: multiple-choice, matching, and true–false. Of the three, multiple-choice questions are clearly the most useful.

Multiple-Choice Questions

Multiple-choice questions are the most difficult to prepare. These questions have two parts: (1) a *stem* that contains the question, and (2) a *response set* that contains both the correct answer, termed the *keyed* response, and one or more incorrect options, termed *distracters*. In preparing multiple-choice questions, teachers should generally follow these guidelines.

- Keep the response options short and of approximately equal length. Students quickly learn that longer options tend to be correct.
- Keep material that is common to all options in the stem. For example, if the first word in each option is "the," it should be put into the stem and removed from the options.
- Avoid grammatical tip-offs. Students can discard grammatically incorrect options. For example, when the correct answer must be plural, alert students will disregard singular options; when the correct answer must be a noun, students will disregard options that are verbs.
- Avoid implausible options. In the best questions, distracters should be attractive to students who do not know the answer. Common errors and misconceptions are often good distracters.
- Make sure that one and only one option is correct. Students should not have to read their teachers' minds to guess which wrong answer is the least wrong or which right answer is the most correct.
- Avoid interdependent questions. Generally, it is bad practice to make the selection of the correct option dependent on getting a prior question correct.
- Vary the position of the correct response in the options. Students will recognize patterns of correct options (for example, when the correct answers to a sequence of questions are a, b, c, d, a, b, c, d) or a teacher's preference for a specific position (usually c).

- Avoid options that indicate multiple correct options (for example, "all the above" or "both a and b are correct"). These options often simplify the question.
- Avoid similar incorrect options. Students who can eliminate one of the two similar options can readily dismiss the other one. For example, if citrus fruit is wrong, lemon must be wrong.
- Avoid using the same words and examples that were used in the students' texts or in class presentations.
- Make sure that one question does not provide information that can be used to answer another question. For example, teachers should not introduce one question with "In 1492, Columbus landed in the Western _____ " and then ask another question requesting the year in which Columbus arrived in the Western hemisphere.

When appropriate, teachers can make multiple-choice questions more challenging by asking students to recognize an instance of a rule or concept, by requiring students to recall and use material that is not present in the question, or by increasing the number of options.[4] In no case should teachers deliberately mislead or trick students.

Matching Questions

Matching questions are a variant of multiple-choice questions in which a set of stems is simultaneously associated with a set of options. Generally, the content of matching questions is limited to simple factual associations (Gronlund, 1985). Teachers usually prepare matching questions so that there are as many options as stems, and an option can be associated only once with a stem in the set. Although we do not recommend their use, there are other possibilities: more options than stems, selection of all correct options for one stem, and multiple use of an option.[5] These additional possibilities increase the difficulty of the question set considerably.

In general, we prefer multiple-choice questions over matching questions. Almost any matching question can be written as a series of multiple-choice questions in which the same or similar options are used. Of course, the correct response will change. However, teachers wishing to use matching questions should consider the following guidelines:

- Each set of matching items should have some dimension in common (e.g., explorers and dates of discovery). This makes preparation easier for the teacher and provides the student with some insight into the relationship required to select the correct option.

---

4. For younger children, three options are generally difficult enough. Older students can be expected to answer questions with four or five options.
5. Scoring for these options is complicated. Generally, separate errors are counted for selecting an incorrect option and failing to select a correct option. Thus, the number of errors can be very large.

- Keep the length of the stems approximately the same, and keep the length and grammar used in the options equivalent. At best, mixing grammatical forms will eliminate some options for some questions; at worst, it will provide the correct answer to several questions.
- Make sure that one and only one option is correct for each stem.
- Vary the sequence of correct responses when more than one matching question is asked.
- Avoid using the same words and examples that were used in the students' texts or in class presentations.

It is easier for a student when questions and options are presented in two columns. When there is a difference in the length of the items in each column, the longer item should be used as the stem. Stems should be placed on the left and options on the right, rather than stems above with options below them. Moreover, all the elements of the question should be kept on one page. Finally, teachers often allow students to draw lines to connect questions and options. Although this has the obvious advantage of helping students keep track of where their answers should be placed, erasures or scratch-outs can be a headache to the person who corrects the test. There is a commercially available product (Learning Wrap Ups) that has cards printed with stems and answers and a shoelace with which to "lace" stems to correct answers. The correct lacing pattern is printed on the back, so it is self-correcting. Teachers could make such cards fairly easily, as an alternative to trying to correct tests with lots of erasures.

True–False Statements

In most cases, true–false statements should simply not be used. Their utility lies primarily in assessing knowledge of factual information, which can be better assessed with other formats. Effective true–false items are difficult to prepare. Because guessing the correct answer is so likely—it happens 50 percent of the time—the reliability of true–false tests is generally low. As a result, they may well have limited validity. Nonetheless, if a teacher chooses to use this format, a few suggestions should be followed:

- Avoid specific determiners such as "all," "never," "always," and so on.
- Avoid sweeping generalizations. Such statements tend to be true, but students can often think of minor exceptions. Thus, there is a problem in the criterion for evaluating the truthfulness of the question. Attempts to avoid the problem by adding restrictive conditions (for example, "with minor exceptions") either render the question obviously true or leave a student trying to guess what the restrictive condition means.
- Avoid convoluted sentences. Tests should assess knowledge of content, not a student's ability to comprehend difficult prose.
- Keep true and false statements approximately the same length. As is the case with longer options on multiple-choice questions, longer true–false statements tend to be true.

- Balance the number of true and false statements. If a student recognizes that there are more of one type of statement than of the other, the odds of guessing the correct answer will exceed 50 percent.

Special Considerations for Students with Disabilities

In developing and using items that employ a select format, teachers must pay attention to individual differences among students, and particularly to disabilities that might interfere with performance. For example, students who have skill deficits in remembering things for short periods of time, or who do not attend well to verbally or visually presented information, may have difficulty with multiple-choice items. Students who have difficulty figuring out the organization of visually presented material will have difficulty with matching items.

Supply Formats

It is useful to distinguish between items requiring a student to write one- or two-word responses (such as fill-in questions) and those requiring more extended responses (such as essay questions). Both types of items require careful delineation of what constitutes a correct response (that is, criteria for scoring). It is generally best for teachers to prepare criteria for a correct response at the time they prepare the question. In that way, they can ensure that the question is written in such a way as to elicit the correct types of answers—or at least not to mislead students—and perhaps save time when correcting exams. (If teachers change criteria for a correct response after they have scored a few questions, they should rescore all previously scored questions with the revised criteria.)

Fill-in Questions

Aside from mathematics problems that require students to calculate an answer and writing spelling words from dictation, fill-in questions require a student to complete a statement by adding a concept or fact—for example, "_____ arrived in America in 1492." Fill-ins are useful in assessing knowledge and comprehension objectives; they are not useful in assessing application, analysis, synthesis, or evaluation objectives. Teachers preparing fill-in questions should follow these guidelines:

- Keep each sentence short. Generally, the less superfluous information in an item, the clearer the question will be to the student and the less likely it will be that one question will cue another.
- If a two-word answer is required, teachers should use two blanks to indicate this in the sentence.
- Avoid sentences with multiple blanks. For example, the item, "In the year _____, _____ discovered _____" is so vague that practically any date, name, and event can be inserted correctly, even ones that are irrelevant to the content; for example, "In 1999, Henry discovered girls."

- Keep the size of all blanks consistent and large enough to accommodate the longest answer readily. The size of the blank should not provide a clue about the length of the correct word.

The most problematic aspect of fill-in questions is the necessity of developing an appropriate response bank of acceptable answers. Often, some student errors may consist of a partially correct response; teachers must decide which answers will receive partial credit, full credit, and no credit. For example, a question may anticipate "Columbus" as the correct response, but a student might write "that Italian dude who was looking for the shortcut to India for the Spanish king and queen." In deciding how far afield to go in crediting unanticipated responses, teachers should look over test questions carefully to see whether the student's answer comes from information presented in another question (for example, "The Spanish monarch employed an Italian sailor to find a shorter route to _____.").

Extended Responses

Essay questions are most useful in assessing comprehension, application, analysis, synthesis, and evaluation objectives. There are two major problems associated with extended response questions. First, teachers are generally able to sample only a limited amount of information because answers may take a long time for students to write. Second, extended essay responses are the most difficult type of answer to score. To avoid subjectivity and inconsistency, teachers should use a scoring key that assigns specific point values for each element in the ideal or criterion answer. In most cases, spelling and grammatical errors should not be deducted from the point total. Moreover, bonus points should not be awarded for particularly detailed responses; many good students will provide a complete answer to one question and spend any extra time working on questions that are more difficult for them.

Finally, teachers should be prepared to deal with responses in which a student tries to bluff a correct answer. Rather than leave a question unanswered, some students may answer a related question that was not asked, or they may structure their response so that they can omit important information that they cannot remember or never knew. Sometimes they will even write a poem or a treatise on why the question asked is unimportant or irrelevant. Therefore, teachers must be very specific about how they will award points, stick to their criteria unless they discover that something is wrong with them, and not give credit to creative bluffs.

Teachers should also be very precise in the directions that they give so that students will not have to guess what responses their teachers will credit. Following are a number of verbs (and their meanings) that are commonly used in essay questions. It is often worthwhile to explain these terms in the test directions, to make sure that students know what kind of answer is desired.

- *Describe, define,* and *identify* mean to give the meaning, essential characteristics, or place within a taxonomy.

- *List* means to enumerate and implies that complete sentences and paragraphs are not required unless specifically requested.
- *Discuss* requires more than a description, definition, or identification; a student is expected to draw implications and elucidate relationships.
- *Explain* means to analyze and make clear or comprehensible a concept, event, principle, relationship, or so forth; thus, *explain* requires going beyond a definition to describe the hows or whys.
- *Compare* means to identify and explain similarities among two or more things.
- *Contrast* means to identify and explain differences among two or more things.
- *Evaluate* means to give the value of something and implies an enumeration and explanation of assets and liabilities, pros and cons.

Finally, unless students know the questions in advance, teachers should allow students sufficient time for planning and rereading answers. For example, if teachers believe that 10 minutes are necessary to write an extended essay to answer a question that requires original thinking, they might allow 20 minutes for the question. The less fluent the students, the greater the proportion of time that should be allotted.

Special Considerations in Assessing Students with Disabilities

In developing items that employ a supply format, teachers must pay attention to individual differences among learners, particularly to disabilities that may interfere with performance. For example, students who write very slowly can be expected to have difficulty with fill-in or essay questions. Students who have considerable difficulty expressing themselves in writing will probably have difficulty completing or performing well on essay examinations. Remember, it is important to assess the skills that students have, not the effects of disability conditions.

● ● ● ● ● ● ● ● ● ● ● ● ● ● ● ● ● ● ● ●

Assessment in Core Achievement Areas

The assessment procedures used by teachers are a function of the content being taught, the criterion to which content is to be learned (such as 80% mastery), and the characteristics of the students. With primary-level curricula in core areas, teachers usually want more than knowledge from their students; they want the material learned so well that correct responses are automatic. For example, teachers do not want their students to think about forming the letter *a*, sounding out the word *the*, or using number lines to solve simple addition problems such as "3 + 5 = _____"; they want their students to respond immediately and correctly. Even in intermediate-level materials, teachers seek highly proficient responding from their students, whether that performance involves two-digit multiplication, reading short stories, writing short stories, or writing spelling words from dictation. However, teachers in all grades, but especially in secondary schools, are also interested in their students' understanding of vast amounts of information about their social, cultural, and physical worlds, as well as their acquisition and application of critical-thinking skills. The assessment of skills taught to high degrees of proficiency is quite different from the assessment of understanding and critical-thinking skills.

In the sections that follow, core achievement areas are discussed in terms of three important attributes: the skills and information to be learned within the major strands of most curricula, the assessment of skills to be learned to proficiency, and the assessment of understanding of information and concepts. Critical-thinking skills are usually embedded within content areas and are assessed in the same ways as understanding of information is assessed—with written multiple-choice and extended-essay questions.

Reading

Reading is usually divided into decoding skills and comprehension. The specific behaviors included in each of these subdomains will depend on the particular curriculum and its sequencing.

Beginning Skills

Beginning decoding can include letter recognition, letter–sound correspondences, sight vocabulary, phonics, and, in some curricula, morphology. Automaticity is the goal for the skills to be learned. See–say (for example, "What letter is this?") and hear–say (for example, "What sound does the letter _____ make?") formats are regularly used for both instruction and assessment. During students' acquisition of specific skills, teachers should first stress the accuracy of student responses. Generally, this concern translates into allowing a moment or two for students to think about their responses. A generally accepted criterion for completion for early learning is 90 percent correct. As soon as accuracy has been attained (and sometimes before), teachers change their criteria from accurate responses to fast and accurate responses. For see–say formats, fluent students will need no thinking time for simple material; for example, they should be able to respond as rapidly as teachers can change stimuli to questions such as "What is this letter?" For the most difficult content (for example, recognition of long or visually difficult words such as "through"), no more than a second or two should be needed by a student to verify the stimulus. However, when students have visual or articulation difficulties, these standards are unlikely to be appropriate.

For beginners, *reading comprehension* is usually assessed in one of three ways: by assessing students' retelling, their responses to comprehension questions, or their rate of oral reading. The most direct method is to have students *retell* what they have read without access to the reading passage. Retold passages may be scored on the basis of the number of words recalled. Fuchs, Fuchs, and Maxwell (1988) have offered two relatively simple scoring procedures that appear to offer valid indications of comprehension. Retelling may be conducted orally or in writing. With students who have relatively undeveloped writing skills, retelling should be oral when it is used to assess comprehension, but it may be in writing as a practice or drill activity. Teachers can listen to students retell, or students can retell using tape recorders so that their efforts can be evaluated later.

A second common method of assessing comprehension is to *ask students questions* about what they have read. Questions should address main ideas, important relationships, and relevant details. Questions may be in supply or selection formats, and either hear–say or see–write formats can be used conveniently. As with retelling, teachers should concentrate their efforts on the gist of the passage.

A third convenient, although indirect, method of assessing reading comprehension is to assess the *rate of oral reading*. Although this procedure may initially seem a bit strange, the rate of oral reading does appear to be empirically related to comprehension (Deno, 1985; Fuchs et al., 1988). Moreover, the relationship between rate and comprehension is logical: Slow oral readers must expend their energy decoding words (for example, attending to letters, remembering letter–sound associations, blending sounds, or searching for context cues), rather than concentrating on the meaning of what is written. Therefore, teachers probably should concentrate on the rate of oral reading regularly with beginning readers. To assess reading rate, teachers should have students read for two minutes from appropriate materials. The reading passage should include familiar vocabulary, syntax, and content; the passage must be longer than the amount any student can read in the two-minute period. Teachers have their own copy of the passage on which to note errors. The number of words read correctly and the number of errors made in two minutes are each divided by two to calculate the rate per minute. Mercer and Mercer (1985) suggest a rate of 80 words per minute (with two or fewer errors) as a desirable goal for reading words from lists and a rate of 100 words per minute (with two or fewer errors) for words in text. See Chapter 21 for a fuller discussion of errors in oral reading.

Advanced Skills

Students who have already mastered basic sight vocabulary and decoding skills generally read silently. Emphasis for these students shifts, and new demands are made. Decoding moves from oral reading to silent reading with subvocalization (that is, saying the words and phrases to themselves) to visual scanning without subvocalization; thus, the reading rates of some students may exceed 1,000 words per minute. Scanning for main ideas and information may also be taught systematically. The demands for reading comprehension may go well beyond the literal comprehension of a passage; summarization, drawing inferences, recognizing and understanding symbolism, sarcasm, irony, and so forth may be systematically taught. For these advanced students, the gist of a passage is usually more important than the details. Teachers of more advanced students may wish to score retold passages on the basis of main ideas, important relationships, and details recalled correctly and the number of errors (that is, ideas, relationships, and details omitted plus the insertion of material not included in the passage). In such cases, the different types of information can be weighted differently, or the use of comprehension strategies (for example, summarization) can be encouraged. However, read–write assessment formats using multiple-choice and extended-essay questions are more commonly used.

Informal Reading Inventories

When making decisions about referral or initial placement in a reading curriculum, teachers often develop *informal reading inventories* (IRIs), which assess decoding and reading comprehension over a wide range of skill levels within the specific reading curricula used in a classroom.[6] Thus, they are top-down assessments that span several levels of difficulty.

IRIs are given to locate the reading levels at which a student reads independently, requires instruction, and is frustrated. Techniques for developing IRIs and the criteria used to define independent, instructional, and frustration reading levels vary. Teachers should use a series of graded reading passages that range from below a student's actual placement to a year or two above the actual placement. If a reading series prepared for several grade levels is used, passages can be selected from the beginning, middle, and end of each grade. Students begin reading the easiest material and continue reading until they can decode less than 85 percent of the words. Salvia and Hughes (1990) recommend an accuracy rate of 95 percent for independent reading and consider 85 to 95 percent accuracy the level at which a student requires instruction.

Mathematics

Eight major components are usually considered in comprehensive mathematics curricula: readiness skills, vocabulary and concepts, numeration, whole-number operations, fractions and decimals, ratios and percentages, measurement, and geometry (Salvia & Hughes, 1990). At any grade level, the specific skills and concepts included in each of these subdomains will depend on the particular curriculum and its sequencing. Mathematics curricula usually contain both problem sets that require only computations and word problems that require selection and application of the correct algorithm as well as computation. The difficulty of application problems goes well beyond the difficulty of the computation involved and is related to three factors: (1) the number of steps involved in the solution (for example, a student might have to add and then multiply; Caldwell & Goldin, 1979); (2) the amount of extraneous information (Englert, Cullata, & Horn, 1987); and

---

6. Some authors may include reading interest as a subdomain.

(3) whether the mathematical operation is directly implied by the vocabulary used in the problem (for example, words such as *and* or *more* imply addition, whereas words such as *each* may imply division; see Bachor, Stacy, & Freeze, 1986). Although reading level is popularly believed to affect the difficulty of word problems, its effect has not been clearly established (see Bachor, 1990; Paul, Nibbelink, & Hoover, 1986).

Beginning Skills

The whole-number operations of addition, subtraction, multiplication, and division are the core of the elementary mathematics curriculum. Readiness for beginning students includes such basics as classification, one-to-one correspondence, and counting. Vocabulary and concepts are generally restricted to quantitative words (for example, *same, equal, larger*) and spatial concepts (for example, *left, above, next to*). Numeration deals with writing and identifying numerals, counting, ordering, and so forth.

See–write is probably the most frequently used assessment format for mathematical skills, although see–say formats are not uncommon. For content associated with readiness, vocabulary and concepts, numeration, and applications, matching formats are commonly used. Accuracy is stressed, and 90 to 95 percent correct is commonly used as the criterion. For computation, accuracy and fluency are stressed in beginning mathematics; teachers do not stop their instruction when students respond accurately, but they continue instruction to build automaticity. Consequently, a teacher may accept somewhat lower rates of accuracy (that is, 80%).

When working toward fluency, teachers usually use probes.[7] Perhaps the most useful criterion for math probes assessing computation is the number of correct digits (in an answer) written per minute, not the number of correct answers per minute. The actual criterion rate will depend on the operation, the type of material (for example, addition facts versus addition of two-digit numbers with regrouping), and the characteristics of the particular students. Students with motor difficulties may be held to a lower criterion or assessed with see–say formats. For see–write formats, students may be expected to write answers to addition and subtraction problems at rates between 50 and 80 digits per minute and to write answers to simple multiplication and division problems at rates between 40 and 50 digits per minute (Salvia & Hughes, 1990).

Advanced Skills

The more advanced mathematical skills (that is, fractions, decimals, ratios, percentages, and geometry) build on whole-number operations. These skills are taught to levels of comprehension and application. Unlike those for beginning skills, assessment formats are almost exclusively see–write, and accuracy is

---

7. *Probes* are small samples of behavior. For example, in assessing skill in addition of single-digit numbers, a student might be given only five single-digit addition problems.

stressed over fluency, except for a few facts such as "$\frac{1}{2}$ equals 0.5 equals 50 percent." Teachers must take into account the extent to which specific student disabilities will interfere with performance of advanced skills. For example, difficulties in sequencing information and in comprehension may interfere with students' performance on items that require problem solving and comprehension of mathematical concepts.

Spelling

Although spelling is considered by many to be a component of written language, in elementary school, it is generally taught as a separate subject. Therefore, we treat it separately in this chapter.

Spelling is the production of letters in the correct sequence to form a word. The specific words that are assigned as spelling words may come from several sources: spelling curricula, word lists, content areas, or a student's own written work. In high school and college, students are expected to use dictionaries and to spell correctly any word they use. Between that point and fourth grade or so, spelling words are typically assigned, and students are left to their own devices to learn them. In the first three grades, spelling is usually taught systematically, using phonics, morphology, rote memorization, or some combination of the three approaches.

Teachers may assess mastery of the prespelling rules associated with the particular approach they are teaching. For example, when a phonics approach is used, students may have to demonstrate mastery of writing the letters associated with specific vowels, consonants, consonant blends, diphthongs, and digraphs. Teachers assess mastery of spelling in at least four ways:

1. *Recognition response.* The teacher provides students with lists of alternative spellings of words (usually three or four alternatives) and reads a word to the student. The student must select the correct spelling of the dictated word from the alternatives. Emphasis is on accuracy.

2. *Spelling dictated single words.* Teachers dictate words, and students write them down. Although teachers often give a spelling word and then use it in a sentence, students find the task easier if just the spelling word is given (Horn, 1967). Moreover, the findings from 1988 research suggest that a seven-second interval between words is sufficient (Shinn, Tindall, & Stein, 1988).

3. *Spelling words in context.* Students write paragraphs using words given by the teacher. This approach is as much a measure of written expression as of spelling. The teacher can also use this approach in instruction of written language by asking students to write paragraphs and counting the number of words spelled correctly.

4. *Students' self-monitoring of errors.* Some teachers teach students to monitor their own performance by finding and correcting spelling errors in the daily assignments they complete.

Written Language

Written language is no doubt the most complex and difficult domain for teachers to assess. Assessment differs widely for beginners and advanced students. Once the preliminary skills of letter formation and rudimentary spelling have been mastered, written-language curricula usually stress both content and *style* (that is, grammar, mechanics, and diction).

Beginning Skills

The most basic instruction in written language is *penmanship,* in which the formation and spacing of uppercase (capital) and lowercase printed and cursive letters are taught. Early instruction stresses accuracy, and criteria are generally qualitative. After accuracy has been attained, teachers may provide extended practice to move students toward automaticity. If this is done, teachers will evaluate performance on the basis of students' rates of writing letters. Target rates are usually in the range of 80 to 100 letters per minute for students without motor handicaps.

Once students can fluently write letters and words, teachers focus on teaching students to write content. For beginners, content generation is often reduced to generation of words in meaningful sequence. Teachers may use *story starters* (that is, pictures or a few words that act as stimuli) to prompt student writing. When the allotted time for writing is over, teachers count the number of words or divide the number of words by the time to obtain a measure of rate. Although this sounds relatively easy, decisions as to what constitutes a word must be made. For example, one-letter words are seldom counted.

Teachers also use the percentage of correct words to assess content production. To be considered correct, the word must be spelled correctly, be capitalized if appropriate, be grammatically correct, and be followed by the correct punctuation (Isaacson, 1988). Criteria for an acceptable percentage of correct words are still the subject of discussion. For now, social comparison, by which one student's writing output is compared with the output of students whose writing is judged acceptable, can provide teachers with rough approximations. Teaching usually boils down to focusing on capitalization, simple punctuation, and basic grammar (for example, subject–verb agreement). Teachers may also use multiple-choice or fill-in tests to assess comprehension of grammatical conventions or rules.

Advanced Skills

Comprehension and application of advanced grammar and mechanics can be tested readily with multiple-choice or fill-in questions. Thus, this aspect of written language can be assessed systematically and objectively. The evaluation of content generation by advanced students is far more difficult than counting correct words. Teachers may consider the quality of ideas, the sequencing of ideas, the coherence of ideas, and consideration of the reading audience. In practice, teachers use holistic judgments of content (Cooper, 1977). In addition, they may point out errors in style or indicate topics that might benefit from greater elaboration or clarification.

Objective scoring of any of these attributes is very difficult, and extended scoring keys and practice are necessary to obtain reliable judgments, if they are ever attained. More objective scoring systems for content require computer analysis and at this time are beyond the resources of most classroom teachers.

Potential Sources of Difficulty in the Use of Teacher-made Tests

To be useful, teacher-made tests must avoid three pitfalls: (1) relying on a single summative assessment, (2) using nonstandardized testing procedures, and (3) using technically inadequate assessment procedures. The first two are easily avoided; avoiding the third is more difficult.

First, teachers should not rely solely on a single summative assessment to evaluate student achievement after a course of instruction. Such assessments do not provide teachers with information they can use to plan and modify sequences of instruction. Moreover, minor technical inadequacies can be magnified when a single summative measure is used. Rather, teachers should test progress toward educational objectives at least two or three times a week. Frequent testing is most important when instruction is aimed at developing automatic or fluent responses in students. Although fluency is most commonly associated with primary curricula, it is not restricted to reading, writing, and arithmetic. For example, instruction in foreign languages, sports, and music often is aimed at automaticity.

Second, teachers should use standardized testing procedures. To conduct frequent assessments that are meaningful, the tests that are used to assess the same objectives must be equivalent. Therefore, the content must be equivalent from test to test; moreover, test directions, kinds of cues or hints, testing formats, criteria for correct responses, and type of score (for example, rates or percentage correct) must be the same.

Third, teachers should develop technically adequate assessment procedures. Two aspects of this adequacy are especially important: content validity and reliability. The tests must have *content validity*. There should seldom be problems with content validity when direct performances are used. For example, the materials used in finding a student's rate of oral reading should have content validity when they come from that student's reading materials; tests used to assess mastery of addition facts will have content validity because they assess the facts that have been taught. A problem with content validity is more likely when teachers use tests to assess achievement outside of the tool subjects (that is, other than reading, math, and language arts).

Although only teachers can develop tests that truly mirror instruction, teachers must not only know what has been taught but also prepare devices that test what has been taught. About the only way to guarantee that an assessment covers the content is to develop tables of specifications for the content of instruction and testing. However, test items geared to specific content may still be ineffective (see Chapter 8).

Careful preparation in and of itself cannot guarantee the validity of one question or set of questions. The only way a teacher can know that the questions are good is to field-test the questions and make revisions based on the field-test results. Realistically speaking, teachers do not have time for field testing and revision prior to giving a test. Therefore, teachers must usually give a test and then delete or discount poor items. The poor items can be edited and the revised questions used the next time the examination is needed. In this way, the responses from one group of students become a field test for a subsequent group of students. When teachers use this approach, they should not return tests to students because students may pass questions down from year to year.

The tests must also be *reliable*. Interscorer agreement is a major concern for any test using a supply format but is especially important when extended responses are evaluated. Agreement can be increased by developing precise scoring guides for all questions of this type and by sticking with the criteria. Interscorer agreement should not be a problem for tests using select or restricted fill-in formats. For select and fill-in tests, internal consistency is of primary concern. Unfortunately, very few people can prepare a set of homogeneous test questions the first time. However, at the same time that they revise poor items, teachers can delete or revise items to increase a test's homogeneity (that is, delete or revise items that have correlations with the total score of .25 or less). Additional items can also be prepared for the next test.

- -

Summary

Teachers assess during instruction in order to monitor pupil progress. They need to engage in careful monitoring so that they can modify instruction, correct errors early, and maintain appropriate instructional pacing. Teachers also assess at the end of an instructional sequence to evaluate what their students have learned, assign grades, and select future instructional objectives. Because teacher-made tests are seldom subject to public scrutiny, many test theorists have doubts about their technical adequacy. However, teacher-made tests have several advantages over professionally prepared tests. Most important are (1) the ability of teachers to tailor their tests' content to the content of their teaching and (2) the potential to include many more pertinent test items, thereby allowing teachers to make finer discriminations.

Tests require students to select or supply responses to stimuli. The stimuli are usually auditory or visual, and student responses are usually vocal or written. For testing in core academic areas (that is, reading, mathematics, spelling, and written language), testing formats will vary, depending on the criteria that teachers use to evaluate learning and the level at which objectives are prepared. When fluent responses are sought by teachers, student performances in reading, math, and spelling are directly evaluated by supply formats. Select formats (that is, multiple choice and matching) are useful in assessing instructional objectives prepared at the levels of knowledge, comprehension, and application. They are not well suited to higher-level objectives. Supply formats (that is, fill-in or extended essay) have varying utility. Fill-in questions can be used in much the same way as questions prepared in select formats. Extended essays can be used to assess objectives prepared at any level higher than knowledge, although they are probably best reserved for objectives stressing analysis, synthesis, and evaluation. Teacher-made tests are most useful when they are administered during and after instruction, are carefully standardized, have content validity, and are reliable.

Questions for Chapter Review and Thought

1. Explain the advantages and disadvantages of multiple-choice, matching, and true–false questions.

2. Explain the advantages and disadvantages of teacher-made tests.

3. List four of the eight major components that are usually considered in comprehensive mathematics curricula.

4. Why is written language the most complex and difficult domain for teachers to assess?

5. Describe bottom-up and top-down formats, as used in teacher-made tests, and indicate when it would be appropriate to use each format.

Resources for Further Investigation

Project

Interview a teacher about tests that he or she has developed and used. Attempt to find out how the teacher decides what to test and how to test. Write a brief report on these answers. Then compare your interviewed teacher's responses with the responses of other teachers interviewed by your classmates. Are similar procedures used by different teachers?

Print Resources

Gronlund, N. (1990). *Measurement and evaluation in teaching* (6th ed.; Part 2, Constructing classroom tests). New York: Macmillan.

Salvia, J., & Hughes, C. (1990). *Curriculum-based assessment: Testing what is taught* (Chapter 4, Development of appropriate assessment procedures: Collection and summarization of results). New York: Macmillan.

Tindal, G. A., & Marston, D. B. (1990). *Classroom-based assessment. Evaluating instructional outcomes* (Chapter 15, Individual-referenced evaluation). Columbus, OH: Merrill.

Technology Resources

The Teachers Network

http://www.teachnet.org/docs.cfm

This web site is sponsored by IMPACT II—The Teachers Network, a nonprofit organization that supports teachers with innovative ideas. It provides a resource of classroom projects available that covers a wide range of subject areas.

Alternatives to Standardized Tests

http://ericae.net/db/edo/ED286938.htm

This ERIC document looks at alternatives to standardized tests, including teacher-made tests and criterion-referenced tests.

Performance and Portfolio Assessment

M ost educational and psychological assessments of humans are assessments of performances. As we have discussed throughout this text, performances can be assessed in a variety of ways: through direct observation, analysis of permanent products (such as projects or papers), and interviews with others who have observed behavior or rated permanent products. One type of performance (responses to short-answer or multiple-choice questions) has come under increased scrutiny since the mid-1980s, and a number of new assessment practices have been developed in response to this scrutiny. Journals directed at educators have devoted entire issues to alternative assessment, and hundreds of papers and numerous books addressing alternative assessment have been published. Among the approaches proposed to supplement or replace short-answer and multiple-choice achievement tests are curriculum-based assessment (Fuchs & Fuchs, 1986; Salvia & Hughes, 1990), judgment-based assessment (Bagnato & Neisworth, 1990), dynamic assessment (Lidz, 1991), and authentic assessment (Archbald & Newman, 1988; Maeroff, 1991; Meyer, 1992).

These assessment alternatives share three common goals. First, they emphasize a more direct examination of student performance. Second, they seek to improve the validity of assessment by basing assessment on student performances and products that relate more directly to the curriculum and to society at large. Third, they seek to link assessment and instruction more directly.

Some of the alternative approaches to assessing performance (for example, curriculum-based assessment) clearly fall within a psychometric tradition and are quite consistent with the stance we have taken throughout this text. Other alternatives fall within a more holistic approach to assessment, which differs substantially from more traditional approaches to assessment. These nontraditional alternatives often favor subjective or qualitative approaches to measurement instead of objective and quantitative measurement. These more qualitative approaches have been referred to as informal assessment, alternative assessment, performance (or performance-based) assessment, authentic assessment, and portfolio assessment. Generally, these approaches require students to create an answer or product to demonstrate their knowledge and skills. Usually, these approaches require students to demonstrate more than recognition and understanding of information; they require higher-order skills such as synthesis and evaluation.

In this chapter, we address the assessment of student learning through the use of more holistic methods and the collection of the products of student learning into portfolios. As typically advocated (see Gillespie, Ford, Gillespie, & Leavell, 1996), portfolio assessment contains most of the elements favored in holistic approaches to measurement. Thus, many of the concepts and concerns in this chapter also apply to alternative approaches other than portfolio assessment. Finally, a number of different models of portfolio assessment have been advocated, and the profession is far from consensus about what constitutes a portfolio or about how a portfolio should be used in assessment. For example, the content of student portfolios for science will differ from the content of those used for basic literacy education. Moreover, even a single academic discipline (for example, literacy education) allows a variety of approaches. Given the heterogeneity of positions and beliefs about how to assemble and use portfolios, characterizations of portfolio assessment are necessarily general.

Concerns About Current Assessment Practices

The impetus for portfolio assessment comes in part from concerns about current assessment practices, many of which are, indeed, imperfect. We discuss three concerns that seem to us most important and widespread: (1) overreliance on norm-referenced achievement tests, (2) confusion regarding what can be assessed versus what should be assessed, and (3) overreliance on objective and quantifiable measures.

Overreliance on Norm-referenced Achievement Tests

Norm-referenced tests provide a snapshot of general student achievement and can provide a point of departure for more intensive and extensive assessment of an individual student. When these tests are misused or misapplied, those responsible for assessment are appropriately criticized. Two misuses of norm-referenced achievement tests are especially noteworthy: using such tests as a means of assessing whether a student can profit from instruction, and using them to guide instruction.

Assessing a Student's Ability to Profit from Instruction

We have argued in this and previous editions that when norm-referenced (or any other type of) achievement tests do not correspond to a student's curriculum, educators cannot infer that low scores indicate the student's failure to profit from instruction. Test scores that students earn on norm-referenced achievement tests are related to the degree of curricular match (Good & Salvia, 1989). Students earn higher scores when tests match what has been taught and lower scores when tests do not reflect the curriculum. Considerable research suggests that norm-referenced achievement tests do not correspond well to specific curricula, especially in mathematics and reading (see, for example, Chapters 20 and 21). Thus, a low test score, in and of itself, does not necessarily suggest a student's failure to profit from instruction.

Guiding Instruction

For a variety of reasons, norm-referenced achievement tests are not suitable for guiding day-to-day instruction. First, these tests are specifically designed to produce stable scores. In practice, the stability of scores makes these tests insensitive to small but important changes in student learning. Thus, students who are developing slowly may show no gains in tested performance. For these students, standardized, norm-referenced tests may not be valid measures of progress.

Second, the results of group-administered, machine-scored tests are frequently unavailable to teachers until weeks after administration. Thus, by the time a teacher knows the scores, they may not be pertinent to students' current levels of functioning. Moreover, when only test scores are reported, teachers have no opportunity to analyze errors or ascertain patterns of strength and weakness within an academic area (for example, decoding in reading); scores are aggregations of strengths and weaknesses.

Third, even when a teacher administers and scores a norm-referenced achievement test, there are problems. Most norm-referenced tests do not contain enough test items to allow judgments about a student's understanding or mastery of specific elements of the curriculum that can guide instructional decision making. Test authors include enough items to assure general content validity, to discriminate among test takers, and to provide reliable scores. Their intent is not to provide enough items for fine-grain analyses.

Fourth, tests assess knowledge about a subject, not ability to acquire such knowledge. Thus, group-administered achievement tests are unlikely to be useful to teachers in making day-to-day instructional decisions—and we know of no professional educators or test authors who would claim that these tests are suitable for this purpose.

Confusion Regarding What Can Be Assessed Versus What Should Be Assessed

Some critics of current testing practices believe that tests determine curricula. These critics contend that the contents of tests are incorrectly viewed as valuable educational outcomes and determine what should be taught. Thus, instead of achievement tests reflecting valued educational outcomes, curricula reflect the content of achievement tests, which may not be valuable. This phenomenon is readily illustrated.

Suppose that a district wanted its students to understand how European imperialism created modern sub-Saharan African nations where traditional enemies were frequently included within a single nation. The students in that district could be expected to earn higher scores on tests that assessed the role of European imperialism on the development of African countries than they would earn on tests that assessed basic geographical facts (such as the capitals and specific locations of sub-Saharan countries). If a districtwide achievement test asked students basic geographical facts, individual teachers (or the district administration) might alter the thrust of the curriculum. Changing the emphasis of the curriculum could result in higher student scores on the test. While the higher scores might make the teachers and district look better and might make parents and taxpayers happier, the curriculum would have been altered. What the district values (that is, an understanding of how the composition of modern African countries is a by-product of European imperialism) would have been displaced by what the test authors value (that is, the capitals and locations of African countries).

Multiple-choice and short-answer (that is, objective) test formats are criticized for determining not only what is learned, but also how learning occurs. Thus, some critics believe that objective testing formats lead curricula away from contextualized information upon which students reflect critically; according to this view, tests—and multiple-choice tests in particular—restrict instruction in higher-order thinking skills (see, for example, Camp, 1993). Some even blame the poor achievement of U.S. students (when compared with students from Europe and Asia) on multiple-choice tests, noting that European and Asian systems rely more heavily on written essays, oral presentations, and exhibits of student work that put knowledge in context and require higher-order thinking skills (Hacker & Hathaway, 1991).[1]

For many, education reform goes hand in hand with reforms in assessment. Without reforms in assessment, reforms in curriculum and instruction may be impeded. For example, the National Council of Teachers of Mathematics (NCTM) has noted that

> objective tests, first developed in the 1910s, were once considered an example of the application of "modern" scientific techniques. Today, we are both technologically and intellectually equipped to improve on outdated methods and instruments—*the continued use of which would be counterproductive to the needed reforms in school mathematics.* (1993, p. 13)

Certainly, if current assessment procedures do not reflect curricula, students may earn lower test scores. Thus, "unless corresponding changes are made in assessment practices, promising new programs developed by teachers and schools will certainly crash as they come into contact with outdated, but often-used and revered, tests" (NCTM, 1993, p. 14). Not only might objective testing formats

---

1. Obviously, there are other important differences between U.S. educational systems and those in Europe and Asia. For example, the responsibility for education tends to be more decentralized in the United States.

impede educational reform, but alternative assessment formats are believed to promote educational reform. For example, Fredricksen and Collins have written that a "systematically valid test is one that induces in the education system curricular and instructional changes that foster the development of cognitive skills that the test is designed to measure" (1989, p. 27).

Overreliance on Objective and Quantifiable Measures

Some proponents of alternative assessment believe that more subjective and qualitative approaches are better for assessing many important educational outcomes (for example, writing for specific audiences or using the scientific method). Many teachers already use such methods to assess student performance in music, art, photography, drafting, writing, wood shop, and so forth. Teachers also draw inferences and make judgments in more concrete domains. For example, teachers examine student computations to judge whether pupils have used correct mathematical algorithms. Thus, subjective and qualitative judgments can provide valuable additional information for use in educational decision making.

However, today the role of qualitative and subjective appraisals has broadened and, in some circles, is replacing more objective and quantitative assessment procedures. Dwyer (1993) noted an increased tolerance for subjectivity and a valuing of human judgment and intuition over precise decision rules and logical operations. Some advocate that student work be assessed more within the context of who students are. For example, Gitomer (1993) has noted the belief that the more assessors know about students, the more accurate their judgments.

Yet subjective appraisals present some serious problems for those charged with conducting educational and psychological evaluations. For good reason, examiners and teachers historically have aspired to be objective, impartial, and disinterested appraisers. As Bennett points out, human judgment "seems to be distrusted because it has so often been a historical companion to bias" (1993, p. 17). Bennett's observation is particularly apropos in special education, where disability labels can bias and distort subjective evaluations (see, for example, Salvia & Meisel, 1980). This inherent weakness in subjective evaluation partly explains the emphasis that interscorer reliability (see Chapter 7) has received in professional literature, as well as the legal mandates for objective criteria for evaluating the progress of students with disabilities.[2]

● ●

Portfolio Assessment

Portfolios go beyond a simple display of sample products; they are intended to facilitate judgments about student performance. As collections of products used to

---

2. As one example, federal regulations require IEPs to contain "appropriate objective criteria . . . for determining whether the short-term instructional objectives are being achieved" (34 CFR §300.46(a)(5)).

demonstrate what a person has done they imply what a person is capable of doing. Collecting a variety of products into a portfolio has allowed artists and craftspeople to show the range and depth of their creative accomplishment. For a long time, portfolios have played an integral part in the evaluation process in fields such as art, music, photography, journalism, commercial arts, and modeling (Winograd & Gaskins, 1992). In these contexts, where judgments of quality are personal and subjective, a portfolio allows potential employers or customers to decide for themselves whether they like an artisan's work.

The use of work samples is neither new nor innovative in U.S. classrooms. We are all familiar with student work displayed in classrooms. Teachers frequently show parents samples of their children's work on back-to-school nights. These samples are tangible proof for students, parents, and building visitors of what pupils create—stories, poems, drawings, and mechanical devices.

However, the use of portfolios is no longer confined to school subjects where creative activities are taught and evaluated. Now, portfolios are being used in more traditional academic areas such as reading, mathematics, and science to document student effort, growth, and achievement. Portfolio assessment projects have been initiated statewide in some states (for example, in Vermont, Kentucky, and California) and are recognized as an assessment option in others (for example, Pennsylvania). Some educators believe portfolio assessment is useful in special education. For example, Salend (1998) asserts that portfolios help teachers make decisions and recommendations about instructional and educational programs and mastery of IEP goals.

Portfolio Assessment Defined

Although different authors stress different components of portfolio assessment (for example, Arter & Spandel, 1992; Camp, 1993; Dwyer, 1993; Gelfer & Perkins, 1998; Grace & Shores, 1992; Katz & Johnson-Kuby, 1996; Kearns, Kleinert, Clayton, Burdge, & Williams, 1998; Salend, 1998) six elements are generally highlighted in the literature advocating this form of assessment.

1. *Targeting valued outcomes for assessment.* Generally, valued outcomes include those that require higher levels of understanding (that is, analysis, synthesis, and evaluation), those that require applying specific processes or strategies to reach answers, and those that are complex and challenging.

2. *Using tasks that mirror work in the real world.* Authentic assessments require students to solve the types of problems found in the real world. These problems may be ill structured (open ended), require significant amounts of student time to solve, or require students to integrate knowledge and skills, rather than treat them as discrete entities.

3. *Encouraging cooperation among learners and between teacher and student.* Outcomes to be assessed should include products or performances created by groups of students, as well as by individual students.

4. *Using multiple dimensions to evaluate student work.* In portfolio assessment, teachers should evaluate more than content knowledge. They should also con-

sider content-specific strategies, methods of inquiry, and work processes that are essential components of student learning.

5. *Encouraging student reflection.* Students should think critically about what they and their peers have created or accomplished, and they should strive to improve their products. Thus, teachers should encourage students to revise and polish their work, rather than turning in a one-shot test, essay, or project.

6. *Integrating assessment and instruction.* Assessment must serve instructional purposes from which it is inseparable. Thus, assessment should do more than provide accurate information about student performance on a continuous basis; it should also motivate students and facilitate teaching.

Portfolio Content

Portfolios should be tailored for a specific purpose. Without a predetermined purpose, a portfolio is just a pile of papers or projects placed in a folder. Thus, portfolio contents should be consistent with the purposes for collecting work and should bear logically on the decision that is to be reached.

Depending on its purpose, a portfolio might include classroom assignments, work developed especially for the portfolio, a list of books that have been read, tests, checklists, journal entries, completed projects, response logs, artwork, and so forth (Polin, 1991). Portfolios can also be dedicated to a single project. For example, a portfolio for a story might include outlines, drafts, revisions, and the final copy (see, for example, Katz & Johnson-Kuby, 1996). Increasingly, teachers are using electronic media to index and archive portfolios (see, for example, Stiggins, 1997).

Collaboration of students and teachers is integral to the creation of portfolios. Thus, decisions about what to include in a portfolio are made in consultations between students and their teachers, frequently during regularly scheduled conferences. (Notes from these conferences may also be included in portfolios.) The guidelines for student participation that have been suggested in the professional literature, however, tend to be conflicting. For example, some advocate having students select a product that they think is particularly good or of which they are particularly proud; others advocate having students select a product that they do not like.

Some educators believe that what students select and the rationales for their selections are as important as the pieces themselves (Arter & Spandel, 1992; Frazier & Paulson, 1992; Hebert, 1992; Mills, 1989; Paulson, Paulson, & Meyer, 1991; Wolf, 1989).[3] Portfolios often include the students' self-evaluations and reflections. Advocates of portfolio assessment encourage the inclusion of reflective statements in which students express their feelings about the specific contents and topics in their portfolios. Teachers can ask students why they have chosen to include certain products, why a product was important, and how they went about

3. This belief suggests that portfolio assessment requires sophisticated understanding of students' motivation and ability to think critically.

completing their work. In addition, students can comment on what they have learned, whether they have met their goals, and what future goals they would like to accomplish.[4]

Using Portfolios to Evaluate Student Work

Advocates of the use of portfolios as assessment tools frequently discuss four aspects of assessment: responsibility for developing performance standards, dimensions to be evaluated, dimension scaling, and responsibility for actual evaluation of portfolios.

Responsibility for Developing Performance Standards

Conflicting advice about who should set performance standards is offered in the literature. Dwyer (1993) notes that teachers should not let politicians or other external groups set standards. Others (such as Tierney, Carter, & Desai, 1991; Winograd & Gaskins, 1992) have urged teachers to let students develop their own personal criteria. According to Gitomer (1993), others have advocated that teachers and students share responsibility for setting standards. It is interesting that parents are seldom mentioned as stakeholders in decisions about performance standards—although when students have disabilities, their parents must be included in the decision-making process for establishing goals and performance criteria. Finally, despite the competing proposals for who should set standards, everyone seems to agree that the standards should be public.

Dimensions to Be Evaluated

A decision must be made about specific dimensions to be rated. The specific dimensions are generally intended to assess a student's effort (sometimes termed *commitment* or *purposefulness*), use of specific strategies or problems (for example, the scientific method), problem solving, and overall quality of the product (usually evaluated holistically). Some (see Tierney et al., 1991) advocate having the entire class select the dimensions; others advocate using evaluation dimensions developed outside the classroom (LeMahieu, Eresh, & Wallace, 1992). The specific dimensions to be evaluated are, of course, a function of the subject matter and the purpose of the assessment.

Dimension Scaling

All scoring systems of which we are aware use ordinal scaling. First, the number of points on the scale must be determined; typically, from 3 to 9 points are used. Next, the endpoints of the scale are *anchored*—given a verbal description of student performance. These anchors may be generic (for example, from novice through master performance or from weak through strong performance), or they may be more focused (for example, there is evidence of serious effort and personal

---

4. Although this type of information can be collected easily, its use is not clearly explained in the literature on portfolio assessment.

commitment within the portfolio). Intervening points on the scale may or may not have verbal descriptors.

Responsibility for Portfolio Evaluation

Obviously, teachers are responsible for the evaluation of portfolios. However, many believe that the evaluation process should be broadened to include evaluations by the students themselves, their classmates, their parents, and even other family members (see, for example, Adams, 1991; Arter & Spandel, 1992; Hansen, 1992; Herbert & Schultz, 1996; Polin, 1991; Salend, 1998; Tierney et al., 1991; Winograd & Gaskins, 1992). While the (hypothesized) enormous benefit of having different people participate in the evaluation of portfolios is regularly extolled, little is usually said about preparing these individuals, step by step, to do an evaluation. Essentially, teachers are left to their own devices when if comes to training students to evaluate portfolios. The situation is exemplified by Keefe (cited by Salend, 1998, p. 41), who suggests that students and family members can "write or dictate a note or letter to the portfolio highlighting what they feel is the most meaningful information included in the portfolio, as well as their beliefs about what the portfolio indicates about the student's progress and educational program." Obviously, no preparation or training is required when feelings and beliefs are the basis of an evaluation.

Because the evaluation of portfolios is frequently subjective, moderation is sometimes used in grading students. *Moderation* is the practice of using several scores for the same performance—not unlike the procedure used for judging Olympic ice skating. The scores awarded to an individual performance may be tempered by discarding scores at the extreme (that is, the highest and lowest scores) or by averaging (or summing) the raters' scores. In this way, idiosyncratic scores have less of a distorting effect, and the average rating should more closely approximate the performer's true score. However, moderation requires several raters or judges.

An Example of a Scoring System for Writing

Scoring systems for writing portfolios are among the most extensively described. The scheme used by the Pittsburgh Public Schools (LeMahieu et al., 1992) is representative. As shown in Table 13.1, the writing assessment is organized around three major dimensions with several characteristics. Each characteristic is scored on a 6-point Likert scale, ranging from inadequate performance to outstanding performance.

Scoring Systems Used in Mathematics and Science

Scoring systems in mathematics education frequently assess *process* (such as solving problems, making valid arguments, explaining reasoning used to arrive at solutions, and using technology appropriately) and *content* (for instance, the type of arithmetic used in the problem, such as addition or quadratic equations) (compare National Council of Teachers of Mathematics, 1993, p. 114; Pandey & Smith, 1991).

TABLE 13.1 ● *Dimensions and Characteristics Used in the Pittsburgh Portfolio Project*

Accomplishment as a Writer	Use of Process and Strategies for Writing	Development as a Writer
Meeting worthwhile challenges Establishing/maintaining purpose Using technique and genre Control of conventions, vocabulary, and sentence structure Awareness of audience needs Using language, sound, images, tone, voice, humor, metaphor, and playfulness	Effective use of prewriting strategies Using drafts to discover and shape ideas Using conferencing opportunities to refine writing Effective use of revision (reshaping, refocusing, refining)	Investing in writing tasks Increasing engagement in writing Developing a sense of self as a writer Evolving personal criteria and standards for writing Seeing strengths and needs in own writing Risk taking and innovation in interpreting writing tasks Progression in use of writing for various purposes, genres, and audiences from early to late pieces

In science, a scoring system may use both technical and substantive criteria. When written records of experiments (or "doing science") are kept, Collins (1993)[5] has described some *technical criteria* that can be used:

> (1) Is there a goal statement? (2) Is there a rationale for the goal statement? (3) Is there a guide that helps the assessor find his/her way through the evidence? (4) Does each piece of evidence have a caption that states what the document is and why it is evidence? (5) Is there a final reflection? (6) Are all prescribed pieces of evidence present? (7) Is there variety among the evidence? And (8) has all redundant evidence been removed? (p. 126)

For Collins (1993), *substantive criteria* address two issues: "(1) Is the assessor convinced by this collection of evidence that the person who has developed the portfolio has achieved or made progress toward the goal? And, (2) if not, what additional evidence would be needed to convince me?" (p. 126). Shavelson, Baxter, and Pine (1991) also gives examples of scoring rubrics for some specific science projects.

● ●

Issues and Concerns to Be Resolved

The use of portfolios, either as an addition to other assessment procedures or as a replacement for other forms of assessment done by teachers, has considerable intuitive appeal. However, portfolio assessment is a new approach, and assessment specialists still need to resolve issues related to the assembling and scoring

---

5. Although Collins's paper focuses on teaching science to undergraduate college students, the descriptions are applicable, with modification, to general education.

of portfolios, veracity of items included, bias, instructional utility, efficiency, and use in actual practice.

Assembling Portfolios

General Issues

What goes into a portfolio is of fundamental concern because educational decisions will be based, at least in part, on these student products. Teachers have been urged to structure portfolios according to the type of decision that they will make. Yet, the literature on portfolio assessment offers little practical guidance about (1) the types of decisions teachers should be making, (2) the characteristics (for example, amount) of the content used for specific decisions, or (3) criteria to guide decision making about any of the following:

1. Grading

2. Identification and remediation of a student's academic weaknesses

3. Instructional improvement and staff development

4. Eligibility for entitlement programs (such as special education)

5. Assessing educational outcomes

6. Educational reform

This absence of theory and empirical research to guide practice in portfolio assessment stands in stark contrast to the situation for other approaches to classroom assessment (for example, curriculum-based assessment).

    Portfolio assessment has developed largely outside the field of special and remedial education. A consequence, perhaps, is that many of the decisions made on behalf of students in special education do not appear to have been considered. Similarly, advocates of portfolio assessment do not appear to have considered the processes and criteria on which these decisions are based. Many decisions in special and remedial education rely, at least in part, on interstudent comparisons. For example, a student may be referred for prereferral intervention on the bases of both failing to meet standards of performance and being substantially behind other students in class; a boy with a learning disability might be mainstreamed in a regular classroom when his achievement is commensurate with that of a nondisabled student in the classroom. Because the content of portfolios is not standardized from student to student, interstudent comparisons based on portfolio assessment are extremely difficult. Thus, portfolios, in the form advocated by most supporters, are unlikely to gain widespread acceptance in special education.[6]

    If portfolios replace tests, educators will need to address some issues of record maintenance. Portfolios can be maintained for a specific marking period, a semester, a year, or a career. When portfolios are used to make long-term decisions

---

6. We note that many advocates of portfolio assessment (as well as advocates of other alternative forms of assessment) oppose interstudent comparisons on philosophical grounds (see, for example, NCTM, 1993.)

(such as determining eligibility, documenting attainment of outcomes required for graduation, documenting the provision of high-quality education, and so forth), some guidelines for maintenance of records will have to be established (see Chapter 3). Storage and retrieval of portfolios may present problems even with digital technology. Although it is possible to maintain electronic copies of portfolios on compact disk, the costs are currently prohibitive.

Specific Issues

Content Selection   Will a student's portfolio include everything a student has done in an area or just a sample of products? For example, should the portfolio contain all or some of the notes, outlines, drafts, corrected copies, and rewrites of every product a student has created for a semester or year? When portfolios contain everything students have created during a year, their contents become more variable, but teachers spend no time deciding what to include. However, teachers will spend more time in evaluation if they evaluate all products in their students' portfolios.

Quality of Student Work   Conflicting advice is offered in the literature about what student work to include. In the absence of research, we can only speculate about the usefulness of different criteria for including student work in portfolios. Some advocate including the student's best work. *Best-work portfolios* show what a student is capable of producing; they are likely to be the most useful in assessing a student's attainment of specific educational goals or outcomes. However, these portfolios fail to provide information about the variability of student work and the quality of typical work. Others advocate including a student's typical work in the portfolio. Although *typical-work portfolios* may be the most useful in making decisions, they do not provide information about the variability of student work or about the best and worst of a student's work. Finally, some recommend including a range of quality in a student's portfolio. Such portfolios provide the most information, but they may not be pertinent to some decisions.

Student Participation in Selection   Student participation in content selection is frequently recommended in the professional literature. As mentioned earlier, students may be asked to select pieces that they think are particularly good or pieces that they do not like. The diagnostic and instructional implications of including products chosen for such reasons are unclear. For example, it is not established that products that a student likes lead to the same instructional and diagnostic decisions as products that the student dislikes; we do not know whether there are interactions between student criteria for selection and the quality of various decisions that are made in schools. Finally, we can locate no evidence to suggest that students, let alone students with cognitive disabilities, can determine what content is pertinent to the multitude of decisions that teachers must make.

Sufficient Information for Decision Making   It is axiomatic that accurate and valid information is the basis for good educational decision making. The psychometric theories on which achievement tests are based allow users to estimate a student's true score on the domain of interest. When these tests do not contain enough items to draw reliable inferences about a student's true score, test authors can estimate (with the Spearman–Brown formula) the number of additional items needed to make their tests reliable.

Psychometricians have yet to develop the necessary theories to allow similar estimation of true scores from portfolios. Most would agree that portfolios should contain enough products to allow reliable appraisal, but at this time, it is unclear how educators are to know what the minimum number of pieces should be.[7] What does seem to be clear is that many who write about portfolios urge teachers to base their assessments on untimed, extended projects (see, for example, Camp, 1993). Such projects require multiple collections of skills that vary considerably across tasks; successful products depend on context-situated skills, as well as knowledge of the context itself (Bennett, 1993, p. 9). Thus, generalizations from one constructed response or performance to other constructed responses are problematic. Teachers cannot assume that because a child performed poorly (or well) on one project, other performances will be similarly poor (or good). It is important that educational decisions be based on more than one pertinent product in a student's portfolio, but when individual products in a portfolio require extended time to create, it is unlikely that multiple products will be available.

Scoring Portfolios

The majority of articles on portfolio assessment elaborate on the importance of scoring and evaluation systems and the philosophical bases for establishing criteria for judging a portfolio's merit; little attention is devoted to the specifics of scoring student work. Evaluation processes are loosely defined, if they are explained at all (Arter & Spandel, 1992; Polin, 1991). Yet, the scoring of projects and of constructed responses is neither simple nor straightforward.

Score Interpretation

Meaning of Evaluative Descriptions   Whether products are evaluated for the presence or absence of specific attributes or on some dimension, interpretation of the resulting scores is likely to present some problems. Consider a science project described by Shavelson, Baxter, and Pine (1991). A teacher asks students to determine which of three paper towels holds the most water. If the students saturate and weigh the towels, the care with which they weigh the towels can be evaluated on a 3-point scale (that is, *yes, no,* or *a little sloppy*). However, the meanings of *yes, no,* and *a little sloppy* are undefined.

---

7. The bromide "the more, the better" is no doubt correct but fails to address the issue of threshold of adequacy. Additionally, the more pieces included in a portfolio, the more time is required for assessment. Therefore, when efficiency is a consideration, portfolios should not contain more products than are needed to make reliable decisions.

Instead, consider the evaluation of a student's written-language project in which various elements are scored as *novice, apprentice, proficient,* and *distinguished.* These terms are likely to lack meaning to anyone unfamiliar with the context-specific meanings developed by a teacher in the classroom. Indeed, we find no evidence to suggest that teacher (or student) ratings of portfolio products are meaningful to anyone outside the classroom or school. Thus, parents and policymakers may find them less useful than other types of descriptions or scores.

Generalizability of Scores   Generalizability of scores presents two problems. First, we know very little about the number of products necessary to estimate a student's ability accurately. For example, Shavelson, Gao, and Baxter (1991) found that from 8 to 20 performances were needed to estimate a student's problem-solving ability in mathematics and science accurately. Yet such estimates will probably vary by the content area (that is, physics, general science, algebra, and so forth), the specific curriculum, and the grade level at which the material is taught. Second, there is some evidence that evaluation context[8] affects student performance (for example, see Gearhart, Herman, Baker, & Whittaker, 1992). What students are asked to do and the circumstances under which they are asked to perform will affect the outcome and, necessarily, inferences about what students have learned and what they are capable of doing.

Lack of Interstudent Comparisons   Although advocates of portfolio assessment often eschew interstudent comparisons, these comparisons are invariably part of the information needed to qualify students for special or remedial services. In schools where interindividual comparisons are based on portfolios with variable contents, making valid comparisons will be a formidable undertaking. In schools where interindividual comparisons are avoided, portfolio assessment is unlikely to provide useful information for a variety of special-education decisions.

Student Reflections   The role of student reflections, often suggested for inclusion in portfolio assessment, is unclear. Although student reflections and self-evaluations may be motivational, it remains to be demonstrated how these reflections facilitate or contribute to assessments of academic or behavioral development. Because student ratings can be influenced by a desire to please the teacher, these ratings may not be independent (or particularly meaningful).

Score Aggregation

Portfolio ratings are aggregated both within individual pieces and across pieces in a portfolio. When one piece of student work is evaluated on several dimensions and then given a summary rating, the summary rating represents an aggregate of the ratings of the component dimensions. For example, suppose a teacher was evaluating a student's accomplishment as a writer—one dimension used in the Pittsburgh Portfolio Project discussed earlier. Further suppose that the student's

8. Some writers use the term *context* to refer to a specific domain (for example, history or mathematics).

performance varied on the six characteristics of that dimension. Each characteristic would be rated on a 6-point Likert scale along a continuum ranging from inadequate performance to outstanding performance. Having rated each characteristic, how would the teacher determine the overall rating? If the rating scale were ordinal, scores from the characteristics should not be added or averaged. If the scores were assumed to be equal-interval, should they be weighted equally? Unless the scores from characteristics were converted to z-scores before weighting, they would be weighted by their variance.

When the summary scores from several pieces are aggregated to arrive at a portfolio score, there are additional problems. Portfolios are intended to include a variety of work. For example, a writing portfolio may consist of poetry, reactions to short stories or news items, journal entries, drafts of extended pieces of prose, and so forth. Insofar as different scoring rubrics are used for different types of writing, summary ratings will be based on different considerations. Thus, the summary ratings will compare apples and oranges, and interpretation of these aggregates will be very challenging.

To illustrate, consider the following scenario. A teacher wishes to make a decision about a student's literacy progress over the course of a semester, using the student's portfolio as the basis of the decision. The portfolio contains 17 items produced during the semester:

- A videotape of the student's classroom presentation on Harriet Tubman (a project prepared during the first nine weeks of the semester)
- One group paper about dinosaurs and some drawings (a project prepared during the last nine weeks of the semester)
- Six biweekly journal entries, completed at home, giving personal reactions to poems read during the first six weeks of the semester.
- Three weekly journal entries, completed in school, giving personal reactions to short stories read in class during the middle six weeks of the semester
- Six weekly journal entries, completed at home and in school, giving personal reactions to articles appearing in a student newspaper (completed during the last six weeks of the semester)

Further assume that the teacher uses Pittsburgh's scoring rubric to judge 20 characteristics associated with the three dimensions. Each of the scores ranges ordinally from 1 to 6. How does the teacher combine the scores? Does the teacher aggregate scores from journal entries with group projects? Does the teacher combine scores across different reading materials (that is, poetry, short stories, and articles from the student newspaper)? How would a teacher incorporate judgments on progress over time, since the materials and tasks vary systematically over the semester? One thing is certain: Different aggregation procedures will yield different summary evaluations.

Guidelines for aggregating ratings are seldom provided to teachers, and there is no evidence that teachers (or students) who invent their own guidelines apply them consistently. Thus, the meanings of summary ratings of individual pieces and of the portfolio as a whole are likely to be idiosyncratic and inconsistently applied.

Score Reliability

Without clear and objective scoring rubrics to guide the evaluation of multiple skills and complex attributes, portfolio assessment is prone to unreliable scoring. Moreover, the products that students construct or create and that are put into portfolios are, by their very nature, difficult to score consistently, whether individual pieces in a portfolio are evaluated separately or aggregated. Part of the difficulty lies in subjective scoring. As Dwyer (1993) noted, efforts at educational reform, and particularly reform of assessment, have celebrated subjectivity: There are "clear indications that [reformers'] orientation includes increasing tolerance for subjectivity, and a valuing of human judgment—and even intuition—over precise decision rules and logical operations" (p. 269). However, precise decision rules and logical operations bring consistency to scoring.

What happens without precise scoring rules is well documented. The research literature on evaluating written language is the most extensive, although written language is difficult to score under any system. In several studies dealing with holistic scoring of writing samples, Breland and colleagues found interscorer agreement ranging from .52 to .65 (Breland, 1983; Breland, Camp, Jones, Morris, & Rock, 1987). In the National Assessment of Educational Progress's portfolio study (Educational Testing Service, 1990), interscorer agreement was computed for ratings of three types of writing (narrative, informative, and persuasive) on a 6-point scale. Interscorer reliabilities ranged from .76 to .89, probably because the scorers had received intensive training just before evaluating the portfolios.

Consistent scoring of student writing is even more difficult when students can select topics and genres. As Dorans and Schmitt (1993, p. 135) have noted, "to the extent that a constructed-response item is unconstrained and examinees are free to produce any response they wish, the test scorer has a difficult and challenging task of extracting information from examinee responses. To date the psychometrics for dealing with this unconstrained response type have lagged behind the development and administration of these items." As Breland and colleagues (Breland, 1983; Breland et al., 1987) have found, interscorer agreement drops from the range of .52 to .65 to a range of .36 to .46 when the writing tasks vary.

Experience in evaluating writing portfolios in Vermont also reflects this tendency. Camp (1993) noted that writing teachers received considerable training before scoring portfolios.

> The criteria for evaluating the portfolios were developed by a statewide committee of writing teachers and applied to sample portfolios by fourth- and eighth-grade teachers in regional meetings throughout the state. They were refined as a result of these experiences. The five portfolio criteria focus on characteristics of writing that are sufficiently generic to be observable in pieces written for different purposes and audiences: clarity of purpose; organization of ideas or information; use of specific detail; personal expression or voice; and appropriate usage, mechanics, and grammar. In the process of applying the portfolio criteria and examining them in relation to the design for the portfolio, the teachers begin to internalize the criteria and to refine their understanding of the portfolio's purpose. (pp. 201–202)

These portfolios were assessed using 4-point scales. "Depending on the grade and subject, the average correlation between raters (across the five or seven scales) ranged from .33 to .43" (Koretz, 1993, p. 2).

Similar findings have been reported in other content areas. For example in a study dealing with scoring science notebooks, Baxter, Shavelson, Goldman, & Pine (1992) found similarly low interscorer agreement (.66), although direct observations were more reliable. Consistent problems have also been noted in the scoring of mathematics portfolios (Koretz, Klein, McCaffrey, & Stecher, 1993). Thus, the evidence to date suggests that level of agreement when teachers score portfolios, especially when the portfolios contain constructed responses, is likely to be below the generally accepted criterion for reliable assessment (.90).

Although research dealing with consistent scoring of portfolios by students is lacking, some indirect evidence is available. Gordon (1990) found that teachers' criteria for judging good stories were often quite different from the criteria used by students. Thus, to the extent that students' evaluations are included in assessment, systematic variation will be introduced. Also, because the literature on portfolio assessment fails to address special training for students who self-evaluate, it is likely that students' criteria and scoring will produce more error than is produced by teachers specifically trained in scoring performances and constructed performances.

Finally, research on behavioral observation, in which definitions of target behaviors are considerably more precise and objective, strongly suggests that as the complexity of observation increases, interscorer agreement decreases (Salvia & Hunt, 1984). Consistent monitoring of and feedback about accuracy can reduce or prevent drifting of criteria, which contributes to lack of reliability (Salvia & Hunt, 1984). These issues remain unaddressed by advocates of portfolio assessment.

In summary, the very nature of portfolio assessment makes reliable scoring extremely difficult. Thus, different teachers should be expected to award different scores to the same piece of work or portfolio. As Bennett has noted, constructed responses "by their very nature will produce less reliable scores. Lower reliability will make the measurement of new constructs relatively inaccurate, limiting the ability to generalize performance beyond the administered tasks and the specific raters grading them" (1993, p. 9). Although advocates of portfolio assessment have downplayed or ignored these problems, the problems have not gone away and will not go away until scoring procedures, as well as procedures for training scorers, are improved.

Veracity of Products

Teachers must determine that their students actually created the products in their portfolios (Gearhart, Herman, Baker, & Whittaker, 1993). For example, how does a teacher know whether students completed the work or handed in someone else's work under their own names? Did a parent, sibling, or friend do the homework? Similarly, if a student revises a paper based on the teacher's formal review of a draft, is the revision considered the student's work or the teacher's? Teachers will need some way to authenticate or weigh the student's contribution to each product. The easiest solution is to use only work completed in class, but this criterion severely restricts a teacher's options.

Bias

Many advocates of portfolio assessment seem to believe that if subjective appraisal replaced objective assessment in the schools, prejudice and bias would be somehow reduced.[9] Assertions that subjectively scored portfolios are less biased appear to be based on ignorance of or cavalier disregard of a substantial research literature. As noted in Chapter 2, researchers have repeatedly shown the susceptibility of subjective decision making to stereotypes associated with race, ethnicity, social class, and gender. Especially pertinent to those working with students with disabilities is the substantial research literature demonstrating that subjective teacher evaluations are quite susceptible to the biasing effects of disability labels (such as mental retardation). Thus, all the relevant research seems to argue against subjective methods of appraisal when more objective methods are available. Snow (1993) has pointed out that bias can be determined objectively and eliminated from objectively scored tests. At this juncture, we cannot say the same of portfolio assessment.

Of course, assessment procedures may be biased in ways other than through their scoring. In addition to content considerations, test format may produce systematic advantage (or disadvantage) for some groups. For example, students of different ethnicities vary in their willingness to attempt open-ended types of questions (Koretz, Lewis, Skewes-Cox, & Burstein, 1992). Snow (1993) has summarized other relevant findings:

- Extended responses (for example, essay questions) produce greater anxiety in students; objective formats seem to help more anxious students.
- The less structured the instruction (a condition associated with portfolio assessment), the greater is the effect of a student's intelligence. Structure facilitates learning for students with lower ability.
- Women do better on tests requiring constructed responses.

Instructional Utility

Portfolios supposedly have two instructional advantages. First, portfolios are favored because they are believed to promote higher-order thinking skills. This belief has yet to be supported empirically. Baker, O'Neil, Jr., & Linn's 1993 summary of the current state of affairs in assessing extended student performances (the preferred form of material to be included in portfolios) remains true today.

---

9. Problems with biased scoring standards are tacitly recognized when moderation is used to overcome different internal criteria and biases in subjective ratings. However, moderation assumes that most of the judges are free of bias.

Advocates of performance-based assessment have been remarkably remiss in providing clear-cut conceptual frameworks for their efforts. Many rather loosely link their exemplars to measurement of higher order thinking without documenting the cognitive processes that students use. Neither explicit frameworks for generating assessments nor detailed descriptions of student learning are offered. Most of the arguments in favor of performance-based assessment, therefore, are based on single instances, essentially hand-crafted exercises whose virtues are assumed because they have been developed by teachers or because they are thought to model good instructional practice. (p. 1211)

Later in the same article, they also point out that the

student's instructional experiences (and the nature of practice on the task) can subvert intentions to measure higher order thinking. With repeated instructional exposure, nominally higher order tasks, such as constructing analyses of a drama or a geometric proof, can be transformed into rote tasks, a fact that may go undetected without collateral information about instructional processes. (Baker et al., 1993, p. 1211)

Similarly, Snow (1993) has noted that when students expect essay examinations, they try to learn how text authors have structured the material, as well as the content. Thus, students do not tend to construct their own structure; instead, they try to memorize someone else's.

Second, portfolios are favored because they are believed to facilitate instructional decision making. Clearly, student products accumulated in portfolios are instructionally relevant. Unlike the empirical validity associated with other forms of alternative assessment (for example, curriculum-based assessment), however, the evidence supporting the role of portfolios, apart from bold and unsupported assertions or testimonials from teachers, remains largely intuitive or unreported. The research that is reported suggests that the relationship of student performance to instructional decision making is neither a simple nor a straightforward matter. For example, Fleischer (1997) found that teachers who were given writing samples collected over an entire year were inconsistent in their recognition of achievement problems and their ability to judge educational progress. Moreover, because portfolio assessment has developed largely outside of special and remedial education, it may not be well suited for some of the decisions that must be made in these contexts. These decisions are discussed in detail in Chapters 14 and 29, but a few examples illustrate this context.

- How are portfolio contents related to the criterion used to decide whether a student is making satisfactory progress?
- How are portfolio contents related to the criterion used to decide whether a student should be referred to ascertain eligibility for special education?
- How are portfolio contents related to decisions to alter instruction when a student is not making satisfactory progress?
- How can a student's portfolio be used to make decisions about mainstreaming and inclusion?
- How can a student's portfolio be used to determine current instructional levels?
- How can a student's portfolio be used to determine rates of acquisition and retention?

Besides the issues of scoring and bias, which clearly impinge on classroom decision making, there are two additional indications that portfolios may lack instructional utility: insensitivity to change and infrequency of assessment. One potentially serious issue is sensitivity to change. For any classroom assessment to be useful, it must be sufficiently sensitive to small but important student changes. We find no empirical evidence for the ability of portfolio scoring systems to detect important changes in student development (unlike the empirical validity associated with other forms of alternative assessment). If portfolio scoring systems do not detect important changes, then teachers cannot gauge the effectiveness of their instruction over relatively short periods of time. Indeed, as Linn and Baker (1993, p. 8) have noted, global scores "would not help teachers to improve teaching and learning. They would function like a qualitative stanine."

A second potentially serious issue is the frequency with which assessments can be conducted. Unlike other forms of assessment, which rely on one- or two-minute probes to assess student progress, portfolios frequently contain extended projects. Teachers may find it difficult to use extended projects to adjust instruction on a daily or weekly basis. Thus, students who are not progressing satisfactorily may experience prolonged periods of failure before their difficulties become apparent to their teachers.

Efficiency

Efficiency is always an issue in assessment. Two issues are especially pertinent when considering portfolio assessment: (1) time and money, and (2) additional training needs.

Time and Money

The first issue is the actual *time* devoted to assessment activities. In those models of portfolio assessment in which assessment is the shared responsibility of both teacher and student and in which assessment occurs during conferences, the instructional value of the evaluation may be worth the added time that must be invested. However, this remains an empirical question.

The evaluation of an extended project is, by its very nature, labor intensive. Yet to produce generalizable estimates of student ability and learning, teachers must have several projects. According to the estimates offered by Shavelson, Gao, and Baxter (1991), teachers will need from 8 to 20 projects to evaluate each student's ability in mathematics and science. Clearly, this is a substantial investment of teacher time; the impact of this time investment on instruction remains unclear. However, educators should expect some reasonable trade-off between depth of coverage and breadth of coverage. Thus, in those classrooms where portfolios are used to collect extended projects, there is likely to be narrowed curricular content.

In those models of portfolio assessment using moderation, inordinate amounts of time could be diverted from teaching. Consider the use of portfolio assessment to assign semester grades in English at the secondary level, where teachers have five classes of 25 or 30 students each. If three teachers score each portfolio, each teacher would be required to evaluate between 375 and 450 portfolios, instead of 125 to 150 without moderation. Even highly dedicated teachers might find this prospect burdensome.

An issue related to time is *cost*. Because portfolio assessment is labor intensive and requires considerable teacher time, cost can be a factor. Moreover, when high-stakes scores are moderated, the costs can soar (Nuttall, 1992).

Additional Training

The second issue is *training*. Even when given considerable training in methods of subjective appraisal, raters typically produce unreliable ratings. Yet, even assuming for the sake of argument that the current amounts of training were adequate, additional training to maintain high levels of agreement in portfolio assessment will be necessary. Retraining requires a considerable investment of time and resources. To date, advocates of portfolio assessment have infrequently considered the costs of training, retraining, and maintenance of scoring standards.

Use of Portfolios in Practice

In practice, portfolio assessment falls far short of even the modest standards recommended by portfolio advocates. In 1993, Calfee and Perfumo conducted a national survey seeking information about portfolio practices and visited several schools and classrooms where portfolios were used. Their findings suggest a state of anarchy in which inconsistent practice was the rule. They found the following:

- No clear indication of how achievement was measured
- No guidelines to help teachers analyze, score, or grade portfolios
- Use of normative rather than developmental procedures
- An absence of procedures to establish reliability
- An absence of procedures to establish validity

In their surveys and site visits, they found that the popularity of portfolios appeared to be a local reaction to external control—the perception seemed to be that the *rebels* do portfolios (p. 536).

In 1995, the Educational Testing Service (ETS) echoed these concerns in an *ETS Packet* on performance testing and portfolio assessment. ETS noted that "Performance assessment is in its infancy, and there are currently more questions than answers about its potential" (p. 14). ETS went on to note the following challenges to be overcome (pp. 14–19).

- Tasks that demand complex performances and also promote learning are difficult to develop.
- Teacher involvement and substantial training are required if performance assessment is to be effective.
- Reliable scoring is difficult to achieve.
- Performance assessment is expensive because of the time required to develop tasks and materials, to train teachers, and to conduct the assessment.

Concluding Comments

The rhetoric used by many advocates of portfolio assessment suggests that portfolio assessment is widely accepted, is sweeping the country, and is the wave of the future. This was probably never the case. Moreover, as educators and parents gain experience with portfolio assessment, many difficulties are being recognized (see, for example, Madaus, 1993). Indeed, it now appears that some districts and states may be pulling back from their initial unqualified enthusiasm. Especially in special and remedial education (with its roots firmly established in federal law, empirical research, and psychometric theory), portfolio assessment will require more than slogans and rhetoric to win converts. Satisfactory solutions must be found for problems associated with content selection, scoring, validity, and efficiency.

Improving Portfolio-Assessment Practices

Those who wish to use portfolios for assessment purposes should give serious consideration to the assembly and evaluation of portfolios. Greater objectivity, less complexity, more scorer training, and greater comparability of portfolio contents are the keys to better practice.

Collecting Student Products

The content of a portfolio should be tailored to the purpose of assessment, but teachers seldom know, at the beginning of the year, all the decisions they will have to make throughout the year. For example, they may not know that Mary will be referred to the school assistance team late in the first semester. Because retrieval of papers and projects can be difficult (and live performances are unretrievable if not recorded), it is probably a good idea to collect all potentially useful student work into the portfolios. Teachers can then assemble decision-specific portfolios.

Teachers *can* be sure that certain types of decisions (for example, grading) will be made during a semester or year. In these cases, teachers should carefully plan the semester's activities to ensure that there will be enough products at appropriate times in the term to make anticipated decisions. If teachers intend to assess progress, they should plan to include in portfolios comparable products from throughout the term. Teachers should also include the criteria for scoring each type of product in the portfolio so that these criteria remain consistent over time.

Using portfolios to make high-stake decisions requires considerably more structure. For meaningful comparisons of a student's progress over time or for comparisons of students, portfolios must have comparable content. For example, it is very difficult for a teacher to judge student progress in writing from diverse products such as a poem, observations from a science walk, a letter, and a story; it is similarly difficult for teachers to compare the progress of two students when one student's portfolio contains persuasive prose and the other student's portfolio contains haiku. The products themselves are not comparable. Generally, the more comparable the products, the less prone to error are the assessments.

Objective Scoring of Portfolios

Since the 1950s, a substantial research literature on consistent rating and scoring has developed. The scoring of portfolios requires essentially the same processes as are used for conducting systematic observations. Specifically, careful preparation is necessary for the scoring of portfolios to be reliable and valid. Criteria should be specified clearly to allow different scorers to agree on whether specific target outcomes have occurred; references to internal process should be minimized (see Chapter 10). Finally, consistent scoring requires instances and noninstances of what meets criteria.

Unfortunately, current practices in portfolio assessment contradict most of what we have learned from research. To be minimally acceptable, portfolio scoring schemes must be sufficiently objective to withstand parent and student disagreement with scores (and grades) and potential court challenges about fairness (Davis & Felknor, 1994). Historically, subjective scoring systems have failed to meet minimum standards. The obvious alternative is more objective scoring systems. One place to start objectifying scoring is to anchor scales in observable and objective characteristics of a performance or product. Without observable anchors, scale values such as *novice performance, strong performance,* and *evidence of serious effort* have no objective referents and are likely to defy consistent judging. A second way to increase consistency is to simplify scoring rubrics. Indeed, Koretz (1993) mentioned scoring rubrics that were too complex or unclear as a possible cause of the unreliable evaluations found in the initial Vermont portfolio studies.

Training and Retraining of Scorers

Even when clear scoring standards have been developed, educators should not assume that teachers will apply the scoring standards consistently without training. The scoring of constructed responses (for example, essays) is *very* difficult. Therefore, teachers should be provided with direct and systematic instruction until they are able to score portfolios consistently.[10]

Training should not end once teachers have mastered the scoring system. There is a strong tendency for scorers to lose their accuracy over time. For example, with experience, a teacher may develop idiosyncratic scoring rules or may stop using some scoring criteria. Thus, scoring criteria drift. To maintain consistency over time, scorers require periodic retraining.

---

10. In addition to helping scorers achieve consistency, training has the added benefit of uncovering scoring criteria that are unclear. Moreover, inconsistent scoring following training strongly suggests that the scoring criteria should be revised. Thus, training acts as a field test for scoring criteria and procedures.

· ·

Concluding Comments

Currently, there appears to be more conviction than empirical support for the use of portfolios. The lack of empirical support can be partly attributed to a rejection of quantitative methods and an empirical orientation; many advocates of portfolio assessment staunchly believe in the superiority of qualitative approaches to assessment. Thus, the published literature created by these advocates consists essentially of testimonials about what is wrong with tests of all kinds (but especially objectively scored tests), rejection of quantitative methods of assessing students, and advice about constructing portfolios. Even given the most optimistic interpretation of the validity of portfolio assessment, we believe that the current literature provides an insufficient basis for acceptance of portfolio assessment on any basis other than experimental. More pessimistically, we concur with Siegler's (1989, p. 15) observation that "if cognitive assessment techniques contain biases that jeopardize the validity of their outcomes, the time does not seem ripe to advocate their use in classrooms." At this time, portfolios offer great research opportunities. Yet, educators must also remember the requirements of the Buckley Amendment (see Chapter 3), which mandates informed consent before students can participate in research. We conclude with Dwyer's (1993) observation about assessment:

> It is the unfortunate tendency, in education as well as in other complex systems, for bad practice to drive out good. This tendency means that for innovative as well as traditional assessment systems, we must anticipate ways in which the system is likely to be debased. Safeguards against bad practice, to the extent that such practices can be reasonably anticipated, must be designed into the assessment system. Also implied is an obligation, as part of on-going validation, to ensure the integrity of the system. (p. 287)

· ·

Summary

Interest in portfolio assessment stems from general concern about the validity and utility of norm-referenced achievement tests, the potential negative effects that standardized tests may have on learning, dissatisfaction in some circles with objective appraisal, and the belief that reform in the area of assessment can drive or support broader efforts in educational reform. Six elements define portfolio assessment: targeting valued outcomes for assessment, using tasks that mirror the work in the real world, encouraging cooperation among learners and between teacher and student, using multiple dimensions to evaluate student work, encouraging student reflection, and integrating assessment and instruction.

Depending on its purpose, the contents of a portfolio can vary considerably. Despite an initial surge of interest in the use of portfolios, several concerns and limitations have not been systematically addressed: selecting the criteria for including work in a student's portfolio, determining the nature of student participation in content selection, ensuring sufficient content generated by a student to reach valid decisions, and finding a way to make portfolio assessment more reliable, with consistency of scoring and breadth of sampling of student performances. In addition, there are concerns about biased scoring, instructional utility, and efficiency. Portfolio assessment will remain difficult and expensive for schools, and educators who wish to pursue this alternative should give serious attention to how portfolios are assembled and evaluated. Objectivity, less complexity, and comparability are the keys to better practice.

Questions for Chapter Review and Thought

1. Why is interscorer agreement important in portfolio assessment?

2. How might a scoring rubric be developed to increase objective scoring of portfolios?

3. How might portfolios of disabled students be used to determine the students' eligibility for special educational services?

4. Identify and discuss assumptions made in norm-referenced assessment and in portfolio assessment that are in direct opposition to each other.

Resources for Further Investigation

Project

Conduct a review of the educational and psychological literature about portfolio assessment. Catalog the titles of articles, scan each article, and give a rating (positive, negative, neutral) that reflects the general attitude of each article about performance assessment.

Print Resources

Black, L., Daiker, D. A., Sommers, J., & Stygall, G. (Eds.). (1994). *New directions in portfolio assessment: Reflective practice, critical theory, and large-scale scoring.* Portsmouth, NH: Boynton/Cook.

Educational Testing Service. (1995). *Performance assessment: Different needs, difficult answers—ETS Trustee's Colloquy.* Princeton, NJ: Educational Testing Service. (Complimentary copies can be ordered by calling 609-734-5050.)

Fleischer, K. (1997). *The effects of structured rating paradigms on the reliability of teacher ratings of written language samples over time.* Unpublished doctoral dissertation, Pennsylvania State University.

Gillespie, C. S., Ford, K. L., Gillespie, R. D., & Leavell, A. G. (1996). Portfolio assessment: Some questions, some answers, some recommendations. *Journal of Adolescent & Adult Literacy, 39,* 480–91.

Technology Resources

New Assessment Methods for School Counselors

http://www.uncg.edu/~ericcas2/assessment/diga08.html

Look here to read about how school counselors can help teachers incorporate portfolios into their assessment repertoires.

Portfolios for Assessment and Instruction

http://www.uncg.edu/~ericcas2/assessment/diga10.html

At this web site, the authors explain the purposes of portfolios in both assessment and instruction. They also discuss the controversial issues surrounding the use of portfolios.

The ACCESS INDIANA Teaching & Learning Center

http://tlc.ai.org/portaidx.htm

This web site contains links to several other web sites that analyze portfolio assessment in depth. Links include the U.S. Department of Education, ERIC, and many universities.

chapter

14

Teacher Decision Making

Each regular and special-education teacher makes literally hundreds of professional decisions every day. Some decisions affect classroom management, whereas others affect instructional management. Some types of decisions occur infrequently; others occur several times each day. In this chapter, we are concerned with the decisions that teachers make about the adequacy and appropriateness of instruction for students who need special assistance, students who are at risk, and students who are exceptional.

The lines of responsibility for students who are exceptional are fluid, and regular teachers are taking increased responsibility for the education of students with disabilities who are mainstreamed or included in their classrooms. Nonetheless, some responsibilities clearly remain those of general educators, while others largely remain the responsibility of special educators. Regular educators are largely responsible for identifying students with sufficiently severe learning or behavioral difficulties to be considered for special education. Special-education teachers are largely responsible for providing education for students with disabilities. In mainstream and inclusive settings, regular and special educators share responsibility for the education of both students who are gifted and talented and students who have disabilities.

Decisions Prior to Referral

The vast majority of students are presumed to be normal when they begin school, and most complete their schooling under the same presumption. However, approximately 40 percent of all students will experience difficulty during their school careers, and approximately 10 to 12 percent of all students who actually enter school will experience sufficient difficulty to be identified as handicapped at some time during their school careers. Most of the students identified as disabled will receive special-education services because they need special instruction. Some students with disabilities (such as students with certain chronic health impairments) will not need special education but will require special related services that must be provided under Section 504 of the Rehabilitation Act of 1973.

In this portion of the chapter, we deal with those decisions that precede entitlement to special education. Before referring students for possible identification as exceptional, regular educators take several steps, some of which are mandated by state regulations. The first step is to recognize that a problem exists; the remaining steps may vary in sequence, depending on the state or district.

Decision: Is There a Problem?

At some point in the school year, regular educators may come to believe that some students have such different academic or behavioral needs that they will require special assistance if they are to achieve desired educational outcomes. The threshold of recognition varies from teacher to teacher and may be a function of several factors: teacher skill and experience, class size, availability of alternative materials and curriculum, ability and behavior of other students in the class, and the teacher's tolerance for atypical progress or behavior. Generally, when a student is performing at a rate that is between 20 and 50 percent of the rate of other students, a teacher has reason to be concerned.

Academic Needs

A teacher's recognition of academic need is usually triggered in one of two ways. First, the teacher may recognize that a student has special academic needs when that student cannot be maintained in the lowest instructional groups in a class—that is, the student becomes an instructional isolate. For example, Mr. Santos may see that Alex is not acquiring skills, information, or processes at a fast enough rate to keep up with even the slowest students in the class. Second, the teacher may recognize that a student has special academic needs when that student performs adequately in most academic areas but has extreme difficulty in one or more important core skills. For example, Sally may be a good student in every subject but reading and writing. *Why* a student is having difficulty is seldom clear at this point in the decision-making process. Obviously, not all achievement problems require special education. There are multiple reasons for school failure, and these reasons may often interact with one another. Generally, these reasons may be classified as being related to ineffective instruction or to individual differences.

Ineffective Instruction

Some students make progress under almost any instructional conditions. When students with emerging skills and a wealth of information enter a learning situation, such students merely need the opportunity to continue learning and developing skills. These students will learn in spite of ineffective instructional methodology.

However, many students enter a learning situation with far less developed skills and require much better instruction. Without effective instruction, these students are in danger of becoming casualties of the educational system because they make progress only when they have sufficient opportunity to learn and when the approaches used to teach them are effective. Some of these students may fail to learn because they are given only limited opportunity to learn. This situation can occur in at least five ways:

1. *Students' lack of prerequisite knowledge or skill.* Some students may lack the prerequisites for learning specific content. In such cases, the content to be learned may be too difficult because the student must learn the prerequisites and the new content simultaneously. For example, Mr. Santos may give Alex a reader in which he knows only 70 percent of the words. Alex will be forced to learn sight vocabulary that he lacks while trying to comprehend what he is reading. The chances are that he will not comprehend the material because he must read too many unknown words (Salvia & Hughes, 1990).

2. *Insufficient instructional time.* The school curriculum may be so cluttered with special events and extras that sufficient time cannot be devoted to core content areas. Students who need more extensive and intensive instruction in order to learn may suffer from the discrepancy between the amount of instruction (or time) they need and the time allocated to teaching them.

3. *Teachers' lack of subject-matter knowledge.* The teacher may lack the skills to teach specific subject matter. For example, in some rural areas, it may not be possible to attract physics teachers, so the biology teacher may have to teach the course and try to stay one or two lectures ahead of the students.

4. *Teachers' lack of pedagogical knowledge.* A teacher may lack sufficient pedagogical knowledge to teach students who are not independent learners. Although educators have known for a long time about teaching methods that promote student learning (see Stevens & Rosenshine, 1981), this information is not as widely known to teachers and supervisors as one would hope. Thus, some educators may not know how to present new material, structure learning opportunities, provide opportunities for guided and independent practice, or give effective feedback. Also, given the number of families in which all adults work, there is less opportunity for parents to provide supplementary instruction at home to overcome faulty instruction in school.

5. *Teachers' use of ineffective methods.* A teacher may be committed to ineffective instructional methods. A considerable amount of effort has gone into the empirical evaluation of various instructional approaches. Yet much of this research fails

to find its way into the classroom. For example, a number of school districts have rejected systematic instruction in phonics. However, the empirical research is more than clear that early and systematic phonics instruction leads to better reading (Adams, 1990; Foorman, Francis, Fletcher, Shatschneider, & Mehta, 1998; Pflaum, Walberg, Karegianes, & Rasher, 1980; Stanovich, 1986).

Before investing in expensive and extensive assessment of the student, it is almost always preferable to examine the effectiveness of the curriculum and the instruction. If a student begins to make better progress with more effective instructional procedures, there is no need to refer her or him. A few students make little progress in spite of systematic application of sound instructional principles that have been shown to be generally effective. These are the students who should be considered for special instruction.

Individual Differences

Even the best general teaching methods and curricula do not work well with every student. Although the research on how different individual characteristics interact with learning is far from clear, there is some reason to believe that students have different learning styles that cause teaching methods to be differentially effective (Cronbach & Snow, 1977). For example, students with relatively high IQs tend to learn mathematics somewhat better when discovery approaches are used, although more direct methods are equally effective with students with lower IQs (see Maynard & Strickland, 1969). As another example, some students appear to learn rote material easily but have difficulty with more conceptual material (see Jensen, 1974). Similarly, whereas some students may find particular content interesting and therefore are likely to be intrinsically motivated to learn, other students may find the same content boring.

Cultural differences also affect academic learning. For example, reading is an interactive process in which an author's writing is interpreted on the basis of a reader's experience and knowledge. To the extent that students from different cultures have different experiences, their comprehension of some written materials may differ. Thus, students from different cultural groups may have different understandings of, for example, "all men are created equal." Similarly, cultural norms for instructional dialogues between teacher and student may also vary, especially when the teacher and student are of different sexes. Boys and girls may be raised differently, with different expectations, in some cultures. Thus, it may be culturally appropriate for women and girls to be reticent in their responses to male teachers. Similarly, teachers may feel ill equipped to teach students from different cultures. For example, teachers may be hesitant to discipline students from another culture, or they may not have culturally relevant examples to illustrate concepts and ideas.

Thus, generally effective instruction may be ill suited to a particular student. It is impossible to be certain whether a student's difficulties are the result of different learning styles, inadequate motivation, or cultural differences without modifying instruction and observing the effect of the modifications. If a student begins

to make better progress with modified instruction, the reasons for the initial difficulties are not particularly important. Because antecedents cannot always be inferred from consequences, we cannot assume that the teacher has isolated the
source of the difficulty. However, the teacher has solved the problem.

Behavioral Needs

Regular educators may also come to believe that a student has such different behavioral needs that he or she will require special assistance to achieve desired educational outcomes. As discussed in Chapter 10, any behavior that falls outside
the range typically expected—too much or too little compliance, too much or too
little assertiveness, too much or too little activity, and so forth—can be problematic in and of itself. In other cases, a behavior may be problematic because it in-
terferes with learning. For example, failing to pay attention, sleeping in class, or
being unable to work cooperatively could all impede learning. As is true with academic learning problems, *why* a student is having difficulty may be unclear. The
problem may lie in the teacher's inability to manage classroom behavior, the individual student's distinctive behavior, or a combination of both.

Ineffective Classroom Management

A teacher may lack sufficient knowledge, skill, or willingness to structure and
manage a classroom effectively. Many students come to school with well-
developed interpersonal and intrapersonal skills, and such students are well behaved and easily directed or coached in almost any setting. Other students enter
the classroom with far less developed skills. For these students, a teacher needs
much better management skills. In a classroom in which the teacher lacks these
skills, the behavior of such students may interfere with their own learning and the
learning of their peers. Thus, a teacher must know how to manage classroom behavior and be willing to do so.

   Classroom management is one of the more emotional topics in education, and
often teachers' personal values and beliefs affect their willingness to control their
classrooms. Although there has been extensive empirical research supporting the
effectiveness of various management techniques for some time (see Alberto &
Troutman, 1990; Bleckman, 1985; O'Leary & O'Leary, 1972), these techniques
may be rejected by some teachers, on philosophical grounds. Occasionally, teachers may know how to manage behavior and be willing to do so generally but be
unwilling to deal with specific students for some reason. For example, some
European-American teachers may be hesitant to discipline minority students.

Individual Differences

Even when teachers use generally effective management strategies, they may be
unable to control some students effectively. For example, some students may be
difficult to manage because they have never had to control their behavior before,
because they reject women as authority figures, or because they seek any kind of

attention—positive or negative. Other students may not get enough sleep or nutritious food to be alert and ready to participate and learn in school.

Thus, generally effective management strategies may be ill suited to a particular student. Because there is seldom a perfect relationship between undesirable behavior and its cause, it is impossible to know a priori whether a student's difficulties are the result of different values, lack of learning, or flawed management techniques without modifying some of the management strategies and observing the effect of the modifications. If a student begins to behave better with the modifications, the reasons for the initial difficulties are not particularly important (and no one should assume that the teacher has found the cause of the difficulty).

● ● ● ● ● ● ● ● ● ● ● ● ● ● ● ● ● ● ● ●

Prereferral Decisions

Early on, special educators adopted the term *referral* to designate a request that a student be evaluated for special-education eligibility and entitlement. Subsequently, an additional step was added to the process. Because the term *referral* had already gained widespread acceptance, the new step was called *prereferral,* although this step clearly involves referral, too. We use the term *prereferral* to describe assessment and intervention activities that occur prior to formal referral to determine eligibility for special education.

Decision: Does the Student Need Extra Help?

Because so many academic and behavioral problems can be remediated or eliminated by classroom teachers, the first decision that a teacher should make is to provide students who are experiencing difficulties with a little extra help. Frequently, this special assistance will take the form of more of the same instruction, attempts to obtain parental help, and occasionally informal consultation with other teachers or building specialists. The special help can also take the form of Title I services. If the student responds to the extra help and the problems are solved, no further action is required (with the exception of perhaps more careful monitoring).

Decision: Should the Student Be Referred to an Intervention Assistance Team?

When teachers are unable to address a student's academic or behavioral problems effectively, they often seek formal help from a specialist or staff support team. Staff support teams are known by different names in different states; for example, in Pennsylvania they are called *instructional support teams.* Often, they are called *teacher assistance teams* (Chalfant, Pysh, & Moultrie, 1979), although they may also be known as *mainstream assistance teams, building-based teams, intervention-assistance teams,* or *schoolwide assistance teams.* Stokes (1982, p. 3), defined a *staff support team* as

> a school-based problem-solving group whose purpose is to provide a vehicle for dis-cussion of issues related to specific needs of teachers or students and to offer consulta-tion and follow-up assistance to staff. The team can respond to staff needs in a variety of ways. It can provide immediate crisis intervention, short-term consultation, continuous support, or the securing of information, resources, or training for those who request its services. By providing problem-specific support and assistance to individuals and groups, the team can help teachers and other professionals to become more skillful, gain confidence, and feel more efficacious in their work with students.

The makeup of the teams varies by state. Although job titles of team members may vary considerably from state to state or within states, team members should be skilled in areas of learning, assessment, classroom management, curriculum modification, and interpersonal communication.

Obviously, students should not receive special education simply because they are casualties of a certain teaching style or curriculum. Nor should students re-ceive special education when better teaching or management would allow them to make satisfactory progress in regular education. Thus, when a teacher seeks help in addressing the special needs of a student, the first form of help offered should be providing the regular classroom teacher with additional strategies and materi-als. The goals of prereferral assessment and intervention are (a) to remediate, if possible, student difficulties before they become disabling; (b) to provide remedi-ation in the least restrictive environment; and (c) to verify that, if the problems cannot be resolved effectively, the problems are not caused by the school (that is, to establish that the problems reside within the child or the family). Typically, there are five stages of prereferral activities (Graden, Casey, & Bonstrom, 1983): (1) making a formal request for services, (2) clarifying the problem, (3) designing the interventions, (4) implementing the interventions, and (5) evaluating the in-terventions' effects.

Making the Request

Because prereferral intervention is a formalized process, a formal request for ser-vices may be required and might be made on a form similar to that shown in Figure 14.1. When a prereferral form is used, it should contain identifying infor-mation (such as teacher and student names), the specific problems for which the teacher is seeking consultation, the interventions that have already been at-tempted in the classroom, the effectiveness of those interventions, and current academic instructional levels. This information allows those responsible for pro-viding consultation to decide whether the problem warrants their further atten-tion.

● ● ●   **FIGURE 14.1**   Request for Prereferral Consultation

Request for Prereferral Consultation

Student _____ Sex _____ Date of Birth _____

Referring Teacher _____ Grade _____ School _____

Specific Educational/Behavioral Problems:

_____

_____

_____

_____

Current Level or Materials in Deficit Areas:

_____

_____

_____

Specific Interventions to Improve Performance in Deficit Areas and Their Effectiveness:

_____

_____

_____

_____

What Special Services Does the Student Receive (e.g., Title I Reading, Speech Therapy)?

_____

_____

Most Convenient Days and Times for Consultation:

_____

_____

Clarifying the Problem

In the initial consultation, the team works with the classroom teacher to specify
the nature of a problem or the specific areas of difficulty. These difficulties should
be stated in terms of observable behavior, not hypothesized causes of the problem.
For example, the teacher may specify a problem by saying that "Heather does not
recognize the letters of the alphabet" or that "Matthew does not complete home-

work assignments." The focus is on the discrepancy between actual and desired performance.

The team may seek additional information. For example, the referring teacher may be asked to describe in some detail the contexts in which problems occur, the student's curriculum, the way in which the teacher interacts with or responds to the student, the student's interactions with the teacher and with classmates, the student's instructional groupings and seating arrangements, and antecedents and consequences of the student's behaviors. The referring teacher may also be asked to specify the ways in which the student's behavior affects the teacher or other students and the extent to which the behavior is incongruent with the teacher's expectations. When multiple problems are identified, they may be ranked in order of importance for action.

Finally, as part of the consultation, a member of the staff support team may observe the pupil in the classroom to verify the nature and extent of the problem. In relevant school settings, a designated member of the team observes the student, notes the frequency and duration of behaviors of concern, and ascertains the extent to which the student's behavior differs from that of classmates. At this point (or later in the process), the perceptions of the student and the student's parents may also be sought.

Designing the Interventions

Next, the team and the referring teacher design interventions to remediate the most pressing problems. The team may need to coach the referring teacher on how to implement the interventions. Initially, the interventions should be based on empirically validated procedures that are known to be generally effective. In addition, parents, other school personnel, and the student may be involved in the intervention.

A major factor determining whether an intervention will be tried or implemented by teachers is feasibility. Those who conduct assessments and make recommendations about teaching must consider the extent to which the interventions they recommend are doable. (Unfortunately, too often, feasibility is determined on the basis of how much of a hassle the intervention planning will be or how much work it will take to implement a given program.) Phillips (1990) identified eight major considerations in making decisions about feasibility, which we suggest that assessors address:

1. *Degree of disruption.* How much will the intervention I recommend disrupt school procedures or teacher routines?

2. *Side effects.* To what extent are there undesirable side effects for the student (for example, social ostracism), peers, home and family, and faculty?

3. *Support services required.* How readily available are the support services required, and are the costs reasonable?

4. *Prerequisite competencies.* Does the teacher have the necessary knowledge, motivation, and experience to be able to implement the intervention? Does the teacher have a philosophical bias against the recommended intervention?

5. *Control.* Does the teacher have control of the necessary variables to ensure the success of the intervention?

6. *Immediacy of results.* Will the student's behavioral change be quick enough for the teacher to be reinforced for implementing the intervention?

7. *Consequences of nonintervention.* What are the short- and long-term prognoses for the student if the behaviors are left uncorrected?

8. *Potential for transition.* Is it reasonable to expect that the intervention will lead to student self-regulation and generalize to other settings, curriculum areas, or even to other students who are experiencing similar difficulty?

The intervention plan should include a clear delineation of the skills to be developed or the behavior to be changed, the methods to be used to effect the change, the duration of the intervention, the location of the intervention, and the names of the individuals responsible for each aspect of the intervention. Moreover, the criterion for a successful intervention should be clear. At a minimum, the intervention should bring a student's performance to an acceptable or tolerable level. For academic difficulties, this usually means accelerating the rate of acquisition. For an instructional isolate, achievement must improve sufficiently to allow placement in an instructional group. For example, if Bernie currently cannot read the material used in the lowest reading group, the team would need to know the level of the materials used by the lowest instructional group. In addition, the team would need to know the probable level of materials that the group will be using when Bernie's intervention has been completed. For students with more variable patterns of achievement, intervention is directed toward improving performance in areas of weakness to a level that approximates performance in areas of strength.

Setting the criterion for a behavioral intervention involves much the same process as setting targets for academic problems. When the goal is to change behavior, the teacher should select two or three students who are behaving appropriately. These students should not be the best behaved students but those in the middle of the range of acceptable behavior. The frequency, duration, latency, or amplitude of their behavior should be used as the criterion. Usually the behavior of the appropriate students is stable, so the team does not have to predict where they will be at the end of the intervention.

Implicit in this discussion is the idea that the interventions will reach the criterion for success within the time allotted. Thus, the team not only desires progress toward the criterion, but also wants that progress to occur at a specific rate—or faster. Finally, it is generally a good idea to maintain a written record of these details. This record might be as informal as a set of notes from the team meeting, or it might be a formal document such as the one shown in Figure 14.2.

Implementing the Interventions

The interventions should then be conducted as planned. Occasionally, a member of the team will observe the teacher using the planned strategy or special materials, to ensure that the intervention is being carried out faithfully.

● ● ● **FIGURE 14.2**   *An Intervention Plan*

Prereferral Intervention Plan

Complete one form for each targeted problem.

Student _____ Sex ____ Date of Birth _____

Referring Teacher _____ Grade ___ School _____

Intervention Objectives:

Behavior to be changed:

Criterion for success/termination of intervention:

Duration of intervention:

Location of intervention:

Person responsible for implementing the intervention:

Strategies:

Instructional methods:

Instructional materials:

Special equipment:

Signatures:

_____   _____
(Referring Teacher)   (Date)

_____   _____
(Member, Teacher Assistance Team)   (Date)

Evaluating the Effects of the Interventions

The effects of the interventions should be evaluated frequently enough to allow fine-tuning of the teaching methods and materials. Frequently, student performance is graphed to create learning pictures (Salvia & Hughes:, 1990). Effective programs designed to increase desired behavior produce results like those shown

● ● ● **FIGURE 14.3**   A Successful Learning Intervention

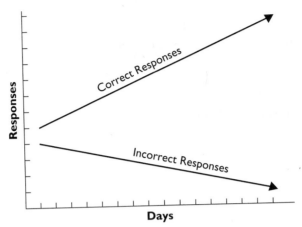

in Figure 14.3: The student usually shows an increase in the desired behavior (correct responses) and a decrease in the number of errors (incorrect responses). It is also possible for successful programs to produce only increasingly correct responses or only a decrease in errors. Ineffective programs show no increase in the desired correct responses or no decrease in the unwanted errors, or both.

To assess a student's rate of behavior change, we graph the acceleration of a desired behavior (or the deceleration of an undesired behavior) as a separate line termed an *aimline*, as shown in Figure 14.4. The aimline connects the student's current level of performance with the point that represents both the desired level of behavior and the time at which the behavior is to be attained. The student's progress is compared with the aimline. When behavior is targeted for increase, we expect the student's progress to be above the aimline (as shown in Figure 14.4); when behavior is targeted for decrease, we expect the student's progress to be below the aimline (not shown). Thus, a teacher, the intervention assistance team, or the student can look at the graph and make a decision about the adequacy of progress.

When adequate progress is being made, the intervention should obviously be continued until the criterion is reached. When better-than-anticipated progress is being made, the teacher or team can decide to set a more ambitious goal (that is, raise the level of desired performance) without changing the aim date, or they can set an earlier target for achieving the criterion without changing the level of performance.

When inadequate progress is being made, teachers can take several steps to fine-tune the student's program. Salvia and Hughes (1990, pp. 121–122) offer various suggestions for instructional modification, depending on the pattern of student performance in relation to the aimline. Although a discussion of instructional methods is beyond the scope of this text, some examples can illustrate the kinds of things a teacher might do when faced with inadequate progress. When a

● ● ● **FIGURE 14.4**   *Student Progress with an Aimline*

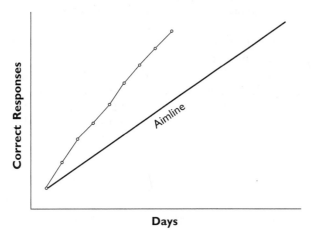

student demonstrates no correct responses (or too few), the goal may be too difficult; the team should consider changing the goal to include attainment of a prerequisite skill. When a student demonstrates correct responses but too many errors, the teacher should consider modeling or prompting and more closely monitoring practice. When a student demonstrates accurate but slow responding, the teacher can encourage faster performance by providing incentives or additional practice. When performance is consistently below the aimline (three days is generally considered a significant amount of time), the teacher might consider varying the instructional methods or incentives. Finally, when a student's performance worsens, the teacher should question the motivational value of the task, vary any drill or practice activities, or discuss the performance directly with the student.

Decision: Should the Student Be Referred for Multidisciplinary Evaluation?

When several attempted interventions have not led to sufficient success, the student is likely to be referred for psychoeducational evaluation to ascertain eligibility for special education. Determination of eligibility requires further assessment by specialists, such as school psychologists, who use commercially prepared instruments. These instruments are discussed in Chapters 16 through 27. Eligibility and related decision making are discussed in Chapters 28 and 29.

● ●

Decisions Made in Special Education

After students have been determined to be eligible for special education, special-education decisions revolve around design and implementation of their individualized educational plans (IEPs).[1] An IEP is a blueprint for instruction and specifies the goals, procedures, and related services for an individual eligible student. Assessment data are important for such planning. Numerous books and hundreds of articles in professional and scientific journals discuss the importance of using assessment data to plan instructional programs for students. The Individuals with Disabilities Education Act requires a thorough assessment that results in an IEP. Pupils are treated differentially on the basis of their IEPs. Moreover, most educators would agree that it is desirable to individualize programs for students in special and remedial education because the regular education programs have not proved beneficial to them.

Decision: What Should Be Included in a Student's IEP?

The Individuals with Disabilities Education Act of 1997 and regulations published in June 1999 set forth the requirements for IEPs. Instructionally, an IEP is a road map of a student's one-year trip from point A to point B. This road map is prepared collaboratively by an IEP team composed of the parents and student (when appropriate), at least one regular-education teacher of the child (if the child is, or may be, participating in regular education), at least one of the student's special-education teachers, a representative of the school administration, an individual who can interpret the instructional implications of evaluation results, and other individuals who have knowledge or special expertise regarding the student.

The IEP begins with a description of the student's current educational levels—the starting point of the metaphoric trip. Next, the IEP specifies measurable annual goals (the student's destination) and short-term objectives (the first stops along the way). The IEP identifies the special-education and related services the student needs in order to reach the goals (the method of transportation and provisions that make the trip possible). Finally, the IEP requires measurement, evaluation, and reporting of the student's progress toward the annual goals (periodic checks to make sure the student is on the right road and traveling fast enough).

Current Levels

A student's current level of performance is not specifically defined in the regulations. However, because current levels are the starting points for instruction, a current level must be instructionally relevant and expressed quantitatively. Although legally permissible, scores from standardized achievement are not particularly useful. The fact that Sandy is reading less well than 90 percent of students in her grade is not useful information about where Sandy's teacher should begin

---

1. The IEPs developed for preschoolers are termed *IFSPs* (individualized family service plans); the IEPs developed for students who are 14 years or older are termed *ITPs* (individualized transition plans). The specific requirements for these plans are somewhat different than those governing IEPs. However, IFSPs, ITPs, and IEPs are all instructional blueprints with specified related services for eligible students.

instruction. If Henry is physically aggressive in his third-grade classroom, that alone is too vague to allow his teacher, his parents, and Henry himself to tell whether he is making progress toward acceptable behavior. We think a current educational level in an academic area should be the level at which a student is appropriately instructed. For example, Javier reads beginning third-grade material with 90 percent accuracy; Mary completes two-digit addition with regrouping with 88 percent accuracy. We think that current educational level in a nonacademic area should be quantified. For example, Ben is out of his seat 25 percent of the time; Maria volunteers answers 15 percent of the time.

Goals and Objectives

IEPs must contain a statement of measurable annual goals, including benchmarks or short-term objectives, that meet each educational need arising from the student's disability and that ensure the student's access to the general-education curriculum (or appropriate activities if a preschooler). Thus, for each area of need, parents and schools must agree on (1) what should be a student's level of achievement after a year of instruction, and (2) what are the major milestones along the way to that level of achievement.

The Context of Goal Setting

In part, the selection of long-term goals is based on the aspirations and prognosis for a student's postschool outcomes. Although these are not formally required until a special-education student reaches 14 years of age, the expected or desired postschool outcomes shape the special education a student receives. For students with pervasive and severe cognitive disabilities, the prognosis may be assisted living without employment. With this prognosis, educational goals are likely to be daily living and leisure rather than academic areas. For students with more moderate disabilities, the prognosis may be independent living and unskilled or semi-skilled employment. With this prognosis, educational goals are likely to be academic and vocational. For students with mild disabilities, the prognosis may be professional or highly skilled employment. For these students, educational goals are likely to lead to the college or technical preparatory curriculum.

In part, the selection of long-term goals is based on the degree to which the educational deficit caused by the disability is remediable. All students receiving special education will lag significantly behind their nondisabled peers.[2] Except when students have severe and pervasive disabilities, special educators and parents generally try to remediate the educational deficits first. The benefit of this approach is that it allows the student the fullest access to later school and postschool opportunities. When remediation repeatedly fails, parents and teachers usually turn

---

2. Some gifted students have learning disabilities. Thus, these gifted students will also have significant deficits.

to compensatory mechanisms so that the student can attain the more generally desired educational outcomes. For example, if Kareem just cannot learn the math facts, he may be allowed to use a calculator. The advantage of this option is that it allows Kareem to move to higher curricular goals; the disadvantage is that the deficits will always be with Kareem, and he will always behave to compensate for them. When a student cannot master the curriculum with compensatory mechanisms, parents and teachers may adapt the curriculum by reducing the complexity of some components. For example, in social studies all students might be required to learn about taxes, but Lashaun might not have to learn about the constitutional issues surrounding the creation of the federal income tax. If reducing the complexity is not appropriate, areas of the curriculum may be eliminated for individual students with disabilities.

Obviously, this option is the last resort, but it may be appropriate when a child's disabilities are profound. For example, we would not expect all deaf students to be fluent oral communicators, although we would expect them to attain other generally prescribed educational outcomes; we would not expect quadriplegics to pass a swimming test, although we might well expect them to meet other educational outcomes.

Specific Goals and Objectives

Annual goals are derived directly from a student's curriculum and a student's current instructional levels. When continued academic integration is the desired educational outcome, a student's goals are mastery of the same content at the same rate as nondisabled peers. Thus, after one year, the student would be expected to be instructional in the same materials as his or her peers. When reintegration is the desired educational outcome, a student's goal depends on where the regular class peers will be in one year. For students pursuing alternative curricula, the IEP team makes an educated guess about where the student will be after one year of instruction.

Objectives or benchmarks lie between a student's current instructional level and the annual goal. They are the instructional targets immediately following mastery of a student's current instructional level.

Specially Designed Instruction

The Individuals with Disabilities Act defines special education, in part, as specially designed instruction that is provided in classrooms, the home, or other settings (see §300.26). It includes the adaptation of instructional content, methods, or delivery to meet the needs of a student with disabilities.

Historically, psychologists and educators have been interested in how a student's abilities affect instructional methods, in the belief that, if instruction can be matched to specific abilities, students will learn better. In special education, this approach led to a search for test-identified strengths and weaknesses and, subsequently, to the development of instructional procedures that capitalized on areas of strength or avoided weaker abilities. For example, test scores from the first edition of the Developmental Test of Visual Perception (Frostig, Maslow, Lefever, & Whittlesey, 1964), the Illinois Test of Psycholinguistic Abilities (Kirk, McCarthy, & Kirk, 1968), and the Purdue Perceptual–Motor Survey (Roach & Kephart, 1966) were at one time believed to have instructional meaning. In part because test-identified abilities were frequently unreliable and in part because special instructional methods did not result in better learning, this approach to instruction gradually lost favor, although some educators today still cling to a belief in it.

In the 1980s, attempts to match instruction to specific student attributes resurfaced. However, hypothetical cognitive structures and learning processes replaced the hypothetical abilities of the 1960s (for example, see Resnick, 1987). Although this approach offers promise, it is far from validated. As one advocate of the approach noted, "widespread adoption and application will require much more work and is likely more than a few years away" (Bruer, 1993, p. 263). We concur.

At present, the best way to teach handicapped learners appears to rely on generally effective procedures. Teachers can do several things to make it easier for their pupils to learn facts and concepts, skills, or behavior. They can model the desired behavior. They can break down the terminal goal into its component parts and teach each of the steps and their integration. They can teach the objective in a variety of contexts with a variety of materials to facilitate generalization. They can provide time for practice, and they can choose the schedule on which practice is done (in other words, they can offer distributed or massed practice). Several techniques that are under the direct control of the teacher can be employed to instruct any learner effectively. To help pupils recall information that has been taught, teachers may organize the material that a pupil is to learn, provide rehearsal strategies, or employ overlearning or distributed practice. There are also a number of things that teachers can do to elicit responses that have already been acquired: Various reinforcers and punishers have been shown to be effective in the control of behavior.

Assessment personnel can help teachers identify specific areas in which instructional difficulties exist, and they can help teachers plan interventions in light of information gained from assessments. Certain procedures (Ysseldyke & Christenson, 1987b; Ysseldyke, Christenson, & Kovaleski, 1994) can aid assessment personnel in determining the nature of students' instructional environments. Procedures such as the Instructional Environment System–II (Ysseldyke & Christenson, 1993) may be used both to pinpoint the extent to which a student's academic or behavioral problems are a function of factors in the instructional environment and to identify likely starting points for designing appropriate interventions for individual students. Yet, there is just no way to know for certain ahead of time how best to teach a specific student.

We recommend that teachers first rely on general principles that are known and demonstrated to be effective in facilitating learning for handicapped students. However, we can seldom find validated translations of these principles into actual classroom activities and procedures. Moreover, even if we did find studies that demonstrated that a particular application of a learning principle worked for a research sample, we still could not be certain that it would work for specific students in a specific classroom. The odds are that it will, but we cannot be sure. Consequently, we must treat our translation of these principles, known to be effective, as tentative. In a real sense, we hypothesize that our treatment will work, but we need to verify that it has worked. The point was made years ago by Deno and Mirkin (1977, p. 11) and remains true today:

> At the present time we are unable to prescribe specific and effective changes in instruction for individual pupils with certainty. Therefore, changes in instructional programs which are arranged for an individual child can be treated only as hypotheses which must be empirically tested before a decision can be made whether they are effective for that child.

Teaching is experimental in nature. Generally, there is no database to guide our selection of specific tasks or materials. Decisions are made about particular strategies, methods, and materials to use in instruction, but these decisions must be tentative. The decision maker makes some good guesses about what will work and then implements an instructional program. We do not know whether a decision is correct until we gather data on the extent to which the instructional program actually works. We never know the program *will* work until it *has* worked.

Tests do provide some very limited information about how to teach. Tests of intelligence, for example, yield information that gives a teacher some hints about teaching. Generally, the lower a pupil's intelligence, the more practice the student will require for mastery—but a score of 55 on the WISC-III does not tell the teacher whether a pupil needs 25 percent or 250 percent more practice, although it does alert the teacher to the likelihood that the pupil will need more practice than the average student will. Other tenuous hints can be derived, but we feel that it is better to rely on direct observation of how a student learns in order to make adjustments in the learning program. Thus, to see whether we had provided enough practice, we would observe Sally's recall of information rather than looking at Sally's IQ. We cannot do anything about Sally's IQ, but we can do something about the amount of practice she gets.

Least Restrictive Appropriate Environment

Federal law expresses a clear preference for educating students with disabilities as close as possible to their homes and with their nondisabled peers to the maximum extent appropriate. Education in "special classes, separate schooling or other removal of children with disabilities from the regular educational environment occurs only if the nature or severity of the disability is such that education in regular classes with the use of supplementary aids and services cannot be achieved satisfactorily" (*Federal Register*, 1999, §300.550).

Placement Options

A hierarchy of placements ranges from the least restrictive (educating students with disabilities in a regular-education classroom with a regular teacher who receives consultative services from a special-education teacher) to the most restrictive (educating students with disabilities in segregated residential facilities that provide services only to students with disabilities). Between these two extremes are at least five other options.

1. *Instructional support from a special-education teacher in the regular classroom.* In this arrangement, eligible students remain in the regular classroom in their neighborhood schools, and the special-education teacher comes to the student to provide whatever specialized instruction is necessary.

2. *Instructional support from a special-education teacher in a resource room.* In this arrangement, eligible students remain in a regular classroom for most of the day. When they need specialized instruction, they go to a special-education resource room to receive services from a special-education teacher. Because districts may not have enough students with disabilities in each school to warrant establishing a resource-room program at each school, a student may be assigned to a regular-education classroom that is not in the student's neighborhood school.

3. *Part-time instruction in a special-education classroom.* In this arrangement, eligible students have some classes or subject matter taught by the special-education teacher and the rest taught in the regular classroom. As is the case with resource rooms, the regular-education classroom may not be in the student's neighborhood school.

4. *Full-time instruction in a special-education classroom, with limited integration.* In this arrangement, eligible students receive all academic instruction from a special-education teacher in a special classroom. Eligible students may be integrated with nondisabled peers for special events or activities (such as lunch, recess, and assemblies) and nonacademic classes (such as art and music).

5. *Full-time instruction in a special-education classroom, without integration.* In this arrangement, eligible students have no interaction with their nondisabled peers, and their classrooms may be in a special day school that serves only students with disabilities.

Factors Affecting the Placement Choice

The selection of a particular option should be based on the intensity of education needed by the eligible student: The less intensive the intervention needed by the student, the less restrictive the environment; the more intensive the intervention needed by the student, the more restrictive the environment. The procedure for determining the intensity of an intervention is less than scientific. Frequently, there is some correspondence between the severity of disability and the intensity of service needed, but that correspondence is not perfect. Therefore, special-education teachers and parents should consider the frequency and duration of the needed interventions. The more frequent an intervention is (for instance, every morning versus one morning per week) and the longer its duration (for example, 30 minutes versus 15 minutes per morning), the more likely it is that the intervention will be provided in more, rather than less, restrictive settings. When frequent and long interventions are needed, the student will have less opportunity to participate with nondisabled peers, no matter what the student's placement. Obviously, if students require round-the-clock intervention, they cannot get what they need from a resource-room program.

In addition to the nature of needed interventions, parents and teachers may also reasonably consider the following factors when deciding on the type of placement.

1. *Disruption.* Bringing a special-education teacher into a regular classroom or pulling a student out of a regular classroom may be disruptive. For example, some students with disabilities cannot handle transitions: They get lost between classrooms, or they forget to go to their resource rooms. When eligible students have a lot of difficulty changing schedules or making transitions between events, then less restrictive options may not be appropriate.

2. *Well-being of nondisabled individuals.* Eligible students will seldom be integrated when they present a clear danger to the welfare of nondisabled peers or teachers. For example, assaultive and disruptive students are likely to be placed in more restrictive environments.

3. *Well-being of the disabled student.* Many students with disabilities require some degree of protection—in some cases, from nondisabled peers who may tease or physically abuse a student who is different; in other cases, from other students with disabilities. For example, the parents of a seriously withdrawn student may decide not to place their child in a classroom for emotionally disturbed students when those students are assaultive.

4. *Labeling.* Many parents, especially those of students with milder handicaps, reject disability labels. They desire special-education services, but they want these services without having their child be labeled. Such parents often prefer consultative or itinerant services for their children.

5. *Inclusion.* Some parents are willing to forgo the instructional benefits of special education for the potential social benefits of having their children educated exclusively with nondisabled peers. For such parents, full inclusion is the only option.

There are also pragmatic considerations in selecting the educational setting. One very real consideration is that a school district may not be able to provide a full range of options for economic reasons. In such districts, parents are offered a choice among existing options unless they are willing to go through a due-process hearing or a court trial. A second consideration is instructional efficiency. When several students require the same intervention, the special-education teacher can often form an instructional group. Thus, it will probably cost less to provide the special-education services. A third consideration is the specific teachers. Some teachers are better than others, and parents may well opt for a more highly regarded teacher who works in a more restrictive setting.

Parents and special-education teachers must realize that selecting a placement option is an imprecise endeavor. Thus, although federal regulations are clear in their preference for less restrictive placements, the criteria that guide the selection of one option over another are unclear. Choices among placement options should be regarded as best guesses.

Related Services

In addition to special instruction, eligible students are entitled to developmental, corrective, and other supportive services if such services are needed in order for the students to benefit from special education; federal legislation uses the term *related services*, which has been widely adopted by states and school districts. Related services include both those not typically provided by schools and those typically provided (*Federal Register*, 1999, §300.24).

Types of Services

Schools must provide to students with disabilities a variety of services to which nondisabled students are seldom entitled. Services include, but are not limited to, the following types:

1. *Audiology.* Allowable services include evaluation of hearing, habilitation (e.g., programs in auditory training, speech reading, and speech conservation), amplification (including the fitting of hearing aids), and hearing conservation programs.

2. *Psychological services.* Psychological services allowed include testing, observation, and consultation.

3. *Physical and occupational therapy.* These therapies can be used to (a) improve, develop, or restore functional impairments caused by illness, injury, or deprivation; and (b) improve independent functioning. These therapies may also be used with preschool populations to prevent impairment or further loss of function.

4. *Recreational therapy.* Allowable programs include those located in the schools and community agencies that provide general recreation programs, therapeutic recreation, and assessment of leisure functioning.

5. *Counseling services.* Either group or individual counseling may be provided for students and their parents. Student counseling includes rehabilitation counseling that focuses on career development, employment preparation, achievement of independence, and integration in the workplace and community; it also includes psychological counseling. Parental counseling includes therapies addressing problems in the student's living situation (that is, home, school, and community) that affect the student's schooling. Parental counseling also includes assistance to help parents understand their child's special needs, as well as information about child development.

6. *Medical services.* Diagnostic and evaluative services required to determine medically related disabilities are allowed.

The schools must also provide to students with disabilities the services they typically provide to all children. Thus, schools must provide to students with disabilities, as needed, speech and language services, school health and school social-work services, and transportation. School-provided transportation includes whatever is needed to get students to and from school, as well as between schools or among school buildings, including any required special equipment, such as ramps. Although these related services are mandatory for students who need them to profit from their special education, there is nothing to prohibit a school from offering other services. Thus, schools may offer additional services free of charge to eligible students.

Establishing Need for Related Services

Although federal law is very clear about the need to provide related services to students with disabilities, how that need should be established remains unclear. In practice, most schools or parents seek an evaluation by a specialist. The specialist notes a problem and expresses a belief that a specific therapy could be successful and benefit the student. Thus, need is frequently based on professional opinion.

We must also note that related services can be very costly, and some school districts try to avoid providing them. We have heard of districts maintaining that they do not offer a particular service, even though that service is mandated by law for students who need it.

Summary

Both regular and special educators have responsibilities for students with disabilities. These responsibilities vary as a function of the severity of a student's disability and the way in which individual states and school districts provide educational services. However, both regular- and special-education personnel will necessarily be involved in decision making with regard to students with exceptional needs. Regular educators may be involved in identifying students with severe learning or behavioral problems who are believed to be in need of special-education services. They may be involved in providing extra assistance to students who are experiencing difficulties in the regular classroom. When the extra assistance is insufficient to meet the students' needs, regular educators are involved in referrals for psychoeducational evaluation.

When this evaluation indicates that a student is entitled to special education or related services, a number of other decisions must be made. All students receiving special education must have IEPs. As part of the process of developing an IEP, educators and parents (as well as other individuals) participate on decision-making teams to select appropriate educational or habilitative goals, instructional methods, related services, and the setting in which the student will receive special education. The decisions made by educators should be based on accurate and meaningful data.

Questions for Chapter Review and Thought

1. Give five examples of why classroom instruction may be ineffective for a specific student.

2. Explain the concept of *least restrictive environment*. What are the most important components of this concept, and on what types of information would educators base decisions regarding their choice of environment?

3. List three related services that a special-education student might need to receive.

4. Jerome is a second-grade student who has enrolled in Blake School during early December. He has moved into the area from another state. No records were sent from the school his mother said that he previously attended, and calls by Blake School personnel to that school indicate that he was not enrolled there. Within the first few weeks of his entry into her class, Ms. Jones has noticed that Jerome is far behind his classmates in reading and math skills. Describe what would be the best practice in addressing this problem.

Resources for Further Investigation

Project

Talk to two teachers, each of whom is from a different school district, about the prereferral process and how it works in their schools. Explore whether each process is formalized or informal. Ask parents, students, or teachers at each school for their opinions about how well that school's process works.

Print Resources

Farlow, L. J., & Snell, M. E. (1989). Teacher use of student performance data to make instructional decisions: Practices in programs for students with moderate to profound disabilities. *Journal of the Association for Persons with Severe Handicaps, 14*(1), 13–22.

Rosenshine, B. (1995). Advances in research on instruction. *Journal of Educational Research, 88,* 262–268.

Salvia, J., & Hughes, C. (1990). *Curriculum-based assessment: Testing what is taught* (Chapter 2, Specify reasons for assessment). New York: Macmillan.

Technology Resource

IEP: Involving the Student Is Important for a Successful Plan

http://www.nfb.org/involve.htm

This article discusses the benefits of involving students in the planning of their own IEP.

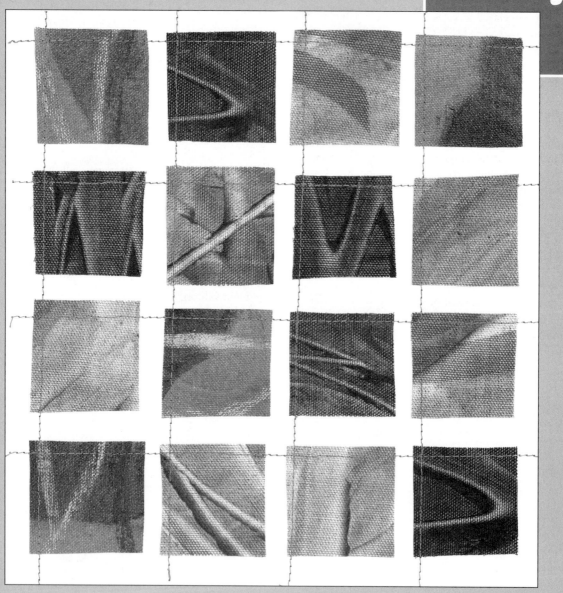

part 4

Assessment Using Formal Measures

art 4 deals with tests and scales used for making decisions entitling students to special-educational services. The first chapter in this section (Chapter 15, on making entitlement decisions) deals specifically with criteria for providing special education and related services to students with disabilities. The remaining chapters describe the most common domains in which assessment of processes (or abilities) and products are conducted. With the exception of Chapter 16 (an overview of intelligence), each chapter in this part focuses on a different process or skill domain and opens with an explanation of why the domain is assessed. We next provide a general overview of the components of the domain (that is, the behaviors that are usually assessed) and then discuss the more commonly used tests within the domain. Each chapter concludes with some suggestions for coping with problems in assessing the domain and a general summary of chapter content.

The criteria we used in selecting and reviewing specific tests warrant some discussion. First, in selecting tests, we could not, and did not, include all the available measures for each domain. Rather, we tried to select representative and commonly used devices in each area. Readers interested in tests not reviewed in this book may want to consult books devoted entirely to test reviews, such as *Tests: A Comprehensive Reference for Assessments in Psychology, Education, and Business* (Sweetland & Keyser, 1991) or *Buros' Mental Measurements Yearbooks*.

Second, in evaluating the technical adequacy of each test, we restricted our evaluation to information in the test manuals. There were two reasons for this decision: (1) As stated in the *Standards for Educational and Psychological Tests* (APA et al., 1999), test authors are responsible for providing all necessary technical information in their test manuals. The test authors must have some basis for claiming that their tests are valid. Therefore, we searched the manuals for technical information that supports the test authors' contentions. (2) An attempt to include the vast body of research literature on commonly used tests would have resulted in a multivolume opus that would be impossible to publish as a current work. Entire books have been written on the subject of using and interpreting single tests.

In reviewing each test, we always use the same format. We describe the general format of the test and the specific behaviors that the test is designed to sample; these descriptions allow the reader to evaluate the extent to which specific tests sample the domain. Next, we describe the kinds of scores that the test provides for the practitioner; this gives information about the meaning and interpretation of those scores. Subsequently, we examine the standardization sample for each test; this enables the reader to judge—recalling the discussion in Chapter 6—the adequacy of the norm group and to evaluate the appropriateness of each test for use with specific populations of students. After that, we evaluate the evidence of reliability for each test, using the standards set forth in Chapter

7, and then we examine evidence of validity for each device, and we evaluate the adequacy of the evidence in light of the standards set forth in Chapter 8. Finally, we give a summary of each test.

We urge our readers to examine the research on tests in which they might be interested. Test users are ultimately responsible for test selection and interpretation. Thus, if you are considering using a particular test that has incomplete or inadequate technical characteristics, it is your responsibility to demonstrate its validity. Current research may provide the support you need to demonstrate the validity of your assessment. Therefore, we urge our readers to go beyond our reviews.

Making Entitlement Decisions

W e are all classified within several types of systems. Sociologists may assign us to particular socioeconomic classes, according to our education, occupation, and income. Government classifies individuals in several ways: as adult or minor, citizen or noncitizen, voter or nonvoter, felon or nonfelon or adjudicated delinquent, and so forth. When we are ill, a physician classifies our sickness: cold, strep throat, or herpes simplex. Psychiatrists may classify clients according to the *Diagnostic and Statistical Manual of Mental Disorders—4th edition* (DSM-IV).

The term *entitlement* has come to be associated with benefits derived from classification; individuals who meet various criteria are entitled to the benefits specified in the law. Thus, for individuals who meet legal criteria for eligibility, classification systems can bring benefits: Social Security benefits, food stamps, veterans' benefits, and so forth. Indeed, these benefits are a substantial portion of federal and state budgets. Of importance for us in special and remedial education is entitlement to special-education services. Individuals who meet the legal criteria are classified as eligible for special and remedial services, and this is one of the primary reasons for classifying students in the public schools.

● ●

Rationale for Entitlement

Think about all the students in preschool, elementary, and secondary educational systems. Except in the Lake Wobegon School District,[1] most students have one

1. Lake Wobegon is a mythical community in which, according to Garrison Keillor, "all the children are above average."

problem or another at some time during their school careers: Some students are unhappy to be in school, some are defiant, some drop out of school, some persist but do not achieve desired educational outcomes, some do not learn as much as is predicted by their intellectual ability, and some have recurrent "bad hair" days. Most of these problems do not entitle a student to special assistance. The bases for policies to provide special help for some students but not for others are seldom made explicit. However, at least three appear to operate: (1) lack of academic success, (2) no-fault failure, and (3) political action.

Lack of Academic Success

The first criterion for providing special help is that a student experiences a lack of academic success. This criterion is either implicit or explicit in the federal definition of disability in educational regulations. (See, for instance, *Federal Register,* 1999, §300.7.) For example, autism, hearing impairment, mental retardation, and six other disabling conditions are defined as adversely affecting a child's educational performance. Multiple disabilities (such as deaf–blindness) cause "severe educational needs." Learning disability, according to *Federal Register,* 1999, §300.7, results in an "imperfect ability to . . . read, write, spell, or do mathematical calculations."

No-Fault Failure

Poor educational performance is a necessary, but insufficient, condition for entitlement to special education. The poor educational performance must be caused by one or more official disabilities.[2] Not every cause of poor educational performance qualifies as a disability. Two sets of circumstances appear to exclude some problems: The problems are not sufficiently severe, or the problems are of the student's (or family's) own making. For example, a considerable amount of research shows that unattractive people are at a disadvantage in U.S. society: They receive lower grades (Salvia, Algozzine, & Sheare, 1977), have lower self-concepts and peer acceptance (Salvia, Sheare, & Algozzine, 1975), and so forth. Yet, there are no special educational services for students with cosmetic disabilities. Similarly, there is no question of the role in learning played by motivation. Yet, there are no special educational services for students with motivational deficits—perhaps because motivation is widely believed to be volitional. Finally, there are no special educational services for students who fail to make academic progress because of poor instruction or faulty curriculum—perhaps because society is unwilling to acknowledge officially that students may be harmed by the educational system.

Federal legislation catalogues the problems required for entitlement. These problems share two characteristics: (1) They are all believed to be severe enough

2. Both federal and state legislation provide for educational entitlement *not* based on educational need, but these entitlements are not part of special education.

to preclude school success without substantial intervention or accommodation, and (2) they are all beyond the control of students and their families. Thus, this criterion relieves students, their families, and schools of any culpability for academic failure.

Political Action

When new disabilities are recognized as more or less distinct entities, they are added to the list of disabilities that carry entitlements and legal protections (for example, learning disabilities and autism). The process for adding disabilities to the approved list of exceptionalities requires more than scientific awareness. The process is usually political. Frequently, coalitions of parents and professionals lobby the U.S. Congress and their state legislatures to include specific exceptionalities. For example, until the late 1980s, students with attention-deficit disorder were not usually covered under special-education regulations. Parents lobbied legislatures and argued successfully in court that their children should be covered. In 1999, attention-deficit disorder was specifically included in the regulations for IDEA. Finally, we note that in some states, advocates have succeeded in mandating programs for students who are gifted, whereas in other states, programs for gifted students are permissive (not mandatory). To our knowledge, once a group has been entitled to special-education services, entitlement has never been removed.

Problems Associated with the Criteria

Four problems with the criteria used to determine eligibility for special services are especially noteworthy. First, we find the prevalent (but mistaken) belief that special-educational services are for students who could benefit from them. Thus, in many circles, educational need is believed to be sufficient for entitlement. Clearly, this belief is contradicted by pertinent law, regulations, and litigation. Nonetheless, educators usually have strong humanitarian beliefs, so when they see students with problems, they want to get those students the services that they believe are needed. Too often, the regulations may be bent so that students fit entitlement criteria.

Second, the definitions that appear in state and federal regulations are frequently very imprecise. The imprecision of federal regulations creates variability in standards among states, and the imprecision of state regulations creates variability in standards among districts within states. Thus, students who are eligible in one state or district may not be eligible in other states or districts. Nowhere is this lack of precision more notable than in the definition of learning disability. How do educators assess an "imperfect ability to listen, think, speak, read, write, spell, or to do mathematical calculations"? In practice, this imperfect ability is defined as a severe discrepancy between measured intellectual ability and actual school achievement. However, there is no consensus about the meaning of "severe discrepancy"; certainly, there is no widely accepted mathematical formula to ascertain severe discrepancy. To some extent, discrepancies between achievement and intelligence are determined by the specific tests used. Thus, one test battery might produce a significant discrepancy, whereas another battery would not produce such a discrepancy for the same student.

Third, the definitions treat disabilities as though they were discrete categories. However, most diagnosticians are hard pressed to distinguish between primary and secondary mental retardation or between primary and secondary emotional disturbance. Also, for example, distinctions between autistic individuals and individuals with severe mental retardation and autistic-like behaviors are practically impossible to make with any certainty.

Fourth, parents may often prefer the label associated with one disability (for example, autistic or learning disabled) over the label associated with another (for example, mentally retarded). Because of the procedural safeguards afforded students with special needs and their parents, school districts may become embroiled in lengthy and unnecessarily adversarial hearings in which each side has an expert testifying that a particular label is correct, and the labels cited by the two sides are contradictory and often mutually exclusive. School personnel find themselves in a no-win situation because the definitions and their operationalizations are so imprecise. As a result, school districts frequently give parents the label and program they want, rather than what educators, in their best professional judgments, believe the student needs. Districts are reluctant to risk litigation because parents can frequently find an expert to contradict the district staff members.

● ●

Entitlements

Once society has decided that government should come to the aid of individuals whose achievement is seriously impeded by a few select disabilities, those individuals become entitled to special treatment. Special education has four components: the special services provided, different expectancies and outcomes, procedural safeguards, and special fiscal arrangements.

Special Services

The federal and state governments extend special benefits to each student entitled to special education. Especially pertinent is the guarantee of a free and appropriate public education that includes specially designed instruction (as detailed in each student's IEP [Individualized Education Plan]), special materials, special equipment and technology, and the provision of a variety of related services that are believed necessary if the student is to profit from special education. Other benefits include (a) formal education continuing until the student graduates or reaches 21 years of age, (b) instruction by teachers who have had special coursework and practicum experiences and may have special certification, (c) instruction in smaller classes than those for regular education, and (d) testing accommodations (see Chapter 9).

Different Outcome Expectancies

Students receiving special education are frequently exempted from various curricular requirements that are established for students in general education. For example, students who complete their individual transition plans are eligible for a high school diploma, regardless of whether they have completed the general graduation requirements mandated for all other students. Further, these students may also be asked to achieve very different outcomes. For example, students with more severe disabilities may be taught skills associated with daily living, using public transportation, building and maintaining interpersonal relationships, and using social services.

Procedural Safeguards

Students who are eligible for special education (or are believed to be eligible) are afforded several procedural safeguards beyond those offered to all other students. These safeguards are discussed in detail in Chapter 3. Here, we only reiterate the safeguards usually associated with special-education entitlement:

- Prior notice and parental consent prior to identification, evaluation, or educational placement
- Parental participation in multidisciplinary teams to determine exceptionality
- Parental participation in IEP meetings to ascertain eligibility and to plan educational programs
- Protection from unfair, biased, and inappropriate evaluation
- Right to an independent evaluation
- Recourse to administrative due-process proceedings to redress conditions specifically guaranteed

Special Fiscal Arrangements

Special educational services generally cost more than the educational services provided for most students in regular education. Part or all of the additional costs are borne by state and federal governments. Determining that Johnny is not succeeding in school because of mental retardation dictates, in essence, that part of his special education will be paid for under special provisions of federal and state law. Thus, in the schools, eligibility decisions are also decisions about whether a child is entitled to additional help paid for by special funds earmarked for children with specific disabilities.

● ● ● ● ● ● ● ● ● ● ● ● ● ● ● ● ● ● ● ●

Determining Eligibility for Special Services

The determination of eligibility for special educational services is based on a multi-disciplinary evaluation (MDE) conducted by a team of professionals, usually called a multidisciplinary team (MDT). The team assembles and evaluates information (that is, conducts an MDE) to determine whether a student meets two criteria: First, the student must be in need of special education,[3] and second, the student must be exceptional.

Establishing Educational Need

Students with milder academic and behavioral disabilities and without obvious sensory or motor disabilities usually are presumed to be normal when they enter school. However, during their education, it becomes clear to school personnel that these students have significant problems. They demonstrate marked discrepancies from mainstream expectations or from the achievement and behavior of typical peers. These discrepancies are usually verified by normative comparisons (that is, use of norm-referenced assessment devices) or peer referencing.[4] The magnitude of a problem that is necessary in order to consider that a student for special education is not codified, and there are many opinions on this issue. Whereas some say that a student should be performing at half the level of his or her peers, others believe that only a 20 percent discrepancy is necessary. Marston and Magnusson (1985) recommend that students receive special-education services when they are two years behind their peers.

The presence of a discrepancy alone does not establish need, because there are many causes for a discrepancy. Thus, school personnel usually engage in a number of remedial and compensatory activities designed to reduce or eliminate the discrepancy. As discussed in Chapter 14, interventions initially may be designed and implemented by the classroom teacher. When the teacher's interventions are unsuccessful, then the student is referred to a teacher assistance team that designs and may help implement further interventions.

Need for special educational services for students with mild disabilities is established when one of two conditions is met. First, if the interventions of the student assistance team have not reduced (or eliminated) the discrepancy in achievement or behavior, there is a strong possibility that the student needs spe-

---

3. Under the requirements of Section 504 of the 1973 Rehabilitation Act, students with disabilities are entitled to related services even when they do not need special education. For example, a student in the early stages of muscular dystrophy may require physical therapy, but the disease may not have progressed to such an extent that special education is required. In such cases, a school district is required to provide the needed services, but the funding for these services does not come from special-education budgets.

4. In *peer referencing,* a target student's performance is compared with the performance of satisfactorily performing peers. See Chapter 14 or Deno (1985).

cial education. Obviously, if the interventions are poorly conceptualized or haphazardly implemented, the case for special education is not made. Thus, failures of interventions only suggest need. However, when well-conceived and carefully implemented interventions fail, the possibility of special need is strong. Second, interventions by the special assistance team might remediate the student's academic or behavioral deficits, but these interventions might be so intrusive, labor intensive, or specialized that a regular classroom teacher cannot continue them without seriously detracting from the education of other students in the classroom. Thus, successful interventions may be too intensive or extensive for use in regular education.

For students with severe disabilities, the process of demonstrating need for special education is easier. From accumulated research and professional experience, educators know that students with certain disabilities (for example, blindness, deafness, severe mental retardation, autism, and so on) will not succeed in school without special education. Thus, educators (and relevant legislation) assume that the presence of a severe disability is sufficient to demonstrate the need for special educational services.

Establishing Exceptionality

When educational need is established, the student is referred to an MDT. The MDT determines whether a student is exceptional.

Composition of the Multidisciplinary Team

IDEA requires that the team have members with the same qualifications as those who must serve on IEP teams and "other qualified professionals, as appropriate" (34 CFR §300.533). Thus, the team must include the student's parents (and the student, if appropriate), a regular-education teacher, a special-education teacher, a representative of the school administration, and an individual who can interpret the instructional implications of evaluation results. If the student is suspected of having a learning disability, the team must also include "at least one person qualified to conduct individual diagnostic examinations of children, such as a school psychologist, speech-language pathologist, or remedial reading teacher" (34 CFR §300.540). In practice, school psychologists are usually members of all teams.

Responsibilities of the Multidisciplinary Team

The team is responsible for gathering information and making a recommendation about a student's exceptionality. In theory, the decision-making process is straightforward. The MDT assesses the student's performance to see whether it meets the criteria for a specific exceptionality. Thus, it must collect, at minimum, information required by the definition of exceptionality. Federal regulations (34 CFR §300.532) require that a student be "assessed in all areas related to the suspected disability, including, if appropriate, health, vision, hearing, social and emotional status, general intelligence, academic performance, communicative status, and motor abilities." Regulations (34 CFR §300.535) also require the team to do the following:

- Draw on information from a variety of sources, including aptitude and achievement tests, teacher recommendations, physical condition, social or cultural background, and adaptive behavior.
- Ensure that information obtained from all these sources is documented and carefully considered.

Official Exceptionalities

Several classification systems are used in U.S. schools today. Different terms are used in different states to specify the handicapping conditions that entitle a student to special-education services. The most frequently used terms and criteria are those required for reporting under the regulations of the Individuals with Disabilities Education Act (IDEA). The definitions used in regulations for IDEA (34 CFR §300.7) are given in the following sections, in italics.

Autism   Autistic students are those who demonstrate *developmental disability significantly affecting verbal and nonverbal communication and social interaction, generally evident before age 3, that adversely affects a child's educational performance. Other characteristics often associated with autism are engagement in repetitive activities and stereotyped movements, resistance to environmental change or change in daily routines, and unusual responses to sensory experiences. The term [autism] does not apply if a child's educational performance is adversely affected primarily because the child has an emotional disturbance.* Students with suspected autism are usually evaluated by speech and language specialists and psychologists. When the student has limited intellectual ability, it is often very difficult to distinguish autism from severe forms of mental retardation.

Mental Retardation   Mentally retarded pupils are those who demonstrate *significantly subaverage intellectual functioning, existing concurrently with deficits in adaptive behavior and manifested during the developmental period, that adversely affects a child's educational performance.* Students who are eventually labeled "mentally retarded" are often referred because of generalized slowness: They lag behind their agemates in most areas of academic achievement, social and emotional development, language ability, and perhaps physical development. This slowness must be demonstrated on an individually administered test of intelligence that is appropriate for the student being assessed. Thus, the test must be appropriate not only for the age of the student but also for his or her acculturation and physical and sensory abilities. However, a test of intelligence is not enough. The pupil must also demonstrate slowness in adaptive behavior. An assessment for mental retardation should always contain an assessment of achievement, intelligence, and adaptive behavior.

Specific Learning Disability   Learning-disabled pupils are those who demonstrate *a disorder in one or more of the basic psychological processes involved in understanding or in using language, spoken or written, that may manifest itself in the imperfect ability to listen, think, speak, read, write, spell, or to do mathematical calculations, including conditions such as perceptual disabilities, brain injury, minimal brain dysfunction, dyslexia, and developmental aphasia. . . . The term does not include learning problems that are primarily the result of visual, hearing, or motor disabilities, of mental retardation, of emotional disturbance, or of environmental, cultural, or economic disadvantage.* Students who are eventually labeled "learning disabled" are often referred because of inconsistent performance; they are likely to have pronounced patterns of academic and cognitive strengths and weaknesses. For example, Jason may grasp mathematics and social concepts quite well, but he may not learn to read, no matter what his teacher tries; Jeanine may be reading at grade level, be a good speller, and have highly developed language skills, but not be able to master addition and subtraction facts.

Criteria for eligibility for services for the learning disabled vary considerably from state to state. Generally, a pupil must demonstrate normal (or at least nonretarded) general intellectual development on an individually administered test of intelligence. The student must also demonstrate, on an individually administered test of achievement, some areas that are within the normal range, while demonstrating significantly delayed development in other areas of achievement, and demonstrate (corrected) hearing and vision within normal limits. Eligible pupils would not have significant emotional problems or cultural disadvantage. Finally, the basic process disorder that causes the learning disability may or may not have to be tested, depending on the particular state's education code. If it is assessed, measures of visual and auditory perception, as well as measures of linguistic and psycholinguistic abilities, could be administered.

Emotional Disturbance   Emotionally disturbed pupils exhibit *one or more of the following characteristics over a long period of time and to a marked degree that adversely affects a child's educational performance: (a) an inability to learn that cannot be explained by intellectual, sensory, or health factors; (b) an inability to build or maintain satisfactory interpersonal relationships with peers and teachers; (c) inappropriate types of behavior or feelings under normal circumstances; (d) a general pervasive mood of unhappiness or depression; [or] (e) a tendency to develop physical symptoms or fears associated with personal or school problems.* Emotional disturbance includes students with schizoprenia but excludes students who are socially maladjusted, unless, they are also emotionally disturbed. Students who are eventually labeled "emotionally disturbed" are often referred for problems in interpersonal relations (for example, fighting or extreme noncompliance) or unusual behavior (for example, unexplained episodes of crying or extreme mood swings). Requirements for establishing a pupil's eligibility for special-education services for the emotionally disturbed vary markedly among the states. Some or all of the following sources of information may be used in determining eligibility: observational data, behavioral rating scales, psychological evaluations, and examination by a board-certified psychiatrist or psychologist.

Traumatic Brain Injury   Students with traumatic brain injury have *an acquired injury to the brain caused by an external physical force, resulting in total or partial functional disability or psychosocial impairment, or both, that adversely affects a child's educational performance. The term applies to open or closed head injuries resulting in impairments in one or more areas, such as cognition; language; memory; attention; reasoning; abstract thinking; judgment; problem-solving; sensory, perceptual and motor abilities; psychosocial behavior; physical functions; information processing; and speech. The term does not apply to brain injuries that are congenital or degenerative, or brain injuries induced by birth trauma.* Students with traumatic brain injury have normal development until they sustain a severe head injury. As a result of this injury, they are disabled. Most head injuries are the result of an accident (frequently an automobile accident), but they may also occur as a result of physical abuse or intentional harm (for example, being shot). Traumatic brain injury will be diagnosed by a physician, who is usually a specialist (a neurologist), and educators identify the school-based deficits.

Speech or Language Impairment   A student with a speech or language impairment has *a communication disorder such as stuttering, impaired articulation, a language impairment, or a voice impairment that adversely affects a child's educational performance.* Many children will experience some developmental problems in their speech and language. For example, children frequently have difficulty with the *r* sound and say "wabbit" instead of "rabbit." Similarly, many children will use incorrect grammar, especially with internal plurals; for example, children may say, "My dog has four foots." Such difficulties are so common as to be considered a part of normal speech development. However, when such speech and language errors continue to occur beyond the age when most children have developed correct speech or language, there is cause for concern. School personnel identify the educational disability, while speech and language specialists use a variety of assessment procedures (norm-referenced tests, systematic observation, and criterion-referenced tests) to identify the speech and language disability.

Visual Impairment   A student with a visual impairment *has an impairment in vision that, even with correction, adversely affects a child's educational development.* [Visual impairment] *includes both partial sight and blindness.* Students with severe visual impairments are usually identified before they enter school, although some partially sighted students may not be identified until they reach school age, when visual demands increase. Assessments of previously undiagnosed visually impaired students may indicate gross- and fine-motor problems or variable visual performance (that is, performance that varies with the size of print, amount of light, and fatigue, for example). Visual acuity and visual field are usually assessed by an ophthalmologist. A specialist usually assesses functional vision through systematic observation of a student's responses to various types of paper, print sizes, lighting conditions, and so forth.

Deafness and Hearing Impairment   Deafness is an impairment in hearing *that is so severe that the child is impaired in processing linguistic information through hearing, with or without amplification,* [and] *that adversely affects the child's educational performance.* A student with a hearing impairment has *an impairment in hearing, whether permanent or fluctuating, that adversely affects a child's educational performance but this is not included under the definition of deafness.* Even severe hearing impairments may be difficult to identify in the first years of life, and students with milder hearing impairments may not be identified until school age. Referrals for undiagnosed hearing-impaired students may indicate both expressive and receptive language problems, variable hearing performance, problems in attending to aural tasks, and perhaps problems in peer relationships. Diagnosis of hearing impairment is usually made by audiologists, who identify the auditory disability, in conjunction with school personnel, who identify the educational disability.

Orthopedic Impairments   An orthopedic impairment is a severe impairment that *adversely affects a child's educational performance. The term includes impairments caused by congenital anomaly (clubfoot, absence of some member, etc.), impairments caused by disease (poliomyelitis, bone tuberculosis, etc.), and impairments from other causes (cerebral palsy, amputations, and fractures or burns that cause contractures).* Pupils with physical disabilities are generally identified prior to entering school. However, accidents and disease may impair a previously normal student. Medical diagnosis establishes the presence of the condition. The severity of the condition may be established in part by medical opinion and in part by systematic observation of the particular student.

Other Health Impairments   Other health impairment means having limited *strength, vitality or alertness, including a heightened alertness to environmental stimuli, that results in limited alertness with respect to the educational environment, that (a) is due to chronic or acute health problems such as asthma, attention deficit disorder or attention deficit hyperactivity disorder, diabetes, epilepsy, a heart condition, hemophilia, lead poisoning, leukemia, nephritis, rheumatic fever, and sickle cell anemia; and (b) adversely affects a child's educational performance.* Diagnosis of health impairments is usually made by physicians, who identify the health problems, and school personnel, who identify the educational disability.

Deaf–Blindness   Deaf-blindness means concomitant hearing and visual impairments, *the combination of which causes such severe communication and other developmental and educational needs that they cannot be accommodated in special education programs solely for children with deafness or children with blindness.*

Multiple Disabilities   Multiple disabilities means concomitant impairments *(such as mental retardation–blindness, mental retardation–orthopedic impairment, etc.), the combination of which causes such severe educational needs that they cannot be accommodated in special education programs solely for one of the impairments. The term does not include deaf-blindness.*

Developmental Delay   Although this is not mandated by IDEA, states may use the category of developmentally delayed for children between the ages of 3 and 9 who need special education and are *experiencing developmental delays, as defined by the State and as measured by appropriate diagnostic instruments and procedures, in one or more of the following areas: physical development, cognitive development, communication development, social or emotional development, or adaptive development.* Diagnosis of developmental delay is usually made by school personnel, who identify the educational disability, and other professionals (such as speech and language specialists, physicians, and psychologists), who identify the delays in the developmental domains.

The Process of Determining Exceptionality

In practice, deciding whether a student is exceptional can be complex. MDT evaluations frequently (and correctly) go beyond the information required by the entitlement criteria to rule out other possible disabling conditions. Sometimes the condition that initiates the referral is not the disabling condition. Those who are responsible for classification of pupils must adopt a point of view that is, in part, *disconfirmatory*—a point of view that looks to disprove the working hypothesis. Assessors must collect information that will allow them to reject the classification if a pupil proves either to be not disabled or to suffer from a different disability. For example, if Lupita were referred for possible classification as a mentally retarded student, we would try to select tests of intelligence and adaptive behavior on which she would do well, to disconfirm the working hypothesis.

As another example, if Tom were referred for inconsistent performance in expressive language, even though his other skills—especially math and science—were average, we might infer that he could have a learning disability. What would it take to reject the hypothesis that he is learning disabled? If we could show that his problem was caused by a sensorineural hearing loss, he would not be considered learning disabled; if his problem arose because his primary language is a dialect of English, he would not be learning disabled; if he suffered from recurrent bouts of *otitis media* (middle-ear infections), he would not be learning disabled. Therefore, the MDT would have to consider other possible causes of his behavior and collect data that would allow them to evaluate these other explanations.

Finally, in attempting to establish that a student should be classified as disabled, we often must choose among competing procedures and tests. For example, to be mentally retarded in Pennsylvania, a pupil must earn a score of 79 or less on an individually administered test of intelligence. However, as we show in Chapter 17, individual tests of intelligence are not interchangeable. They differ significantly in the behaviors they sample and in the adequacy of their norms and reliability and slightly in their standard deviations. A dull, but normal, person may earn an IQ of less than 80 on one or two tests of intelligence but earn scores greater than 80 on two others. Thus, if we had to assess such a student, we could be caught in a terrible dilemma of conflicting information.

The routes around and through the dilemma are easier to state than to accomplish. First, we should choose (and put the most faith in) objective, technically adequate (reliable and well-normed) procedures that have demonstrated validity for the particular purpose of classification. Second, we must consider the specific validity. For example, we must consider the culture in which the student grew up and how that culture interacts with the content of the test. A test's technical manuals may contain information about the wisdom of using the test with individuals of various cultures, or the research literature may have information for the particular cultural group to which a student belongs. Often theory can guide us in the absence of research. Sometimes it is just not possible to test validly, and we must also recognize that fact. Finally, when we find ourselves in a swamp of conflicting data, we must remember why we gathered the data. In this example, we would have gathered the data to learn whether a student met the eligibility requirement, an IQ equal to or less than 79. (Note that the reason for giving an intelligence test was not to see whether the student needed help; we already knew that.)

· ·

Summary

Assessment data are collected to make decisions about a student's need for special educational services and the student's exceptionality. When students are exceptional and have such intense or special instructional needs that these needs cannot be met in regular education, they are classified as entitled to special education. Entitlement is an administrative act. Federal and most state special-education laws contain provisions specifying that students must be classified before they can be declared eligible for services. Criteria for establishing the existence of handicapping conditions are specified in rules or guidelines, and assessment data are used to ascertain the extent to which the criteria are met.

Questions for Chapter Review and Thought

1. List and explain three benefits of classifying handicapped students.

2. How would you go about selecting an assessment battery to see whether a boy (age 8) should be eligible for special-education classes?

3. In establishing educational need for services, it is necessary to document a discrepancy between expected performance and the performance of peers. Discuss two other criteria that must be met for the documentation of need for special educational services.

4. What criteria should be used to select the assessment device for collecting data to make a decision about eligibility or classification?

Resources for Further Investigation

Project

Talk to a parent of a student who receives special-education services. Have the parent tell you about the multidisciplinary team and the process of determining eligibility for services and developing an individualized education plan.

Print Resources

Cromwell, R. L., Blashfield, R. K., & Strauss, J. S. (1975). Criteria for classification systems. In N. Hobbs (Ed.), *Issues in the classification of children* (Vol. 1). San Francisco: Jossey-Bass.

Nelson, J. R., Smith, D. J., Taylor, L., Dodd, J. M., & Reavis, K. (1991). Prereferral intervention: A review of the research. *Education and Treatment of Children, 14,* 243–253.

Reynolds, M. C., & Lakin, K. C. (1987). Noncategorical special education: Models for research and practice. In M. C. Wang, M. C. Reynolds, & H. J. Walberg (Eds.), *The handbook of special education: Research and practice.* Oxford, England: Pergamon Press.

Technology Resources

Introduction to Mental Retardation

http://thearc.org/faqs/mrqa.html

Look here to find more information about mental retardation. The authors describe how mental retardation affects individuals, how it is diagnosed, what causes it, and how it can be prevented.

British Columbia Ministry of Education, Skills and Training: Special Education Branch

http://www.bced.gov.bc.ca/specialed/

This Canadian web site offers explanations of various exceptionalities, including visual impairments, hearing loss, chronic health conditions, and intellectual disabilities.

Learning Disabilities

http://pursuit.rehab.uiuc.edu/pursuit/
dis-resources/accommodations/ld. html

Look here to explore further about students with learning disabilities. The web site describes the characteristics of students and the accommodations that teachers can implement in the classroom.

The Individuals with Disabilities Education Act (IDEA) Amendments of 1997

http://www.ed.gov/offices/OSERS/IDEA/index.html

This web site explains the IDEA amendments that were proposed in 1997 to improve the law.

Assessment of Intelligence:
An Overview

N
o other area of assessment has generated as much attention, controversy, and debate as the testing of what we call "intelligence." For centuries, philosophers, psychologists, educators, and laypeople have debated the meaning of intelligence. Numerous definitions of the term *intelligence* have been proposed, with each definition serving as a stimulus for counterdefinitions and counterproposals. Several theories have been advanced to describe and explain intelligence and its development such as Cattell–Horn, Gardner, Kaufman, Sternberg, and Guilford (Flanagan, Genshaft, & Harrison, 1997). The extent to which intelligence is genetically or environmentally determined has been of special concern. Genetic determinists, environmental determinists, and interactionists have all observed differences in the intelligence test performances of different populations of children.

Both the interpretation of group differences in intelligence measurements and the practice of testing the intelligence of schoolchildren have been topics of recurrent controversy and debate, aired in professional journals, in the popular press, and on television. In some instances, the courts have acted to curtail or halt intelligence assessment in the public schools; in others, the courts have defined what composes intelligence assessment. Debate and controversy have flourished about whether intelligence tests should be given, what they measure, and how different levels of performance attained by different populations are to be explained.

No one, however, has seen a specific thing called "intelligence." Rather, we observe differences in the ways people behave—either differences in everyday behavior in a variety of situations or differences in responses to standard stimuli or sets of stimuli; then we attribute those differences to something termed *intelligence*.

In this sense, intelligence is an inferred entity, a term or construct we use to explain differences in present behavior and to predict differences in future behavior.

We have repeatedly stressed the fact that all tests, including, therefore, intelligence tests—assess samples of behavior. Regardless of how an individual's performance on any given test is viewed and interpreted, intelligence tests—and the items on those tests—simply sample behaviors. A variety of different kinds of behavior samplings are used to assess intelligence; in most cases, the kinds of behaviors sampled reflect a test author's conception of intelligence. The behavior samples are combined in different ways by different authors, usually on the basis of the ways in which they view the concept of intelligence. In this chapter, we review the kinds of behaviors sampled by intelligence tests, with particular emphasis on the psychological demands of different test items, as a function of pupil characteristics.

● ● ● ● ● ● ● ● ● ● ● ● ● ● ● ● ● ● ● ●

Intelligence Tests as Samples of Behavior

There is a hypothetical domain of items that could be used to assess intelligence. In practice, it is impossible to administer every item in the domain to a student whose intelligence we want to assess. The dots in Figure 16.1 represent different items in the domain of behaviors that could be used to assess intelligence. No two tests evaluate identical samples of behavior; some tests overlap in the kinds of behaviors they sample, and others do not. Figure 16.1 shows that tests A and D sample different behaviors. Both tests assess some behaviors sampled by test E. None of the tests sample all the possible behaviors in the domain.

● ● ● ● **FIGURE 16.1**   Intelligence Tests as Samples of Behavior from a Larger Domain of Behaviors

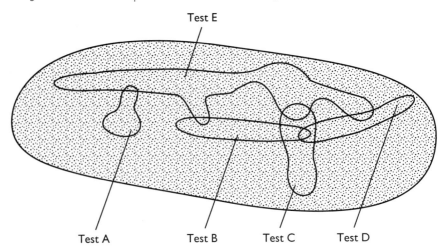

The characterization of behaviors sampled by intelligence tests is complex. Some persons have argued, for example, that intelligence tests assess a student's capacity to profit from instruction, whereas others argue that such tests assess merely what has been learned; some have characterized intelligence tests as either verbal or nonverbal; some characterize intelligence tests as either culturally biased or culturally fair. In actuality, nearly any contention regarding what intelligence tests measure can be supported. The relative merit of competing opinions, theories, and contentions is primarily a function of the interaction between the characteristics of an individual and the psychological demands of items in an intelligence test. It is also a function of the stimulus and response requirements of the items.

There are many kinds of nonverbal behavior samples. A test might require children (a) to point to objects in response to directions read by the examiner, (b) to build block towers, (c) to manipulate colored blocks in order to reproduce a design, or (d) to copy symbols or designs on paper. Similarly, there are many kinds of verbal behavior samples. We could, for example, ask students factual questions, such as "Who wrote *The Adventures of Huckleberry Finn?*" We could ask them to define words or to identify similarities and differences in words or objects. We could ask them to state actions that they would take in specific social situations or to repeat sequences of digits. Test items may be presented orally, or the test takers may have to read the items.

Similar behaviors may be assessed in different ways. In assessing vocabulary, for example, the examiner may ask pupils to define words, to name pictures, to select a synonym of a stimulus word, or to point to pictures depicting words read by the examiner. All four kinds of assessments are called "vocabulary tests," yet they sample different behaviors. The psychological demands of the items change with the ways the behavior is assessed.

In evaluating the performance of individuals on intelligence tests, teachers, administrators, counselors, and diagnostic specialists must go beyond test names and scores to look at the kinds of behaviors sampled on the test. They must be willing to question the ways test stimuli are presented, to question the response requirements, and to evaluate the psychological demands placed on the individual.

● ●

The Effect of Pupil Characteristics on Assessment of Intelligence

Acculturation is the most important characteristic to consider in evaluating performance on intelligence tests. *Acculturation* refers to an individual's particular set of background experiences and opportunities to learn in both formal and informal educational settings. This, in turn, depends on the experiences available in the person's environment (that is, culture) and the length of time the person has had to assimilate those experiences. The culture in which an individual lives and the length of time that the person has lived in that culture effectively determine the psychological demands presented by a test item. Simply knowing the kind of behavior sampled by a test is not enough, for the same test item may create different psychological demands for different people.

Suppose, for example, that we assess intelligence by asking children to tell how *hail* and *sleet* are alike. Children may fail the item for very different reasons. Mitch, for example, does not know what hail and sleet are, so he stands little chance of telling how hail and sleet are alike; he will fail the item simply because he does not know the meanings of the words. Lupita may know what hail is and what sleet is, but she fails the item because she is unable to integrate these two words into a conceptual category (precipitation). The psychological demand of the item changes as a function of the children's acculturation. For the child who has not learned the meanings of the words, the item assesses vocabulary. For the child who knows the meanings of the words, the item is a generalization task.

In considering how individuals perform on intelligence tests, we need to know how acculturation affects test performance. Items on intelligence tests range along a continuum, from items that sample fundamental psychological behaviors that are relatively unaffected by the test taker's learning history to items that sample primarily learned behavior. To determine exactly what is being assessed, we need to know the essential background of the student. Consider for a moment the following item:

> Jeff went walking in the forest. He saw a porcupine that he tried to take home for a pet. It got away from him, but when he got home, his father took him to the doctor. Why?

For a student who knows what a porcupine is, that a porcupine has quills, and that quills are sharp, the item can assess comprehension, abstract reasoning, and problem-solving skill. The student who does not know any of that information may very well fail the item. In this case, failure is due not to an inability to comprehend or solve the problem but to a deficiency in background experience.

Similarly, we could ask a child to identify the seasons of the year. The experiences available in children's environments are reflected in the way they respond to this item. Children from central Illinois, who experience four discernibly different climatic conditions, may well respond, "summer, fall, winter, and spring." Children from central Pennsylvania, who also experience four discernibly different climatic conditions but who live in an environment where hunting is prevalent, might respond, "buck season, doe season, rabbit season, and squirrel season." Within specific cultures, both responses are logical and appropriate; only one is scored as correct.

Items on intelligence tests also sample different behaviors as a function of the age of the child assessed. Age and acculturation are positively related; older children in general have had more opportunities to acquire the skills assessed by intelligence tests. The performances of 5-year-old children on an item requiring them to tell how a cardinal, a blue jay, and a swallow are alike are almost entirely a function of their knowledge of the word meanings. Most college students know the meanings of the three words; for them, the item assesses primarily their ability to identify similarities and to integrate words or objects into a conceptual category. As children get older, they have increasing opportunities to acquire the elements of the collective intelligence of a culture.

The interaction between acculturation and the behavior sampled determines the psychological demands of an intelligence-test item. For this reason, it is impossible to define exactly what intelligence tests assess. Identical test items place different psychological demands on different children. Thirteen kinds of behaviors sampled by intelligence tests are described in the next section of this chapter. For the sake of illustration, let us assume that there are only three discrete sets of background experiences, which we identify as m. (This is a very conservative estimate; there are probably many times this number in the United States alone.) To further simplify our example, let us consider only the 13 kinds of behaviors sampled by intelligence tests, identified as n, rather than the millions of items that could be used to sample each of the 13 kinds. Even with these very restrictive conditions, there are still $(mn)!/m!n!$ possible interactions between behavior samples and types of acculturation, or $(3 \times 13)!/3!13!$. (The exclamation marks are mathematical symbols for "factorial"; for example, 3! is $3 \times 2 \times 1 = 6$.) This very restrictive estimate produces more than 1.35×10^{32} interactions. No wonder there is controversy about what intelligence tests measure! They measure more things than we can conceive of, and they measure different things for different children.

Used appropriately, intelligence tests can provide information that can lead to the enhancement of both individual opportunity and protection of the rights of students. Used inappropriately, they can restrict opportunity and rights. Chapters 17 and 18 review commonly used individually administered and group-administered intelligence tests, with particular reference to the kinds of behaviors sampled by those tests and to their technical adequacy.

Behaviors Sampled by Intelligence Tests

Regardless of the interpretation of measured intelligence, it is a fact that intelligence tests simply sample behaviors. This section describes the kinds of behaviors sampled, including discrimination, generalization, motor behavior, general knowledge, vocabulary, induction, comprehension, sequencing, detail recognition, analogical reasoning, pattern completion, abstract reasoning, and memory.

Discrimination

Intelligence-test items that sample skill in discrimination usually present a variety of stimuli and ask the student to find the one that differs from all the others. Figural, symbolic, or semantic discrimination may be assessed. Figure 16.2 illustrates items assessing discrimination: Items a and b assess discrimination of figures; items c and d assess symbolic discrimination; items e and f assess semantic discrimination. In each case, the student must identify the item that differs from the others. The psychological demand of the items differs, however, depending on the student's age and particular set of background experiences.

● ● ● **FIGURE 16.2**   Items That Assess Figural, Symbolic, and Semantic Discrimination

Figural Discrimination

a. ● ● ▲ ●

b.

Symbolic Discrimination

c.   **4**   **A**   **Q**   **W**

d.

Semantic Discrimination

e.	elephant	horse	monkey	truck
f.	Hispanic	French	Arabian	Germanic

Generalization

Items assessing generalization present a stimulus and ask the student to identify which of several response possibilities goes with the stimulus. Again, the content of the items may be figural, symbolic, or semantic; the difficulty may range from simple matching to a more difficult type of classification. Figure 16.3 illustrates several items assessing generalization. In each case, the student is given a stimulus element and is required to identify the one that is like it or that goes with it.

Motor Behavior

Many items on intelligence tests require a motor response. The intellectual level of very young children, for example, is often assessed by items requiring them to throw objects, walk, follow moving objects with their eyes, demonstrate a pincer grasp in picking up objects, build block towers, and place geometric forms in a recessed-form board. Most motor items at higher age levels are actually visual-motor items. The student may be required to copy geometric designs, trace paths through a maze, or reconstruct designs from memory. Obviously, because motor responses can be required for items assessing understanding and conceptualization, many items assess motor behavior at the same time that they assess other behaviors.

● ● ● **FIGURE 16.3** Items That Assess Figural, Symbolic, and Semantic Generalization

Figural Generalization

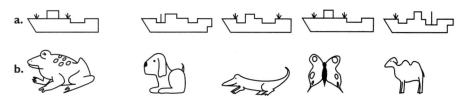

a.

b.

Symbolic Generalization

c.	J	H	8	6	9
d.	81	21	23	26	25

Semantic Generalization

e.	tree	car	man	horse	walk
f.	salvia	flashlight	frog	tulip	banana

General Knowledge

Items on intelligence tests sometimes require a student to answer specific factual questions, such as, "In what direction would you travel if you were to go from Poland to Argentina?" and "What is the cube root of 8?" Essentially, such items are like the kinds of items in achievement tests; they assess primarily what has been learned.

Vocabulary

Many different kinds of test items are used to assess vocabulary. In some cases, the student must name pictures, and in others, she or he must point to objects in response to words read by the examiner. Some vocabulary items require the student to produce oral definitions of words, whereas others call for reading a definition and selecting one of several words to match the definition. Some tests score a student's definitions of words as simply pass or fail; others use a weighted scoring system to reflect the degree of abstraction used in defining words. The Wechsler Intelligence Scale for Children–III, for example, assigns 0 points to incorrect definitions, 1 point to definitions that are descriptive (an orange is round) or functional (an orange is to eat), and 2 points to more abstract definitions (an orange is a citrus fruit).

Induction

Induction items present a series of examples and require the student to induce a governing principle. For example, the student is given a magnet and several different cloth, wooden, and metal objects and is asked to try to pick up the objects with the magnet. After several trials, the student is asked to state a rule or principle about the kinds of objects that magnets can pick up.

Comprehension

There are three kinds of items used to assess comprehension: items related to directions, to printed material, and to societal customs and mores. In some instances, the examiner presents a specific situation and asks what actions the student would take (for example, "What would you do if you saw a train approaching a washed-out bridge?"). In other cases, the examiner reads paragraphs to a student and then asks specific questions about the content of the paragraphs. In still other instances, the student is asked questions about social mores, such as, "Why should we keep promises?"

Sequencing

Items assessing sequencing consist of a series of stimuli that have a progressive relationship among them. The student must identify a response that continues the relationship. Four sequencing items are illustrated in Figure 16.4.

Detail Recognition

In general, not many tests or test items assess detail recognition. Those that do evaluate the completeness and detail with which a student solves problems. For example,

● ● ● **FIGURE 16.4**   Items That Assess Sequencing Skill

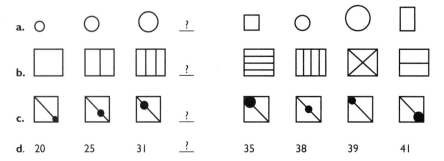

certain drawing tests, such as the Goodenough–Harris Draw-A-Person Test, evaluate a student's drawing of a person on the basis of inclusion of detail. The more details in a student's drawing, the more credit the student earns. In other instances, items require a student to count the blocks in pictured piles of blocks in which some of the blocks are not directly visible, to copy geometric designs, or to identify missing parts in pictures. To do so correctly, the student must attend to detail in the stimulus drawings and must reflect this attention to detail in making responses.

Analogical Reasoning

"A is to B as C is to ____" is the usual form for analogies. Element A is related to element B. The student must identify the response having the same relationship to element C as B has to A. Figure 16.5 illustrates several different analogy items.

Pattern Completion

Some tests and test items require a student to select from several possibilities the missing part of a pattern or matrix. Figures 16.6 and 16.7 (p. 310) illustrate two different completion items. The item in Figure 16.6 requires identification of a missing part in a pattern. The item in Figure 16.7 calls for identification of the response that completes the matrix by continuing the horizontal, vertical, and diagonal sequences.

Abstract Reasoning

A variety of items on intelligence tests sample abstract reasoning ability. The Stanford–Binet Intelligence Scale, for example, presents absurd verbal statements and pictures and asks the student to identify the absurdity. It also includes a series of proverbs, the essential meanings of which the student must state. In the Stanford–Binet and other scales, arithmetic-reasoning problems are often thought to assess abstract reasoning.

● ● ● ● **FIGURE 16.5**   Analogy Items

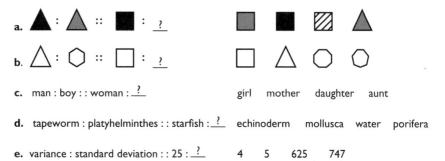

● ● ● **FIGURE 16.6**   A Pattern-Completion Item

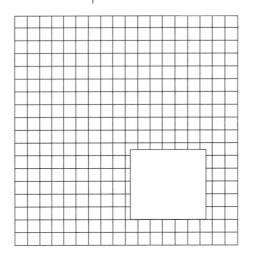

● ● ● **FIGURE 16.7**   A Matrix-Completion Item

a.   b.   c.   d.

Coping with Dilemmas in Current Practice

The practice of assessing children's intelligence is currently marked by controversy. However, much of that controversy could be set aside if intelligence tests were viewed appropriately. Intelligence tests simply assess samples of behavior, and different intelligence tests sample different behaviors. For that reason, it is wrong to speak of a person's IQ. Instead, we can refer only to a person's IQ on a specific test. An IQ on the Stanford–Binet IV Intelligence Scale is not derived from the same samples of behaviors as an IQ on any other intelligence test. Because the behavior samples are different for different tests, educators and others must always ask,

"IQ on what test?" It is helpful to understand that, for the most part, the particular kinds of items or subtests found on an intelligence test are a matter of the way in which a test author defines intelligence and thinks about the kinds of items and subtests that assess it.

The same test may make different psychological demands on various test takers, depending on their ages and acculturation. Test results mean different things for different students. It is imperative that we be especially aware of the relationship between a person's acculturation and the acculturation of the norm group with which that person is compared.

Memory

Several different kinds of tasks assess memory: repetition of sequences of digits presented orally, reproduction of geometric designs from memory, verbatim repetition of sentences, and reconstruction of the essential meaning of paragraphs or stories. Simply saying that an item assesses memory is too simplistic. We need to ask, Memory for what? The psychological demand of a memory task changes in relation to both the method of assessment and the meaningfulness of the material to be recalled.

Summary

Many different kinds of behaviors are sampled by intelligence tests; this chapter has described 13 kinds: discrimination, generalization, motor behavior, general knowledge, vocabulary, induction, comprehension, sequencing, detail recognition, analogical reasoning, abstract reasoning, memory, and pattern completion.

Questions for Chapter Review and Thought

1. Describe at least three kinds of behaviors sampled by intelligence tests.

2. Using the categorization of behavior samplings described in this chapter, identify the kind or kinds of behaviors sampled by the following test items.

    a. How many legs does an octopus have?

    b. In what way are *first* and *last* alike?

    c. Find the one that is different: (1) table (2) bed (3) pillow (4) chair

    d. Who wrote *Macbeth?*

    e. Window is to sill as door is to ____. (1) knob (2) entrance (3) threshold (4) pane

    f. Define *hieroglyphic.*

    g. Identify the one that comes next: 3, 6, 9, ____. (1) 12 (2) 11 (3) 18 (4) 15

3. What role does acculturation play in the assessment of intelligence? How is acculturation related to age?

4. Compare and contrast the behaviors of sequencing, pattern completion, and memory.

Resources for Further Investigation

Project

Examine your own state's special-education regulations and guidelines, or examine criteria used in a local school district, to determine whether specific intelligence tests are required or recommended. If specific tests are required or recommended, are data provided on the technical adequacy of those tests?

Print Resources

Carroll, J. B., & Horn, J. L. (1981). On the scientific basis of ability testing. *American Psychologist, 36,* 1012–1020.

Flanagan, D. P., Genshaft, J. L., & Harrison, P. L. (1997). *Contemporary intellectual assessment: Theories, tests, and issues.* New York: Guilford Press.

Keith, T. Z. (1994). Intelligence *is* important, intelligence *is* complex. *School Psychology Quarterly, 9,* 209–221.

Technology Resources

APA News Release: APA Task Force Examines the Knowns and Unknowns of Intelligence

http://www.apa.org/releases/intell.html

This news release includes the results of the APA task force that examined the concept of intelligence and how it can be measured.

Traditional Intelligence in Education

http://k12.cnidr.org:90/edref.mi.histschl.html

The theory of multiple intelligences is presented as an alternative view of traditional intelligence. Look here to find out more information about the theory and its implications for education.

chapter

17

Assessment of Intelligence:
Individual Tests

*I*n Chapter 16, we discussed the various kinds of behaviors sampled by intelligence tests and indicated that different tests sample different behaviors. In this chapter, we review the most commonly used individually administered intelligence tests, with special reference to the kinds of behaviors they sample and to their technical adequacy.

Although some individual intelligence tests may be appropriately administered by teachers, counselors, or other specialists, the intelligence tests on which school personnel rely most heavily must be given by psychologists. All intelligence tests yield scores of relative standing (and some still provide developmental scores) that provide information about a test taker's performance relative to the performances of other similar test takers. This comparative information is usually critical in reaching a decision about a student's eligibility for special educational services. However, other aspects of a test taker's performance (for example, what are the psychological implications of a low score?) as well as interpretations of a student's behavior during testing require much greater understanding of cognitive development if the interpretations are to be appropriate. As mentioned previously, one of the basic assumptions underlying psychoeducational assessment is that the person who uses a test should be adequately trained to administer, score, and interpret it. The correct administration, scoring, and interpretation of individual intelligence tests is complex. Despite the claims of test developers, we believe that intelligence tests should be used only by licensed or certified psychologists who have received specific training in their use.

In this chapter, we review commonly used measures of global intelligence: the Stanford-Binet Intelligence Scale–IV, the four Wechsler scales, the Detroit Tests of Learning Aptitude–4, and the Cognitive Assessment System. In general, these tests sample the 13 different kinds of behavior described in Chapter 16. We conclude the chapter with a discussion of more specialized tests: the Comprehensive Test of Nonverbal Intelligence, the Leiter International Performance Scale–Revised, the Test of Nonverbal Intelligence–3, the Universal Nonverbal Intelligence Test, the Naglieri Nonverbal Ability Test, and the Peabody Picture Vocabulary Test–Revised. Two other frequently used measure of global intelligence (that is, the Woodcock Johnson Psycho-educational Battery–Revised and the Kaufman Assessment Battery for Children) are parts of diagnostic systems and are reviewed in Chapter 27.

In previous editions of *Assessment,* other individually administered intelligence tests were also reviewed: the McCarthy Scales of Children's Abilities, the Quick Test and the Full-Range Picture Vocabulary Test, the Pictorial Test of Intelligence, the Blind Learning Aptitude Test, the Detroit Tests of Learning Aptitude–Primary 2, the Slosson Intelligence Test, and the Nebraska Test of Learning Aptitude. The norms for most of these tests are now so old that use of the tests should be discouraged.

● ●

Why Do We Give Individual Intelligence Tests?

Individually administered intelligence tests are most frequently used for making exceptionality, eligibility, and educational-placement decisions. State special-education eligibility guidelines and criteria typically specify that the collection of data about intellectual functioning must be included in the decision-making process for eligibility and placement decisions and that these data must come from individual intellectual evaluation by a certified school psychologist.

General Intelligence Tests

Stanford–Binet Intelligence Scale, Fourth Edition (SB)

The fourth edition of the Stanford–Binet (SB; Thorndike, Hagen, & Sattler, 1985) is the latest version of the scale originally developed by Alfred Binet in 1905 and revised for American children by Terman and Merrill (1916, 1937). The 1960 version of the scale combined the best items from earlier forms into one form (L–M) and provided new norms with deviation IQs. Although the scale was renormed for the 1972 normative edition (Terman & Merrill, 1973), this edition was not truly a revision because the 1960 items were used.

The fourth edition maintains some continuity with the past but also brings the SB up to date. It eliminates age scores because—even though the concept of mental age played an important role in earlier editions of the scale—age scales have several drawbacks. Like its predecessors, the new SB is an individually administered, norm-referenced measure of general intelligence that can be given to persons between the ages of 2 and 23 years.

Fifteen subtests are grouped into four areas: verbal reasoning, quantitative reasoning, abstract/visual reasoning, and short-term memory. The authors retained as many types of items from the 1960 version as could be fit into one of these four areas. Because of the extended range of ages, not all test takers are given all subtests; a complete battery requires from 8 to 13 subtests. Nevertheless, under certain circumstances (for screening, the identification of gifted students, or the assessment of students with school-learning difficulties), various abbreviated test batteries may be used. These subtests are listed here, according to the behavior sampled.

Verbal Reasoning

Vocabulary   There are 46 vocabulary items. The first 14 use a picture vocabulary format. The remainder are presented orally and visually (on a printed form) and are answered orally.

Comprehension   The 42 comprehension items require a test taker to explain why something is done or what should be done (for example, the sample items are "Why do buildings have fire escapes?" and "Why should lawyers be licensed?").

Absurdities   This 32-item subtest requires a test taker to explain why the pictures presented are absurd (for example, a picture of a fish being walked).

Verbal Relations   The test taker is presented with four concepts and must explain in what way three of them are alike and the fourth is different. (For example, in response to the sample item "Jim, Bob, Kate, not John," the test taker is expected to answer that the first three names are nicknames, or informal names, and the last is not.)

Quantitative Reasoning

Quantitative   This subtest assesses computation skills using 48 problems in two formats. The first 12 questions, designed for youngsters, require the test taker to use a counting tray and blocks to answer mathematical questions (for example, questions about counting). Questions geared to older individuals take the form of pictures or written questions.

Number Series   The test taker is presented with a series of numbers and is expected to induce the rule that governs the series. (For example, a student presented with the sample sequence 4, 9, 16, 25, 36, _____ is expected to complete the series with 49, because $4 = 2^2$, $9 = 3^2$, $16 = 4^2$, $25 = 5^2$, $36 = 6^2$, and $49 = 7^2$.) There are 26 problems in this subtest.

Equation Building   The test taker is presented with a sequence of numbers and mathematical symbols and is instructed to arrange them in a way that forms a valid equation. (For example, a student given the sample series 2, 2, 8, 4, $\times$, $+$, $=$ is expected to reformulate the sequence as $2 \times 2 + 4 = 8$.) There are 18 equations.

Abstract/Visual Reasoning

Pattern Analysis   Because the SB covers a wide range of ages, two sets of materials are used in this subtest. A three-hole form board is used with very young children, who must place geometric forms in the correct holes or must combine parts to make the geometric forms and then place them in the correct holes. Older individuals are given up to nine cubes with various geometric patterns; they are then shown a stimulus design and asked to reproduce it with the cubes. Credit is awarded on the basis of accuracy and completion within the time limits.

Copying   The 28 items on this subtest consist of designs of increasing complexity to be copied by the test taker. The type of copying required depends on the level of the test. At the lower levels, the designs are copied with blocks. At the higher levels, the designs are drawn with a pencil.

Matrices   Two types of problems are given in this subtest. The first 22 problems, designed for younger children, are multiple-choice matrix-completion problems. The first 12 involve 2×2 matrices; the next 10 involve 3×3 matrices. The last four problems, for older children, require the test taker to complete the matrices by writing the correct responses. The format of each of these problems is the same: a 3×3 matrix in which each of the nine stimuli is actually a smaller 3×3 matrix.

Paper Folding and Cutting   This is an 18-item, multiple-choice subtest that consists of pictures. Each item has two parts: an item stem and some response options. The item stem shows how a rectangular sheet of paper is folded and cut; the response options include one that correctly shows what the paper would look like after it had been cut and unfolded. The most difficult item has three folds and one area cut out.

Short-Term Memory

Bead Memory   Beads of different colors (red, white, blue) and shapes (flat, round, spherical, conical, cylindrical) are used in this subtest. The types of items used depend on the level at which testing occurs. On lower-level items, the subject is required to look at one bead for two seconds (or two beads for three seconds) and then correctly identify the bead (or beads) on a card containing assorted pictures of beads. At higher levels, the subject looks for five seconds at a picture of colored beads of different shapes strung on a stick and then must reproduce the design with his or her own beads and stick.

Memory for Sentences   The examiner reads a sentence, and the test taker must repeat that sentence verbatim. The 42 sentences range from simple (of the type, "Marv walked the cat") to complex (of the type, "Books and reading were now a very important part of Rosemary's everyday plans, opening new worlds and bringing new adventures her way").

Memory for Digits   After listening to a sequence of digits, the test taker must repeat it. Half of the sequences are to be repeated backward.

Memory for Objects   This subtest assesses visual sequential memory with 14 items. After showing a picture of a common object for one second and then another picture of a different object for one second, the examiner shows a picture containing several objects, including the two that were shown previously. The test taker must select the previously shown pictures in the order in which they were shown. At the highest level, a subject may be shown eight objects and asked to recall them in order.

Scores

Raw scores for each subtest are converted to standard age scores (SAS). These scores have a mean of 50 and a standard deviation of 8. Subtest scores are combined into area scores and an overall composite score, each with a mean of 100 and a standard deviation of 16. Extensive tables are provided for these conversions. The procedures for extrapolating scores at the extremes are carefully reported and appear appropriate.

Norms

The normative sample was selected on the basis of five variables: age, sex, ethnicity (white, black, Hispanic, and Asian/Pacific Islander), geographic region, and community size. Extensive tables provided in the technical manual indicate reasonably good correspondence on each of these variables. When an appropriate number of subjects with particular characteristics could not be located, those who were tested were weighted so as to count for more than one; similarly, when there were too many subjects with a particular characteristic, each was weighted so as to count for less than one.

Reliability

Internal-consistency (KR-20), SEMs, and stability coefficients are reported for each subtest, for each area, and for the composite at each age level. As would be expected, subtest reliabilities are lower than composite reliabilities. The test authors recommend that the composite score "be used as the primary source of information for making decisions" (Thorndike, Hagen, & Sattler, 1986, p. 38). All KR-20s for the SAS composites are excellent; they range from a low of .95 to a high of .99. Test–retest data were available for two groups of children: 5-year-olds ($n = 57$) and 8-year-olds ($n = 55$). Stability coefficients for these two groups were .91 and .90.

KR-20s for the areas are based on different numbers of subtests. The more subtests, the higher the reliability. For abstract reasoning, all reliabilities exceed .90, except when two subtests are used at ages 2 and 3 years. For quantitative reasoning, internal consistencies based on one subtest are all lower than .90; those based on two or more subtests are all higher than .90, with the exception of those for 7-year-olds when a two-test composite is used. For short-term memory, all area scores have reliabilities exceeding .90 when three or four subtests are used. When only two subtests are used, 9 of the 17 age groups have reliabilities for the short-term memory area in the high .80s; the rest are in the low .90s. Stabilities for areas ranged from a low of .51 (quantitative reasoning at age 5 years) to a high of .88 (verbal reasoning, also at age 5).

Validity

The authors explain the SB within the context of current theoretical formulations about intelligence, justifying the development of a scale that assesses g, a general factor. The primary validity of interest for an intelligence scale is its construct validity. For the new SB, construct validity was established by conducting factor analyses to confirm a g factor and factors for each of the areas. Although g held up across ages, the factor structure varied for different age groups. For example, the quantitative factor did not emerge until after age 11 years.

Several concurrent validity studies were also conducted with the new SB. In one study, using a sample of children between about 2 and 10 years of age, the old SB (form L–M) correlated with the new composite IQ ($r = .81$). In another study, using a sample of children between about 6 and 13 years of age, the Wechsler Intelligence Scale for Children–Revised, Full Scale IQ was highly correlated with the SB composite IQ ($r = .83$). The correlation of the new SB was .80 with the Wechsler Preschool and Primary Scale of Intelligence and .91 with the Wechsler Adult Intelligence Scale–Revised. For a sample of children (mean age = 7-0, standard deviation = 2-5), the correlation of the SB with the Mental Processing Composite of the Kaufman Assessment Battery for Children was .89.

Finally, eight studies examined the performance of previously identified gifted, learning disabled, and mentally retarded students on the SB. These studies are difficult to interpret because criteria vary dramatically from state to state. No data are presented to indicate the degree of correspondence between decisions based on the new SB and the original decisions based on other devices. As would be expected, students classified as gifted received higher than average composite IQs (mean composite IQ = 123.3, S = 11.2); students classified as learning disabled received lower than average composite IQs (mean composite IQ = 85.1, S = 14.6); and students classified as mentally retarded received the lowest composite IQs (mean composite IQ = 54.9, S = 16.2).

Summary

The fourth edition of the Stanford–Binet Intelligence Scale is a marked improvement over previous editions. The behavior sample is psychologically interesting, and the materials are appealing. Not only does the SB provide the technical data needed to evaluate the adequacy of its reliability and norms, but the data indicate a well-normed and highly reliable device. There is also ample evidence of content and concurrent validity and some evidence of construct validity. It is unclear how effective the new SB will be in identifying students who are exceptional. It is becoming clear, however, that the SB requires significantly more time to administer than do other individually administered tests of intelligence.

The Wechsler Scales (WAIS-III, WISC-III, WPPSI-R, WASI)

Four different measures of intelligence have been constructed by David Wechsler. Wechsler summarized his views on the concept of intelligence by stating that "intelligence is the overall capacity of an individual to understand and cope with the world around him" (Wechsler, 1974, p. 5). The definition is consistent with his original one, in which he stated that intelligence is "the capacity of the individual to act purposefully, to think rationally, and to deal effectively with his or her environment" (1974, p. 3). Wechsler (1974, p. 5) stated that his definition of intelligence differs from the conceptions of others in two important respects:

1. It conceives of intelligence as an overall or global entity—that is, a multidetermined and multifaceted entity rather than an independent, uniquely defined trait.

2. It avoids singling out any ability (e.g., abstract reasoning), however esteemed as crucial or overwhelmingly important. In particular, it avoids equating general intelligence with intellectual ability.

The original Wechsler scale, the Wechsler-Bellevue Intelligence Scale (Wechsler, 1939), designed to assess the intelligence of adults, was revised in 1955 and named the "Wechsler Adult Intelligence Scale." Now in its third edition, the scale is typically referred to as the WAIS-III. In 1949, Wechsler developed the Wechsler Intelligence Scale for Children (WISC). This scale was revised and restandardized in 1974 and again in

1991. Its present form, the Wechsler Intelligence Scale for Children–III (WISC-III), was developed by personnel at the Psychological Corporation. In 1967, Wechsler developed a downward extension of the WISC, the Wechsler Preschool and Primary Scale of Intelligence (WPPSI). The WPPSI was revised and restandardized in 1989 and is now called the WPPSI-R. In 1999, personnel at the Psychological Corporation developed the Wechsler Abbreviated Scale of Intelligence (WASI) to provide a "short and reliable measure of intelligence in clinical, psychoeducational, and research settings" (Psychological Corporation, 1999, p. 1). The WASI is composed of four subtests that are similar to subtests on both the WISC-III and WAIS-III.

Although the four Wechsler scales are similar in form and content, they are distinct scales. The WAIS-III is designed for use with individuals over 16 years of age, the WISC-III is designed to assess the intelligence of persons 6 through 16 years of age, the WASI is designed for persons between 6 and 89, and the WPPSI-R is used with children between 3 and 7 years of age. All four scales include verbal and performance subtests, as shown in Table 17.1.

Although the Wechsler scales differ in terms of age-level appropriateness, they sample similar behaviors. Descriptions of the behaviors sampled by each of the verbal and performance subtests follow; differences in format among the three Wechsler scales are noted where appropriate.

Verbal Subtests

Information   This subtest assesses ability to answer specific factual questions. The content is learned; it consists of information that a person

TABLE 17.1 ● Subtests of the Four Wechsler Scales

	WAIS-III	WISC-III	WPPSI-R	WASI
Verbal subtests				
Information	X	X	X	—
Comprehension	X	X	X	—
Similarities	X	X	X	X
Arithmetic	X	X	X	—
Vocabulary	X	X	X	X
Digit Span	X	S[b]	—	—
Sentences	—	—	S	—
Letter–Number Sequencing	I[c]	—	—	—
Performance subtests				
Picture Completion	X	X	X	—
Picture Arrangement	X	X	—	—
Block Design	X	X	X	X
Object Assembly	S	X	X	—
Coding[a]	X	X	X	—
Symbol Search	I	S	—	—
Mazes	—	S	X	—
Geometric Design	—	—	X	—
Matrix Reasoning	X	—	—	X

[a] This subtest is called Digit Symbol on the WAIS-III and Animal Pegs on the WPPSI-R.
[b] S indicates a supplemental subtest.
[c] I indicates a subtest that is not required to calculate IQ but is required for other indexes.

is expected to have acquired in both formal and informal educational settings. The examinee is asked questions such as, "Which fast food franchise is represented by the symbol of golden arches?"

Comprehension   This subtest assesses ability to comprehend verbal directions or to understand specific customs and mores. The examinee is asked questions such as, "Why is it important to wear boots after a large snowfall?"

Similarities   This subtest requires identification of similarities or commonalities in superficially unrelated verbal stimuli.

Arithmetic   This subtest assesses ability to solve problems requiring the application of arithmetic operations. Individual items range from relatively simple counting tasks on the WPPSI to conceptually and computationally more difficult problems on the WISC-III and the WAIS-III.

Vocabulary   Items on this subtest assess ability to define words. For the WPPSI-R, the Vocabulary subtest is a two-part test. At the lower age levels, children are required to name pictured objects. At higher age levels, the child defines words.

Digit Span   This subtest assesses immediate recall of orally presented digits. There is no Digit Span subtest for the WPPSI-R.

Sentences   This subtest is included only in the WPPSI-R. It assesses ability to repeat sentences verbatim.

Letter–Number Sequencing   This WAIS-III subtest assesses a person's ability to sequence numbers and letters that are mixed together and presented orally. For example, the examiner might say, "Y 9 H 4." The examinee must sort the numbers and letters and respond, "4 9 H Y." This subtest is required for index scores but optional for IQs.

Performance Subtests

Picture Completion   This subtest assesses the ability to identify missing parts in pictures.

Picture Arrangement   This subtest assesses comprehension, sequencing, and identification of relationships by requiring a person to place pictures in sequence to produce a logically correct story.

Block Design   This subtest assesses ability to manipulate blocks in order to reproduce a stimulus design that is presented visually.

Object Assembly   This subtest assesses ability to place disjointed puzzle pieces together to form complete objects. The WPPSI-R now includes an Object Assembly subtest; the subtest was not included in the WPPSI.

Coding   This subtest assesses the ability to associate certain symbols with others and to copy them onto paper. On the WAIS-III, this subtest is called "Digit Symbol–Coding" and has a second (optional) part called "Digit Symbol–Incidental Learning." This part of the subtest is administered immediately after the Digit Symbol–Coding subtest and assesses the examinee's incidental learning of the association between symbols. One part of the subtest assesses the examinee's ability to write the symbols when the number is presented; the second part assesses the examinee's ability to recall the symbols without the number being present. The WPPSI-R uses the Animal Pegs subtest in place of Coding; instead of copying symbols on paper, a child must match colored cubes to specific animals.

Symbol Search   This supplementary subtest appears on only the WISC-III and WAIS-III, and it can be used only to substitute for the Coding subtest. The test consists of a series of paired groups of symbols, each pair including a target group and a search group. The child scans the two groups and indicates whether the target symbol appears in the search group.

Mazes   This subtest assesses the ability to trace a path through progressively more difficult mazes.

Geometric Design   This subtest appears on only the WPPSI-R. Two distinct types of tasks are included. The first section is a visual-recognition task. The child looks at a simple design and, with the stimulus in full view, picks one like it from a response array. The remaining items require the child to copy a geometric design by drawing.

Matrix Reasoning   This WAIS-III performance subtest assesses a person's ability to solve pattern-completion, classification, analogy, and serial-reasoning problems. The stimuli consist of geometric figures and designs.

Scores

Raw scores obtained on the four Wechsler scales are transformed to scaled scores with a mean of 10 and a standard deviation of 3. The scaled scores for verbal subtests, performance subtests, and all subtests combined are added and then transformed to obtain Verbal (VIQ), Performance (PIQ), and Full-Scale (FSIQ) IQs. IQs for the Wechsler scales are deviation IQs with a mean of 100 and a standard deviation of 15. For the WPPSI-R and the WISC-III, but not for the WAIS-III and WASI, raw scores may be transformed to test ages. *Test ages* represent the average performance on each of the subtests by individuals of specific ages. Four factor scores may be obtained for the WISC-III: Verbal Comprehension, Perceptual Organization, Freedom from Distractibility, and Processing Speed.

The Wechsler intelligence scales employ a differential scoring system for some of the subtests. Responses for the Information, Digit Span, Sentences, Picture Completion, and Geometric Design subtests are scored pass–fail. A weighted scoring system is used for the Comprehension, Similarities, and Vocabulary subtests. Incorrect responses receive a score of 0, lower-level or lower-quality responses are assigned a score of 1, and more abstract responses are assigned a score of 2. The remainder of the subtests are timed. Individuals who complete the tasks in relatively short periods of time receive more credit. These differential weightings of responses must be given special consideration, especially when the timed tests are used with

children who demonstrate motor impairments that interfere with the speed of response.

Norms

All three Wechsler intelligence scales were standardized by selecting stratified samples and having individual examiners around the country administer the tests to specified kinds of individuals.

The WAIS-III was standardized on 2,450 adults between 16 and 89 years of age. This age range was divided into 13 groups: 16–17, 18–19, 20–24, 25–29, 30–34, 35–44, 45–54, 55–64, 65–69, 70–74, 75–79, 80–84, and 85–89. Except for the 85–89 group, which had 100 subjects, and the 80–84 group, which had 150 subjects, all groups had 200 participants. The sample contains equal numbers of men and women until age 64; after 64, more women were included so that the sample would correspond to the U.S. Census. The standardization sample appears representative in terms of race, educational level, and geographic region— variables used to stratify the sample.

The WISC-III was standardized on 2,200 children ages $6\frac{1}{2}$ to $16\frac{1}{2}$. The standardization group was stratified on the basis of age, race/ethnicity, geographic region, and parent education (used as a measure of socioeconomic status), according to 1988 U.S. Census information. Extensive tables in the manual are used to compare sample data with census data. Although the sample looks representative overall, there are some matters of concern. The sample is stratified, but insufficient attention was paid to cross-tabulations. For example, although 51 percent of the European American group had some college education, 27.9 percent of the African American group and 19.9 percent of the Hispanic group had some college education. The majority of the European and African American samples came from the north central and the south regions of the country, whereas the majority of the Hispanic and other groups came from the south and the west of the United States.

The WPPSI-R was administered to more than 2,100 children, including 1,700 children used for norming and an oversample of 400 minority children used to investigate item bias. The sample was stratified by age, and within age, it was stratified on the basis of sex, geographic region, ethnicity, and parental education and occupation. The standardization sample is made up of 100 boys and 100 girls at each age, in half-year age intervals. Tables in the manual show the match of proportions in the standardization sample to proportions in 1986 census data. The sample is representative of the U.S. population of children ages 3 to 7 years.

The WASI was standardized on 2,245 children and adults between the ages of 6 and 89 years. There are 50 males and 50 females in each of the 11 age groups for children (that is, 6, 7, . . . 15, 16); there are also 50 males and 50 females in 9 multiage groups for adults (that is, 17–19, 20–24, 25–29, 30–34, 35–44, 45–54, 55–64, 65–69, and 70–74). For the three oldest age ranges (that is, 75–79, 80–84, and 85–89), there are more women than men in the normative samples. The sample appears to approximate the 1997 census data better for ethnicity than for education.

Reliability

Because the Digit Symbol–Coding and Symbol Search subtests are timed, reliability was estimated using test–retest calculations. These reliability estimates are incompletely reported for the WISC-III and WAIS-III. All other reliability estimates for the four scales use split-half reliability coefficients corrected by the Spearman–Brown formula. All reliability estimates differ by subtests and age level. Ranges of reliability for the four scales are listed in Table 17.2.

On the WAIS-III, verbal subtest reliabilities range from .77 to .95; performance subtest reliabilities range from .50 to .94. Reliabilities for all IQs (i.e., VIQ, PIQ, and FSIQ) exceed .90. On the WISC-III, verbal subtest reliabilities range from .71 to .91, while performance subtest reliabilities range from .61 to .92. The reliabilities for the VIQ and FSIQ all exceeded .90, while the reliabilities of the PIQ range from .80 to .94. On the WPPSI-R, verbal subtest reliabilities range from .54 to .90,

and the performance subtest reliabilities range from .54 to .89. All estimates are less than .90 except Information at ages 3 and 4–5 and Picture Completion at age 4–5; they are especially low at age 7. The reliabilities of the FSIQ all equal or exceed .90. The reliabilities of the VIQ range from .86 to .96, while the reliabilities of the PIQ range from .85 to .93. Finally, the reliabilities of the two verbal subtests on the WASI range from .86 to .98, and reliability estimates on the performance subtests range from .88 to .98. All reliability estimates for the three IQs exceed .90. The overall pattern is for subtests in general to lack sufficient reliability for use in making important educational decisions. The VIQ and PIQ on the WISC-III and WPPSI-R may or may not be sufficiently reliable to use in making important educational decisions. The FSIQ and the VIQ and PIQ on the WAIS-Ill and WASI are always reliable enough to use in making important educational decisions.

Stability estimates for the WISC-III are reported at three age levels for all subtests and range from .54 to .89. Stability estimates for the WAIS-III are reported for four age groups (i.e., 16–29, 30–54, 55–74, and 75–89) and range from .48 to .94 for individual subtests. All obtained stabilities for the VIQ and FSIQ exceed .90; half the obtained stabilities for the PIQ exceed .90. Stability estimates for the WASI are reported for two groups of children (that is, 6–11 and 12–16) and two groups of adults (that is, 17–54 and 55–89). Only the obtained stabilities of the FSIQ using all four subtests exceeded .90 for both groups of children and both groups of adults.

Validity

The WAIS-III contains more evidence of validity than its predecessors. To ensure content validity, the authors reviewed the literature on previous editions, and consultants reviewed the content of WAIS-R items and new items that were proposed. Criterion-related validity was examined in several ways. Scores from the WAIS-III were correlated with scores from the WAIS-R and WISC-III. Not surprisingly, because there is substantial overlap in

TABLE 17.2 ● Split-Half Reliabilities for Subtests of the Four Wechsler Scales[a]

	WAIS-III	WISC-III	WPPSI-R	WASI
Verbal subtests				
Information	89–93	73–88	62–90	—
Comprehension	79–87	72–85	59–88	—
Similarities	81–89	74–84	54–89	86–96
Arithmetic	77–91	71–82	66–81	—
Vocabulary	90–95	79–91	74–87	90–98
Digit Span	84–93	79–91	—	—
Sentences	—	—	73–88	—
Letter–Number Sequencing	75–88	—	—	—
Performance subtests				
Picture Completion	76–88	72–84	72–89	
Picture Arrangement	66–81	70–84	—	
Block Design	76–90	77–92	79–88	90–94
Object Assembly	50–78	65–76	54–70	—
Coding	81–87	70–90	58	—
Symbol Search	74–82	—	—	—
Mazes	—	61–80	65–85	—
Geometric Design	—	—	68–86	—
Matrix Reasoning	84–94	—	—	88–96
Verbal IQ	96–98	92–96	86–96	92–98
Performance IQ	93–96	80–94	85–93	92–97
Full Scale IQ	97–98	94–97	90–97	95–98

[a] Decimals omitted.

content, scores were highly correlated. WAIS-III scores were also correlated with scores on the Raven's Standard Progressive Matrices and the fourth edition of the Stanford–Binet Intelligence Scale. Finally, WAIS-III scores were correlated with scores on the Wechsler Individual Achievement Test (WIAT). The obtained correlations support the validity of the WAIS-III. Limited evidence of construct validity comes from factor-analytic studies and correlations with scales measuring attention and concentration, memory, language, motor speed and fine motor dexterity, spatial processing, and problem solving.

Most of the information presented in the WISC-III manual in support of the validity of the test consists of information on the validity of the WISC-R. The two measures are not the same. The authors do present evidence for convergent and discriminant validity: They show that the

verbal subtests correlate more highly with one another than with the performance subtests, and that the performance subtests correlate more highly with one another than with the verbal subtests. Evidence that the WISC-III correlates highly with the WISC-R is used as evidence in support of the contention that the two tests are measuring the same constructs. Finally, the WISC-III was correlated with the Otis–Lennon School Ability Test. Correlation of the full-scale WISC-III IQ and the Otis–Lennon IQ was .73. A study of correlation of the WISC-III and the Differential Ability Scales (Elliott, 1990) is reported. The sample consisted only of 27 children ages 7 to 17 years. Moderate to high correlations (.70s to .80s) are reported.

Evidence for the validity of the WPPSI-R is presented in the manual. Much of the WPPSI-R evidence is actually evidence for the validity of the WPPSI. Because 50 percent of the items on the

WPPSI-R are new and it has been restandardized, evidence for the validity of the WPPSI is irrelevant to the validity of the WPPSI-R.

The WPPSI-R is shown to correlate very highly with the WISC-R for 50 students ages 72–86 months living in Jacksonville, Florida. Correlations with the Stanford–Binet–IV were shown to be moderate. Performance on the WPPSI-R is more closely related to performance on the McCarthy Scales than to performance on the Stanford–Binet–IV. Correlations between performance on the WPPSI-R and on the Kaufman Assessment Battery for Children are low.

Scores earned by children on the WPPSI-R are generally lower than scores they earn on other measures. The test manual reports that student scores on the WPPSI-R Full Scale IQ are 8 points lower than their scores on the WPPSI, 7 points lower than their scores on the WISC-R, 2 points lower than their scores on the Stanford–Binet–IV, and 6 points lower than their scores on the Kaufman Assessment Battery for Children.

The WASI manual contains a considerable amount of information intended as evidence of the test's validity as a quick screener. The most compelling evidence is the WASI's ability to predict WISC-III and WAIS-III IQs and achievement. After correction for the constricted range of ability, the correlations between FSIQs (using four subtests) was .92 with the WAIS-III (using a sample of 248 adults between the ages of 16 and 89) and .87 with the WISC-III (using a sample of 176 individuals between the ages of 6 and 16). Correlations using two WASI subtests are lower (that is, .87 with the WAIS-III and .81 with the WISC-III). The variability of correlations by age is not reported. Correlations between the WASI and the WIAT are similar to the correlations between the WICS-III or WAIS-III and the WIAT.

Summary

The four Wechsler intelligence scales (WAIS-III, WISC-III, WPPSI-R, WASI) are widely used individually administered intelligence tests. Although they are designed for different age levels, the four scales are similar in content and format. Evidence for the reliability of the scales is good. Reliabilities are much lower for subtests, and so subtest scores should not be used in making placement decisions. Evidence for validity, as presented in the manuals, is limited.

The Detroit Tests of Learning Aptitude–4 (DTLA-4)

The Detroit Tests of Learning Aptitude–4 (DTLA-4; Hammill, 1998) are the most recent version of Baker and Leland's test, originally published in 1935. To Hammill's credit, the 1985, 1991, and current revisions have systematically strengthened weaker areas of the test and risen to the increasingly rigorous standards of educators and psychologists. This edition of the test has more attractive stimulus materials, better-described norms, more reliability information, and additional validity information. The Picture Fragments subtest has also been dropped.

The test is described as a measure of developed abilities, a concept first used by Anastasi (1980). She argued that the considerable confusion created by using the terms *aptitude, intelligence,* and *achievement* could be reduced by substituting for each the word *abilities.* Hammill (1991) adopts Anastasi's notion of developed abilities and a fundamental assumption that goes along with the term. Anastasi (1988, p. 413) stated that

All ability tests—whether they be designed as general intelligence tests, multiple aptitude batteries, special aptitude tests, or achievement tests—measure the level of development attained by the individual in one or more abilities. No test reveals how or why the individual reached that level.

There are four principal uses for the test: "(a) to determine strengths and weaknesses among developed mental abilities, (b) to identify children and youths who are significantly below their peers in important abilities, (c) to make predictions about future performance, and (d) to serve as a measurement device in research studies investigating aptitude, intelligence, and cognitive behavior" (Hammill, 1998, p. 24). The DTLA-4 consists of ten subtests that measure different but interrelated developed abilities in individuals ranging in age from 6-0 to 17-11.[1] The DTLA-4 takes between 50 minutes and 2 hours to administer.

Subtests

Word Opposites   A stimulus word is read aloud, and the student is asked to state a word that means the opposite of the stimulus word.

Design Sequences   A student is shown a card with a sequence of designs for five seconds. The card is then removed, and the student uses cubes to reproduce the designs from memory.

Sentence Imitation   The examiner reads a sentence without inflection, and the student must repeat the sentence.

Reversed Letters   The examiner says a series of letter names at the rate of one letter per second, and the subject then writes each letter in the series in reversed order.

Story Construction   The student is shown pictures and is asked to make up and tell stories in response to the pictures.

---

1. The Hammill Multiability Intelligence Test, a special version of the DTLA-4, uses eight of the ten subtests and yields verbal, nonverbal, and overall Qs. The Detroit Test of Learning Aptitude–Primary 2 was reviewed in the previous edition.

Design Reproduction   Geometric forms are presented for specified time intervals and then removed. The student must draw the forms from memory.

Basic Information   The student must answer specific factual questions that assess knowledge of everyday situations, rather than knowledge acquired in school.

Symbolic Relations   The student is shown a design and then must select from among six possible responses the pattern that completes the design.

Word Sequences   The student is required to repeat a series of unrelated and isolated words read by the examiner.

Story Sequences   The examinee is shown a series of cartoonlike pictures and must put these into sequence in order to depict a story. The student indicates the order by putting numbered chips under the pictures.

An examiner administers all items of the Design Sequences, Reversed Letters, Story Construction, and Story Sequences subtests. On the remaining subtests, examiners start testing at a specified point and continue until a ceiling is reached. On all tests with ceilings except Design Reproduction, the ceiling is that point at which the student has failed five consecutive items. On Design Reproduction, the ceiling is reached when the student has received a score of zero on three consecutive drawings.

Subtests can be combined into 6 different composites. All subtests are combined to form the General Mental Ability Composite. The Optimal Composite is composed of the four subtests on which a student earned the highest scores; these subtests, of course, vary from person to person. As shown in Table 17.3, subtests can be combined into 14 other composites. Three pairs of DTLA-4 composites contrast verbal and nonverbal, attention-enhanced and attention-reduced, and motor-enhanced and motor-reduced abilities. The remaining eight composites are intended to represent the theoretical aspects of intelligence formulated by other theorists. Specifically, there are

TABLE 17.3 • *Relationship between DTLA-4 Subtests and Composites*

Composite/Subtests[a]	WO	DS	SI	RL	SC	DR	BI	SR	WS	SS
DTLA-4 Domain Composites										
General Mental Ability	X	X	X	X	X	X	X	X	X	X
Verbal	X		X		X		X		X	
Nonverbal		X		X		X		X		X
Attention-Enhanced		X	X	X		X			X	X
Attention-Reduced	X				X		X	X		
Motor-Enhanced		X		X		X				X
Motor-Reduced	X		X		X		X	X	X	
Theoretical Composites										
Fluid Intelligence		X		X		X		X		
Crystallized Intelligence	X		X		X		X		X	X
Simultaneous Processing	X		X		X	X	X	X		
Successive Processing		X		X					X	X
Associative Level		X	X	X		X			X	
Cognitive Level	X				X		X	X		X
Verbal Intelligence	X		X		X		X		X	
Performance Intelligence		X		X		X		X		X

[a]WO = Word Opposites; DS = Design Sequences; SI = Sentence Imitation; RL = Reversed Letters; SC = Story Construction; DR = Design Reproduction; BI = Basic Information; SR = Symbolic Relations; WS = Word Sequences; SS = Story Sequences.

separate composites intended to reflect Cattell's crystallized and fluid intelligences, Das's simultaneous and successive processing abilities, Jensen's associative and cognitive levels of intelligence, and Wechsler's verbal and performance abilities.

Scores and Norms

Raw scores on each subtest can be converted to age equivalents, percentiles, and standard scores with a mean of 10 and a standard deviation of 3. Composite scores can be converted to percentiles and quotients with a mean of 100 and a standard deviation of 15.

DTLA-4 norms combine the individuals from two groups. The first group consists of the 922 students from the DTLA-3's norms who were tested in 1989–1990. The second group consists of 428 students tested in 1996–1997. Students in the 1996–1997 sample were located using a sampling plan similar to the plan used to identify part of the 1989–1990 sample. Four sites (one in each geo-

graphic region of the United States) were selected, and classrooms within each area were identified. Thus, students came from intact classrooms. Students with disabilities are included in the norms to the extent that they were enrolled in these classes. The remainder of the 1989–1990 sample came from individuals across the United States who agreed to participate by testing 10–30 students. The number and location of these participants are not reported. The overall sample closely resembles the U.S. population in 1996.

While the description of the normative sample is substantially better than in previous editions, it remains less than complete. For example, geographic area, sex, race, ethnicity, urban/rural residence, and parental income resemble the U.S. population for four age groups (6–8, 9–11, 12–14, and 15–17). No data are presented to show that the sample is representative at each age. An appropriate sampling plan might provide the basis for a reader's inferring that the DTLA-4 samples at each age are representative because the samples for age groups are representative. However, the description of the sampling plan is too incomplete to make such an inference with much confidence. For example, it is not possible to tell if the "primary standardization sites" were restricted to the communities named or if they included the surrounding suburban and rural areas. It is also unclear how one primary standardization site (for example, South Wales, NY, or New Orleans, LA) is representative of an entire geographic region.

Reliability

The DTLA-4 manual contains information about internal consistency, stability, interscorer agreement, and differences between subtests and between composites. Internal consistency for each subtest at each age was estimated from the performance of the normative sample. The 120 *coefficient alphas* (10 subtests at 12 ages) range from .71 (Story Sequences at age 6 and Basic Information at age 7) to .97 (Design Sequences at age 10). Of 120 alphas, 9 (7.5%) are less than .80 and 41 (34.2%) equal or exceed .90. The internal consistency of all composites, with one exception, equals or exceeds .90. (The exception is when a 6-year-old's optimal composite uses the four most unreliable subtests; in that case, the optimal composite's internal consistency is .87.) Internal consistency was also examined separately for specific subgroups within the normative samples (males [$n = 687$] and females [$n = 663$]; Euro-Americans [$n = 976$], African Americans [$n = 198$], Asian Americans [$n = 27$], and Hispanic Americans [$n = 133$]; students with learning disabilities [$n = 63$] and students with mental retardation [$n = 37$]). A similar pattern of coefficients was found. With two exceptions, about half of the subtest reliabilities were in the .80s and half were in the .90s; the reliability of every composite equaled or exceeded .90. Although these coefficients are somewhat higher than the age group coefficients, they were calculated across ages.

To investigate stability, 96 students (from grades 3 to 12) from Austin, TX, were tested twice within one week. The students are described in the manual as multicultural and of low socioeconomic status. Test–retest coefficients are presented for all subtests for three groups: 24 children in grades 1 through 3 (although the manual indicates elsewhere that there were no students in first or second grade), 36 students in grades 4 through 6, and 36 students in grades 7 through 12. Of the stability estimates, 10 were in the .70s, 11 were in the .80s, and 9 were in the .90s. No estimates of the composites for the three age groups are presented; presumably, they are higher. Stability estimates for the pooled groups are also presented; it is unclear why these estimates are substantially higher.

To investigate the interscorer reliability, two individuals independently scored 30 completed protocols (that is, answer forms) and converted the raw scores to standard scores. These standard scores were then correlated. Interscorer agreement for all subtests and composites equaled or exceeded .95. However, as described in the DTLA-4 manual, the examiners apparently did not evaluate the students' responses, but instead dealt with protocols that had already been scored. Thus, the coefficients seem more likely to reflect the degree to which basal and ceiling rules are applied, correct responses summed, and derived scores found for the subtotals and totals.

Finally, the author presents the critical values needed to evaluate the reliability of a difference between any two subtests or between any two composites. However, these values are based on the average reliability (across ages), not on the actual age of the student whose scores are being compared.

Validity

The DTLA-4 manual contains considerable information about various aspects of the test's validity. Because the DTLA-3 and DTLA-4 are quite similar, much of the evidence for the present edition is actually from the previous edition. Rather than separate the studies by edition, we refer to the test as the DTLA when evidence from the two editions is combined.

Evidence for content validity is of two types. First, the author justifies the inclusion of the content of each subtest with a paragraph or two in which he shows that other tests of intelligence use similar types of items and/or provides a brief rationale for the content. Second, the author also shows how the items and subtests on the DTLA-4 cover the aspects or elements of intelligence that are most often incorporated into the various theories or descriptions of intelligence.

Evidence for criterion-related validity rests in part on the validity of the previous edition and in part on new research. Several studies (with sample sizes ranging from 25 to 50) correlated the DTLA and various measures of intelligence (the Kaufman Assessment Battery for Children, the Scholastic Aptitude Scale, the Peabody Picture Vocabulary Test–Revised, the Wechsler Intelligence Scale for Children–III, and the revised Woodcock-Johnson Psycho-Educational Battery). The correlations between the General Mental Ability Quotient of the DTLA-4 and these measures varied from .55 to .91. Moreover, the pattern of correlations also tends to support the theoretical composites. For example, the WISC-III verbal IQ correlates more highly with the DTLA's verbal scale than with the nonverbal scale, while the WISC-III performance IQ correlates more highly with the DTLA's nonverbal scale than with its verbal scale.

A variety of evidence for construct validity is presented. First, the DTLA-4 subtests appear to measure the same constructs for African Americans, Hispanics, and females. Moreover, the means for males and females and for students from various ethnic groups are remarkably similar. Second, subtest scores increase with age, as would be expected. Third, students identified as mentally retarded by independent criteria earn substantially lower scores; students identified as learning disabled by independent criteria earn scores between those earned by mentally retarded students and students who are not identified as disabled.

The results of several studies indicate that the DTLA predicts school achievement as measured by the Wide Range Achievement Test–Revised, the Diagnostic Achievement Test–2, the Diagnostic Achievement Battery for Adolescents–2, and the Diagnostic Achievement Battery–2. The DTLA also predicts teacher ratings on the Comprehensive Scales of Student Abilities.

Finally, several factor-analytic investigations were conducted. Two factors appear to underlie the entire scale: verbal ability and nonverbal ability. Confirmatory factor analyses indicate that the other composite scores are tenable.

Summary

The Detroit Tests of Learning Aptitude–4 are intended to measure developed abilities. The test contains 10 subtests that can be formed into 16 composites. The sampling plan for the development of the norms is incompletely described. However, the resulting sample does approximate the U.S. population in terms of geographic area, race, sex, parental income, and urban–rural residence. The internal consistency of composites at all ages is excellent. Stability data are incompletely reported and weaker. Ample evidence suggests that the DTLA-4 provides an unbiased measure of general intelligence as well as other ways of looking at intellectual functioning.

Cognitive Assessment System

The Cognitive Assessment System (CAS; Naglieri & Das, 1997) is an individually administered, norm-referenced test of cognitive processing.

Within the authors' theory, intellectual functioning is the interaction between a person's store of basic knowledge and his or her ability to plan, pay attention, and process (simultaneously or successively). Naglieri (1999, p. 13) explains the major components of the theory in essentially this way: Planning is composed of developing a plan of action, monitoring its effectiveness, revising the plan as things change, and controlling impulses to act without careful consideration. Attention is focused, selective, and sustained on a particular activity. In simultaneous processing, an individual synthesizes all of the parts into a meaningful whole. In successive processing, an individual connects parts serially to form a chain or sequence of the parts. The CAS is composed of four components, each having three subtests. Administration of all 12 subtests is called the Standard Battery; administration of 8 subtests is called the Basic Battery.

Planning Subtests

Matching Numbers   Each of the four items on this timed subtest consists of eight rows of six numbers each. The student is to find the two numbers in each row that are the same. The numbers range from one-digit integers to seven-digit integers. The rows of multidigit numbers were prepared in order to facilitate particular strategies; for example, each number in a row may start with a different integer or each number may end with one or two different integers. Children between 5 and 7 years old are given the first two items; individuals between 8 and 17 years of age are administered the last three items. An item is scored as the number correct (of 8) divided by the number of seconds required to complete the item (or the maximum time). After the final item is administered, students are asked what strategy they used to find the identical integers. The subtest raw score is the rounded sum of the item raw scores; item raw scores are quotients of the square of the number correct plus 10 divided by the number of seconds (measured in three-second intervals).

Planned Codes   There are two items on this timed subtest. On each item, a code associates Xs and Os with A, B, C, or D; for example, OX is as-

sociated with A on item 1. The test taker is to write the correct two-letter code for each letter. On the first item, the eight columns always contain the same letter and are in alphabetic sequence, with A following D (that is, A, B, C, D, A, B, C, D). Thus, the eight rows are identical. On the second item, the rows remain in alphabetical sequence, but the first letter is not always A. The letters are arranged so that a letter forms a diagonal. For example, the first row begins with A; A is the second letter in row two, the third letter in row 3, and so forth. After the last item in the subtest is completed, students are asked to explain how they completed the problem. The subtest raw score is the rounded sum of item raw scores; item raw scores are quotients of the square of the number correct plus 10 divided by the number of seconds (measured in three-second intervals).

Planned Connections   The eight items on this timed subtest require a student to connect lettered and/or numbered boxes sequentially. Children between 5 and 7 years old are given the first five items, which consist of numbers. Older children begin with item 5 and progress to items that require test takers to alternate between numbers and letters (for example, 1, A, 2, B, 3, C, and so forth). With the last item still exposed, test takers are asked to explain how they completed the problem. Raw scores are the total number of seconds needed to complete the items.

Simultaneous Subtests

Nonverbal Matrices   The 33 items on this untimed subtest require the selection of the one option that completes a relational matrix from an array of six choices. The raw score is the number of correct responses.

Verbal–Spatial Relations   The 27 items in this untimed subtest require the selection of the one option that answers a question read by the examiner from an array of six choices. A difficult item would be similar to this: Which picture shows an arrow over a circle in a square under a cross? The raw score is the number of correct responses.

Figure Memory   The 57 items on this untimed test each consist of two parts. The first part is a stimulus (geometric design), which is shown for five seconds. The second part is a more complicated geometric design in which the stimulus is embedded. Test takers must trace the stimulus design in the embedded design. The raw score is the number of correct responses.

Attention Subtests

Expressive Attention   For children from 5 to 7 years of age, the test items contain drawings of eight animals. Four animals depicted in the drawings are classified as large (for example, dinosaur and bear), and four are classified as small (for example, butterfly and mouse). Children are presented with an array of drawings of these animals and must say big or small for each. Children then must identify drawings of large animals as large, and drawings of small animals as small. On the test item, large animals are represented by small drawings, and small animals, by large drawings. For test takers who are 8 or older, the stimuli are colors or color names. Test takers first read the names of colors and name colors. On the test item, the names of colors are printed in different colors (for example the word *red* might be printed in blue ink). Test takers must name the color in which the word is printed (not read the word). The subtest raw score is the quotient of the square of the number correct plus 10, all divided by the number of seconds (measured in three-second intervals).

Number Detection   Children from 5 to 7 years of age must determine if each number in a 10 by 18 array of single digits is one of three stimulus numbers. Test takers who are 8 or older must base their determination on both the integer and the style in which it is printed. The subtest raw score is the rounded quotient of the square of the number correct less the number incorrect plus 10, divided by the number of seconds (measured in three-second intervals).

Receptive Attention   For children from 5 to 7 years of age, each item consists of 10 rows of 5 pairs of drawings. Children must underline the two drawings in a pair when they are the same. Items that are more difficult require children to identify different examples of the same concept as the same; for example, a Cape Cod–style house and a ranch-style house are both houses. For test takers who are 8 or older, the stimuli are letters. On easier items, the letter and case are the same. On more difficult items, test takers must recognize that letters are the same whether they are upper- or lowercase; for example, r and R must be recognized as the same, whereas R and S must be recognized as different. The subtest raw score is the rounded quotient of the square of the number correct less the number incorrect plus ten, divided by the number of seconds (measured in three-second intervals).

Successive Subtests

Word Series   The 27 items on this subtest require the repetition of a series of two to nine nouns spoken by the examiner at one-second intervals. The same nine nouns are used in all 27 items. The raw score is the number of correct responses.

Sentence Repetition   The 20 items on this subtest require the repetition of "sentences" ranging from 3 to 19 words. Sentences are composed of color names used as verbs, nouns, and adjectives— for example, "The blue yellowed the purple green." The raw score is the number of correct responses.

Speech Rate   This subtest is administered to children between 5 and 7 years of age. Each of the eight items consists of 3 one- or two-syllable words (for example, girl–dog–purple). Children must say the sequence correctly ten times as fast as they can within a maximum time of 30 seconds. Scores are based on the time it takes to repeat each sequence ten times. Raw scores are the total number of seconds needed to complete the items.

Sentence Questions   This subtest is administered to individuals 8 and older. The 21 items consist of declarative "sentences" composed of color names used as verbs, nouns, and adjectives. The examiner reads the sentence, and then asks a question—for example, "The red and blue browned the yellow; who browned the yellow?" The raw score is the number of correct responses.

Scores

For each age group, subtest raw scores are converted to scaled scores, which are standard scores (mean = 10 and standard deviation = 3) that have been normalized and smoothed. Subtest scaled scores are combined to obtain PASS Scale Scores (that is, scale scores for Planning, Attention, Simultaneous Processing, and Successive Processing); PASS Scale Scores have a mean of 100 (standard deviation = 15). The CAS (Standard) Full Scale is based on all 12 subtests, and the CAS (Basic) Full Scale does not include 4 subtests (Planned Connections, Figure Memory, Receptive Attention, and Speech Rate or Sentence Questions). Both Full Scales have a mean of 100 (standard deviation = 15).

Norms

The CAS was normed on 2,200 individuals (150 males and 150 females at each age) who were tested by 274 examiners at 68 sites from 1993 through 1996. At each age, the sample has appropriate proportions from each region of the country, with different levels of parental education, of Hispanic and non-Hispanic individuals, and of individuals who identify themselves racially as black, white, or other. Although this is somewhat unclear, subjects apparently were located through schools. If so, the samples of children younger than 7 and older than 16 (who are not subject to compulsory attendance laws in many states) may be less representative.

Reliability

Corrected split-half reliabilities for the Simultaneous and Successive subtests are presented for each age. These reliability estimates range from .70 to .96; 18 of the 78 age × subtest coefficients equal or exceed .90. Test–retest correlations were used to estimate reliability of the subtests on the Planning

and Attention Scales. These estimates range from .63 to .93; 3 of these 78 age × subtest coefficients equal or exceed .90. For the Basic Battery, the Planning and Attention Scales are reliable enough for screening. For only 2 (ages 5 and 6) of the 13 age groups do Planning reliabilities equal or exceed .90, and no age group has an Attention reliability that equals or exceeds .90. On both the Simultaneous and Successive Scales, 9 of the 13 reliability estimates equal or exceed .90. Only 2 reliability estimates for the Full Scale Score equal or exceed .90. For the Standard Battery, the Planning and Attention Scales continue to be less reliable than the Simultaneous and Successive Scales. For only 3 of the 13 age groups do Planning reliabilities equal or exceed .90; the same is true for Attention. The Simultaneous and Successive Scales are generally reliable. At only 2 of 13 ages for the Simultaneous Scale and 1 of 13 ages for the Successive Scale are reliability estimates less than .90. The estimated reliabilities of the Standard Battery Full Scale Score exceed .90 at all ages.

Additional information about the stability of standard scores is presented for 215 individuals in three age ranges: 5–7, 8–11, and 12–17. The retest interval ranged from 9 to 73 days; the median interval was 21 days. For children 5–7, the highest obtained correlation was .88. There was a mean gain of 7 points (almost half a standard deviation) between test and retest on the Full Scale Score of the Standard Battery. For children 8–11, only for the Full Scale Scores on the Standard and Basic Batteries and the Successive Scale on the Standard Battery did the test–retest correlation equal or exceed .90. The mean gain between test and retest on the Full Scale Score of the Standard Battery was 6 points. For adolescents 12–17, the highest obtained correlation was .89. There was a mean gain of 5 points between test and retest on the Full Scale Score of the Standard Battery.

Given these estimates of reliability, the Basic Battery appears better suited for screening and research purposes. Examiners using the Standard Battery should interpret scores, especially on the Planning and Attention Scales, cautiously. The authors provide tables that should greatly aid in the interpretation of CAS scores. They provide tables containing 90 and 95 percent confidence intervals for each CAS score. In addition, they provide tables for the significance and meaningfulness (that is, degree of unusualness) of the differences between each PASS Scale Score and the mean PASS Scale Score. Finally, they also provide tables for the significance and meaningfulness of differences between each subtest scaled score and the mean scaled score for the PASS Scale.

Validity

Evidence for the content validity of the CAS is problematic because many practitioners and scholars do not view cognitive processing as synonymous with intelligence. Indeed, most of the subtests assess behavior that is not usually assessed on other tests of intelligence. This is both a strength (CAS is different) and a weakness (CAS is really different).

Some evidence for the CAS's criterion-related validity is presented. In one study, the relationship between CAS Scale Scores and verbal and math scores on the Scholastic Aptitude Test was examined. Planning and Attention are unrelated to SAT verbal scores; Successive Processing is unrelated to SAT math scores. The other correlations are significant, with the Full Scale Score having the highest correlations with SAT verbal (.49) and math (.56). In another study, the relationship of scores on the CAS and two Wechsler scales was examined. With younger children, the Simultaneous and Successive Scales were well correlated with the three WPPSI-R IQs (r's ranged from .52 to .76). The CAS Full Scale was not significantly correlated with the PIQ, and the Planning and Attention Scales were uncorrelated with any of the WPPSI-R IQs. The relationship between CAS Scale Scores and WISC-III scores was investigated with three different samples of students: students in regular education, students with learning disabilities, and students with mental retardation. The WISC-III VIQ was not significantly correlated with Planning or Attention for regular-education

students or students with mental retardation; the WISC-III PIQ was uncorrelated with Successive Processing for students with learning disabilities. All other correlations were significant.

The authors offer four types of evidence to support the CAS's construct validity. First, CAS scores increase with age. Second, the CAS predicts scores on the Woodcock Johnson Revised Tests of Achievement. The Basic and Standard Full Scale Scores correlate highly (r's in the high .60s) with the WJ-R clusters and subtests, while individual scales correlate moderately (r's typically in the .5 to .6 range). Third, groups of students with disabilities (that is, attention-deficit hyperactivity disorder, mental retardation, traumatic brain injury, reading disability, and serious emotional disturbance) earn lower scores on some PASS Scales and subtests. However, the rationale for why these differences are meaningful is unclear in some instances. Finally, and most important, factor-analytic techniques generally support CAS's theoretical model. Depending on the statistical technique and age of the test takers, three or four factors underlie the CAS. Regardless of technique, Simultaneous and Successive Processing clearly emerge. Attention and Planning may or may not be distinct factors.

Summary

The Cognitive Assessment System is an individually administered norm-referenced test of cognitive processing—that is planning, attending, simultaneous processing, and successive processing. The test consists of 12 subtests divided equally among the four processes. Subtest raw scores are converted to normalized scaled scores; subtest scaled scores are combined to obtain PASS Scale Scores and Full Scale Scores with a mean of 100 (*S* = 15). The CAS (Standard) Full Scale is based on all 12 subtests, whereas the CAS (Basic) Full Scale does not include four subtests. At each age, CAS's normative sample has appropriate proportions of students from each region of the country, with different levels of parental education, and from different ethnic groups. The reliabilities of PASS Scale Scores on the Standard Battery are high enough to use in making important decisions on behalf of individual students. The Basic Battery appears better suited for screening purposes. Evidence for CAS's validity is difficult because the model of intelligence is so different from the models used by other tests of intelligence. Factor-analytic studies generally support the presence of four subscales that appear to be measuring the intended abilities. CAS does correlate well with other intelligence measures, and it does predict scores on standardized achievement tests.

Nonverbal Intelligence Tests

Nonverbal Intelligence Tests

A number of nonverbal tests are among the most widely used tests for assessment of intelligence. Some are designed to measure intelligence broadly; others are called "picture-vocabulary tests." Before we describe an individual *picture-vocabulary test,* we believe it is important to state what these devices measure. The tests are not measures of intelligence per se; rather, they measure only one aspect of intelligence: receptive vocabulary. In picture-vocabulary tests, pictures are presented to the test taker, who is asked to identify those pictures that correspond to words read by the examiner. Some authors of picture-vocabulary measures state that the tests measure receptive vo-

cabulary; others equate receptive vocabulary with intelligence and claim that their tests assess intelligence. Because the tests measure only one aspect of intelligence, they should not be used to make eligibility decisions. Some commonly used picture-vocabulary tests were reviewed in earlier editions of this textbook. They have not been updated for so long that they are no longer useful. We review only one picture-vocabulary test (the Peabody Picture Vocabulary Test–III) in this section of the chapter. Other measures used to assess receptive vocabulary are reviewed in Chapter 23, on the assessment of language.

Comprehensive Test of Nonverbal Intelligence (CTONI)

The Comprehensive Test of Nonverbal Intelligence (CTONI; Hammill, Pearson, & Wiederholt, 1997) is designed to measure those intellectual abilities that exist independent of language. Designed as a measure of "higher-order" nonverbal abilities (generalization, discrimination, sequencing) rather than "lower-order" abilities like copying, the CTONI is basically a measure of the figural and symbolic domains described in the previous chapter.

The test is designed to measure three kinds of abilities: Analogies, Classification, and Sequencing. Each is measured in two ways: through the use of pictures (representational artwork) and of figures (abstract icons and symbols). There are six subtests (Pictorial Analogies, Geometric Analogies, Pictorial Categories, Geometric Categories, Pictorial Sequences, and Geometric Sequences). In the Analogies subtests, the student is given figures

or pictures in an A:B::C:? format. The correct response must be selected from five response alternatives. In the categories subtests, the student is shown two members of a category and must pick from a five-item response bank another member of the category. In the sequencing subtests, the student is given sequences of pictures or figures with a relationship among them and must pick from a response bank the one that continues the relationship. The authors of the CTONI developed a chart showing the behaviors we describe in Chapter 16, which are sampled by subtests of the CTONI. The chart is reproduced in Table 17.4.

The CTONI is designed for use with children 6-0 through 18-11 years of age. It can be administered using either oral or pantomime directions. Thus, its authors argue that it is a useful device in assessing the learning aptitude of deaf, hearing-impaired, or non–English-speaking students. In

TABLE 17.4 ● CTONI Subtests Organized According to Salvia and Ysseldyke's Classification System

Classification System	CTONI Subtest					
	Pictorial Analogies	Pictorial Categories	Pictorial Sequences	Geometric Analogies	Geometric Categories	Geometric Sequences
Discrimination	X	X	X	X	X	X
Generalization	X	X	X	X	X	X
Induction	X	X	X	X	X	X
Comprehension	X	X	X	X	X	X
Sequencing				X		X
Detail Recognition	X	X	X	X	X	X
Analogies	X			X		
Abstract Reasoning	X	X	X	X	X	X
Memory	X	X	X	X	X	X
Pattern Completion	X	X	X	X	X	X
General Information	not appropriate to CTONI					
Vocabulary	not appropriate to CTONI					
Motor	not appropriate to CTONI					

SOURCE: From D. Hammill, N. Pearson, & J. L. Wiederbolt (1997). *Comprehensive Test of Nonverbal Intelligence* (CTONI), p. 53. Copyright © 1997 by Pro-Ed. Reprinted by permission of the publisher.

administering the test, the test giver begins at Item 1 and continues until the student misses three of five items.

Scores

Scores available for the CTONI include raw scores, standard scores, percentiles, and age equivalents. In addition, three kinds of IQ scores are provided: Pictorial Nonverbal IQ, Geometric Nonverbal IQ, and Nonverbal IQ.

Norms

The CTONI was standardized on 2,129 people in 23 states. Two methods were used to select the standardization sample. First, the authors selected primary sites in each of four geographic regions. There is no indication of the extent to which the sites selected were representative of the regions from which they were selected. Test coordinators in each site coordinated the collection of data on

1,156 students. For a second method, names were selected from the file of test purchasers at Pro-Ed publishers. Letters were sent, asking people to give a number of CTONIs. As a result, 53 testers tested 973 students. The authors show the percentage breakdown of the sample for region, gender, race, residence, ethnicity, family income, educational attainment of parents, and disability status. They show how sample statistics compare with census statistics, and there is good agreement. They show stratification of the sample on age but do not provide cross-tabulations on other characteristics.

A strong case is made for use of this measure with students who are hearing impaired and those who speak English as a second language. Yet, the authors did not specifically standardize the test on these two populations. It would have helped to oversample individuals with these characteristics, so that differential item-response curves could be compared.

There are two alternative procedures for administering the CTONI, yet only one set of norms.

The authors do provide limited data showing the equivalence of scores earned under pantomime versus verbal administration of the test. Nonetheless, separate norms should be provided for the two alternative procedures.

Reliability

Three kinds of reliability data are reported. Internal-consistency coefficients for all subtests exceed .80 and for all composites exceed .90. There is good evidence for the internal consistency of this test.

Results of a test–retest reliability study are reported. They are limited to the performance of 33 third-grade and 30 eleventh-grade students who are not described, but who attended a single school in Llano, Texas. The tests were given pantomime on the first administration and oral on the second. The reliabilities reported are greater than .80. However, the sample is not described, is limited to two grade levels, and is very limited in size. There is no evidence of test–retest reliability at other age levels.

To establish interscorer reliability, the authors had two staff people score 50 protocols for students ages 11–14 years. The coefficients all exceeded .95. However, the sample size and age range of the norm group are both incredibly small.

Validity

It is our contention that one of the most important kinds of validity for a measure of intelligence is *predictive validity,* evidence that test performance predicts performance in school. There is no evidence for the predictive validity of the CTONI.

As evidence of content validity, the authors show that the CTONI measures the behaviors we describe in Chapter 16, on intelligence. They show the chart reproduced in Table 17.4.

Evidence for criterion-related validity is limited. The authors compare performance on the CTONI, the TONI, the WISC-III, and the PPVT. The sample reported on is a group of 43 learning-disabled (LD) students attending a separate private school in Dallas, Texas. Correlations among subtests are

moderate. We were surprised to learn that performance on the CTONI (Pictorial Nonverbal IQ, Geometric Nonverbal IQ, and Nonverbal IQ) correlated more highly with WISC-II Verbal than with WISC-II Performance IQs. The authors do not discuss this finding.

The authors also report on the comparative performance of 32 deaf students attending two Texas regional day schools. They show correlations between CTONI subtest scores and WISC-III performance subtest scores of from .39 to .88 and correlations for composites of from .67 to .90.

As evidence of construct validity, the authors show that scores on the CTONI increase with age. In the table they provide, we see an alarming fact. Scores do get higher with increasing age, but the mean score at each age changes little, if at all. For example, the average CTONI score on Pictorial Analogies is the same (15) for students who are 15, 16, and 17 years old. There is a 1-point difference in the average score earned on Geometric Categories by students who are 13 and by those who are 18 years old. We think this is illustrative of one of two difficulties with this test: a limited behavior sample (number of items), and virtually no discrimination ability in items.

Summary

The CTONI is an assessment of students' classification, analogies, and sequencing ability. Nonverbal stimuli (representational pictures and geometric figures) are used. The test can be administered using pantomime or verbal directions, but we think that the norms are for verbal directions only. We do not know in how many instances examiners used pantomime versus verbal directions during the norming of this test. We also raised some issues about the ways in which the standardization was carried out, and about the reporting of cross-tabulation information. Data on reliability and validity are very limited. The CTONI may be an adequate measure of nonverbal intelligence, but judgment about whether it is will need to await evidence of its reliability and both its construct and its predictive validity.

Leiter International Performance Scale–Revised (Leiter-R)

The Leiter International Performance Scale–Revised (Leiter-R; Roid & Miller, 1997) is a new revision of the Leiter International Performance Scale (LIPS) and the Arthur Adaptation of the Leiter International Performance Scale (AALIPS). The LIPS, first published in 1929, was one of the original nonverbal measures of intelligence and has been used for more than 65 years. Grace Arthur renormed the test in 1950, although the items remained unchanged. Both the LIPS and the AALIPS used wooden blocks that were manipulated by children to match sequences of figures and pictures depicted on a wooden frame that would hold the reordered blocks. The Leiter-R is a nonverbal measure of intelligence, requiring no speaking or writing on the part of either the examiner or the test taker. For this reason, the test has been very popular for use with students with hearing impairments, cerebral palsy, communication disorders, and non–English-language backgrounds. Because the test's authors regularly claim that the measure is culture free, it is popular for use with students whose acculturation differs from that of public-school students from the dominant culture.

Subtests

The Leiter-R is now available with stimulus items in easel format, and with lightweight, laminated response cards rather than wooden blocks. The test is now in color rather than the black-and-white format of earlier versions. The test is used with individuals 2-0 to 20-11 years of age; there is no indication of how long it takes to give the Leiter-R. The test measures intellectual performance in four domains: Reasoning, Visualization, Memory, and Attention. It includes the following 20 subtests.

Reasoning

Classification. This subtest assesses skill in categorization of objects or geometric designs.

Sequencing. This test measures skill in identifying the stimulus that comes next in a sequence.

Repeated Patterns. Students must identify which of several stimuli fill in missing parts in repeated sequences of pictures or figures.

Design Analogies. Students must identify geometric shapes that complete matrix analogies.

Visualization (Spatial)

Matching. Testees must match response cards to easel pictures.

Figure–Ground. Students must identify designs embedded in complex backgrounds.

Form Completion. Students are given randomly displayed parts of designs and must select the whole design from several alternatives.

Picture Context. Students must use visual-context clues to identify a part of a picture that has been removed from a larger picture.

Paper Folding. This test measures skill in viewing an unfolded object in two dimensions and then matching it to a picture of the whole object.

Figure Rotation. Students must identify rotated pictures of original nonrotated objects.

Memory

Immediate Recognition. Students are shown five pictures or figures for five seconds, and after these items are removed and re-presented, students must identify the one item that is missing.

Delayed Recognition. After a 20-minute delay, students must identify the objects presented in the Immediate Recognition subtest.

● ● ● **FIGURE 17.1**   Materials for Leiter International Performance Scale–Revised

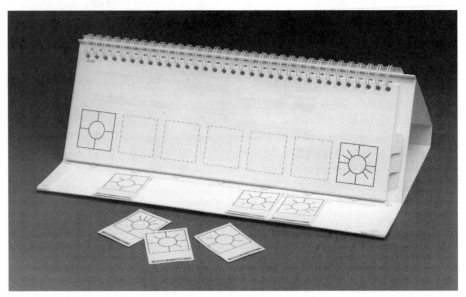

CREDIT: Courtesy of the Stoelting Company, Wood Dale, Illinois.

Associated Pairs. Students are shown pairs of objects for five to ten seconds, and after the objects are removed, students must make meaningful associations for each pair.

Delayed Pairs. This is a 20-minute delay measure of the items in the Associated Pairs subtest.

Forward Memory. Students must remember pictured objects to which the examiner points and must repeat the sequence in which the examiner points to the objects.

Reversed Memory. The examiner points to pictures or figures in order, and the student must point to the same pictures in reverse order.

Spatial Memory. The student is shown increasingly complex stimulus displays, arranged in matrix format, and the student must then place cards in order on a blank matrix display.

Visual Coding. This is a nonverbal task requiring matching of pictures and geometric objects to numbers.

Attention

Attention Sustained. Students are given large numbers of stimuli and must identify those that are alike. They mark all squares containing a geometric shape. There are three parallel forms of increasing difficulty for ages 2–5, 6–10, and 11–21.

Attention Divided. Students must divide attention between a moving display of pictures and the sorting of playing cards.

Scores

Several scores are available for the Leiter-R, including full-scale IQ, brief screening IQ, brief ADHD screening score, brief gifted screening score, and scaled scores for the Reasoning, Visualization, Memory, and Attention subtests. In addition, scaled scores can be obtained for each subtest, and all scaled scores can be converted to age- and grade-equivalent scores.

Norms

Restandardization of the Leiter-R took place between 1993 and 1995. The test was tried out by 60 field researchers on 550 so-called typical children, of whom 325 either had communication disorders or cognitive impairments or spoke English as a second language. Based on the performance of these students, 17 subtests were retained, and items were redesigned. The final version of the test was standardized on 1,800 children considered "normal" and 725 children and adolescents designated clinical/atypical, stratified on the basis of gender, race, parent educational level, and geographic region, using data from the 1993 census. The authors show that the percentages in various gender, race, and other categories closely match the 1993 census data, but no cross-tabulations are presented.

Reliability

The authors provide extensive information about the reliability of the Leiter, and for each kind of reliability they provide a good description of the sample. Internal-consistency reliability coefficients are provided for the Visualization/Reasoning Battery, the Attention/Memory Battery, and the Attention/Memory Battery Special Diagnostic Scales. Fewer than half the coefficients are above .80. Reliabilities are also provided for IQ and composite scores. Most of these exceed .80. The subtests have limited application in making important decisions about individuals. IQs and composite scores are more reliable for this purpose. Evidence is also provided for test–retest reliability. Coefficients are high for composites and (except above age 11) low for subtests.

Validity

Evidence of content validity is based on mapping of the test to theoretical models of intelligence presented by Gustafson (1984) and by Carroll (1993). Evidence of criterion-related validity was based on the performance of diagnostic groups. Representative mainstream students earned an average brief IQ of 101, severely hearing-impaired students averaged 94, students with severe cognitive disabilities averaged 56, students who were gifted and talented averaged 115, and ESL students averaged 95. In addition, the Leiter brief IQ correlated .83 with full-scale IQs on the WISC-III and the original Leiter. Studies of correlations with other batteries are underway.

Evidence of construct validity is based on completion of factor analyses showing a match between the scale and the theoretical model that guided its development. In addition, the authors argue that demonstration of comparable performance across several racial groups is evidence of construct validity.

Summary

The Leiter-R is a measure of intelligence that requires no verbalization on the part of the examiner or the examinee. The test measures intellectual skill development in four domains. The test is adequately standardized, and there is good evidence that IQs and composite scores are reliable. Reliabilities of subtests are too low for use in making diagnostic decisions about individuals.

Test of Nonverbal Intelligence–3 (TONI-3)

The Test of Nonverbal Intelligence–III (TONI-3; Brown, Sherbenou, & Johnson, 1997) is the third edition of a test that was first published in 1982 and revised in 1990. The test is an individually

● ● ● **FIGURE 17.2** Representative Items from the TONI-3

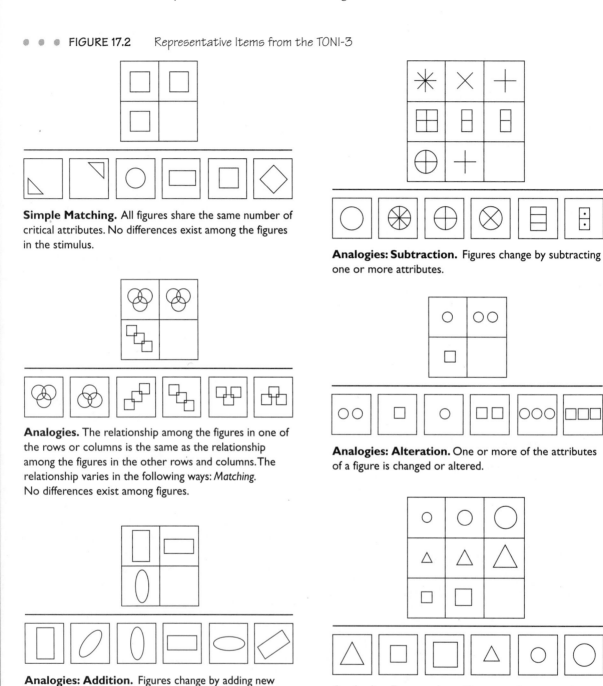

Simple Matching. All figures share the same number of critical attributes. No differences exist among the figures in the stimulus.

Analogies: Subtraction. Figures change by subtracting one or more attributes.

Analogies. The relationship among the figures in one of the rows or columns is the same as the relationship among the figures in the other rows and columns. The relationship varies in the following ways: *Matching.* No differences exist among figures.

Analogies: Alteration. One or more of the attributes of a figure is changed or altered.

Analogies: Addition. Figures change by adding new attributes or additional figures.

Analogies: Progressions. The same change continues between or among figures.

● ● ● ● FIGURE 17.2 *(continued)*

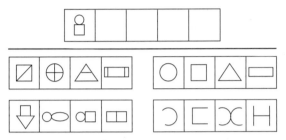

Classification. The figure in the stimulus is a member of one of the sets of figures in the response alternatives.

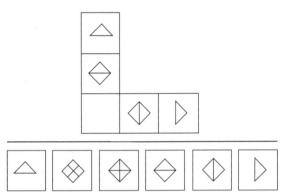

Intersections. A new figure is formed by joining parts of figures in the rows and columns.

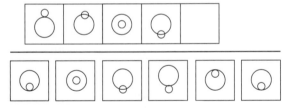

Progressions. The same change continues between or among figures.

SOURCE: From *Test of Non-Verbal Intelligence–3* (TONI-3). Copyright © 1997 by Pro-Ed. Reprinted by permission of the publisher.

administered measure of the aptitude of children and adults who require a language-free, motor-reduced, or culture-reduced test of abstract/figural problem solving. The test includes pantomimed di-

rections and requires no verbal response by the examinee. So, the authors describe the TONI-3 as a language-free measure, one that in its content, instructional format, and response format requires no reading, writing, speaking, or listening. It is designed to be used in both screening and diagnosis with individuals between 5-0 and 85-11 years of age. The test is untimed and takes about 15 minutes to administer.

There are two forms of the TONI-3; each has 45 items (10 less than the TONI-2). All TONI-3 items require test takers to solve problems by identifying relationships among abstract figures. The subject must point to the one response among several alternatives that best fits a missing part in a pattern or matrix. There are five types of problem-solving items: simple matching, analogies, classification, intersections, and progressions. The test items shown in Figure 17.2 are examples of the kinds of items used in the TONI-3. The authors claim that the test is particularly useful with "subjects whose test performance may be confounded by language and motor impairments arising from such conditions as aphasia, hearing impairments, lack of proficiency with spoken or written English, cerebral palsy, stroke, head trauma, and lack of familiarity with the culture of the United States" (Brown et al., 1997, p. 32).

Scores

Two kinds of scores—percentile ranks and TONI quotients—may be obtained. TONI quotients are standard scores with a mean of 100 and a standard deviation of 15.

Norms

The authors developed a set of new norms for this third edition of the TONI. The TONI-3 was standardized on a sample of 3,451 people residing in 28 states. The authors selected six primary standardization sites, using data on geographic regions reported in the U.S. Census. A total of 2,060 individuals were tested at these sites. The remaining standardization sample was chosen by contacting professionals who had purchased earlier versions of the test. Cross-tabulations are shown in the manual for age and other sample characteristics, but not for the other characteristics with one another (for example, race by geographic region).

Reliability

The authors report internal-consistency reliability coefficients for both forms of the test. All coefficients equal or exceed .89, and all but four are in the .90s, the criterion for using the test to make important decisions about individuals. Correlations between performance on the two forms exceed .80, and means and standard deviations on the two forms are nearly identical at all age intervals. One-week test–retest reliabilities exceeded .90 for a group of 170 individuals between 13 and 40 years of age.

Validity

The authors report the results of correlations of the TONI-3 with scores on the CTONI, WISC-III, and WAIS-R (now the WAIS-III). Correlations were within expected ranges. Surprisingly, the correlations between the TONI-3 and the WISC-III were about the same for verbal and nonverbal scales of the WISC-III. This was not true for the WAIS-R, where correlations with the nonverbal scale significantly exceeded those for the verbal scale.

Summary

The TONI-3 is an individually administered nonverbal measure of problem-solving ability. This third edition was renormed. Evidence for the reliability and validity of this test is good.

Universal Nonverbal Intelligence Test

The Universal Nonverbal Intelligence Test (UNIT; Bracken & McCallum, 1998) is a set of individually administered tasks designed to measure the cognitive abilities of children and adolescents (ages 5–17) who may be at a disadvantage in responding to traditional verbal or language-loaded tests. The test was designed to measure two primary kinds of intelligence, memory and reasoning. The authors define intelligence as the ability to solve problems using memory and reasoning. These two intellectual abilities are assessed through two underlying types of processes that facilitate nonverbal problem solving: symbolic and nonsymbolic. Symbolic processes include stimuli that symbolize people, analogies, or concepts, whereas the nonsymbolic processes resemble the nonverbal or performance portions of tests like the Wechsler scales and the Stanford–Binet. The UNIT comprises six subtests, each designed to be a mea-

sure of complex short-term memory or a measure of reasoning and to assess aspects of symbolic and nonsymbolic processing. The six subtests are called Symbolic Memory, Spatial Memory, Object Memory, Cube Design, Analogic Reasoning, and Mazes. The first three make up the Memory scale; the second three make up the Reasoning scale.

The descriptions of the UNIT scales are very general. For example, Reasoning is described as "The cornerstone of intelligence: As the core thinking ability it includes the ability to use information to solve problems" (Bracken & McCallum, 1998, p. 16). Subtests require the student to engage in the following activities:

Symbolic Memory: Students are shown sequences of symbols for five seconds; the symbols are then removed, and the student must reproduce the symbols using response cards.

Spatial Memory: Students are shown patterns of green and black dots for five seconds; these are then removed, and the student must reproduce the patterns using green and black chips.

Object Memory: Students are shown a random pictorial array for five seconds; the stimulus array is then removed, and students indicate from a response bank the ones that were included in the stimulus.

Cube Design: Examinees are shown two-color abstract geometric designs and must reconstruct the designs using one-inch cubes. The stimulus remains present during performance.

Analogic Reasoning: Students are shown incomplete conceptual or geometric analogies in matrix format and must select from four response options the one that completes the analogy.

Mazes: The student uses paper and pencil to create a path from the middle of a maze to a correct exit.

Users of the UNIT may decide to use the Standard Battery (Symbolic Memory, Cube Design, Spatial Memory, and Analogic Reasoning subtests), an Abbreviated Battery (Spatial Memory and Cube Design), or an Extended Battery (all six subtests).

Scores

Raw scores on subtests of the UNIT may be transformed to scaled scores with a mean of 10 and a standard deviation of 3. In addition, users may obtain age equivalents, standard scores for sums of scaled scores (mean = 100, standard deviation = 15), and confidence intervals for raw scores. Separate intellectual quotients are obtained for Memory, Reasoning, Symbolic, and Nonsymbolic scales.

Norms

The UNIT was standardized on a sample of 2,100 children that matched the demographic characteristics of the U.S. population as reported in the 1995 census. The sample was stratified on the basis of gender, race, geographic region, community setting (urban/suburban, rural), classroom placement (full-time regular, full-time self-contained, or some combination thereof), special-education classification, and parental educational attainment. Tables in the manual show cross-tabulations on age, geographic region, and gender and race with other variables. The extensive tables in the manual enable users to understand quite clearly the nature of the group to which students are being compared. A major strength of this test is the fact that students with disabilities were included in the norm group in the proportions of their presence in the U.S. student population.

Reliability

The UNIT manual includes data on internal-consistency and test–retest reliability. Internal-consistency coefficients across ages for the subtests of the UNIT range from .50 to. 95. The reliabilities of Mazes are quite low (. 50 to .76). Reliabilities for the Analogic Reasoning, Object Memory, and Mazes subtests are too low for use in individual decision making. The reliabilities of scales (Memory, Reasoning, Symbolic, and Nonsymbolic), on the other hand, exceed .87 and are sufficient for use in individual decision making.

Test–retest reliability of the UNIT is based on only one study, which included 197 participants (15 at each age level). More than two-thirds of the coefficients are below the .90 coefficient necessary for making decisions about individuals.

Validity

The authors of the UNIT provide evidence of correlation with other measures of intelligence and with measures of academic achievement. They show that, overall, the correlations are high. However, they also provide evidence that at least in some instances, measures of Nonsymbolic Reasoning (defined as primarily nonverbal in nature) correlate more highly with verbal than with performance scales of other measures.

Summary

The UNIT is an individually administered intelligence test that requires no verbal directions and no verbal response on the part of the student. The test is designed to provide information about student use of symbolic and nonsymbolic information-processing skills to solve memory and reasoning tasks. The test is appropriately standardized, and there is good evidence for internal-consistency reliability. Evidence for test–retest reliability is limited, and validity evidence is sufficient for use of IQ scores obtained for the full battery only. Reliance on subtest scores or subscale scores for diagnostic purposes is precarious.

Naglieri Nonverbal Ability Test

The Naglieri Nonverbal Ability Test (NNAT; Naglieri, 1997) is an individually administered measure that uses shapes and designs in a progressive matrix format to assess the nonverbal ability of students from kindergarten through grade 12. The test is an extension and revision of the Matrix Analogies Test (Naglieri, 1985). The test is organized into seven levels, each level for use in specific grades. The test includes pattern completion, analogy, sequencing, and spatial visualization items. The NNAT is suggested as a measure of general ability and a predictor of scholastic achievement. The author says it is appropriate for students from diverse cultural and language backgrounds, and in identification of students with learning disabilities. It is said to be fair for use with students with hearing, language, or motor impairments.

Scores

Scaled scores, normal-curve equivalents, nonverbal ability indexes (mean = 100, standard deviation = 15), stanines, and grade-based percentiles are available for the NNAT. In addition, users can obtain content cluster scores for student performance on pattern completion, analogy, sequencing, and spatial visualization clusters of items.

Norms

The NNAT was standardized on 22,600 children in grades K–12 in the fall of 1995, and on 67,000 children in K–12 in the spring of 1996. Demographic characteristics of the NNAT standardization are shown in comparison to national proportions. Students from urban environments and African American students look underrepresented in the sample. Students from rural environments are overrepresented. No cross-tabulations (indications, for example, of the numbers of African American students from the Northeast) are shown in the manual.

Reliability

Internal-consistency reliability coefficients for the total raw score on the NNAT range from .81 to .89. Reliability coefficients for cluster scores are much lower, ranging from .24 to .80. The test meets reliability criteria for making decisions about groups of students, but not for making decisions about individuals. Most of the cluster coefficients are too low to be used for any purpose.

Validity

One index of validity is provided. The author correlated scores on the NNAT with scores on the SAT-9 and APRENDA2 for unspecified kinds of students who participated in the standardization of the three tests. The correlations were moderate for both measures, with the exception of APRENDA2 for kindergarten and beyond grade 9. Very low correlations were obtained. There are no studies of the relationship of NNAT scores to other measures of either verbal or nonverbal ability. The author identifies a number of purposes for the NNAT and indicates its usefulness with many different populations of students. However, evidence of validity for the many purposes, and for use with the many groups, is not provided.

Summary

The NNAT, a derivative of the earlier published Matrix Analogies Test, is a measure of nonverbal intellectual ability presented entirely in matrix analogy format. The test was standardized on a very large group of students who are not well described. Evidence for reliability of the scale is limited, and the evidence reported indicates low reliability, especially for cluster scores. Evidence for validity is restricted to correlations with achievement tests.

Peabody Picture Vocabulary Test–III (PPVT-III)

The Peabody Picture Vocabulary Test–III (PPVT-III; Dunn & Dunn, 1997) is an individually administered, norm-referenced test of listening comprehension for the spoken word in standard English. The authors of the PPVT-III identify two uses for the test:

The PPVT-III is designed as a measure of an examinee's receptive (hearing) vocabulary acquisition, and the PPVT-III serves as a screening test of verbal ability, or as one element in a comprehensive test battery of cognitive processes. (Dunn & Dunn, 1997, p. 2)

The PPVT-III is a revision of the Peabody Picture Vocabulary Test, which originally appeared in 1959 and later in 1981. Many of the features of the earlier editions were retained in the third edition. For example, the test still consists of two parallel forms, is used with a wide age range of examinees, is untimed, requires no reading by the examinee, and includes training items. New features of the third edition include an increase to 204 items in each form of the test, an extension of national norms to ages 2½ years to 90 plus, modernized content, and new packaging. There are two forms of the PPVT-III (IIIA and IIIB). Each has a separate test kit, which contains an examiner's manual, performance records, and a norms booklet. Each test kit includes four training items and 17 sets of picture plates. In a separate publication,

Technical References to the Peabody Picture Vocabulary Test, Third Edition (Williams & Wang, 1997) considerable detail is given about development of the test, standardization, reliability, and validity.

The PPVT-III is administered in easel format, with the examiner showing the test taker a series of plates on which four pictures are drawn. The examiner reads a stimulus word for each plate, and the person being tested points to the picture that best represents the stimulus word. The PPVT-III is an untimed power test, and it usually takes about 15 minutes to administer. There are 17 sets of items, and those sets that are too easy or too difficult are not administered. On average, the test involves 5 sets of 12 items each, or 60 test items out of 204 (30 percent). The authors provide recommended start items, based on the age of the examinee.

Scores

The student's raw score is the number of pictures correctly identified between the basal and the ceiling items. The test employs a multiple-choice format. The *basal* is the lowest set administered in which the respondent makes one (1) or no errors. The *ceiling* is the highest set in which the examinee makes eight (8) or more errors. Raw scores are obtained by subtracting the total number of errors from the ceiling item. Two types of derived scores can be obtained: deviation-type scores (standard scores, percentiles, stanines, and normal-curve equivalents), and developmental scores (age scores). Procedures are included in the manual for calculating confidence intervals for obtained scores.

Norms

The development of the PPVT-III began with an item tryout program in 1994. A total of 908 persons (ages 2½ to 21) were tested at 73 sites, using 480 items. Of the 480 items, 242 were retained from the PPVT-R, and 238 new items were created. Both traditional item analysis and Rasch–Wright latent-trait methods were used to select final items for the two forms of the test.[2] As a result of the national tryout, 75 items were dropped from the item pool.

The PPVT-R was standardized on a representative national sample of 3,726 individuals. An effort was made to include 100 individuals at each half-year interval from ages 2½ to 7 years, 100 at each year interval from ages 7 to 14, 150 at each 2-year interval from ages 15 to 24, and 125 at each 10-year interval from ages 31 to 60. An effort was made to include an additional 100 people over 61 years of age. A table is included in the manual showing the actual numbers of individuals at each age level included in the standardization.

The standardization sample for the PPVT-III was selected by recruiting examiners in each of four geographic areas. Test coordinators at a total of 268 sites in the four regions selected the subjects to participate in the standardization. They sent questionnaires to parents of individuals between 2½ and 24 years of age, and they received returned questionnaires from more than 8,000 parents. The parents indicated the child's age, gender, and ethnicity/race, and their own (the parents') educational level. The questionnaires were sent to the publisher, and examiners were given lists of individuals to assess. The sample was selected on the basis of 1994 census data. Extensive numbers of tables are included in the manual, showing sample breakdown by geographic region, race, ethnicity, age, and parent or examinee educational level. Sample proportions match census proportions very well.

Reliability

Extensive reliability data are provided in the technical manual for the PPVT-III. There is also a separate section on the equivalency of the PPVT-R and the PPVT-III. Three kinds of reliability data are reported for the PPVT-III: coefficient alpha and split-half indexes of internal consistency; immediate test–retest reliability using alternative forms; and delayed test–retest reliability (8–203 days delay) using alternative forms. Coefficient alpha reliabilities ranged from .92 to .98, with a median of .95 for each form. Split-half reliability coefficients ranged from .86 to .97, with a median of .94 for both forms. Alternative-forms reliabilities ranged from .88 to .96 with a median of .94, while test–retest reliabilities for four age samples (2-6 to 5-11, 6-0 to 10-11, 12-0 to 17-11, and 26-0 to 57-11) ranged from .91 to .93. Reliabilities for the PPVT-III are exceptionally high.

Validity

Extensive information is provided on the validity of the PPVT-III. Four studies are reported in which scores on the PPVT-III are compared with performance on measures of oral vocabulary and cognitive ability. The studies were carried out in conjunction with standardization of the test, and this facilitated selection of representative samples of subjects. Correlations with the WISC-III, Kaufman Adolescent and Adult Intelligence Test, and Kaufman Brief Intelligence Test (Kaufman & Kaufman, 1990) are reported. The correlations are higher with verbal than with performance measures, and they are within expected ranges. Correlations with a measure of oral language (Oral and Written Language Scales) are reported. Again, correlations are within an expected range.

2. See Appendix 4 for a general description of Rasch scaling and item-response theory.

Coping with Dilemmas in Current Practice

The biggest difficulty encountered in trying to use individual intelligence tests is a problem of definition. What is *intelligence*? We noted in Chapter 16 that intelligence is an inferred construct. No one has seen a thing called "intelligence." Yet there are many tests of this thing that no one has seen, and assessors are regularly required to assess it. Most of the definitions of conditions that indicate need or eligibility for special education include reference to cognitive functioning, intelligence, or capability. Students who are mentally retarded are said to have too little of it, students who are gifted have more than most. Students with learning disabilities are said to have average intelligence but fail to demonstrate school performance commensurate with the amount that they have.

Those who assess intelligence—and most diagnostic personnel are required to do so—must recognize that they can only infer intelligence from a sample of behavior derived through testing. Assessors must pay special attention to the kinds of behaviors sampled by intelligence tests. Two considerations are especially important. First, intelligence tests are usually administered for the purpose of making a prediction about future academic performance. In selecting an intelligence test, test givers must always ask, "What is the relationship between the kind(s) of behavior sampled by the test and the kind(s) of behavior I am trying to predict?" The closer the relationship, the better the prediction. It is wise to try to select tests that sample behaviors that are related as closely as possible to the behaviors to be predicted.

Second, test givers must always consider what behaviors or attributes are being assessed by intelligence-test items. In particular, when different kinds of intelligence tests are used to assess students with disabilities, it is very important to be aware of the stimulus and response demands of the items. The descriptions of the kinds of behaviors sampled by intelligence tests that were provided in the last chapter should be helpful. When we assess students' intelligence, we want the test results to reflect intelligence, not sensory dysfunction.

It is important to remember that intelligence is not a fixed thing that we measure. Rather, it is an inferred entity, one that is understood best by evaluating the ways in which individuals who have different kinds of acculturation perform several different kinds of tasks. Intelligence tests differ markedly; individuals differ markedly. Evaluations of the intelligence of an individual must be understood as a function of the interaction between the skills and characteristics the individual brings to a test setting and the behaviors sampled by the test.

The authors include studies of the performance on the PPVT-III of seven special populations: students with speech impairment, language delay, language impairment, mental retardation, learning disability in reading, and hearing impairment, and also gifted students. Individuals who participated in the studies were matched (on the basis of gender, age, race/ethnicity, SES, and geographic region) with individuals in the standardization sample. Results of the seven studies were as would be expected and show the value of the PPVT-III in differentiating representatives of special populations from other individuals.

Summary

The PPVT-III is an individually administered, norm-referenced measure of receptive vocabulary.

The test is well developed and adequately standardized. Data in the technical manual indicate adequate reliability and validity for screening purposes. Overall, the technical characteristics of this scale far surpass those of other picture-vocabulary tests. If used properly and with the awareness that it samples only receptive vocabulary, the PPVT-III can serve as a useful screening device.

● ●

Summary

In this chapter, we have reviewed individually administered intelligence tests that are commonly used or that offer new approaches to assessment. The tests reviewed are the Stanford–Binet Intelligence Scale–IV, four Wechsler scales, the Detroit Tests of Learning Aptitude–4, the Cognitive Assessment System, the Comprehensive Test of Nonverbal Intelligence, the Leiter International Performance Scale–Revised, the Test of Nonverbal Intelligence–3, the Universal Nonverbal Intelligence Test, the Naglieri Nonverbal Ability Test, and the Peabody Picture Vocabulary Test–Revised. Two other measures, the Woodcock-Johnson Psychoeducational Battery–Revised and the Kaufman Assessment Battery for Children, are reviewed in Chapter 27. The kinds of behaviors sampled differ among the various measures of intelligence because test authors have differing theories of intelligence. Thus, it is critical for test users to go beyond global scores and consider the actual behavior sampled by tests.

Questions for Chapter Review and Thought

1. Why is it more appropriate to use an individual test than a group test to assess intelligence?

2. The Stanford–Binet Intelligence Scale and the Wechsler Intelligence Scale for Children–III are two intelligence tests frequently used with school-age children. Identify similarities and differences in the domains of behavior sampled by these two tests.

3. Explain why it is more appropriate to use the Stanford–Binet Intelligence Scale and the WISC-III for making placement decisions than to use tests such as the Peabody Picture Vocabulary Test–III.

4. You have just joined a school system and have been asked to become involved in the triennial review process for a 10-year-old youngster with a learning disability. Your supervisor asks your opinion about using the Peabody Picture Vocabulary Test in the test battery. How would you respond?

Resources for Further Investigation

Project

Using information found in the text, write a summary for three individually administered tests used in the assessment of intelligence. When you have finished, compare your summary with the text summary. Then go to the *Mental Measurements Yearbook,* and compare and contrast your summaries with the reviews of the tests you selected. If your summary is different, has the reviewer used different information and different standards?

Print Resources

Buros, O. K. (1972). *The seventh mental measurements yearbook* (NTLA, pp. 410). Highland Park, NJ: Gryphon.

Carroll, J. G. (1993). *Human cognitive abilities: A survey of factor-analytic studies.* New York: Cambridge University Press.

Conoley, J. C., & Impara, J. C. (1995). *The twelfth mental measurements yearbook* (WISC-III, pp. 1090-1105; DTLA-3, pp. 275–278). Lincoln, NE: University of Nebraska Press.

Conoley, J. C., & Kramer, J. J. (1989). *The tenth mental measurements yearbook* (SB, pp. 768–775). Lincoln, NE: University of Nebraska Press.

Dunn, L., & Dunn, M. (1997). *Peabody Picture Vocabulary Test–III.* Circle Pines, MN: American Guidance Services.

Gustafson, J. E. (1984). A unifying model for the structure of intellectual abilities. *Intelligence, 8,* 179–203.

Hammill, D., Pearson, N., & Wiederholt, J. L. (1997). *Comprehensive Test of Nonverbal Intelligence.* Austin, TX: Pro-Ed.

Kamphaus, R. W. (1994). *Clinical Assessment of Children's Intelligence* (Chapter 10, Stanford-Binet–4th ed.; Chapter 6, Wechsler Intelligence Scale for Children–3rd ed.) Boston: Allyn & Bacon.

Kaufman, A., & Kaufman, N. (1990). *Kaufman Brief Intelligence Test.* Circle Pines, MN: American Guidance Services.

Kramer, J. J., & Conoley, J. C. (1992). *The eleventh mental measurements yearbook* (TONI-2, pp. 969–972). Lincoln, NE: University of Nebraska Press.

Mitchell, J. V. (1985). *The ninth mental measurements yearbook* (PPVT, pp. 1123–1128). Lincoln, NE: University of Nebraska Press.

Roid, G. & Miller, N. (1997). *Leiter International Performance Scale-Revised.* Chicago: Stoelting.

Roid, G. H. (1996, August). *The Leiter International Performance Scale–Revised: Preliminary Report on Validity.* Toronto: Paper presented at the annual meeting of the American Psychological Association.

Wechsler, D. (1939). *Wechsler-Bellevue Intelligence Scale.* New York: Psychological Corporation.

Technology Resources

Pro-ed Catalog Information for Products

http://www.proedinc.com

Find product and ordering information about the *Detroit Tests of Learning Aptitude* (4th ed., 3rd ed., 2nd ed., and Primary ed.) and the *Test of Nonverbal Intelligence–3.*

Psychological Corporation

http://www.psychcorp.com/

Under featured products there is information on the various Wechsler scales of intelligence as well as information on other tests of assessment.

Riverside Publishing

http://www.riverpub.com/

Go to products and services; under clinical and special needs you will find information on the *Das–Naglieri Cognitive Assessment System* (CAS), the *Stanford–Binet Intelligence Scale,* and the *Universal Nonverbal Intelligence Test.*

Welcome to AGS On-line Products and Services

http://www.agsnet.com/

Look for product and ordering information about the instruments available from American Guidance Service. Search by product title for the *Peabody Picture Vocabulary Test–III* and the *Kaufmann Brief Intelligence Test.*

Assessment of Intelligence:
Group Tests

Group intelligence tests differ from one another in three ways: in format, in the kinds of scores they provide, and in their emphasis on speed versus power. First, whereas some group tests consist of a single battery to be administered in one sitting, others contain a number of subscales or subtests and are administered in two or more sittings. Second, some provide IQs or mental ages based on a global performance; others provide the same kinds of scores but differentiate them into subscale scores (for example, verbal, performance, and total; language, nonlanguage, and total). Third, some group intelligence tests are *speed tests,* which are timed, and others are *power tests,* which are untimed.

Why Do We Administer Group Intelligence Tests?

Group intelligence tests are used for one of two purposes: as screening devices for individual students, or as sources of descriptive information about groups of students. Most often, they are routinely administered as screening devices to identify those students who differ enough from average to warrant further assessment. In these cases, the tests' merit is that teachers can administer them relatively quickly to large numbers of students. The tests suffer from the same limitations as any group test: They can be made to yield qualitative information only with difficulty, and they require students to sit still for about 20 minutes, to mark with a pencil, and, often, to read.

Group intelligence tests are also used to provide descriptive information about the level of capability of students in a classroom, a district, or even a state. They are, on occasion, used to track students, in place of or in addition to achievement tests. When used in this way, the tests set expectations; they are thought to indicate the level of achievement to be expected in individual classrooms or districts.

As we prepared this eighth edition of *Assessment,* it was becoming increasingly common for school districts to drop the practice of group intelligence testing. When administrators are asked why they are doing so, they cite (a) the limited relevance of knowing about students' capability, as opposed to knowing about the subject matter skills (such as for reading and math) that students do and do not have; (b) the difficulty teachers experience in trying to use the test results for instructional purposes; and (c) the cost of a schoolwide intellectual screening program. At the same time, many school districts continue to use these measures as an index of the capability of the students in their schools. In this chapter, we review the two most commonly used group intelligence tests: the Cognitive Abilities Test (CogAT) and the Otis–Lennon School Ability Test (seventh edition: OLSAT 7).

Specific Group Tests of Intelligence

Cognitive Abilities Test (CogAT)

The Cognitive Abilities Test (CogAT; Thorndike & Hagen, 1994) is a further development of the Lorge–Thorndike Intelligence Tests, which first appeared in 1954. The Iowa Tests of Basic Skills, the Tests of Achievement and Proficiency, and the CogAT compose the Riverside Basic Skills Assessment Program.

There are ten levels of the CogAT. Levels 1 and 2 make up the primary battery. Level 1 is appropriate for use in kindergarten and first grade, and Level 2 is to be used in second and third grades. The other eight levels of the test (levels A through H) are published in a multilevel edition in a single test booklet. Items in the multilevel edition range from easy third-grade items to very difficult items at the twelfth-grade level. Examinees start and stop at different points, depending on the level being administered. The inclusion of eight levels of the test in a single multilevel edition allows teachers to administer levels of difficulty appropriate to the ability of their students. The scales increase in difficulty in very small steps. For students who attain little more than chance-level performance, the next easier level of the scale may be administered; for those who get nearly every item correct, the next more difficult level may be administered. Practice tests are available for all subtests in the scale.

Levels 1 and 2 are designed for assessing the extent to which the child has developed the ability to reason inductively, to solve problems, to comprehend verbal statements, to scan pictorial and figural stimuli to obtain either specific or general information, to compare stimuli and detect similarities and differences in relative size, to classify or order familiar objects, and to use quantitative and special relationships and concepts, as well as for assessing the child's store of general information and concepts.

The multilevel edition of the CogAT was constructed to provide a variety of tasks that require the student to discover and use relationships to solve problems. The tasks use verbal, numerical, and nonverbal symbols.

Although both Levels 1 and 2 and the multilevel edition include three separate batteries—verbal, quantitative, and nonverbal—the subtests included in the two editions differ. The various subtests are described here.

Verbal Battery—Levels 1 and 2

Oral Vocabulary The examiner reads a word or phrase aloud, and the student must mark the picture that illustrates it.

Verbal Reasoning Students are asked to make inferences, transformations, or judgments in response to common situations.

Quantitative Battery—Levels 1 and 2

Quantitative Concepts The examiner asks the child to solve simple story problems or to solve a serious problem based on a mathematical principle. All the problems can be solved by using counting strategies that the majority of children develop before entering kindergarten.

Relational Concepts The examiner asks the child to mark the picture illustrating a particular relational concept (for example, biggest, tallest, or beside) read aloud by the examiner.

Nonverbal Battery—Levels 1 and 2

Matrices   The student must select from among four response choices the one that best completes a stimulus figure.

Figure Classification   The child is shown three figures that are alike in some way and must select from four response possibilities the one figure that is like the three stimulus figures.

Verbal Battery—Multilevel Edition

Sentence Completion   The student reads a sentence with a missing word and must select the response word that most appropriately fills the blank.

Verbal Classification   The student is given three or four words that are members of a conceptual category and must identify which response word best fits into the same category as the stimulus words.

Verbal Analogies   The student must complete verbal analogies of the form A:B::C:_____.

Quantitative Battery—Multilevel Edition

Quantitative Relations   The student must make judgments about relative sizes or amounts of material. Given two quantities (for example, $2 + 4$ and 2×4), the student must identify which one is greater.

Number Series   Given a series of numbers that have a progressive relationship to one another, the student must select the number that best completes the relationship.

Equation Building   The student must construct correct equations using numbers and symbols for mathematical operations.

Nonverbal Battery—Multilevel Edition

Figure Classification   Given three figures that are alike in some way, the student must identify the response figure that best fits into the same conceptual category.

Figure Analogies   The student must deduce the relationship between a pair of figures and must then select the last element of a second pair so that it accurately completes the analogy.

Figure Analysis   The student is given parts of figures and must identify the whole figure that could be formed by putting the parts together.

Levels 1 and 2 Versus Multilevel Edition

Levels 1 and 2 require no reading. These two levels are administered in three sessions, ranging from 35 to 40 minutes each. Total working time is 98 minutes for each level. The multilevel edition is also administered in three sessions. Though administration time necessarily is longer, actual working time is 90 minutes for the three batteries of the multilevel edition.

Scores

Four scores are provided for each level of the CogAT, one for each battery (verbal, quantitative, and nonverbal) and a composite. Scores are not obtained for subtests within each battery. Among the scores available for each battery are number of items marked, raw score, standard age score, national grade and age percentile ranks, and grade and age stanines. Normal-curve-equivalent tables are provided in the norms booklet.

Norms

The CogAT was standardized concurrently with the Iowa Tests of Basic Skills (Hoover, Hieronymus, Frisbie, & Dunbar, 1996) and the Tests of Achievement and Proficiency (Scannell, Haugh, Lloyd, & Risinger, 1993). These measures were standardized on a carefully selected stratified national sample of about 170,000 students. All public school districts in the United States were stratified first on the basis of geographic region and then on the basis of size of enrollment. Districts were then stratified on the basis of socioeconomic status within the district, based on the percentage of students in the district falling below the federal government's poverty guideline. One district was randomly selected from each socioeconomic stratum. Once districts had been selected and had agreed to participate, further sample selection was accomplished when buildings were selected that would be representative of the distribution of achievement within the selected districts. Data provided in the test manuals show the breakdown of the sample by district size, region of the country, and district socioeconomic status. In addition to the public-school norm sample, norms are provided for Catholic schools and for private non-Catholic schools. There are eight separate sets of norms—national, interpolated, local, large city, Catholic/private school, high socioeconomic, low socioeconomic, and international—so that student performance can be compared across different groups.

Reliability

Data on internal-consistency reliability are reported for the verbal, quantitative, and nonverbal batteries, based on the performance of students in the fall and spring standardization sample. All reliability coefficients exceeded .80, with reliabilities higher for the multilevel edition than for Levels 1 and 2. There is good evidence of the internal consistency of the CogAT. No other reliability data are reported in the technical manual.

Validity

There are no data on the validity of the 1993 CogAT.

Summary

The CogAT consists of three batteries (verbal, quantitative, and nonverbal) designed to measure the intelligence of students in kindergarten through grade 12. The procedures used in standardizing this test are exemplary. Evidence for internal-consistency reliability is good, but there are no data on other forms of reliability. There are currently no data on the validity of the CogAT.

Otis–Lennon School Ability Test, Seventh Edition (OLSAT 7)

The seventh edition of the Otis–Lennon School Ability Test (OLSAT 7; Otis & Lennon, 1996) is the latest in a series of intelligence tests that date back to 1918. The OLSAT 7 requires a student to perform tasks such as detecting similarities and differences, following directions, solving analogies and matrices, classifying, and sequencing as a measure of those verbal, quantitative, and figural reasoning skills that are most closely related to school achievement. The test is designed to assess "the examinees' ability to cope with school learning tasks, to suggest their possible placement for school learning functions, and to evaluate their achievement in relation to the talents they bring to school learning situations" (Otis & Lennon, 1996, p. 5).

Seven levels of the OLSAT 7 (designated A through G) are used to assess the abilities of students in grades K–12. There are separate tests for each grade from K–3; one test for grades 4–5, one for grades 6–8, and one for the high school grades. At levels A and B (kindergarten and first grade), the entire test is dictated. Level C (second grade) contains two self-administered subtests, with the remainder of the test dictated. All other levels (D–G) are self-administered.

Subtests

The 21 different types of items that compose the OLSAT fall into five clusters: verbal comprehension, verbal reasoning, pictorial reasoning, figural reasoning, and quantitative reasoning. The clusters, in turn, make up the verbal and nonverbal scales. Table 18.1 shows the types of items at the seven levels of the test. Behavioral samples for each of the item types in the clusters are as follows.

Verbal Comprehension   Items in this cluster assess knowledge of vocabulary, skill in identifying relationships among words, ability to derive meaning from words, and skill in identifying subtle differences between similar words and phrases.

Verbal Reasoning   Items in this cluster assess skill in inferring relationships among words, including verbal math problems; in making verbal classification; and identifying similarities and differences between words.

Pictorial Reasoning   Items in this cluster all use pictures and require students to classify pictures, complete sequences, and solve analogies.

Figural Reasoning   Items in this cluster assess skill in using geometric figures to identify analogies and to complete matrices and sequences.

Quantitative Reasoning   Items in this cluster assess reasoning, completion of sequences, and completion of matrices using numbers.

Scores

Raw scores earned on verbal, nonverbal, and total test sections of the OLSAT may be converted to one or more derived scores: scaled scores, school ability indexes (with a mean of 100 and a standard deviation of 16), percentile ranks, stanines, or normal-curve equivalents (NCEs).

Norms

The OLSAT was standardized in both fall and spring of 1995. The spring standardization sample consisted of 175,000 students from 1,000 school districts; the fall standardization used 135,000 students. The sampling of students took into account socioeconomic status (SES), region of the country, environment (urban or rural), and ethnicity. There was no specific stratification on the basis of age, grade, or gender. The sampling distribution is reported, but cross-tabulations are not. The sample is not a stratified sample; for example, we do not know how many students from the Northeast were from urban environments.

Reliability

At each level, KR-20s are reported for each age and grade. Most reliability coefficients range from .80 to .89, but some are as low as .63 (specifically, nonverbal scales of level D for individuals 11 years, 0–2 months). Reliabilities for students who are 11 years, 0–2 months are lower than for other, even adjacent age ranges; the verbal scale at this level has a reliability of .68. There are no data on test stability.

Validity

The authors of the OLSAT argue that construct validity of the measure is shown by the high consistency of scores across all levels of the test. This is more a reliability than a validity argument. Evidence for validity is presented in the form of high correlations between the OLSAT and the Stanford Achievement Test (SAT). The test authors show that scores on the verbal subtests of the OLSAT, as compared with the nonverbal, are better predictors of performance on verbal (language and reading) subtests of the SAT, and performance on the nonverbal section is more predictive of scores on the SAT mathematics subtests.

Summary

The OLSAT is a quickly administered group test of intelligence for which there is reasonable evidence of internal consistency. There is no support for stability. Evidence for validity is limited. The authors do not report the stratification of the standardization sample.

TABLE 18.1 ● Types of Items from the OLSAT 7

Cluster/Item Type	Test Level						
	A (Kindergarten)	B (Grade 1)	C (Grade 2)	D (Grade 3)	E (Grades 4–5)	F (Grades 6–8)	G (Grades 9–12)
VERBAL							
Verbal Comprehension							
Following Directions	X	X	X				
Antonyms				X	X	X	X
Sentence Completion				X	X	X	X
Sentence Arrangement				X	X	X	X
Verbal Reasoning							
Aural Reasoning	X	X	X				
Arithmetic Reasoning	X	X	X	X	X	X	X
Logical Selection				X	X	X	X
Word/Letter Matrix				X	X	X	X
Verbal Analogies				X	X	X	X
Verbal Classification				X	X	X	X
Inference					X	X	X
NONVERBAL							
Pictorial Reasoning							
Picture Classification	X	X	X				
Picture Analogies	X	X	X				
Picture Series	X						
Figural Reasoning							
Figural Classification	X	X	X	X			
Figural Analogies	X	X	X	X	X	X	X
Pattern Matrix	X	X	X	X	X	X	X
Figural Series	X	X	X	X	X	X	X
Quantitative Reasoning							
Number Series					X	X	X
Numeric Inference					X	X	X
Number Matrix					X	X	X

Coping with Dilemmas in Current Practice

A number of specific limitations are inherent in the construction and use of group intelligence tests. The first limitation is that most tests have many levels designed for use in specific grades (for example, level A for kindergarten through third grade, level B for third through sixth grade). Tests are typically standardized by grade, but students of different ages are enrolled in the same grade, and students of the same age are enrolled in different grades. Further, students with disabilities are often in ungraded programs. Test authors then use interpolation and extrapolation to compute mental ages for students based on grade sampling. In earlier discussions, an age score was defined as the average score earned by individuals of a given age. Let us now consider a problem.

Suppose that an intelligence test has a level Q, which is designed to measure the intelligence of students in grades 6 through 9. As is typical of group intelligence tests, the test is standardized on students in grades 6 through 9, students who range in age from approximately 10 or 11 to 14 or 15 years. Norms are based on this age range. The test is later administered to Stanley, age 10-8, who earns a mental age of 7-3. How can this be? Stanley, who is 10 years, 8 months old, could not possibly earn the same score as is typically earned on the test by students who are 7 years, 3 months old because *no* students 7 years and 3 months old were included in the normative sample. The score is based on an extrapolation.

The second limitation is that most group intelligence tests, although standardized on large numbers of students, often are not standardized on representative populations. Most are standardized on school districts, not on individual students. An effort is made to select representative districts, but these may not necessarily include a representative population of individuals. Yet, the normative tables for group intelligence tests typically provide scores for individuals, not for groups.

The third limitation is that most group intelligence tests are standardized on volunteer samples. In the process of standardizing the test, representative districts are selected and are asked to participate. Districts that refuse, for any of a number of reasons, are replaced by what are believed to be comparable districts. This process of replacement may introduce bias into the standardization.

A final limitation is that when tests are standardized in public schools, those students who are excluded from school are also excluded from the standardization population. Students who are severely retarded or severely disturbed or who have dropped out of school are excluded from the norms. Similarly, most authors of group intelligence tests do not describe the extent to which they included students enrolled in special-education classes in their standardization samples. Exclusion of students with low IQs biases the norms; the range of performance of the standardization group is reduced, and the standard deviation is decreased. It is extremely important for the authors of group tests to provide tables in test manuals illustrating the composition of the standardization sample. Such tables should include descriptions of the kinds of individuals on whom a test was standardized, rather than descriptions of districts.

In spite of their limitations and problems, group intelligence tests are still used. Those who use the tests must recognize that the tests are sampling behaviors and must be aware of the behaviors sampled by the tests. School personnel give group intelligence tests to predict future performance, usually future achievement. It is wise, therefore, to use group intelligence tests and group achievement tests that have been standardized on the same population. We recommended that school personnel first select the group achievement test to be used and then choose the group intelligence test that has been standardized on the same population. The following pairs of tests have been standardized on identical groups of students: the OLSAT 7 and the Stanford Achievement Test 9; the CogAT and the Iowa Tests of Basic Skills; the OLSAT 7 and the Metropolitan Achievement Tests 7; and the CogAT and the Tests of Achievement and Proficiency.

Summary

Group intelligence tests are used primarily as screening devices; they are designed to identify those whose intellectual development deviates significantly enough from normal to warrant individual intellectual assessment. Many different group intelligence tests are currently used in the schools. A review of the most commonly used group tests illustrates the many kinds of behaviors sampled in the assessment of intelligence. When teachers evaluate students' performances on group intelligence tests, they must go beyond obtained scores to look at the kinds of behaviors sampled by the tests. When selecting group intelligence tests, teachers must evaluate the extent to which specific tests are standardized on samples of students with whom they want to compare their pupils and the extent to which the tests are technically adequate for their own purposes.

Questions for Chapter Review and Thought

1. Obtain a copy of any group intelligence test, and identify the domains of behaviors sampled by at least ten items. Use the domains described in Chapter 16.

2. Identify at least four major factors that a teacher must consider when administering a group intelligence test to students.

3. Suppose you had to decide which group intelligence test to give in your school. What factors would you consider in selecting a test? Which test might you select? Justify your answer.

4. You have just been hired as a classroom teacher. On your first day, you were told that one of your students had recently been evaluated and identified as having a learning disability. The school psychologist provides you with her test results, and you note that the youngster had difficulty with generalization, spatial relationships, and sentence-completion subtests. With what classroom activities might this youngster have difficulty?

Resources for Further Investigation

Project

Using information found in the text, write a summary for one of the group intelligence tests. Upon completion, compare your summary with the text summary. Then go to the *Mental Measurement Yearbook* (see "Print Resources"), and compare and contrast your summary with the review of the test you selected. If your summary is different, has the reviewer used different information and different standards?

Print Resources

Kramer, J. J., & Conoley, J. C. (1992). *The eleventh mental measurements yearbook* (OLSAT, pp. 632–639). Lincoln, NE: University of Nebraska Press.

Otis, A., & Lennon, R. (1996). *Otis–Lennon School Ability Test, Seventh Edition.* San Antonio: Psychological Corporation.

Technology Resources

Riverside Publishing

http://www.riverpub.com/

Go to products and services, and then under educational assessments in the index of products you will find information on the *Cognitive Abilities Test.*

Harcourt Educational Measurement

http://www.hbem.com/trophy/ability/olsat7.htm

Here you will find information and a description of the *Otis–Lennon School Ability Test,* Seventh Edition.

chapter

19

Assessment of Sensory Acuity

T he first thing to check when a child is having academic or social difficulties is whether that child is adequately and properly receiving environmental information. In efforts to identify why children experience difficulties, too often we overlook the obvious in search of the subtle. Vision and hearing difficulties interfere with the educational progress of a significant number of schoolchildren.

The teacher's role in assessment of sensory acuity is twofold. First, the teacher must be aware of behaviors that may indicate sensory difficulties and thus must have at least an embryonic knowledge of the kinds of sensory difficulties that children experience. Second, the teacher must know the instructional implications of sensory difficulties. Communication with *vision specialists* (teachers of students with visual impairments, ophthalmologists, optometrists, and orientation and mobility specialists) and *hearing specialists* (teachers of students with hearing impairments, audiologists, speech and language pathologists, and otolaryngologists) is the most effective way to gain such information. The teacher must have basic knowledge about procedures used for assessing sensory acuity in order to comprehend and use data from specialists. This chapter, therefore, differs from previous chapters. It provides basic knowledge about the kinds of vision and hearing difficulties pupils experience, as well as an overview of procedures and devices used to assess sensory acuity.

Why Do We Assess Sensory Acuity?

Difficulties in seeing or hearing are among the most obvious reasons that students experience academic and behavioral difficulties in school. They also generally are the kinds of difficulties most easily corrected or compensated for. The link between sensory difficulties and academic problems is easy to appreciate. The fact that sensory difficulties may cause behavioral problems, while not so obvious, has also been established.

Visual Difficulties

Types of Visual Impairment

There are three ways in which vision may be limited: (1) Visual acuity may be limited; (2) the field of vision may be restricted; or (3) color vision may be imperfect. The first two are the most significant. *Visual acuity* refers to the clarity or sharpness with which a person sees. The method of measuring visual acuity is derived from the use of the Snellen Wall Chart. A person is described as having normal vision (20/20 in both eyes) if, at 20 feet from the chart, that person is able to distinguish letters that an average person can distinguish at 20 feet. A rating of 20/200 means that the person can distinguish letters at 20 feet that the average person can distinguish at 200 feet. Conversely, 20/10 vision means the person is able to distinguish letters at 20 feet that the average person can distinguish only at 10 feet. The former demonstrates limited vision, whereas the latter demonstrates better than average visual acuity.

A person's field of vision may be restricted in either of two ways. First, a person may demonstrate normal central visual acuity with a restricted peripheral field; this is usually referred to as *tunnel vision*. Second, a person may have a *scotoma*, a blind or dark spot in the visual field. If the spot occurs in the middle of the eye, it may result in central vision impairment, particularly if both eyes are impaired.

Color vision is determined by the discrimination of three qualities of color: *hue* (such as red vs. green), *saturation* (that is, pure vs. muddied colors), and *brightness* (that is, vibrant vs. dull reflection of light). The essential difference between colorblind and normal persons is that hues that appear different to normal persons look the same to a colorblind person. Colorblind persons frequently do not know that they are colorblind unless they have been tested and told so. Colorblindness is not usually an all-or-nothing condition. Most colorblindness is partial; the person has difficulty distinguishing certain colors, usually red and green. Total colorblindness is extremely rare. Colorblindness is an inherited trait found in about 1 out of 12 males and about 1 out of 200 females. There is no cure for colorblindness, but the condition is not usually regarded as a disability.

Impaired Visual Acuity

Blindness may be either congenital or acquired. Congenital blindness or blindness acquired prior to age 5 years has the most serious educational implications. Few people are totally blind. Many can at least perceive some light (versus total darkness) and some objects; any perception of light or of objects helps for mobility. Blindness, for legal purposes, is defined as

> central visual activity of 20/200 or less in the better eye, with correcting glasses, or central visual acuity of more than 20/200 if there is a field defect in which the peripheral field has contracted to such an extent that the widest diameter of visual field subtends an angular distance no greater than 20 degrees.[1] (Hurlin, 1962, p. 8)

It has been said that more people are blinded by definition (the legal definition cited here) than by any other cause (Greenwood, 1963, cited in Barraga, 1976). According to Taylor (cited in Barraga, 1976, p. 13; italic emphasis added),

> the term *visually handicapped* is being used widely at present to denote the total group of children who have impairments in the structure or functioning of the visual sense organ—the eye—irrespective of the nature and extent of the impairment. The term has gained acceptance because the impairment causes a limitation that, even with the best possible correction, interferes with incidental or normal learning through the sense of vision.

When we deal with children, we are concerned primarily with the educational implications of reduced acuity. Educational needs resulting from low acuity lead to students being declared eligible for special-education services. Barraga (1976, p. 14) differentiates among three categories of visual disabilities:

> Blind. This term [is] used to refer to children who have only light perception without projection, or those who are totally without the sense of vision (Faye, 1970). . . . Educationally, the blind child is one who learns through Braille and related media without the use of vision (Halliday, 1970), although perception of light may be present and useful in orientation and movement.
> Low Vision. Children who have limitations in distance vision but are able to see objects and materials when they are within a few inches or at a maximum of a few feet away are another subgroup. Most low-vision children will be able to use their vision for many school learning activities, a few for visual reading perhaps, whereas others may need to use tactual materials and possibly even Braille to supplement printed and other visual materials. . . .
> Visually Limited. This term refers to children who in some way are limited in their use of vision under average circumstances. They may have difficulty seeing learning materials without special lighting, or they may be unable to see distant objects unless the objects are moving, or they need to wear prescriptive lenses or use optical aids and special materials to function visually. Visually limited children will be considered for all educational purposes and under all circumstances as seeing children.

---

1. Tunnel vision.

Estimates of the number of school-age children who experience some form of visual difficulties range from 5 to 33 percent. Obviously, estimates differ as a function of the definition used and the screening devices employed.

Teachers must be consistently on the lookout for symptoms and signs of visual difficulty. When children complain of symptoms such as frequent headaches, dizziness, sensitivity to light, or blurred vision, efforts must be made to evaluate the extent to which they are seeing properly. Obvious signs of possible visual difficulty include crossed eyes or turned-out eyes (*strabismus*); red, swollen, or encrusted eyelids; constant rapid movement of the eyes; watery eyes or discharges from the eye; and haziness in the pupils. These symptoms and signs should receive special attention in the form of referral for vision screening (U.S. Public Health Service, 1971).

Certain behaviors also may indicate visual difficulties. According to the U.S. Public Health Service (1971), behaviors indicative of potential visual difficulties include holding books unusually close to or far from the eyes while reading; frequent blinking, squinting, or rubbing of the eyes; abnormal tilting or turning of the head; inattention during blackboard lessons; poor alignment of letters in written work; unusual choice of colors in artwork; confusion of certain letters of the alphabet in reading (*o*'s and *a*'s, *e*'s and *c*'s, *b*'s and *h*'s, *n*'s and *r*'s); inability or reluctance to participate in games requiring distance vision or visual accuracy; and irritability when doing close work.

• •

Vision Screening and Assessment

Schools conduct vision screening, whereas vision testing is done clinically by ophthalmologists and optometrists. When youngsters experience learning difficulties, or when routine vision screening indicates visual difficulties, the child is referred for a clinical vision exam. If the clinical exam indicates 20/20 vision, no additional visual assessment needs to be done by educational personnel. Similarly, if visual acuity is limited but can be corrected by glasses, no visual assessments need be conducted by education personnel. However, if vision is 20/70 or less with best correction, or if there is a limited visual field, educational personnel must ensure that a clinical low-vision exam, functional-vision assessment, or learning-media assessment is conducted. The purpose of these tests is intervention planning.

Most schools now have vision-screening programs, but the effectiveness of these programs varies. Two fundamentally different kinds of tests are used: those that screen only central visual acuity at a distance and those that assess both central visual acuity and a number of other visual capabilities. Most preschool screening programs also include screening for *amblyopia,* often called "lazy eye."

Basic Screening

The standard Snellen Wall Chart is the most commonly used screening test to assess visual acuity. The test consists simply of a wall chart of standard-sized letters that a child is asked to read at a distance of 20 feet. The test provides limited information about vision, assessing only central visual acuity at a distance of 20 feet. Specific difficulties may be encountered in using the test with some school-age children. First, children may be unable to read the letters or to discriminate between letters such as *F* and *P*. Second, children can often memorize the letters ahead of time. Third, the letters of the alphabet differ in legibility, which leads to guessing. The practical criterion for referral using this test is acuity of 20/40 or less in either eye for children in kindergarten through third grade, and 20/30 or less in either eye for older children and juveniles (National Society for the Prevention of Blindness, 1961).

An adaptation of the Snellen Wall Chart, the Snellen E Test, is the most commonly used test with preschool children and those who are unable to read. The letter *E* is presented with its arms facing in one of four directions, and the person being tested is asked either to name the direction, to point, or to hold up a letter E to match the stimulus. Again, this test assesses only central visual acuity at a distance.

Both of the Snellen tests fail to identify students with near-vision problems, the kinds of problems that are often the most critical to reading. They also miss physical difficulties and problems in the internal structure of the eye (such as the retina). Some schools use the Keystone Telebinocular, a device that assesses 14 different visual skills. Visual functioning is assessed at both a near point (16 inches) and a far point (20 inches). The distances are produced optically, and children remain seated in front of the instrument throughout testing.

Clinical Low-Vision Exams

More and more, educators are recognizing the limitations of assessing visual acuity with traditional measures. They note that low-vision students with similar ratings on measures of acuity vary considerably in their actual classroom functioning. For example, some children have vision but are unable to use it spontaneously. Others can use their vision in certain situations (for example, during one-to-one instruction in a controlled setting) but not for incidental learning. Still other students choose, consciously or unconsciously, not to use their vision (Corn, 1983). Corn (1983) outlined a theoretical model that can be used to think about vision and to assist professionals in eliciting vision behaviors or maximizing function in individuals with low vision. She points out that low vision results from differing visual disabilities (that is, retinal acuity, retinal field, or cortical brain functions), and that these interact with other individual differences (such as cognition and physical makeup, including motor development and health) and also with environmental factors (such as poor lighting or highly complex visual field) to influence visual functioning. She illustrates why so much of the assessment of students with visual impairments is individualized and clinical. In essence, educators use whatever methods they can to try to elicit visual behaviors in students who are not demonstrating them spontaneously. (For example, they might use a penlight, and if that did not work, they might use a large white dot on a television screen, to try to elicit a response to light.) Also, educators assess the extent to which educational adaptations (such as large print) optimize the functioning of students with low vision.

Functional-Vision Assessment

A significant effort is under way to develop in-school measures of residual vision and of functional vision. Unfortunately, most of the assessment procedures available are informal, nonstandardized sets of procedures or are more formal standardized procedures that are still under development (and have been for a very long time). Researchers at the University of Minnesota have been working on the Minnesota Functional Vision Assessment (MFVA; Knowlton, 1988). They have produced eight subtests, each designed to assess an aspect of functional vision: acuity, binocular coordination, contrast, color, motion, functional fields, accommodation, and illusion. This assessment instrument is for use in the regular school environment.

Others have been working on assessment of functional vision. Jose, Smith, and Shane (1988) outline a set of procedures for gathering information on the following aspects of functional vision: pupillary response, muscle imbalance (the tendency for the eyes to deviate), blink reflex, eye preference, central and peripheral fields, visual field preference, tracking ability, responses to lights and to objects (reaching for or shifting attention to them), scanning ability, matching, ability to follow moving objects, imitation, object concept (response to objects and pictures), and object permanence. Langley and DuBose (1989) provide a set of procedures for functional vision testing and a checklist for diagnostic personnel to use in evaluating responses to visual stimuli, responses to objects on the basis of their size and distance, integration of visual and cognitive processing, and integration of visual and motor processing.

Learning-Media Assessment

Learning-media assessment is an objective process of systematically selecting learning and literacy media for students with visual impairments. Koening and Holbrook (1993), at the Texas School for the Blind and Visually Impaired, developed this informal assessment method for gathering data on general learning media and literacy media. General learning media include *instructional materials* (such as rulers, worksheets, pictures) and *instructional methods* (such as demonstration, modeling). *Literacy media* are the tools for reading and writing.

Koening and Holbrook (1993) indicate that three types of information are gathered on the student in learning-media assessment:

1. The efficiency with which the student gathers information from various sensory channels

2. The types of learning media the student uses or will use to accomplish learning tasks

3. The literacy media the student will use for reading and writing

Braille Assessment Inventory

In Minnesota, teachers of students with visual impairments have been developing the Braille Assessment Inventory (BAI; Sharpe, McNear, & McGrew, 1996). This is an empirically based scale to be used by child study teams that are charged with the task of designing interventions for students with visual impairments. The scale is used to decide the appropriateness of Braille instruction for students who are blind and visually impaired. Composed of 43 items grouped into five scales, the test is used to decide whether students should begin or continue to receive Braille instruction. The BAI was developed by a national sample of teachers of students who were blind or visually impaired. The three subscales of this measure are object recognition, visual orientation, and tactual orientation. Behaviors measured by the subscales are as follows:

Object recognition. A measure of the student's skill in recognizing objects, people, and letters at varying distances

Visual orientation. A measure of functional vision in skills such as the student's using and reading printed materials and reading her or his own handwriting, as well as a means of detecting signs of visual fatigue

Tactual orientation. A measure of a student's skill in discriminating symbols and objects, in using tactual materials, and in perceiving various objects

The scoring of this measure is functional. It is recommended that students who obtain raw scores greater than 96 be taught using print materials. For those who score lower than 85, Braille instruction is recommended, while for those who earn scores between 86 and 95, the preferred mode of instruction is not certain. Reliability of this scale (based on interrater reliability computation) exceeds .90.

● ●

Hearing Difficulties[2]

Signs of Hearing Loss

Early detection of hearing problems in preschool and school-age children is imperative, so that appropriate remedial or compensatory procedures can be instituted. Children with hearing problems characteristically fail to pay attention, provide wrong answers to simple questions, frequently ask to have words or sentences repeated, and hear better in quiet conditions and when watching the teacher's face. Such children often function below their educational potential, are withdrawn, or exhibit behavior problems. Children who are repeatedly sick, having frequent earaches, colds or other upper respiratory infections, allergies, or

2. This section was written especially for this book by Dr. Tom Frank, Professor of Audiology, Department of Communication Disorders, College of Health and Human Development, The Pennsylvania State University.

fluid draining from their ears, may also have a concomitant hearing problem. Further, children who do not speak clearly or who show other types of speech or language problems, and children who fail to discriminate between sounds or words with similar vowels but different consonants may also have hearing problems. Finally, some preschool and school-age children are more at risk for hearing problems, including children with craniofacial anomalies such as cleft palate or Down syndrome; children from a lower socioeconomic class; Native Americans and Eskimos, who may not be receiving appropriate and routine health care (Northern & Downs, 1991, pp. 22–24); and learning-disabled or retarded children who cannot express that they have trouble hearing.

Any child, regardless of age, who has one or more of the aforementioned hearing-loss symptoms and any child at risk for hearing loss should be referred for a hearing test. Depending on the school system, the hearing test may be given by the school nurse, a speech–language pathologist, a hearing therapist, an audiologist, or a trained technician. In a preschool setting, support personnel for assessing hearing problems may not be available. Children in such a setting should be referred to their family physician or directly to a hearing specialist.

If a hearing problem is detected or if the child is difficult to test, making the results questionable, the child should be referred to a physician specializing in disorders of the ear, called an "otologist" or an "otolaryngologist," or to a specialist in hearing evaluation and rehabilitation, called an "audiologist." The otologist and the audiologist often work together as a team. An *otologist* has expertise in physical examination of the ears and in diagnosing and treating ear disorders. If a child has a correctable hearing loss, the otologist can provide the appropriate treatment (such as drug therapy or surgery). The *audiologist* has expertise in hearing assessment and rehabilitation. If a child has an educationally significant and noncorrectable hearing loss, the audiologist can prescribe, fit, and monitor the use of hearing aids. Further, the audiologist can make recommendations to teachers, hearing therapists, speech–language pathologists, and parents concerning the child's hearing ability in different listening environments.

Modes of Hearing

The sensation of hearing can be initiated through two modes: air conduction and bone conduction. *Air-conduction hearing* occurs when the sense of hearing is initiated by an airborne sound that enters the outer ear, passes through the middle and inner ear and the brainstem, and is processed in the central auditory system. The vast majority of our everyday hearing experiences occur by air conduction—for example, listening to a teacher's voice or a television. To test hearing, air-conduction signals can be transmitted to the ear via either a loudspeaker or, more commonly, an earphone placed on the outer ear.

Bone-conduction hearing occurs when the head is mechanically vibrated, so that the sense of hearing is initiated in the inner ear, with little or no participation of the outer or middle ear. Hearing by bone conduction occurs when we listen to ourselves speak. To test hearing by bone conduction, signals are transmitted to the ear via a small vibrator, commonly placed behind the outer ear on the mastoid bone. It is very important to note that normal hearing by air conduction depends on the normal functioning of the outer, middle, and inner ear and the neural pathways, whereas normal hearing by bone conduction depends solely on the normal functioning of the inner ear and neural pathways.

Hearing-screening tests initiate the sense of hearing using the air-conduction mode of hearing. Diagnostic hearing tests, which require the measurement of hearing thresholds, initiate the sense of hearing by both air and bone conduction. This is done to define the type and severity of a hearing loss, the *severity* of a hearing loss being generally defined as the average air-conduction hearing thresholds. Hearing screening, hearing-threshold testing, and other types of hearing tests are conducted with an electronic instrument termed an *audiometer*.

Types of Screening and Assessment

The identification of preschool and school-age children with hearing problems usually falls within the realm of a *hearing-screening program*, which may also be called a "hearing-conservation program," a "hearing-loss identification program," or "identification audiometry." All states have laws requiring hearing screening of school-age children. Unfortunately, hearing screening for many children in preschool programs is not mandated by state or federal laws. Therefore, many preschool children who have educationally significant hearing losses are not being identified and may become educationally delayed. Hearing-screening programs generally have three components: the actual hearing screening, follow-up hearing-threshold tests for those who fail the screening, and referral for those diagnosed with hearing impairment.

Hearing Screening

The primary purpose of hearing screening in a school situation is to identify children with educationally significant hearing problems. Experience has indicated that teachers and parents may not be able to identify a child with an educationally significant hearing loss. Further, teachers and parents sometimes identify a normal child as having hearing loss. Thus, subjective estimates of a child's hearing ability are not always reliable, and more objective testing must be conducted. This is the purpose of hearing screening.

Hearing screening should be conducted for one child at a time. Screening a large number of children individually is more effective in identifying children with hearing problems and in the long run is more cost-efficient than screening groups of children.

Typically, hearing-screening guidelines require that hearing screening include (1) a case history and visual inspection of the outer ear, the ear canal, and the eardrum; (2) pure-tone hearing screening; and (3) tympanometry (discussed later in this chapter). Hearing should be screened annually for children functioning at a developmental level of 3 years through third grade and for high-risk children regardless of grade. *High-risk children* are those who have repeated a grade; require special education; are new to the school; are absent during the hearing screening; have failed previous hearing screenings; have speech, language, or communication problems; are suspected of having a hearing impairment or have a medical problem associated with hearing impairment (for example, chronic earaches or allergies); or are involved in coursework in which they are around loud noise (such as band, woodworking, and auto repair).

The case history and visual inspection of the ear must be done by a qualified individual, such as a school nurse, speech–language pathologist, or audiologist. If a child has a significant case history for ear problems or if inspection of the ear reveals abnormalities (such as wax blocking the ear canal, fluid draining from the middle ear, or an eardrum perforation), the child is removed from the screening and should be referred for medical evaluation or treatment. Even though the case history and ear inspection should be the first step in hearing screening, this step is often bypassed, and hearing screening using air-conducted pure tones becomes the first step.

When pure-tone hearing screening is conducted, the child is instructed to respond, even if the tone is very soft, by raising his or her hand. Older children may use a response button. Some preschool and younger school-age children must be taught or conditioned to respond. The tester then places earphones directly over the child's ears, making sure that there is no hair in between the earphone and the opening to the ear canal, that eyeglasses have been removed, and that earrings are removed if they cause a problem. The child should be seated so that he or she cannot see the examiner. Because earphones are employed, the child's entire auditory system is being stimulated. That is, the child's hearing is being tested by air conduction.

Typically for hearing screening, the frequencies 500, 1,000, 2,000, and 4,000 Hz are presented at a hearing level (HL) of 20 dB. However, if tympanometry screening is also conducted, screening at 500 Hz can be excluded. The choice of frequencies relates to the fact that hearing sounds in the range of 500 to 4,000 Hz is crucial for understanding speech, and 20 dB HL is the upper range of normal hearing for children. Many states have regulations pertaining to hearing screening that also specify hearing-screening frequencies and hearing levels. Needless to say, all hearing testing should be done in a very quiet room, separated not only acoustically but also by distance from noisy parts of the school. If hearing testing is done in the presence of excessive external noise, the noise will cover up, or mask, a pure tone. Consequently, many children who have normal hearing will fail the hearing screening because the external noise will prevent them from hearing the pure tone, especially at the lower pitches.

A frequent criterion for failing is the failure to respond at the hearing-screening level at any frequency in either ear. However, state hearing-screening regulations may have different criteria for failure. Regardless of the failure criteria, all failures should be retested immediately, after the child is given a more careful set of instructions.

Hearing-Threshold Testing

Children who fail both the initial hearing screening and the repeat screening should receive a more detailed hearing test and be referred to an audiologist or an otologist. The more detailed test is known as the *pure-tone threshold test,* or *pure-tone audiometry.* The purpose of this test is to determine the child's hearing thresholds for different-frequency pure tones in each ear. For this testing, hearing is measured using both earphones (air conduction) and a bone vibrator (bone conduction). Bone conduction should never be assessed in a school setting because many variables may influence the results. A *hearing threshold* is usually defined as the lowest hearing level at which the child responds to a minimum of two out of three pure tones.

In some situations, hearing thresholds must be obtained for one ear while a noise signal is directed to the other ear. This is called "masking," and the resultant hearing threshold for the ear being tested is called a "masked threshold." Masking is necessary so that the ear not being tested does not respond and the true hearing threshold of the test ear can be obtained. Masked thresholds should be obtained only by an audiologist or otologist.

The hearing-threshold levels obtained as a result of the pure-tone threshold test can be expressed numerically. However, it is more common to plot the hearing thresholds on a graph termed an *audiogram,* as shown in Figure 19.1. On the audiogram, frequency in Hz is shown along the top, in octave and half-octave intervals from 125 to 8,000 Hz. Hearing level in dB is shown along the side of the audiogram, from −10 to 120 dB in 10-dB steps. The symbols plotted on the audiogram correspond to the hearing threshold for each ear at each frequency tested, using earphones (air conduction) or a bone vibrator (bone conduction) when the thresholds were unmasked or masked. Each audiogram contains an adjacent legend that defines the meaning of the symbols used on it. An audiogram legend is shown in Figure 19.2. A circle indicates an unmasked air-conduction threshold for the right ear, and an X indicates an unmasked air-conduction threshold for the left ear. It is also common practice to mark thresholds for the right ear in red and for the left ear in blue. The criteria for failing a pure-tone threshold test are generally the same as for the hearing screening.

Tympanometry Screening

Even though the pure-tone air-conduction screening and the threshold test are commonly used to identify children with educationally significant hearing loss, they have a number of drawbacks. Both the amount of external noise in the test environment and the rapport between the child and the examiner influence the results. Also, some children with normal-hearing may fail these tests because they are immature or inattentive or because they do not understand the instructions. Moreover, some children may pass these tests but have a minor hearing problem or a fluctuating hearing loss, usually due to abnormal conditions of the middle ear. Consequently, several school systems and states have initiated another type of

● ● ● **FIGURE 19.1**   Audiogram Showing Frequency in Hertz (Hz) (Top) and Hearing Level in Decibels (dB) (Side)

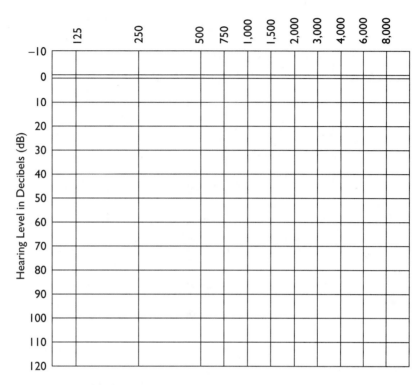

Average normal hearing is 0 dB HL at each frequency, and the normal range is from −10 to 20 dB, regardless of frequency.

SOURCE: "Guidelines for Audiometric Symbols," Figure 1. *ASHA, 32,* 25–30, 1990. Reprinted by permission of the American Speech-Language-Hearing Association.

screening test, used alone or in conjunction with pure-tone screening. This test, known as *tympanometry,* is the third step in the guidelines for hearing screening. Tympanometry has also been called "impedance audiometry," "admittance audiometry," "oto-admittance," "middle-ear screening," and "tympanometric screening." *Tympanometry* can be defined as a method for detecting normal, as well as abnormal, conditions of the eardrum and middle ear. Overall, tympanometry screening is designed to detect abnormal conditions, not to detect educationally significant hearing losses. Disorders of the middle ear are the largest cause of

● ● ● **FIGURE 19.2**   Audiogram Legend Showing the Meaning of Symbols Plotted on an Audiogram

Audiogram Legend

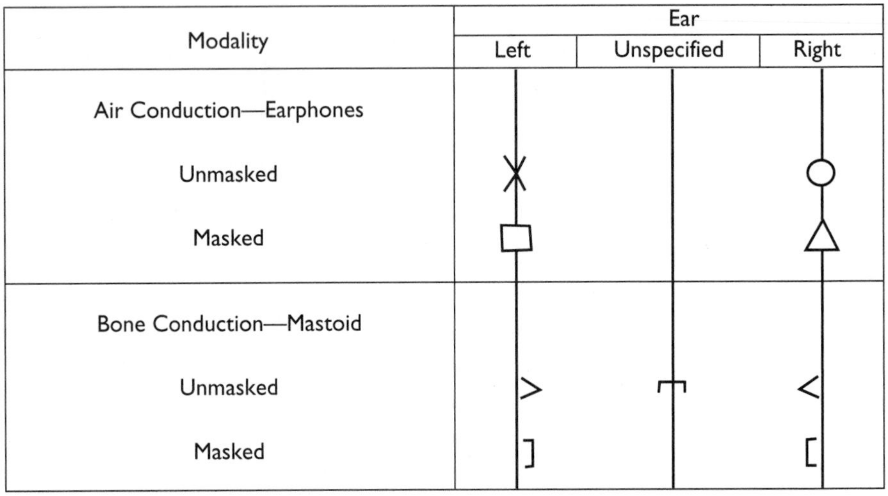

Modality	Ear		
	Left	Unspecified	Right
Air Conduction—Earphones Unmasked Masked	✕ ☐		◯ △
Bone Conduction—Mastoid Unmasked Masked	>]	⊓	< [

This legend shows the symbols for air-conduction unmasked and masked thresholds and for bone-conduction unmasked and masked thresholds when a bone vibrator is placed on the mastoid bone behind the ear. There are many other symbols that can be used to plot hearing thresholds. The symbols shown in this figure are the most commonly used.

SOURCE: Adapted from "Guidelines for Audiometric Symbols," Table 1. *ASHA,* *32,* 25–30, 1990. Reprinted by permission of the American Speech-Language-Hearing Association.

educationally significant hearing loss in children, especially for preschool and young school-age children.

Tympanometry is done using an instrument known as a *middle-ear screener, tympanogram screener, middle-ear analyzer,* or *impedance* or *admittance meter.* Middle-ear screening instruments are automatic, so that the procedure takes less than 10 seconds per ear.

The results of tympanometry are plotted on a graph known as a *tympanogram,* which shows eardrum movement on the *y*-axis, as a function of air pressure in the ear canal on the *x*-axis. Figure 19.3 shows tympanograms for a normal middle ear and for middle ears that have various pathologic conditions.

Children who fail tympanometry (that is, have abnormal tympanograms) but pass the pure-tone air-conduction screening should be rescreened (with both a pure-tone test and tympanometry) in four to six weeks. If they fail either re-screening procedure, they should be referred for additional testing and diagnosis. However, depending on the type of tympanogram, an immediate referral for further diagnosis or treatment should be made.

● ● ● ● **FIGURE 19.3** Tympanogram Configurations for a Normal Middle Ear (a) and for Middle Ears Having a Pathologic Condition (b to e)

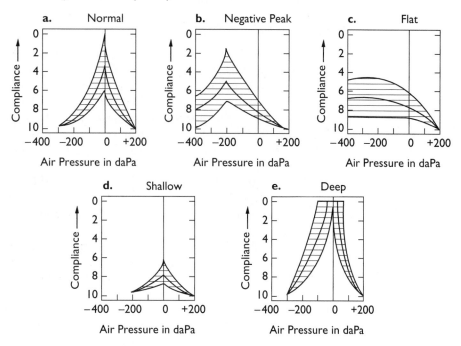

Each tympanogram shows eardrum mobility, called compliance, on the *y*-axis, air pressure on the *x*-axis, and a shaded area used for interpreting the tympanogram. Tympanogram (a) is normal. Tympanogram (b) is called "negative peak" and is observed in children having negative pressure in their middle ear. Tympanogram (c) is called "flat" and is commonly observed in children having middle-ear fluid. Tympanogram (d) is called "shallow" and is observed when the middle ear is stiffer than normal but does not contain fluid. Tympanogram (e) is called "deep" and is observed in children who have a flaccid eardrum or dysarticulation of the middle-ear bones.

SOURCE: From F. H. Bess and L. E. Humes, *Audiology: The Fundamentals*, 1st edition, Copyright Williams and Wilkins, 1990. Reprinted by permission of Lippincott Williams & Wilkins.

It is important to recognize that screening for middle-ear disorders is not the same as screening for hearing loss, because a child could have a middle-ear disorder but pass the pure-tone screening. To differentiate, note that the primary goal of pure-tone screening is to identify children with educationally significant hearing loss, whereas the primary goal of tympanometry screening is to identify children with middle-ear disorders. Even though some states require only pure-tone screening, it is in the best health interests of preschool and school-age children to have both a pure-tone and a tympanometry (middle-ear) screening in the same session. Further, criteria for failure and consequential referral should include the screening results for both air-conduction hearing (pure-tone screening) and middle-ear disorders (tympanometry).

Other Types of Hearing Testing

In addition to tympanometry and pure-tone audiometry, audiologists conduct several other hearing and middle-ear-function tests. These tests aid in diagnosis and hearing-aid fitting and are beyond the scope of this section. However, there are two important and routine tests that employ speech as the test signal. One test, known as a *speech-recognition threshold* (*SRT*), is used to determine a hearing threshold for speech. The other test, known as a *word-recognition score* (*WRS*), is used to determine word-recognition ability. (Word-recognition tests were once known as "speech-discrimination" or "speech-intelligibility tests.") Generally, both the SRT and the WRS are obtained both via earphones for each ear separately and via a loudspeaker located in an audiometric test booth. When testing is done via the loudspeaker, only the better-hearing ear responds. In cases where each ear hears at the same level, the advantage of *binaural* (both ears) hearing, compared with *monaural* (one ear) hearing, can usually be demonstrated.

The SRT is determined by having the child repeat back or point to printed *bisyllabic words* (for example, hot dog, baseball, snowman), spoken with a *spondaic stress pattern* (that is, equal stress on both syllables) while the hearing level is varied. The SRT is defined as the lowest hearing level at which the child responds to 50 percent of the words. The SRT is used to check the validity of the air-conducted pure-tone hearing thresholds, to provide an estimate of the child's threshold for speech, and to adjust and fit hearing aids.

A WRS is usually determined by having the child repeat back or point to printed words when the words are presented at a hearing level loud enough to produce maximum recognition. A WRS is simply the percentage of words correctly heard. A WRS can also be determined by presenting the words through a loudspeaker at a hearing level corresponding to the level of normal conversational speech. This testing is very important for estimating the child's hearing handicap for speech. For example, if a child had a WRS of 90 percent in his or her better-hearing ear when speech was presented loud enough to be heard but had a WRS of only 20 percent when speech was presented at a normal level, the child would be very educationally handicapped for hearing speech. This result would also indicate that if speech were made louder through the use of hearing aids or if the hearing loss were medically corrected to normal, the child's WRS would increase from 20 percent to about 90 percent, drastically decreasing the educational significance of the child's hearing loss.

Types of Hearing Loss

As noted previously, the sense of hearing can be stimulated by both air and bone conduction. When hearing thresholds are obtained for both air- and bone-conducted pure tones, the type of hearing loss can be defined.

FIGURE 19.4   Audiogram for a Six-Year-Old Girl Having Normal Air-Conduction Hearing in Each Ear from 250 to 8,000 Hz

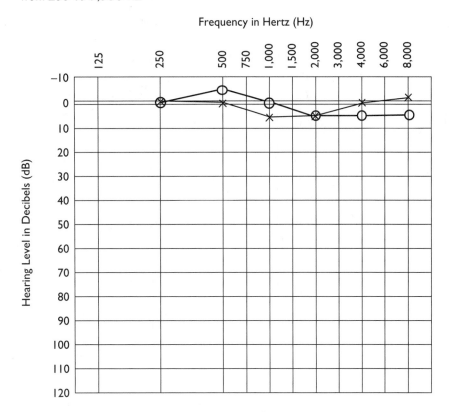

Normal hearing for preschool and school-age children is usually defined within a range around 0 dB HL, from −10 to 20 dB HL. The audiogram in Figure 19.4 shows the air-conduction thresholds for a 6-year-old girl with normal hearing in each ear, from 250 to 8,000 Hz. Note that the right- and left-ear air-conduction symbols show about average normal hearing (0 dB HL) and lie within the normal range of −10 to 20 dB HL. In this case, bone-conduction thresholds were not measured, because the child had normal air-conduction hearing.

Conductive Hearing Loss

If a child has a hearing loss caused by an abnormal condition or pathology in the outer ear, such as an excessive buildup of wax (*cerumen*) in the ear canal, or an abnormal condition of the middle ear, such as fluid in the middle ear (*otitis media*) or a perforation in the eardrum, bone-conduction hearing will be normal, because the inner ear is not affected. However, the child's hearing by air conduction will be abnormal, because the dysfunction is due to a pathology in the outer or middle ear or both. This type of hearing loss, evidenced by normal bone-conduction

● ● ● FIGURE 19.5   Audiogram for a Five-Year-Old Girl Having a Mild, Bilateral (Both Ears), Conductive Hearing Loss Due to Middle-Ear Fluid in Each Middle Ear

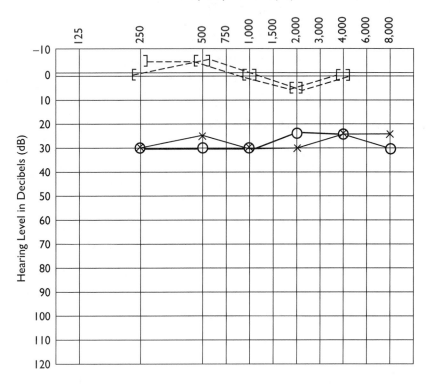

Note that her bone-conduction thresholds were normal and were obtained when masking was directed to the nontest ear. However, her air-conduction thresholds were abnormal and demonstrated an educationally significant hearing loss.

but abnormal air-conduction hearing, is known as a *conductive hearing loss* because the pathology has affected the sound-conducting mechanisms of the outer or middle ear or both. The audiogram in Figure 19.5 shows the air- and bone-conduction thresholds of a 5-year-old girl with a mild, *bilateral* (both ears), conductive hearing loss due to middle-ear fluid. Note that bone-conduction masked thresholds are normal but the air-conduction thresholds are abnormal (>20 dB HL). This child failed the pure-tone screening and threshold test and had an abnormal tympanogram. She was classified as having an educationally significant hearing loss in each ear and was referred to an otologist for treatment. After the middle-ear fluid problem was resolved by medication, her air-conduction hearing and tympanogram returned to normal.

The most common type of hearing problem in preschool and school-age children is a conductive hearing loss due to the presence of middle-ear fluid. This condition is commonly known as *otitis media with effusion* (fluid) and can have several causes. However, almost all the causes are related to dysfunction of the Eustachian tube. Some children have many episodes of otitis media and earaches, especially in early childhood. These children might be categorized as being otitis media–prone. Hearing loss due to otitis media is usually mild to moderate in degree; may fluctuate, with more hearing loss on some days than on others; and is usually temporary, lasting until the fluid dissipates and the eardrum and middle ear return to normal. Generally, otitis media is treated by drug therapy. If this is not successful, the fluid can be removed surgically. This is done by making an incision in the lower part of the eardrum, removing the fluid, and then placing a small plastic tube in the eardrum incision. This surgical procedure is termed a *myringotomy with tubal insertion*. The small tube, called a "pressure-equalization (PE) tube," temporarily takes over the function of the Eustachian tube by allowing air to enter the middle-ear space. A PE tube usually works its way out of the eardrum over time and can be removed, if necessary.

Educators are starting to identify the associations among otitis media, speech and language development, attention, and learning ability. Many researchers (Feagans, Sanyal, Henderson, Collier, & Appelbaum, 1986; Friel-Patti & Finitzo, 1990; Northern & Downs, 1991, pp. 18–28) have suggested that children who have chronic otitis media have more speech and language, attention, and learning problems than children who do not suffer middle-ear disease. After appropriate treatment for conductive hearing loss, hearing ability can almost always be restored to normal. When this is not possible, if the hearing loss is educationally significant, the use of hearing aids should be seriously considered. However, children with long-standing conductive hearing loss probably will need additional instruction to make up for what they missed when their hearing loss was present.

Sensorineural Hearing Loss

If a child has a hearing loss due to a dysfunction of the inner ear, both bone- and air-conduction hearing will be equally abnormal. This type of loss (abnormal bone- and equally abnormal air-conduction hearing) is known as a *sensorineural, cochlear,* or *neurosensory hearing loss*. There are many causes of sensorineural hearing loss, such as noise exposure, inheritance, ototoxic drugs, mumps, measles, and head trauma. The audiogram in Figure 19.6 is for a 7-year-old boy with a mild to moderate, bilateral, high-frequency, sensorineural hearing loss, probably due to a very high fever in infancy. Note that for the higher frequencies, the bone- and air-conduction thresholds are equally abnormal (>20 dB HL). This child failed the pure-tone screening and threshold test and was classified as having an educationally significant hearing loss in each ear. Because the child's hearing loss was not due to an outer- or middle-ear problem, he passed the middle-ear screening (with a normal tympanogram). The child was referred to an audiologist and otologist and was fitted with a behind-the-ear hearing aid for each ear.

An educationally significant moderate or more severe sensorineural hearing loss will almost always be detected before a child enters preschool. On the other hand, other problems—such as educationally significant sensorineural hearing

Audiogram for a Seven-Year-Old Boy Having a Mild to Moderate, Bilateral, High-Frequency, Sensorineural Hearing Loss

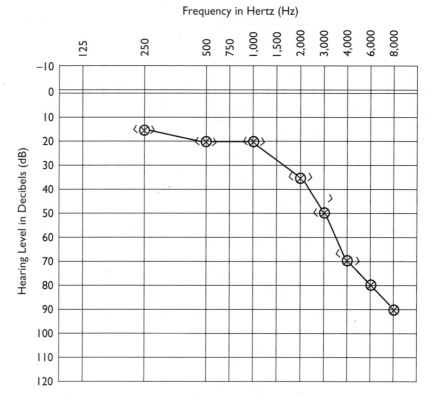

Note that his air- and bone-conduction thresholds were equally abnormal for the higher pitches.

losses in just one ear (unilateral), bilateral losses in the very high frequencies, or bilateral and very mild losses in all frequencies—are usually detected by hearing screening when a child enters kindergarten or first grade. At present, a sensorineural hearing loss will not respond to medical or surgical treatment. For the vast majority of children with sensorineural hearing loss, hearing aids are very helpful.

Mixed Hearing Loss

A hearing loss can also be a combination of conductive and sensorineural hearing loss. This type is known as a *mixed hearing loss* (abnormal bone- and even more abnormal air-conduction hearing). For example, a mixed loss could arise if a child had a problem both with the middle ear (due to middle-ear fluid) and with the inner ear (hair-cell dysfunction due to a very high fever). Generally, mixed hearing losses in children are the result of a pathology that creates a conductive loss on top of an existing sensorineural hearing loss. An otologist can usually alleviate the conductive part of the hearing loss through medical or surgical treatment. However, in some cases, the conductive part of the mixed loss cannot be corrected. If a mixed hearing loss is educationally significant following medical or surgical treatment, the use of hearing aids is warranted.

Central Auditory Hearing Loss

Another type of hearing problem can occur in preschool and school-age children with either normal hearing or hearing loss. This type of hearing problem is related to the function and processing capabilities of the central auditory system and is generally termed a *central auditory-processing dysfunction* or *central auditory hearing loss*. Children who have a central auditory processing dysfunction generally pass hearing screenings, threshold tests, and tympanometry because they have normal air-conduction hearing and middle-ear function. Further, they respond to whispers or speech spoken at a normal level when there is little background noise. However, these children may have difficulty understanding speech against a noisy background, as would occur in a classroom, and have problems with short- and long-term auditory memory, auditory sequential memory, sounding out words (phonetics), or reading comprehension. A central auditory-processing problem can be very educationally significant and frustrating not only to the child but also to the teacher and parents. Any child who passes a hearing screening but is still suspected of having a hearing problem should be considered a candidate for central auditory-processing testing. Testing for central auditory processing also should be considered for children with a reading or visual-perception problem.

Several standardized tests have been developed for the sole purpose of determining a child's central auditory-processing ability. Some of these tests can be administered by a school psychologist, a speech–language pathologist, or an audiologist. Testing for central auditory processing is very complex, and the results are often difficult to interpret. Children suspected of having a central auditory-processing problem should be evaluated by a team of professionals representing many disciplines. If a central auditory problem is diagnosed, new teaching and learning strategies may need to be developed to reduce the educational significance of the problem. These strategies can be provided by special-education teachers, speech–language pathologists, and school psychologists.

Severity of Hearing Loss

Besides providing a way to judge the type of hearing loss, a pure-tone threshold test also provides valuable information regarding the severity of hearing loss for individual frequencies and frequency regions. This information is very important for fitting students' hearing aids and for helping students to understand speech. There are many ways to calculate hearing-loss severity and many classification schemes to categorize it. The most common method for determining severity is based on the average better-ear air-conduction hearing threshold. This is calculated by determining the lowest air-conduction hearing threshold, regardless of ear, at 500, 1,000, and 2,000 Hz, and then determining the average hearing level. This measure is usually referred to as the *better-ear three-frequency average*. The frequencies of 500, 1,000, and 2,000 Hz—termed the *speech frequencies*—were chosen because several speech sounds needed for understanding speech occur between 500 to 2,000 Hz. (However, it is important to realize that many speech sounds also needed for understanding speech are located in frequencies higher than 2,000 Hz. These speech sounds include many of the voiceless consonants, such as *f, s,* and *sh.*)

The average hearing loss can be described or classified in reference to a severity category and in relation to hearing and understanding speech. Figure 19.7 shows an audiogram that classifies hearing impairment by both severity and handicap for hearing speech. For example, a child with an average hearing loss of 35 dB would be classified as having a mild hearing loss and would have difficulty

● ● ● ● **FIGURE 19.7**   Classification of the Severity of Hearing Impairment in Relation to Hearing Handicap for Speech Recognition, Shown on an Audiogram

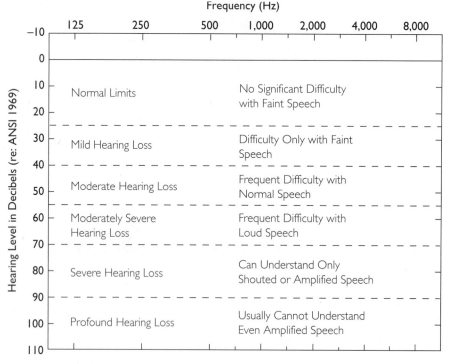

SOURCE: From F. H. Bess and L. E. Humes, *Audiology: The Fundamentals*, 1st edition, Copyright Williams and Wilkins, 1990. Reprinted by permission of Lippincott Williams & Wilkins.

hearing whispered or faint speech. A child with a hearing loss of 80 dB would be classified as having a severe hearing impairment and could understand only shouted or amplified speech.

Speech Understanding and Hearing Loss

Recall that children with a conductive hearing loss have a normal inner ear. Such children can perceive speech normally if it is loud enough to overcome the hearing loss. The effect of a 30- to 40-dB conductive hearing loss can be simulated by wearing a tight-fitting earplug in each ear. If you had such a loss, you would be able to hear normal conversational speech but at a very reduced level. You would have to strain to understand what had been said and would not be able to hear people talking at a distance. In addition, you might not be able to hear yourself walk or hear whispers. Imagine what it is like for a child to sit in a classroom all day every day, perhaps for months, without being able to hear and understand everything that is being said!

Children with a sensorineural hearing loss have abnormal function of the inner ear, and the severity of the hearing loss usually increases as the sound frequency

Coping with Dilemmas in Current Practice

The accurate assessment of sensory acuity poses fewer difficulties than other kinds of assessment. Those who assess vision or hearing acuity are assessing relatively stable human characteristics, for the most part. There are well-accepted objective standards of performance for making decisions about the nature and extent of vision or hearing difficulties. With the exception of color vision, the relationship between sensory difficulties and performance in the curriculum is well understood and established. Also, there are known treatments (corrective lenses or hearing aids) for most mild vision or hearing problems. There are also methods for coping with severe vision or hearing problems.

The major dilemma in assessment of sensory acuity is that, with the exception of routine screening, assessment is done by people outside the school. Students who have serious vision problems are assessed by optometrists or ophthalmologists. Those who have serious hearing problems are assessed by audiologists or ear, nose, and throat specialists. Communication between specialists outside the school and school personnel may be difficult—specialists may not be familiar with the curriculum, understand the educational relevance of their diagnoses, or take the necessary time to speak with school personnel about their findings for individual children. Difficulty may also arise when school personnel do not understand the vocabulary used by those who assess vision and hearing problems. Problems are most effectively overcome when there is very good communication and ongoing interaction among school personnel and out-of-school specialists.

increases. These children often report that they can hear someone talking, but they cannot always understand what is said, sometimes even with the use of hearing aids. This occurs because the child can hear low-frequency vowel sounds, which carry the power of speech, but cannot hear the high-frequency consonant sounds, which carry the intelligibility of speech. It is difficult to simulate the effects of a sensorineural hearing loss. However, try listening to a radio station when your radio is slightly mistuned, then turn down the level and increase the bass. You will notice that you can hear speech but not understand what is being said.

Children who have sensorineural hearing loss have extreme difficulty hearing in a noisy environment. In most classrooms, the teacher's voice is only about 6 to 10 dB louder than the background noise. Research has clearly demonstrated that if the teacher's voice is about 15 to 20 dB louder than the classroom noise, children with sensorineural loss—and, for that matter, normal-hearing children—will have better speech understanding. In other words, improving the *signal-to-noise ratio* (teacher's voice to classroom noise) will improve speech understanding for all children in the classroom.

There are many ways to improve the signal-to-noise ratio. One way is for the teacher simply to talk louder. Another way is to reduce the level of classroom noise by fitting the classroom with carpeting, acoustic ceiling tile, and window drapes. An audiologist can recommend additional ways to improve the signal-to-noise ratio so as to increase speech understanding. Research has also demonstrated that a child with sensorineural hearing loss will have improved understanding for speech when speech is more distinctly articulated, spoken directly to the child, and spoken at a slightly slower rate.

Summary

Vision and hearing difficulties can have a significant effect on the performance of children in educational environments. School personnel can more readily decide how to intervene when they have a basic overview of the kinds of vision and hearing difficulties children experience and of the procedures used to assess sensory acuity. Screening tests of both visual and auditory acuity must be individually administered. This chapter reviewed individually administered screening tests that are appropriate and reasonably effective. The actual diagnosis of sensory difficulties must be completed by specialists: ophthalmologists, optometrists, audiologists, and otologists. Teachers of visually impaired, deaf, and hard-of-hearing students are very helpful in facilitating communication with such specialists.

Questions for Chapter Review and Thought

1. Identify several characteristics (behaviors) a student might demonstrate that would make you question whether that individual is seeing adequately.

2. Identify several characteristics (behaviors) a student might demonstrate that would make you question whether that individual is hearing adequately.

3. After a complete visual examination, the doctor reported that "Raul demonstrates 20/20 corrected vision, and the visual field subtends an angular distance of 15 degrees." Glasses were prescribed. Translate the report into nontechnical

terms. Will Raul's vision have any implications for instructional procedures?

4. Amy's hearing test, administered in November, showed a 35-dB loss on a pure-tone audiometric sweep in the speech range. In December, she was assessed using the WISC-III and the Test of Adolescent Language and scored very poorly on subtests requiring auditory reception. In April, the audiologist reported a 10-dB loss in the speech range. In July (and following several months of intensive remediation), Amy was reevaluated in the school and performed substantially better on both intelligence measures and tests of oral language. What conclusions can be drawn about Amy's performance?

Resources for Further Investigation

Project

Contact your local school district and find out what provisions are made for educating students with sensory disorders. What factors determine when the child will be sent to a special school for the blind or the deaf?

Print Resources

Bess, F. H., & Hall, J. W. (1992). *Screening children for auditory function.* Nashville, TN: Bill Wilkerson Center Press.

Chase, J. B. (1985). Assessment of the visually impaired. *Diagnostique, 10,* 144–160.

Sharpe, M., McNear, D., & McGrew, K. (1996). *Braille assessment inventory.* Columbia, MO: Hawthorne Educational Services.

Technology Resources

American Council of the Blind

http://www.acb.org/

The American Council of the Blind's home page provides general information about the council and resources and information about blindness.

Visual Impairments

http://www.ed.gov/databases/ERIC_Digests/ed349774.html

This ERIC document contains a description of visual impairments, characteristics of individuals with visual impairments, and the educational implications of visual impairments.

Deaf World Web

http://dww.deaFworldweb.org/

This is the web site of the International Web Publication of the Deaf. It contains links to a large resource of information for those interested in knowing more about deafness.

All You Wanted to Know About Deafness—DEAF-L FAQ WWW Site

http://www.weizmann.ac.il/deaf-info/home.html

Link to information regarding the education of students with hearing impairments by clicking on the *Education* button.

Assessment of Academic Achievement with Multiple-Skill Devices

Achievement tests are the most frequently used tests in educational settings. Multiple-skill achievement tests evaluate knowledge and understanding in several curricular areas, such as reading and math. These tests are intended to assess the extent to which students have profited from schooling and other life experiences, compared with other students of the same age or grade. Consequently, most achievement tests are norm-referenced, although some are criterion-referenced or performance measures. Norm-referenced, criterion-referenced, and performance tests are designed in consultation with subject-matter experts and are believed to reflect national curricula and national curricular trends in general.

Achievement tests can be classified along several dimensions; perhaps the most important one describes their specificity and density of content. Diagnostic achievement tests have dense content; they have many more items to assess specific skills and concepts and allow finer analyses to pinpoint specific strengths and weaknesses in academic development. Tests with fewer items per skill allow comparisons among test takers but do not have enough items to pinpoint students' strengths and weaknesses. These tests may still be useful for estimating a student's current general level of functioning in comparison with other students, and they estimate the extent to which an individual has acquired the skills and concepts that other students of the same age have acquired.

Another important dimension is the number of students who can be tested at once. Achievement tests are designed to be given to groups of students or to individual students. Generally, group tests require students to read and either write or mark answers; individually administered tests may require an examiner to read questions to a student and may allow students to respond orally. The primary advantage of individually administered tests is that they afford examiners the opportunity to observe students working and solving problems. Therefore, examiners can glean valuable qualitative information in addition to the quantitative information that scores provide. Finally, a group test may be appropriately given to one student at a time, but individual tests should not be given to a group of students.

Table 20.1 shows the different categories of achievement tests. The Stanford Achievement Test, for example, is both a norm-referenced and a criterion-referenced (objective-referenced), group-administered screening test that samples skill development in many content areas. The Stanford Diagnostic Reading Test (SDRT), detailed in Chapter 21, is both a norm-referenced, group-administered test and a criterion-referenced, individually administered diagnostic test that samples skill-development strengths and weaknesses in the single skill of reading. The SDRT is intended to provide a classroom teacher with a more detailed analysis of students' strengths and weaknesses in reading, which may be of assistance in program planning and evaluation.

The most obvious advantage of multiple-skill achievement tests is that they can provide teachers with data showing the extent to which their pupils have acquired information and skills. By using group-administered, multiple-skill batteries, teachers can obtain a considerable amount of information in a relatively short time.

In selecting a multiple-skill achievement test, teachers must consider three factors: content validity, stimulus/response modes, and relevant norms. First, teachers must evaluate evidence for content validity, the most important kind of validity for achievement tests. Many multiple-skill tests have general content validity—the tests measure important concepts and skills that are generally part of most curricula. This validity makes their content suitable for assessing general attainment. However, if a test is to be used to assess the extent to which students have profited from school instruction—that is, to measure student achievement— more than general content validity is required: The test must match the instruction provided. Tests that do not match instruction lack content validity, and decisions based on such tests should be restricted. When making decisions about content validity for students with disabilities, educators must consider the extent to which the student has had an opportunity to learn the content of the test. Many students with disabilities are assigned to a curriculum (often a functional curriculum) that differs from the curriculum to which nondisabled students are exposed.

Second, educators who use achievement tests for students with disabilities need to consider whether the stimulus/response modes of subtests may be exceptionally difficult for students with physical or motor problems. Tests that are timed may be inappropriately difficult for students whose reading or motor difficulties cause them to take more time on specific tasks. (Many of these issues were described in greater detail in Chapter 9.)

Third, teachers must evaluate the adequacy of each test's norms by asking whether the normative group is composed of the kinds of individuals with which they wish to compare their students. If a test is used to estimate general attainment, a representative sample of students from across the nation is preferred. However, if a test is used to estimate achievement in a school system, local norms are probably better. Finally, teachers should examine the extent to which a total

TABLE 20.1 ● Categories of Achievement Tests

	Norm-Referenced		Criterion-Referenced	
	Single Skill	*Multiple Skill*	*Single Skill*	*Multiple Skill*
Group-Administered Screening Devices	Gates–MacGinitie	California Achievement Test Iowa Tests of Basic Skills Metropolitan Achievement Tests (Survey Battery) Stanford Achievement Test Series Terra Nova	None	California Achievement Test Iowa Tests of Basic Skills Metropolitan Achievement Tests (Instructional Batteries) Stanford Achievement Test Series
Individually Administered Screening Devices	Test of Mathematical Abilities–2	Kaufman Test of Educational Achievement–Revised Peabody Individual Achievement Test–Revised Wide Range Achievement Test–3 Woodcock–Johnson Psychoeducation Battery–Revised Kaufman Assessment Battery for Children Mini-Battery of Achievement	None	
Group-Administered Diagnostic Devices	Stanford Diagnostic Reading Test Stanford Diagnostic Mathematics Test	None	Stanford Diagnostic Mathematics Test	None
Individually Administered Diagnostic Devices	Gray Oral Reading Test–3 Durrel Analysis of Reading Difficulty Gates–McKillop–Horowitz Reading Diagnostic Tests Woodcock Reading Mastery Tests–Revised Test of Written Language–3 Test of Written Spelling 4 Test of Reading Comprehension–3 Formal Reading Inventory Standardized Test for Assessment of Reading Standardized Test for Assessment of Math Test of Language Development I2 Test of Language Development P2 Test of Adolescent Language 2	Diagnostic Achievement Battery–2	Key Math–Revised Stanford Diagnostic Reading Test Standardized Reading Inventory	

test and its components have the reliability necessary for making decisions about what students have learned.

· ·

Why Do We Assess Achievement?

The very term *screening device* reflects the major purpose of achievement tests. These tests are used most often to screen students, to identify those who demonstrate low-level, average, or high-level attainment in comparison with their peers. Achievement tests provide a global estimate of academic skill development and may be used to identify individual students for whom educational intervention is necessary, either in the form of remediation (for those who demonstrate relatively low-level skill development) or in the form of academic enrichment (for those who exhibit exceptionally high-level skill development). However, screening tests have limited behavior samples and lower requirements for reliability. Therefore, students who are identified with screening tests should be further assessed with diagnostic tests to verify their need for educational intervention.

Although multiple-skill, group-administered achievement tests are usually considered to be screening devices, they are occasionally used in eligibility or entitlement decisions. In principle, such a use is generally inappropriate, although it may be justifiable and even desirable when the group tests (for example, the Stanford Achievement Test Series or the Metropolitan Achievement Tests) contain behavior samples that are more complete than those contained in some individually administered tests of achievement used for placement (such as the Wide Range Achievement Test 3). Use of an achievement test with a better behavior sample is desirable if the tester goes beyond the scores earned to examine performance on specific test items.

Multiple-skill achievement tests may also be used for progress evaluation. Most school districts have routine testing programs at various grade levels to evaluate the extent to which pupils in their schools are progressing in comparison with some national standard. Scores on achievement tests provide communities, school boards, and parents with an index of the quality of schooling. Schools and the teachers within those schools are often subject to question when pupils fail to demonstrate expected progress.

Finally, achievement tests are used to evaluate the relative effectiveness of alternative curricula. For instance, Brown School may choose to use the Scott, Foresman Reading Series in third grade, while Green School decides to use the Lippincott Reading Program. If school personnel can assume that children were at relatively comparable reading levels when they entered the third grade, then achievement tests may be administered at the end of the year to ascertain the relative effectiveness of the Scott, Foresman and the Lippincott programs. Educators must, of course, avoid many assumptions in such evaluations (for example, that the quality of individual teachers and the instructional environment are comparable in the two schools) and many research pitfalls if comparative evaluation is to have meaning.

Specific Tests of Academic Achievement

The remainder of this chapter addresses specific multiple-skill devices and examines four popular group-administered multiple-skill batteries (the California Achievement Tests, the Iowa Tests of Basic Skills, the Metropolitan Achievement Tests, and the Stanford Achievement Test Series); five individually administered multiple-skill batteries (the Basic Achievement Skills Individual Screener, the Kaufman Test of Educational Achievement, the Mini-Battery of Achievement, the Peabody In-

dividual Achievement Test–Revised, and the Wide Range Achievement Test 3); one individually administered, norm-referenced measure that is conormed with intelligence tests (Wechsler Individual Achievement Test); and one individually administered, norm-referenced, multiple-skill measure (Diagnostic Achievement Battery–2). Later chapters discuss both screening and diagnostic tests that are devoted to specific content areas, such as reading and mathematics.

California Achievement Tests (CAT/5)

The California Achievement Tests (CAT/5; CTB/ Macmillan/McGraw-Hill, 1993) are a set of norm-referenced tests from which mastery scores for specific instructional objectives can also be obtained. The CAT/5 contains 13 overlapping levels that measure academic achievement in grades K through 12. The tests include measures of skill development in reading, spelling, language, mathematics, study skills, science, and social studies. The CAT/5 has two test configurations: a survey battery and a complete battery. The survey battery is two thirds as long as the complete battery and provides only norm-referenced information. The survey can be used at only 10 of the 13 levels. The complete battery is available in two alternative forms and provides curriculum-referenced information as well as norm-referenced scores. The complete battery requires from 1 hour 27 minutes at level K to 5 hours 16 minutes at Levels 14–21/22. The survey requires 2 hours 47 minutes or less for each level.

A locator test is also available; it may be used as a pretest to determine the appropriate level of the test to administer. Use of the locator test facilitates *functional-level testing*—assessment of stu-

dents at their functional level rather than their grade-placement level. The CAT/5 also has six practice exercises, which are designed to give students practice in taking standardized tests. The authors recommend giving the practice exercises a day or two before the first testing session. A class-management guide is provided that includes instructions for norm-referenced and criterion-referenced use and interpretation of the test results, as well as selected instructional activities matched to the objectives assessed by the test. Technical information is included in separate technical bulletins.

The CAT/5 is organized into three broad areas: Reading/Language Arts, Mathematics, and Supplementary Content Areas. The students included in specific levels of the CAT are shown in Table 20.2. A description of each subtest follows.

Reading/Language Arts

This content area was revised in the fifth edition of the CAT to reflect recent changes in education theory and practice regarding reading and language arts.

TABLE 20.2 ● *Subtests at Each Level of the CAT/5*

Test	K	10	11	12	13	14	15	16	17	18	19	20	21/22
Visual Recognition	×												
Word Analysis (Sound Recognition at Level K)	×	×	×	×	×								
Vocabulary	×	×	×	×	×	×	×	×	×	×	×	×	×
Comprehension	×	×	×	×	×	×	×	×	×	×	×	×	×
Spelling			×	×	×	×	×	×	×	×	×	×	×
Language Mechanics			×	×	×	×	×	×	×	×	×	×	×
Language Expression			×	×	×	×	×	×	×	×	×	×	×
Mathematics Computation			×	×	×	×	×	×	×	×	×	×	×
Mathematics Concepts and Applications	×	×	×	×	×	×	×	×	×	×	×	×	×
Study Skills						×	×	×	×	×	×	×	×
Science			×	×	×	×	×	×	×	×	×	×	×
Social Studies			×	×	×	×	×	×	×	×	×	×	×

SOURCE: *Subtests at Each Level of the CAT/5 from The California Achievement Tests™, 5th Edition. Technical Bulletin 1.* (CTB/Macmillan/ McGraw-Hill, © 1992). Reproduced with permission of The McGraw-Hill Companies, Inc.

Visual Recognition   In this subtest, students must distinguish letters by recognizing single letters that are orally presented, recognizing uppercase and lowercase forms of the same letter, and matching letter groups.

Sound Recognition   This subtest assesses students' skill in recognizing sounds in spoken words. Students must (a) identify pictures of objects that have the same initial or final consonant sounds as words read by the examiner and (b) identify pictures of objects, the names of which rhyme with words read by the examiner.

Word Analysis   This subtest measures students' skill in decoding and in using structural clues to identify the proper pronunciation and meaning of unfamiliar words.

Vocabulary   This subtest measures students' understanding of word meaning. Students must identify words that fit categories, that have the same meaning, or that have opposite meanings. Stu-

dents are also required to use context clues to identify the intended meaning of words that have multiple meanings.

Comprehension   This subtest assesses literal, inferential, and evaluative comprehension; students derive meaning from written sentences and passages.

Spelling   The single subtest in this content area—which is not given at levels K, 10, and 11—assesses students' skill in identifying incorrectly spelled words used in written sentences.

Language Mechanics   This subtest measures capitalization and punctuation skills. Students are required to edit passages presented in differing formats.

Language Expression   This subtest assesses students' skill in effective written expression, including the use of various parts of speech and the formation and organization of sentences and paragraphs.

Mathematics

The two subtests in this content area have been revised to meet the standards set by the National Council of Teachers of Mathematics (NCTM).

Mathematics Computation   This subtest assesses students' skill in solving addition, subtraction, multiplication, and division problems involving whole numbers, fractions, mixed numbers, decimals, and algebraic expressions.

Mathematics Concepts and Applications   This subtest assesses students' skill in understanding and applying a wide range of mathematical concepts involving numeration, number sentences, number theory, problem solving, measurement, and geometry.

Supplementary Content Areas

Study Skills   Items in this subtest relate to parts of books, dictionary conventions, library skills, graphic information, and study techniques. The subtest measures students' skill in finding and using information.

Science   The subtest in this content area measures students' understanding of scientific language, concepts, and methods of inquiry. Item content is drawn from each of the major areas of science.

Social Studies   Items in the subtest in this content area measure understanding of the social sciences, including geography, economics, history, political science, and sociology.

Scores

Five types of norm-referenced scores may be obtained for the CAT/5: percentile ranks, stanines, grade equivalents, normal-curve equivalents, and scale scores (ranging from 000 to 999). Two types of curriculum-referenced information can be derived from the test: an objective performance index (OPI) and a mastery band. An *OPI* describes a student's percentage correct on a specific test objective. A *mastery band* can be computed, based on the error of measurement of the test and the student's score; the mastery band is designed to give a graphic representation of students' actual level on each objective. An anticipated achievement score is provided if the CAT/5 is given along with the Test of Cognitive Skills (TCS/2), a measure of learning aptitude.

The tests may be either hand scored or submitted to the publisher for machine scoring. A variety of information systems is available, including individual test records, graphic frequency distributions, summary reports, error analyses, and class test records. Schools may obtain criterion-referenced data on objectives mastered by individuals or by classes, norm-referenced data comparing pupil performance with national norms, or demographic norm reports comparing class or school performance with the performances of schools of comparable demographic makeup.

Norms

The CAT/5 has norms for the fall, winter, and spring. The test was standardized in January (winter norms), April (spring norms), and October (fall norms) of 1991. The winter standardization was for Level 11 only and consisted of 4,161 students. Stratification information was not provided for this group. The spring standardization involved 115,888 students, and the fall standardization used 109,825 participants.

Three separate sampling designs were used in norming the CAT/5: public, private, and Catholic. The number of students from each setting was not reported in *Technical Bulletin 1* (CTB/Macmillan/McGraw-Hill, 1992). Although the authors state that the public-school samples were stratified on the basis of geographic region, community type (urban, rural, suburban), district size, and socioeconomic status, the extent of stratification and counterbalancing could not be determined from the data provided. The norms are therefore questionable.

Reliability

Data on reliability are restricted to KR-20 internal-consistency estimates. The authors provide internal-consistency coefficients for each of the subtests at each level of the CAT/5. The survey is less reliable than the complete battery and may not be suitable for screening. Several of the reliability coefficients for the subtests of the survey are below .80. The reliability coefficients for the complete battery subtests are generally above .80. The exceptions are at grades 1 and 2 (Levels 11 and 12) for science and social studies, which fall below the .80 level. Data are not reported on test–retest reliability or alternate-forms reliability.

Validity

Although the authors made an effort to ensure content validity and eliminate cultural bias from the test items, users must decide whether the CAT/5 measures the objectives of their school or class curriculum. Data on other forms of validity of the CAT/5 are limited to an illustration that the percentage of students mastering objectives increases with age and a report of correlation of the CAT/5 with the TCS/2.

Summary

The CAT/5 is a set of group-administered, norm-referenced measures of pupils' skill development in reading, spelling, language, mathematics, science, and social studies. The tests are composed of a survey and a complete battery. The information about standardization of the CAT/5 is incomplete. Data on reliability are limited to evidence of internal consistency and suggest that the CAT/5 survey may not be suitable for screening. The complete battery appears to have sufficient reliability to support both educational decisions about groups of students and reports of data on group performance. The reliabilities of some subtests are too low for use in making decisions about individual students. Data on validity are very limited.

Riverside 2000 Assessment Series: ITBS, TAP, ITED

The Riverside Assessment Series consists of three tests: the Iowa Tests of Basic Skills (ITBS; Hoover, Hieronymus, Frisbie, & Dunbar, 1996), the Tests of Achievement and Proficiency (TAP; Scannell, 1996), and the Iowa Tests of Educational Development (ITED; Feldt, Forsyth, Ansley, & Alnot, 1996). The ITBS is intended for pupils in grades K–8, while both the TAP and the ITED are intended for grades 9–12. Users of the Riverside series can adopt a K–12 testing program including the ITBS/TAP or the ITBS/ITED. All three tests are norm-referenced and criterion-referenced tests de-signed to assess broad general functioning rather than specific facts and content. The tests serve as continuous measures of growth in fundamental skills necessary to academic and later life success. Table 20.3 shows the three tests, the grade levels for which they are appropriate, and the subtests included at each level. Tests that appear in shaded format are supplementary listening or writing assessments, or performance tests in math, science, and social studies. In the three sections that follow, we separately review each of the three tests (ITBS, TAP, and ITED).

TABLE 20.3 ● Riverside's Integrated Assessment Program

Curriculum Area	Grade → Level →	Iowa Tests of Basic Skills®										Tests of Achievement and Proficiency	Iowa Tests of Educational Development®
	Grade	K.1–1.5	K.8–1.9	1.7–2.6	2.5–3.5	3 4 5 6 7 8						9 10 11 12	9 10 11 12
	Level	5	6	7	8	9 10 11 12 13 14						15 16 17 18	15 16 17/18
Vocabulary		Vocabulary				Vocabulary						Vocabulary	Vocabulary
Reading		Word Analysis				Reading Comprehension						Reading Comprehension	Ability to Interpret Literary Materials
			Reading										
		Listening				Listening Assessment						Listening Assessment	
Language		Language				Spelling						Written Expression	Correctness and Appropriateness of Expression
						Capitalization							
						Punctuation							
						Usage and Expression							
						Integrated Writing Skills						Iowa Writing Assessments	
						Iowa Writing Assessments							
Integrated Language Arts		Performance Assessments										Performance Assessments	
Mathematics		Mathematics		Math Concepts		Math Concepts and Estimation						Math Concepts and Problem Solving	Ability to Do Quantitative Thinking
				Math Problems		Math Problem Solving and Data Interpretation							
				Math Computation		Math Computation						Math Computation	
		Performance Assessments										Performance Assessments	
Social Studies				Social Studies		Social Studies						Social Studies	Analysis of Social Studies Materials
		Performance Assessments										Performance Assessments	
Science				Science		Science						Science	Analysis of Science Materials
		Performance Assessments										Performance Assessments	
Using Information				Sources of Information		Maps and Diagrams						Information Processing	Use of Sources of Information
						Reference Materials							

TABLE 20.3 ● Riverside's Integrated Assessment Program (continued)

Ability Area	Cognitive Abilities Test™	
	Levels 1 and 2 (Grades K–3)	*Levels A–H (Grades 3–12)*
Verbal	Verbal Reasoning Oral Vocabulary	Verbal Classification Sentence Completion Verbal Analogies
Quantitative	Relational Concepts Quantitative Relations	Quantitative Concepts Number Series Equation Building
Nonverbal	Figure Classification Matrices	Figure Classification Figure Analogies Figure Analysis

NOTE: The shaded areas indicate the tests that are included in the Complete Battery booklets for the *Iowa Tests of Basic Skills,* the *Tests of Achievement and Proficiency,* and the *Iowa Tests of Educational Development.* A Complete Battery booklet for *ITBS* contains *either* Spelling, Capitalization, Punctuation, and Usage and Expression *or* Integrated Writing Skills.
SOURCE: Copyright © 1996 by The University of Iowa. All rights reserved. Reproduced from the *Iowa Test of Basic Skills, Interpretive Guide for Teachers and Counselors,* Complete and Survey Battery, Form M, Levels 9–14 with permission of the publisher.

Iowa Tests of Basic Skills (ITBS)

There are three forms of the Iowa Tests of Basic Skills: forms K and L, first published in 1994, and form M, published in 1996. Our review focuses on form M, which is an updated-norms version of forms K and L. It is important to recognize that there are actually two versions of form M available, with essentially the same name. In one version, language is tested, as it always has been with the ITBS, using four subtests: Spelling, Capitalization, Punctuation, and Usage and Expression. In the other version, called the "Integrated Writing Skills Edition," language is tested in a single Integrated Writing Skills Version. Table 20.3 has listed the names of the subtests that make up the ITBS at each grade level. Form M is published in a complete battery booklet (13 subtests) for each level; in machine-scorable complete, core, and survey battery booklets for Level 9 (grade 3); and in a survey battery booklet (3 subtests) for Levels 10–14 (grades 4–8). Testing times are shown in Table 20.4. Note that the survey battery takes from 1½ to nearly 2 hours to administer, whereas the complete battery can take 5 hours to administer.

The ITBS was designed to provide information about individual student competence in the basic school subject-matter areas. The test is to be used for (a) general instructional (whole class) planning, (b) planning individualized instruction (adapting instruction), (c) monitoring of individual progress, (d) program evaluation, and (e) providing reports to parents, which will help parents and the school work together. The authors of the

TABLE 20.4 ● Testing Levels, Batteries, and Times for the ITBS, Form M

Level	Battery	Time
5	Complete	2 hours
6	Complete	2 hours, 43 minutes
7	Complete	4 hours, 30 minutes
	Core	2 hours, 30 minutes
	Survey	1 hour, 30 minutes
8	Complete	4 hours, 35 minutes
	Core	2 hours, 35 minutes
	Survey	1 hour, 30 minutes
9–14	Complete	5 hours, 10 minutes
	Core	2 hours, 55 minutes
	Survey	1 hour, 51 minutes

ITBS stress the fact that the test was designed to measure critical-thinking skills (often referred to as higher-order thinking skills) that are more complex than the recall of factual material. The test is designed to assess the complex skills involved in interpretation, inference, classification, analysis, and making comparisons.

Following is a list of the subtests of the ITBS and the skills they assess.

Listening   This subtest, included at Levels 5–8 of the ITBS, assesses skill in comprehending literal meaning and inferential meaning; following directions; understanding sequence; comprehending numerical, spatial, and temporal relationships; predicting outcomes; understanding linguistic relationships; and understanding a speaker's purpose, point of view, and style. An optional listening assessment is offered for Levels 9–14, but the score for this subtest is not included in the composite score.

Vocabulary   At Levels 5 and 6, this stand-alone subtest measures students' listening vocabulary. Reading vocabulary is assessed at Levels 7 and 8. At the highest levels, students' skill in identifying words in context is assessed.

Writing   A supplemental writing subtest, available at Levels 9–14, contains four different prompts to which students respond. The score on this supplemental subtest is not included in the composite score.

Word Analysis   This subtest is available only at the levels of the test intended for use in kindergarten through third grade. At the lower levels (Levels 5 and 6), the subtest provides information about skill development in letter recognition and letter–sound correspondence. At Levels 7 and 8, this subtest assesses students' knowledge of letter–sound relationships.

Reading Comprehension   At Level 6, this subtest assesses word recognition, word attack, and literal and inferential comprehension. At higher levels, the subtest assesses skill development in constructing factual meaning (understanding factual information and deducing the literal meaning of words or phrases), constructing inferential/interpretive meaning (drawing conclusions, making inferences or deducing meaning, inferring feelings, generalizing), and constructing evaluative meaning (determining main ideas; identifying an author's viewpoint; recognizing mood, tone, and style; and interpreting nonliteral content).

Language Skills   We noted that the ITBS offers two ways in which to assess language skills. In the first way, language skills are tested in four subareas: spelling, capitalization, punctuation, and usage. The spelling section is a measure of recognition; students identify one of four words as the correct spelling of a word read by the teacher. The capitalization section requires students to identify words that should be capitalized in sentences or paragraphs. The punctuation section requires students to identify places in sentences that need specific punctuation marks. The usage section assesses knowledge of grammatical rules by requiring students to identify which of three alternative sentences employs correct usage.

The alternative way to assess language is to use the version of the test called the Integrated Writing Skills Version. Most of the questions in the Integrated Writing Skills Test are embedded in a story, letter, or report. The authors indicate that the methodology parallels the editing and revision stages that students experience in their classroom work.

Mathematics Skills   Three kinds of math tests are included in the ITBS: The first kind assesses knowledge of mathematical concepts, the second requires students to solve written problems and interpret data, and the optional third test requires students to solve computational problems. At lower levels of the test, the directions are read to the students; at upper levels, students must read the directions themselves. The content of this subtest was heavily influenced by the new math standards published by the NCTM.

Science   This subtest, available for Levels 7–14 of the ITBS, assesses students' factual and conceptual knowledge and understanding of science, as well as their ability to evaluate facts and concepts in the content areas of life science, earth and space science, and physical science.

Social Studies   This subtest, available for Levels 7–14 of the ITBS, includes an assessment of students' factual and conceptual knowledge and understanding of social studies, as well as their ability to evaluate facts and concepts in economics, geography, history, political science, sociology, anthropology, and related social sciences.

Maps and Diagrams   This subtest, included only at Levels 7–14, measures students' skills in reading maps, charts, and diagrams.

Reference Materials   This subtest, also available only at Levels 7–14, measures students' knowledge and use of references. Students must demonstrate knowledge of how to alphabetize, read tables of contents, and use an index, dictionary, encyclopedia, and other general reference materials.

Tests of Achievement and Proficiency (TAP)

The Tests of Achievement and Proficiency (TAP; Scannell, 1996) are available only in form M. This form of the test is a 1995 updated-norms version of forms originally standardized in 1992. The test is appropriate for use with students in grades 9–12 and is available in two booklet formats: a complete battery and a survey battery. The complete battery takes 4 hours, 35 minutes to administer, while the survey battery takes 1 hour, 40 minutes. The authors indicate five purposes for administering the TAP: (1) identifying skill-development strengths and weaknesses for both individuals and classes, (2) monitoring student progress, (3) deciding which secondary-school courses students should take, (4) providing a basis for progress reports to parents, and (5) evaluating programs and curricula. The subtests of the TAP and the skills they assess are as follows.

Vocabulary   This subtest assesses students' working vocabulary, free of contextual cues. The student identifies synonyms of words drawn from the content of secondary-school curricula in science, math, and so forth.

Written Expression   This subtest emphasizes complete written composition and assesses the skills necessary for expressing ideas in writing. It includes questions on spelling, sentence structure, and the correct use of pronoun references and measures student skill in writing letters, reports, and anecdotes and in analyzing sentences and paragraphs.

Reading Comprehension   This subtest assesses students' skill in constructing three kinds of meaning from prose: factual meaning, interpretive meaning, and evaluative meaning. The content of the reading selections is general, from literature, from science, and from social studies.

Information Processing   This subtest assesses the extent to which students can read and use various types of maps, charts, and graphs and use references to locate information.

Mathematics   Two types of mathematics tests are included in the TAP. The first measures both the understanding of mathematical principles and the use of basic mathematics in managing the quantitative aspects of everyday living. The second, optional test assesses computational skills.

Social Studies   This subtest assesses students' knowledge of issues and problems associated with interactions both among people and between people and the environment.

Science   This subtest measures problem solving and the interpretation of scientific information. Content is drawn from the life sciences and the earth and space sciences.

Iowa Tests of Educational Development (ITED)

The Iowa Tests of Educational Development (ITED; Feldt, Forsyth, Ansley, & Alnot, 1996) is a norm-referenced and curriculum-referenced test intended for use with students in grades 9–12. It is available only in form M, but this form has two formats: a complete battery and a survey battery. Subtests included in the complete battery are listed in Table 20.3. The survey battery includes three subtests: Reading, Correctness and Appropriateness of Expression, and Ability to Do Quantitative Thinking. The Reading test consists of items from the Vocabulary, Ability to Interpret Literary Materials, Analysis of Social Studies Materials, and Analysis of Science Materials subtests of the complete battery. All test questions are in multiple-choice format. There is an optional 44-item questionnaire included in both batteries, designed to assess students' educational and occupational interests and goals. The complete battery takes 3 hours, 55 minutes to administer, whereas the survey battery takes just 90 minutes. The questionnaire adds 15 minutes to each testing time. The

authors indicate three major purposes for the ITED: (1) assessment of student competence in the major goals of secondary education, (2) monitoring of student progress, and (3) program evaluation. Subtests included in the complete battery and the behaviors they sample are as follows.

Vocabulary   In this measure of general vocabulary development, the words are those encountered in general communication rather than content-specific words. They are presented in phrases, and students must identify synonyms.

Ability to Interpret Literary Materials   This test reflects changes in the way reading and literature are taught, using high-quality literature rather than traditional reading texts. The test measures students' ability to derive meaning from prose, and it assesses their construction of factual, nonliteral, and inferential meaning. In addition, items are included that measure student competence in drawing generalizations about themes and ideas and in recognizing literary techniques and tone.

Correctness and Appropriateness of Expression This subtest measures students' skill in recognizing correct and effective use of standard American English in writing. Students are required to edit and revise prose.

Ability to Do Quantitative Thinking This subtest measures problem-solving skill, rather than computational ability. Based on the NCTM standards, it measures problem-solving skills based on realistic situations. Interestingly, there are separate norms for students who do and do not use calculators in solving the problems.

Analysis of Social Studies Materials This subtest requires students to respond to multiple-choice questions by evaluating and analyzing social-studies information. The kinds of behaviors assessed include making inferences or predictions, distinguishing facts from opinions, recognizing an author's purpose, and judging the adequacy of information for reaching conclusions.

Analysis of Science Materials This subtest requires students to evaluate and analyze science information. Behaviors assessed include making inferences or predictions based on observed data; defining the problem in a scientific experiment; distinguishing among hypotheses, assumptions, data, and conclusions; and selecting the best evidence for answering a question.

Use of Sources of Information This subtest measures students' ability to use important sources of information. One of the difficulties the authors encountered in building this subtest was the fact that different schools use different computerized periodical guides. They have used a generic approach in which items are portrayed on a computer screen but are not reliant on a particular research approach.

Scores

The ITBS, TAP, and ITED provide six types of scores: raw scores, developmental standard scores, grade equivalents, national percentile ranks, national stanines, and normal-curve equivalents. The *developmental standard score* provides an estimate of a student's location on an academic-achievement continuum. The median standard score for each grade is computed and placed along the continuum of scores. The standard score can then be interpreted, based on the typical performance of students in each grade. For example, the development standard score for students in grade 1 is 130, and the median score for students in grade 7 is 239. The ITBS, TAP, and ITED can be hand or machine scored. A software package, *Keyscore Norm Look-Up,* is available to assist the hand-scoring process. The program will convert raw scores to each of the five other types of scores and will provide interpolated norms and graphs of national percentile ranks.

Norms

The ITBS, TAP, and ITED were standardized concurrently in 1992 with the CogAT (Thorndike & Hagen, 1994). These measures were standardized on a carefully selected stratified national sample of about 170,000 students. All public-school districts in the United States were stratified, first on the basis of geographic region, and then on the basis of size of enrollment. Districts were then stratified on the basis of socioeconomic status, using the percentage of students in the district falling below the federal government's poverty guideline. Within each socioeconomic stratum, one district was randomly selected. Once districts had been selected and had agreed to participate, further sample selection was accomplished by selecting buildings that would be representative of the distribution of achievement within the selected districts. Data provided in the test manuals show the breakdown of the sample by district size, region of the country, and district socioeconomic status.

In addition to the public-school norm sample, norms are provided for Catholic schools and for private non-Catholic schools. Catholic schools were selected on the basis of geographic region and size of the diocesan school system of which they were members. Private non-Catholic schools were selected on the basis of region and type of school—Baptist, Lutheran, Seventh Day Adventist, other church related, and non-church related. There are eight separate sets of norms—national, interpolated, local, large city, Catholic/private school, high socioeconomic, low socioeconomic, and international—so that student performance can be compared with that of various groups.

The 1996 editions of the ITBS, TAP, and ITED are identical in item content to the 1994 editions of these same tests. The 1996 versions are updated-norms versions. The authors built new norms tables based on the change in performance (up *or* down) between the 1992 and the 1995 samples of students in what they consider to be representative samples of school districts. Statistical procedures were used to build new norms.

Reliability

Internal-consistency reliability data are based on the performance of the fall and spring 1992 standardization samples. Because major areas of the tests (for example, reading total and mathematics total) are most often used in norm-referenced interpretation, these are the reliabilities of greatest concern. Reliabilities for the ITBS raw scores range from .65 to .94 at the kindergarten and first-grade levels, and from .61 to .93 for the other levels of the test. At the kindergarten level, the Language and Word Analysis subtests are the only subtests with reliabilities that are sufficient for the tests to be used in making screening decisions about individuals (that is, the reliabilities for these subtests exceed .80). At the first-grade level, only the Language, Word Analysis, and Mathematics subtests have reliabilities high enough for the tests to be used in making screening decisions about individuals. At the second- and third-grade levels, the reliability of the Listening, Mathematics Concepts, Social Studies, and Science subtests is too low for these tests to be used in making screening decisions about individuals.

Data on internal-consistency reliability of the TAP and the ITED are based on the performance of the fall and spring 1992 standardization sample. The reliability coefficients for the TAP and the ITED raw scores all exceed .80. New internal-consistency studies have been conducted on the new norms, and all reliabilities exceed .80. There are no data on the stability of raw scores on the ITBS, ITED, or TAP.

Validity

The authors of the ITBS, TAP, and ITED attempted to ensure content validity by following a number of steps in the development of the tests. Curriculum guides, textbooks, and research were consulted in writing the items. Potential items were reviewed by experts for content fit and item bias. Then the items were tried out on more than 100,000 students from 30 states plus Guam and the Virgin Islands. Item selection was based on the performance of this sample group. There are no data on the construct validity or the criterion validity of the ITBS, TAP, or ITED.

Summary

The ITBS, the TAP, and the ITED make up the Riverside 2000 Assessment Program. The tests are a comprehensive battery designed to assess broad critical-thinking skills in grades K through 12. Development and standardization of the tests appear exemplary. From the internal-consistency data presented in the manual, reliability is variable. Test users should check the manual to ascertain the reliability for the grades and subtests they are considering. There are no data on the long-term stability (test–retest reliability) of either the ITBS, the TAP, or the ITED. Users must judge the content validity of these tests for their particular use. There are no data on either the construct validity or the criterion-related validity of the ITBS, TAP, or ITED.

Metropolitan Achievement Tests (MAT7)

The Metropolitan Achievement Tests, seventh edition (MAT7; Balow, Farr, & Hogan, 1992) are standardized group achievement tests designed to measure student achievement in reading, language, mathematics, science, and social studies. The tests have been completely revised to address recent changes in school curricula. Leading textbooks, curriculum guidelines, and course syllabi were analyzed to create test specifications and blueprints. The MAT7 includes 14 levels, spanning kindergarten through twelfth grade. Two levels were created for kindergarten and one level for each remaining grade. Two forms were developed, one of which is a secure form and has limited release. Depending on the test level, the complete battery requires from 1 hour, 35 minutes to 4 hours, 10 minutes to administer (see Table 20.5). Besides the five content areas, the MAT7 also assesses research skills and thinking skills. The subtests of the MAT7 are described next.

Subtests

Word Recognition   This subtest measures skill in identifying consonant sounds, vowel sounds, and word parts.

Reading Vocabulary   This subtest, which must be read by the pupils, assesses skill in deriving meaning from words in context.

Reading Comprehension   This subtest assesses students' skill in recognizing detail and sequence; inferring meaning, cause and effect, main idea, and character analysis; and drawing conclusions.

Prereading   This subtest appears only at the preprimer and primer levels. All directions are read to the students. The test is a measure of auditory discrimination, visual discrimination, and letter recognition.

Mathematics   This subtest, which appears at the preprimer and primer levels only, assesses basic concepts of number and units, shapes, and money. The NCTM standards were used in the development of the mathematics tests. Scores can be derived from the mathematics tests that reflect the NCTM core areas.

Prewriting/Composing/Editing   These subtests use a multiple-choice format that is designed to emulate the process of writing. Students must evaluate sections of a text and are asked questions related to the three stages of writing. Spelling items are also included in these subtests, which begin at the elementary Level 1.

Language   A single language composite is produced for preprimer through primary Level 2. Skill development in listening comprehension and basic prewriting skills are measured at the lower levels of the test.

Concepts and Problem Solving   This subtest assesses the students' ability to determine which problem-solving strategies should be selected and used. The items require students to carefully analyze the problem, synthesize the information, and attend to detail.

Procedures   This subtest is optional and is not used at the preprimer, primer, and secondary levels. It includes traditional computation problems and word problems.

Science   This subtest assesses students' knowledge of basic science facts and concepts derived from physical, earth and space, and life sciences. Also assessed are inquiry skills and skill in critical analysis.

Social Studies   This subtest assesses knowledge and comprehension of facts and concepts from the

TABLE 20.5 • Subtests and Levels of the MAT7

	PP		PR		P1		P2		E1		E2		I1		I2		I3		I4		S1		S2		S3		S4	
	Grade K-0–K-5		Grade K-5–1-5		Grade 1-5–2-5		Grade 2-5–3-5		Grade 3-5–4-5		Grade 4-5–5-5		Grade 5-5–6-5		Grade 6-5–7-5		Grade 7-5–8-5		Grade 8-5–9-5		Grade 9		Grade 10		Grade 11		Grade 12	
	K	T	K	T	K	T	K	T	K	T	K	T	K	T	K	T	K	T	K	T	K	T	K	T	K	T	K	T
Word Recognition					30	20	24	15																				
Reading Vocabulary					24	20	24	20	30	20	30	20	30	20	30	20	30	20	30	20	30	20	30	20	30	20	30	20
Reading Comprehension					40	35	45	40	55	50	55	50	55	50	55	50	55	50	55	50	55	50	55	50	55	50	55	50
Prereading/Total Reading	50	35	50	35	94	75	93	75	85	70	85	70	85	70	85	70	85	70	85	70	85	70	85	70	85	70	85	70
Concepts and Problem Solving					32	35	36	35	40	40	40	40	48	50	54	50	54	50	54	50								
Procedures					20	20	20	20	24	25	24	25	24	25	24	25	24	25	24	25								
Mathematics/Total Mathematics	30	30	38	40	52	55	56	55	64	65	64	65	72	75	78	75	78	75	78	75	52	50	52	50	52	50	52	50
Prewriting									15		15		15		15		15		15		15		15		15		15	
Composing									15		15		15		15		15		15		15		15		15		15	
Editing									24		24		24		24		24		24		24		24		24		24	
Language	40	30	40	30	46	40	46	40	54	45	54	45	54	45	54	45	54	45	54	45	54	45	54	45	54	45	54	45
Science					30	25	30	25	35	25	35	25	40	30	40	30	40	30	40	30	40	30	40	30	40	30	40	30
Social Studies					30	25	30	25	35	25	35	25	40	30	40	30	40	30	40	30	40	30	40	30	40	30	40	30
Research Skills									31		36		41		42		42		42		41		41		43		43	
Thinking Skills									78		83		100		103		103		110		116		117		119		120	
Basic Battery	120	95	128	105	192	170	195	170	203	180	203	180	211	190	217	190	217	190	217	190	191	165	191	165	191	165	191	165
Complete Battery	120	95	128	105	252	220	255	220	273	230	278	230	291	250	297	250	297	250	271	250	271	225	271	225	271	225	271	225
Total Testing Time	1 hr. 35 min.		1 hr. 45 min.		3 hrs. 40 min.		3 hrs. 40 min.		3 hrs. 50 min.		3 hrs. 50 min.		4 hrs. 10 min.		4 hrs. 10 min.		4 hrs. 10 min.		4 hrs. 10 min.		3 hrs. 45 min.		3 hrs. 45 min.		3 hrs. 45 min.		3 hrs. 45 min.	

K = Number of items

T = Time in minutes

SOURCE: Metropolitan Achievement Tests: Seventh Edition. Copyright © 1993 by Harcourt Inc. Reproduced by permission. All rights reserved. "Metropolitan Achievement Tests" and "MAT7" are trademarks.

subject-matter areas of geography, economics, history, political science, sociology, anthropology, and psychology.

Research Skills/Thinking Skills   These subtests, which are included in levels of the test intended for use beyond third grade, measure skill development both in using library resources and other methods of collecting data and in properly analyzing and applying information in a variety of contexts.

Scores

Raw scores and several types of derived scores can be obtained for subtests and components of the MAT7. Derived scores include scaled scores, percentile ranks, grade equivalents, normal-curve equivalents, functional reading levels, content-cluster performance categories, proficiency statements, and predicted Scholastic Aptitude Test and American College Test performance ranges. Achievement–ability comparisons can also be derived if students are given the Otis–Lennon School Ability Test.

Content-cluster performance indicators are used to describe each student's performance on each content cluster of the MAT7, relative to the performance of a nationwide sample of students at the same grade level. Three types of functional reading level are provided: instructional, independent, and frustration. *Instructional reading levels* are indexes of the highest level at which pupils can read without experiencing frustration. *Independent reading levels* are criterion-referenced scores indicating the level of material students can read with ease and efficiency. *Frustration reading levels* are criterion-referenced scores showing the level at which students will find materials too difficult to comprehend, even with instruction. Proficiency statements describe what type of tasks students should be able to complete, based on their MAT7 scores.

The MAT7 may be hand scored or submitted to the publisher for computerized scoring. The scoring service may be used to obtain class summary reports, norm-referenced analyses for classes and for individual pupils, and criterion-referenced analyses for classes and for individuals.

Norms

The MAT7 was standardized during the spring and fall of 1992. The spring standardization consisted of 100,000 students from 300 schools; the fall standardization contained 79,000 students. The authors state that the sample was stratified originally by geographic region, socioeconomic status (SES), community type (urban or rural), and ethnicity and then statistically weighted to match the 1990 U.S. Census Bureau data when they became available.

Reliability

Three forms of internal-consistency reliability data were computed. Alternate-form, KR-20, and KR-21 reliability coefficients generally exceed .80 across the 14 levels of the test, although several cluster scores drop well below the .80 mark. The test appears to be adequate for group reporting and screening but should not be used to make decisions about individuals. Test–retest data were not reported.

Validity

Although the content validity of an achievement test must ultimately be determined by the user, the authors of the MAT7 rigorously attempted to match the test with current school curricula. An effort was also made to eliminate cultural bias from the test items, mostly by asking individuals from different cultural groups to review the items. Data on the construct validity of the MAT7 are limited to an illustration that growth occurs across levels of the test and that items can discriminate across grade levels.

Summary

The MAT7 is a norm-referenced and criterion-referenced achievement test designed for use in grades K through 12. The test was adequately standardized and is reliable for group reporting and screening purposes. The test was redesigned to match current school curricula. Judgments about content validity must be made by users, who must consider the extent to which the test samples what they teach.

Stanford Achievement Test Series (SESAT, SAT, TASK)

Three separate measures make up the Stanford Achievement Test Series. The Stanford Early School Achievement Test (SESAT; Harcourt Brace Educational Measurement, 1996b) is in its fourth edition and is intended for use in kindergarten and first grade. The Stanford Achievement Test (SAT) (Harcourt Brace Educational Measurement, 1996a) is in its ninth edition and is used in first through ninth grades. The Test of Academic Skills (TASK) (Harcourt Brace Educational Measurement, 1996c) is in its fourth edition and is used in ninth grade through community college. The name *Stanford 9* is used to designate the entire series of tests.

All forms and levels of the test are group administered. The test is both norm-referenced and criterion-referenced, and there are multiple ways in which the criterion-referenced information can be interpreted. In Stanford 9, two testing approaches—multiple-choice and open-ended subtests—have been combined into one assessment system. In developing the multiple-choice items for this new edition, the authors framed the items within classroom or real-life situations, attempted to elicit actual performance from students, and increased the number of items that measure processes or strategies.

There are 13 levels of the Stanford Achievement Test Series and 5 to 13 subtests at each level. Subtests at each level of the series, as well as number of items per subtest and the administration time, are listed in Table 20.6. No subtest occurs at all levels.

Assessors must decide whether to use a basic battery or a complete battery. At all levels, the basic battery includes all subtests except the Environment, Science, and Social Science subtests. Assessors may also decide to assess students in only reading or mathematics. The publishers have provided separate booklets including all reading tests and all mathematics tests. Total administration time for the basic battery ranges from 1 hour, 45 minutes to 4 hours, 35 minutes. Administration time for the complete battery ranges from 2 hours, 15 minutes to 5 hours, 25 minutes.

Subtests

Following is a description of subtests of the Stanford series and the behaviors these subtests sample.

Sounds and Letters This subtest, included only in SESAT 1 and 2, assesses these abilities: to match beginning or ending sounds in words, to recognize letters, and to match sounds to letters.

Word Study Skills This subtest, available only at the primary levels, measures students' skills in decoding words and in identifying relationships between sounds and letters.

Word Reading This subtest, available only at the SESAT and the primary 1 levels, measures students' ability to recognize words by (1) matching spoken words to pictures, (2) identifying printed words that name particular illustrations, and (3) identifying printed words that describe or are associated with a picture.

Sentence Reading This subtest, used at the SESAT 2 level only, assesses students' skill in iden-

TABLE 20.6 ● Stanford 9 Scope and Sequence

K = No. of items   T = Time in Minutes

COMPLETE BATTERY–MULTIPLE-CHOICE SUBTESTS

Test Levels	SESAT 1 (K.0–K.5)		SESAT 2 (K.5–1.5)		Primary 1 (1.5–2.5)		Primary 2 (2.5–3.5)		Primary 3 (3.5–4.5)		Intermediate 1 (4.5–5.5)		Intermediate 2 (5.5–6.5)		Intermediate 3 (6.5–7.5)		Advanced 1 (7.5–8.5)		Advanced 2 (8.5–9.9)		TASK 1 (9.0–9.9)		TASK 2 (10.0–10.9)		TASK 3 (11.0–13.0)	
	K	T	K	T	K	T	K	T	K	T	K	T	K	T	K	T	K	T	K	T	K	T	K	T	K	T
Sounds and Letters	48	30	40	25																						
Word Study Skills	30	15	40	25	36	20	48	25																		
Word Reading			30	30	30	25																				
Sentence Reading																										
Reading Vocabulary					40	40	30	20	30	20	30	20	30	20	30	20	30	20	30	20	30	20	30	20	30	20
Reading Comprehension									54	50	54	50	54	50	54	50	54	50	54	50	54	40	54	40	54	40
Total Reading	78	45	110	80	106	85	118	85	84	70	84	70	84	70	84	70	84	70	84	70	84	80	84	60	84	80
Mathematics	40	30	40	30																	48	45	48	45	48	45
Mathematics: Problem Solving					44	50	46	50	46	50	48	50	48	50	48	50	50	50	52	50						
Mathematics: Procedures					25	30	28	30	30	30	30	30	30	30	30	30	30	30	30	30						
Total Mathematics					69	80	74	80	76	80	78	80	78	80	78	80	80	80	82	80						
Language Form S					44	40	44	40	48	45	48	45	48	45	48	45	48	45	48	45	48	40	48	40	48	40
Spelling					30	25	30	25	30	25	30	25	30	25	30	25	30	25	30	25	30	20	30	20	30	20
Study Skills											30	25	30	25	30	25	30	20	30	20	30	20	30	20	30	20
Listening to Words and Stories	40	30	40	30																						
Listening					40	30	40	30	40	30	40	30	40	30	40	30	40	30	40	30						
Environment	40	30	40	30	40	30	40	30																		
Science									40	25	40	25	40	25	40	25	40	25	40	25	40	20	40	20	40	20
Social Science									40	25	40	25	40	25	40	25	40	25	40	25	40	20	40	20	40	20
Basic Battery	158	105	190	140	289	260	306	290	278	250	310	235	310	275	310	275	312	270	314	270	240	185	240	185	240	185
Complete Battery	198	135	230	170	329	290	346	290	358	300	390	325	390	325	390	325	392	320	394	320	320	225	320	225	320	225
Total Testing Time	2 hrs	15 mins	2 hrs	50 mins	4 hrs	50 mins	4 hrs	50 mins	5 hrs		5 hrs	25 mins	5 hrs	25 mins	5 hrs	25 mins	5 hrs	20 mins	5 hrs	20 mins	3 hrs	45 mins	3 hrs	45 mins	3 hrs	45 mins
Language Form SA					46	40	46	40	54	45	54	45	54	45	54	45	54	45	54	45	54	45	54	45	54	45

ABBREVIATED BATTERY–MULTIPLE-CHOICE SUBTESTS

Test Levels	SESAT 1		SESAT 2		Primary 1		Primary 2		Primary 3		Intermediate 1		Intermediate 2		Intermediate 3		Advanced 1		Advanced 2		TASK 1		TASK 2		TASK 3	
	K	T	K	T	K	T	K	T	K	T	K	T	K	T	K	T	K	T	K	T	K	T	K	T	K	T
Word Study Skills	20	11	20	11																						
Word Reading			20	17																						
Reading Vocabulary											20	14	20	14	20	14	20	14	20	14	20	14	20	14	20	14
Reading Comprehension					30	30	30	30	30	28	30	28	30	28	30	28	30	28	30	28	30	28	30	28	30	28
Mathematics					30	34	30	33	30	33	30	31	30	31	30	31	30	30	30	29	30	28	30	28	30	28
Mathematics: Problem Solving					20	24	20	22	20	20	20	20	20	20	20	20	20	20	20	20						
Mathematics: Procedures					20	20	20	20	20	20	20	20	20	20	20	20	20	20	20	20						
Language Form S					30	27	30	27	30	28	30	28	30	28	30	28	30	28	30	28	30	25	30	25	30	25

tifying pictures that illustrate sentences the students read.

Reading Vocabulary   In this subtest, students are asked to select words that best fit definitions read by the examiner. The measure thus provides an assessment of students' word knowledge independent of their ability to read definitions.

Reading Comprehension   In this subtest, students read passages that assess textual, functional, and recreational reading skills; at the end of each passage, students answer questions that assess literal and inferential comprehension. This subtest includes a variety of new items that assess important reading processes such as initial understanding, interpretation, critical analysis, and use of reading strategies. In an alternative format, this test is available as an open-ended reading assessment, which consists of a narrative reading selection followed by nine questions.

Listening to Words and Stories   This subtest assesses students' ability to remember details, follow directions, identify cause and effect, identify main ideas, and understand aspects of language structure. Students must demonstrate knowledge of word meanings and skill in comprehending what is read to them.

Listening   This subtest assesses students' ability to process information that is read to them. The students are expected to take notes on the material as the tester reads it.

Language   This subtest is available in two versions. One version measures proficiency in both mechanics and expression, along with content and organization and sentence structure. An alternative version, called the "integrated language subtest," measures prewriting, composing, editing, and spelling in a holistic fashion. Mechanics such as spelling and punctuation are measured by having students edit in context. When the alternative version is used, there are no separate study skills and spelling subtests.

Study Skills   This subtest measures the skills used in the process of investigation.

Spelling   In this subtest, students must identify the correct spelling of words.

Mathematics   The SAT contains both multiple-choice and open-ended assessments in two subtests: Mathematics: Problem Solving and Mathematics: Procedures. There are optional calculator norms for the Mathematics: Problem Solving subtest. The math subtests were developed in alignment with the NCTM standards for school mathematics (NCTM, 1993).

Science   This subtest measures students' understanding of the facts and concepts of the biological and physical sciences. In addition, it assesses students' processing of science information and their inquiry skills in science. The test includes both open-ended and multiple-choice items, which are derived from and matched to *Science for All Americans, Benchmarks for Science Literacy,* and the *National Science Education Standards*.

Social Science   This subtest measures students' skill development in geography, history, anthropology, sociology, political science, and economics, as well as students' ability to interpret data presented in graphic form. The open-ended social science questions require students to apply concepts and to make inferences at a level beyond that required by the multiple-choice questions.

Environment   The Science and Social Science subtests are combined at the early levels of the test, to form an assessment of concepts about the social and natural environment.

Special Editions

There are two special editions of the Stanford Achievement Test: one for assessing blind or partially sighted students and one for assessing deaf students. The edition for use with blind or partially sighted students can be obtained in either

Braille or large print from the American Printing House for the Blind, and the edition for hearing-impaired students may be obtained from Gallaudet College. Both special editions were standardized on the respective populations of individuals with disabilities.

Scores

A variety of transformed scores are obtained for the Stanford series: stanines, grade-equivalent scores, percentiles, and various standard scores. The tests may be scored by hand or submitted to the publisher for machine scoring. When protocols are submitted to the publisher's scoring service, the publisher can provide record sheets for individual students, forms for reporting test results to parents, item analyses, class profiles, profiles comparing individual achievement with individual capability, analyses of each student's performance in attainment of specific objectives, local norms, and so forth.

In addition, a variety of performance scores can now also be obtained. Performance standards were developed through the expert judgment of national panels of educators in each content area. Users can also set their own standards. The performance standards are available for items in reading and mathematics, the Stanford Writing Assessment, and open-ended assessments in each content area. Performance is scored as below satisfactory, partial mastery of knowledge and skills, solid academic performance, and superior performance.

Norms

The ninth edition of the Stanford Achievement Test Series was standardized simultaneously with the OLSAT 7 in both the fall and spring of 1995. Separate norms are thus provided for schools in which students must be tested at specific times of the year. Standardizing the series along with the OLSAT 7 enabled the authors to account for the ability levels of the students in the standardization population and also to develop a set of tables for comparison of ability level to achievement.

Sample selection was based on several variables, including geographic region, socioeconomic status, community type (urban or rural), and public/nonpublic status. About 250,000 students participated in the standardization of the series. The technical manual includes a table showing the percentages of different types of students who participated and comparing those percentages to national census data. There is close correspondence between standardization-sample makeup and the makeup of the 1992–1993 census. Cross-tabulations are not shown, so we do not know, for example, the number of males from the northeast region.

Performance standards were set by having approximately 200 teachers representing school districts from around the country participate in a three-week series of standard-setting meetings and set scoring standards for the test.

Reliability

Reliability data for the SESAT, SAT, and TASK consist of KR-20 and KR-21 internal-consistency coefficients and alternate-forms coefficients for each level of the test. KR-20 coefficients ranged from .78 to .98, with only two coefficients below .80. Alternate-forms reliability estimates ranged from .58 to .93. Extensive tables listing reliability coefficients and standard errors of measurement are included in the technical manual for the test. With only a few exceptions, the scores for subtests are reliable enough for group decision making and reporting.

Validity

As for any achievement test, the validity of the Stanford series rests primarily on its content validity. Items for the series were originally written by the test authors and submitted to a group of subject-matter experts to establish the content accuracy. Measurement experts examined and edited the items, and the items were reviewed by general editors for writing clarity. The test items were submitted to a group of people representing minority groups, who screened the items in terms of the appropriateness of content for various cultural groups. In addition, teachers from the schools participating in the standardization process evaluated the clarity of both the instructions and the items.

Empirical validity was established on the basis of three factors: the increasing difficulty of items with higher grade levels, a moderate to high relationship with the eighth edition of the Stanford series, and intercorrelations between Stanford subtests and the OLSAT 7.

Summary

The Stanford Achievement Test Series is composed of the SESAT, the SAT, and the TASK. The tests provide a comprehensive continuous assessment of skill development in a variety of areas. Standardization, reliability, and validity are adequate for screening purposes.

Terra Nova

The Terra Nova (CTB/McGraw-Hill, 1997), a group-administered multiple-skill battery that provides norm-referenced and objective-mastery scores, is the most recent edition of the Comprehensive Test of Basic Skills. The test includes selected-response items (multiple-choice) and extended open-ended items. The Terra Nova is available in multiple formats called CTBS Complete Battery, CTBS Survey Battery, and CTBS Multiple Assessment. For both the complete battery and the survey battery, users may administer the basic test, consisting of four subtests, or the basic test plus supplemental tests. All items in the survey battery are selected-response items. In addition to the off-the-shelf test, states and school districts may order custom-built performance tests. Subtests included in the three batteries, grade levels, and testing times are shown in Table 20.7.

Subtests

Reading/Language Arts   Skills assessed in this subtest include listening comprehension; basic understanding; text analysis, including drawing conclusions; evaluation; identification of reading strategies; knowledge of sound/symbol and structural relationships in letters, words, and signs; understanding of sentence structure, including punctuation and capitalization; sentence writing and connected prose writing; and editing skills.

Mathematics   Measured skills include number recognition and number relations, computation and estimation, basic mathematics operations, measurement, geometry, data analysis, statistics and probability, algebra and math functions, problem solving and reasoning, and math vocabulary and terminology.

Science   Skills assessed include understanding of the fundamental concepts of scientific inquiry; understanding of fundamental concepts and principles of physical science, life science, and earth and space science; understanding of how technology and science interact; and the history and nature of science.

Social Studies   Geography, cultural perspectives, history, civics, government, and economics are tested.

Word Analysis   A measure of word skill consists of recognizing consonants, blends, digraphs, sight

Table 20.7 ● Terra Nova Subtests, Grade Levels, and Testing Times

Battery	Subtests	Grades	Testing Time
Complete	Reading/Language Arts	K–12	3:30 @ K; 2:40 @ grade
	Mathematics	K–12	1, to 4:10 @ grades 9–12
	Science	1–12	
	Social Studies	1–12	
Complete with	Word Analysis	1–12	3:30 @ grade 1 to 5:15
Supplemental	Vocabulary	1–12	@ grades 9–12
Subtests	Language Mechanics	2–12	
	Spelling	2–12	
	Mathematics Computation	1–12	
Survey	Reading/Language Arts	2–12	2:15 @ grade 2 to 2:40
	Mathematics	2–12 @ grades 9–12	
	Science	2–12	
	Social Studies	2–12	
Survey with	Word Analysis	2–12	3:35 @ grade 2 to 3:45
Supplemental	Vocabulary	2–12	@ grades 9–12
Subtests	Language Mechanics	2–12	
	Spelling	2–12	
	Mathematics Computation	2–12	
Multiple	Reading/Language Arts	1–12	4:00 @ grade 1 to 5:20
Assessment	Mathematics	1–12	@ grades 9–12
	Science	1–12	
	Social Studies	1–12	

words, vowels, contractions and compounds, roots, and affixes.

Vocabulary   This subtest is an assessment of skill in understanding word meanings and relationships, including the use of context to infer words missing from passages.

Language Mechanics   The appropriate use of capitalization and punctuation and writing conventions are assessed.

Spelling   Students identify the correct spelling of words presented in sentences and paragraphs.

Mathematics Computation   Skills assessed in this subtest include addition, subtraction, multiplication, and division; use of decimals, fractions and percent; and algebraic operations.

Norms

The standardization sample for the Terra Nova was stratified on the basis of geographic region, community type, school size, socioeconomic status, and school type (public, Catholic, private non-Catholic). The test was standardized on more than 171,000 students in kindergarten through grade 12. Cross-tabulations in the manual show the stratification of the sample. Sample proportions closely approximate census proportions.

Scores

Those who use the Terra Nova may receive a variety of reports. The Individual Profile Report provides the teacher with specific information about student strengths and weaknesses in both norm-referenced and criterion-referenced terms. Teachers can quickly identify their students' instructional needs. The Home Report gives parents information about student performance, and a Performance Level Summary Report gives educators standards-based information about academic achievement. Administrators receive summary information about student performance in the form of an Evaluation Summary, whereas school-board members can get data in the form of a Board Report. For all reports, norm-referenced scores are in the form of national percentiles, and standards-referenced scores indicate relative standing on specific objectives.

Reliability

Internal consistency coefficients for the Terra Nova Survey Plus, Complete Battery Plus, and Multiple Assessments are shown in the test manual. Internal-consistency coefficients are from .72 to .94 for subtests of the survey battery, .76 to .97 for the complete battery, and .76 to .96 for the multiple assessments. There are no data on test–retest reliability or on alternate-form reliability. Reliabilities

of some of the separate subtests are too low for use in making decisions about individuals.

Validity

There is limited evidence for the validity of the Terra Nova batteries. The authors indicate that they ensured content validity by anchoring the test to curricula used in schools and will establish criterion-related validity by correlating performance on the test with performance on the National Assessment of Educational Progress as soon as scores on that test are available. The authors attempt to support construct validity by correlating performance on the Terra Nova with performance on the Test of Cognitive Skills–2 (TCS/2). Yet, our examination of tables in the manual indicated that correlations between measures of cognitive skills (TCS/2) and achievement are about the same as correlations among Terra Nova subtests. It could be argued that the test is a measure of cognition as much as of achievement.

Summary

The Terra Nova is one of several multiple-skill achievement batteries available to schools and districts. Those who must make a decision about which test to use should examine carefully the match between their curriculum and the various tests. There is less evidence for the technical adequacy of the Terra Nova than for that of other comparable achievement batteries.

Kaufman Test of Educational Achievement–Normative Update (K-TEA-NU)

The Kaufman Test of Educational Achievement was originally published in 1985. In 1998 the authors updated the norms for the test, and it is now called the Kaufman Test of Educational Achievement–Normative Update (K-TEA-NU; Kaufman

& Kaufman, 1998a, 1998b). The test is an individually administered norm-referenced multiple-skill achievement test that can be used with students in the first through twelfth grades. The K-TEA comes in two different forms: the comprehensive form (Kaufman & Kaufman, 1998b) and the brief form (Kaufman & Kaufman, 1998a). The brief form requires from 10 to 25 minutes to administer and the comprehensive form from 20 to 75 minutes, depending on the child's grade. Both forms of the test are intended for use in program planning, research, placement, student self-appraisal, personnel selection, and measurement of adaptive functioning. The comprehensive form is said to be useful in analyzing strengths and weaknesses and error analysis. The brief form is designed for use in screening.

All items and subtests remained the same for the normative updates of the two forms of the K-TEA. Although the comprehensive and brief forms bear the same name (K-TEA), they include quite different items and subtests. Thus, we treat the two forms separately in our review.

Subtests

The comprehensive form (CF) contains five subtests.

Reading Decoding   This 60-item subtest requires a student to identify letters and then to read phonetic and nonphonetic words of increasing difficulty.

Reading Comprehension   This subtest contains two types of items. For 12 questions, the student must respond gesturally or orally to commands given in printed sentences. For the remaining 38 questions, the student must read material and then answer literal and inferential questions about it. The complexity and variety of language structures increase over the course of the subtest.

Mathematics Applications   This subtest assesses a student's "ability to solve real-world problems by the application of mathematics knowledge" (Kaufman & Kaufman, 1985c, p. 196). The 60 items are of two types: math concepts and applications in practical situations. All problems are read to the student, who can refer to various visual materials (illustrations, graphs, and so forth).

Mathematics Computation   This 60-item subtest assesses a student's skill in solving problems involving basic operations, exponents, symbols, abbreviations, and algebraic equations.

Spelling   This subtest assesses a student's ability to spell 50 words. The tester says each word and uses each in a sentence. (A student who is unable to write is allowed to spell orally.)

The brief form (BF) includes three subtests that provide global assessment of skill in reading, mathematics, and spelling.

Reading   This subtest contains 52 items. The first 23 items require letter identification and word decoding; the remaining items are similar to those on the CF Reading Comprehension subtest.

Mathematics   This subtest contains 52 items that assess arithmetic concepts, applications, reasoning, and computational skill. The first 25 problems require written computation. The remaining problems are read to the student, who can refer to various visual materials (such as illustrations, graphs, and so forth).

Spelling   This 40-word subtest is similar in form to the CF Spelling subtest.

Scores

For individual subtest scores and composite scores (reading, mathematics, and battery), normalized standard scores are available by grade or age and can be compared with either the spring or the fall norm sample. (For the CF, mean = 100 and standard deviation = 15; the values are approximately the same for the BF.) Composites are based on raw-score totals; thus, subtests are not equally weighted within composites. Percentile ranks, stanines, and normal-curve equivalents are also available, as are age and grade equivalents.

Finally, a teacher can conduct an error analysis of each subtest of the CF. Errors made consistently by a student are noted, and the number of errors is compared with the number made by students in the norm sample.

Norms

When the K-TEA was originally developed, it was standardized on a spring sample of 1,409 students and a fall sample of 1,067 students, with no fewer than 100 students per grade. The authors did an exemplary job of describing and documenting the characteristics of the normative sample. Norms for the brief form were equated to the norms for the comprehensive form by testing 589 students with both forms and then equating their scores.

The 1998 normative update was completed in conjunction with normative updating of the Peabody Individual Achievement Test–Revised, the Key Math–Revised, and the Woodcock Reading Mastery Tests–Revised. The sample for the normative updates was 3,184 students in kindergarten through grade 12. A stratified multistage sampling procedure was used to ensure selection of a nationally representative group at each grade level. Students in the norm group did not take each of the five tests. Rather, one fifth of the students took each test, along with portions of each of the other tests. Thus, the norm groups for the brief and comprehensive forms consist of about 600 students. There are as few as 91 students at three-year age ranges. Because multiple measures were given to each student, the authors could use linking and equating to increase the size of the norm sample.

The authors (Kaufman & Kaufman, 1998b) report that "approximately twelve years separate the data-collection periods for the original K-TEA norms and the updated norms. Changes during that time in curriculum and educational practice, in population demographics, and in the general cultural environment may have affected levels of academic achievement" (p. 257). The authors also include descriptions of the extent to which scores on the various subtests have changed. For example, this is what they say about changes in Reading Decoding for the Comprehensive Form:

The average level of performance has increased slightly. Each grade shows greater variation in reading decoding scores: the lower end of the score distribution has dropped slightly, while the upper end has increased more dramatically, especially at grades 1 through 4. (p. 257).

Reliability

All data on reliability of the K-TEA-NU are for the original K-TEA. The performance of students on the two measures has changed, and so the authors should have conducted a few reliability studies on students in the late 1990s. Generalizations from the reliability of the original K-TEA to reliability of the K-TEA-NU are suspect.

Validity

All data on validity of the K-TEA-NU are for the original K-TEA. The performance of students on the two measures has changed, and so the authors should have conducted a few validity studies on students in the late 1990s. Generalizations from the validity of the original K-TEA to validity of the K-TEA-NU are suspect. This is especially true for measures of external validity, where the measures (such as the Wide Range Achievement Test or the Peabody Picture Vocabulary Test) have been revised.

Summary

The K-TEA-NU is an individually administered achievement test that is available in both comprehensive and brief formats. The test was renormed in 1998. Reliability and validity information is based on studies of the original (1985) test. As with any achievement test, the most crucial concern is content validity. Users must be sensitive to the correspondence of the content of the K-TEA-NU to a student's curriculum.

Mini-Battery of Achievement (MBA)

The Mini-Battery of Achievement (MBA; Woodcock, McGrew, & Werder, 1994) is an individually administered, brief, and comprehensive measure of academic achievement designed to assess a broad cross section of skills across a wide age range. The authors indicate that the MBA is designed for educational, clinical, vocational placement, and research purposes. The test is applicable for individuals from 4 to 90-plus years of age, and it takes about 30 minutes to administer. No special training is required for those who administer the test. The MBA includes measures of academic competence in reading, math, writing, and factual knowledge (in science, social studies, and humanities). Test items are printed in an easel format, and the examiner uses the easel and a test record with worksheet in administering the test. There is a computer scoring program that accompanies the test, and use of it yields a one-page interpretive report. The MBA is essentially a short form of the Woodcock–Johnson Psychoeducational Battery (see Chapter 27). Willis, Dumont, and Cruse (in press) conducted an analysis of test-item overlap. They report that 82 percent of the items on the MBA are from the two forms of the Woodcock–Johnson–Revised (WJ-R). The remaining items came from the original item pool for the WJ-R.

Subtests

The following behaviors are sampled by the subtests of the MBA.

Reading   The reading subtest is a three-part measure. Letter- and word-identification skills are assessed in Part A, in which the test taker must read isolated letters and words. In Part B (Vocabulary), the test taker must identify an antonym of a word read by the examiner. Part C (Comprehension) of the test is a cloze measure of reading in which the

test taker must identify missing words in short passages.

Writing   The writing subtest is a two-part measure. In Part A (Dictation), the test taker must write words or sentences—and by doing so demonstrate knowledge of letter forms, spelling, punctuation, capitalization, and word knowledge. In Part B (Proofreading), the test taker is required to correct mistakes in capitalization, punctuation, spelling, or word usage.

Math   Math is also a two-part subtest. Part A (Calculation) is an assessment of skill in performing basic math operations plus geometry, algebra, trigonometry, and calculus on problems that involve whole numbers, fractions, and decimals. The test taker completes responses on a worksheet, so this is not a problem-solving assessment in which the person must decide what to add, subtract, and so on. Rather, the items are given to the test taker. In Part B (Reasoning and Concepts), the test taker must analyze and solve practical problems. This requires deciding what data to use and how to solve the problems.

Factual Knowledge   This subtest is like the general information subtest on other measures and includes an assessment of knowledge of facts and concepts drawn from social studies, science, and humanities.

Scores

Scores on Reading, Math, and Writing are combined into a basic skills cluster. Raw scores on the MBA may be converted to grade scores, age equivalents, standard scores, percentile scores, normal-curve equivalents, and *T*-scores. There are no norm tables in the manual. Rather, the computerized scoring program is used to obtain all scores.

Norms

The MBA and the WJ-R are standardized on a common norming sample. The MBA was never administered. Rather, performance by the WJ-R norm sample on items used to construct the MBA makes up the norming sample for the MBA. The MBA was standardized on 6,026 subjects aged 4 to 95 years. The sample was stratified on the basis of census region, community size, gender, race, national origin, distribution of education of adults in the community, adult occupational status (employed, not employed, not in workforce), and distribution of occupations; in addition, college students were stratified as to whether the college was public or private and its type. The manual for the MBA does not include information illustrating the extent to which the norm sample is representative of the general population. Test givers must refer to the technical manual of the WJ-R (McGrew, Werder, & Woodcock, 1991) for this information.

Reliability

The authors report data on internal-consistency and test–retest reliability for the MBA. They report internal-consistency reliability by age with large numbers of subjects (125 to 715 at each age level). With the exception of mathematics at age 5 years (reliability = .70), all reliability coefficients exceed .90, although reliabilities for Factual Knowledge are lower than those for other subtests. The MBA has good internal-consistency reliabilities.

A study of test–retest reliability was completed on subjects at three age levels (sixth grade, college, and adult). The sample is not described, so we have no idea whether it is representative of the population. The test–retest interval is not de-

scribed. There were 52–56 people in the sample at each age level. Reliabilities exceeded .85, but the limited size of the sample weakens the argument for test–retest reliability.

Validity

The authors report content-, concurrent-, and construct-validity studies. In arguing for content validity, the authors say that the items were selected "carefully" and cover many levels of difficulty. They do not provide a rationale for selection of the items and do not indicate the curricular match for items. The manual includes the report of a concurrent-validity study using the same sample as that used in establishing test–retest reliability. Again, the sample is not described. Correlations of performance between the basic skills cluster and each MBA subtest, each composite score, and each total score are reported. Performance on the basic skills cluster consistently correlated in excess of .80 with performance on other composite or total scores. Evidence for construct validity also comes from this study. The authors show that performance on similar-content subtests (such as reading with reading) correlates more highly than that on different-content subtests (such as reading with math).

Summary

The MBA is a brief measure of academic achievement that is more comprehensive than similar brief measures. It includes an assessment of performance in Reading, Mathematics, Writing, and Factual Knowledge. The test is a short form of the Achievement Portion of the Woodcock–Johnson Psychoeducational Battery–Revised. The MBA was adequately standardized and has good internal-consistency reliability. Evidence for test–retest reliability and for concurrent and construct validity is based on very limited samples. The test is a good screening measure of academic achievement.

Peabody Individual Achievement Test–Revised–Normative Update (PIAT-R-NU)

The most recent edition of the Peabody Individual Achievement Test (PIAT-R-NU; Markwardt, 1998) is not a new edition of the test but a normative update of the 1989 edition of the PIAT-R. The test is an individually administered norm-referenced instrument designed to provide a wide-ranging screening measure of academic achievement in six content areas. It can be used with students in kindergarten through twelfth grade. PIAT-R test materials are contained in four easel kits, one for each volume of the test. Easel-kit volumes present stimulus materials to the student at eye level; the examiner's instructions are placed on the reverse side. The student can see one side of the response plate, whereas the examiner can see both sides. The test is recommended by the author for use in individual evaluation, guidance, admissions and transfers, grouping of students, progress evaluation, and personnel selection.

The original PIAT (Dunn & Markwardt, 1970) included five subtests. The PIAT-R added a written expression subtest. The 1989 edition updated the content of the test. The 1998 edition is identical to the 1989 edition. Behaviors sampled by the six subtests of the PIAT-R-NU are as follows.

Subtests

Mathematics This subtest contains 100 multiple-choice items, ranging from items that assess such early skills as matching, discriminating, and recognizing numerals to items that assess advanced concepts in geometry and trigonometry. The test is a measure of the student's knowledge and application of math concepts and facts.

Reading Recognition This subtest also contains 100 items, ranging in difficulty from preschool level through high-school level. Items assess skill development in matching letters, naming capital and lowercase letters, and recognizing words in isolation.

Reading Comprehension This subtest contains 81 multiple-choice items assessing skill development in understanding what is read. After reading a sentence, the student must indicate comprehension by choosing the correct picture out of a group of four.

Spelling This subtest consists of 100 items sampling behaviors from kindergarten level through high-school level. Initial items assess the student's ability to distinguish a printed letter of the alphabet from pictured objects and to associate letter symbols with speech sounds. More difficult items assess the student's ability to identify, from a response bank of four words, the correct spelling of a word read aloud by the examiner.

General Information This subtest consists of 100 questions presented orally, which the student must answer orally. Items assess the extent to which the student has learned facts in social studies, science, sports, and the fine arts.

Written Expression This subtest assesses written-language skills at two levels. Level I, appropriate for students in kindergarten and first grade, is a measure of prewriting skills such as skill in copying and writing letters, words, and sentences from dictation. At Level II, students write a story in response to a picture prompt.

Scores

All but one of the PIAT-R subtests are scored in the same way: The student's response to each item is rated pass–fail. On these five subtests, raw scores are converted to grade and age equivalents, grade- and age-based standard scores, percentile ranks, normal-curve equivalents, and stanines. The Written Expression subtest is scored differently from the other subtests. The examiner uses a set of scoring criteria included in an appendix in the test manual. At Level I, the examiner scores the student's writing of his or her name and then scores 18 items pass–fail. For the more difficult items at Level I, the student must earn a specified number of subcredits to pass the item. Methods for assigning subcredits are specified clearly in the manual. At Level II, the student generates a free response, and the assessor examines the response for certain specified characteristics. For example, the student is given credit for each letter correctly capitalized, each correct punctuation, and absence of inappropriate words. Scores earned on the Written Expression subtest include grade-based stanines and developmental scaled scores (with mean = 8 and standard deviation = 3).

Three composite scores are used to summarize student performance on the PIAT-R: total reading, total test, and written language. Total reading is described as an overall measure of "reading ability" and is obtained by combining scores on Reading Recognition and Reading Comprehension. The total test score is obtained by combining performance on the General Information, Reading Recognition, Reading Comprehension, Mathematics, and Spelling subtests. A third composite score, the written language composite score, is optional and is obtained by combining performance on the Spelling and Written Expression subtests.

Norms

The 1989 edition of the PIAT-R was standardized on 1,563 students in kindergarten through grade 12. The 1998 normative update was completed in conjunction with normative updating of the Kaufman Test of Educational Achievement, the Key Math–Revised, and the Woodcock Reading Mastery Tests–Revised. The sample for the normative updates was 3,184 students in kindergarten through grade 12. A stratified multistage sampling procedure was used to ensure selection of a nationally representative group at each grade level. Students in the norm group did not all take each of the five tests. Rather, one fifth of the students took each test, along with portions of each of the other tests. Thus, the norm groups for the brief and comprehensive forms consist of about 600 students. There are as few as 91 students at three-year age ranges. Because multiple measures were given to each student, the authors could use linking and equating to increase the size of the norm sample.

Approximately ten years separate the data-collection periods for the original PIAT norms and the updated norms. Changes during that time in curriculum and educational practice, in population demographics, and in the general cultural environment may have affected levels of academic achievement.

Reliability

All data on the reliability of the PIAT-R-NU are for the original PIAT-R. The performance of students on the two measures has changed, and so the authors should have conducted a few reliability studies on students in the late 1990s. Generalizations from the reliability of the original PIAT-R to reliability of the PIAT-R-NU are suspect.

Validity

All data on validity of the PIAT-R-NU are for the original PIAT-R. The performance of students on the two measures has changed, and so the authors should have conducted a few validity studies on students in the late 1990s. Generalizations from the validity of the original PIAT-R to validity of PIAT-R-NU are suspect. This is especially true for measures of external validity where the measures (for example, the Wide Range Achievement Test or the Peabody Picture Vocabulary Test) have been revised.

Summary

The PIAT-R is an individually administered achievement test that was renormed in 1998. Reliability and validity information is based on studies of the 1989 edition of the test. As with any achievement test, the most crucial concern is content validity. Users must be sensitive to the correspondence of the content of the PIAT-R to a student's curriculum. The test is essentially a 1970 test that was revised and renormed in 1989 and then renormed again in 1998.

Wide Range Achievement Test 3 (WRAT3)

The Wide Range Achievement Test 3 (WRAT3; Wilkinson, 1993) is designed to measure the "codes which are needed to learn the basic skills of reading, writing, spelling and arithmetic" (p. 10). The author states that an attempt was made to eliminate the effect of comprehension. This was done to enable diagnosticians to determine whether an academic problem is caused by an inability to learn specific codes or by an inability to derive meaning from the codes.

The WRAT3 is a single-level, individually administered test that can be used with individuals aged 5 to 75 years. Two forms were developed; these can be either used individually or combined to give a more comprehensive evaluation. The author suggests using the alternative forms for pre- and posttesting situations. The test contains three subtests.

Subtests

Reading This subtest assesses skill in letter recognition, letter naming, and pronunciation of words in isolation.

Spelling This subtest assesses students' skills in copying marks onto paper, writing their names, and writing single words from dictation.

Arithmetic This subtest assesses skills in counting, reading numerals, solving problems presented orally, and performing written composition of arithmetic problems.

Scores

Six kinds of scores can be derived from the WRAT3: raw, absolute, standard, grade equiva- lent, percentile, and normal-curve equivalent. The absolute score provides an interval-based estimate of an individual's performance level, which can be used to make comparisons across scales or between individuals. The standard scores have a mean of 100 and a standard deviation of 15. A profile analysis form is provided, which can be used to compare WRAT3 scores with intelligence test scores; it gives a picture of the degree of difficulty of the items passed by the test taker.

Norms

The WRAT3 was standardized on 4,443 individuals. The sample was stratified and counterbalanced by age, regional residence, gender, and ethnicity, based on 1990 U.S. census data. The author controlled for socioeconomic level based on the occupational category of the individual or of his or her caregiver. The author states that a minimum of four states per region were used, but the total number of states and settings (rural, urban, suburban) is not reported.

Reliability

The WRAT3 appears to be internally consistent. Three forms of internal consistency were provided. Coefficient alphas for each of the 23 age groups were computed for each form. The median coefficient alphas for the individual forms ranged from .85 to .91. The combined-form coefficients all exceeded .90. Alternate-forms correlations were also computed. The median correlations for the Reading, Spelling, and Arithmetic subtests are .92, .93, and .89, respectively. Rasch Person Separation indexes, a form of internal consistency, ranged from .98 to .99. (See Appendix 4.) The stability of the WRAT3 appears to be more than adequate. Corrected test–retest reliability coefficients for a sample of 142 individuals between the ages of 6 and 16 years were all greater than .91.

Validity

The author argues that because the Rasch Item Separation indexes are all 1.00, the test has content validity. However, information is not provided regarding the match between the WRAT3 content and that of a typical curriculum; therefore the content validity is questionable. Several forms of support for construct validity are provided. The mean scores of the subtests increase with age, which is in accordance with the developmental nature of basic academic skills. Moderate correlations exist between the WRAT3 and two measures of intelligence: the WISC-III and the WAIS-R. Moderate correlations were found between the WRAT3 and three standardized group achievement tests: the California Achievement Test–Form E, the California Test of Basic Skills–4, and the Stanford Achievement Test. The WRAT3 was able to discriminate among 222 regular- and special-education students. The test was able to group students labeled gifted, learning disabled, educably mentally handicapped, and general education with 68 percent success.

Summary

The WRAT3 is an individually administered achievement test designed to assess the basic academic skills necessary in reading, spelling, and arithmetic. The test is well standardized and has adequate reliability. There are two forms of the test. Data on standardization are incomplete. The test has sufficient reliability to be used in making decisions about individuals. Several forms of construct validity are provided in the manual that accompanies the test, but the test's content validity is questionable.

Wechsler Individual Achievement Test (WIAT)

The Wechsler Individual Achievement Test (WIAT; Psychological Corporation, 1992d) is an individually administered, norm-referenced achievement test designed to be used with students in grades K through 12 who are between 5 and 19 years old. The WIAT was conormed with the Wechsler series of intelligence tests: the WPPSI-R, the WISC-III, and the WAIS-R. This characteristic makes the WIAT especially useful for educational planning and placement decisions that use ability–achievement discrepancies. The use of conormed ability and achievement tests provides more reliable estimates of a student's aptitude–achievement discrepancy.

Another unique characteristic of the WIAT is its design. The test's authors created subtests that parallel and comprehensively cover the seven areas of learning disability specified in Public Law 94-142: basic reading skill, reading comprehension, mathematics reasoning, mathematics calculation, listening comprehension, oral expression, and written expression. These seven domains, plus spelling, compose the eight subtests of the WIAT. Three of the subtests—Basic Reading, Mathematics Reasoning, and Spelling—compose the WIAT Screener, which is a 10- to 15-minute academic achievement screening instrument. The WIAT can be completed in 30 to 50 minutes for younger children and approximately 55 minutes for adolescents. The behaviors sampled by the WIAT subtests are described in Table 20.8.

TABLE 20.8 ● *Description of the WIAT Subtests*

Subtest	Description
Basic Reading	A series of pictures and printed words for assessing decoding and word-reading ability—For early items, the child is to point to responses; later items require the child to respond orally.
Mathematics Reasoning	A series of problems for assessing the ability to reason mathematically—Many items include visual stimuli (e.g., graphs). The text for each item is presented orally and in most cases is also printed on the child's Stimulus Booklet page. The child is to respond in a variety of ways.
Spelling	A series of dictated letters, sounds, and words for measuring encoding and spelling ability—The child is to write responses.
Reading Comprehension	A series of printed passages and orally presented questions designed to tap skills such as recognizing stated detail and making inferences—Passages consist of one or more sentences, some of which are accompanied by a picture. The child is to respond orally.
Numerical Operations	Sets of problems for assessing the ability to write dictated numerals and solve calculation problems and equations involving all basic operations (addition, subtraction, multiplication, and division)—The child is to write responses.
Listening Comprehension	A series of items for assessing listening comprehension skills such as listening for detail—Items focus on the child's ability to identify the picture that corresponds to an orally presented word and on the child's comprehension of orally presented passages accompanied by pictures. For early items, the child is to respond by pointing; for later items, the child is to respond orally.
Oral Expression	A series of items focusing on the ability to express words, describe scenes, give directions, and explain steps—Items consist of pictures accompanied by orally presented instructions. The child is to respond orally.
Written Expression	For grades 3–12 only, writing prompts for assessing various writing skills such as development and organization of ideas, capitalization, and punctuation—Two prompts are provided, but only one is used in any one WIAT administration. The child's response can be evaluated analytically and holistically.

Scores

Five types of scores—standard, percentile rank, age equivalent, normal-curve equivalent, and stanine—can be derived from each of the subtests and six composites. The reading, mathematics, language, and writing composites are each based on two subtests. Three subtests form the screening composite, and the total composite is based on all the subtests. The standard score, which has a mean of 100 and a standard deviation of 15, can be computed by age or grade. Ability–achievement scores based on the WIAT standard scores and one of the three Wechsler ability tests (WPPSI-R, WISC-III, or WAIS-R) are also provided. The test authors provide two methods of computing discrepancy scores—simple-difference and predicted achievement—and provide information regarding the limitations of each approach.

Norms

The WIAT was standardized on 4,252 children in grades K through 12. A sample of 1,289 children was used to link the WIAT with the WPPSI-R, the WISC-III, and the WAIS-R. The information collected from the linking studies was used to develop the ability–achievement discrepancy statistics. The sample selection was based on 1988 U.S. Census Bureau data. The sample was randomly selected and stratified on age, grade, gender, race/ethnicity, geographic region, and parent education. Economic status was not used as a stratification variable. The extent of stratification and the national representativeness of the sample cannot be determined from the information provided in the technical manual.

Reliability

Three forms of reliability data were calculated for the WIAT. Split-half reliability coefficients based on age and grade standard subtest scores generally exceed .80. The Basic Reading coefficient for the fall norm group and the coefficients for Numerical Operations and Written Expression for certain ages fall below .80. The split-half coefficients for the six composites are all greater than .80. A sample of 367 students in grades 1, 3, 5, 8, and 10 was selected to determine the test–retest reliability of the WIAT. The subtest scores are generally above .80, but scores for Oral Expression and Written Expression are below .80 for most of the grades in the sample. Scores on the language composite for grades 5, 8, and 10 are the only composite test–retest scores below .80. Interrater agreement was calculated with 50 protocols for the four subtests that require subjective scoring. The correlation between raters for Reading Comprehension and raters for Listening Comprehension ranges from .89 to .99, with an average correlation of .98. The interrater agreement for Oral Expression was .93. Interrater agreement for Prompt 1 of the Written Expression subtest was .89, and for Prompt 2, it was .79.

Validity

The WIAT has excellent content, construct, and criterion-related validity. Expert judgment and a large-scale item tryout were used to establish the content validity of the instrument. Experts analyzed the extent to which the items measured specific curriculum objectives and were related to current instructional methodology and content. Empirical item analysis was used to eliminate poorly constructed items and to prevent gender or race bias. The construct validity of the WIAT was documented through analysis of subtest intercorrelations, correlations with ability measures, and expected developmental differences across age and grade groups.

Several forms of support for criterion-related validity are provided. There are moderate correlations between the WIAT and the Kaufman Test of Educational Achievement (KTEA), the Basic Achievement Skills Individual Screener (BASIS), the Wide Range Achievement Test–Revised (WRAT-R), the achievement test of the Woodcock–Johnson Psychoeducational Battery–Revised (WJ-R ACH), the Differential Ability Scales (DAS), and the Peabody Picture Vocabulary Test–Revised (PPVT-R). The WIAT was also correlated with several group-administered achievement tests, which produced moderate correlations. The correlation between the WIAT and school grades was generally low, but this is no different from what would be expected, given the low reliability of school grades.

Summary

The WIAT is an individually administered achievement test that is conormed with the Wechsler series of intelligence tests. The subtests are designed to measure the seven areas of learning disability defined in Public Law 94-142. The test has an adequate standardization sample and appears to be very reliable and valid. Two methods and statistical tables for computing ability–achievement discrepancies are provided, along with a description of the limitations of each method.

Diagnostic Achievement Battery–2 (DAB-2)

The Diagnostic Achievement Battery–2 (DAB-2) (Newcomer, 1990) is an individually administered measure of children's skills in listening, speaking, reading, writing, and mathematics. Although the test is called "diagnostic," it is essentially similar to the PIAT-R, WRAT3, and KTEA. Test givers do not use this test to "diagnose" skill strengths and weaknesses in individual content areas, but rather to obtain profile scores across areas. The test is designed to meet four purposes: (1) to identify students who are significantly below their peers in spoken language (listening and speaking), written language (reading and writing), and mathematics; (2) to ascertain an individual student's skill-development strengths and weaknesses; (3) to document intervention progress for individual students; and (4) to conduct research.

The DAB-2 is based on a specific conceptual model of academic achievement; that model is shown in Figure 20.1. (You may find it helpful to refer to the figure while reading the following description of the individual subtests and composites.) Subtests are divided into five areas: listening (Story Comprehension, Characteristics), speaking (Synonyms, Grammatic Completion), reading (Reading Comprehension, Alphabet/Word Knowledge), writing (Capitalization, Punctuation, Spelling, Writing Composition), and mathematics (Mathematics Calculation and Mathematics Reasoning). Behaviors sampled by the subtests are as follows.

Subtests

Story Comprehension   The student must listen to the examiner read a story and then answer oral questions about the story.

Characteristics   After listening to the examiner read brief statements, the student must indicate whether the statements are true or false.

Synonyms   The student must provide synonyms for words read by the examiner.

Grammatic Completion   The student must supply missing words or phrases in sentences read by the examiner.

Reading Comprehension   The student must read short stories silently and then answer questions about them.

Alphabet/Word Knowledge   The student must read letters or words.

Punctuation   The student must indicate appropriate punctuation in a set of 30 sentences.

Capitalization   The student must indicate appropriate placement of capital letters in a set of 30 sentences.

Spelling   The student must write and spell correctly 20 dictated words.

Writing Composition   The student must write a story in response to three pictures that represent a modified version of the classic fable "The Tortoise and the Hare." The story is evaluated for the presence of words that have seven or more letters and for thematic content.

Mathematics Calculation   The student must solve 36 written calculation problems.

Mathematics Reasoning   The student is given mathematical information in the form of pictures (for a young child) or statements presented orally and must use the information to solve math problems.

Test Administration

The DAB-2 is an untimed test. The examiner begins and ends the test using specific rules for basals and ceilings. The test takes from one to two hours

● ● ● ● **FIGURE 20.1**   *Conceptual Model Underlying the DAB-2*

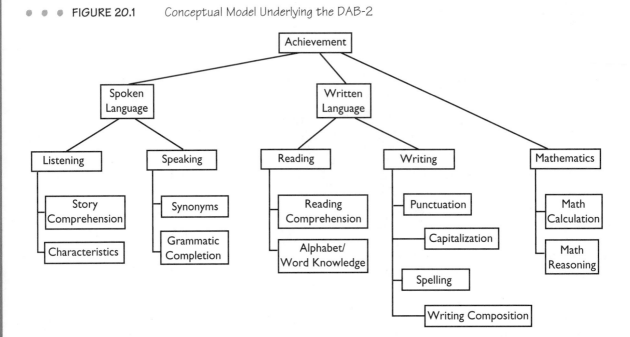

to administer. The DAB-2 is a mixture of eight subtests that were retained from the original DAB (Newcomer, 1983) and four new subtests. The new subtests consist of three revised DAB subtests (Capitalization, Punctuation, and Reading Comprehension) and one new subtest (Writing Composition). Items for DAB-2 were tried out and selected on the basis of the performance of a limited and geographically restricted sample of 100 children in San Antonio, Texas.

Norms

The DAB-2 norms are a mixture of new norms and norms retained from the standardization of the original DAB. The total standardization population was 2,623 students from 40 states. The norms were obtained by (a) keeping the 1983 norms for the eight subtests that are unchanged, and (b) adding data on these original eight and the four new subtests. The new data were obtained by asking users of the test to administer the test to 20–30 children representative of their area. The author argues that

a population representative of the 1985 census was obtained. Comparative percentages are shown, but there is no information on cross-tabulations. That is, we do not know, for example, if all the black children were from urban areas in the Northeast, rural areas in the South, and so forth.

Scores

Four kinds of scores are obtained for performance on the DAB-2. The examiner can compute standard scores (with mean = 10 and standard deviation = 3), composite scores (quotients with mean = 100 and standard deviation = 15) for each of the composites, percentile ranks for students and composites, and grade equivalents.

Reliability

Data on reliability are for either the original DAB or the DAB-2. Most of the data are for the DAB. Data on internal consistency of the DAB-2 were computed by examining performance on 50 protocols at each level. Of the 99 coefficients reported for subtests, 91 exceed .80. All reliability coefficients for composite scores exceed .80. Information on test–retest reliability of the DAB-2 is limited to the performance of 52 children in a private school in Los Angeles on three of the four new subtests of the DAB-2. Reliability coefficients for Capitalization, Punctuation, and Written Composition exceeded .80.

Validity

The author reports considerable data on validity of the DAB-2. Criteria for content and item selection are specified, and evidence for construct and criterion-related validity is presented. There is good evidence for the validity of this test.

Summary

The DAB-2 is a revision of the 1983 DAB, which was changed by modifying three subtests and adding one new one. The test was standardized on a population of students drawn in 1982–1983 and 1988. The norm sample is described in the manual, but evidence on the extent to which it was stratified is limited. There is limited evidence for the reliability of this test, but good evidence for its validity.

Getting the Most Out of an Achievement Test

The achievement tests described in this chapter provide the teacher with global scores in areas such as word meaning and work-study skills. Although global scores can help in screening children, they generally lack the specificity to help in planning individualized instructional programs. The fact that Emily earned a standard score of 85 on the Mathematics Computation subtest of the ITBS does not tell us what math skills Emily has. In addition, a teacher cannot rely on test names as an indication of what is measured by a specific test. For example, a reading score of 115 on the WRAT tells a teacher nothing about reading comprehension or rate of oral reading.

A teacher must look at any screening test (or at any test, for that matter) in terms of the behaviors sampled by that test. Here is a case in point. Suppose Richard earned a standard score of 70 on a spelling subtest. What do we know about Richard? We know that Richard earned enough raw-score points to place him two standard deviations below the mean of students in his grade. That is all we know without going beyond the score and looking at the kinds of behaviors sampled by the test. The test title tells us only that the test measures skill development in spelling. However, we still do not know what Richard did to earn a score of 70.

First, we need to ask, "What is the nature of the behaviors sampled by the test?" Spelling tests can be of several kinds. Richard may have been asked to write a word read by his teacher, as is the case in the Spelling subtest of the WRAT. Such a behavior sampling demands that he recall the correct spelling of a word and actually produce that correct spelling in writing. On the other hand, Richard's score of 70 may have been earned on a spelling test that asked him just to recognize the correct spelling of a word. For example, the Spelling subtest of the PIAT presents the student with four alternative spellings of a word (for example, *empti, empty, impty, emity*), and the teacher asks a child to point to the word *empty*. Such an

Coping with Dilemmas in Current Practice

Two limitations affect the use of achievement tests as screening devices: the match of the test to the content of the curriculum, and the fact that the tests are group administered. Unless the content assessed by an achievement test reflects the content of the curriculum, the results are meaningless. Students will not have had a formal opportunity to learn the material tested. When students are tested on material they have not been taught, or tested in ways other than those by which they are taught, the test results will not reflect their actual skills. Jenkins and Pany (1978) compared the contents of four reading-achievement tests with the contents of five commercial reading series at grades 1 and 2. Their major concern was the extent to which students might earn different scores on different tests of reading achievement, simply as a function of the degree of overlap in content between tests and curricula. Jenkins and Pany calculated the grade scores that would be earned by students who had mastered the words taught in the respective curricula and who had correctly read those words on the four tests. Grade scores are shown in Table 20.9. It is clear that different curricula result in different performances on different tests.

The data produced by Jenkins and Pany are now over 20 years old. Yet the table is still the best visual illustration of test–curriculum overlap. Shapiro and Derr (1987) showed that the degree of overlap between what is taught and what is tested varied considerably across tests and curricula. Also, Good and Salvia (1989) demonstrated significant differences in test performance for the same students on different reading tests. They indicate the significance of the test–curriculum overlap issue, stating,

Curriculum bias is undesirable because it severely limits the interpretation of a student's test score. For example, it is unclear whether a student's reading score of 78 reflects deficient reading skills or the selection of a test with poor content validity for the pupil's curriculum. (p. 56)

item demands recognition and pointing, rather than recall and production. Thus, we need to look first at the nature of the behaviors sampled by the test.

Second, we must look at the specific items a student passes or fails. This requires going back to the original test protocol to analyze the specific nature of skill development in a given area. We need to ask, "What kinds of items did the child fail?" and to look for consistent patterns among the failures. In trying to identify the nature of spelling errors, we need to know, "Does the student consistently demonstrate errors in spelling words with long vowels? with silent *e*'s? with specific consonant blends?" and so on. The search is for specific patterns of errors, and we try to ascertain the student's relative degree of consistency in making certain errors. Of course, finding error patterns requires that the test content be sufficiently dense to allow a student to make the same error at least two times.

Similar procedures are followed with any screening device. Quite obviously, the information achieved is not nearly as specific as the information obtained

TABLE 20.9 • *Grade-Equivalent Scores Obtained by Matching Specific Reading-Test Words to Standardized Reading-Test Words*

| Curriculum | PIAT | MAT | | SDRT | WRAT |
		Word Knowledge	*Word Analysis*		
Bank Street Reading Series					
Grade 1	1.5	1.0	1.1	1.8	2.0
Grade 2	2.8	2.5	1.2	2.9	2.7
Keys to Reading					
Grade 1	2.0	1.4	1.2	2.2	2.2
Grade 2	3.3	1.9	1.0	3.0	3.0
Reading 360					
Grade 1	1.5	1.0	1.0	1.4	1.7
Grade 2	2.2	2.1	1.0	2.7	2.3
SRA Reading Program					
Grade 1	1.5	1.2	1.3	1.0	2.1
Grade 2	3.1	2.5	1.4	2.9	3.5
Sullivan Associates Programmed Reading					
Grade 1	1.8	1.4	1.2	1.1	2.0
Grade 2	2.2	2.4	1.1	2.5	2.5

SOURCE: Grade-Equivalent Scores Obtained by Matching Specific Reading Test Words to Standardized Reading Test Words. From "Standardized Achievement Tests: How Useful for Special Education?" by J. Jenkins & D. Pany, *Exceptional Children*, 44, (1978), 450. Copyright 1978 by The Council for Exceptional Children. Reprinted with permission.

from diagnostic tests. Administration of an achievement test that is a screening test gives the classroom teacher a general idea of where to start with any additional diagnostic assessment.

Summary

Screening devices used for assessing academic achievement provide a global picture of a student's skill development in academic content areas. Screening tests must be selected on the basis of the kinds of behavior each test samples, the adequacy of its norms, its reliability, and its validity. When selecting an achievement test or when evaluating the results of a student's performance on an achievement test, the classroom teacher needs to take into careful consideration not only the technical characteristics of the test but also the extent to which the behaviors sampled represent the goals and objectives of the student's curriculum. The teacher can adapt certain techniques for administering group tests and for getting the most mileage out of the results of group tests.

Questions for Chapter Review and Thought

1. Identify at least four important considerations in selecting a specific achievement test for use with the third-graders in your local school system.

2. Describe the major advantages and disadvantages of group-administered multiple-skill achievement tests.

3. A new student is assessed in September using the WRAT3. Her achievement-test scores (using the PIAT-3) are forwarded from her previous school and place her in the nineteenth percentile overall. However, the latest assessment places her only in the seventy-seventh percentile. Give three possible explanations for this discrepancy.

4. Ms. Epstein decides to assess the achievement of her fifth-grade pupils. She believes that they are unusually "slow" learners and estimates that, in general, they are functioning on about a third-grade level. She decides to use Primary Level III of the SAT. What difficulties will she face?

5. Mr. Fitzpatrick has used the results of a group-administered achievement test to make a placement decision concerning John. What facts about group-administered achievement tests has Mr. Fitzpatrick failed to attend to? Under what conditions could he use an achievement test designed to be administered to a group?

Resources for Further Investigation

Project

Assume that you wish to use one of the tests reviewed in this text as a screening test for achievement. What test would be your first choice? Why? Compare your answer with a classmate's answer. Reconcile your differences.

Print Resources

Conoley, J. C., & Impara, J. C. (1995). *The twelfth mental measurements yearbook* (MAT7, pp. 601–610; WRAT3, pp. 1106–1111; DAB-2, pp. 294–296). Lincoln, NE: University of Nebraska Press.

Conoley, J. C., & Kramer, J. J. (1989). *The tenth mental measurements yearbook* (CAT, pp. 123–133; KTEA, pp. 410–413). Lincoln, NE: University of Nebraska Press.

CTB/Macmillan/McGraw-Hill (1993). California Achievement Test/5. Monterey, CA: CTB/McGraw-Hill.

Feldt, L. S., Forsyth, R. A., Ansley, T. N., & Alnot, S. D. (1996). *Iowa tests of educational development*. Chicago: Riverside Publishing Company.

Good, R. H. & Salvia, J. A. (1989). Curriculum bias in published, norm-referenced reading tests: Demonstrable effects. *School Psychology Review, 17*(1), 51–60.

Gronlund, N. E. (1982). *Constructing achievement tests*. Englewood Cliffs, NJ: Prentice-Hall.

Harcourt Brace Educational Measurement (1996a). *Stanford Achievement Test* (9th Ed.). San Antonio, TX: Psychological Corporation.

Harcourt Brace Educational Measurement (1996b). *Stanford Early School Achievement Test*. San Antonio, TX: Psychological Corporation.

Harcourt Brace Educational Measurement (1996c). *Test of Academic Skills*. San Antonio, TX: Psychological Corporation.

Hoover, H. D., Hieronymus, A. N., Frisbie, D. A., & Dunbar, S. B. (1996). *Iowa Tests of Basic Skills*. Chicago: Riverside Publishing Company.

Kramer, J. J., & Conoley, J. C. (1992). *The eleventh mental measurements yearbook* (ITBS, pp. 419–424; SAT, pp. 859–865; PIAT-R, pp. 647–654).

McGrew, K., Werder, J., & Woodcock, R. (1991). *Woodcock–Johnson Psychoeducational Battery–Revised: Technical Manual*. Chicago: Riverside Publishing Company.

Mitchell, J. V. (1985). *The ninth mental measurements yearbook* (BASIS, pp. 134–136). Lincoln, NE: University of Nebraska Press.

Scannell, D. P. (1996). *Tests of achievement and proficiency*. Chicago: Riverside Publishing Company.

Shapiro, E. S., & Derr, T. (1987). An examination of overlap between reading curricula and standardized reading tests. *The Journal of Special Education, 21* (2), 59–67.

Woodcock, R., McGrew, K., & Werder, J. (1994). *Mini-Battery of Achievement*. Chicago: Riverside Publishing Company.

Technology Resources

Welcome to AGS On-line Products and Services

http://www.agsnet.com

Look for product and ordering information about the instruments available from American Guidance

Service. Search by product title to find information about the *Kaufman Test of Educational Achievement* and the *Peabody Individual Achievement Test–Revised.*

Pro-Ed Catalog Information for Products

http://www.proedinc.com

Find product and ordering information about the *Wide Range Achievement Test–3, the Diagnostic Achievement Battery–2,* and the *Diagnostic Achievement Test for Adolescents–2.*

Psychological Corporation

http://www.psychcorp.com

This site contains information on the many Wechsler assessments of achievement as well as other tests of assessment.

Riverside Publishing

http://www.riverpub.com/

o to products and services. Under educational assessments in the index of products you will find information on the *Iowa Tests of Basic Skills,* the *Tests of Achievement and Proficiency,* and the *Iowa Tests of Educational Development* as well as other tests of academic achievement.

chapter

21

Assessment of Reading

I n Chapter 20, we described multiple-skill achievement tests, which provide global information about a student's achievements. Often, school personnel need more specific information. In this chapter, we give detailed descriptions of the kinds of behaviors sampled by reading tests and then describe commonly used reading tests, both norm-referenced (comparative) and criterion-referenced (performance) measures.

● ● ● ● ● ● ● ● ● ● ● ● ● ● ● ● ● ● ●

Why Do We Assess Reading?

Reading is one of the most fundamental skills that students learn. For poor readers, life in school is likely to be difficult even with appropriate curricular and testing accommodations and adaptations, and life after school is likely to have constrained opportunities and less personal independence and satisfaction. Moreover, students who have not learned to read fluently by the end of third grade are unlikely ever to read fluently (Adams, 1990). For these reasons, students' development of reading skills is closely monitored in order to identify those with problems early enough to enable remediation.

Diagnostic tests are used primarily to improve two educational decisions. First, they are administered to children who are experiencing difficulty in learning to read. In this case, tests identify a student's strengths and weaknesses so that educators can plan appropriate interventions. Second, they are given to ascertain a student's initial or continuing eligibility for special services. Tests given for this purpose are used to compare a student's achievement with the achievement of other students. Diagnostic reading tests may also be administered to evaluate the effects of instruction. However, this use of diagnostic reading tests is generally unwise. Individually administered tests are an inefficient way to evaluate instructional effectiveness for large groups of students; group survey tests are generally more appropriate for this purpose. Diagnostic tests are generally too insensitive to identify small but important gains by individual students. Teachers should monitor students' daily or weekly progress with direct performance measures [such as having a student read aloud currently used materials to ascertain accuracy (percent correct) and fluency (rate of correct words per minute)].

The Ways in Which Reading Is Taught

For about 150 years, educators have been divided (sometimes acrimoniously) over the issue of teaching the language code (letters and sounds). Some educators favor a "look/say" (or whole-word) approach, in which students learn whole words and practice them by reading appropriate stories and other passages. Proponents of this approach stress the meaning of the words and usually believe that students learn the code incidentally (or with a little coaching). Finally, proponents of this approach offer the opinion (frequently contradicted by empirical research) that drilling children in letters and sounds destroys their motivation to read. Other educators favor systematically teaching the language code: how letters represent sounds and how sounds and letters are combined to form words—both spoken and written. Proponents of this approach argue that specifically and systematically teaching phonics produces more skillful readers more easily; they also argue that reading failure destroys motivation to read.

For the first hundred years or so of the debate, observations of reading were too crude to indicate more than that the reader looked at print and said the printed words (or answered questions about the content conveyed by those printed words). Consequently, theoreticians speculated about the processes occurring inside the reader, and the speculations of advocates of whole-word instruction dominated the debate until the 1950s. Thereafter, phonics instruction (systematically teaching beginning readers the relationships among the alphabetic code, phonemes, and words) increasingly became part of prereading and reading instruction. Some of that increased emphasis on phonics may be attributable to *Why Johnny Can't Read* (Flesch, 1955), a book vigorously advocating phonics instruction; more importantly, the growing body of empirical evidence increasingly showed phonics instruction's effectiveness. By 1967, there was substantial evidence that systematic instruction in phonics produced better readers, and that the effect of phonics instruction was greater for children of low ability or from disadvantaged backgrounds. With phonics instruction, beginning readers had better word recognition, better reading comprehension, and better reading vocabulary (Bond & Dykstra, 1967; Chall, 1967). Subsequent empirical evidence leads to the same conclusions (Adams, 1990; Foorman, Francis, Fletcher, Schatschneider, & Mehta, 1998; Pflaum, Walberg, Karegianes, & Rasher, 1980; Stanovich, 1986).

While some scholars were demonstrating the efficacy of phonics instruction, others began unraveling the ways in which beginners learn to read. Today, that process is much clearer than it was even in the 1970s. Students must be able to discriminate the letters of the alphabet and name them quickly and accurately; those who cannot will have difficulty learning to read (Tunmer, Herriman, & Nesdale, 1988). Students also must be able to process the sounds in the language they speak and read (that is, they must be skilled phonologically). There are three components of this skill. Beginning readers must have sufficient phonemic awareness to discriminate the individual sounds in English (see, for example, Torgesen, Morgan, & Davis, 1992). Students must also be able to associate phonemes and letters. Finally, students must be able to recall these associations fluently (see, for example, Wolf, 1991). Readers who can fluently retrieve letter–phoneme associations are better able to use them to decode (see, for example, Bowers & Wolf, 1993). These findings suggest that beginning readers read letter by letter, but they do so rapidly. After students become fluent decoders, they read more difficult material—that is, material with more challenging vocabulary, more complex sentence structure, more condensed and abstract ideas, and less literal and more inferential sentence meanings. At this point, understanding what is read depends not so much on the ability to change the visual symbols into words and sentences as on linguistic and cognitive competence.

While learning more about how students begin to read, we also learned that some long-held beliefs were not valid. For example, it is incorrect to say that poor readers read letter by letter, but skilled readers read entire words and phrases as a unit. Actually, skilled readers read letter by letter and word by word, but they do it so quickly that they appear to be reading words and phrases (see, for example, Snow, Burns, & Griffin, 1998). It is also incorrect to say that good readers do not rely heavily on context cues to identify words (Share & Stanovich, 1995). Good readers do use context cues to verify their decoding accuracy. Poor readers rely on them heavily, however, probably because they lack skill in more appropriate word-attack skills (see, for example, Briggs & Underwood, 1984).

Today, despite clear evidence indicating the essential role of phonics in reading and strong indications of the superiority of reading programs with direct instruction in phonics, some professionals continue to reject phonics instruction. Perhaps this may explain why most students who are referred for psychological assessment are referred because of reading problems, and why most of these students have problems changing the symbols (that is, alphabet letters) into sounds and words. The obvious connection between phonics instruction and beginning reading has not escaped the notice of many parents, however. They have become eager consumers of educational materials (such as "Hooked on Phonics" and "The Phonics Game") and private tutoring (for example, instruction at a Sylvan Learning Center).

Educators' views of how students learn to read and how students should be taught will determine their beliefs about reading assessment. Thus, diagnostic testing in reading is caught between the opposing camps. If the test includes an assessment of the skills needed to decode text, it is attacked by those who reject analytic approaches to reading. If the test does not include an assessment of decoding skills, it is attacked by those who know the importance of those skills in beginning reading.

* *

Skills Assessed by Diagnostic Reading Tests

Reading is a complex process that changes as readers develop. Beginning readers rely heavily on a complex set of decoding skills that can be assessed holistically by having a student read orally and assessing his or her accuracy and fluency. Decoding skills may also be measured analytically by having students apply these skills in isolation (for example, using phonics to read nonsense words). Once fluency in decoding has been attained, readers are expected to go beyond the comprehension of simple language and simple ideas to the process of understanding and evaluating what is written. Advanced readers rely on different skills (that is, linguistic competence and abstract reasoning) and different facts (that is, vocabulary, prior knowledge and experience, and beliefs). Comprehension may be assessed by having a student read a passage that deals with an esoteric topic and is filled with abstract concepts and difficult vocabulary; moreover, the sentences in that passage may have complicated grammar with minimal redundancy.

Assessment of Oral-Reading Skills

A number of tests and subtests are designed to assess the accuracy or fluency of a student's oral reading. Oral-reading tests consist of a series of graded paragraphs that are read sequentially by a student. The examiner notes reading errors and behaviors that characterize the student's oral reading. The Gray Oral Reading Test–3[1] was specifically designed to assess oral reading; other commonly used tests (for example, the Stanford Diagnostic Reading Test 4) include oral-reading subtests.

Errors and Miscues

Rate and fluency of oral reading are based on correct reading. Therefore, it is necessary to define what constitutes an error. Different oral-reading tests record different behaviors as errors (also sometimes called miscues). Following are descriptions of commonly recorded errors.

Teacher Pronunciation or Aid   If a student either hesitates for a time without making an audible effort to pronounce a word or appears to be attempting for ten seconds to pronounce the word, the examiner pronounces the word and records an error.

---

1. In earlier editions we also reviewed the Gilmore Oral Reading Test, the Gates–McKillop–Horowitz Reading Diagnostic Tests, the Formal Reading Inventory, and the Durrell Analysis of Reading Difficulty.

Hesitation   The student hesitates for two or more seconds before pronouncing a word.

Gross Mispronunciation of a Word   A gross mispronunciation is recorded when the pupil's pronunciation of a word bears so little resemblance to the proper pronunciation that the examiner must be looking at the word to recognize it. An example of gross mispronunciation is reading the word *encounter* as "actors."

Partial Mispronunciation of a Word   A partial mispronunciation can be one of several different kinds of errors. The examiner may have to pronounce part of a word for the student (an aid); the student may phonetically mispronounce specific letters (for example, by reading the word *red* as "reed"); or the student may omit part of a word, insert elements of words, or make errors in syllabication, accent, or inversion.

Omission of a Word or Group of Words   Omissions consist of skipping individual words or groups of words.

Insertion of a Word or Group of Words   Insertions consist of the student's putting one or more words into the sentence being read. The student may, for example, read *the dog* as "the mean dog."

Substitution of One Meaningful Word for Another   Substitutions consist of the replacement of one or more words in the passage by one or more different meaningful words. The student might read *dense* as "depress." Students often replace entire sequences of words with others, as illustrated by the replacement of *he is his own mechanic* with "he sat on his own machine." Some oral-reading tests require that examiners record the specific kind of substitution error. Substitutions are classified as *meaning similarity* (the words have similar meanings), *function similarity* (the two words have syntactically similar functions), *graphic/phoneme similarity* (the words look or sound alike), or a combination of the preceding.

Repetition   Repetition occurs when students repeat words or groups of words while attempting to read sentences or paragraphs. In some cases, if a student repeats a group of words to correct an error, the original error is not recorded, but a repetition error is. In other cases, such behaviors are recorded simply as spontaneous self-corrections.

Inversion, or Changing of Word Order   Errors of inversion are recorded when the child changes the order of words appearing in a sentence; for example, *house the* is an inversion.

Nonerrors

Examiners may note characteristics of a student's oral reading that are not counted as errors. Self-corrections are not counted as errors. Disregarded punctuation marks (for example, failing to pause for a comma or to inflect vocally to indicate a question mark) are not counted as errors. Repetitions and hesitations due to speech handicaps (for example, stuttering or stammering) are not counted as errors. Dialectic accents are not counted as mispronunciations. Examiners may also note various characteristics of a student's oral reading that are problematic (although not errors) or that may have contributed to a student's errors. Commonly noted indicators include poor posture, inappropriate head movement, finger pointing, loss of place, lack of expression (for example, word-by-word reading, lack of phrasing, or monotone voice), and strained voice.

Assessment of Reading Comprehension

Diagnostic tests assess five different types of reading comprehension.

1. *Literal comprehension* entails understanding the information that is explicit in the reading material.

2. *Inferential comprehension* means interpreting, synthesizing, or extending the information that is explicit in the reading material.

3. *Critical comprehension* requires analyzing, evaluating, and making judgments about the material read.

4. *Affective comprehension* involves a reader's personal and emotional responses to the reading material.

5. *Lexical comprehension* means knowing the meaning of key vocabulary words.

In our opinion, the best way to assess reading comprehension is to give readers access to the material and have them restate or paraphrase what they have read.

Poor comprehension has many causes. The most common is poor decoding, which affects comprehension in two ways. First, if a student cannot convert the symbols to words, he or she cannot comprehend the message conveyed by those words. The second issue is more subtle. If a student expends all of his or her mental resources on sounding out the words, he or she will have no resources left to process their meaning. For that reason, increasing reading fluency frequently eliminates problems in comprehension.

Another problem is that students may not know how to read for comprehension (Taylor, Harris, Pearson, & Garcia, 1995). They may not actively focus on the meaning of what they read or know how to monitor their comprehension (for example, by asking themselves questions about what they have read or whether they understand what they have read). Students may not know how to foster comprehension (for example, by summarizing material, determining the main ideas and supporting facts, and integrating material with previous knowledge). Finally, individual characteristics can interact with the assessment of reading comprehension. For example, in an assessment of literal comprehension, a reader's memory capacity can affect comprehension scores unless the reader has access to the passage while answering questions about it or retelling its gist. Inferential comprehension depends on more than reading; it also depends on a reader's ability to see relationships (a defining element of intelligence) and on background information and experiences.

Assessment of Word-Attack Skills

Word-attack, or word-analysis, skills are those used to derive the pronunciation or meaning of a word through phonic analysis, structural analysis, or context cues. *Phonic analysis* is the use of letter–sound correspondences and sound blending to identify words. *Structural analysis* is a process of breaking words into *morphemes,* or meaningful units. Words contain free morphemes (such as *farm, book,* and *land*) and bound morphemes (such as *-ed, -s,* and *-er*).

Because lack of word-attack skills is the principal reason that students have trouble reading, a variety of subtests of commonly used diagnostic reading tests specifically assess these skills. Subtests that assess word-attack skills range from such basic assessments as analysis of skill in associating letters with sounds to tests of syllabication and blending. Generally, for subtests that assess skill in associating letters with sounds, the examiner reads a word aloud, and the student must identify the consonant-vowel-consonant cluster or digraph that has the same sound as the beginning, middle, or ending letters of the word. Syllabication subtests present polysyllabic words, and the student must either divide the word orally into syllables or circle specific syllables.

Blending subtests, on the other hand, are of three types. In the first method, the examiner may read syllables out loud ("wa-ter-mel-on," for example) and ask the student to pronounce the word. In the second type of subtest, the student may be asked to read word parts and to pronounce whole words. In the third method, the student may be presented with alternative beginning, middle, and ending sounds and asked to produce a word. Figure 21.1 illustrates the third method, used with the Stanford Diagnostic Reading Test 4.

Assessment of Word-Recognition Skills

Subtests of diagnostic reading tests that assess a pupil's word-recognition skills are designed to ascertain what many educators call "sight vocabulary." A student learns the correct pronunciation of letters and words through a variety of experiences. The more a student is exposed to specific words and the more familiar those words become to the student, the more readily he or she recognizes those words and is able to pronounce them correctly. Well-known words require very little reliance on word-attack skills. Most readers of this book immediately recognize the word *hemorrhage* and do not have to employ phonetic skills to pronounce it. On the other hand, words such as *nephrocystanastomosis* are not a

● ● ● **FIGURE 21.1**   An Item That Assesses Blending Skill

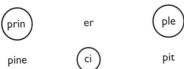

part of the sight vocabulary for most of us. Such words slow us down; we must use phonetics to analyze them.

Word-recognition subtests form a major part of most diagnostic reading tests. Some tests use paper tachistoscopes to expose words for brief periods of time (usually one-half second). Students who recognize many words are said to have good sight vocabularies or good word-recognition skills. Other subtests assess letter recognition, recognition of words in isolation, and recognition of words in context.

Assessment of Rate of Reading

Reading rate is generally played down in the diagnostic assessment of reading difficulties. There are, however, some exceptions. Two levels of the Stanford Diagnostic Reading Test have subtests to assess rate of reading. On the other hand, tests such as the Gray Oral Reading Test–3 (GORT-3) are timed, with time affecting the score a pupil receives. A pupil who reads a passage on the GORT-3 slowly but makes no errors in reading may earn a lower score than a rapid reader who makes one or two errors in reading.

Assessment of Other Reading and Reading-Related Behaviors

A variety of subtests that fit none of the aforementioned categories are included in diagnostic reading tests as either major or supplementary subtests. Examples of such tests include oral vocabulary, spelling, handwriting, and auditory discrimination. In most cases, such subtests are included simply to provide the examiner with additional diagnostic information.

Oral Reading Tests

Gray Oral Reading Test, Third Edition (GORT-3)

The Gray Oral Reading Test–3 (GORT-3) is the second revision of the Gray Oral Reading Test by Wiederholt and Bryant (1992). The GORT-3 remains an individually administered, norm-referenced measure of oral reading and comprehension. Each of the two forms (A and B) of the GORT-3 contains 13 reading passages of increasing difficulty. Students are required to read paragraphs orally and to respond to a set of five comprehension questions for each paragraph. The test is intended for use with students between the ages of 7-0 and 18-11. Specific basal and ceiling rules are used to limit time, which typically ranges from 15 to 30 minutes.

The authors of the GORT-3 state four purposes for the test: "(a) to help identify those students who are significantly below their peers in oral reading proficiency and who may profit from supplemental help; (b) to aid in determining the particular kinds of reading strengths and weaknesses that individual students possess; (c) to document students' progress in reading as a consequence of special intervention programs; and (d) to serve as a measurement device in investigations where researchers are studying the abilities of school-age students" (Wiederholt & Bryant, 1992, p. 6).

In the manual, the authors go into considerable detail in describing the extensive care with which the oral reading passages for the GORT-3 were developed. They describe the great care taken to ensure that the comprehension questions that follow each passage were written to assess literal, inferential, critical, and affective comprehension. In fact, the two forms of the GORT-3 are identical in every way to the two forms of the GORT-R, which are, in turn, identical to forms B and D of the Formal Reading Inventory (FRI; Wiederholt, 1986). The FRI differs from the GORT-R in that the FRI examiner obtains only a classification of oral-reading miscues; the GORT-R examiner can obtain a composite oral reading quotient, separate indexes of oral reading and comprehension, and a percentage score for each of the specific kinds of miscues. The GORT-3 differs from the GORT-R in that the GORT-3 provides separate percentiles and standard scores for rate and accuracy, whereas the GORT-R provides percentiles and standard scores for rate and accuracy combined.

Scores

The examiner (a) records the number of seconds that the student needed to read the passage aloud and (b) tallies the number of deviations from the text (that is, any deviation from print is scored as an oral-reading miscue, unless the deviation is the result of normal speech variations). At the bottom of the test protocol is a matrix. The top row of the matrix has a 6-point scale (0–5); the next row of the matrix has six time ranges corresponding to the 6-point scale; and the third row has six error ranges that also correspond to the 6-point scale. The examiner awards points (0–5) for the speed and for the accuracy with which the passage is read. For each passage, the sum of the rate and accuracy scores is called a "passage score." The rate, accuracy, passage, and comprehension scores for the stories read are then summed to yield total scores for rate, accuracy, passage, and comprehension. From these total scores, corresponding grade equivalents, percentiles, and standard scores (mean = 10, standard deviation = 3) can be found in various tables in the manual. The passage and comprehension standard scores are added and then transformed into a standard score called the "oral reading quotient," which has a mean of 100 and a standard deviation of 15.

The examiner also records both the number and the kinds of miscues. The number is also converted into a percentage. (On the FRI, the examiner simply records the number of errors of a given type.)

Norms

The GORT-R was standardized on 1,401 students from 15 states. The GORT-3 combines 1,259 of the original 1,401 students tested in the 1980s with 226 newly tested students.[2] The GORT-3 norms are better described than the GORT-R norms and appear to be generally representative of the U.S. population in terms of sex, place of residence (urban, rural), race, ethnicity, and geographic region; no data describing the socioeconomic status of the standardization sample are provided.

Reliability

The internal consistency for five scores (rate, accuracy, passage, comprehension, and oral reading quotient) at 12 ages (6–7 years through 17–18 years) was estimated from the performances of 50 students in each age group, who were randomly selected from the standardization sample. The 96 alphas for subtests ranged from .79 to .96; 54 of the 96 coefficients equaled or exceeded .90. Alpha for the oral reading quotient equaled or exceeded .95 at all ages. Test–retest reliability using the alternate forms was also estimated. These coefficients ranged from .62 to .90, but users should understand that these estimates include error attributable to content sampling, as well as error attributable to different rates. Overall, the oral reading quotient of the GORT-3 appears suffi-

ciently reliable for making important decisions for individual students; use of other scores for this purpose will depend on the age of the student and the particular score.

Validity

As mentioned previously, early in the manual for the GORT-3, the authors list several purposes of the test. They do not, however, provide evidence of the validity of the scale for those purposes. Rather, data are provided on the general content, criterion-related, and construct validity of the test. The authors argue that the test has good content validity because of the procedures followed in test construction. Specifically, they argue that the reading passages were written to control for "density of words, length of words and sentences, complexity of sentence structure, structure of sentences, logical connections between sentences and clauses, and coherence of topics" (p. 37).

With two exceptions, the concurrent validity of GORT-3 is based on studies previously reported on GORT-R. Relying on the validity of a previous edition is often problematic; in this case, however, this reliance is appropriate because the content of the test is unchanged and the norms are essentially unchanged. In the GORT-R studies, concurrent validity was examined by taking scores earned on other tests from the files of students who participated in the standardized population. Thus, the other test scores are for students from a variety of school districts who took the test at various times. The GORT-R scores of 30 students were correlated with the scores on form C of the FRI; correlations ranged from .44 to .66. Three elementary teachers rated the overall reading of 37 students on a 5-point scale. The correlations between their judgments and GORT-R scores ranged from .47 to .78. Data are reported on the correlation of the scores of 108 students in grades 9 through 12 on the GORT-R and the Iowa Tests of Educational Development. Correlations ranged from .28 to .47. The GORT-3 scores for form A earned by 74 students in grades 3 and 4 were correlated with their reading subtest scores on the California

2. The norms for the two editions are, therefore, almost identical. Approximately 85 percent of the 1992 norm group (1,259 of 1,485) came from the 1986 normative sample. The manual offers no explanation for the deletion of 142 students from the 1986 standardization.

Achievement Test; the correlations ranged from .35 to .60. A final study reported in the manual involved the scores of 34 students who were tested with form A and also tested with the reading subtest of the Screening Children for Related Early Educational Needs and the reading subtests of the Diagnostic Achievement Battery—second edition. In all, approximately 180 correlation coefficients were calculated, the median of which was .57.

The authors examined the construct validity of the GORT-3 by showing that GORT-3 scores increase with age and are highly correlated with measures of other language abilities and total achievement. The GORT-3 also distinguishes groups of students identified as having reading deficits from groups of students without deficits.

Summary

The GORT-3 is an individually administered, norm-referenced measure of oral reading and comprehension for use with students between the ages of 7-0 and 18-11. Multiple scores are derived from a student's reading (rate, accuracy, and rate plus accuracy); a single score is derived for com-prehension; and a composite score based on rate, accuracy, and comprehension can be calculated. The standardization sample used for the GORT-3 appears to be generally representative of the U.S. population in terms of sex, place of residence (urban, rural), race, ethnicity, and geographic region; there were no data on the socioeconomic status of the standardization sample. Overall, the oral reading quotient of the GORT-3 appears sufficiently reliable for making important decisions for individual students; use of other scores for this purpose will depend on the age of the student and the particular score. The GORT-3 appears to have satisfactory validity.

Although we have used the authors' terminology in calling the test the GORT-3, the GORT-3 is the same test as the GORT-R. Test users would have been better served by the publication of modified test protocols and a brief supplement to the GORT-R manual. The supplement to the manual might have included (a) separate standard scores and percentiles for rate and accuracy, (b) better-described norms with 84 more students, and (c) better descriptions of the test's reliability.

Diagnostic Reading Tests

Stanford Diagnostic Reading Test 4 (SDRT4)

The 1995 Stanford Diagnostic Reading Test (Karlsen & Gardner, 1996) is the fourth edition (SDRT4) of a test originally published in 1966. The SDRT4 is a group-administered diagnostic test designed to identify specific strengths and weaknesses in reading. It provides detailed coverage of skills in phonetic analysis, vocabulary, comprehension, and scanning. Because the test is intended for use with low achievers, it contains easier questions than most achievement tests do.

An interesting feature of this test is the way in which the items are ordered. Most diagnostic tests have the items within a subtest arranged in order of difficulty, from the easiest to the most difficult. The items in the SDRT4 are arranged so that difficult items are interspersed among easier items. The easier items cushion student performance and help alleviate the frustration experienced when students fail many items in a row.

There are six levels of the SDRT4, with one form at each of the first three levels and two alternative and equivalent forms at each of the upper three levels. The levels and the grades for which they are intended are shown in Table 21.1.

TABLE 21.1 ● Levels and Grades of the SDRT4

Levels	Grades
Red	1.5–2.5
Orange	2.5–3.5
Green	3.5–4.5
Purple	4.5–6.5
Brown	6.5–8.9
Blue	9.0–13.0

SOURCE: *Stanford Diagnostic Reading Test: Fourth Edition.* Copyright © 1995 by Harcourt, Inc. Reproduced by permission. All rights reserved.

Sampled Behaviors

The SDRT4 can be group-administered by a classroom teacher. Four skill domains are sampled by the test, although not all domains are sampled at all levels. Subtests and skill domains sampled by the SDRT4 are reported in Table 21.2. Behaviors sampled are as follows.

Phonetic Analysis   This domain is sampled only at the red, orange, and green levels of the test (prior to grade 4.5). Items in this domain sample students' skill in associating letters and word segments with consonant and vowel sounds.

Vocabulary   This subtest appears at all levels of the test and is a measure of listening vocabulary, skill in identifying synonyms, and verbal classification. Knowledge of synonyms is assessed by asking students to choose the printed word that means the same as the tested word. Knowledge of the relationships among words is assessed by having students classify words into categories.

Comprehension   Comprehension is assessed using three kinds of materials: recreational, informational, and functional text. Four kinds of comprehension are assessed:

1. *Initial understanding.* Students must recognize ideas and relationships that are directly stated.

2. *Interpretation.* Students must show skill in making inferences and predictions based on what is read.

3. *Critical analysis.* Students must show skill in evaluating what is read.

4. *Reading strategies.* Students are asked to show skill in recognizing and using reader strategies, text structures, and types of text.

TABLE 21.2 ● Subtests, Objectives, and Numbers of Items of the SDRT4

	Red Level 1.5–2.5	Orange Level 2.5–3.5	Green Level 3.5–4.5	Purple Level 4.5–6.5	Brown Level 6.5–8.9	Blue Level 9.0–12.9
Phonetic Analysis	40	30	30			
Consonants	24	18	15			
Single	8	6	5			
Blends	8	6	5			
Digraphs	8	6	5			
Vowels	16	12	15			
Short	10	6	5			
Long	6	6	5			
Other			5			
Vocabulary	40	40	40	30	30	30
Word Reading	10					
Listening Vocabulary	30	10	10			
Nouns	8					
Verbs	13					
Others	9					
Reading Vocabulary		30	30	30	30	30
Synonyms		25	25	19	18	14
Classification		5	5	5	4	3
Word Parts				3	4	5
Content Area Words				3	4	8
Comprehension	40	40	45	54	54	54
Sentences	8					
Riddles	8					
Cloze	8	8				
Paragraphs with Questions	16	32	45	54	54	54
By Type of Text:						
Recreational Reading		13	15	18	18	18
Textual Reading		10	15	18	18	18
Functional Reading		9	15	18	18	18
By Mode of Comprehension:						
Initial Understanding			18	18	18	18
Interpretation			21	25	25	25
Critical Analysis and Reading Strategies			6			
Critical Analysis				6	6	6
Reading Strategies				5	5	5
Scanning				30	30	30

Scanning   This subtest measures a student's skill in scanning a text for important information. The new fourth edition of the SDRT includes three optional informal assessment instruments: a Reading Strategies Survey, a Reading Questionnaire (a measure of attitudes toward reading, reading interests, and familiarity with concepts that appear in the comprehension subtest), and a measure of Story Retelling.

Scores

The SDRT4 is both norm-referenced and criterion-referenced. It can be used to assess a pupil's performance relative to the performance of others, and it can be used to pinpoint individual pupils' strengths and weaknesses in specific reading skills.

Students respond either in the test booklets or on machine-readable answer sheets. The test can, therefore, be either hand scored or machine scored. Six kinds of scores can be obtained: (1) Raw scores are obtained for each subtest and can be transformed into (2) "progress indicators," (3) percentile ranks, (4) stanines, (5) grade equivalents, or (6) scaled scores. Which scores are useful depends on the purpose for which the test has been administered. Progress indicators are criterion-referenced scores, whereas the other four derived scores are norm-referenced. Progress indicators are + or − indications as to whether a pupil achieved a predetermined cutoff score in a specific skill domain; they show whether a pupil demonstrates mastery of specific skills that are important to the various stages in the process of learning to read effectively. The manual reports that "in setting the Progress Indicator cutoff scores, the SDRT4 authors were guided by the relative importance of each skill to the reading process, by the location of these skills in the developmental sequence, and by the performance of students at different achievement levels on the items measuring these skills" (Karlsen & Gardner, 1996, p. 15). The manual for each level of the SDRT4 includes an appendix that lists specific instructional objectives assessed by each level of the test.

The norm-referenced scores obtained by administering the SDRT4 can be used for a variety of purposes. The authors provide a detailed table in the test manual showing the recommended uses of each of the kinds of scores and the extent to which scores are comparable across subtests, forms, levels, and grades. The scores on the test can be used to make setting decisions, identify reading strengths and weaknesses, evaluate pupil progress, and identify trends in reading achievement at the class, school, and district level.

A number of reports can be generated from the SDRT4 by making use of the publisher's computer-scoring service. Examiners can obtain an individual diagnostic report, which contains a detailed analysis of the performance of a single pupil. They can also obtain a class summary report, which shows the average scores earned by the pupils on each of the subtests. It also provides an analysis of skill development for the class by indicating the number of students in the class who obtained a progress indicator of + and of −. Examiners can obtain a master list report, which consists of a listing of scores for all students in a class. They can obtain a parent report, classified specifically for sending test results home to parents. Additionally, they can obtain a pupil item analysis, showing the raw scores earned by a particular student on each subtest and cluster, as well as the student's response to each item.

Norms

In preparing this fourth edition of the SDRT, the authors wrote or rewrote all items. In selecting the standardization sample for the SDRT4, the authors used a stratified random-sampling technique. Socioeconomic status, urbanicity, ethnicity, and geographic region were the stratification variables. School-system data were obtained from the U.S. Office of Education's 1990 census tapes. Age and gender were not controlled in standardizing the SDRT4.

School districts within each of the stratified cells were invited to participate in standardization of the test. A random sample of consenting districts within each cell was selected. The SDRT4 was standardized during the fall of 1994 and spring of 1995. Four hundred school systems participated in the fall standardization (33,000 students). The test was standardized on about 60,000 students. The authors provide a table in their manual showing the relationship of sample characteristics to census characteristics. The numbers are a close match. There is no report of cross-tabulations. Thus, we don't know how many low-SES students were from urban versus suburban settings.

Reliability

Two kinds of reliability data are provided for the SDRT4. Data on internal consistency are provided for all students in the standardization sample. Data on alternate-forms reliability are reported for three levels of the test at which there are alternate forms (purple, brown, and blue). All but one of the internal-consistency coefficients exceed .80. The reliability of the Vocabulary subtest is .79 at grade 1. Alternate-forms reliabilities are generally lower. These range from .62 to .88.

Validity

Data are provided on content validity and criterion-related validity. As test items were written, they were reviewed by content experts, who made sure that the items were actually assessing the content objectives they were intended to assess. Measurement experts reviewed items for appropriate test-item properties, and more than twice as many items were tried as were retained. The item tryout phase of the standardization program was on 150 districts from 32 states; about 16,000 students participated. The authors appropriately indicate that judgments about content validity must ultimately be made at the local school level by comparing the content of the test to the content of the local curriculum. Criterion-related validity was established by correlating performance on subtests of the SDRT4 with performance on their counterparts on the SDRT3. There is a strong relationship between performance on the two editions.

Summary

The SDRT4 is a group-administered device that is both norm-referenced and criterion-referenced. The device was exceptionally well standardized and is reliable enough to be used in pinpointing specific domains of reading in which pupils demonstrate skill-development strengths and weaknesses. Validity for the SDRT4, as for any achievement measure, must be judged relative to the content of local curricula. The test is one of the more carefully designed and developed diagnostic reading measures available.

Woodcock Reading Mastery Tests–Revised, Normative Update (WRMT-Rnu)

The normative update of the Woodcock Reading Mastery Tests–Revised (WRMT-Rnu; Woodcock, 1998) is a battery of six individually administered tests to assess the development of readiness skills, basic reading skills, and reading comprehension of individuals from kindergarten through 75 years of age. Test results can be used in clinical and educational assessment and diagnosis, planning of educational programs, and research. The complete materials for the test are contained in an easel kit. There are two forms of the test, G and H. Form G includes all six tests; form H includes only the four reading-achievement tests (it does not include the readiness measures).

Subtests and Clusters

The six tests that make up the WRMT-Rnu battery are described next.

Visual–Auditory Learning In a miniature learning-to-read task, the student is required to associate unfamiliar visual stimuli (rebuses) with familiar oral words and to translate sequences of rebuses into sentences. The test is the same as the Visual-Auditory Learning subtest of the Woodcock–Johnson Psychoeducational Battery.

Letter Identification This test assesses skill in naming or pronouncing (the student is permitted to do either) letters of the alphabet. Both upper- and lowercase letters are used, and the letters are presented in a variety of type styles.

Word Identification This test measures skill in pronouncing words in isolation.

Word Attack This test assesses skill in using phonic and structural analysis to read nonsense words.

Word Comprehension Three subtests make up this test: Antonyms, Synonyms, and Analogies. In the Antonyms subtest, the student must read a word and then provide a word that means its opposite. In the Synonyms subtest, words with meanings similar to those of the stimulus words must be provided. In the Analogies subtest, the student must read a pair of words, ascertain the relationship between the two words, read a third word, and then supply a word that has the same relationship to the third word as exists between the initial pair of words read. Separate scores can be obtained for comprehension of words in different content areas: General Reading Vocabulary, Science–Mathematics Vocabulary, Social Studies Vocabulary, and Humanities Vocabulary.

Passage Comprehension This test uses a modified cloze procedure.[3] The student's task is to read silently a passage that has a word missing and then tell the examiner a word that could appropriately fill the blank space. The passages are drawn from actual newspaper articles and textbooks.

The six tests of the WRMT-Rnu are organized into three clusters. The readiness cluster is composed of the Visual–Auditory Learning and Letter Identification tests. The Word Identification and Word Attack tests make up the basic skills cluster. The Word Comprehension and Passage Comprehension tests make up the reading comprehension cluster.

Scores

Raw scores can be converted into commonly understood derived scores: percentiles, standard scores (with a mean of 100 and a standard deviation of 15), T-scores, normal-curve equivalents, and age and grade equivalents. Raw scores can also be converted to W-scores (a Rasch ability score[4]) and to a Relative Performance Index (RPI), which is a ratio of the test taker's mastery of material to that mastered at 90 percent by the normative sample.[5]

Norms

In 1998 new norms were published for the WRMT-Rnu. Because item-response theory was used to develop the tests, the normative sample plays a less central role. (See Appendix 4.) Students in the norm sample are used to calibrate the test items.

---

3. The cloze procedure is a technique in which words are omitted from a sentence, and for each omission the test taker supplies a word that is appropriate in terms of both meaning and grammar. In a modified cloze procedure, the test taker selects the correct word from a multiple-choice array.

4. See Appendix 4 for a brief explanation of item-response theory.

5. For example, if a student earned an RPI of 30/90, that student performs the tasks with 30 percent mastery while average individuals perform them with 90 percent mastery.

The norms for the WRMT-Rnu are based on the performances of 3,184 students in first through twelfth grade and 245 individuals between 18 and 22 years of age who were tested as part of an effort to develop new norms for this test and also Key Math–Revised, the Peabody Individual Achievement Test–Revised, and the comprehensive and brief forms of the Kaufman Test of Educational Achievement. The sampling plan to locate individuals willing to participate in the renorming effort is well described. Actual participants were selected from a pool of volunteers using stratified random-sampling techniques. At each grade, the sample appears representative in terms of sex, geographic region, parental education, race and ethnicity (that is, African American, Hispanic, white, and other), and placement in special-education programs for students with disabilities and for gifted students. However, only portions of the total sample were used to calibrate the items in each subtest. The numbers of individuals range from 2,662 (Word Reading) to 721 (Word Comprehension); the representatives of these subsamples varies by grade for each subtest, as well as from subtest to subtest.

Reliability

Data are provided on the internal-consistency reliability of the WRMT-Rnu. These data are for all tests and clusters and are provided separately for grades 1, 3, 5, 8, and 11 and for college and adult groups. Reliabilities for clusters exceed .80; in all but three cases, they exceed .90. With one exception, reliabilities for the six tests exceed .80; most exceed .90. There are no data on the test–retest reliability of the WRMT-Rnu.

Validity

Several kinds of validity are discussed in the manual for the WRMT-Rnu. The case for content validity is made on the basis of expert judgment and the Rasch scaling procedures used in constructing the test. Users of the test will have to make judgments about the extent to which the test measures mastery of the content of their curriculum. Evidence for concurrent validity is good. Data are presented showing correlations of the WRMT-Rnu with the reading subtests of the Woodcock–Johnson Psychoeducational Battery. Correlations among subtests measuring similar behaviors are high. There is good evidence for the *convergent validity* of the scale; that is, performance on specific tests correlates more highly with performance on other measures of similar reading behaviors than with performance on measures of different reading behaviors.

Summary

The WRMT-Rnu, a revision of a scale that was originally published in 1973, includes six separate measures of pupil skill development in reading and reading comprehension. The WRMT-Rnu has expanded and updated norms and now includes a readiness component. The test is also normed on college students and adults. The several new diagnostic aids that have been developed appear to be useful. The test is appropriately and adequately normed, and evidence for internal-consistency reliability is good. There are no data on test–retest reliability. Evidence for validity of the tests is good. This is one of the better diagnostic reading measures.

Woodcock Diagnostic Reading Battery (WDRB)

The Woodcock Diagnostic Reading Battery (WDRB; Woodcock, 1997) is a set of individually administered tests used to measure ten aspects of reading achievement and a set of closely related abilities. The ten subtests for this test are identical to ten subtests contained in the cognitive and achievement batteries of Woodcock–Johnson Psychoeducational Battery–Revised (Woodcock & Johnson, 1989). In that sense, this is not a new test, but rather one formed by combining some of the parts of a more extensive cognitive and achievement battery.

The WDRB is based on a model of reading performance illustrated in Figure 21.2. Woodcock views reading performance as a result of a combination of prior knowledge, basic reading skills, reading comprehension, other cognitive factors, and noncognitive factors. Basic reading skills are seen as the direct result of the application of phonological awareness skills, while reading comprehension is derived from application of oral comprehension.

The WDRB is used with individuals between 5 and 90 years of age. It is used to diagnose strengths and weaknesses in five areas: basic reading skills, reading comprehension, phonological awareness, oral-language comprehension, and reading aptitude. The author claims that the test is useful in making eligibility decisions and provides a method for computing an ability–achievement discrepancy in reading. The test is also designed for use in instructional planning, progress monitoring, and research.

Subtests

The ten subtests of the WDRB are combined to provide cluster scores in seven areas. The tests and the ways in which they are combined into clusters are illustrated in Figure 21.3. The subtests and the behaviors they sample follow.

● ● ● **FIGURE 21.2**   The Reading Performance Model

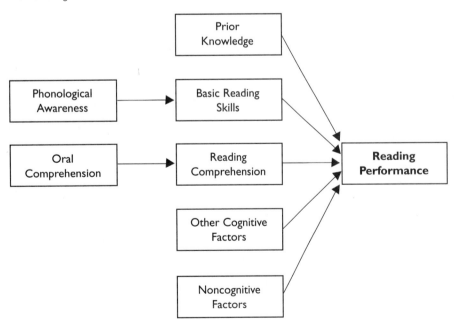

● ● ● FIGURE 21.3   WDRB Selective Testing Table

TESTS	READING				RELATED ABILITIES		
	Total Reading	Broad Reading	Basic Reading Skills	Reading Comprehension	Phonological Awareness	Oral Comprehension	Reading Aptitude
1. Letter-Word Identification	●	●	●				
2. Word Attack	●		●				
3. Reading Vocabulary	●			●			
4. Passage Comprehension	●	●		●			
5. Incomplete Words					●		
6. Sound Blending					●		●
7. Oral Vocabulary						●	●
8. Listening Comprehension						●	
9. Memory for Sentences							●
10. Visual Matching							●

SOURCE: Copyright © 1997 by The Riverside Publishing Company. Reproduced from *Woodcock Diagnostic Reading Battery, Examiner's Manual*, By Richard W. Woodcock with permission of the publisher. All rights reserved.

Letter–Word Identification   Items in this subtest include those measuring ability to match photographic representations of words (rebuses) with actual pictures of objects, and items that assess letter and word recognition.

Word Attack   This measure of phonic and structural analysis requires students to pronounce nonwords or unfamiliar words.

Reading Vocabulary   This subtest measures students' skill in gaining meaning from the words they read. Both synonyms and antonyms are included.

Passage Comprehension   Students read phrases or short passages and either point to pictures that illustrate what they read or identify missing words in the phrases or short passages.

Incomplete Words   This subtest has words with one or more missing phonemes that the individual must identify.

Sound Blending   This is a measure of the individual's skill in synthesizing syllables into words.

Oral Vocabulary   The individual gives synonyms or antonyms in response to stimulus words read by the examiner.

Listening Comprehension   This is an oral cloze test; the individual listens to a passage and supplies the last word.

Memory for Sentences   This subtest consists of phrases and sentences that are presented individually on audiotape and must be repeated by the individual.

Visual Matching   This subtest consists of 70 sets of numbers; each set consists of six numbers that range from single digits to three-digit numbers. An individual's score is based on the number of sets that are matched correctly within three minutes.

Subtest Clusters   The ten subtests are combined into the following clusters: total reading, broad reading, basic reading skills, reading comprehension, phonological awareness, oral comprehension, and reading aptitude. The WDRB is available in easel format, with stimulus pictures or words facing the individual being tested, and test directions facing the examiner. An audiotape is provided for use in administering some of the subtests.

Scores

Scores are available for each subtest and cluster. Raw scores may be converted to standard scores, percentile ranks, *W*-scores, age equivalents, grade equivalents, relative performance indexes (RPIs), and cluster difference scores. RPIs are expressed as ratios of percentage of success relative to peers. An RPI of 60/90 indicates that the individual achieves 60 percent success on a task on which peers achieve 90 percent success. Percentile ranks and standard scores are peer-comparison scores. RPIs are descriptions of proficiency or quality of performance, while age and grade equivalents describe developmental level.

Norms

The norms for the WDRB are a subset of the norms for the Woodcock–Johnson Psychoeducational Battery. The sample comprised 6,026 individuals who were assessed during 1986 to 1988. The sample was drawn from 100 geographically diverse settings, stratified on the basis of ten community and subject variables: census region, community size, gender, race, Hispanic/non-Hispanic, funding of college or university, education of adults, occupational status of adults (employed/unemployed), and occupation of adults (white collar, blue collar/farm, service). The sample is representative of the U.S. census.

Reliability

Data on both internal-consistency and test–retest reliability are reported in the manual for the WDRB. Table 21.3 lists the median internal-consistency reliabilities for students ages 5–18 years and for adults. Test–retest reliabilities are based on the performance of 504 students and range from .62 (Incomplete Words) to .92 (Letter–Word Identification). With the exception of those for the Incomplete Words subtest, reliabilities look sufficiently high to use the test for making decisions about individuals.

Validity

Extensive evidence on validity is presented in the manual. In supporting content validity, Woodcock shows how reading skills to sample, from simple to complex, were selected and matches these to a model of reading. In supporting concurrent validity, he illustrates appropriately high correlations with the Peabody Individual Achievement Test, Basic Academic Skills Individual Screener, Kaufman Assessment Battery for Children, Kaufman Test of Education Achievement, Wide Range Achievement Test–Revised, Stanford–Binet Intelligence Scale, and Wechsler Intelligence Scale for Children–Revised. Also, good evidence for construct validity is provided.

Summary

The WDRB is a test that was built by pulling a subset of tests from the Woodcock–Johnson Psychoeducational Battery–Revised (WJPB-R). In that sense, the test is not new. The strength of this measure is that it puts in one place the reading subtests

TABLE 21.3   ●   Median Reliabilities for WDRB Subtests and Clusters

Subtests	Median Reliability in 5–18 Age Range	Median Reliability in Adults
Letter–Word Identification	.94	.95
Word Attack	.91	.90
Reading Vocabulary	.92	.93
Passage Comprehension	.88	.92
Incomplete Words	.72	.87
Sound Blending	.86	.91
Oral Vocabulary	.88	.92
Listening Comprehension	.80	.83
Memory for Sentences	.86	.88
Visual Matching	.78	.84
Clusters		
Total Reading	.98	.98
Broad Reading	.95	.96
Basic Reading Skills	.96	.96
Reading Comprehension	.95	.96
Phonological Awareness	.88	.93
Oral Comprehension	.91	.95
Reading Aptitude	.93	.96

SOURCE: Copyright © 1997 by The Riverside Publishing Company. Reproduced from *Woodcock Diagnostic Reading Battery, Examiner's Manual*, by Richard W. Woodcock with permission of the publisher. All rights reserved.

and clusters from the WJPB-R. The test is used to measure behaviors in ten subtests and clusters, and it is intended to be used for diagnostic and instruc-tional planning purposes. The test is among the best-normed diagnostic reading tests, and there is good evidence for its reliability and validity.

Measures of Reading Comprehension

Test of Reading Comprehension–3 (TORC-3)

The Test of Reading Comprehension–3 (TORC-3; V. Brown, Hammill, & Wiederholt, 1995) is an individually administered, norm-referenced measure of students' understanding of written language. The authors of the TORC identify four purposes for using the test:

(1) to identify students whose scores are significantly below their peers and who might need interventions designed to improve reading comprehension, (2) to determine relative strengths and weaknesses in areas of reading comprehension, (3) to document student progress in reading comprehension, and (4) [to aid] in research. (p. 8)

Changes were made in the third edition of this test to address concerns that we and others had raised regarding earlier editions. Specifically, we had raised concerns about the way the norm sample was stratified, the description of the sample, and the validity. In developing this third edition, the authors collected all new normative information, stratified the norm sample by age (but not by other student characteristics), reported on studies of gender and race bias, provided new test–retest reliability data, and provided updated and expanded information on criterion-related and content validity. The content of the test remains as in the first edition.

TORC-3 may be given to individuals, groups of three to five students, or entire classes. It is appropriate for use with students ages 7-0 to 17-11. In developing the TORC-3, the authors set out (a) to construct a measure of comprehension of written language that was independent of any instructional program; (b) to use multiple formats or styles to assess reading comprehension; (c) to minimize the likelihood of obtaining correct responses

solely as a result of general information, memorization, or guessing; (d) to use a silent rather than an oral reading format; and (e) to avoid overuse of vocabulary from any specific content area. For the most part, they were successful. The authors clearly state that any results obtained from this measure are to be treated as instructional hypotheses to be confirmed through more individualized, behaviorally focused strategies.

Subtests

The TORC-3 is made up of eight subtests: Four are combined to form a general reading comprehension core, three are measures of content-specific vocabularies, and one is a measure of the student's skill in reading directions in schoolwork. Following is a brief description of each subtest.

General Vocabulary The student is required to read three stimulus words that are related in some way and then to select from four response words the two that are related to the three stimulus words.

Syntactic Similarities The student is given five sentences and must select the two that are most closely related in meaning.

Paragraph Reading The student is required to read paragraphs and then answer five multiple-choice questions for each paragraph. The questions differ in their demands: One question requires the selection of a "best title" for the paragraph, two require the literal recall of story details, one requires the inference of meaning, and one requires a negative inference.

Sentence Sequencing Each item consists of five randomly ordered sentences, which the student must order in such a way that they make a meaningful story.

Mathematics Vocabulary   The format of this subtest is identical to that of the General Vocabulary subtest. The words are taken from recent mathematics textbooks.

Social Studies Vocabulary   The format of this subtest is identical to that of the General Vocabulary subtest. The words are taken from recent social studies textbooks.

Science Vocabulary   The format of this subtest is identical to that of the General Vocabulary subtest. The words are taken from recent science textbooks.

Reading the Directions of Schoolwork   This subtest is designed for younger and remedial readers. The student must read a set of directions and then implement the instructions on an answer sheet.

Subtest Items   The TORC-3 contains a relatively limited number of items for a measure spanning a 10-year age range. Six of the subtests contain 25 items each, the Sentence Sequencing subtest contains 10 items, and the Paragraph Reading subtest contains 6 reading passages, each of which is followed by 5 questions. Item selection was based on the performance of 120 elementary school students in grades two through sixth in one school district in Austin, Texas. The authors used the performance of these students to reduce the test from an initial 358 items to the 190 items that make up the test.

Scores

Raw scores, percentiles, and standard scores may be obtained for each subtest. In addition, an overall reading comprehension quotient may be calculated. Standard scores have a mean of 10 and a standard deviation of 3. The reading comprehension quotient is obtained by adding the standard scores for the General Vocabulary, Syntactic Simi-

larities, Paragraph Reading, and Sentence Sequencing subtests. These four subtests compose the general reading comprehension core. The reading comprehension quotient has a mean of 100 and a standard deviation of 15.

The authors provide grade-equivalent scores for the TORC-3 but appropriately caution readers about their use. They indicate that the reason for including grade scores is because they are required in many SEAs and LEAs. Throughout the manual, they warn users about the limitations and potential misuse of grade scores.

Norms

The TORC-3 was standardized on a sample of 1,962 students from 19 states. The norm population was selected in two ways. First, the authors picked one or two cities from each of four U.S. census regions, and used a test coordinator in each city to coordinate the collection of data on a total of 950 students. They do not specify the reason for the selection of the specific city within each region. Second, people who had purchased reading tests from the publisher were contacted and asked to assess 20 students each. Fifty-one people volunteered, and they collectively tested 1,012 students. The authors provide a table showing the gender, residence (urban versus rural), race, ethnicity, geographic region, and disabling condition of students in the norm sample, and they contrast these data with census information. They provide stratification information for age with other variables (such as 12-year-old females) but not with other variables (such as number of African American students who were from urban environments, or number of males from the South). These data are necessary to make judgments concerning the representativeness of the norm group.

Reliability

The authors of the TORC-3 provide data on three kinds of reliability: internal consistency, test–retest, and interscorer. Internal-consistency coefficients were computed for each of the individual subtests at each age. Eighty-nine percent of those coefficients exceed .90, and all but one of the coefficients exceed the desirable standard of .80.

Validity

The authors have not done a convincing job of demonstrating that the TORC-3 is, indeed, a measure of reading comprehension. First, the rationale for inclusion of the eight subtests as measures of reading comprehension is not convincing. This is especially true for the subtests that measure content-specific vocabulary in mathematics, social studies, and science. The authors report that they selected vocabulary for these subtests by sampling textbooks in science, social studies, and math. Yet, the textbooks sampled were all published prior to 1978. It is our contention that textbooks in these subject areas have changed in the more than 20 years since the authors sampled them.

The results of six criterion-related validity studies reported by the authors raise some major questions. The investigations were conducted with very specific samples (for example, 54 boys and girls attending second and third grade in Norman, Oklahoma; 28 adolescent girls attending a residential treatment center in Austin, Texas). Sample size ranged from 28 to 94, and performance on the TORC-3 was correlated with performance on other measures of reading, intelligence, mathematics, and language arts. The measures are all old and no longer published. Correlations of TORC-3 subtests with measures of intelligence and measures of mathematics achievement were as high as correlations with other measures of reading, language arts, and reading comprehension.

Summary

The Test of Reading Comprehension–3 is a norm-referenced measure designed to provide an evaluation of students' comprehension of written language. In addition to a reading comprehension quotient, which is based on pupil performance on four subtests, the test provides users with an assessment of pupil performance in content-specific vocabulary and in following the directions of schoolwork. There is some question about the adequacy of the norms. In general, TORC-3 appears sufficiently reliable for making important individual decisions about students, but the extent to which the test measures reading comprehension is uncertain.

Criterion-Referenced Testing in Reading

The tests we have discussed to this point are norm-referenced tests, which are designed to compare individuals with their peers. Criterion-referenced diagnostic testing in reading is a practice that dates from the late 1960s. Criterion-referenced diagnostic reading tests are designed to analyze systematically an individual's strengths and weaknesses without comparing that individual with others. The principal objective of criterion-referenced tests is to assess the specific skills a pupil has, to determine those skills the pupil does not have, and to relate the assessment to curricular content. Criterion-referenced assessment is tied to instructional objectives, and individual items are designed to assess mastery of specific objectives.

Although all criterion-referenced reading tests are based on task analyses of reading, the particular skills assessed and their sequences differ from test to test. This is because different authors view reading in different ways and see the sequence of development of reading skills differently. For this reason, it is especially important with criterion-referenced tests (as with norm-referenced tests) that teachers pay special attention to the behaviors and sequences of behaviors sampled by the tests.

Because normative comparisons are not made in criterion-referenced assessment, no derived scores are calculated. For that reason, many authors of criterion-referenced tests downplay the importance of reliability for their scales. Nonetheless reliable assessment is important in criterion-referenced tests. Although we are not concerned with the consistency of derived scores, we are concerned with the consistency of responses to items when all items in the domain are assessed. If a different pattern of item scores is obtained each time an individual takes the test, we begin to question the reliability of the device. Because criterion-referenced devices generally contain relatively limited samples of behavior, it is important that test authors report the consistency with which their tests assess each specific behavior. Test authors can and should report test–retest reliabilities for each item. It is important to note the consistency with which the test samples the domain of possible test items when the domain is not exhausted. When alternative forms of a criterion-referenced test are available, the authors should report correlations between performances on the two forms.

Standardized Reading Inventory (SRI)

The Standardized Reading Inventory (SRI; Newcomer, 1986) is an individually administered measure of skill development in oral and silent reading, appropriate for use with students whose reading competence does not exceed the eighth-grade level. The test provides information on both word recognition and reading comprehension and is designed to be used to diagnose the nature of the reading difficulties of students who are experiencing reading problems. The author indicates that the test can be administered in 15 to 45 minutes but recommends that users allot 1 hour for testing. Materials for this scale consist of a test manual; a student booklet containing word lists, reading passages, and comprehension questions; and summary/record sheets. After reading the word lists, the student reads passages orally and then silently. There are two forms of the test, form A and form B.

In administering the SRI, the examiner first asks the student to read the words from the word list that is two grades below the student's estimated reading level. If the student misreads three or more words, the examiner drops down to an easier list. The student continues reading words in isolation until three or more words on a list are misread. The student then is required to read passages, beginning with the passage that corresponds to the highest grade level at which the student attained an independent level in reading the word lists. The student reads each passage aloud, and the examiner records errors in oral reading. The student then reads the same passages silently and responds to a set of comprehension questions for each passage.

In developing the SRI, the author first compiled lists of new words that are included as typical words in five popular basal reading series: Scott, Foresman Basics in Reading; Houghton Mifflin Reading Series; HBJ Bookmark Reading Program; Macmillan Reading Series; and Ginn Reading Series. Words presented at the same grade level in two or more reading series were designated as key words, and these words were then used in writing the reading passages. The author states, "In composing the passages, the total number of words, [the] total number of sentences, and the number of words per sentence were held relatively constant for the forms of the passages at each grade level; but the number of key words and novel words varied" (Newcomer, 1986, p. 6). Words considered "typical" in 1986 may no longer be "typical" today, however.

Scores

The SRI is scored in such a way that examiners obtain an indication of whether word-recognition skills and reading comprehension are at an independent, instructional, or frustration level. An *instructional level* is defined as a score that is plus or minus one standard deviation from the mean; an *independent level* is defined as a score that is more than one standard deviation above the mean; and a *frustration level* is defined as a score that is more than one standard deviation below the mean. In practice, for word-recognition skills, an independent level is the level at which the student misreads fewer than two words; the instruction level is the level at which two words are misread; and the frustration level is the level at which the student misreads three or more words. For the oral-reading passages, there are specified criteria for independent, instructional, and frustration levels for both word recognition and comprehension.

Norms

There are no norms for the SRI. The author argues that the SRI is a criterion-referenced test that is standardized. She uses Hammill's definition of standardized assessment instruments as instruments that possess "(a) set administration procedures, (b) objective scoring criteria, and (c) specified guidelines for interpreting results" (Newcomer, 1986, p. 1).

Reliability

Three types of reliability are presented for the SRI: test–retest, alternate-form, and interscorer. Test–retest reliability data are based on the performance of 30 third-grade students in a single school district at Levels 2, 3, and 4 of the SRI. The test was given twice at an interval of one week. Test–retest reliabilities ranged from .83 for Level 2 of form A to .92 for Level 4 of form B.

Alternate-form reliability was established by correlating performance on forms A and B for the 288 children who took the test as part of the standardization process. This sample included 24 students reading at the preprimer level, 24 at the primer level, and 30 each at Levels 1 through 8. The students took the test so that the difficulty of the passages could be calibrated. Alternate-form coefficients ranged from .70 to .97 for Word Recognition and from .71 to .96 for Reading

Comprehension. For Word Recognition, acceptable levels of reliability were obtained only after the grade 1 level.

To establish interscorer reliability, the author and a colleague scored 30 completed protocols. There was 97 percent agreement for both Word Recognition and Reading Comprehension. The author and a colleague also scored tape-recorded performances of 20 students. Interscorer agreement on the instructional level exceeded 90 percent. The reliability coefficients for the SRI indicate satisfactory reliability, although the coefficients are based on limited samples of students.

Validity

The author goes to considerable trouble to demonstrate the content validity of the SRI. This is as it should be for criterion-referenced measures. Yet, passages were selected for the test and placed at specified grade levels based on the performances of 288 children from a single school district in suburban Philadelphia. Designated reading levels were established by getting data on the performance of students on end-of-book tests at specified levels and, in some instances, performance on the Stanford Achievement Test.

Criterion-related validity was established by correlating the results of performance on the SRI with the results of performance on the reading section of the Stanford Achievement Test. Subjects were 30 fifth-graders from a suburban Philadelphia school district. Correlation of the Stanford Achievement Test reading score was .74 with the SRI Word Recognition score and .74 with the SRI Reading Comprehension score.

Further evidence for validity of the test is provided: Scores on the SRI increase with age, performance on the test is highly correlated with intelligence, and good readers perform significantly better than poor readers.

Summary

The SRI is a criterion-referenced measure of pupil skill development in both oral and silent reading. The test provides users with an assessment of both the nature of oral-reading errors and the comprehension of material read silently. There are no norms for this test; the author argues that the test is a standardized criterion-referenced measure. Reliability coefficients are variable, so test users must consult the manual to determine the test's suitability for various educational decisions at specific ages. There is good evidence for the validity of the test.

Standardized Test for the Assessment of Reading (S.T.A.R.)

The Standardized Test for the Assessment of Reading (S.T.A.R.; Advantage Learning Systems Inc., 1997) is designed to provide teachers with quick and accurate estimates of students' instructional reading levels and estimates of their reading levels relative to national norms. The test is administered using computer software, so the specific test items each student receives are determined by his or her responses to previous test items. Using computer-adaptive procedures, a branching formula matches test items to student ability and performance level. The test uses a vocabulary in context format in which students must identify the best choice for a missing word in a single-context sentence. Correct answers fit both the semantics and the syntax of the sentence. All incorrect answers either fit the syntax of the sentence or relate to the meaning of something in the sentence.

Scores

Users of S.T.A.R. may obtain grade equivalents, percentile ranks, normal curve equivalents, and scaled scores. In addition, they may obtain information about the zone of proximal development (zpd), an index of the low and high ends of the range at which students can read. The software used to administer the test provides the information, and scores are obtained immediately.

Norms

Items for S.T.A.R. were developed using 13,846 students from 59 schools. The development sample was stratified on the basis of gender, grade, geographic region, district socioeconomic status, school type, and district enrollment. The primary unit of selection was school rather than students. Tables in the manual contrast sample characteristics with national population characteristics. For the most part, sample characteristics approximate population characteristics. Notable exceptions include an underrepresentation of students from the Northeast (9% versus 20% in the population) and of schools with small (<2,500) and large (>25,000) enrollments.

S.T.A.R. was standardized on 42,000 students from 171 schools. The standardization sample was stratified on the basis of geographic region, school system and per-grade district enrollment, and socioeconomic status. Sample characteristics very closely approximate population characteristics. Students from all geographic regions, socioeconomic levels, and school sizes were selected in proportion to their presence in the population. Normative tables in the manual describe the close approximation of the sample to the U.S. population.

Reliability

S.T.A.R. is a computer-adaptive test that offers a virtually unlimited number of test forms, so tradi- tional methods of conducting reliability analyses do not apply. The authors instead conducted reliability analyses using a test–retest methodology with alternative forms. Reliability was tested using both scaled scores and instructional reading levels. A total of 34,446 students were tested twice with S.T.A.R., each taking the second test an average of five days after the first. Test–retest reliabilities ranged from .85 to .95 for scaled scores, and from .79 to .91 for instructional reading level.

Validity

Performance on S.T.A.R. was correlated with performance on a number of different standardized measures of reading skills administered to those in the standardization group. An extensive table in the manual reports these results. Comparison tests included the California Achievement Test, Comprehensive Test of Basic Skills, Degrees of Reading Power, Gates–MacGinitie, Iowa Test of Basic Skills, Metropolitan Achievement Test, Stanford Achievement Test, and several state custom-built tests (Connecticut, Texas, Indiana, Tennessee, Kentucky, North Carolina, and New York). Performance on S.T.A.R. is related closely to performance on the other measures of reading.

Summary

S.T.A.R. is a norm-referenced, computer-adaptive reading test that provides teachers with information about students' instructional levels as well as their level of performance relative to a national sample. S.T.A.R. enables users to sample a wide range of reading behaviors in a relatively limited period of time. The test was standardized on a large and representative group of students. Evidence for reliability and validity is satisfactory. The test should be very useful to those who want immediate scoring and information about appropriate student instructional level.

Comprehensive Test of Phonological Processing (CTOPP)

Comprehensive Test of Phonological Processing (CTOPP; Wagner, Torgesen, & Rashotte, 1999) is an individually administered, norm-referenced test that is appropriately used with individuals ranging in age from 5 to 25 years. In addition to use in research, CTOPP is intended for identifying individual strengths and weaknesses in phonological processing, for diagnosing individuals who lag significantly behind their peers in phonological skills, and for documenting development of these skills.

Subtests

CTOPP is composed of 13 subtests in three areas of phonology: phonological awareness, phonological memory, and rapid naming. As show in Table 21.4, the required and supplemental subtests differ for two age groups, children 5 and 6 years of age and individuals 7 years of age and older.

Elision   This subtest measures the ability to delete sounds from spoken words in order to create new words. Test takers repeat a word read by the examiner and then say the word again without a particular sound. For example, "Say *cold*. Now say *cold* without saying *k*."

Blending Words   This subtest measures the ability to synthesize sounds into words. Test takers listen to syllables and then say what word the syllables make. For example, "can–dy" requires a response of "candy."

Sound Matching   This subtest measures the ability to discriminate words with the same beginning or ending sounds by having test takers point to a drawing depicting a word that starts (or ends) with the same sound as a stimulus word.

Blending Nonwords   This subtest measures the ability to synthesize sounds into units like words

by requiring test takers to listen to separate sounds and then blend them into a nonsense word. For example, "flib–bo" is "flibbo."

Segmenting Nonwords   This subtest measures the ability to separate the sounds in nonwords by having test takers listen to a nonsense word (like flibbo), repeat the word, then repeat the nonsense word one syllable at a time (flib–bo).

TABLE 21.4 ● *CTOPP Subtests by Age and Phonological Process*

	Age Group	
Subtest	**5–6**	**7–21**
Phonological Awareness		
Elision	C[a]	C
Blending Words	C	C
Sound Matching	C	
Blending Nonwords[b]	S	S
Segmenting Nonwords[b]		S
Phonological Memory		
Memory for Digits	C	C
Nonword Repetition	C	C
Rapid Naming		
Rapid Color Naming	C	S[c]
Rapid Object Naming	C	S[c]
Rapid Digit Naming		C
Rapid Letter Naming		C
Additional Diagnostic Subtests		
Phoneme Reversal		S
Segmenting Words		S

[a]C indicates that the subtest is used in the composite, and S indicates the subtest is supplemental.
[b]Subtest is part of the Alternate Phonological Awareness composite.
[c]Subtest is part of the Alternate Rapid Naming composite.

Memory for Digits   This subtest measures the ability to recall a sequence of numbers by having test takers repeat a series of digits in the same order as presented. The digit sequences range in length from two to eight.

Nonword Repetition   This subtest measures the ability to recall nonwords by having test takers listen to a stimulus composed of 3 to 15 sounds and then repeat it.

Rapid Color Naming   This subtest measures the ability to recall and fluently say the names of colors by having test takers name blocks printed in one of six different colors. The blocks are arranged in two matrices, each on a separate page. Each matrix consists of 4 rows and 9 columns of randomly arranged colors. The score is the number of seconds needed to name the colors of the 72 blocks.

Rapid Object Naming   This subtest measures the ability to recall and fluently say the names of familiar objects by having test takers name drawings of them. The drawings are arranged in two matrices, each on a separate page. Each matrix consists of 4 rows and 9 columns of randomly arranged drawings. The score is the number of seconds needed to name the 72 objects.

Rapid Digit Naming   This subtest measures the ability to recall and fluently say the names of numbers by having test takers say the names of six different integers. The integers are arranged in two matrices, each on a separate page. Each matrix consists of 4 rows and 9 columns of randomly arranged integers. The score is the number of seconds needed to name the 72 integers.

Rapid Letter Naming   This subtest measures the ability to recall and fluently say the names of letters by having test takers say the names of six different letters. The letters are arranged in two matrices, each on a separate page. Each matrix consists of 4 rows and 9 columns of randomly arranged letters, and the score is the number of seconds needed to name the 72 letters.

Phoneme Reversal   This subtest measures the ability to say phonemes in reverse order to create a meaningful word by having test takers listen to a nonword, repeat the nonword, and then reorder the sounds to form a word. For example, a child might hear "o-g" and be required to make the word *go* from the two sounds.

Segmenting Words   This subtest measures the ability to separate the sounds in words by having test takers listen to a word (like *it*), repeat the word, then repeat the word one phoneme at a time ("i-t").

Scores

Subtest raw scores can be converted to percentiles, standard scores with a mean of 10 and standard deviation of 3, and age and grade equivalents. In addition, selected subtests can be combined to form composites. As shown in Table 21.4 the subtests used to form the three usual composites (that is, Phonological Awareness, Phonological Memory, and Rapid Naming) differ for students of different ages. Two alternative composites are also available for older test takers (that is, Alternate Phonological Awareness and Alternate Rapid Naming). Composites can be converted to percentiles and to standard scores with a mean of 100 and a standard deviation of 15.

Norms

The CTOPP was normed on 1,656 individuals residing in 30 states. The sampling plan consists of three poorly described strategies to locate individuals. The authors present data to show that the standardization sample has approximately the same proportions of individuals as the U.S. population in 1997. However, there are two problems. First, there is no discussion of the criteria used for categorization into urban–rural resident, ethnic group, or race. Second, the data presented do not correspond to the specific normative comparisons. Separate norms tables are provided for individuals in whole-year groups (that is, for individuals from

5 years 0 months to 5 years 11 months, and so on) except for persons aged 18 through 24. However, the data describing the norms are presented in two-year intervals, and no data are presented for the normative groups for individuals aged 18 through 24.

Reliability

Coefficient alpha was used to estimate the reliability of item samples for all untimed subtests. The authors state on page 68 of the manual that they estimated the reliability of item samples for the timed tests (that is, Rapid Color Naming, Rapid Object Naming, Rapid Digit Naming, and Rapid Letter Naming) by alternate-form procedures. Although not explained in the manual, the procedures do not appear to be the usual alternate-form method of estimating reliability because the test has no alternate forms. The reported estimates of item reliability for the individual subtests are generally too low to be used in making decisions on behalf of individual children. Of the 165 subtest by age group estimates, only 34 (almost 21 percent) equal or exceed .90, while 42 (about 25 percent) are less than .80. Estimates of the reliability of item samples for composites vary by age. For 5- and 6-year-olds, the reliability of Phonological Awareness equals or exceeds .95; the other composites are less than .90. For older individuals, reliability estimates equal or exceed .90 for 8 of the 12 age groups on the Phonological Awareness composite and for 9 of the 12 age groups on the Rapid Naming composite; on the Phonological Memory composite, the highest estimated item reliability, is .86. Reliability estimates equal or exceed .90 for 9 of the 12 age groups on the Alternate Phonological Awareness composite and for 1 of the 12 age groups on the Alternate Rapid Naming composite.

Stability of CTOPP scores was estimated using 91 Floridians who were tested within a two-week period. For children 5 to 7 years of age, only the Phonological Memory composite has a test–retest correlation equaling or exceeding .90.[6] For individuals 8 to 17 years of age, only Rapid Object Naming and the Alternate Rapid Naming composite have a test–retest correlation of .90 or more. Finally, for the 18 and older group, Rapid Digit Naming, the Phonological Memory composite, and the Alternate Rapid Naming composite have test–retest correlations of .90 or more.

To investigate the interscorer reliability, two individuals independently scored 30 completed protocols (that is, answer forms) for 5- and 6-year-olds and 30 completed protocols for individuals 7 through 24. All 60 protocols were selected randomly from the normative sample. The scorers summed the number correct and converted the raw scores to standard scores. Correlations between scores were uniformly high, equaling or exceeding .95. However, the scorers apparently did not evaluate the students' actual responses to ascertain whether they were correct or incorrect. Thus, the high coefficients only reflect the degree to which adults can apply ceiling rules, sum correct responses, and look up scores.

Validity

The three aspects of phonological processing were selected by the authors because of their relationship to academic achievement (especially in reading and mathematics) and the comprehension of oral and written language, and because of their implication in learning disability. The behaviors used to assess the three aspects of phonological processing are based on experimental tasks.

Several studies demonstrating CTOPP's criterion-related predictive validity are reported in the test manual. Illustrative is one study that used the three composites to predict decoding scores on the Woodcock Reading Mastery Tests–Revised administered one year later. The correlations with

---

6. Rapid Digit Naming and Rapid Letter Naming also had stabilities over .90, but these subtests are not given to children in this age range and no norm tables are available to convert raw scores.

decoding scores are impressive for kindergartners and first graders: $r = .71$ and $.80$ for Phonological Awareness, $r = .66$ and $.70$ for Rapid Naming, and $r = .42$ and $.52$ for Phonological Memory. Overall, there is considerable evidence that CTOPP predicts decoding.

Evidence for CTOPP's construct validity comes from several sources. Confirmatory factor analyses support the test's organization and conceptual model. Scores on most subtests increase with age, supporting the developmental nature of the skills being assessed. Students with independently identified speech disabilities, language disabilities, or learning disabilities earn lower scores than nondisabled students. CTOPP scores show neither racial, ethnic, nor gender bias. Finally, CT0PP scores appear to be sensitive to intervention; that is, improved skills following intervention are reflected in increased test scores.

Summary

The Comprehensive Test of Phonological Processing is an individually administered, norm-referenced test intended to assess phonological awareness, phonological memory, and rapid naming. Different combinations of the 13 subtests are used to assess these abilities for test takers of different ages. The number of individuals in the CTOPP normative sample (1,656) is adequate, and the overall sample appears representative of the nation. However, questions about the representativeness of the sample remain because the sampling plan is poorly described and the data presented in the manual do not correspond to the actual normative comparisons. Except for Phonological Awareness, reliability estimates are generally too low for making decisions concerning individuals. There is strong evidence for CTOPP's validity.

Coping with Dilemmas in Current Practice

There are five major problems in the diagnostic assessment of reading strengths and weaknesses. The first is the problem of curriculum match. Students enrolled in different reading curricula have different opportunities to learn specific skills. Reading series differ in the skills that are taught, in the emphasis placed on different skills, in the sequence in which skills are taught, and in the time at which skills are taught. Tests differ in the skills they assess. Thus, it can be expected that pupils studying different curricula will perform differently on the same reading test. It can also be expected that pupils studying the same curriculum will perform differently on different reading tests. Diagnostic personnel must be very careful to examine the match between skills taught in the student's curriculum and skills tested. Most teachers' manuals for reading series include a listing of the skills taught at each level in the series. Many authors of diagnostic reading tests now include in test manuals a list of the objectives measured by the test. At the very least, assessors should carefully examine the extent to which the test measures what has been taught. Ideally, assessors would select specific parts of tests to measure exactly what has been taught. To the extent that there is a difference between what has been taught and what is tested, the test is not a valid measure.

The second problem is also a test–curriculum match problem. Most reading instruction now takes place in regular classrooms, using the content of typical reading textbooks. This is true for developmental reading instruction, remedial reading instruction, and the teaching of reading to students with disabilities. Most diagnostic reading tests measure student skill-development competence in isolation. Also, they do not include assessments of the comprehension strategies, such as the metacognitive strategies that are now part of reading instruction.

A third problem is the selection of tests that are appropriate for making different kinds of educational decisions. We noted that there are different types of diagnostic reading tests. In making classification decisions, educators must administer tests individually. They may either use an individually administered test or give a group test to one individual. For making instructional-planning decisions, the most precise and helpful information will be obtained by giving individually administered criterion-referenced measures. Educators can, of course, systematically analyze pupil performance on a norm-referenced test, but the approach is difficult and time-consuming. It may also be futile because norm-referenced tests usually do not contain enough items on which to base a diagnosis.

When evaluating individual pupil progress, assessors must consider carefully the kinds of comparisons they want to make. If they want to compare pupils with same-age peers, norm-referenced measures are useful. If, on the other hand, they want to know the extent to which individual pupils are mastering curriculum objectives, criterion-referenced measures are the tests of choice.

The fourth problem in the assessment of reading strengths and weaknesses is that there are few technically adequate tests. We have noted that for many norm-referenced reading tests, there is no adequate description of the groups on which the tests were standardized. Other tests were inadequately standardized. There is no evidence of the reliability or validity of many diagnostic reading tests. The reliability of other tests is not sufficient to allow valid decisions about individuals. Diagnostic personnel should refrain from using technically inadequate measures. At the very least, they must operate with full awareness of the technical limitations of the devices they use.

The fifth problem is one of generalization. Assessors are faced with the difficult task of describing or predicting pupil performance in reading. Yet, reading itself is difficult to describe, being a complex behavior composed of numerous subskills. Those who engage in reading diagnosis will do well to describe pupil performance in terms of specific skills or subskills (such as recognition of words in isolation, listening comprehension, specific word-attack skills, and so on). They should also limit their predictions to making statements about probable performance of specific reading behaviors, not probable performance in reading.

Summary

In this chapter, we have reviewed the kinds of behaviors sampled by diagnostic reading tests. Several specific norm-referenced and criterion-referenced tests have been evaluated in terms of the kinds of behaviors they sample and their technical adequacy. Most of the norm-referenced devices clearly lack the technical characteristics necessary for use in making specific instructional decisions. Many do not present evidence of reliability and validity. In fact, some tests present the assessor with numerous normative tables for interpreting test data without describing the nature of the normative population.

The criterion-referenced test described in this chapter is designed to pinpoint skill-development strengths and weaknesses, provide teachers with instructional objectives, and direct teachers to materials that help teach to those objectives. We do not yet have sufficient empirical evidence to judge the extent to which criterion-referenced tests meet their stated objectives. Teachers need to judge for their own purposes the sequences of the behavior samplings and the sequences of behaviors sampled. The systems still contain many rough spots that need to be smoothed out.

How, then, do teachers and diagnostic specialists assess skill development in reading and prescribe developmental, corrective, or remedial programs? Reliance on scores provided by diagnostic reading tests is indeed precarious. Teachers and diagnostic specialists must rely on the qualitative information obtained in testing. Some tests provide checklists of observed difficulties, and these may be of considerable help in identifying an individual pupil's reading characteristics. Also, teachers and diagnostic specialists must rely on data they obtain by watching students read texts and by asking students questions about the reading strategies the students use.

In assessing reading strengths and weaknesses, teachers must first ask themselves what kinds of behaviors they want to assess. Specific subtests of larger batteries can then be used to assess those behaviors. Teachers should choose the subtests that are technically most accurate. Interpretation must be in terms of behaviors sampled rather than in terms of subtest names.

Questions for Chapter Review and Thought

1. Reading tests assess six types of comprehension skills. A skill deficit in each type could have significant implications for learning. What are the implications of deficits in listening and lexical comprehension?

2. In assessing reading strengths and weaknesses, what options do teachers have?

3. What are the relative merits and limitations in using criterion-referenced diagnostic reading tests and in using norm-referenced tests?

4. Dierdre, a student in Mr. Albert's fifth-grade class, has considerable difficulty reading. Mr. Albert wants to know at what level to begin reading instruction. Given the state of the art in diagnostic testing in reading, describe some alternative ways for Mr. Albert to identify a starting point.

5. When teachers use criterion-referenced reading tests, they often find that the sequence in which specific individuals learn reading skills differs from the sequence of skills assessed by the test. How might this difference be explained?

Resources for Further Investigation

Project

Using information found in the text, write a summary for three diagnostic reading tests. Upon completion, compare your summary with the text summary. Then go to the *Mental Measurements Yearbook* (see "Print Resources") and compare and contrast your summaries with the reviews of the tests you selected. If your summary differs from the review, has the reviewer used information and standards different from those you used?

Print Resources

Beck, I. (1993). On reading: A survey of recent research and proposals for the future. In A. P. Sweet & J. I. Anderson (Eds.), *Reading research into the year 2000* (pp. 65–88).

Brown, V., Hammill, D., & Wiederholt, J. L. (1997). *Test of Reading Comprehension–3.* Austin, TX: Pro Ed.

Conoley, J. C., & Impara, J. C. (1995). *The twelfth mental measurements yearbook* (GORT-3, pp. 422–425). Lincoln, NE: University of Nebraska Press.

Conoley, J. C., & Kramer, J. J. (1989). *The tenth mental measurements yearbook* (WRMT-R, pp. 909–916; TORC, pp. 850–855). Lincoln, NE: University of Nebraska Press.

Elliott, S. N., & Piersel, W. C. (1982). Direct assessment of reading skills: An approach which links assessment to intervention. *School Psychology Review, 11,* 267–280.

Karlsen, B., & Gardner, E. F. (1996). *Directions for Administering the Stanford Diagnostic Reading Test, Forms J/K* (pp. 7–8). San Antonio, TX: Harcourt Educational Measurement.

Kramer, J. J., & Conoley, J. C. (1992). *The eleventh mental measurements yearbook* (Gates–MacGinitie, pp. 348–354). Lincoln, NE: University of Nebraska Press.

Mitchell, J. V. (1985). *The ninth mental measurements yearbook* (SDRT, pp. 1462–1465). Lincoln, NE: University of Nebraska Press.

Palincsar, A. M., & Brown, A. L. (1984). Reciprocal teaching of comprehension-fostering and comprehension-monitoring activities. *Cognition and Instruction, 1,* pp. 117–175.

Taylor, B., Harris, L., Pearson, P. D., & Garcia, G. (1995). *Reading difficulties: Instruction and assessment* (2nd ed.). New York: McGraw-Hill.

Woodcock, R. (1997). *Woodcock Diagnostic Reading Battery.* Chicago, IL: Riverside Publishing Company.

Technology Resources

Riverside Publishing

http://www.riverpub.com/

Go to products and services, and then under clinical and special needs you will find information on the *Woodcock Reading Mastery Tests–Revised* and the *Woodcock Diagnostic Reading Battery.*

Pro-Ed Catalog Information for Products

http://www.proedinc.com

Find product and ordering information about the *Gray Oral Reading Test, Third Edition; Formal Reading Inventory; Test of Reading Comprehension, Third Edition; Standardized Reading Inventory;* and various other measures.

chapter

22

Assessment of Mathematics

*D*iagnostic testing in mathematics is designed to identify specific strengths and weaknesses in skill development. We have seen that all major achievement tests designed to assess multiple skills include subtests that measure mathematics competence. These tests are necessarily global and attempt to assess a wide range of skills. In most cases, the number of items assessing specific math skills is insufficient for diagnostic purposes. Diagnostic testing in mathematics is more specific, providing a detailed assessment of skill development within specific areas.

There are fewer diagnostic math tests than diagnostic reading tests, but math assessment is more clear-cut. Because the successful performance of some mathematical operations clearly depends on the successful performance of other operations (for example, multiplication depends on addition), it is easier to sequence skill development and assessment in math than in reading. Diagnostic math tests generally sample similar behaviors. They sample various mathematical contents, concepts, and operations, as well as applications of mathematical facts and principles. Some now also include assessment of students' attitudes toward math.

Why Do We Assess Mathematics?

There are several reasons to assess mathematics skills. First, we are often interested in evaluating a student's competence in math. We may use diagnostic tests in mathematics to assess a student's readiness for instruction (in mathematics and other subjects) or to determine eligibility for employment. Second, all public-school programs, with the exception of programs for students with profound disabilities, teach math facts and concepts. Thus, teachers need to know whether pupils have mastered those facts and concepts. Diagnostic math tests are intended to provide sufficiently detailed information so that teachers and intervention-assistance teams can plan and evaluate instructional programs. Finally, diagnostic math tests are occasionally used to make exceptionality and eligibility decisions. Individually administered tests are usually required for eligibility and placement decisions. Therefore, we often see diagnostic math tests used to establish special learning needs and eligibility for programs for children with learning disabilities in mathematics.

● ●

Behaviors Sampled by Diagnostic Mathematics Tests

Behaviors sampled by diagnostic math tests have been classified by Connolly (1988) and are described here, in terms of content, operations, applications, and attitudes.

Content

A number of content areas are assessed by diagnostic math tests. Facts, knowledge, and concepts necessary for the successful performance of mathematical operations and for meaningful applications of math are assessed in each of the following content areas.

Numeration   Diagnostic math subtests assess knowledge of the number system. Items include those that assess identification of quantities and set value, rounding, identification of missing numbers in sequences, and counting.

Fractions   In nearly all cases, and especially in tests designed to be used with students beyond fourth grade, tests assess understanding of basic concepts about fractions, decimals, and percentages.

Geometry   Items that assess knowledge of geometry typically measure skill in recognizing specific shapes and, in some cases, understanding of theorems.

Algebra   Some diagnostic math tests include subtests or items designed to assess knowledge and understanding of principles involved in the solution of linear and quadratic equations.

Operations

Subtests and items designed to assess students' skill in carrying out fundamental arithmetic operations include measures of counting, computation, and arithmetic reasoning.

Counting   Items designed to assess skill in counting usually require the student to count dots or objects and to select or write numerals to represent the number of objects counted.

Computation   Items and subtests designed to assess computational skills range from those that sample the traditional arithmetic operations of addition, subtraction, multiplication, and division to those that require the student to complete as many as four computational operations in each of various problem-solving tasks. Items designed to assess specific operations generally range from those that require use of the operation in solving word problems to those that require the written solution of relatively complex computational problems.

Arithmetic Reasoning   Arithmetic-reasoning subtests require the solution of problems with missing number facts.

Applications

Diagnostic math tests assess students' skills in applying mathematical facts and concepts to the solution of problems. Tasks generally include the following kinds of behavior samplings.

Measurement   Items assessing measurement require the recognition and application of common measurement units and the practical application of length, weight, and temperature measures.

Reading Graphs and Tables   The application of mathematical skills and concepts may be assessed by requiring the student to read graphs and tables in order to solve problems.

Money and Budgeting   The application of mathematical skills and concepts may be assessed by requiring the student to solve money problems. Items include those that assess the extent to which the student can (a) make value judgments about purchasing articles, (b) interpret budgets, and (c) comprehend checks and checking accounts.

Time   The application of mathematical facts and concepts to the solution of problems involving time includes test items requiring the student to read clocks and to identify time intervals, holidays, and seasons.

Problem Solving   Problem-solving tasks require students to solve story problems that are read to them or that they read themselves. Four kinds of problems are generally included: (1) those requiring only a one-step mathematical operation; (2) those requiring more than one computational operation; (3) those requiring the student to differentiate between essential and nonessential information in solving problems; and (4) those requiring the student to demonstrate logical thinking by solving problems with missing elements.

Attitudes

Some math tests include survey questions asking students about their attitudes toward math. Students are asked the extent to which they enjoy math, the extent to which their friends like math more than they do, and so on.

Specific Diagnostic Mathematics Tests

This chapter reviews four diagnostic mathematics tests: the KeyMath–Revised, the Stanford Diagnostic Mathematics Test 4, the Test of Mathematical Abilities–2, and STAR Math.

KeyMath–Revised–Normative Update (keyMath-R-NU)

KeyMath–Revised. A Diagnostic Inventory of Essential Mathematics (KeyMath–R; Connolly, 1998) is an individually administered, norm-referenced test. The 1998 edition is a normative update only. The basic testing materials consist of two easels that contain testing items and directions for presenting and scoring items. Four uses are suggested for the test: (1) instructional planning, (2) comparison of students, (3) evaluation of educational progress, and (4) curriculum evaluation.

There are two forms of KeyMath-R (forms A and B), and each contains 258 items. Total math performance is divided into three areas. The area of basic concepts comprises three subtests: numeration, rational numbers, and geometry. The operations area consists of addition, subtraction, multiplication, division, and mental computation. The area of applications contains items assessing measurement, time and money, estimation, interpretation of data, and problem solving. Each subtest in turn, comprises various domains. A *domain* is a subdivision of a subtest; for example, in the measurement subtest, there are four domains: comparisons, using nonstandard units, using standard units of length and area, and using standard units of weight and capacity. The subtest of rational numbers consists of three domains: fractions, decimals, and percentages. There are 3 or 4 domains per subtest (for the 13 subtests), for a total of 43 domains. Written computation is permitted only on some of the subtests in the operations area.

Scores

For each subtest, both percentiles and standard scores (with a mean of 10 and a standard deviation of 3) are available. For area performance and total test performance, six derived scores are provided: standard scores (with a mean of 100 and standard deviation of 15), normal-curve equivalents, stanines, percentiles, age equivalents, and grade equivalents. Finally, KeyMath-R provides a rather unusual score for domains. Domain-performance scores divide student performances into strong (top quartile), average (middle quartiles) or weak (bottom quartile); the usefulness of domain scores for instructional planning is unclear. A computer program is available to convert raw scores and to construct student profiles.

Norms

The 1998 normative update was completed in conjunction with normative updating of the Peabody Individual Achievement Test–Revised, the Kaufman Test of Educational Achievement–Revised, and the Woodcock Reading Mastery Tests–Revised. The sample for the normative updates was 3,184 students in kindergarten through grade 12. A stratified multistage sampling procedure was used to ensure selection of a nationally representative group at each grade level. Students in the norm group did not each take all five tests. Rather, one fifth of the students took each test, along with portions of each of the other tests. Thus, the norm group for KeyMath consists of about 600 students. There are as few as 91 students at three-year age ranges. Because multiple measures were given to each student, the authors could use linking and equating to increase the size of the norm sample.

Reliability

Alternate-forms reliability was estimated by retesting about 70 percent of the students in grades K, 2, 4, 6, and 8 at two- and four-week intervals. However, Connolly does not report estimated reliability by grade; rather, he reports pooled (across-grade) coefficients. Only the total score may be sufficiently reliable for making important educational decisions for students; all subtest and area estimates of reliability are less than .85.

Split-half reliabilities (using odd–even splits and Spearman–Brown correction) were also estimated by grade and age.[1] For students in kindergarten through second grade, total scores are consistently reliable enough to use in making decisions for individuals; area subtests fluctuate, so the test user must determine whether a particular age–area combination is sufficiently reliable for interpretation. After second grade, area scores have acceptable reliability, and total scores have excellent reliability; however, because basal and ceiling rules were applied to the test scores, the obtained split-half estimates are likely to be inflated.

A third method of estimating reliability based on item-response theory was used. The results of this analysis are essentially the same as those obtained using split-half estimates.

1. We believe that the reliability estimates based on age are somewhat misleading because several age groups are contained within any grade. Consequently, the range of ability would probably be extended.

No reliability data are provided for domain scores. No stability coefficients are reported, although stability can be inferred from the alternate-forms reliability coefficients.

Validity

Little evidence of construct validity is presented. What is offered is a demonstration of mean-score progressions from grade to grade. No evidence of concurrent validity is presented. However, for most achievement tests, these indexes of validity are less important than evidence of content validity. Limited evidence for KeyMath-R's content validity comes from the careful development of a table of specifications to guide item development. As is always the case, however, test users should inspect the test's content to make sure that it conforms to the curriculum followed by the students who are being assessed.

Summary

Based on its full title and the claims made in its manual, KeyMath-R is intended as a diagnostic test. The standardization of the test appears to be generally adequate. For grades before third grade, only the total score is sufficiently reliable for diagnostic purposes; for third grade and later, area and total scores are sufficiently reliable. Because of the low reliabilities of subtests and the absence of reliability information for domains, users should avoid making inferences about a student's instructional strengths and weaknesses based on subtest and domain scores. Of the four uses that are proffered for the test, no evidence of KeyMath-R's validity for instructional planning, evaluation of educational progress, or curriculum evaluation is presented. Some evidence for the validity of comparing students' global performances is presented.

Stanford Diagnostic Mathematics Test 4 (SDMT4)

The Stanford Diagnostic Mathematics Test 4 (SDMT4; Harcourt Brace Educational Measurement, 1996b) is the fourth edition of a widely used test that was first developed and published in 1966. The SDMT4 is a group-administered diagnostic test designed to identify specific strengths and weaknesses in math. It emphasizes general problem-solving and math-specific problem-solving strategies while measuring student competence in those basic math skills and concepts that are prerequisite to mathematics problem solving. SDMT4 subtests and levels and the grades for which they are appropriate are shown in Table 22.1. The test includes both multiple-choice and free-response items.

Skill Domains

The SDMT4 can be group-administered by a classroom teacher. Two skill domains are sampled: concepts and applications, and computation. The following are the kinds of skills assessed in each of the domains.

Concepts and Applications   Items in this domain measure the degree to which students have mastered fundamental concepts and skills and the extent to which they are able to integrate and apply the skills to solve grade-level-appropriate problems. The kinds of concepts assessed include place value, size, geometric properties, math vocabulary, fractions, and decimals. Skills assessed include rounding, measurement, number recognition, recognition and interpretation of alternative representations in graphs and tables, spatial reasoning, and application of math skills and concepts to solve problems.

Computation   Computation items assess the extent to which students have mastered addition, subtraction, multiplication, and division skills.

Scores

The SDMT is both norm- and criterion-referenced. It can be used to assess a pupil's performance relative to the performance of others, and it can be used to pinpoint individual pupils' strengths and weaknesses in specific math skills. Students respond either in the test booklets or on machine-readable answer sheets. The test, therefore, can be either hand scored or machine scored. Six kinds of scores can be obtained; which scores are useful depends on the purpose for which the test has been administered.

Raw scores are obtained for each subtest and can be transformed into "Progress Indicators," percentile ranks, stanines, grade equivalents, and scaled scores. *Progress indicators* are criterion-referenced scores, whereas the other four scores are norm referenced. Progress indicators are + or − indications as to whether a pupil achieved a predetermined cutoff score in a specific skill domain; they show whether a pupil demonstrates mastery of specific skills important to progress in learning to solve math problems. The manual reports that "in setting the Progress Indicator cutoff scores, the following factors were taken into account: the relative importance of each skill to mathematics, by the location of these skills in the developmental sequence, and by the performance of students at different achievement levels on the items measuring these skills" (Harcourt Brace Educational Measurement, 1996, p. 15). The manual for each level of the SDMT4 includes an appendix that lists specific instructional objectives assessed by each level of the test.

The norm-referenced scores obtained by administering the SDMT4 can be used for a variety of purposes. The manual includes a detailed table showing the recommended uses of each of the kinds of scores and the extent to which scores are comparable across subtests, forms, levels, and

TABLE 22.1 ● *Subtests and Objectives of the Stanford Diagnostic Mathematics Test,* Fourth Edition

Multiple Choice	Red Level 1.5–2.5	Orange Level 2.5–3.5	Green Level 3.5–4.5	Purple Level 4.5–6.5	Brown Level 6.5–8.9	Blue Level 9.0–12.9
Concepts and Applications	32	32	32	32	32	32
Numeration	12	12	12	10	10	10
Patterns and Functions	3	3	3			
Probability and Statistics				4	4	4
Graphs and Tables	3	3	3	4	4	4
Problem Solving	6	6	8	8	8	8
Geometry and Measurement	8	8	6	6	6	6
Computation	20	20	20	20	20	20
Addition of Whole Numbers	12	9				
Subtraction of Whole Numbers	8	11				
Addition and Subtraction of Whole Numbers			10	8	4	4
Multiplication of Whole Numbers			7	6	4	
Division of Whole Numbers			3	6	3	
Multiplication and Division of Whole Numbers						4
Operations with Fractions and Mixed Numbers					3	4
Operations with Decimals and Percents					3	5
Equations					3	5

grades. The scores on the test can be used to make setting decisions, identify math strengths and weaknesses, evaluate pupil progress, and identify trends in math achievement at the class, school, and district level.

A number of reports can be generated from the SDMT by making use of the publisher's computer-scoring service. Examiners can obtain an individual diagnostic report, which contains a detailed analysis of the performance of a single pupil. They can also obtain a class summary report, which shows the average scores earned by the pupils on each of the subtests. It also provides an analysis of skill development for the class by indicating the number of students in the class who obtained a progress indicator of + and the number who obtained a progress indicator of −. Examiners can obtain a master-list report, which consists of a list-

ing of scores for all students in a class. They can obtain a parent report, designed specifically for sending test results home to parents. In addition, they can obtain a pupil item analysis, showing the raw scores earned by a particular student on each subtest and cluster, as well as the student's response to each item.

Norms

In preparing this fourth edition of the SDMT, the authors wrote or rewrote all items. Both multiple-choice and free-response items were written. About 3,000 items were tried out on about 27,000 students in 150 districts from 32 states and the District of Columbia. To eliminate bias in assessment, extensive work went into item review and into statistical review of the performance of differ-

TABLE 22.1 (*continued*)

Free Response	Red Level 1.5–2.5	Orange Level 2.5–3.5	Green Level 3.5–4.5	Purple Level 4.5–6.5	Brown Level 6.5–8.9	Blue Level 9.0–12.9
Concepts and Applications	30	30	30	30	30	30
Numeration	8	8	8	8	8	8
Patterns and Functions	3	3	3	4	4	4
Probability and Statistics				3	3	3
Graphs and Tables	3	3	3	3	3	3
Problem Solving	6	6	6	6	6	6
Geometry and Measurement	10	10	10	6	6	6
Computation	20	20	20	20	20	20
Addition of Whole Numbers	12	9				
Subtraction of Whole Numbers	8	11				
Addition and Subtraction of Whole Numbers			10	8	4	4
Multiplication of Whole Numbers			7	6		
Division of Whole Numbers			3	6		
Multiplication and Division of Whole Numbers					7	4
Operations with Fractions and Mixed Numbers					3	4
Operations with Decimals and Percents					3	5
Equations					3	3

ing groups of students. In selecting the standardization sample for the SDMT4, the authors used a stratified-random-sampling technique. Socioeconomic status, urbanicity, ethnicity, and geographic region were the stratification variables. School-system data were obtained from the U.S. Office of Education's 1990 census tapes. Age and gender were not controlled in standardizing the SDMT4.

School districts within each of the stratified cells were invited to participate in standardization of the test. A random sample of consenting districts within each cell was selected. The SDMT4 was standardized during the fall of 1994 and spring of 1995. In the fall standardization (48,000 students), 425 school systems participated. The spring standardization included about 40,000 students, yielding about 88,000 students for both samples. The

authors provide a table in their manual showing the relationship of sample characteristics to census characteristics. The numbers are a close match. There is no report of cross-tabulations. Thus, we do not know how many low-SES students were from urban versus suburban settings.

Reliability

Three kinds of reliability information for the SDMT4 are provided: internal-consistency, alternate-forms, and—for the free-response version—interscorer reliability. Internal-consistency reliabilities were computed on the 40,000 students who participated in the spring 1995 standardization. Reliability coefficients are reported by subtest for the six levels of the test and for each of the alternative forms for the three higher levels of the test; about 98 percent (195 of 199) of the reliability coefficients exceed .80.

Alternate-forms reliability coefficients are reported based on the performance of 7,000 students in the fall 1994 standardization. Of the 27 coefficients, 21 exceed the desirable .80. Reliabilities for the multiple-choice computation test are consistently in the mid-.70s range at all levels of the test. Interrater reliabilities were all in excess of .97. There is good evidence for the reliability of the SDMT4.

Validity

Data are provided on the content validity, criterion-related validity, and construct validity of the SDMT4. As test items were written, they were reviewed by content experts, who made sure that the items were actually assessing the content objectives they were intended to assess. The manual includes an extensive list of the objectives measured by the items. Criterion-related validity was established by correlating performance on SDMT3 with SDMT4. There is a strong relationship between performance on the two editions.

Intercorrelations among subtests and between subtests and performance on the Otis–Lennon School Ability Test are provided as evidence for the construct validity of the SDMT4. This does not indicate construct validity but shows the relationship of performance on SDMT4 and a measure of school ability. Relationships are high. Further evidence of construct validity is provided by showing correlations among performances on the same subtest at adjacent levels. The authors would have done well to correlate performance on SDMT4 with other measures (such as the Stanford Achievement Test 9) of mathematics achievement.

Summary

The SDMT4 is a group-administered device that is both norm-referenced and criterion-referenced. The text was exceptionally well standardized and developed. It is reliable enough to be used in pinpointing math strengths and weaknesses. Validity of the test should be judged relative to the content of local curricula.

Test of Mathematical Abilities–2 (TOMA-2)

The Test of Mathematical Abilities–2 (TOMA-2; V. Brown, Cronin, & McEntire, 1994) is a norm-referenced test intended for use with students between the ages of 8-0 and 18-11. The test differs from other math tests in that it goes beyond computation and solving of story problems to measure three other aspects of math now considered to be crucial: (1) students' attitudes toward math; (2) their understanding of the language of mathematics, as represented in the vocabulary of instruction; and (3) their familiarity with math terms and concepts used in everyday life. The authors indicate that the test is designed to assist school personnel in the following:

making decisions about curriculum placement, assessing the extent to which students have mastered specific math skills, and making normative comparisons of student performance in math. In addition, the test is designed to answer these questions (V. Brown, Cronin, & McEntire, 1994, p. 1):

- What is the student's expressed attitude toward math?
- What is the student's general math vocabulary level?
- How knowledgeable is the student about the functional use of math facts and concepts?

• How do the student's attitudes, vocabulary, and general math information compare with the basic skills shown in the areas of computation and story problems?
• Do the student's math vocabulary and level of general math information differ from those of his or her peers?

Most of this test is identical to the first edition of TOMA. A few items were added to the beginning and end of each of four subtests. The authors indicate that they performed an item analysis on the original TOMA items and retained what they called "good" items. The authors do not indicate the number of items retained but do say that "TOMA-2 contains most of the items found in the original TOMA and additional items added to the top and bottom of each subtest" (p. 33).

Subtests

The 120 test items (13 more than in the original TOMA) are grouped into the following subtests:

Vocabulary   The student must write definitions of each of 25 mathematical terms, such as *volume*, *ratio*, and *ellipse*.

Computation   Students solve 25 problems in their answer booklets. The problems sample basic math skills, as well as advanced fractions, percentages, money, and complex math problems.

General Information   Students respond orally or in writing to questions about math, as used in everyday situations. For example, "Why can a canceled check be your receipt?"

Story Problems   Students solve 25 word problems in their answer booklets.

Attitude Toward Mathematics   This is a 15-item supplemental test in which students respond to questions such as, "It's fun to work math problems" and "My friends like math more than I do," using a 4-point scale: "yes, definitely," "closer to yes," "closer to no," and "no, definitely."

Scores

Raw scores on the TOMA-2 can be converted to age scores, standard scores (with a mean of 10 and a standard deviation of 3), grade equivalents, percentiles, and math quotients.

Norms

The norms of TOMA-2 are a combination of TOMA norms and new norms. Remember that the only new items for TOMA-2 are a few at the beginning and end of four subtests. An undetermined number of items were dropped from the original TOMA. If students in the original norm sample reached a ceiling without taking higher-level items, their scores were included in the norms for TOMA-2. The performances of 336 students were used. In addition, two procedures were used to develop the TOMA-2 norm sample. First, testing sites were identified in four major census districts. Normative data were collected by one of the authors or by a specially trained person in these sites. The authors say that the sites were chosen because the demographic characteristics of the students in the school matched closely those in the region. No data on sample selection are provided. The second method was to go to Pro-Ed customer files and pick people who had purchased TOMA and would be willing to test students in their own school districts. Each willing respondent tested 10 to 50 students. The standardization sample for TOMA-2 is not a stratified sample.

There were 2,082 students in the norm group. Tables in the manual indicate that their characteristics resemble closely the characteristics of students in the general population. No cross-tabulation information is presented, so we do not know whether most of the males came from the East, African American students from the West, and so forth. We believe that it is critical to indicate the makeup of the norm sample beyond one-variable descriptions.

Reliability

The authors report information on internal-consistency and test–retest reliability. Internal consistency was computed using data from the standardization sample. All coefficients exceed the desirable .80. Test–retest reliability is reported for 198 students in New Orleans. The students ranged from 9 through 14 years of age. Given that 72 percent were African American, whereas 14 percent of the norm sample was African American, the sample was not representative. The test–retest reliabilities ranged from .70 (Attitude Toward Math) to .85 (Story Problems). Information about the reliability of this test just is too limited to be useful. More studies need to be completed on larger and more representative samples.

Validity

A major improvement in this second edition of TOMA is seen in the rationale and explanation the authors provide for item selection. This was missing, for the most part, in the original TOMA. The authors claim that the test has good content validity because items are similar to those in other math tests. Yet, they do not report the relationship between items on TOMA-2 and the content of mathematics curricula.

In establishing the criterion-related validity of this test, the authors report studies on both the original TOMA and the TOMA-2. They argue that the tests are "almost identical." To establish comparability, they report correlations in performance on the two scales. Nearly all correlations are above .98. The results of two very limited studies are then reported. The first is a study of the relationship between TOMA performance and performance on now out-of-print versions of the KeyMath Diagnostic Test, Peabody Individual Achievement Test, and Wide Range Achievement Test. The study was completed on only 38 children, all of whom were learning disabled and ranged in age from 9 through 14. The results are essentially meaningless as evidence for the validity of TOMA-2. The second study of criterion-related validity was also completed on the original TOMA. The scores of an unspecified (age, grade, gender, ethnicity, SES?) sample of 290 students attending school in Illinois and Louisiana were correlated with their performance on the math subtests of the Science Research Associates (SRA) achievement test. Correlations were moderate, but we do not know what they mean.

Evidence for construct validity is provided. The authors demonstrate that scores increase with age and that performance on the subtests is moderately intercorrelated. They demonstrate that the test correlates moderately with out-of-print versions of the Wechsler Intelligence Scale for Children and the Slosson Intelligence Test. There is no description of the group on whom this study was conducted, and the study is not referenced. As further evidence of construct validity, the authors again report the results of the study of 39 learning-disabled students. They show that the students earned lower-than-average scores.

In our opinion, the validity studies conducted on TOMA-2 do not provide evidence of the test's validity. The studies are on very limited samples, which are not described; when samples are described, the age range is limited to older students; and when correlations with other measures are reported, the other measures are out-of-print editions of currently used tests. There is no evidence for the validity of the one unique subtest, Attitude Toward Math.

Summary

The TOMA-2 is designed to measure skill development in math and, in addition, attitude toward math. The authors contend that the test is virtually unchanged from its original version. In standardizing this measure, the authors did not use a stratified normative sampling approach. Thus, we do not know the extent to which the norms are representative. Evidence for reliability is limited to evidence of internal consistency. There is no evidence of test–retest reliability. Evidence of validity is limited to content validity. The remaining reliability and validity studies had major design problems. The SDMT4 appears to be a better diagnostic mathematic test.

STAR Math

STAR Math (Advantage Learning Systems, 1998) is designed to provide teachers with quick and accurate estimates of students' math achievement levels relative to national norms. The test also can be used to monitor student progress in math over time. It is appropriate for use with students in grades 3 through 12. Using computer-adaptive procedures, a branching formula matches test items to students' ability and performance level. In other words, the specific test items that students receive depend on how well they perform on previous items. Thus, each test is unique, tailored to the individual student, and students can be given the test as many as five times in one year without being exposed to the same item more than once. The test is timed. Students have up to three minutes to solve each item and are given a warning when 30 seconds remain.

Items on STAR Math consist of some of the major strands of math content: numeration concepts, computation, word problems, estimation, statistics, charts, graphs, geometry, measurement, and algebra. Responses are four-item multiple-choice responses. The test consists of two parts; concepts of numeration and computation are addressed in the first part, while the other content areas are addressed in the second part.

Scores

Users of STAR Math can obtain grade equivalents, percentile ranks, normal-curve equivalents, and scaled scores. The software provided with the test is used to score the test and give users immediate feedback on student performance.

Norms

STAR Math was standardized on 25,800 students who attended 256 schools in 42 states. Norming was completed in spring 1998, using a sample that was stratified on the basis of geographic region, school location (urban, rural, suburban), gender, and ethnicity. The sample is representative of the U.S. population, as are the proportions of the various kinds of students in the sample.

Reliability

Reliability was calculated using a test–retest method with 1,541 students, who took alternative forms of the test because of its computer-adaptive nature. Reliabilities at grades 3 through 6 are in the high .70s, while at higher grades they are in the .80s. The test has sufficient reliability for use as a screening test, but not for making eligibility and placement decisions.

Validity

Performance on STAR Math was correlated with performance on a number of standardized math tests administered during standardization of the test. An extensive table in the manual reports these results. Comparison tests included the California Achievement Test, Comprehensive Test of Basic Skills, Iowa Tests of Basic Skills, and Metropolitan Achievement Test. Scores were moderately high, and about as would be expected.

Summary

STAR Math is a norm-referenced, computer-adaptive math test that gives teachers information about students' instructional levels as well as their level of performance relative to a national sample. The test was standardized on a large representative sample. It provides teachers with immediate diagnostic profiles on student performance. Evidence for reliability is limited, but evidence for validity is good.

Coping with Dilemmas in Current Practice

There are three major problems in the diagnostic assessment of math skills. The first problem is the recurring issue of curriculum match. There is considerable variation in math curricula. This variation means that diagnostic math tests will not be equally representative of all curricula or even appropriate for some commonly used ones. As a result, great care must be exercised in using diagnostic math tests to make various educational decisions. Assessment personnel must be extremely careful to note the match between test content and school curriculum. This should involve far more than a quick inspection of test items by someone unfamiliar with the specific classroom curriculum. For example, a diagnostician could inspect the teacher's manual to ensure that the teacher assesses only material that has been taught and that there is reasonable correspondence between the relative emphasis placed on teaching the material and testing the material. To do this, the diagnostician might have to develop a table of specifications for the math curriculum and compare test items with that table. However, once a table of specifications has been developed for the curriculum, a better procedure would be to select items from a criterion-referenced system to fit the cells in the table exactly.

The second problem is selecting an appropriate test for the type of decision to be made. School personnel are usually required to use individually administered norm-referenced devices in classification decisions. Decisions about a pupil's eligibility for special services, however, need not be based on detailed information about the pupil's strengths and weaknesses, as provided by diagnostic tests; diagnosticians are interested in a pupil's relative standing. In our opinion, the best mathematical achievement survey tests are subtests of group-administered tests. A practical solution is not to use a diagnostic math test for eligibility decisions but to administer individually a subtest from one of the better group-administered achievement tests.

The third problem is that most of the diagnostic tests in mathematics do not test a sufficiently detailed sample of facts and concepts. Consequently, assessors must generalize from a student's performance on the items tested to his or her performance on the items that are not tested. The reliabilities of the subtests of diagnostic math tests are often not high enough for educators to make such a generalization with any great degree of confidence. As a result, these tests are not very useful in assessing readiness or strengths and weaknesses in order to plan instructional programs. We believe that the preferred practice in diagnostic testing in mathematics is for teachers to develop criterion-referenced achievement tests that exactly parallel the curriculum being taught.

Summary

In this chapter, we have reviewed the kinds of behaviors sampled by diagnostic mathematics tests and have evaluated the most commonly used tests in terms of the kinds of behaviors they sample and their technical adequacy. The four tests reviewed in this chapter are designed to provide teachers and diagnostic specialists with specific information on those math skills that pupils have or have not mastered. Compared with diagnostic testing in reading, diagnostic testing in math puts less emphasis on scores.

The tests described in this chapter differ in their technical adequacy for use in making instructional decisions for students. Knowledge of pupil mastery of specific math skills gained from administration of one or more of the tests, along with knowledge of the general sequence of development of math skills, can help teachers design curricular content for individual students.

Questions for Chapter Review and Thought

1. Identify four ways in which a teacher can interpret a pupil's performance on the KeyMath-R diagnostic test.

2. How can the diagnostician overcome the problem of curriculum match in the diagnostic assessment of mathematical competence?

3. List and describe the major areas in which behaviors are sampled in diagnostic mathematics tests.

4. Discuss the three major problems in the diagnostic assessment of mathematical competence.

Resources for Further Investigation

Project

Assume that you wish to use one of the tests reviewed in this text to diagnose strengths and weaknesses in mathematics. Which test would be your first choice? Why? Compare your answer with a classmate's answer. Reconcile any differences.

Print Resources

Harcourt Brace Educational Measurement. (1996). *Stanford Diagnostic Mathematics Test 4*. San Antonio, TX: Psychological Corporation.

Kramer, J. J., & Conoley, J. C. (1992). *The eleventh mental measurements yearbook* (KeyMath-R, pp. 436–439). Lincoln, NE: University of Nebraska Press.

Reisman, F. (1982). Strategies for mathematics disorders. In C. Reynolds & T. Gutkin (Eds.), *Handbook of school psychology*. New York: Wiley.

Tindal, G., & Marston, D. (1990). Math assessment. In G. A. Tindal & D. B. Marston, *Classroom-based assessment: Evaluating instructional outcomes* (pp. 233–272). Columbus, OH: Merrill.

Technology Resources

Welcome to AGS Online Products and Services

http://www.agsnet.com/

Look for product and ordering information about the instruments available from American Guidance Service. Search for information about *KeyMath–Revised: A Diagnostic Inventory of Essential Mathematics*.

Pro-Ed Catalog Information for Products

http://www.proedinc.com

Find product and ordering information about the *Test of Early Mathematical Ability, Second Edition* and the *Test of Mathematical Abilities, Second Edition*.

NCTM: National Council of Teachers of Mathematics

http://www.nctm.org/

This web site is designed for teachers of mathematics and contains information and resources related to the subject of math.

Assessment of Oral and Written Language

T he assessment of language competence should include evaluation of a student's ability to process, both in comprehension and in expression, language in a spoken or written format. There are four major communication processes: oral comprehension (listening and comprehending speech), written comprehension (reading), oral expression (speaking), and written expression (writing). These are illustrated in Figure 23.1.

In assessing language skills, it is important to break language down into processes and measure each one, because each process makes different demands on the person's ability to communicate. Performance in one modality does not always predict performance in the others. For example, a child who has normal comprehension does not necessarily have normal production skills. Also, a child with relatively normal expressive skills may have problems with receptive language. Therefore, a complete language assessment will include examination of both oral and written reception (comprehension) and expression (production).

● ● ● ● ● ● ● ● ● ● ● ● ● ● ● ● ● ● ● ●

Terminology

Educators, psychologists, linguists, and speech–language pathologists often have different perspectives on which skills make up language. These different views have resulted in the development of a plethora of language-assessment tests, each with an apparently unique method of assessing language. The terminology used to describe the behaviors and skills assessed can be confusing as well. Words like *morphology, semantics, syntax, metalinguistics,* and *supralinguistic functioning*

● ● ● ● **FIGURE 23.1**   *The Four Major Communication Processes*

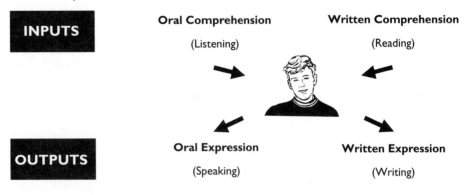

are used, and sometimes different test authors use different terms to mean the same thing. One author's vocabulary subtest is another's measure of "lexical semantics."

We define language as a code for conveying ideas—a code that includes phonology, semantics, morphology, syntax, and pragmatics. This is how we define these terms:

Phonology: The hearing and production of speech sounds. The term *articulation* is considered a synonym for phonology.

Semantics: The study of word meanings. In assessment, this term is generally used to refer to the derivation of meaning from single words. The term *vocabulary* is often used interchangeably with semantics.

Morphology: The use of affixes (prefixes and suffixes) to change the meaning of words used in sentences. Morphology also includes verb tense (John *is* going versus John *was* going).

Syntax: The use of word order to convey meaning. There typically are rules for arranging words into sentences. In language assessment, the word *grammar* is often used to refer to a combination of morphology and syntax.

Pragmatics: The social context in which a sentence occurs. Context influences both the way a message is expressed and the way it is interpreted. For example, the sentence "Can you close the door?" can have different meanings to a student sitting closest to an open door in a classroom and a student undergoing physical therapy to rehabilitate motor skills. According to Carrow-Woolfolk (1995), contexts that influence language comprehension and production include

- Social variables, such as the setting and the age, roles, relationship, and number of participants in a discourse

- Linguistic variables produced by the type of discourse (which might be a conversation, or narrative, lecture, or text)
- The intention, motivation, knowledge, and style of the sender

Supralinguistic: A second order of analysis required to understand the meaning of words or sentences. For example, much language must be interpreted in a nonliteral way (sarcasm, indirect requests, and figurative language). Dad may say that the lawn looks like a hay field when he is actually implying that he wants his child to cut the grass. Mother may say that the weather is "great" when she really means that she is tired of all the cloudy and rainy weather.

Throughout this chapter, we use the term *comprehension* as a synonym for receptive language, and the term *production* as a synonym for expressive language. In Table 23.1 we define each of the basic language components for receptive and expressive modalities.

Why Assess Oral and Written Language?

There are two primary reasons for assessing language abilities. First, well-developed language abilities are desirable in and of themselves. The ability to converse and express thoughts and feelings is a goal of most individuals. Those who have difficulties with various aspects of language are often eligible for special services from speech and language specialists or from special educators. Second, various language processes and skills are believed to underlie subsequent development. Stu-

TABLE 23.1 ● *Language Subskills for Each Channel of Communication*

Language Component	Channel of Communication	
	Reception (Comprehension)	*Expression (Production)*
Phonology	Hearing and discrimination of speech sounds	Articulation of speech sounds
Morphology and syntax	Understanding the grammatical structure of language	Using the grammatical structure of language
Semantics	Understanding vocabulary, meaning, and concepts	Using vocabulary, meaning, and concepts
Pragmatics and supralinguistics	Understanding a speaker's or writer's intentions	Using awareness of social aspects of language
Ultimate language skill	Understanding spoken or written language	Speaking or writing

dents who experience language difficulties have also been shown to experience behavior disorders, learning disabilities, and reading disorders.

Written language and spelling are regularly taught in school, and these areas are singled out for assessment in the Individuals with Disabilities Education Act. Written- and oral-language tests are administered for purposes of screening, instructional planning, entitlement, and progress evaluation.

Considerations in Assessing Oral Language

Those who assess oral language must necessarily give consideration to cultural diversity and the developmental status of those they assess.

Cultural Diversity

Cultural background must be considered in assessing oral-language competence. Although most children in the United States learn English, the form of English they learn depends on where they were born, who their parents are, and so on. For example, in central Pennsylvania, a child might say, "My hands need washed" instead of the standard "My hands need to be washed." In New York City, a child learning Black English might say "birfday" instead of "birthday," or "he be running" instead of "he is running." These and other culturally determined alternative constructions and pronunciations are not incorrect or inferior; they are just different. Indeed, they are appropriate within the child's surrounding community. Children should be viewed as having a language disorder only if they exhibit disordered production of their own primary language or dialect.

Cultural background is particularly important when the language-assessment devices that are currently available are considered. Ideally, a child should be compared with others in the same language community. There should be separate norms for each language community, including standard American English. Unfortunately, the norm samples of most language tests are heterogeneous, and scores on these tests may not be valid indicators of a child's language ability. Consider Plate 25 of the original Peabody Picture Vocabulary Test. This plate contained four pictures, and the examiner said, "Show me the wiener." There are many places in this country where the only word for that item is *hot dog* or *frankfurter*. Yet, because the test was standardized using *wiener*, the examiner was required to use that term. If a child had never heard the word *wiener*, he or she was penalized and received a lower score, even though the error was cultural and not indicative of a semantic or intellectual deficiency. If there are a number of such items on a language test, the child's score can hardly be considered a valid indicator of language ability.

Developmental Considerations

Age is a major consideration in assessment of the child's language. Language acquisition is developmental; some sounds, linguistic structures, and even semantic elements are correctly produced at an earlier age than others. Thus, it is not unusual or indicative of language disorder for a 2-year-old child to say "Kitty house" for "The cat is in the house," although the same phrase would be an indication of a disorder in a 3-year-old. It is important to be aware of developmental norms for language acquisition and to use those norms when making judgments about a child's language competence.

Considerations in Assessing Written Language

There are two major components of written language: content and form. The *content* of written expression is the product of considerable intellectual and linguistic activity: formulating, elaborating, sequencing, and then clarifying and revising ideas; choosing the precise word to convey meaning; and so forth. Moreover, much of what we consider to be content is the result of a creative endeavor. Our ability to use words to excite, to depict vividly, to imply, and to describe complex ideas is far more involved than simply putting symbols on paper.

The *form* of written language is far more mechanistic than its content. For writer and reader to communicate, three sets of conventions or rules are used: penmanship, spelling, and style rules. The most fundamental rules deal with *penmanship,* the formation of individual letters and letter sequences that make up words. While letter formation tends to become more individualistic with age, there are a limited number of ways, for example, that the letter *A* can be written and still be recognized as an *A*. Moreover, there are conventions about the relative spacing of letters between and within words.

Spelling is also rule-governed. Although American English is more irregular phonetically than other languages, it remains largely regular, and students should be able to spell most words by applying a few phonetic rules. For example, we have known since the mid-1960s that about 80 percent of all consonants have a single spelling (Hanna, Hanna, Hodges, & Rudoff, 1966). Short vowels are the major source of difficulty for most writers.

The third set of conventions involves style. Style is a catchall term for rule-governed writing, which includes grammar (such as parts of speech, pronoun use, agreement, and verb voice and mood) and mechanics (such as punctuation, capitalization, abbreviations, and referencing).

The conventions of written language are tested on many standardized achievement tests. Spelling is assessed as part of the current forms of the California Achievement Tests, the Iowa Tests of Basic Skills and Tests of Achievement and Proficiency, the Metropolitan Achievement Tests, the Stanford Achievement Test, the Wide Range Achievement Test, the Peabody Individual Achievement Test, and the Woodcock–Johnson Psychoeducational Battery. However, the spelling words that students are to learn vary considerably from curriculum to curriculum. For examples, Ames (1965) examined seven spelling series and found that they introduce an average of 3,200 words between the second and eighth grades. However, only about 1,300 words were common to all the series; about 1,700 words were taught in only one series. Moreover, those words that are taught in several series varied considerably in their grade placement, sometimes by as many as five grades.

Language *mechanics* (capitalization and punctuation) are also assessed on the current forms of several achievement batteries: the California Achievement Tests, the Iowa Tests of Basic Skills and Tests of Achievement and Proficiency, the Metropolitan Achievement Tests, the Stanford Achievement Test, and the Woodcock–Johnson Psychoeducational Battery. Again, standardized tests are not well suited to measuring achievement in these areas because the grade level at which these skills are taught varies so much from one curriculum to another. To be valid, the measurement of achievement in these areas must be closely tied to the curriculum being taught. For example, pupils may learn in kindergarten, first grade, second grade, or later that a sentence always begins with a capital letter. They may learn that commercial brand names are capitalized in the sixth grade or several grades earlier. Students may be taught in the second or third grade that the apostrophe in "it's" makes the word a contraction of "it is" or may still be studying "it's" in high school. Finally, in assessing word usage, organization, and penmanship, we must take into account the emphasis that individual teachers place on these components of written language and when and how students are taught.

The more usual way to assess written language is to evaluate a student's written work and to develop vocabulary and spelling tests that parallel the curriculum. In this way, teachers can be sure that they are measuring precisely what has been taught. Most teacher's editions of language-arts textbook series contain scope-and-sequence charts that specify fairly clearly the objectives that are taught in each unit. From these charts, teachers can develop appropriate criterion-referenced and curriculum-based assessments.

. . . .

Observing Language Behavior

There has been some disagreement among language professionals about the most valid method of evaluating a child's language performance, especially in the expressive channel of communication. In all, there are three procedures used to gather a sample of a child's language behavior: spontaneous, imitative, and elicited.

Spontaneous Language

One school of thought holds that the only valid measure of a child's language abilities is one that studies the language the child produces spontaneously (for example, see Miller, 1981). Using this approach, the examiner records 50–100 consecutive utterances produced as the child is talking to an adult or playing with toys. With older children, conversations or storytelling tasks are often used. The child's utterances are then analyzed in terms of phonology, semantics, morphology, syntax, and pragmatics in order to provide information about the child's conversational abilities. Because the construct of pragmatics has been developed only recently, there are few standard assessment instruments available to sample this domain. Therefore, spontaneous language sampling procedures are widely used to evaluate pragmatic abilities (see Prutting & Kirshner, 1987). Although analysis of a child's spontaneous language production is not the purpose of any standard oral-language assessment instruments, some interest has been shown in standard assessment of handwriting and spelling skills in an uncontrived, spontaneous situation (for example, the revised Test of Written Language by Hammill and Larsen, 1996).

Imitation

Imitation tasks require a child to repeat directly the word, phrase, or sentence produced by the examiner. It might seem that such tasks bear little relationship to spontaneous performance, but some evidence suggests that such tasks are valid predictors of spontaneous production. In fact, many investigators have demonstrated that children's imitative language is essentially the same in content and structure as their spontaneous language (R. Brown & Bellugi, 1964; Ervin, 1964; Slobin & Welsh, 1973). Evidently, children translate adult sentences into their own language system and then repeat the sentences using their own language rules. A young child might imitate "The boy is running and jumping" as "Boy run and jump." Imitation thus seems to be a valuable tool for providing information about a child's language abilities. We note one caution, however: Features of a child's language systems can be obtained using imitation only if the stimulus sentences are long enough to tax the child's memory, because a child will imitate any sentence perfectly if the *length* of that sentence is within the child's *memory capacity* (Slobin & Welsh, 1973).

The use of imitation does not preclude the need for spontaneous sampling because the examiner also needs information derived from direct observation of conversational skills. Rather, imitation tasks should be used to augment the information obtained from the spontaneous sample, for such tasks can be used to elicit forms that the child did not attempt in the conversations. Standardized imitation tasks are widely used in oral-language assessment instruments (such as the Test of Language Development and the Illinois Test of Psycholinguist Abilities). Assessment devices that use imitation usually contain a number of grammatically loaded words, phrases, or sentences that children are asked to imitate. The examiner records and transcribes the children's responses and then analyzes their phonology, morphology, and syntax. (Semantics and pragmatics are rarely assessed using an imitative mode.) Finally, imitation generally is used only in assessing expressive oral language.

Elicited Language[1]

Using a picture stimulus to elicit language involves no imitation on the part of the child, but the procedure cannot be classified as totally spontaneous. In this type of task, the child is presented with a picture or pictures of objects or action scenes and is asked to do one of the following: (a) point to the correct object (a receptive vocabulary task), (b) point to the action picture that best describes a sentence (receptive language, including vocabulary), (c) name the picture (expressive vocabulary), or (d) describe the picture (expressive language, including vocabulary).

Advantages and Disadvantages of Each Procedure

There are advantages and disadvantages to all three methods of language observation (spontaneous, imitative, and elicited). The use of spontaneous language samples has two major advantages. First, a child's spontaneous language is undoubtedly the best and most natural indicator of everyday language performance. Second, the informality of the procedure often allows the examiner to assess children quite easily, without the difficulties sometimes associated with a formal testing atmosphere.

The disadvantages associated with this procedure relate to the nonstandardized nature of the data collection. Although some aspects of language sampling are stable across a variety of parameters, this procedure shows much wider variability than is seen with other standardized assessments. Additionally, language sampling requires detailed analyses across language domains; such analyses are more time-consuming than administering a standardized instrument. Finally, because the examiner does not directly control the selection of target words and phrases, he or she may have difficulty understanding a young child, or there may be several different interpretations of what a child intended to say. Moreover, the child may have avoided, or may not have had an opportunity to attempt, a particular structure that is of interest to the examiner.

The use of imitation overcomes many of the disadvantages inherent in the spontaneous approach. An imitation task will often assess many different language elements and provide a representative view of a child's language system. Also, because of the structure of the test, the examiner knows at all times what elements of language are being assessed. Thus, even the language abilities of a child with a severe language disorder (especially a severe phonological disorder) can be quantified. Finally, imitation devices can be administered much more quickly than can spontaneous language samples.

Unfortunately, the advantages of the spontaneous approach become the disadvantages of the imitative method. First, a child's auditory memory may have some effect on the results. For example, an echolalic child may score well on an imitative test without demonstrating productive knowledge of the language structures

---

1. Although only stimulus pictures are described in this section, some tests use concrete objects rather than pictures to elicit language responses.

being imitated. Second, a child may repeat part of a sentence exactly because the utterance is too simple or short to place a load on the child's memory. Therefore, accurate production is not necessarily evidence that the child uses the structure spontaneously. However, inaccurate productions often do reflect a child's lack of mastery of the structure. Thus, test givers should draw conclusions only about a child's *errors* from an imitative test. A third disadvantage of imitative tests is that they are often quite boring to the child. Not all children will sit still for the time required to repeat 50–100 sentences without any other stimulation, such as pictures or toys.

The use of pictures to elicit language production is an attempt to overcome the disadvantages of both imitation and spontaneous language. Pictures are easy to administer, are interesting to children, and require minimal administration time. They can be structured to test desired language elements and yet retain some of the impromptu nature of spontaneous language samples because children have to formulate the language on their own. Because there is no time limit, results do not depend on the child's word-retention skills. Despite these advantages, a major disadvantage limits the usefulness of picture stimuli in language assessment: It is difficult to create pictures guaranteed to elicit specific language elements. Even though it is probably easiest to create pictures for object identification, difficulties arise even in this area. Thus, the disadvantage seen in spontaneous sampling is evident with picture stimuli as well—the child may not produce or attempt to produce the desired language structure.

To summarize, all three methods of language observation have advantages and disadvantages. The examiner must decide which elements of language should be tested, which methods of observation are most appropriate for assessing those elements, and which assessment devices satisfy these needs. It should not be surprising that more than one test is often necessary to assess all components of language (phonology, semantics, morphology, syntax, and pragmatics), both receptively and expressively. As noted, standardized instruments should be supplemented with measures of conversational abilities within any oral-language assessment. Additionally, the different language domains are often best assessed by different procedures. For example, picture stimuli are particularly well suited for assessment of phonological abilities because the examiner should know the intended production. Similarly, imitation tasks are often employed to assess morphological abilities, as the child having difficulty with this component will often delete suffixes and prefixes during imitation. Finally, because assessment of pragmatics involves determining the child's conversational use of language, this domain should be assessed with spontaneous production.

Oral-Language Tests

Goldman–Fristoe Test of Articulation (GFTA)

The Goldman–Fristoe Test of Articulation (GFTA; Goldman & Fristoe, 1986) is one of the more popular tools developed to assess phonology. It is an individually administered, norm-referenced device in which most consonant sounds and 11 common consonant blends (*st,* for example) are elicited in differing levels of complexity (word, sentence) and in a variety of word positions (beginning, middle, and end of word). Familiarity with the International Phonetic Alphabet (IPA) and experience in identifying and transcribing disordered speech are useful for administering and scoring the GFTA. Although the device does not specifically measure vowels, the examiner can observe the child's vowel production, because all vowels and diphthongs are used at least once within the stimulus words.

Subtests

The GFTA is divided into three sections.

Sounds-in-Words   In this subtest, 35 pictures of familiar objects are presented to the child, who must either name the picture or answer questions pertaining to it. In all, 44 responses are elicited, including 11 common consonant blends and all single consonant sounds (except *zh*); medial position *h, w, wh,* and *y;* and final position voiced *th* (as in *bathe*).

Sounds-in-Sentences   This subtest is designed to elicit a sample of a child's speech in a more complex, spontaneous context. The examiner reads two stories aloud to the child while presenting four or five pictures illustrating each story. After the story is read, the examiner again presents the pictures to the child, who recounts the story. The story is loaded with the sounds most commonly misarticulated by children, and the examiner appraises the child's speech–sound production in the more complex context of sentences.

Stimulability   After the first two subtests are completed, the examiner returns to the sounds the child has misarticulated and tries to stimulate correct production by means of a three-step procedure explained in the instructions. The purpose of this subtest is to find out how stimulable a child is to intervention. This clinical information then leads to a decision regarding prognosis for and length of intervention.

Unlike some other articulation tests, the GFTA assesses more than one speech sound in many of the test items. This places a greater load on the listening abilities of the examiner, although many individuals using this test seem to have no problem listening for more than one sound in a given word. The stimulus pictures are large and colorful, making the test very motivating for young children. However, older children might find the device too juvenile, especially compared with the black-and-white pictures of a test such as the Arizona Articulation Proficiency Scale (Fudala, 1970).

Scores

Percentile ranks are available for school-age students for the Sounds-in-Words and Stimulability subtests (ages 6-6 through 16-10). Percentile ranks are also available for children between 2 and 6 years of age. These norms are from the 1983 sample used to standardize the Khan–Lewis Phonological Analysis. Pertinent characteristics of the children making up these norms are not described.

Reliability

Percentage of agreement data are presented in the manual for three types of reliability. The stability of a child's correct production of each sound on two subtests (Sounds-in-Words and Sounds-in-Sentences) was assessed with a one-week interval between assessments. Data were collected on 37 children between the ages of 4 and 8 years, who were assessed by eight certified (Certificate of Clinical Competence) clinicians. Only median stabilites for each subtest are presented; neither data for each sound nor ranges of values are reported. For Sounds-in-Words, the median reliability was .95; for Sounds-in-Sentences, it was .94; and for the specific type of error made (such as omission or distortion) on Sounds-in-Words, it was .89.

Intrarater agreement (stability of the rater over time) was assessed by having six judges, described only as having had "at least one semester of experience" using the test, evaluate the tape-recorded responses of four individuals who had articulation problems judged to range from mild to severe. Only medians are presented. For presence or absence of error and for the type of error, the median stability was .91.

Interrater agreement was also assessed for Sounds-in-Words. As with intrarater agreement, six judges, described only as having had "at least one semester of experience" using the test, evaluated the tape-recorded responses of four individuals who had articulation problems judged to range from mild to severe. Again, only medians are presented for percentage of agreement. For presence or absence of error for the sounds, the median was .92; for type of error, the median was .88.

Validity

Only content validity is discussed in the manual. The authors argue that the test is a valid sampling of English consonants and that the productions are representative of the child's use. Although the test items include an adequate sample of consonant speech sounds, there are no objective measures of validity reported. This lack of validity data is a weakness in the instrument.

Summary

The GFTA is an individually administered norm-referenced device that has supplemental norms. The norms are more than 20 years old for all ages except the 2- to 6-year-olds. Reliability data are inadequately reported but do appear adequate for at least half of the sample. Validity data are lacking.

Comprehensive Receptive and Expressive Vocabulary Test (CREVT)

The Comprehensive Receptive and Expressive Vocabulary Test (CREVT; Wallace & Hammill, 1994) is a norm-referenced instrument designed to assess receptive and expressive vocabulary in children aged 4-0 through 17-11 (5-0 through 17-11 for expressive vocabulary). It combines receptive and expressive vocabulary assessment into one instrument; these two communication channels have traditionally been assessed using two instruments, such as the Peabody Picture Vocabulary Test–Revised and the Expressive One-Word Picture Vocabulary Test–Revised (EOWPVT-R). High-quality photographs are included in the stimulus materials. Two forms of the test (A and B) are available.

Receptive Vocabulary   In this 6-item subtest, the child points to one of six pictures in response to the verbal presentation of words by the examiner. Unlike the PPVT-R or the Test of Auditory Comprehension of Language–Revised (TACL-R), which require one response per page (plate), CREVT requires four to seven responses on each plate. Therefore, the 61 items are represented on ten plates (pages).

Expressive Vocabulary   This 25-item subtest uses a format similar to that of the Test of Language Development 2, Primary (TOLD-P2). The child is required to tell the examiner "what a word means" in response to a verbal presentation of the word.

Scores

The CREVT yields standard scores with a mean of 100 and a standard deviation of 15 for each subtest. A composite score (general vocabulary) is generated by combining the two subtests and yields a transformed standard score with identical parameters (mean = 100, standard deviation = 15).

Norms

Normative data are provided for receptive vocabulary at six-month intervals for each year from 4-0 to 12-11 and at one-year intervals from 13-0 through 17-11; for expressive vocabulary, data are given at six-month intervals from 5-0 through 10-11 and at one-year intervals from 11-0 through 17-11.

Reliability

Coefficient alpha was computed for forms A and B for each level for each subtest and for the composite. In contrast with the standard scores, coefficients are reported at one-year intervals for all age levels. Also unlike the standard scores, a coefficient for 4-0 is provided for expressive vocabulary. This yields a total of 84 alpha coefficients (14 age groups with two forms across two subtests and one composite). All are above .80, with 60 above .90 (24 between .80 and .90). Composites (general vocabulary) at all age levels are above .90. Also,

alpha coefficients are presented for children with learning disabilities, speech–language disabilities, and mental retardation. Although many of these were pooled across age levels, so that it is difficult to determine what proportion of subjects was at each age level, these coefficients are routinely high (ranging from .83 to .98). Alternate-forms reliability was assessed by computing correlations at each age level for test forms A and B in the entire normative sample. The results of this analysis indicate that r_{AB} ranged from .84 (age 6) to .97 (age 17) with a mean of .92 for Receptive Vocabulary, and r_{AB} ranged from .74 (age 6) to .96 (age 16 and 17) with a mean of .90 for Expressive Vocabulary.

Test–retest reliability was assessed by readministering the instrument to 27 kindergartners after two months and to 28 twelfth-graders after two weeks. Both groups were selected from the Austin, Texas, area. Coefficients are reported for each group for both forms (A and B) of the expressive and receptive subtests and for the composite (general vocabulary) scores. These correlations ranged from .79 to .87 for the kindergartners and from .79 to .94 for the twelfth-graders. Although this test–retest reliability is lower than the alpha coefficients, which is somewhat surprising given the likelihood of both samples being derived from presumably homogeneous populations, all reliability coefficients are within acceptable ranges.

Validity

The manual includes sections on content, concurrent, and construct validity. Content validity was evaluated qualitatively by simply reporting the rationale for selecting the test format and the procedures for selecting the pool of items that ultimately were included in the test.

Concurrent validity was evaluated by correlating the scores on the CREVT with the PPVT-R, the EOWPVT-R, the Clinical Evaluation of Language Function–Revised (CELF-R), and the TOLD-P2. Although the authors indicate that these correlations are based on a subset of children in the normative sample who were also assessed using one or more of these other instruments, it is not clear what the sample size or selection criteria were for these data. Therefore, it is difficult to interpret the correlation coefficients presented in the manual.

Although a number of the correlation coefficients would suggest a high degree of concurrent validity, a number of them are surprisingly low. For example, the correlation between the CREVT Expressive Vocabulary subtest and the EOWPVT-R is .36 for form A and .44 for form B. Although, arguably, the different formats (one-word responses for the EOWPVT-R, multiword descriptions for the CREVT) might result in a lower correlation, this distinction appears to be a relatively minor difference in response format, as compared with tests showing higher correlation (for example, the TOLD-P2 syntax composite has correlations of .75 and .76 for forms A and B, respectively). Similarly, we had expected very high correlations between the PPVT-R and the Receptive Vocabulary subtest of the CREVT because these tests are sampling identical domains (receptive vocabulary). Instead, however, these correlations were only in the acceptable range (.76 and .72 for forms A and B of the CREVT). Thus, we need additional information, including sampling procedures, correlations with relevant subtests, and a more detailed explanation of the observed coefficients (particularly for the EOWPVT-R), before we can be assured that the CREVT displays adequate concurrent validity.

Evidence of construct validity is also included in the manual. Four basic constructs underlying the CREVT are presented and evaluated: (1) The test is constructed to be developmentally ordered. (2) Expressive and receptive vocabulary should be highly related to each other. (3) The CREVT is designed to differentiate normal children and adolescents from those with deficiencies in vocabulary skills. (4) Each item within a subtest should relate to the overall score for that subtest. Although, arguably, a larger language construct might be included because vocabulary is an essential building block for overall language competence, these four constructs are reasonable.

The evidence for construct validity addresses each of the four constructs: (1) presentation of correlational relationships between chronological age and CREVT scores; (2) intercorrelations between the subtests (Receptive and Expressive); (3) comparison to the normative sample for mean performance on the CREVT for three groups of children with disabilities (32 with mental retardation, 33 with speech and language problems, and 37 with learning disabilities); and (4) reference to item-analysis data. With the exception of the data on group differentiation, this evidence of construct validity appears to be adequate. In addition to the group means, information about the percentage of students who actually fell below the normal range on the CREVT would be helpful to researchers and practitioners. Speech pathologists, special educators, and psychometricians often identify children as qualifying for services if their score on one or more standardized instruments falls below a cutoff score. Given the relatively high means evident on the CREVT for the children with speech and language disabilities and with learning disabilities, it is not clear that this instrument would, in practice, be useful in distinguishing these groups from the normal population. Presentation of individual scores, or at least median and range values, would be useful.

Summary

The CREVT is an individually administered receptive and expressive vocabulary test. A primary strength of the instrument is that expressive and receptive vocabulary can be assessed in a relatively short time across a wide age range of children and adolescents. Psychometric data on reliability and validity are provided. Weaknesses include a lack of information on key psychometric parameters and a potential lack of sensitivity due to the relatively low number of items on the instrument (particularly on the Expressive subtest). Despite these weaknesses, the CREVT appears to be potentially useful as a quickly administered vocabulary screening instrument, to be followed up with more detailed vocabulary assessment, as needed.

Test of Adolescent Language–3 (TOAL-3)

The third revision of the Test of Adolescent Language: A Multidimensional Approach to Assessment (TOAL-3; Hammill, Brown, Larsen, & Wiederholt, 1994) is a norm-referenced device designed for adolescents between the ages of 12 and 25. It is intended to identify areas of relative strength and weakness, document academic progress, and identify those who might profit from programs of language intervention. Six of the subtests may be administered to groups; two (Speaking/Vocabulary and Speaking/Grammar) must be administered individually. The TOAL-3 was designed to assess receptive and expressive spoken and written vocabulary (semantics) and grammar (morphology and syntax).

Subtests

The TOAL-3 has the following eight subtests:

Listening/Vocabulary   In this 35-item picture-vocabulary subtest, the adolescent must select two pictures that relate to the stimulus word read by the examiner. Credit for an item is awarded only if both correct items are selected.

Listening/Grammar   Each of the 35 items in this subtest contains three sentences that are read aloud to the adolescent, who must select the two sentences that have the same meaning.

Speaking/Vocabulary   In this subtest, the examiner reads a stimulus word, and the adolescent must say a meaningful sentence that includes appropriate use of the target word. The subtest contains 25 stimulus words.

Speaking/Grammar   In this 30-item subtest, the examiner reads a sentence to the adolescent, who must then repeat it.

Reading/Vocabulary   The adolescent is presented with up to 30 items in this subtest. Each item has three stimulus words and a multiple-choice array containing four additional words. The adolescent must select from the array two words that go with the stimulus words.

Reading/Grammar   The adolescent is presented with up to 25 items, each of which contains five sentences. He or she must read all five sentences and then find the two that mean "almost the same thing."

Writing/Vocabulary   The adolescent is required to read a stimulus word and to write a meaningful sentence using that word. The stimulus word must be used correctly in the exact form in which it is given. The subtest contains 30 items.

Writing/Grammar   Each of the 30 items in this subtest contains two to six sentences of varying complexity. The adolescent is instructed to combine the sentences into one. The simple sentences prompt grammatically more complex constructions. This subtest is analogous to the Sentence Combining subtest of the Test of Language Development, Intermediate 3 (TOLD-I3), but requires written rather than verbal responses.

Scores

Several types of scores are available. The eight subtest scores can be transformed into standard scores (mean = 10, standard deviation = 3). Standard scores (mean = 100, standard deviation = 15) are also available for each of the following 11 composite scores:

1. Listening (Listening/Vocabulary and Listening/Grammar)

2. Speaking (Speaking/Vocabulary and Speaking/Grammar)

3. Reading (Reading/Vocabulary and Reading/Grammar)

4. Writing (Writing/Vocabulary and Writing/Grammar)

5. Spoken language (Listening/Vocabulary, Listening/Grammar, Speaking/Vocabulary, and Speaking/Grammar)

6. Written language (Reading/Vocabulary, Reading/Grammar, Writing/Vocabulary, and Writing/Grammar)

7. Vocabulary (Listening/Vocabulary, Speaking/Vocabulary, Reading/Vocabulary, and Writing/Vocabulary)

8. Grammar (Listening/Grammar, Speaking/Grammar, Reading/Grammar, and Writing/Grammar)

9. Receptive Language (Listening/Vocabulary, Listening/Grammar, Reading/Vocabulary, and Reading/Grammar)

10. Expressive language (Speaking/Vocabulary, Speaking/Grammar, Writing/Vocabulary, and Writing/Grammar)

11. General language

Norms

The TOAL-3 was normed on a total of 3,056 adolescents between 12 and 25 years of age, selected from 26 states. Of this total, 1,512 were from the original TOAL sample, 957 were added for the TOAL-2, and 587 were added for the TOAL-3. All the subjects in the TOAL-3 group were from 18-0 to 24-11 years old and were added to extend the TOAL-3 norms upward from the 18-year level on the TOAL-2. Because each version of the TOAL has included some modifications (for example, the TOAL-3 includes extensive modifications of the Writing/Grammar subtest), combining norms from three different versions may not be appropriate.

The manual includes sample characteristics of the normative group, but these data are reported for two-year intervals, and so the information is not consistent with the scoring norms, and it is impossible to determine whether adequate sample sizes were included in the scoring norms. For example, a total of 319 thirteen-year-olds were included in the normative sample, but the authors do not indicate how many were in the 13-0 to 13-6 and 13-7 to 13-11 age ranges that are included in the scoring norms. Tables in the TOAL-3 manual show that the normative sample corresponds closely to the overall population of adolescents at the time of the 1990 census. There is no more than a 3 percent difference between the TOAL-3 sample and the population with respect to sex, residence (urban/rural), race, ethnicity, and geographic region (four U.S. regions).

Reliability

Three types of reliability data are presented. First, coefficient alpha was computed for each subtest, each composite, and the total score for each age group. Again, these data are not presented for the age groups for the reported standard scores; rather, data are given for ages 12, 13, 14, 15, 16, 17/18, 19/20, 21/22, and 23/24 for each subtest. Of the 72 age-by-subtest coefficients (9 age groups × 8 subtests), 22 are less than .90, but none is lower than .80. All 99 of the composite-by-age coefficients (9 age groups × 11 composites) exceed .90.

Second, two stability coefficients were computed. The first was on 52 adolescents attending different grades in a parochial school in Kansas City, Missouri. These adolescents took TOAL, not the revised version (TOAL-3), and 19 of the subjects were below the normative age range. In this sample, coefficients for three subtests (Listening/Vocabulary, Listening/Grammar, and Speaking/Grammar) were greater than .70 but less than .80. On four subtests (Speaking/Vocabulary, Reading/Vocabulary, Reading/Grammar, and Writing/Grammar), coefficients were greater than .80 but less than .90. On one (Writing/Vocabulary), the coefficient was .90. The listening and speaking composites were greater than .80 but less than .90, whereas the remaining composites exceeded .90.

The second measure of stability was completed on 59 college students from Austin, Texas, who were retested following a two-week interval. These college students ranged in age from 19 to 24 years. The results indicated that stability coefficients for two subtests (Reading/Grammar and Writing/Grammar) were greater than .70 but less than .80, and those for the remaining subtests fell between .80 and .90. The Listening, Speaking, Reading, and Writing composites all fell between .80 and .90, and the remaining composites were greater than .90.

Finally, reliability data are presented on interscorer agreement of six raters on the three subtests that use subjective scoring. For Writing/Vocabulary, the correlations between raters ranged from .70 to .95; for Speaking/Vocabulary, correlations ranged from .86 to .99; and for Writing/Grammar, they ranged from .91 to .99. Calculations of the percentage of interscorer agreement, based on the same data, yielded different results. Only the Speaking/Vocabulary subtest attained a minimum of 90 percent agreement among all raters. Because several items presented difficulties in scoring, the authors revised the criteria for scoring those items. Unfortunately, the revised scoring criteria were not empirically tested, and the revised items were not identified. Also, these data appear to have been gathered on an earlier version of the TOAL.

Validity

The authors provide a discussion of the selection of formats for subtests. Content validity is discussed in terms of the procedures and theoretical rationale for test construction. No empirical studies of content validity are presented. It would be useful to see the results of survey data from professionals, as were presented for the related tests in the series (TOLD-P2 and TOLD-I2).

Evidence of criterion-related validity for the first edition of the test is presented. Moderate correlations are reported between TOAL and the PPVT, a subtest of the DTLA, the reading and language totals from the CTBS, the total score from the Test of Written Language, and the Test of Language Competence. Because the TOAL, TOAL-2, and TOAL-3 are very highly correlated, the authors assume that these correlations are for TOAL-3 as well as for TOAL and TOAL-2. Additionally, the authors note that the TOAL correlated with intelligence and that students previously identified as mentally retarded or learning disabled attained lower scores. No data are provided to indicate that the TOAL-3 is sufficiently sensitive to monitor a student's progress, and no data are provided to demonstrate that the TOAL-3 identifies students who might profit from programs of language intervention (predictive validity.)

Summary

TOAL-3 is a norm-referenced device that assesses three aspects of language (semantics, morphology, and syntax) via both the receptive and the expressive channels. Expressive and receptive skills are sampled using both oral and written modes of communication. The composite scores have good internal consistency, and the reported stability and interscorer reliability are adequate, although it is difficult to interpret these data because different versions of the test are pooled in the normative sample, and the standard score groups are not consistent with normative sample information. Evidence of criterion-related validity is presented, as well. Despite the limitations noted, the TOAL-3 appears to be a useful instrument and is widely used.

Test of Auditory Comprehension of Language–Revised (TACL-R)

The Test of Auditory Comprehension of Language–Revised (TACL-R; Carrow-Woolfolk, 1985) is an individually administered, norm-referenced test designed to assess the language comprehension of children between the ages of 3 years, 0 months, and 9 years, 11 months. TACL-R consists of 120 test items in which a child selects, from a set of three pictures, the one picture that best represents a word or sentence read to the child by the examiner. An oral response is not required. Basal and ceiling criteria speed the administration of the test.

Test items are arranged in three categories. Category I assesses the literal meaning of various words and basic word relations (for example, "riding a little bicycle"). Category II assesses grammatical morphemes (for example, past tense, noun and verb agreement). Category III assesses the ability to derive meaning from spoken sentences (for example, active and passive voices, direct and indirect objects). The author states that TACL-R scores are useful for identifying children with language problems, for measuring school readiness, for program planning, and for program monitoring.

Scores

Various tables are provided in the examiner's manual (Carrow-Woolfolk, 1985) for converting raw scores to percentile ranks and age equivalents. A student's performances are compared with those of the most appropriate of ten age groups: 6 six-month norm groups (from age 3-0 to 5-11) and 4 one-year norm groups (from age 6-0 to 9-11). In addition, a table is presented for converting percentile ranks to z-scores, T-scores, deviation quotients (mean = 100, standard deviation = 15), and normal-curve equivalents. This table is based on the assumption that the raw scores are normally distributed. However, no data are presented to indicate whether this assumption is valid.

Norms

A stratified sample of 1,003 children was selected to correspond to the population at the time of the 1980 U.S. census. Stratification variables within each age group included family occupation, ethnic/racial background, sex, and geographical factors

(such as region of the United States and community size). The obtained sample was differentially weighted (for instance, some children were counted as more than one child) in order to adjust the norm characteristics so that they would correspond exactly to the census data.

Reliability

Forty split-half estimates of internal consistency (corrected by the Spearman–Brown formula) were computed (ten age groups on three category scores and a total score). For Category I, coefficients ranged from .73 to .95, with half of the coefficients equaling or exceeding .90. Category II coefficients ranged from .82 to .95; four of the ten coefficients were less than .90. For Category III, the coefficients ranged from .86 to .96, with only two coefficients less than .90. As expected, the reliability of the total score was higher; except for one age group—8-0 to 8-11—all coefficients exceeded .91. The reliability for this age group was consistently low. Stability coefficients for the four scores equaled or exceeded .90, except for Category III ($r_{xx} = .89$).

Validity

Evidence is presented for the content validity of TACL-R. A wide variety of language elements are assessed. The author also presents evidence for construct validity by demonstrating that the TACL-R is correlated with age and hence is developmental. Also, performances of the children in the normative sample corresponded to the expected progression of subtest difficulty (Category I was easier than Category II, which in turn was easier than Category III). The performances of the children in the norm sample also were better than the performances of children with language disorders. The results of several studies are presented to establish the criterion-related validity of the TACL-R. However, the data in these studies are difficult to interpret.

Finally, no data are presented to demonstrate that TACL-R scores are useful for identifying children with language problems, for determining school readiness, for planning educational or therapeutic programs, or for monitoring the therapeutic program of an individual student.

Summary

TACL-R is an individually administered device intended to assess receptive morphological, syntactic, and semantic abilities of children between 3 and 12 years of age. Reliability data for total scores are high, but category-score reliability is variable. Some evidence of validity is presented. The total score appears to be the most reliable and valid indicator of comprehension ability.

Test of Language Development, Primary: Third Edition (TOLD-P:3)

The Test of Language Development, Primary: third edition (TOLD-P:3; Newcomer & Hammill, 1999) is a norm-referenced, individually administered test intended to (1) measure children's expressive and receptive competencies in the major components of linguistics, (2) identify children with language problems, (3) provide examiners with a comparative index of children's language strengths and weaknesses, and (4) measure progress in language development. TOLD-P:3 is designed for use with children aged 4-0 through 8-11. The test contains assessments of semantics (vocabulary), syntax (grammar), and phonology. These competencies are assessed through measures of receptive, expressive, and integrating (mediating) skills. The two-dimensional model used to generate the TOLD-P:3 subtests is shown in Table 23.2.

Subtests

Nine specific subtests make up the TOLD-P:3. Six subtests are considered core or primary in that their results are combined to form composite scores. These are measures of semantics and syntax. The three phonology subtests are considered supplementary and optional. The authors argue that this was done to provide a clear separation of language (semantics and syntax) and speech (phonology). The nine subtests are described as follows.

Picture Vocabulary   This 30-item subtest requires a child to point to the one picture in a group of four that best represents the stimulus word spoken by the examiner.

Relational Vocabulary   This 30-item subtest requires the child to identify similarities or differences between items or objects whose names are spoken by the examiner. No pictures or other supports are provided.

Oral Vocabulary   This 28-item subtest requires the child to define words that are spoken by the examiner. No pictures or other stimulus supports are provided.

Grammatic Understanding   This 25-item subtest requires a child to select from a group of three pictures the one that best represents a sentence spoken by the examiner. The task requires no verbalization.

Sentence Imitation   This 30-item subtest requires a child to repeat, verbatim, sentences that vary in length from 5 to 12 words and that vary considerably in grammatical form.

Grammatic Completion   This 28-item subtest uses a cloze prompting procedure and requires the

TABLE 23.2 ● *The Two-dimensional Theoretical Model Used to Develop TOLD-P:3*

Linguistic Feature	Linguistic System		
	Listening (Receptive Skills)	Organizing (Integrating–Mediating Skills)	Speaking (Expressive Skills)
Semantics	Picture Vocabulary	Relational Vocabulary	Oral Vocabulary
Syntax	Grammatic Understanding	Sentence Imitation	Grammatic Completion
Phonology	Word Discrimination	Phonemic Analysis	Word Articulation

SOURCE: From Hammill, D., & Newcomer, P., *Test of Language Development-Primary* (Third Edition), Austin, TX: Pro-Ed. Reprinted by permission.

child to complete sentences by supplying appropriate plurals, possessives, tenses, comparative and superlative adjective forms, and so forth.

Word Discrimination   This 20-item subtest requires a child to say whether two words read by the examiner are the same or different. The words differ from each other only in the beginning, middle, or ending phoneme. Six "foil" items with identical words are included to ensure that the child is not simply responding "different" to all items.

Phonemic Analysis   This 14-item subtest is an assessment of the child's skill in breaking words into smaller phonemic units. The child is given specific commands to follow. For example, the examiner says, "Say *government*. Now say it again, but don't say *ment.*"

Word Articulation   This 20-item subtest uses pictures of familiar things to prompt speech. Phonemic transcriptions of the child's production of the words are completed, and speech errors are noted.

Scores

Subtest raw scores can be transformed into language ages (based on mean performances), percentiles, and standard scores (mean = 10, standard deviation = 3). Each of the subtests of the TOLD-P:3 is made up of a linguistic system (listening, organizing, or speaking) and a linguistic feature

(semantics, syntax, or phonology). The subtests can be combined into the following six composites:

1. Listening (Picture Vocabulary and Grammatic Understanding)

2. Organizing (Relational Vocabulary and Sentence Imitation)

3. Speaking (Oral Vocabulary and Grammatic Completion)

4. Semantics (Picture Vocabulary, Relational Vocabulary, and Oral Vocabulary)

5. Syntax (Grammatic Understanding, Sentence Imitation, and Grammatic Completion)

6. Spoken Language (Picture Vocabulary, Relational Vocabulary, Oral Vocabulary, Grammatic Understanding, Sentence Imitation, and Grammatic Completion)

Norms

The TOLD-P:3 was standardized on a sample of 1,000 students in 28 states. This complete renorming of the test is a significant advance over earlier versions, in which a small number of students were added for the new edition rather than restandardizing. The norm sample was chosen on the basis of geographic region, gender, race, residence (rural/urban/suburban), ethnicity, family income, educational attainment of parents, and disabling condition. Tables in the manual show the relationship between sample makeup and the makeup of the 1997 census population. There is good correspondence.

Reliability

Internal-consistency reliability was calculated for both the students in the standardization sample and subgroups (e.g., boys, students who live in the Northeast). All coefficients exceeded .80. Test-retest reliability was investigated by twice testing 33 students in an elementary school in Austin, Texas, over a 4-month interval. Although all but one coefficient exceeded .80, this study is very limited in both sample size and representativeness. Interscorer reliability was studied by having two people in the publisher's research department score the test. Their scoring correlated .99. Evidence for reliability is good, but very limited.

Validity

The authors provide extensive evidence on the content validity of the TOLD-P:3. They show how the procedures they used in selecting test items represent time-honored approaches to assessment of language abilities, and they describe in detail the approaches they used to select items for each subtest. The argument is convincing. They also used classical item-analysis procedures to demonstrate the item characteristics of the final version of the test. The resulting item-discrimination coefficients and item difficulties are reported and provide evidence of content validity.

Correlations of the performance of 30 children from an Austin, Texas, elementary school on the TOLD-P:3 and the Bankson Language Test–Second Edition (Bankson, 1990) are reported. The correlations are significant and as expected. The sample is very small and nonrepresentative.

Several indices of construct validity are described and discussed. The authors show that performance on the test is correlated with age, that it differentiates between people known to be average and those known to be below average in linguistic ability, that subtests correlate with one another, that test performance is like that expected based on the way in which the test was developed, and that item performance is correlated with total score. There is good evidence for the construct validity of the test.

Summary

TOLD-P:3 is an individually administered, norm-referenced test designed to assess expressive, mediating, and receptive semantics, syntax, and phonology. This third edition of the test was completely renormed, and the norms appear representative of the U.S. population of schoolage children. Evidence for reliability is limited to data on the internal consistency of the test. There is good evidence for content and construct validity, while evidence for concurrent validity is very limited. The test seems most appropriate for identification of students experiencing language difficulty and for intervention planning. The item sample is too limited for the test to be used for either program planning or accountability purposes.

Test of Language Development–Intermediate:3 (TOLD-I:3)

The Test of Language Development–Intermediate:3 (TOLD-I:3; Hammill & Newcomer, 1999) is the third edition of this test, originally published in 1977. TOLD-I:3 is a norm-referenced, individually administered measure designed for use with children between the ages of 8-6 and 12-11. The test is designed to be used in the same ways as TOLD-P:3: to (1) measure children's expressive and receptive competencies in the major components of linguistics, (2) identify children with language problems, (3) provide examiners with a comparative index of children's language strengths and weaknesses, and (4) measure progress in language development.

A specific theoretical framework was used to develop TOLD-I:3. The framework is illustrated in Table 23.3. The test includes semantic and syntactic measures of both speaking and listening.

Subtests

The six subtests of TOLD-I:3 are described as follows.

Sentence Combining In this 25-item subtest, a child must combine two or more simple sentences into a compound or complex sentence that incorporates all the essential information from the original simple sentences.

Picture Vocabulary The child is required to make judgments about words presented by the examiner. The examiner says a series of two-word phrases (for example, *telephone user*) and the child must identify which of six pictures best represents the stimulus phrase.

Word Ordering In this 23-item subtest of syntactic ability, a sentence in which the words have been scrambled is presented orally. The child must reorder the words to make a correct English sentence (for example, *party, fun, was, the*).

Generals In this 24-item test, the child must identify the way in which three words read by the examiner are alike. For example, the examiner reads *trout, perch, and bass,* and the child is expected to identify them as *types of fish.*

Grammatic Comprehension In this 38-item subtest, the child must state whether a sentence presented orally is grammatically correct. The incorrect sentences contain errors in noun–verb agreement, pronouns, comparative and superlative adjectives, negatives, plurals, and adverbs.

Malapropisms The child is required to identify an incorrect word in each of the 30 sentences on this subtest and to supply the correct form. For example, the child is required to tell the examiner that the word *photograph* should have been used in the sentence "John took a phonograph of his family." The examiner reads the sentences.

Scores

Subtest raw scores can be transformed into percentiles and standard scores (mean = 10, standard deviation = 3). Subtests can be combined into five composites as follows:

1. Syntax (Grammatic Comprehension, Sentence Combining, and Word Ordering)

TABLE 23.3 ● The Two-dimensional Theoretical Model Used to Develop TOLD-I:3

	Linguistic System	
Linguistic Feature	*Listening (Receptive Skills)*	*Speaking (Expressive Skills)*
Semantics	Picture Vocabulary Malapropisms	Generals
Syntax	Grammatic Comprehension	Sentence Combining Word Ordering

SOURCE: From Hammill, D., & Newcomer, P., *Test of Language Development-Primary* (Third Edition), Austin, TX: Pro-Ed. Reprinted by permission.

2. Semantics (Vocabulary, Generals, and Mala-propisms)

3. Speaking (Sentence Combining, Word Ordering, and Generals)

4. Listening (Vocabulary, Grammatic Comprehension, and Malapropisms)

5. Spoken Language (all subtests)

Composites are appropriately obtained by adding the subtest scaled scores and converting this sum to a scaled score with a mean of 100 and a standard deviation of 15.

Norms

TOLD-I:3 was normed on 779 students in 23 states. This complete renorming of the test is a significant advance over earlier versions, in which a small number of students were added for the new edition rather than restandardizing. The norm sample was chosen on the basis of geographic region, gender, race, residence (rural/urban/suburban), ethnicity, family income, educational attainment of parents, and disabling condition. Tables in the manual show the relationship between sample makeup and the makeup of the 1997 census population. There is good correspondence.

Reliability

Internal-consistency reliability was calculated for both the students in the standardization sample and subgroups (e.g., boys, students who live in the Northeast). All coefficients exceeded .84. Test–retest reliability was investigated by twice testing 55 students in an elementary school in Austin, Texas, over a 4-month interval. Although all coefficients exceeded .80, and coefficients for the composites exceeded .90, this study is very limited in both sample size and representativeness. Interscorer reliability was studied by having two people in the publisher's research department score the test. Their scoring correlated .94. Evidence for reliability is good, but very limited.

Validity

Concurrent validity of the TOLD-I:3 was established by correlating the test performance of 26 elementary school students from Austin, Texas, with their performance on the Test of Adolescent and Adult Language (TOAL-3). Correlations among subtests that measure similar skills were significant. The sample is limited in size and representativeness. Several indices of construct validity are described and discussed. The authors show that performance on the test is correlated with age, that it differentiates between people known to be average and those known to be below average in linguistic ability, that subtests correlate with one another, that test performance is like that expected based on the way in which the test was developed, and that item performance is correlated with total score. There is good evidence for the construct validity of the test.

Summary

TOLD-I:3 is an individually administered, norm-referenced test designed to assess expressive and receptive semantics and syntax. This third edition of the test was completely renormed, and the norms appear to be representative of the U.S. population of schoolage children. Evidence for reliability is limited to data on the internal consistency of the test. There is good evidence for content and construct validity, while evidence for concurrent validity is very limited. The TOLD-I:3, like the TOLD-P:3 and the TOAL-3, meets a higher number of psychometric criteria than many tests designed to evaluate oral language. The test seems most appropriate for identification of students experiencing language difficulty and for intervention planning. The item sample is too limited for the test to be used for either program planning or accountability purposes.

Expressive One-Word Picture Vocabulary Test–Revised (EOWPVT-R)

The Expressive One-Word Picture Vocabulary Test–Revised (EOWPVT-R; Gardner, 1990) is one of the few formal expressive vocabulary tests that has a standardized form for Spanish, in addition to one for English. It provides a standard estimate of a child's spoken vocabulary in a relatively quick assessment and norm-referenced information that is particularly useful for identifying strengths and weaknesses within this construct.

The EOWPVT-R is an individually administered device consisting of 100 test pictures. The stimulus items are developmentally ordered to allow establishment of basal and ceiling levels so that the entire set of test pictures need not be administered. To administer the test, the examiner presents a stimulus picture and asks the child to name that item. Ideally, the child's responses should be taped, so that there can be two levels of analysis: one immediate and one after listening to the tape. This two-step method is advised when the examiner wishes to perform secondary phonological analysis on the named pictures (as suggested by Gardner).

The test itself takes about 20 to 30 minutes to administer, depending on the child's attention span and level of cooperation. Scoring is relatively quick and straightforward, particularly for users who are already familiar with the Peabody Picture Vocabulary Test–III (Dunn & Dunn, 1997), which uses a similar format.

Scores

The number of correctly named pictures is used as a raw score. This raw score is then transformed to a standard score (mean = 100, standard deviation = 15) or a scaled score (mean = 10, standard deviation = 3) appropriate for the child's age level. These can then be converted to stanines or percentile ranks, if desired. A table for converting the raw scores to age equivalencies is also provided.

Norms

The EOWPVT-R was standardized on a restricted group of 1,118 children ages 2-0 through 11-11, residing in the San Francisco Bay area. Approximately equal proportions of males and females were included in the sample at each age level. More than 100 children were included in the normative sample from age 4 through age 11 years, but only 53 children were included at 2 years, and only 77 were included at 3 years. No information was provided regarding the ethnic background of the standardization sample, nor were data on socioeconomic status provided. It is presumed that the standardization sample included only English-speaking children; no standardization data are provided for administration of the instrument in Spanish. It appears that applying the EOWPVT-R to Spanish-speaking individuals requires use of the norms for English speakers, which limits the usefulness of the norms in this group.

Reliability

Split-half reliability was computed for each age level in the standardization sample, and reliability coefficients were generated using the Kuder–Richardsen formula (KR-20). These range from .84 at age 2 to .92 at age 9, with a median reliability coefficient of .90. The manual also includes conversion of reliability to standard error of measurement (SEM) at each age interval for standard scores and for scaled scores. No other reliability data were reported.

Validity

Evidence of concurrent validity is presented in the technical manual. The EOWPVT-R was compared with the various subtests of the WPPSI-R, Vocabulary and Similarities subtests of the WISC-

R, Word Opposites subtest of the DTLA-2, various subtests of the Test of Auditory–Perceptual Skills, and the Reading subtest of the Test of Academic Achievement Skills. These comparisons generally yielded low to moderate correlations (ranging from .19 to .59). In addition, note that the concurrent validity was completed on a restricted age range of the EOWPVT-R because the comparison tests did not uniformly overlap with regard to applicability across age ranges. This is particularly noteworthy for the lower age ranges of the EOWPVT-R, because no concurrent validity was completed for the 2- and 3-year levels.

No additional information on construct or criterion-related validity was provided.

Summary

The EOWPVT-R is an individually administered device designed to measure the expressive vocabulary of children between 2 and 11 years of age. This instrument is useful in providing specific data from the expressive semantics language domain. Reliability and validity data are provided for application to English-speaking 4- to 11-year-olds. Interpretations of results from 2- and 3-year-olds and from Spanish-speaking children should be made with caution because of limited normative and validity data. Norms for the test are representative only of children in San Francisco.

Written-Language Tests

Test of Written Language–3 (TOWL-3)

The Test of Written Language–3 (TOWL-3; Hammill & Larsen, 1996) is a norm-referenced device designed to assess written-language competence of students between the ages of 7-0 and 17-11. Although the TOWL-3 was designed to be individually administered, the authors provide a series of modifications to al low group administration, with minimal follow-up testing of individual students to assure valid testing. The recommended uses of TOWL-3 include identifying students who have sufficient difficulty in writing to warrant special help, determining strengths and weaknesses of individual students, evaluating student progress, and conducting research. Two alternative forms (A and B) are available.

TOWL-3 uses two writing formats (contrived and spontaneous) to evaluate written language. In a contrived format, students' linguistic options are purposely constrained to force the students to use specific words or conventions. TOWL-3 uses these two formats to assess three components of written language (conventional, linguistic, and cognitive). The *conventional component* deals with using the rules of Standard American English in spelling, capitalization, and punctuation. The *linguistic component* deals with syntactic and semantic structures, and the *cognitive component* deals with producing "logical, coherent, and sequenced written products" (Hammill & Larsen, 1996, p. 3)

Subtests

The first five subtests, eliciting writing in contrived contexts, are briefly described here.

Vocabulary This area is assessed by having a student write correct sentences containing stimulus words.

Spelling The TOWL-3 assesses spelling by having a student write sentences from dictation.

Style Competence in this aspect of writing is assessed by evaluating the punctuation in sentences written from dictation.

Logical Sentences Competence in this area is assessed by having students rewrite illogical sentences so that they make sense.

Sentence Combining TOWL-3 requires students to write one grammatically correct sentence based on the information in several short sentences presented visually.

The last three subtests elicit more spontaneous, contextual writing by the student, in response to one of two pictures used as a story starter. After the story has been written (and the other five subtests administered), the story is scored on three dimensions. Each dimension is treated as a subtest. Following are brief descriptions of these subtests.

Contextual Conventions A student's ability to use mechanical conventions (such as punctuation and spelling) in context is assessed using the student's story.

Contextual Language A student's ability to construct grammatically correct sentences and appropriate vocabulary is assessed from the student's story.

Story Construction As described by Hammill and Larsen (1996, p. 6), this subtest evaluates the student's story on the basis of the "quality of its plot, prose, development of characters, interest to the reader, and other compositional aspects."

Scores

Raw scores for each subtest can be converted to percentiles or standard scores. The standard scores have a mean of 10 and a standard deviation of 3. Various combinations of subtests result in three composites: contrived writing (Vocabulary, Spelling, Style, Logical Sentences, and Sentence Combining), spontaneous writing (Contextual Conventions, Contextual Language, and, Story Construction), and overall writing (all subtests). Subtest standard scores can be summed and converted to standard scores and percentiles for each composite. These quotients have a mean of 100 and a standard deviation of 15.

Raw-score conversions are based on age rather than grade. However, written expression is not a trait that develops independently of schooling; much of TOWL-3's content (for example, spelling, punctuation, and paragraph usage) is systematically taught in school. Because students of the same age may receive instruction in two or three different grades, grade conversions should also have been provided.

Norms

Two different sampling techniques were used to establish norms for TOWL-3. First, one site in each of four geographic regions of the United States was selected, and 970 students were tested. Second, an additional 1,247 students were tested by volunteers who had previously purchased materials from the publisher. The total sample of 2,217 students is distributed somewhat unevenly across the 11 age groups, but no age group has fewer than 105 students. The total sample varies no more than 3 percent from the 1990 census on various demographic variables (that is, gender, urban/rural residence, race, geographic region, ethnicity, family income, educational attainment of parents, and disability). The authors also present data for four age ranges (that is, 7 to 8, 9 to 11, 12 to 14, and 15 to 17) showing that each age range also approximates the 1990 census. However, the comparisons of interest (that is, the degree to which each normative group approximates the census) are absent.

Reliability

Three types of reliability are discussed in the TOWL-3 manual: internal consistencies (both coefficient-alpha and alternate-forms reliability), stability, and interscorer agreement.

Two procedures were used to estimate the internal consistency of TOWL-3. First, a series of coefficient alphas were computed. Using the entire normative sample, coefficient alpha was used to estimate the internal consistency of each score and composite on each form at each age. Of the 176 alphas reported (that is, 2 forms × 11 ages × 8 subtests), 101 are in the .80s. Of the remaining 75 alphas, 25 equal or exceed .90, 46 are in the .70s, and 4 are in the .60s. Alphas are consistently higher on the Vocabulary subtest and lowest on the Contextual Conventions subtest. As is typical, coefficient alpha was substantially higher for the composites. Except for spontaneous writing at ages 7 and 8 years, where all three alphas were in the .80s, all coefficients equaled or exceeded .90. Thus, the composites are sufficiently reliable for making important educational decisions about students.

The authors are to be commended for also reporting subtest internal consistencies for several demographic subgroups (that is, males and females, Anglo-Americans, African Americans, Hispanic Americans, and Asian Americans), as well as students with disabilities (that is, learning disabled, speech impaired, and attention deficit/hyperactive). The obtained coefficients for the various demographic: subgroups are comparable to those for the entire normative sample, while those for the students with disabilities, as should be expected, are somewhat lower. Second, alternate-forms reliability was also computed for each subtest and each composite at each age, using the entire normative sample. These coefficients were distributed in about the same way as were the alphas.

The two-week stability of each subtest and each composite on both forms was estimated with 27 second-graders and 28 twelfth-graders. Of the 44 coefficients (that is, 11 subtests and composites × 2 forms × 2 age groups), 3 coefficients equaled or exceed .90, 30 were in the .80s, and 11 were in the .70s. While these coefficients are somewhat lower than would be desirable, the two age groups selected for study probably provide the most conservative estimates of stability because of potential floor and ceiling effects.

To estimate interscorer agreement, 39 TOWL-3 protocols were selected at random and scored. The correlations between scorers was remarkably consistent. Of the 22 coefficients (that is, 2 forms × 11 subtests and composites), 11 were in the .90s, and 11 were in the .80s. As we discussed in Chapter 13, the scoring of written-language samples is quite difficult, and unacceptably low levels of interscorer agreement appear to be the rule rather than the exception. It appears that the scoring criteria contained in the TOWL-3 manual are sufficiently precise and clear to allow for consistent scoring.

Validity

Support for control validity comes from the way the test was developed, the completeness of the dimensions of written language, and the methods by which competence in written language is assessed. The evidence for criterion-related validity comes from a single study in which teacher ratings of writing from the *Comprehensive Scales of Student Abilities* (Hammill & Hresko, 1994) were correlated with each score on the TOWL-3. Correlations ranging from .34 (story construction) to .69 (spelling) provide quite limited support for TOWL-3's validity, because teacher ratings for reading, math, and general facts correlated as well as or better than those for writing.

Construct validity is considered at some length in the TOWL-3 manual. First, the authors present evidence to show that TOWL-3 scores increase with age. The correlations with age are substantially stronger for students between the ages of 7 and 13 years than for students from 13 to 18, for whom

correlations are negligible. Second, in examining either the subtest intercorrelations or the factor structure, TOWL-3 appears to assess a single factor both for the sample as a whole and separately for males, females, Anglo-Americans, African Americans, Hispanic Americans, students with learning disabilities, and students with speech impairments. Thus, while individual subtests (or the contrived and spontaneous composites) may be of interest, they are not independent of the other skills measured on the test. Third, scores on TOWL-3 are moderately (that is, .3 to .6) correlated with scores on the Comprehensive Test of Nonverbal Intelligence (Hammill, Pearson, & Wiederholt, 1996).

The authors were especially careful to examine the possibility of racial or ethnic bias in their assessment of written language. Not only did they examine the factor structure separately for various demographic groups, but they also examined the various reliabilities and the pattern of increasing difficulty of test items for three racial groups. From the data reported, TOWL-3 does not appear to have racial or ethnic bias.

Summary

The TOWL-3 is designed to assess written-language competence of students aged 7-0 to 17-11. Contrived and spontaneous formats are used to evaluate the conventional, linguistic, and cognitive components of written American English. The content and structure of TOWL-3 appear appropriate, and the two forms of the test appear to be equivalent.

While TOWL-3's norms appear representative in general, the adequacy of the norms at each age cannot be evaluated with the data presented in the test manual. Interscorer reliability is quite good for this type of test. The internal consistencies of composite and total scores are high enough for use in making individual decisions; the stabilities of subtests are incompletely reported and are lower.

Although the test's content appears appropriate and well conceived, the validity of the inferences to be drawn from the scores is unclear. Specifically, group means are the only data to suggest that

TOWL-3 is useful in identifying students with disabilities or in determining strengths and weaknesses of individual students. Students with learning disabilities and speech impairments earn TOWL-3 subtest scores that are only 1 standard deviation (or less) below the mean; they earn composite scores that are no more than 1.2 standard deviations below the mean. However, because we do not know whether these students had disabilities in written language, their scores tell us little about TOWL-3's ability to identify students with special needs. Given that TOWL-3 has only two forms and relatively low stability, its usefulness in evaluating pupil progress is also limited.

Test of Written Spelling–4 (TWS-4)

The Test of Written Spelling–4 (TWS-4; Larsen, Hammill, & Moats, 1999) is a norm-referenced test intended to assess the spelling ability of students ranging in age from 6-0 to 18-11. TWS-4 uses a dictation format in which the tester reads a word, uses the word in a sentence, and reads the word a second time in isolation. The student then writes the word. *Basal* and *ceiling levels* (five consecutive correct responses and five consecutive incorrect responses, respectively) allow the test to be administered quickly, usually in less than 25 minutes. Although primarily used as an individually administered test, TWS-4 can also be administered to groups, provided the tester uses the ceiling rules to score the tests after all students have completed testing.

Changes to the fourth edition of this test included doing away with the format of having two separate tests, one each for predictable and unpredictable words, and its replacement with two alternative forms. In addition, the authors conducted one reliability study, examined differential item functioning for different racial or ethnic groups, and examined the extent to which the words included in TWS-4 are still prominent in spelling basal series. No changes were made in items or in norms.

Scores

Raw scores for each form of the TWS-4 may be converted into percentiles and standard scores that have a mean of 100 and a standard deviation of 15. With an apology and a strong warning about the dangers of their use, the authors provide grade and age equivalents because users say they want them.

Norms

Though the test was changed from one with two subtests to one with no subtests, and equivalent forms were developed, the authors did not restandardize the test. The norms are a strange mixture of 3,805 students who made up the TWS-2 norms and 855 students from intact classrooms at only three sites who took the TWS-3. We believe that given the changes in format and administration procedure, and the fact that the majority of norms are more than 20 years old, the authors should have restandardized this test.

Reliability

With one minor exception, all data on reliability are on former editions of the TWS-4. The authors report reliabilities in excess of .90 for the earlier editions of the TWS-4. For this edition, they went back to original normative data and computed reliabilities for gender and racial subgroups. The test has a reliability of .96 for both forms for every subgroup.

A test–retest study was completed on 41 students at one Texas school. The characteristics of the sample are not described. We know only that there were 14 first-, 14 third-, and 13 sixth-grade students. Reliabilities exceeded .94 for each group.

Validity

With one exception, validity data are on earlier forms of the TWS-4. In the seventh edition of our text, we concluded that evidence for concurrent validity is strong. The new study correlated scores on TWS-4 are with scores on three achievement tests (none with a spelling subtest) for the group of 41 students on whom the reliability study was conducted. Corrrelations were low to moderate.

To investigate the extent to which words on TWS-4 are still instructionally relevant, the authors examined their status in each of six spelling basal series. The first two thirds of the words on both forms of the test appear in nearly all series.

Every word on the TWS-4 is in the Steck-Vaughn EDL Core Vocabulary, a series used to select the words.

Summary

The fourth edition of the Test of Written Spelling differs from earlier editions. The words are the same, but they are arranged in two alternative forms rather than two subtests. The test was not restandardized, the norms are more than 20 years old, and only one small new reliability and validity study was completed. Norms are dated, and while evidence for reliability and validity of the test is good, that evidence is based on a different format of the test. Users are cautioned against making norm-referenced comparisons using this test.

Language Tests That Assess both Written and Oral Language

Oral and Written Language Scales (OWLS)

The Oral and Written Language Scales (OWLS; Carrow-Woolfolk, 1995) are an individually administered assessment of receptive and expressive language for children and young adults aged 3 through 21. The test includes three scales: Listening Comprehension, Oral Expression, and Written Expression. Test results are used to determine broad levels of language skills and specific performance in listening, speaking, and writing. The scales are described as follows:

Listening Comprehension Scale   This scale is designed to measure understanding of spoken language. It consists of 111 items. The examiner

reads aloud a verbal stimulus, and the student is to identify which of four pictures is the best response to the stimulus. The scale takes 5 to 15 minutes to administer.

Oral Expression Scale   This scale is a measure of understanding and use of spoken language. It consists of 96 items. The examiner reads aloud a verbal stimulus and shows a picture. The student responds orally by answering a question, completing a sentence, or generating one or more sentences. The scale takes 10 to 25 minutes to administer.

Written Expression Scale   This scale is an assessment of written language for students 5 to 21 years of age. It is designed to measure ability to use conventions (spelling, punctuation, and so on), use syntactical forms (modifiers, phrases, sentence structures, and so on), and communicate meaningfully (with appropriate content, coherence, organization, and so on). The student responds to direct writing prompts provided by the examiner.

The OWLS is designed to be used in identification of students with language difficulties and disorders, in intervention planning, and in monitoring student progress.

Norms

The OWLS standardization sample consisted of 1,985 students chosen to match the U.S. census data from the 1991 Current Population Survey. The sample was stratified within age group by gender, race, geographic region, and socioeconomic status. Tables in the manual show the comparison of the sample to the U.S. population. Cross-tabulations are shown only for age, not for other variables. The 14–21 age group is overrepresented by students in the North Central region, and underrepresented by students from the West.

Scores

The OWLS produces raw scores, which may be transformed to standard scores with a mean of 100 and a standard deviation of 15. In addition, test age equivalents, normal-curve equivalents, percentiles, and stanines can be obtained. Scores are obtained for each subtest, for an oral-language composite, and for a written language composite.

Reliability

Internal-consistency reliability was calculated using students in the standardization. Reliability coefficients ranged from .75 to .89 for Listening Comprehension, from .76 to .91 for Oral Expression, and from .87 to .94 for the oral composite. They range from .77 to .89 for Written Expression. Test–retest reliabilities were computed on a small sample of students who are not described. The coefficients range from .58 to .85 for the oral subtests and composite, and from .66 to .83 for the Written Expression subtest. Reliabilities are sufficient to use this measure as a screening device. They are not sufficient to use it in making important decisions about individual students. This latter, of course, is the use the authors suggest for the test.

Validity

The authors report the results of a set of external validity studies, each consisting of a comparison of performance on the OWLS to performance on other measures. Sample sizes were small, but correlations were in the expected range. The Written Expression subtest was compared to the Kaufman Test of Educational Achievement, the Peabody Individual Achievement Test–Revised, the Woodcock Reading Mastery Test, and the Peabody Picture Vocabulary Test. Student performance on the Oral Expression and Listening Comprehension subtests was compared to performance on the Test for Auditory Comprehension of Language–Revised, the Peabody Picture Vocabulary Test, the Clinical Evaluation of Language Fundamentals–Revised, and the Kaufman Assessment Battery for Children.

Summary

The OWLS is a language test combining assessment of oral and written language. The test was standardized on the same population, so comparisons of student performance on oral and written measures are enhanced. The manual includes data showing that the standardization sample is generally representative of the U.S. population. Reliability coefficients are too low to permit use of this measure in making important decisions for individuals. Evidence for validity is good, although it is based on a set of studies with limited numbers of students.

Coping with Dilemmas in Current Practice

Oral Language

Three issues are particularly troublesome in the assessment of oral language: (1) ensuring that the elicited language assessment is a true reflection of the child's general spontaneous language capacity, (2) using the results of standardized tests to generate effective therapy, and (3) adapting assessment to individuals who do not match the characteristics of the standardization sample. All these dilemmas stem from the limited nature of the standardized tests and must be addressed in practice.

From a practical standpoint, the clinician must use standardized tests to identify a language-impaired child. Yet, as noted earlier in this chapter, such instruments may not directly measure a child's true language abilities. Thus, the clinician must supplement the standard tests with nonstandard spontaneous language sampling. Additionally, if possible, the child should be observed in a number of settings outside the formal testing situation. After the spontaneous samples have been gathered, the results of these analyses should be compared with the performance on the standardized tests.

Selection of targets for intervention is one of the more difficult tasks facing the clinician. Many standardized tests that are useful for identifying language disorders in children may not lend themselves to determining efficient treatment. The clinician must evaluate the results of both the standard and the nonstandard assessment procedures and decide which language skills are most important to the child. Although it is tempting simply to train the child to perform better on a particular test (hence boosting performance on that instrument), the clinician must bear in mind that such tasks are often metalinguistic in nature and will not ultimately result in generalized language skills. Rather, the focus of treatment should be on those language behaviors and structures that are needed for improved language competence in the home and in the classroom.

Finally, in today's language assessment environment, with a plethora of multicultural and socioeconomic variation within caseloads, a clinician is bound to encounter many children who differ in one or more respects from the normative sample of a particular test. Indeed, clinicians are likely to see children who do not match the normative sample of any standardized test. When this occurs, the clinician must interpret the scores derived from these tests conservatively. Information from nonstandard assessment becomes even more important, and the clinician should obtain reports from parents, teachers, and peers regarding their impressions of the child's language competence. The clinician should also determine whether local norms have been developed for the standard and nonstandard assessment procedures. As noted earlier, it is inappropriate to treat multicultural language differences as if they were language disorders. However, the clinician performing an assessment must judge whether the child's language is disordered within his or her language community and what impact such disorders may have on classroom performance and communication skills generally.

Written Language

There are two serious problems in the assessment of written language. The first problem, assessing the content of written expression, was treated in some detail in Chapter 13 (Portfolios). The content of written language is usually scored holistically and subjectively. Holistic evaluations tend to be unreliable. When content on the same topic and of the same genre (such as narratives) is scored, interscorer agreement varies from the .50–.65 range (such as Breland, 1983; Breland, Camp, Jones, Morris, & Rock, 1987) to the .75–.90 range immediately following intensive training (such as Educational Testing Service, 1990). Consistent scoring is even more difficult when topics and genres vary. Interscorer agreement can drop to a range of .35 to .45 when the writing tasks vary (such as Breland, 1983; Breland et al., 1987). In addition, as we noted in Chapter 2, subjective scoring and decision making are susceptible to the biasing effects associated with racial, ethnic, social-class, gender, and disability stereotypes. We believe the best alternative to holistic and subjective scoring schemes is to use a measure of writing fluency as an indicator of content generation. Two options have received some support in the research literature: (1) the number of words written (cf. Shinn, Tindal, & Stein, 1988), and (2) the percentage of correctly written words (cf. Isaacson, 1988).

The second problem is in identifying a match between what is taught in the school curriculum and what is tested. The great variation in the time at which various skills and facts are taught renders a general test of achievement inappropriate. This dilemma also attends diagnostic assessment of written language. Commercially prepared tests have doubtful validity for planning individual programs and evaluating the progress of individual pupils. We recommend that teachers and diagnosticians construct criterion-referenced achievement tests that closely parallel the curricula followed by the students being tested. In cases where normative data are required, there are three choices. Diagnosticians can (1) select the devices that most closely parallel the curriculum, (2) develop local norms, or (3) select individual students for comparative purposes. Care should be exercised in selecting methods of assessing language skills. For example, it is probably better to test pupils in ways that are familiar to them. Thus, if the teacher's weekly spelling test is from dictation, then spelling tests using dictation are probably preferable to tests requiring the students to identify incorrectly spelled words.

Summary

The primary function of standard oral-language tests is to identify language disorders. Assessment sessions should include nonstandard measures such as language sampling to augment the results obtained from standard instruments. In our review of standardized oral- and written-language measures, we have noted a general lack of application of psychometric principles to the construction of these instruments. Additionally, the mismatch between the standard instruments and the content of instruction remains large.

Questions for Chapter Review and Thought

1. Identify and describe the three techniques for obtaining a sample of a child's language.

2. Identify and describe briefly two issues that are particularly troublesome in the assessment of oral language.

3. Design an assessment session that includes information about all aspects of language, both comprehension and production. Include a list of specific tests required to complete the session, as well as language sampling.

4. Identify and explain three limitations on analyzing a pupil's English composition to assess skill in spelling, grammar, and punctuation.

Resources for Further Investigation

Project

Assume that you wish to use one of the tests reviewed in this text to screen for written-language difficulties. Which test would be your first choice? Why? Compare your answer with a classmate's answer. Reconcile any difference.

Print Resources

Camarata, S. (1996). On the importance of integrating naturalistic language, social intervention, and speech-intelligibility training (pp. 333–351). In L. Koegel & G. Dunlap (eds.), *Positive behavior support*. Baltimore: Brookes.

Camarata, S., Nelson, K., & Camarata, M. (1994). A comparison of conversation based to imitation based procedures for training grammatical structures in specifically language impaired children. *Journal of Speech and Hearing Research, 37,* 1414–1423.

Hammill, D., & Hresko, W. (1994). *Comprehensive Scales of Student Abilities*. Austin, TX: Pro-Ed.

Hammill, D., & Larsen, S. (1996). *Test of Written Language, Third Edition: Examiner's Manual*. Austin, TX: Pro-Ed.

Hammill, D., Pearson, N., & Wiederholt, L. (1996). *Comprehensive Test of Nonverbal Intelligence*. Austin, TX: Pro-Ed.

Hanna, P., Hanna, J., Hodges, R., & Rudoff, E. (1966). *Phoneme grapheme correspondence as cues to spelling improvement*. Washington, DC: Department of Health, Education, and Welfare.

Hillerich, R. L. (1985). *Teaching children to write, K–8* (selected chapters on the evaluation of writing). Englewood Cliffs, NJ: Prentice-Hall.

Isaacson, S. (1988). Assessing the writing product: Quantitative and qualitative measures. *Exceptional Children, 54,* 528–535.

Lahey, M. (1988). *Language disorders and language development*. New York: Macmillan.

Larsen, S., & Hammill, D. (1994). *Test of Written Spelling, Third Edition*. Austin, TX: Pro-Ed.

Miller, J. (1981). *Assessing language production in children*. Austin, TX: Pro-Ed.

Moss, P., Cole, N., & Khampalikit, C. (1982). A comparison of procedures to assess written language skills at grades 4, 7, and 10. *Journal of Educational Measurement, 19,* 37–47.

Shinn, M., Tindal, G., & Stein, S. (1988). Curriculum-based measurement and the identification of mildly handicapped students: A review of research. *Professional School Psychology, 3* (1), 69–85.

Technology Resources

Welcome to AGS On-line Products and Services

http://www.agsnet.com/

Look for product and ordering information about the instruments available from American Guidance Service. Here you can find out information about the *Goldman–Fristoe Test of Articulation, Test of Language Development–2,* and other language-development measures.

Pro-Ed Catalog Information for Products

http://www.proedinc.com

Find product and ordering information about the *Goldman–Fristoe Test of Articulation; Comprehensive Receptive and Expressive Vocabulary Test; Test of Adolescent and Adult Language–3; Test for Auditory Comprehension of Language, Revised; Test of Early Language Development, Third Edition; Test of Language Development, Primary:3; Carrow Elicited Language Inventory; Expressive and Receptive One-Word Picture Vocabulary Tests;* and several other instruments that measure oral language.

Welcome to AGS On-line Products and Services

http://www.agsnet.com

Look for product and ordering information about the instruments available from American Guidance Service. Here you can find out information about the *Test of Written Language–2.*

Pro-Ed Catalog Information for Products

http://www.proedinc.com

Find product and ordering information about the *Test of Written Language–3, the Test of Early Written Language–2, the Test of Written Expression, and the Test of Written Spelling–4.*

chapter

24

Assessment of Perceptual–Motor Skills

ducators and psychologists have operated for quite some time under the assumption that adequate perceptual–motor development is important both in and of itself and as a prerequisite to the development of academic skills. A wide variety of devices designed to assess children's perceptual–motor functioning are in use in the public schools today. Many measures of learning aptitude include items designed to assess perceptual or motor skills, and many readiness tests assess aspects of perceptual–motor development. However, this chapter focuses solely on those devices designed specifically and exclusively to assess perceptual–motor skills.

● ●

Why Do We Assess Perceptual–Motor Skills?

Perceptual–motor assessment typically takes place for one of three purposes. First, the perceptual–motor skills of entire classes of students may be assessed to identify students with perceptual–motor difficulties, so that training programs can be instituted to prevent incipient learning difficulties from worsening. Students who perform poorly on these perceptual–motor devices are said to demonstrate perceptual–motor problems, which may then contribute to or cause learning problems. Second, students who are known to have academic difficulties may be assessed with perceptual–motor tests to identify whether perceptual–motor difficulties may be causing these academic difficulties. In both instances, efforts are made to identify perceptual–motor problems so that training programs can be prescribed. Third, perceptual–motor tests are widely used to diagnose brain injury.

The Problem of Perceptual–Motor Assessment

Although perceptual–motor tests have been used for some time to diagnose brain injury, it was not until the 1960s that there was a dramatic and significant increase in the use of various perceptual–motor devices to diagnose learning disabilities. The majority of research has shown, however, that most perceptual–motor tests are unreliable. We do not know what they measure because they do not measure anything consistently. Unlike the majority of intelligence and achievement tests, the tests used to assess perceptual–motor skills in children are technically inadequate. Also, for the most part, they are neither theoretically nor psychometrically sound. For example, they may be designed to assess perceptual–motor abilities under the assumption that such abilities cause academic success or failure (see Ysseldyke & Salvia, 1974). Alternatively, tests may be designed to assess hypothetical constructs such as figure–ground perception and body image and differentiation but do not do so with consistency (see Ysseldyke, 1973; Ysseldyke & Salvia, 1974). Instead, the assessments may be based on criteria that can lead to logical fallacies of undistributed middle terms (for instance, all learning-disabled students have normal intelligence; Esmeralda has normal intelligence; therefore, Esmeralda is a learning-disabled student. All brain-injured people have perceptual–motor problems; Esmeralda has perceptual–motor problems; therefore, Esmeralda is brain-injured).

In short, the majority of the devices currently used to assess children's perceptual–motor skills are extremely inadequate. The real danger is that reliance on such tests in planning interventions for children may actually lead teachers to assign children to activities that do the children no known good. Having said that, we review the devices that are most often used.

Specific Tests of Perceptual–Motor Skills

Bender Visual Motor Gestalt Test (BVMGT)

The Bender Visual Motor Gestalt Test (BVMGT), consisting of nine geometric designs to be copied on paper, was originally developed by Loretta Bender in 1938. Bender used the designs in a test to differentiate brain-injured from non–brain-injured adults and to detect signs of emotional disturbance. The test has gained widespread popularity among clinical psychologists and has become one of the most frequently administered psychometric devices.

Administration of the BVMGT simply consists of presenting nine geometric designs, one at a time, to a subject, who is asked to copy each of them onto a plain sheet of paper. Although Bender provided criteria for scoring the test, a variety of other scoring systems were developed by Elizabeth Koppitz in 1963. The impetus for Koppitz's work arose from her experience in a child-guidance clinic, where she was reportedly impressed with the frequency of perceptual problems among children with emotional difficulties.

The Koppitz scoring system, restricted to use with children between 5 and 11 years of age, is the system most often used by psychologists in school settings. In 1963, Koppitz published a text describing the scoring system, the various uses of the BVMGT with children, normative data for the scoring system, and limited information about reliability and validity. In 1975, Koppitz published the second volume of the *Bender Gestalt Test for Young Children*, a compilation and synthesis of research on the BVMGT between 1963 and 1973. This 1975 book is a commendable effort that eliminates the need to search the literature for research on the test. Our discussion of the BVMGT is based entirely on use of the Koppitz scoring system.

Scores

When scoring according to the Koppitz system, the examiner records the number of errors on each of the nine separate geometric forms. Four kinds of errors are recorded.

1. *Distortion of shape.* Errors are scored as distortion of shape when a child's reproduction of the stimulus design is so misshapen that the general configuration is lost. If a child converts dots to circles, alters the relative size of components of the stimulus drawing, or in other ways distorts the design, errors are recorded.

2. *Perseveration.* Perseveration errors are recorded when a child fails to stop after completing the required drawing—for example, a child is asked to copy 11 dots in a row and then copies significantly more than 11.

3. *Integration.* Integration errors consist of a failure to juxtapose parts of a design correctly, as illustrated in Figure 24.1. In drawing a, the components of the design fail to meet. In drawing b, they overlap.

4. *Rotation.* Rotation errors are recorded when a child rotates a design by more than 45 degrees or rotates the stimulus card and then copies the rotated drawing correctly. Reversals are 180-degree rotations and are scored as rotation errors.

More than one error can be scored on each drawing. The total number of possible errors is 25. The examiner adds the number of errors to obtain a total raw score for the test. The higher the total raw score, the poorer the performance.

The Koppitz manual (1963) contains a normative table reporting means and standard deviations

Two Integration Errors in Koppitz's Scoring of the BVMGT

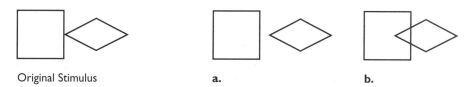

Original Stimulus   **a.**   **b.**

of error scores for specific age levels in half-year intervals. This normative table, based on the 1963 standardization of the test, is used to transform error scores to developmental ages. The 1975 publication reporting research on the BVMGT from 1963 to 1973 includes two features. A new set of examples for scoring individual items has been included to eliminate the scoring difficulties that examiners reported to the author. The publication also includes a new set of normative tables based on a 1974 renorming of the test. This set of tables can be used to convert error scores to age equivalents and to percentile ranks.

Norms

Two sets of norms are available for the Koppitz scoring system. The test was originally standardized on 1,104 children from 46 classes in 12 public schools. The schools were reportedly selected from rural, urban, and suburban areas, in unspecified proportions. The original normative sample included 637 boys and 467 girls. There are no data in the 1963 manual on the geographic areas the sample was drawn from or the demographic characteristics. In Volume II (Koppitz, 1975), Koppitz reports that 98 percent of the original sample was European American.

Koppitz renormed the test in 1974 in an effort to achieve a more representative sample of U.S. schoolchildren. The 1974 normative sample included 975 children between the ages of 5 and 11 years. A geographic cross section was not obtained; 15 percent of the children were from the

West, 2 percent were from the South, and 83 percent were from the Northeast. Racial balance is more nearly representative: 86 percent of the sample was European American, 8.5 percent was African American, 4.5 percent was either Mexican American or Puerto Rican, and 1 percent was Asian American. There is no indication of the socioeconomic level of the sample; Koppitz states that research has demonstrated that socioeconomic status is not an important variable in children's performance on the BVMGT. Community size is adequately described: 7 percent were from rural communities, 31 percent were from small towns, 36 percent were from suburbs, and 26 percent were from large metropolitan areas.

The sample sizes for half-year-interval age groups in both the 1963 and the 1974 norms are unevenly distributed. For the 1963 norms, the norm groups ranged in size from 27 children (at ages 10-0 to 10-5) to 180 children (at ages 6-6 to 6-11). For the 1974 norms, the norm groups ranged in size from 47 children (at ages 5-0 to 5-5, 7-6 to 7-11, and 9-6 to 9-11) to 175 children (at ages 6-0 to 6-5). Another major difficulty was present in the 1963 standardization: After age 8-6, the standard deviations for raw scores exceeded the means. For the 1974 norms, the standard deviations after age 8-6 are about equal to the means.

Those who use the BVMGT as a norm-referenced test are comparing the individuals they assess to an unknown group. Clearly, such comparisons are unwarranted, and the norms are now more than 20 years out of date.

Reliability

Two kinds of reliability data are reported for the BVMGT. Koppitz (1975) summarizes 23 studies of the interscorer reliability for her scoring system. Interscorer reliabilities ranged from .79 to .99, with 81 percent exceeding .89. The revised set of scoring examples, published by Koppitz in 1975, after test users reported scoring difficulties, facilitates interscorer agreement in scoring a child's performance.

In her 1975 addition to the 1963 manual, Koppitz reports research on factors she believes may affect performance on the scale. Her review of research on the effects of motivation, task familiarization, verbal labeling, tracing and copying, and specific perceptual–motor training led to the conclusion that the BVMGT does indeed serve mainly as a measure of children's level of maturation in integration of perceptual and motor functions. Only secondarily does it reflect their various learning experiences with specific perceptual–motor tasks.

The 1975 manual also summarizes the results of nine test-retest reliability studies with normal elementary-school children. Reliability coefficients ranged from .50 to .90 (mean = .71; mode = .76). On the basis of her review, Koppitz made a claim for the essential reliability of the BVMGT scores for normal children. Yet five of the nine reliability studies she reports are on kindergarten children only, and only 1 of 25 reported coefficients exceeds the standard of .90 recommended for tests used to make important decisions. As Koppitz wisely cautions, "Certainly no diagnosis or major decision should ever be made on the basis of a single scoring point, nor for that matter on the basis of a youngster's total Developmental Bender Test score" (1975; p. 29).

Validity

The construct of *visual–motor perception* is never adequately defined in either Koppitz manual. There is no evidence about the extent to which the test assesses visual–motor perception; the copying of nine designs is believed to be a measure of visual perception because some experts say it is.

Koppitz (1975) cites several uses for the BVMGT and reports research on each of the suggested uses. She reports correlations of performance on the BVMGT and performance on measures of intelligence, academic achievement, and visual perception. She also cites evidence for use of the test in diagnosing minimal brain dysfunction and emotional disturbance. The following paragraphs describe some of her findings and recommendations.

In her 1963 manual, Koppitz reported results of tests of the relationship between scores earned on the BVMGT and scores earned on intelligence tests. She concluded that the BVMGT may be substituted "with some confidence" for a screening test of intelligence. She stated,

In clinical and school settings psychologists are constantly faced with the problem of how to use their limited time most economically. . . . The Bender test not only gives the examiner a rough measure of the youngster's intellectual ability, but also serves as a nonthreatening introduction to the interview. (p. 51)

In the 1975 addition to the 1963 manual, Koppitz (1975, p. 47) continues to support the use of the BVMGT as a rough test of intelligence:

The statement "The Bender Gestalt Test can be used with some degree of confidence as a short nonverbal intelligence test for young children, particularly for screening purposes" (Koppitz, 1963, p. 50) has been supported by a number of recent studies. But as I previously suggested, the Bender Test should if possible be combined with a brief verbal test.

The BVMGT is *not* an intelligence test but a measure of a child's skill in copying geometric designs. It provides a very limited sample of behavior; in fact, of the 13 kinds of behaviors described in Chapter 16 as being regularly sampled in intelligence tests, the Bender samples only 1. In our opinion, the BVMGT should never be used as, or substituted for, a measure of intellectual functioning.

Koppitz (1975) reviews numerous investigations of the relationship between children's performance on the BVMGT and their academic achievement. Good students and poor students, she concludes, tend—as groups—to make significantly different total scores on the test. Furthermore, the scores normal children earn show a positive correlation with their academic achievement. Koppitz uses observed differences to conclude that scores earned on the BVMGT appear to be most successful in predicting overall school functioning and rate of progress in total achievement.

Children who perform well in school may in fact do better on the BVMGT than children who experience academic difficulty. However, as Koppitz herself states, the test cannot be used to predict the academic performance of individual children (1975, p. 70). Moreover, Koppitz has not provided evidence to support the contention that the test facilitates individualization of instruction. To do so would require demonstration of an interaction between test performance and success under different methods or techniques of instruction.

Koppitz (1975) reviewed many studies of the use of the BVMGT to diagnose minimal brain dysfunction in schoolchildren. She concluded that the test is a valuable aid for this purpose but should never be used in isolation. Rather, she believes test results are valuable when combined with other medical and behavioral data.

Koppitz (1975) also claims that research gives additional validity to the ten indicators of emotional problems that she delineated in her 1963 text. Although she again provides notes of caution indicating that not all children with poor Bender protocols have emotional problems, she does state that "the presence of three or more emotional indicators on a Bender Test protocol tends to reflect emotional difficulties that warrant further investigation" (p. 92).

Koppitz (1975) provides evidence to support the contention that performance on the BVMGT is significantly related to performance on other visual–perceptual measures. She does not report the extent to which pupils who achieve low scores on the BVMGT perform well on these other tests, or vice versa.

Summary

The BVMGT requires the child to copy nine geometric designs. The test was originally developed by Bender. Koppitz has developed a scoring system for the test, and her system is designed to be used with children aged 5 to 11 years. The BVMGT is today one of the most widely used psychometric devices. The most recent standardization of the test was in 1974, so the norms are more than 20 years old.

Reliability for the BVMGT is relatively low—at least, too low for its use in making eligibility decisions. Yet, performance on the test is used as a criterion in the differential identification of children as brain injured, perceptually handicapped, or emotionally disturbed. Validity for the BVMGT is currently not clearly established. The author has not empirically demonstrated that the test measures visual–motor perception or that it discriminates individual cases of brain injury, perceptual handicap, or emotional disturbance. The test certainly provides a very limited sample of perceptual–motor behavior, and, for this reason if for no other, educators should be extremely cautious in interpreting and using its results.

The BVMGT is, quite simply, a measure of skill development in copying geometric designs. It is not designed as a measure of intelligence, a predictor of achievement, or a measure of emotional disturbance or minimal brain dysfunction. Using it for any of these purposes is risky and unwarranted. A statement by Koppitz is a fitting conclusion to our discussion of her test. "The very fact," she writes, "that the Bender Test is so appealing and is easy to administer presents a certain danger. Because it is so deceptively simple, it is probably one of the most overrated, most misunderstood, and most maligned tests currently in use" (1975, p. 2).

Developmental Test of Visual Perception, Second Edition (DTVP-2)

The second edition of the Developmental Test of Visual Perception (DTVP-2; Hammill, Pearson, & Voress, 1993) is an individually administered, norm-referenced test designed for use with children between the ages of 4 and 10 years. In several ways, the second edition of the DTVP is different from the first edition, published in the 1960s. Two new composite scores have been added (motor-reduced perception and visual–motor integration), the age range of the test has been extended to age 10 years, and the technical characteristics (and their reporting) have been substantially improved.

Subtests

Requiring 30 to 60 minutes to administer, the DTVP-2 has eight subtests, all of which have demonstration items.

Eye–Hand Coordination Four items require children to draw a line on a band that progressively narrows and curves from Item 1 to Item 4. Each band is segmented, and the child receives a point for each segment in which performance is acceptable. Thus, although there are only four items, the child may earn up to 52 points for staying on the band and not picking up the pencil.

Position in Space Twenty-five items require children to match a figure from an array containing the same figure in three to five different rotations.

Copying Twenty items require a child to copy a sample figure of increasing difficulty in a 1.75-inch box. Each drawing is awarded 0, 1, or 2 points on the basis of clear scoring standards.

Figure–Ground Eighteen items require children to identify two or more figures embedded in a stimulus composed of overlapping and overdrawn figures. Each item is scored pass (1) or fail (0). For example, in Item 10 of this subtest, the

child must find all of the figures shown in the boxed area that are included in the stimulus drawing at the top of the item.

Spatial Relations Ten items require children to connect some dots in an array of dots, to reproduce a stimulus pattern.

Visual Closure In these 20 items, children are shown a stimulus picture and are required to select (from a multiple-choice array) the option that could match the stimulus picture if that option were completed. The child does not need to draw the stimulus from the option but needs only to recognize the one option that could be completed.

Visual–Motor Speed On this timed subtest, children are shown four stimuli (large circle, small circle, large square, and small square). The large circle contains two parallel, horizontal lines, and the small square contains two diagonal lines connecting opposite corners. Below these stimuli are 128 figures (32 large circles, 32 small circles, and so on, in random order) that do not contain the internal lines. Children must add the lines to as many other appropriate figures as they can in one minute. One point is awarded for each figure correctly completed without drawing outside the figure.

Form Constancy The 20 items in this subtest each contain a stimulus (a geometric form) and an array of response options. For each item, children are required to identify the two options that are the same shape as the stimulus. However, correct response options may differ from the stimulus in size, rotation, color, or shading.

Scores

All subtests except Visual–Motor Speed have ceiling rules. Subtest raw scores may be converted to age equivalents, percentiles, and normalized standard scores (mean = 10, standard deviation = 3). Subtest standard scores can be summed and converted to three different composite standard scores (each with a mean of 100 and standard deviation of 15): general visual perception quotient (based on all eight subtests), motor reduced visual perception quotient (based on the four subtests that require only a pointing response), and visual–motor integration quotient (based on the four subtests that require drawing).

Norms

To obtain a normative sample, the authors of the DTVP-2 asked those who had purchased other Pro-Ed perceptual–motor tests to test children in their immediate geographic vicinity. The resulting sample of 1,972 children, from 12 states, appears representative of the United States (1990 census) in terms of race, ethnicity, gender, residence (urban/rural), geographic area, and handedness. Approximately 3 percent of the sample were children with disabilities. The number of children at each age appears to be more than sufficient, except for 4-year-olds.[1]

Reliability

Alphas for individual subtests range from .80 (Figure–Ground at three ages) to .97 (Spatial Relations at two ages). Of the 56 subtest-by-age alphas, 30 are in the .80s, and 20 equal or exceed .90. Thus, individual subtests generally do not

have sufficient reliability for making important educational decisions for individual students. The alphas of the three composites are all excellent, ranging from .43 to .98. Similar patterns of results were found for stability. Eighty-eight students, ranging in age from 4 through 10 years, were tested and retested two weeks later.[2] Reliabilities for subtests range from .71 to .86; stabilities for the composites range from .89 to .95. Thus, the composites are quite stable. Finally, interscorer agreement, estimated from the protocols of 88 students, is excellent for subtests and composites.

Validity

The selection of specific subtests is based on classic research and theory in visual perception, and careful and thoughtful item development closely approximates the theoretical constructs on which the subtests are based. Thus, there is strong rationale for the DTVP-2's content validity. Strong evidence of criterion-related validity is also presented in the manual. DTVP-2 scores were correlated with scores from the Motor Free Visual Perception Test (MFVPT) and the Developmental Test of Visual Motor Integration (VMI) (a test that requires copying, discussed in the following section). The correlations between the DTVP-2 subtests and these measures range from .27 to .95. As should occur, DTVP-2 subtests that have a motor component generally correlate more highly with the VMI, whereas subtests without a perceptual component generally correlate more highly with the MFVPT. This pattern is even more pronounced for the composite scores of the DTVP-2.

Some evidence of construct validity is provided by the DTVP-2's relationship with age (as should be expected). More compelling are the results of factor-analytic studies suggesting that two related factors, approximately the same as motor-reduced visual perception and visual–motor integration, underlie the test. In addition, the DTVP-2 appears

---

1. Raw scores are converted to derived scores by six-month intervals. For example, the scores of children from 4-0 through 4-5 are converted using one table; scores of children from 4-6 through 4-11 are converted using a different table. The number of children in whole-year groups (for example, 4-0 through 4-11) is reported, not the number of children in each half-year group. Nonetheless, assuming even a 60 percent–40 percent division of children into the two age subgroups, all age subgroups would have at least 100 children, except for the 4-year-old subgroups, each of which would have around 50 students.

2. The authors report stabilities with the effects of age correctly controlled.

to differentiate between groups of children known to be normal and those known to be below average in visual-perceptual ability. Finally, the DTVP-2 has low correlations with cognitive measures, which supports the notion that visual perception is a discrete ability.

Summary

The revised Developmental Test of Visual Perception is an individually administered, norm-referenced test suitable for use with children between the ages of 4 and 10 years. The DTVP-2 has eight subtests: (1) Eye–Hand Coordination, (2) Position in Space, (3) Copying, (4) Figure–Ground, (5) Spatial Relations, (6) Visual Closure, (7) Visual–Motor Speed, and (8) Form Constancy. Raw scores can be converted to age equivalents, percentiles, or normalized standard scores; subtest standard scores can be combined to form three composite scores: general visual perception quotient, motor reduced visual perception quotient, and visual–motor integration quotient. The second edition of the DTVP represents a significant improvement over the first edition in all technical aspects. The norms appear representative, the test is internally consistent and stable, and the test has good interscorer reliability. The considerable amount of information presented by the authors strongly suggests that the DTVP-2 is a valid measure of visual perception.

Developmental Test of Visual–Motor Integration (VMI)

The Developmental Test of Visual–Motor Integration (VMI; Beery, 1997) is designed to assess the extent to which individuals can integrate their visual and motor abilities. Beery defines *visual–motor integration* as the degree to which visual perception and finger–hand movements are well coordinated (1997, p. 19). He indicates that if a child performs poorly on the VMI, it could be because he or she has adequate visual–perceptual and motor-coordination abilities but has not yet learned to integrate, or coordinate, these two domains (1997, p. 21).

The VMI is a set of geometric forms that are increasingly difficult to copy, which the test taker is to copy with paper and pencil. There are multiple versions of the VMI. The full VMI is intended for use with individuals from age 3 years to adult. It contains all 24 VMI forms, including the initial 3 that are both imitated and copied directly, making a total of 27 items. The short VMI contains the initial 3 and the first 15 forms and is intended for use with children aged 3 to 7 years. Two supplemental subtests are also available: Visual Perception and Motor Coordination. Items for the supplemental tests are identical to items for the full VMI. The VMI may be administered individually or to groups. The test can be administered and scored by a classroom teacher and usually takes about 15 minutes. Scoring is relatively easy, because the designs are scored pass–fail, and individual protocols can be scored in a few minutes.

Scores

The manual for the VMI includes two pages of scoring information for each of the 24 designs. The child's reproduction of each design is scored pass–fail, and criteria for successful performance are clearly articulated. A raw score for the total test is obtained by adding the number of reproductions copied correctly before the test taker has three consecutive failures. Normative tables provided in the manual allow the examiner to convert the total raw score to a developmental age equivalent, grade equivalent, standard score, scaled score, stanine, or percentile. Imitated drawings of the first three forms are included in the total score, so there are 27 possible total points.

Norms

The VMI was originally standardized on 1,030 children in rural, urban, and suburban Illinois. In 1981 the test was cross-validated with samples of children "from various ethnic and income groups in California" (Beery, 1982, p. 10). In 1988 the test was again cross-validated with an unspecified group of students "from several Eastern, Northern and Southern states" (Beery, 1989, p. 10). The 1988 norm sample is not representative of the U.S. population with respect to ethnicity and residence of the students. The VMI and its supplemental tests were normed in 1996 on 2,614 children from 3 to 18 years of age, selected from five major sections of the United States. The sample was selected by contacting school psychologists and learning-disabilities specialists, chosen at random from membership lists for major professional organizations. Those who indicated a willingness to participate tested the subjects. A total of 26 child-care, preschool, private, and public schools participated; these were located in California, Connecticut, New Mexico, New York, North Dakota, Mississippi, Missouri, Oklahoma, South Carolina, and Washington. While the norms collectively were representative of the U.S. population, cross-tabulations are shown only for age by gender, ethnicity, socioeconomic status, and geographic region. Thus, we do not know whether, for example, all the African American students were from middle-SES families, from the East, and so on.

Reliability

The author reports the results of studies of internal consistency on an unspecified sample of individuals. Internal consistency ranged from .71 to .95, with an average of .88. Interscorer reliability was .94 for the VMI, .98 for the visual supplement, and .95 for the motor supplement. Test–retest reliability was assessed by administering the VMI to 122 children between the ages of 6 and 10 years, in regular public-school classrooms. The sample is not further defined. Test–retest reliability was .87 for the VMI, .84 for the visual supplement, and .83 for the motor supplement. The VMI has adequate reliability for screening purposes.

Validity

The author contends that the VMI has good content validity because of the way in which the items were selected. Evidence for concurrent validity comes from comparing results of performance on the VMI to performance on the Copying subtest of the Developmental Test of Visual Perception–2 (DTVP-2) and the Drawing subtest of the Wide Range Assessment of Visual–Motor Abilities. The sample is described only as 122 students attending public schools. Correlations were moderate.

The author provides evidence for construct validity by (1) generating a set of hypotheses about what performance on the test would look like if it were measuring what is intended and (2) providing answers to the hypotheses. He shows that the abilities measured by the VMI are developmental, that they are related to one another, and that the supplements measure a part, but not the whole, of the abilities measured by the VMI. He also shows that performance on the VMI is related more closely to nonverbal than to verbal aspects of intelligence, that performance on the test correlates moderately with performance on academic-achievement tests, and that test performance is related to disabling conditions.

Summary

The VMI is designed to assess the integration of visual and motor skills by asking a child to copy geometric designs. As is the case with other such tests, the behavior sampling is limited, although the 27 items on the VMI certainly provide a larger sample of behavior than is provided by the 9 items on the BVMGT. The VMI has relatively high reliability and validity in comparison with other measures of perceptual–motor skills.

Test of Visual–Motor Integration (TVMI)

The Test of Visual–Motor Integration (TVMI; Hammill, Pearson, & Voress, 1996) measures the ability to relate visual stimuli to motor responses in an accurate, appropriate manner. The test is intended for use with children and adolescents aged 4 to 17 years and takes about 15 to 30 minutes to administer. The authors identify four uses of this test: "(a) to document the presence and degree of visual–motor difficulties in individual children, (b) to identify candidates for referral, (c) to verify the effectiveness of intervention programs, and (d) to serve as a research tool" (1996, p. 3).

The 30 TVMI items each require a student to copy a design. The number of items administered depends on the student's age and proficiency in copying designs. For students younger than 11 years, the test is always started with the first design and continued until the student scores a 0 on three items in a row. Students over 11 years of age begin with Item 13 and continue until they earn a score of 0 on three items in a row.

Scores

Students earn scores of 0, 1, 2, or 3, depending on the quality of their copies of designs. Examples of how to score the test are included in the manual. Raw scores on the TVMI can be transformed to age equivalents, percentiles, and standard scores.

Norms

The TVMI was standardized on 2,478 children in 13 states. Data were collected in 1992 and 1995. Students were tested by 14 examiners, and the sample was stratified for age only. Tables in the manual compare the makeup of the standardization sample to that of the 1990 census on gender, urban/ rural residence, race, geographic region, ethnicity, income, educational attainment of parents, and age. There are cross-tabulations for age only, so we do not know, for example, where the males came from.

Reliability

The authors report the internal-consistency reliability of the TVMI, based on the performance of the entire norm sample. The internal-consistency coefficient was .91. Test–retest reliability is based on the performance of 88 students, ages 4–10 years, attending a private school in Austin, Texas. The students are not described. The test–retest coefficient was .80. Interscorer reliability was established by having two people score 40 protocols. A coefficient of .96 was attained.

Validity

Two important validity questions are, Does this test measure visual–motor integration, and does it predict performance in school? In selecting the content for this test, the authors picked designs from other measures of visual–motor integration. To establish criterion-related validity, they gave it to a limited sample of students. The TVMI, MFVPT, and VMI were given to 99 "students with various neurologic impairments and autism" attending a private school in Pennsylvania. The group is not described further. The TVMI correlated .67 with the MFVPT and .95 with the VMI.

In providing evidence of construct validity, the authors argue, and demonstrate, that the test should (a) correlate more highly with age for younger than for older students, (b) show a low relationship to measures of school achievement, (c) correlate moderately well with broad-based measures of intelligence, and (d) differentiate groups of people known to be average and below average in visual-integration ability. Evidence is based on the performance of limited samples. The TVMI does measure the same skills as other measures of visual–motor integration, but performance on the test does not predict performance in school.

Summary

In the TVMI, students are asked to copy geometric designs. The sample of behavior is limited to 30 items (6 more than on the VMI). Evidence of reliability and validity is very limited.

● ●

Summary

Educational personnel typically assess perceptual–motor skills for one of three reasons: prevention, remediation, or differential diagnosis. First, the preventive use of perceptual–motor tests to identify children who demonstrate perceptual–motor difficulties is based on the assumption that without special perceptual–motor training, these children will experience academic difficulties. Second, tests are used to try to ascertain whether perceptual–motor difficulties are already causing academic difficulties and must therefore be remediated. Third, perceptual–motor tests are used diagnostically to identify brain injury or emotional difficulties.

In this chapter, we reviewed the most commonly used perceptual–motor tests. Most lack the reliability needed in making important instructional decisions.

Coping with Dilemmas in Current Practice

● ●

The assessment of perceptual–motor skills is incredibly problematic, with many obvious problems. First, it is very difficult to define perception and therefore difficult to come up with measures of it. Yet school personnel assume, and in fact insist, that adequate perceptual–motor development is a necessary prerequisite to acquiring reading skills. Often, assessors are asked to find out whether students have perceptual–motor problems. Without an adequate definition of perception, with few technically adequate tests to measure it, and with no evidence that there are specific, effective interventions for students with perceptual–motor problems, the assessor is in a difficult bind.

We believe that if assessments cannot be done properly, they should not be done at all. We believe that this is one domain in which formal assessment using standardized tests is of little value. Rather, we encourage those who are concerned about development of perceptual–motor skills to engage in direct systematic observation in the natural environment in which these skills actually occur.

Likewise, they lack demonstrated validity; we simply cannot say with much certainty that the tests measure what they purport to measure.

The practice of perceptual–motor assessment is linked directly to perceptual–motor training or remediation. There is an appalling lack of empirical evidence to support the claim that specific perceptual–motor training facilitates the acquisition of academic skills or improves the chances of academic success. Perceptual–motor training will improve perceptual–motor functioning. When the purpose of perceptual–motor assessment is to identify specific important perceptual and motor behaviors that children have not yet mastered, some of the devices reviewed in this chapter may provide useful information; performance on individual items will indicate the extent to which specific skills (for example, walking along a straight line) have been mastered. There is no support for the use of perceptual–motor tests in planning programs designed to facilitate academic learning or to remediate academic difficulties.

Questions for Chapter Review and Thought

1. Identify the major difficulties in conducting perceptual–motor skill assessment.

2. Discuss the rationale for using perceptual–motor tests. Discuss the degree to which the rationale is supported by research.

3. Assume that you had to assess a student's perceptual–motor skills. How would you go about doing this in a way that would be appropriate?

4. Homer, age 6-3, takes two visual-perceptual–motor tests, the Developmental Test of Visual Perception-2 and the Developmental Test of Visual–Motor Integration. On the DTVP-2, he earns a developmental age of 5-6, and on the VMI, he earns a developmental age of 7-4. Give two different explanations for the discrepancy between the scores.

5. Performance on the Bender Visual Motor Gestalt Test is used as a criterion in the differential identification of children as brain injured, perceptually handicapped, or emotionally disturbed. Why

must the examiner use caution in interpreting and using test results for these purposes?

Resources for Further Investigation

Project

Using information found in the text, write a summary for one test used in the assessment of perceptual–motor skills. Upon completion, compare your summary with the text summary. Then go to *The Twelfth Mental Measurements Yearbook* (see "Print Resources"), and compare and contrast your summary with the review of the test you selected. If your summary differs from the review, did the reviewer use information and standards different from those that you used?

Print Resources

Arter, J., & Jenkins, J. R. (1979). Differential diagnosis—prescriptive teaching: A critical appraisal. *Review of Educational Research, 49*, 517–556.

Beery, K. E. (1997). *Developmental Test of Visual-Motor Integration.* Cleveland: Modern Curriculum Press.

Bender, L. (1938). *Bender Visual Motor Gestalt Test.* New York: Grune & Stratton.

Conoley, J. C., & Impara, J. C. (1995). *The twelfth mental measurements yearbook,* (DTVP, pp. 289–292; DTVMI, pp. 286–289). Lincoln, NE: University of Nebraska Press.

Hammill, D., Pearson, N., & Voress, J. (1996). *Test of Visual–Motor Integration.* Austin, TX: Pro-Ed.

Mann, L. (1971). Perceptual training revisited: The training of nothing at all. *Rehabilitation Literature, 32*, 322–335.

Technology Resources

Welcome to AGS On-line Products and Services

http://www.agsnet.com/

Look for product and ordering information about the instruments available from American Guidance Service.

Pro-Ed Catalog Information for Products
http://www.proedinc.com
Find product and ordering information about the *Test of Visual–Motor Integration,* the *Developmental Test of Visual Perception,* and the *Developmental Test of Visual–Motor Integration.*

Bender Visual Motor Gestalt Test
http://138.86.6.82/pub2/~bardos/bender.html
This site gives a short description, information on administration, and directions for the test.

Assessment of
Problem Behavior

In Chapter 10, we noted that teachers, psychologists, and other diagnosticians systematically observe behavior that causes concern: behavior that is (a) harmful to students themselves or to other persons, (b) stereotypic, (c) desirable but infrequent or absent, or (d) exhibited in inappropriate contexts. Some behavior is of concern even when it occurs infrequently and in limited contexts. For example, setting fire to an animal is significant even if it rarely occurs—only every year or so. Other behavior is of concern only because it occurs too frequently. For example, most children are late for school once or twice; however, being late for school every day suggests that something is amiss. Finally, some behavior is important only to the extent that it is part of a larger pattern of problem behavior. For example, some patterns of behavior might suggest organic pathology (such as brain damage or hearing loss); other patterns may define a disability (such as emotional disturbance or autism). In this chapter, we discuss the assessment of patterns of behavior that are variously termed *social, emotional,* or *problem behaviors.*

The development and expression of social–emotional behavior is often influenced by each specific environment the student encounters (Bronfenbrenner, 1979). Therefore, when examining problem behavior, we are particularly interested in the extent to which behavior is generalized across contexts. Behavior that is restricted to one or a few contexts is more likely to be under environmental control. For example, there may be discriminative stimuli unique to the few environments that occasion the behavior; there may also be specific contingencies in those environments that increase or at least maintain the behavior. Problem behavior that is generalized to most environments may have multiple determinants, may be biologically based, or may simply be well generalized. Such behavior may be more difficult to modify and therefore of greater concern than behavior isolated to a few contexts.

Ways of Assessing Problem Behavior

Six methods are commonly used, singly or in combination, to gather information about problem behavior: rating scales, observational procedures, self-report measures, interview techniques, situational measures, and projective methods.

Rating Scales

There are several types of rating scales; generally a parent, teacher, peer, or "significant other" in a student's environment must rate the extent to which that student demonstrates certain desirable or undesirable behaviors. Raters are often asked to determine the presence or absence of a particular behavior and may be asked to quantify the amount, intensity, or frequency of the behavior. Rating scales are popular because they are easy to administer and useful in providing basic information about a student's level of functioning. They offer structure to an assessment or evaluation and can be used in almost any environment to gather data from almost any source. The important concept to remember is that rating scales provide an index of someone's perception of a student's behavior. Different raters will probably have different perceptions of the same student's behavior and are likely to provide different ratings of the student; each is likely to have different views of acceptable and unacceptable expectations or standards. Gresham and Elliott (1990) point out that rating scales are inexact and should be supplemented by other data-collection methods.

Observational Procedures

Most observational procedures used to assess emotional characteristics are systematic. As Merrell (1994) notes, "The most direct and desirable way to assess child and adolescent behavior in most cases is through naturalistic observation." H. M. Walker (1983) claims that observation of natural situations reduces the chance of making incorrect assumptions. We most often observe students in school, but there are times when a home or work environment is a more appropriate setting. Sometimes it is necessary to contrive a situation for an observation of a student. Such an observation is called an "analogue" and serves to control the environment to increase the probability that the behavior of concern will be exhibited.

Self-report Measures

A technique commonly used in social–emotional assessment is the self-report measure. Individuals being assessed are asked to reveal common behaviors in which they engage or to identify inner feelings. Martin (1988) maintains that self-reports of "aspirations, anxieties, feelings of self-worth, attributions about the causes of behavior, and attitudes about school are [important] regardless of the theoretical orientation of the psychologist" (p. 230). Self-reports are usually part of a more comprehensive assessment plan and often involve the use of interviews to obtain data.

Interview Techniques

Interviews are most often used by experienced professionals as a source of information about a student's perspective on a variety of issues and to gain insight into overall patterns of thinking and behaving. There are many variations on the interview method—most distinctions are made along a continuum from structured to unstructured or from formal to informal. Regardless of the format, Merrell (1994) suggests that most interviews probe for information in one or more of the following areas of functioning and development: medical/developmental history, social–emotional functioning, educational progress, and community involvement. Increasingly, the family as a unit (or individual family members) is the focus of interviews that seek to identify salient home-environment factors that may be having an impact on the student (Broderick, 1993).

Situational Measures

Situational measures of social–emotional behavior can include nearly any reasonable activity (Walker, 1973), but two well-known methods are peer-acceptance nomination scales and sociometric ranking techniques. Both types of measures provide an indication of an individual's social status and may help describe the attitude of a particular group (such as the class) toward the target student. *Peer-nomination techniques* require that students identify other students whom they prefer on some set of criteria (such as students they would like to have as study partners). From these measurements, *sociograms,* pictorial representations of the results, can be created. Overall, sociometric techniques provide a contemporary point of reference for comparisons of a student's status among members of a specified group.

Projective Methods

To delve more deeply into an individual's personality, projective measures are sometimes used. Projective methods grew out of psychoanalytic and Gestalt psychology. In this method, ambiguous stimuli (such as inkblots) are presented, and individuals are asked to describe what they see. Theoretically, the inner feelings of the students are engaged by the stimuli, and they will project aspects of their personality in their responses. Information about their thoughts, beliefs, expectations, and needs is obtained. Sometimes, projective techniques involve responses requiring a lower level of inference. For example, measures using sentence-completion stimuli may be used to probe about a particular event or time period. In this case, projective methods are somewhat like interviews but still require a great deal of interpretation on the part of the examiner.

Why Do We Assess Problem Behavior?

There are two major reasons for assessing problem behavior: (1) identification and classification, and (2) intervention. First, some disabilities are defined, in part, by inappropriate behavior. For example, the regulations to implement the Individuals with Disabilities Education Act describe in general terms the types of inappropriate behavior that are indicative of emotional disturbance and autism. Thus, to classify a pupil as disabled and in need of special education, educators need to assess social and emotional behavior.

Second, assessment of problem behavior may lead to appropriate intervention. For students whose disabilities are defined by behavior problems, the need for intervention is obvious. However, the development of prosocial behavior and the reduction of problem behavior are worthwhile goals for any student. After intervention, problem behaviors are assessed to learn whether the treatment has been successful and the desired behavior has generalized.

Specific Tests of Social–Emotional Behavior

Attention-Deficit Disorders Evaluation Scale–Second Edition, School Version (ADDES-2, SV)

The Attention-Deficit Disorders Evaluation Scale– Second Edition, School Version (ADDES-2, SV; J. McCarney, 1995b), is a rating scale consisting of 60 items divided into two subscales: Inattentive (29 items) and Hyperactive–Impulsive (31 items). The test was designed to measure the three constructs of attention-deficit/hyperactivity disorder (ADHD) posited in *The Diagnostic and Statistical Manual of Mental Disorders*–fourth edition (DSM-IV): ADHD, combined type; ADHD, inattentive type; and ADHD, hyperactive–impulsive type. The ADDES-2, SV is administered individually; it takes about 20 minutes for an educator familiar with the target student to complete the scale. Appropriately used with students from 4 or 5 years to 18 years of age, the ADDES-2, SV is intended to accomplish the following (J. McCarney, 1995b, p. 5):

1. Screen for characteristics of ADHD

2. Provide a measure of ADHD

3. Contribute to the diagnosis of ADHD

4. Contribute to the development of program goals and objectives

5. Identify intervention activities for ADHD in educational environments

Each item is scored on a 5-point scale:

0 Does not engage in the behavior

1 One to several times per month

2 One to several times per week

3 One to several times per day

4 One to several times per hour

All items on all scales are to be completed; if an item is not appropriate for a particular student, it is scored as "Does not engage in the behavior."

Scores

Raw scores on each subscale can be converted to standard scores (mean = 10, standard deviation = 3). Five score-conversion tables are provided for females, based on their ages: 4 through 6, 7 through 8, 9 through 12, 13 through 15, and 16 through 18. Five score-conversion tables are also provided for males, but the age ranges are different: 4 through 7, 8 through 9, 10 through 13, 14 through 15, and 16 through 18. Subscale standard scores can be summed and converted to percentile ranks.

Norms

The ADDES-2, SV was normed on 5,795 students who ranged in age from 4-0 to 19 years. No age group has fewer than 329 students. In all, 30 states are represented in the norms. The author provides no information about his sampling plan or how students and teachers were recruited.

When compared with 1992 U.S. demographic data, the sample as a whole is generally representative in terms of sex, race, urban/rural residence, and mother's occupation. The North Central region of the country is overrepresented, as are blue-collar workers. However, no information is provided about specific age groups—critical information for judging the adequacy of the scale's norm for the particular student being evaluated.

Reliability

Stability was estimated using 481 individuals randomly selected from the normative sample, who were rerated within 30 days of their initial rating. For total score and each subscale, an estimate of stability is provided for each age group and sex. All stability estimates exceed .90 for the total score and the Inattentive subscale. For the Hyperactive–Impulsive subscale, the stabilities for males all equal or exceed .90; three of the five stabilities for females equal or exceed .90, and the remaining two are in the high .80s.

Interrater agreement was evaluated by having 237 pairs of teachers rate 462 students selected at random from the standardization sample. The two ratings of each subject were correlated by ages (for boys and girls together). With one exception (age 16), all correlations were in the .80s.

Coefficient alpha was used to estimate the internal consistency of each subscale and the total score, based on the performance of the total normative sample.[1] One coefficient alpha (.98) is reported for each subscale and for the total score (.99). However, because this coefficient was calculated across a wide range of ages, internal consistency will be overestimated to the extent that age and ADDES-2, SV scores are correlated.

Validity

Overall, evidence for content validity appears good. Items for the ADDES-2, SV were derived from the literature and input from educational diagnosticians. Items were field-tested prior to standardization. Data from the standardization sample suggest that individual items produce distributions of responses and that individual items are associated with total scores.

Construct validity was investigated in two ways. First, although incompletely reported, factor analyses suggest that the ADDES-2, SV comprises as many as five factors. The first factor (Inattention) is very strong, and the second factor (Hyperactive–Impulsive) is relatively weak. In a two-factor solution, 41 of the 60 scale items are correlated with both factors, and the correlation between subscales exceeds .7. Some evidence of construct validity is provided by a study comparing 72 male and 30 female students previously identified as having ADHD with 72 male and 30 female students drawn at random from the standardization sample. On average, both male and female students with ADHD earned substantially lower scores than the nondisabled students.

To investigate the criterion-related validity, ADDES-2, SV ratings of students previously identified as having ADHD were compared with their ratings on five other scales: the Conners' Teacher Rating Scale–28, the Conners' Teacher Rating scale–39, the ADHD Comprehensive Teacher's Rating Scale, the Children's Attention and Adjustment Survey (school form), and the Child Behavior Checklist (teacher report form). Although incompletely reported, the results of these studies appear to provide good support for concurrent validity. The ADDES-2, SV is highly correlated with subtests measuring inattention, impulsivity, hyperactivity, and so on, but it is essentially uncorrelated with other characteristics (such as withdrawal).

Summary

The ADDES-2, SV is a 60-item rating scale designed for use with students between 4 and 18 years of age. There are two subscales (Inattentive and Hyperactive–Impulsive). Separate norms are provided for boys and girls at five age groups. Although the overall sample appears to be generally representative of the United States, no information about the representativeness of the individual sex–age norm groups is presented. Scores tend to be stable, but interrater agreement is sufficient only

---

1. Although, in the text, the author says that KR-20 was used to estimate internal consistency, the table containing the values reports coefficient "alpha." Because KR-20 can be used only with dichotomously scored data and the items in this scale are scored on a 5-point scale, we assume that "KR-20" is a typographical error.

for screening purposes. Data on internal consistency are inadequately reported. Content and criterion-related validity appear strong. Evidence of construct validity is quite limited.

Attention-Deficit Disorders Evaluation Scale–Home Version (ADDES-HV)

The Attention-Deficit Disorder Evaluation Scale–Home Version (ADDES-HV; J. McCarney, 1995a) is a counterpart of the Attention-Deficit Disorders Evaluation Scale–Second Edition, School Version (ADDES-2, SV). Large portions of the manual, the scale format, and many items are virtually identical to the school version. Intended uses of the device are the same as those for the ADDES-2, SV, except that the home is the target environment for intervention planning. Like items on the school version, items on the ADDES-HV are rated on a 5-point scale:

0 Does not engage in the behavior

1 One to several times per month

2 One to several times per week

3 One to several times per day

4 One to several times per hour

The 46-item scale is divided into two subscales: Inattentive (22 items) and Hyperactive–Impulsive (24 items). Although the ADDES-HV contains fewer items than the school version, item content is similar and is designed to reflect *The Diagnostic and Statistical Manual of Mental Disorders*–third edition (DSM-III-R) definition of attention-deficit/hyperactivity disorder.

Scores

Raw scores are obtained for each subscale by summing the ratings assigned to each item. Subscale raw scores are converted to standard scores (mean = 10, standard deviation = 3) by using gender- and age-specific norm tables. Percentile ranks are available only for the total score (that is, the sum of subscale standard scores).

Norms

The ADDES-HV was normed on 2,415 students who ranged from 3-0 to 20 years of age. In all, 30 states are represented in the norms. The author provides no information about his sampling plan or how students and parents were recruited. When compared with 1992 U.S. demographic data, the sample as a whole is generally representative in terms of sex, race, urban/rural and regional residence, and mother's and father's occupation. However, no information is provided about specific age groups—critical information for judging the adequacy of the scale's norms for the particular student being evaluated.

Because males earn "significantly" higher scores on both subscales than females, separate norms were provided for each sex. For reasons that are not entirely clear, norms are provided in multiyear age ranges (except for 6-year-old boys). For females, the age groups are 3 through 6, 7 through 8, 9 through 10, 11 through 13, and 14 through 18. For males, the age groups are 3 through 5, 6, 7 through 10, 11 through 12, and 13 through 18. Although an unknown number of 19- and 20-year-olds were apparently included in the norm sample, the norm tables for men and women stop at 18 years of age.

Reliability

Stability was estimated using either 86 or 148[2] individuals randomly selected from the normative sample, who were rerated within 30 days of their

---

2. Table 3 of the technical manual reports different numbers from the text (p. 11).

initial rating. Stability coefficients are provided by sex and age, although the age groups are not the same as those used in tables to convert raw scores to standard scores. For subscales, 5 stability coefficients are either .88 or .89, and the remaining 15 equal or exceed .90.

Interrater agreement was estimated by examining the total ratings of 86 students by both of their parents. Four groups were formed: children from 4 through 7 years, from 8 through 10 years, from 11 through 13 years, and from 14 through 20 years. The correlations of interparent ratings ranged from .80 to .84.

Coefficient alpha was used to estimate the internal consistency of each subscale and the total score, based on the performance of the total normative sample.[3] One coefficient alpha (.96) is reported for each subscale and for the total score (.96). However, because this coefficient was calculated across a wide range of ages, internal consistency may be overestimated to the extent that age and ADDES-HV scores are correlated.

Validity

Content validity is based on literature reviews, input from diagnosticians and parents of children with ADHD, and systematic field testing. In addition, item-response distributions and item–total correlations were examined.

Construct validity was investigated in two ways. First, although incompletely reported, factor analyses suggest that the ADDES-HV comprises as many as four factors. The first factor (inattention) is very strong, and the second factor (hyperactive–impulsive) is relatively weak. In a two-factor solution, two thirds of the items corre-

late with both factors, and the correlation between subscales exceeds .7. Some evidence of construct validity is provided by a study comparing 72 male and 30 female students previously identified as having ADHD with 72 male and 30 female students drawn at random from the standardization sample. On average, both male and female students with ADHD earned substantially lower scores than the nondisabled students.

To investigate the criterion-related validity, ADDES-HV ratings of students previously identified as having ADHD were compared with their ratings on four other scales: the Conners' Parent Rating Scale–48, the Conners' Parent Rating Scale–93, the Children's Attention and Adjustment Survey (home form), and the Child Behavior Checklist. Although incompletely reported, the results of these studies appear to provide good support for concurrent validity. The ADDES-HV is highly correlated with subtests measuring inattention, impulsivity, hyperactivity, and so on, but is less correlated with other characteristics (such as withdrawal or somatic complaints).

Summary

The ADDES-HV is a 46-item rating scale designed for use with children and students 3 to 18 years of age. The instrument consists of two subscales: Inattentive and Impulsive–Hyperactive, each of which is supposed to assess ADD characteristics.

Like the ADDES-HV, this instrument was standardized using sufficient numbers of subjects in the norm samples. However, the procedures used to recruit subjects and the characteristics of resulting age–gender norm groups are inadequately described. Scores tend to be stable, but interrater agreement is sufficient only for screening purposes. Data on internal consistency are incompletely reported. Content and criterion-related validity appear to be relatively strong. Evidence of construct validity is quite limited.

---

3. Although in the text, the author says that KR-20 was used to estimate internal consistency, the table containing the values reports coefficient "alpha." Because KR-20 can be used only with dichotomously scored data and the items in this scale are scored on a 5-point scale, we assume that "KR-20" is a typographical error.

Autism Screening Instrument for Educational Planning, Second Edition (ASIEP-2)

The Autism Screening Instrument for Educational Planning, Second Edition (ASIEP-2; Krug, Arick, & Almond, 1993) is an assessment consisting of five separate subtests. Each subtest is designed to assist in one or more of the following areas: screening, diagnosis, placement, program planning, and progress monitoring. The Autism Behavior Checklist, Sample of Vocal Behavior, and Interaction Assessment are listed as screening and diagnostic scales; Educational Assessment and Prognosis of Learning Rate may be used in conjunction with the diagnostic tests as part of a complete intervention-planning battery. The Autism Behavior Checklist is designed for use with any individual who may have autism, whereas the other subtests are appropriate for individuals functioning at a language and social age of between 3 and 49 months.

Subtests

The Autism Behavior Checklist (ABC) consists of 57 differentially weighted behavior statements grouped into five symptom areas: sensory, relating, body and object use, language, and social/self-help. The rater (a professional educator or parent) circles the number (weight) that most accurately describes the student or client with respect to a given behavior statement.

The Sample of Vocal Behavior (SVB) is used to evaluate expressive speech at the preverbal and emerging language levels. The authors recommend that two people share responsibility for conducting this subtest—one to elicit utterances and one to make a verbatim recording. The subtest lasts 30 minutes or until 50 vocalizations are recorded.

The Interaction Assessment (IA) uses a ten-second time-sampling procedure under three conditions (active modeling, passive/no initiation, direct cues), each of which lasts four minutes. Student behaviors are categorized as interactions, indepen-

dent play, no response, or negative aggressive. Two adults (an observer and an interacting adult) are needed for this subtest, which measures spontaneous social reactions and the responses to requests.

The Educational Assessment (EA) probes the student's functioning level in five areas: in-seat behavior, receptive language, expressive language, body concept, and speech imitation. All subparts except in-seat behavior have 12 items. The assessor presents various materials (such as toys, foods, and blocks) and gives cues to the student to elicit certain responses. The EA probes the individual's adaptive-language concepts and requires that the child have some entry-level behaviors (such as staying seated and looking at objects). The authors state also that "an individual must have no disruptive behaviors that are incompatible with test taking" (Krug, Arick, & Almond, 1993, p. 5). The EA takes about 20 minutes and is meant to be useful in intervention planning.

The Progress of Learning Rate (PLR) subtest is used to examine an individual's rate of learning by training the individual on a discrete trial, direct-instruction task, using a differential reinforcement strategy. The learning task on which the student is trained—placing a chip on a tray—consists of three phases: pretraining, random presentation of objects (black-circle chip, white-circle chip, white-square chip), and posttesting for shape and color discriminations. Optional training steps that vary the positioning of the objects may be used.

Scoring Procedures and Scores

The ABC is scored by summing the weighted values first within symptom areas and then across all areas for a total score. Raw scores are plotted on summary profiles that show the area means for the standardization sample. The total score mean of the total sample on the ABC is 77 (standard deviation = 20), and the authors suggest a cutoff score of one-half standard deviation below this point (67) as indicating a high probability of autism (p. 27).

The SVB appears rather complicated to administer and score. The author's suggestion of tape-recording each subtest should be followed. Each of the nine possible speech characteristics is summed individually, and the total score is calculated as the sum of four areas: repetitive, noncommunicative, unintelligible, and babbling. This total score is also called the "autistic speech characteristics" score. All scores are plotted on a summary profile. A language-age equivalency (LAE) score is obtained by first summing some of the characteristics. Percentile scores are available in the IA profile for the total autistic speech characteristics only.

The IA yields raw scores in four areas: interaction, independent play, no response, and negative aggressive. These are plotted on a summary profile the shows mean performance levels of an autistic and a nonautistic subgroup. Raw scores are converted to percentiles using one of two charts defining the two groups by ABC total score, language age, and chronological age. An autistic social score is computed by following a formula on the record form. Care must be taken in using IA scores because two areas are positively oriented (interaction and independent play) and two are negatively oriented (no response and negative aggressive).

The EA is summarized by raw scores in five areas: in-seat, receptive language, expressive language, body concept, and speech imitation. The total score is the sum across these areas. Each raw score is plotted on a summary profile and can be converted to percentiles for either subgroup. The total raw score is converted to percentiles for the IA profile.

The PLR raw scores (number of trials to criterion) for each step of the subtest are translated to percentiles, according to the autistic–nonautistic breakdown. The raw score from the first random-position task is used on the IA profile and is converted to a percentile.

Norms

Autism Behavior Checklist The ABC was normed on three samples of individuals. Sample 1 consisted of persons selected by members of the American Association for the Education of the Severely/Profoundly Handicapped, "teachers of trainable mentally retarded children throughout Oregon, and attenders of several conference presentations in the western United States and Canada" (Krug, Arick, & Almond, 1993, pp. 41–42). Although 3,000 ABCs were distributed, Sample 1 consisted of just 1,049 individuals ranging in age from 18 months to 35 years. Reported diagnoses of the total sample were 172 autistic, 423 severely mentally retarded, 254 emotionally disturbed, 100 deaf–blind, and 100 nondisabled. No other demographic information on these persons is provided, except that the male-to-female ratio across all ages was 2.5 to 1.

Sample 2 consisted of 62 individuals ages 3 to 23 years, all of whom had a diagnosis of autism. The individuals were selected by professionals throughout the United States and Canada. Sample 3 consisted of 953 adults ages 21 to 68 years. Ninety-five percent of these individuals were diagnosed with severe mental retardation. It is not clear how these individuals were selected. No further information about Samples 2 and 3 is presented in the manual.

Given the limitations surrounding these low-incidence populations, the ABC norm samples may be somewhat representative of the autistic, deaf–blind, and severe mental-retardation groups. However, the remaining groups are inadequately sampled. Because very gross age breakdowns are given (such as 21–68 years for Sample 3), and because no other descriptions are provided, educators must be very cautious in making interpretations based on the ABC standardization.

Sample of Vocal Behavior For the SVB, 81 examiners collected data on 157 subjects ages 2 years, 4 months to 20 years; 61 of these persons had autism, and 96 had severe disabilities without autism. Forty of these individuals (24 with autism,

16 without autism) were selected for subgroup analysis to define representative summary profiles on the SVB. Preschool and school-age profiles were developed from samples of 9 and 14 students, respectively. No other information about any of these students is provided.

Interaction Assessment Sixty professionals gathered data for the standardization study of the IA. Subjects were 52 students with autism (as defined by the combination demographics of ABC scores, language age, and chronological age) and 63 individuals who were nonautistic but were otherwise severely disabled. Profiles based on the total sample are provided. No other identifying information on the IA standardization subjects is provided.

Educational Assessment The EA is a criterion-referenced subtest. Standardization was conducted by 80 examiners on 41 students who met the defined demographic criteria for autism and on 91 students who were severely disabled but not autistic. A summary profile on each group was developed.

Prognosis of Learning Rate The PLR was standardized on 124 students who were assessed by 81 examiners. Diagnostic profiles for autistic and nonautistic groups are provided.

Summary The norms for the ASIEP-2 are tenuous at best. The ABC is the best-normed subtest; however, the reader is given very little information other than numbers of subjects per diagnostic group. Hammill, Brown, and Bryant (1992) have suggested that 75 or more subjects in most one-year age intervals for which the test is intended to be used could have been considered appropriate for constructing useful norms. The representativeness of the ABC norm sample along demographic characteristics (such as gender, urban/rural domicile, parental education, geographic region, and ethnicity) is also largely unknown. The remaining four subtests were standardized on not more than 157 students, whose characteristics are mostly unspecified.

Reliability

Two reliability statistics for the ABC are provided. On the full Sample 1 group, split-half reliability was .87. On a subset of 14 children rated by 42 people, 95 percent interrater agreement was reached. No information is provided on the type of raters used.

Test–retest reliabilities on five areas of the SVB for 20 subjects over a three-day period were all above .81. Split-half reliability determined by separation of odd–even utterances was .95. Interrater agreement across the repetitive, babbling, noncommunicative, and unintelligible categories averaged 90 percent.

Eighty-seven observers who watched a videotape of the IA administration obtained a median agreement of 89 percent match to a criterion defined as the ratings of six professionals already familiar with the subtest. A Kuder–Richardson test of item reliability yielded a coefficient of .85.

A test–retest evaluation over an unspecified time period was conducted for the EA. Agreement ranged from 84 to 100 percent, with an average across all data points of 95 percent.

In summary, reliability evidence for the ASIEP-2 is potentially strong; most reported coefficients are above .80. Some reliability studies were on small samples of subjects, and some interrater agreement studies are not described in enough detail for a reader to be able to tell who is doing what comparisons. Finally, no reliability for the PLR is reported in the manual. The evidence on reliability is not strong enough to consider the ASIEP-2 reliable for all of the purposes presented by the authors.

Validity

Evidence for the validity of the ABC begins with the procedures used to establish content validity. The authors first examined many sources (such as instruments, checklists, and literature reviews) for relevant behavior descriptors. Second, 26 experts in the field of autism reviewed an initial ABC device. A revised version containing 57 items was subjected to chi-square analysis using individuals' reported autism as the criterion variable. Results were used to assign the weights for items by forming groups of items with similar predictive coefficients.

Two criterion-related validity studies are reported for the SVB. The autistic speech characteristics scores from the SVB were correlated with the total ABC scores for 185 subjects. Correlations ranged from .32 to .46. The SVB language-age raw score was correlated with the language age provided by examiners. This correlation was .81. The authors (Krug, Arick, & Almond, 1993) report that examiner-identified language ages were "generally from the Sequenced Inventory of Communication Development" (p. 46), although no summary of the examiners' reports is provided. Profiles of performance for the two groups are offered for the SVB.

Arguments for the content validity of the EA are based on the reviews of existing curricula, assessments, and literature related to the needs of individuals with autism. Specific validity studies are not presented for the IA or PLR subtests. Several studies showing differences between students with autism and students with severe disabilities on ASIEP-2 subtests are presented, and cross-validity data are discussed by the authors. It is sometimes unclear which sample participated in these studies. Matched sample studies usually had fewer than 25 students per group (some had 4 or 5). Cross-validity, in this case, refers to correlations among subtests of the instrument and not to analyses of performance of distinct groups on items from the subscales. Because validity for all subtests and their intended purposes must be demonstrated, the authors' treatment of validity issues in the manual provides only limited support for their claims for the instrument and its subscales.

Summary

The ASIEP-2 was developed for use by professionals in identifying persons with autism and in making appropriate educational plans. Five subtests are included: the Autism Behavior Checklist, Sample of Verbal Behavior, Interaction Assessment, Educational Assessment, and Prognosis of Learning Rate. Of these, the ABC is the best-developed, best-normed scale and may be useful for screening purposes. Reliability data for the subtests are sparse, and validity is inadequately demonstrated, for the most part. Validity of an instrument is demonstrated over time; the authors have sound theoretical bases for the instrument and its components, but to date, they have not documented enough evidence to support some of the suggested uses for particular scales. Skilled professionals may still gain useful information from administrations of the ASIEP-2, as the complete battery does yield a great deal of qualitative information about the examinee.

Overview of the Child Behavior Checklist

One of the most frequently used assessments of child and adolescent emotional/behavioral functioning is the Child Behavior Checklist (CBCL) series by Achenbach and his colleagues (Achenbach, 1991a; McConaughy, 1993b). The following overview draws on these sources. Table 25.1 summarizes the domains, groupings, and syndromes of the six forms of the CBCL.

The six forms of the CBCL are the original CBCL and 1992 Profile for Ages 2–3, the CBCL and 1991 Profile for Ages 4–18, the Youth Self-Report (YSR) and 1991 Profile for Ages 11–18, the Teacher's Report Form (TRF) and 1991 Profile for Ages 5–18, the Direct Observation Form (DOF), and the Semistructured Clinical Interview for Children and Adolescents (SCICA). The need for data on children's functioning from multiple sources has led to the development of multiaxial, empirically based assessment (Achenbach, 1991a). Therefore, each Achenbach scale seeks to document the strengths and weaknesses of the same child in different contexts. The instruments are designed to provide *behavioral descriptions* of students, as opposed to diagnostic inferences.

Data from multiple sources are the basis for empirically derived cross-informant syndromes for the CBCL, TRF, and YSR (McConaughy, 1993a). A *syndrome* is composed of items that tend to co-

TABLE 25.1 ● Domains, Groupings, and Syndromes of the CBCL

Test Form	Sections/Domains	Groupings and Syndrome Scales (numbered)
CBCL/4–18	I. Competence items	Extracurricular Activity Social Interaction School Functioning
	II. Problem items	Internalizing (1) Withdrawn (2) Somatic Complaints (3) Anxious/Depressed Externalizing (4) Delinquent Behavior (5) Aggressive Behavior (6) Social Problems (7) Thought Problems (8) Attention Problems (9) Sex Problems
CBCL/2–3		Internalizing (1) Anxious/Depressed (2) Withdrawn Externalizing (3) Aggressive Behavior (4) Destructive Behavior (5) Sleep Problems (6) Somatic Problems

TABLE 25.1 (*continued*)

Test Form	Sections/Domains	Groupings and Syndrome Scales (numbered)
TRF	I. Academic Performance	
	II. Adaptive Characteristics	Working hard
		Behaving appropriately
		Is learning
		Is happy
	III. Problem items	Internalizing
		(1) Withdrawn
		(2) Somatic Complaints
		(3) Anxious/Depressed
		Externalizing
		(4) Aggressive Behavior
		(5) Delinquent Behavior
		(6) Social Problems
		(7) Thought Problems
		(8) Attention Problems
YSR	I. Competence	Activities
		Social
		Total Competence
	II. Problem items	Internalizing
		(1) Withdrawn
		(2) Somatic Complaints
		(3) Anxious/Depressed
		Externalizing
		(4) Delinquent Behavior
		(5) Aggressive Behavior
		(6) Social Problems
		(7) Thought Problems
		(8) Attention Problems
		(9) Self-Destructive/Identity Problems
DOF		On Task
		Problem Behaviors
		Internalizing
		(1) Withdrawn/Inattentive
		(2) Nervous/Obsessive
		(3) Depressed
		Externalizing
		(4) Hyperactive
		(5) Attention Demanding
		(6) Aggressive

occur within one instrument. The *cross-informant syndromes* are composed of items that were found to be in a syndrome for at least two of these three instruments. All scoring profiles have two levels of problem scales: broad scales (Internalizing, Externalizing) and syndrome scales. As you read the descriptions of the Achenbach scales included here, keep in mind that the different scales share many items. Still, each form has its own research base, protocols, and technical manual. Achenbach also publishes overviews and integrative guides to assist professionals in using the various scales.

Child Behavior Checklist and 1991 Profile for Ages 4–18 (CBCL/4–18)

The Child Behavior Checklist and 1991 Profile for Ages 4–18 (CBCL/4–18; Achenbach, 1991b) is an individually administered parent (or surrogate) assessment checklist of a child's competence and problem behaviors. The primary purpose of the CBCL/4–18 is to provide a set of standardized procedures for assessing behavioral and emotional disorders. The current CBCL is a revision of *The Manual for the Child Behavior Checklist and Revised Child Behavior Profile* (Achenbach & Edelbrock, 1983). The CBCL/4–18 can be completed within 10 to 20 minutes. It assumes that the test administrator has fifth-grade reading ability, and it may be self-administered or read by the parent without modifying the results.

The CBCL/4–18 is composed of two main sections: Competence items and Problem items. Discriminations are made between children who are adapting successfully and those in need of additional support to deal with behavioral and emotional problems. The Competence scale includes 20 items that parents rate according to the amount and quality of their child's participation along three dimensions: (1) extracurricular activities (such as participation in sports, hobbies, clubs, and friendships), (2) social interactions, and (3) school functioning. The Problem section includes 118 specific problem items and 2 open-ended items. Problem items include statements such as "Argues a lot," "Deliberately harms self," or "Likes to be alone." On some items, parents are asked to describe the problem behavior—for example, "Hears sounds or voices that aren't there (describe)," or "Nervous movements or twitching (describe)." Two broad groupings of internalizing

and externalizing problems, nine syndrome scales, and a total Problem score are presented on the CBCL/4–18. The first grouping, internalizing, includes three syndrome scales: Withdrawn, Somatic Complaints, and Anxious/Depressed. The externalizing grouping consists of two syndrome scales: Delinquent Behavior and Aggressive Behavior. Four additional syndrome scales—Social Problems, Thought Problems, Attention Problems, and Sex Problems (scored only for ages 6–11)—are provided but are categorized as neither internalizing nor externalizing.

Scores

The Competence items are scored by having parents estimate their child's engagement (both type and quality) across the 20 items and three scales. A 4-point comparative scale ("Don't know," "Less than average," "Average," "More than average") is used to make judgments on a child's engagement in comparison with same-age peers. Problem items are scored using a 3-point response scale: 0, Not true; 1, Somewhat or sometimes true; 2, Very true or often true. Problem scores are computed by summing the item scores for each syndrome (Competence and Problem behaviors). Internalizing, externalizing, and total Problem scores are also computed. A child's score is then evaluated according to percentile ranks and normalized T-scores, to classify scores within a normal, borderline, or clinical range. Decision rules and scoring criteria are included in the manual. The CBCL/4–18 can be scored by hand or via computer.

Norms

The norms for the CBCL/4–18 consist of a national sample that includes children ages 4 through 18 years ($N = 2,368$). Normative data for the CBCL/4–18 are based on children who had not received mental-health or special-education services within one year of standardization. Subjects were recruited to produce a standardization sample representative of the 48 contiguous states, with respect to socioeconomic status (SES), geographic region, and urban, suburban, and rural demographic characteristics. The CBCL/4–18 scales are normed separately for each gender for ages 4–11 and 12–18. Ethnic distribution averaged across gender and age groups was 73 percent European American, 16 percent African American, 7 percent Hispanic American, and 3 percent other.

The CBCL/4–18 syndrome scales were derived from principal-components analyses of clinical samples of boys and girls ages 4–18. These children were from 52 clinical settings located in the Eastern, Southern, and Midwestern areas of the United States. The author claims that a broad distribution of SES, demographic, and other client characteristics was obtained; however, no data are provided to substantiate the claim.

Reliability

Data are reported on inter-interviewer reliability, test–retest reliability, and internal consistency. Achenbach uses intraclass correlation coefficients (ICCs) for several reliability measures. ICCs reflect the proportion of total variance present in item scores and are sensitive to differences in rank order and magnitude of scored items. It should be noted that a significant portion of supporting reliability information from earlier versions of the CBCL is not presented in the 1991 manual.

Inter-interviewer Reliability   To assess differences that may result if the CBCL/4–18 is self-administered or used as a questionnaire, inter-interviewer reliability was computed on results obtained by three interviewers. A total of 241 children were matched for gender, age, ethnicity, and SES to establish matched triads. ICCs obtained for the 20 Competence items and for the 118 specific Problem items were .93 and .96, respectively.

Test–Retest Reliability   A single interviewer visited mothers of 72 nonreferred 4- to 16-year-old children two times, one week apart. Reliabilities were .99 for the 20 Competence items and .95 for the 118 Problem items. Mothers' ratings of 80 children (the aforementioned 72 subjects plus an additional 8 subjects) were compared at two points, seven days apart. Mean correlation for all Competence items was .87, and mean correlation for Problem behavior items was .89.

CBCLs were completed by mothers during a longitudinal study that included low-birth-weight and normal-birth-weight children (ages 6–7 years and 7–8 years) at one- and two-year intervals. Across all Competence items, average mean correlations ranged from .56 to .63. Mean correlations across Problem items ranged from .71 to .74.

The author reports a study of parents' ratings of clinical and general population samples in a longitudinal investigation. Interparent agreement from four age groups ranged from .48 to .79 for the various syndromes. The mean r for total Competence was .79.

Internal Consistency   Internal consistency, using Cronbach's alpha for total Competence scales, ranged from .57 to .64. For total Problem items, alpha was .96 for both boys and girls at both age levels.

Validity

Several types of validity data are reported on the CBCL/4–18. The primary concern in the development of the CBCL/4–18 was to ensure content validity by assembling items that represented a broad range of competencies and problem items of clinical concern. Selection of the original item pool and evaluation of item content were extremely rigorous and included clinical research and literature reviews. In addition, consultations with clinical experts, developmental psychologists, psychiatrists, and psychiatric social workers were completed. The initial item pool was then pilot-tested. Empirical evidence and professional feedback were used to improve the final measure.

Criterion-Related Validity The CBCL/4–18, Conners Parent Questionnaire (1973), and Quay–Peterson Revised Behavior Problems Checklist (1987) were administered to parents of 60 clinically referred students 6 to 11 years old. The children were being seen in 60 separate outpatient settings across the United States and Canada. Correlations between the CBCL and the other measures are reported for scales that are similar or that correspond. Correlations between the CBCL and the Conners syndromes ranged from .56 to .86; total Problem scores correlated at .82. Correlations between the CBCL and the Quay–Peterson ranged from .52 to .88, with total Problem scores correlating at .81.

Achenbach states that a key index of criterion validity is the ability of a measure to identify individuals whose problems arouse enough concern that they are referred for professional help. Criterion validity of the CBCL/4–18 was assessed by determining the degree to which each scale discriminated between children who were selected from the clinical sample and nonreferred children who were demographically matched. All Competence scales were scored higher for nonreferred than for referred persons, and all Problem scales were scored lower for nonreferred than for referred persons.

Achenbach also presents relative-risk odds ratios to indicate the odds of an individual's having a particular condition, given a particular risk factor. This ratio is compared with the odds for individuals who do not have the particular risk factor. For the sake of this comparison, individuals who were scored in the clinical range were identified as having a risk factor. The odds ratios provide evidence that the CBCL/4–18 can help distinguish between these two groups of individuals.

Construct Validity The CBCL/4–18 syndromes were derived empirically, using a principal-components analysis to construct a taxonomy of childhood disorders. Results of discriminant analyses are presented for total scores, scale scores, and individual items. Probabilities for total *T*-scores and referral status are also provided. On the whole, the evidence suggests that if both total Competence and total Problem scores are in the same range (normal or clinical), then the CBCL/4–18 is very effective in making group discriminations. In addition, clinical cutoff points were used to evaluate the discriminant ability of the CBCL/4–18. Overall, 61 percent of the referred children score in the clinical range on the total Competence scale, compared with 16 percent of the nonreferred children. Additionally, 68 percent of the referred children scored in the clinical range on the total Problem score, compared with 18 percent of the nonreferred sample. These data provide evidence that the CBCL/4–18 discriminates between referred and nonreferred children.

Summary

The CBCL/4–18 is used to record in a standardized manner children's competence and problem behaviors as reported by a parent or other informant. Internalizing and externalizing dimensions are used to classify children's emotional and behavioral problems. Nine syndrome scales were derived empirically. Norms are adequate and more representative of the national population than for previous versions of the CBCL. Some of the reliability measures, although described in detail, were conducted on a small subset of the standardization sample. Validity is supported by content, criterion-related, and construct data within the manual. In addition, the author provides a reference to *The Bibliography of Published Studies Using the Child Behavior Checklist and Related Materials* (Achenbach & Brown, 1991), which is a resource that describes numerous studies identifying correlates of CBCL syndromes and other variables. The 1991 revision advances the CBCL assessment system, which continues to be one of the best available assessments for use by clinicians and psychologists.

Child Behavior Checklist and 1992 Profile for Ages 2–3 (CBCL/2–3)

The Child Behavior Checklist and 1992 Profile for Ages 2–3 (CBCL/2–3; Achenbach, 1992) provides information on behavioral and emotional problems evidenced by young children, as seen by parents or other respondents who interact with them. The CBCL/2–3 is a two-page form modeled after the CBCL/4–18. In fact, 59 problem items were taken from the CBCL/4–18. An additional 40 problem items were developed to meet the specific needs of children ages 2–3 years. Informants are asked to rate each item as either representing the child's current behavior or describing the child's behavior over the previous two months.

The CBCL/2–3 yields information on six empirically derived syndromes. These syndromes provide a profile of a child's problem behaviors along two broad groupings of behavior: internalizing and externalizing. The internalizing grouping comprises the Anxious/Depressed and Withdrawn scales. The externalizing grouping is composed of the Aggressive Behavior scale and the Destructive Behavior scale. Two additional scales, Sleep Problems and Somatic Problems, which are part of neither the internalizing nor the externalizing grouping, are provided. Unlike the other Achenbach behavioral scales, the CBCL/2–3 does not include a separate section of scored competence items for extracurricular activities, social interactions, or school functioning.

Scores

The CBCL/2–3 can be scored by hand or by computer. Detailed scoring procedures are described in the manual. Scale scores are computed by summing the scores of items that compose a separate behavioral grouping or scale. In addition, a total problems score is presented on the CBCL/2–3. Percentile ranks and T-scores can be obtained from a profile. Explicit decision rules and scoring criteria are provided in the manual for classifying a child's score on the internalizing or externalizing grouping, and for determining whether the child falls within the normal, borderline, or clinical range.

Norms

A national sample was obtained by identifying 2- to 3-year-old siblings of children who were part of the original standardization sample for the CBCL/4–18. Because gender and age distributions from this sampling procedure were unequal, children were also "randomly selected" from a previous CBCL sample recruited from Massachusetts. A total sample of 368 children was obtained (183 from the national sample and 185 from Massachusetts), with 92 children at each age level for both boys and girls. The author provides demographic breakdowns of the total sample; however, the degree to which these children are representative of the U.S. population at large may be questionable. Whereas the original standardization sample was recruited to produce a representative sample of the 48 contiguous states, no census data are provided to substantiate the author's claim that a representative sample was achieved in this case. It does appear that the Northeastern United States is overrepresented and the West is underrepresented.

The six syndromes for the 1992 profile were derived from (1) the original (1986) Massachusetts sample, (2) characteristics of children from a longitudinal study, and (3) characteristics of children receiving mental-health or special-education services in seven different states. This clinical sample consisted of 367 boys and 273 girls who were initially recruited from the previously named sites. However, to provide an equal number of boys and girls by age, a random subsample of 273 boys was selected, to produce a final clinical sample of 546 children.

Reliability

Interparent Agreement   The CBCL/2–3 was administered to both parents of 64 children at age 2 and of 59 children at age 3. All CBCL scales were evaluated for interparent-agreement correlations. Results indicate that interparent correlations were significant at the .01 confidence level at both ages and that mean correlations were similar (.63 for age 2 and .60 for age 3).

Test-Retest Reliability   Mothers' ratings of 61 nonreferred 2- and 3-year-old children from Massachusetts were compared seven days after their initial rating. Comparisons were calculated to examine the degree to which rank orders and magnitude of scores remained stable. Correlations for all six syndromes, internalizing and externalizing groupings, and total problem scales were significant at the .001 confidence level, with a mean r of .85.

Long-term Stability   Seventy-five children participating in a longitudinal study were rated by their mothers one year after having completed an initial rating. Stability correlations ranged from .50 to .78, with a mean correlation of .64.

Internal Consistency   Internal consistency using Cronbach's alpha was calculated for the matched referred and nonreferred children. The alphas for the six syndrome scales ranged from .65 (Somatic Problems) to .92 (Aggressive Behavior). For internalizing items, Cronbach's alpha was .88, and for externalizing items, .93. The total problems alpha was .96.

Validity

Content Validity   The CBCL/2–3 is an empirically derived scale based on assessment data for actual samples of children. A total of 99 problem items appear on the CBCL/2–3, 59 items from the CBCL/4–18 plus 40 additional items selected to provide differentiating data on emotional and behavioral problems in young children. These additional items were developed from interviews with parents and from previous research. Children who had been referred to a clinic for mental-health services obtained higher total scores than did demographically similar, nonreferred children. The author cautions users of the instrument to judge for themselves whether the content is appropriate for their particular purpose.

Criterion-Related Validity   A study of 642 children (321 children from the clinical standardization and 321 children from the general normative sample) who were matched on demographic characteristics revealed that children who were clinically referred scored significantly higher on all problem scales than did nonreferred children.

Construct Validity   Convergent validity was examined in a study comparing scores obtained on the CBCL/2–3 and the Richman Behavior Checklist (RBCL; Richman, Stevenson, & Graham, 1982), a British measure of problem behavior. Although the structure of the RBCL is different from that of the CBCL/2–3, correlations ranged from .56 to .77.

A second correlational study was conducted to assess the divergent validity of the CBCL/2–3 and common developmental measures. A total of 86 children participating in a low-birth-weight study were examined on the Bayley Mental Scale at age 2, the McCarthy General Cognitive Index at age 3, and the Minnesota Child Development Inventory (MCDI; Ireton & Thwing, 1974). The results of this study indicate no concurrent correlations between the CBCL/2–3 and the Bayley, the McCarthy, or the MCDI. These studies provide support for the CBCL/2–3 as a measure of the construct of early childhood problem behavior.

Further support of construct validity is found in the procedural studies in which the six syndromes and two primary groupings of problem behavior on the CBCL/2–3 were derived empirically, using a principal-components analysis. A clinical sample of 546 boys and girls from seven sites was recruited to obtain CBCL/2–3 data. Three sets of discriminant analyses were performed for each gender-age group. First, internalizing and externalizing scores were used as predictors. Second, the six syndrome scales were used as predictors, followed by all problem items. For boys, externalizing items discriminated between clinically referred and nonreferred children. Although externalizing items were seven times more powerful than internalizing items, the internalizing items also accounted for a significant amount of variance between the two groups. For girls, internalizing items accounted for a majority of the variance. These results suggest that specific items, groupings, and syndromes from the CBCL/2–3 can discriminate between clinically referred and nonreferred children, but the author points out that the degree of influence that sample specificity may have exerted is unknown.

Summary

The CBCL/2–3 is a two-page parent rating form of young children's emotional and behavioral prob-

lems. A total of 99 items are scored, using a 3-point scale. Some items are designed so that parents provide additional written descriptions to add clarity to behavioral concerns. The standardization sample, norms, reliability, and validity are not as well developed as they are for other Achenbach instruments. The author cites *The Bibliography of Published Studies Using the Child Behavior Checklist and Related Materials* (Achenbach & Brown, 1991) as a resource to validate the CBCL/2–3. This reference describes numerous studies identifying correlates of CBCL syndromes and other variables. Overall, the CBCL/2–3 appears to be an adequate adaptation of a well-known system of evaluation and should contribute greatly to the identification and monitoring of young children in need of additional emotional and behavioral supports. As the author mentions, however, the CBCL/2–3 should not be used as the sole data source when making individual diagnostic or placement decisions.

Teacher's Report Form and 1991 Profile for Ages 5–18 (TRF)

The Teacher's Report Form and 1991 Profile for Ages 5–18 (TRF; Achenbach, 1991c) is modeled on the CBCL/4–18 and is designed to obtain a description of a pupil's behavior as observed by teachers in school environments. Like all the Achenbach instruments, the TRF is not meant to be used as the sole basis for diagnostic inferences. Practitioners are encouraged to verify that the teacher is familiar with the student being evaluated and that the student has been enrolled in the class for at least a two-month period.

Description of the Scales

The TRF comprises three major sections. In the first section, a student's Academic Performance relative to grade level is rated by the teacher for

specific content areas. In the second section, ratings of four Adaptive Characteristics (working hard, behaving appropriately, is learning, and is happy) compare the target student with typically developing peers of the same age. Examples of Adaptive items include "How hard is he/she working?" and "How happy is he/she?"

The third section consists of 118 items indicative of childhood and adolescent behavior problems. Problem items include statements such as "Acts too young for his/her age," "Destroys property belonging to others," "Overconforms to rules," and "Withdrawn, doesn't get involved with others." As with the CBCL/4–18, several items require additional information from the teacher to provide a description of the problem behavior—for example, "Behaves irresponsibly (describe)" and "Stores up things he/she doesn't need (describe)." Two groupings (internalizing and externalizing), eight syndrome scales, and a total Problems score are presented on the TRF. The first grouping, internalizing, comprises three scales: Withdrawn, Somatic Complaints, and Anxious/Depressed. The externalizing grouping comprises the Aggressive Behavior scale and the Delinquent Behavior scale. Three additional scales, Social Problems, Thought Problems, and Attention Problems, are not categorized as part of the internalizing or externalizing grouping.

Scores

The Academic Performance items are scored on a 5-point scale from "far below grade level" to "far above grade level." Adaptive Characteristics are rated on a 7-point comparative scale. Problem Behaviors are scored on a 3-point scale (0, Never; 1, Somewhat or sometimes true; and 2, Very true or often true). Scale scores are computed by summing the item scores for each domain (Academic, Adaptive, Problems). Scores are plotted by gender and age (5–11 years and 12–18 years) to provide a graphic display for each scale. Percentiles based on nonreferred pupils and T-scores are obtained from the profile. Internalizing, externalizing, and total Problems scores are also computed. Decision rules and scoring criteria are included in the manual. The TRF can be scored by hand or by computer.

Norms

A subset of subjects assessed on the CBCL/4–18 in 1989 was used to standardize the TRF. Students aged 7 to 18 years were chosen to provide a representative sample of the 48 contiguous states, with respect to SES, ethnicity, region, and urban, suburban, and rural areas. The authors refer the user of the TRF to journal articles that define the census information. Children aged 5 to 6 years were siblings of those in the 7- to 18-year-old sample. A total of 2,113 children were ultimately recruited, and complete data were obtained for 1,613 (76%) of these children. Students who had received

special-education or mental-health services were removed from this group, to provide a normative sample ($N = 1,391$) of "healthy" individuals (Achenbach, 1991c, p. 15). The TRF scales are normed on each gender for ages 5–11 and 12–18. Ethnic distributions are similar to those of the CBCL/4–18.

A clinical sample of 2,550 students was obtained from a recruited sample of 2,815 children who were receiving either special-education services for severe emotional disturbances or mental-health services outside of school. The author reports that these students came from 58 settings that were diverse enough to "minimize selective factors affecting the caseloads of individual services" (p. 26); however, no supporting data are presented. This clinical sample was used (a) to derive the TRF syndrome scales and (b) to conduct validation studies.

Reliability

Test–Retest Reliability   Teachers completed TRF ratings twice on forty-four 8- and 9-year-old students following a waiting period of between 7 and 30 days. All test–retest correlations were found to be significant at the .01 confidence level except for one scale (Thought Problems for girls). Mean correlations between first and second assessments were .90 for Adaptive scales and .92 for all Problem Behaviors scales.

Stability   Teachers completed TRF ratings at two- and four-month intervals for 19 boys who were referred for special services relating to behavioral and emotional problems. The mean correlation was .75 at the two-month interval and .66 at the four-month interval.

Interrater Agreement   A total of 207 children ages 5–18 years were rated by two teachers who were familiar with each student. The mean correlation was .61 for the total Adaptive scale and .60 for the total Problems scale. A second study compared a primary teacher's rating of a child with that of a teacher's aide who worked with the child under similar conditions. Mean correlations were .65 for the total Adaptive and .57 for the total Problems scale.

Internal Consistency Internal-consistency reliability coefficients were reported for total Problems and for the externalizing and internalizing groupings. In addition, coefficients are provided for each of the eight syndrome scales by gender and age. Coefficients for both boys and girls (ages 5–11 years and 12–18 years) on the total Problems scale were approximately .97; on externalizing, the coefficient was .96; on internalizing, the coefficient was .90 for boys and .91 and .92 for girls at the two age levels. For boys, coefficients ranged from .70 (Delinquent Behavior) to .96 (Aggressive Behavior) on syndrome scales; for girls, coefficients ranged from .63 (Thought Problems) to .97 (Aggressive Behavior).

Validity

Content Validity All scale items on the TRF are statements of a student's competencies and problems that are identified concerns of parents, mental-health providers, and educators. The scales have been subjected to extensive research and clinical application. Most of the Problem Behaviors items on the TRF are taken directly from the CBCL/4–18. A total of 25 Problem Behaviors items were replaced with items that are more appropriate for teachers to rate, and an unspecified number of Problem items were altered to make them more appropriate for teachers. Academic Performance and Adaptive Characteristics items were evaluated during field testing for their usefulness in judging children's functioning in schools.

Criterion-Related Validity In a study to establish criterion-related validity, 45 students (38 boys, 7 girls) ages 5–16 years were rated by teachers on the TRF and the Conners Revised Teacher Rating Scale (Goyette, Conners, & Ulrich, 1978). TRF scales correlated from .80 to .83 with the Conners Conduct Problems, Inattention–Passivity, and total Problem scores. The TRF Aggressive Behavior

scale ($r = .67$) and the externalizing grouping ($r = .63$) were the closest counterparts of the Conners Hyperactivity scale. In addition, the closest counterpart of the Conners Hyperactivity Index was the TRF total Problems score (.71). Criterion-related validity of the TRF instrument was also assessed by evaluating two samples of demographically matched referred and nonreferred students who were rated by teachers. Nonreferred students were rated higher on Academic and Adaptive scales and lower on Problem scores, when compared with the referred sample. All comparisons were significant at the .01 confidence level, with the exception of Somatic Complaints for 12- to 18-year-old males.

Achenbach also presents relative-risk odds ratios to indicate the odds of having a particular condition, given that an individual has a particular risk factor. Odds-ratio analyses were conducted on TRF scores and referral status. Students from the matched referred and nonreferred sample were identified as scoring in the clinical range on any of the TRF scales. Next, calculations were made to determine the odds that a clinical score was obtained by a student from the referred sample. All odds ratios were significantly greater than 1.0, and the percentage of children scoring in the clinical range was statistically significant between the two samples at the .01 confidence level.

Construct Validity A study that compared 1,275 students referred for behavioral or emotional problems with 1,275 demographically matched nonreferred students was conducted to evaluate the discriminative validity of the TRF. With referral status as the criterion, results indicated that nonreferred students were rated significantly higher on all items of Adaptive functioning and lower on nearly all TRF Problem items. These data suggest that the TRF content is able to discriminate adequately between referred and nonreferred students.

One of the most efficient and effective ways to discriminate clinical from nonclinical subgroups is to classify students as deviant if their Academic, total Adaptive, and total Problem scores are in the clinical range. Additional findings are presented in the manual that will help practitioners select the most powerful combinations of scale and items to differentiate between clinical and normal samples. Evidence of construct validity is taken from independent studies of the TRF scores and children with clinical diagnoses. All evidence is provided on the pre-1991 measure. Children classified as having ADHD were found to produce higher scores on the TRF Attention Problems items than a control group of other clinically diagnosed children. In a comparison of special-education students, children classified as learning disabled scored significantly lower than those classified as emotionally disordered on Problem scales.

Overall, the TRF appears to be a useful measure of the construct of emotional/behavioral functioning. The TRF appears relatively successful at discriminating among groups of referred and nonreferred students and students with different disability conditions.

Summary

The TRF is a well-developed, empirically based instrument designed to obtain information about a student's performance on Academic, Adaptive, and Problem items in a standardized manner that can be compared with norms established by gender and age. The standardization sample was selected from the overall CBCL/4–18 sample. Three types of reliability data were reported. Test–retest coefficients were within an acceptable range, stability and interrater reliability are marginal, and internal consistency of scale items is based on factor-analytic studies. Validity rests primarily on CBCL/4–18 validity.

Overall, the TRF is a well-researched instrument that appears to measure what it is supposed to measure—the overall emotional/behavioral status of children and youth. The TRF is an important component of assessment that will well serve professionals in the field, as part of Achenbach's five-axis assessment systems.

Youth Self-Report and 1991 Profile for Ages 11–18 (YSR)

The Youth Self-Report (YSR; Achenbach, 1991d) is a self-administered rating scale designed to be completed in approximately 15 minutes by adolescents ages 11 to 18 years with at least a fifth-grade reading level. The YSR was developed primarily to assess a student's interests, feelings, and behaviors. It is a revision of the Manual for the Youth Self-Report and Profile (Achenbach & Edelbrock, 1987). The current revision incorporates new national norms and changes in the scoring profile and includes new provisions for integrating self-report data with the CBCL/4–18 and the TRF.

Description of the Scales

Two broad areas are assessed: Competence and Problem Behaviors. The Competence scales include activities (such as sports, hobbies, and extracurricular activities), social (such as total number of friends and activities with friends), and total competence, which includes self-ratings of academic performance. Problem scales include two groupings of syndromes: internalizing (Withdrawn, Somatic Complaints, Anxious/Depressed) and externalizing (Delinquent Behavior, Aggressive Behavior). Four additional syndromes are not part of either the internalizing or the externalizing grouping (Social Problems, Thought Problems, Attention Problems, and Self-Destructive/Identity Problems). (The Self-Destructive/Identity Problems syndrome is relevant for boys only).

The Problem Behaviors items are very similar to the items from the CBCL/4–18 but are written in the first person. An additional 16 items that were deemed to reflect socially undesirable behavior are also included on the Problem items scale. For example, items include statements such as "I argue a lot," "I destroy my own things," and "I set fires." Some items provide open-ended questions that allow the student to list additional physical problems or to provide further descriptions of scored items. Examples include "I do things other people think are strange (describe)" and "I have trouble sleeping (describe)." Respondents are encouraged to provide descriptions of these items so that the items will not be scored improperly.

Scores

Detailed scoring procedures are provided in the administration manual. Students rate their competence across different points of interest, using a 3-point scale—that is, they determine whether the amount of time or number of activities is "Less than average," "Average," or "More than average," as compared with their same-age peers. The 102 Problem items, plus an open-ended item, are rated on a 3-point scale (0, Not true; 1, Somewhat or sometimes true; 2, Very true or often true).

Raw scores are tallied for all items within individual scales and are plotted on the YSR profile by gender. Percentile rank and normalized *T*-scores are presented for all scales; no differentiation is made by gender or age. As with the other Achenbach instruments, scores may be classified within the normal, borderline, or clinical range.

Norms

A subsample of the CBCL standardization sample was recruited by targeting children and adolescents between 11 and 18 years of age. To create a normative sample that was representative of regular-education students, students who had not received mental-health services or special-education services within the preceding 12 months were selected from this group; the resulting YSR normative sample contained 1,315 subjects. Ethnic distributions were similar to those of the CBCL/4–18. The YSR scales are normed separately for

each gender for ages 11–18. A clinical sample of 709 boys and 563 girls ages 11–18 years was also assessed on the YSR. These subjects were from 26 settings, primarily in the Eastern United States. The author claims that a wide distribution of socioeconomic, demographic, and other client characteristics were obtained on all samples, although no national census data are provided for comparison.

Reliability

Test–Retest Reliability   Fifty subjects completed the YSR two times, with a seven-day time lapse. Correlations between the two administrations are presented for each scale by gender and age. Most scale correlations were significant at the .05 confidence level, although ratings by 11- to 14-year-olds were somewhat less reliable. The range of coefficients was from .37 (Activities for boys and Thought Problems for ages 11–14) to .91 (internalizing, externalizing, and total Problems for ages 15–18). The total Competence mean correlation was .80, and the total Problems scale mean correlation was .79.

Long-term Stability   Children selected from the general population sample completed the YSR on two occasions, seven months apart. A total of 111 children (49 boys, 62 girls) ages 11–14 years participated. Results are presented by gender and age groupings. Total Competence scores produced a mean correlation of .62, and the total Problems scale produced a mean correlation of .56. In a study of a nondefined clinical sample of 12- to 17-year-olds, total Problems scores correlated at .69 over a six-month interval (Achenbach & Edelbrock, 1987).

Internal Consistency   Internal consistency for the total Competence scale was .46; for total Problems, alpha was .95. Both the internalizing and externalizing groupings had internal consistencies of .89. Alphas for syndrome scales ranged from .59 (Withdrawn) to .86 (Aggressive Behavior and Anxious/Depressed).

Validity

Content Validity   A majority of YSR items were taken directly from the previously validated CBCL/4–18. The author describes the process used to revise some items and to delete others from certain scores.

Criterion-Related Validity   As with the other measures, referral status is used as the validity criterion. In a study of 2,108 subjects, the author evaluated the relationship between scale scores and concurrent referral status. Significantly higher Competence scores and lower Problem scores were obtained by the nonreferred group, compared with the referred group. For both girls and boys, the largest effects of referral status were found for Delinquent Behavior and for total Problems. The Problem scales appear to function well in discriminating between referred and nonreferred students; however, the YSR Competence scales are not strong discriminators of referral status.

Construct Validity   Achenbach does not present explicit evidence of construct validity for the YSR as he does for other measures. He offers the cur-rent lack of suitable (and similar) measures to employ in convergent and divergent validity studies as the reason for limited available evidence. Some indirect evidence is provided in the form of correlations among the other Achenbach instruments. The mean coefficient is .50 (with a range of .27 to .62). Ratings such as these are not unexpected and fall in the low to moderate range for validity coefficients.

Summary

The YSR is a self-administered report on an adolescent's competence and problem concerns. The instrument's scales provide indications of the student's overall emotional/behavioral status. Because of the empirical underpinnings of the YSR, its technical features are advanced for this particular type of assessment. However, they are not sufficiently defined and described to warrant extensive trust in the device. Reliability and validity studies are mixed but generally supportive. Still, the YSR should be considered a useful adjunct in screening and a key component in a multiaxial assessment process.

Direct Observation Form (DOF)

The Direct Observation Form (DOF; Achenbach, 1986) is designed to record behavior problems exhibited by a child during ten-minute observations. No age-range guidelines are given, although the clinical sample included children ages 5–14 years. Observations are conducted in group settings such as in classrooms and at recess. A detailed list of 96 specific problem behaviors and an open-ended item for entering additional problems are provided. In general, observers are asked to describe a child's behavior in a narrative during a ten-minute observation. The observer is advised to refer to the DOF items during the observation to organize the narrative description. In addition, a child's on-task behavior is recorded and included in the final description of his or her performance. After watching a child and completing the narrative, an observer rates the child on each of the 96 items and provides information on the open-ended question. Whereas the DOF provides supplemental information on a child's performance, direct links with the other Achenbach instruments are enhanced by the fact that 72 of the 96 Problem items have counterparts on the CBCL/4–18, and 85 items directly correspond to items on the TRF. Examples of Problem items include "Acts too young for age," "Argues," "Disturbs other children," "Shows off or clowns," and "Unhappy, sad, or depressed."

Like the other Achenbach instruments, the DOF can be scored by hand or by computer. Detailed rules for scoring each item are printed on the DOF form. Scores are provided on four broad scales and six syndromes. Broad scales include on task, total Problems, internalizing, and externalizing. The syndromes include Withdrawn/Inattentive, Nervous/Obsessive, Depressed, Hyperactive, Attention Demanding, and Aggressive. Unlike those for other instruments, the syndrome scores for the DOF can be obtained only when the computer-scoring program is used, because of the complexity of producing these scores.

Scores

The on-task intervals are tallied at the end of the observation and reported as a score ranging from 0 to 10. The 96 Problem Behaviors are also rated by the observer along a 4-point scale (0 to 3). This 4-point scale is different from those used in the other Achenbach instruments, in that the author claims that the additional gradation of the scale allows "a slight or ambiguous occurrence" of a behavior to be scored as a 1, "a definite occurrence with a mild to moderate intensity and less than three minutes duration" to be scored as a 2, and "a definite occurrence with severe intensity or greater than three minutes duration" to be scored as a 3.

Mean scores are computed based on the number of observations conducted. Scores can be plotted on the DOF profile, and percentiles and T-scores can be obtained to determine whether a target student's performance is within clinical or normal ranges. The same scoring profile is used for both boys and girls. The author suggests that the DOF should be completed on three to six occasions to obtain a stable index of a child's performance. In addition, to provide direct peer comparisons, it is suggested that two randomly selected peers be observed immediately prior to and immediately after observing the target child. The two peer observations can be averaged to provide a standard against which the target child's performance can be compared.

Norms

All scale scores and syndromes identified on the DOF are empirically derived using principal-components analyses on data obtained from a sample of 212 clinically referred individuals (5–14 years old). The DOF was then normed on 287 regular-education students recruited from 45 schools located in three states (Vermont, Nebraska, and Oregon). No additional demographic characteristics are provided.

Reliability and Validity

Reliability and validity information are not provided in a separate manual for the DOF. Rather, users of the DOF are referred to the following sources for technical data in support of the scale: Achenbach and Edelbrock (1983); McConaughy, Achenbach, and Gent (1988); and Reed and Edelbrock (1983).

Summary

The DOF provides practitioners with an observational tool that can be used to record on-task behavior and problem behaviors across 96 items that are highly similar to those included in other Achenbach instruments. Although the correspondence of items across the CBCL/4–18 and the TRF may be helpful in coordinating data, the overall technical adequacy of the DOF by itself is not well substantiated. The norms of the DOF are not well defined, and users of the scale who want information on reliability and validity must seek outside references to obtain this evidence. Overall, the DOF should be considered as an ancillary tool to substantiate behavioral problems in classroom or group settings, rather than as an independent instrument.

Additional Behavioral Assessment Scales

Additional Behavioral Assessment Scales

Behavior Evaluation Scale–2 (BES-2)

The Behavior Evaluation Scale–2 (BES-2; S. B. Mc-Carney & Leigh, 1990) is a 76-item rating scale developed for students enrolled in kindergarten through grade 12. The manual provides a brief description of the rationale for and importance of assessing emotional/behavioral disorders. The manual also provides clear administration, scoring, and interpretation guidelines, as well as technical information about the standardization process. Five scale scores are provided on the BES-2: Learning Problems, Interpersonal Difficulties, Inappropriate Behavior, Unhappiness/Depression, and Physical Symptoms/Fears. Educators who have had at least one month of interaction with a student may complete the BES-2 rating scale. Estimated time to complete the rating form is 15 to 20 minutes. The author suggests six primary uses of this scale:

1. Screen for behavior problems

2. Assess the behavior of students who are referred

3. Assist in the diagnosis of behavior disorders or emotional disturbance

4. Contribute to the development of individual educational programs

5. Document progress resulting from behavioral interventions

6. Collect data for research purposes

All items on the BES-2 are stated in observable and measurable terms. In addition, great effort has been made to link behavioral descriptions to federal guidelines established by Public Law 94-142, as well as to Bower's (1981) widely used definition of emotionally disturbed/behaviorally disordered children. To reduce the subjective nature of teachers' ratings, a 7-point scale is provided: 1, Never

or not observed; 2, Less than once a week; 3, Approximately once a month; 4, Approximately once a week; 5, More than once a week; 6, Daily at various times; 7, Continuously throughout the day. The authors claim that rating the frequency of behaviors can reduce the need for more expensive methods of direct and continuous observation by school personnel.

Scores

Five types of scores can be obtained from the BES-2: weighted scores of individual items, subscale raw scores, subscale standard scores, a quotient representing performance on the total scale, and percentile ranks for each subscale and total scale. Scale scores are computed by transferring ratings for each of the 76 items to a data-summary sheet on the rating protocol. Each subscale lists the specific item numbers that compose the five individual scales. Item ratings are multiplied by a preestablished weighting factor and summed by scale. The sums of the weighted scores for each of the five subscales are converted to standard scores (mean = 10, standard deviation = 3) and percentile ranks. A total quotient score (mean = 100, standard deviation = 15) and percentile rank are computed by summing the five subscale standard scores and using appropriate conversion tables provided in the appendix.

Norms

The BES-2 was standardized on a completely new standardization sample. A total of 2,272 students from 31 states were selected to represent four geographic regions of the United States. A sample of

568 regular-education teachers administered the BES-2 to randomly selected students from their classes. The number of participating children was distributed fairly equally across the K–12 grade levels (range = 137–207). Demographic characteristics of the sample provide a good match to the U.S. (1980) census data for gender, race, ethnicity, geographic area, and educational status of parents. A notable exception appears to be an underrepresentation of Hispanic American and Asian American students within the standardization sample.

Reliability

Two types of reliability data are offered for the BES-2: internal consistency and test–retest. Internal-consistency coefficients range from .75 to .95, with 20 of 24 calculated coefficients exceeding a coefficient alpha of .88. Total-scale coefficients were either .97 or .98 across all grade levels. Stability of scores obtained on typically developing children ($N = 82$) from 10 states and on emotionally disturbed/behaviorally disordered children ($N = 108$) from 13 states was assessed at an interval of 10–14 days. Spearman correlation coefficients between two sets of obtained scores (test and retest) exceed or round to .90 (range = .89–.97). All correlations were found to be statistically significant at the .001 level of confidence. No evidence of interrater agreement is provided.

Validity

Studies were conducted to provide evidence of validity for the BES-2. Three types of validity are presented: content validity, criterion-related validity, and construct validity. Appropriateness of scale items (content validity) was initially evaluated by a large sample of classroom teachers and special-education personnel with expertise in the area of behavioral disorders. In addition, during the revision process, a sample of 675 professionals from 31 states reviewed each item to determine its appropriateness for describing educational behavioral problems. All items on the final version were

judged by 95 percent of the experts as appropriate descriptors of problem behavior.

To evaluate concurrent criterion-related validity, the BES-2 was compared with the Teacher Rating Scale of the Behavior Rating Profile (BRP; L. Brown & Hammill, 1978). Twenty-six students from elementary and secondary grades, identified as behaviorally disordered and receiving special education services in Missouri, were assessed on both measures. Five of six scores on the BES-2 produced coefficients that were statistically significant at the .01 and .05 confidence levels (range = .44–.81). One subscale, Learning Problems, did not correlate at all with the BRP ($r = .01$). In another study, teachers' professional judgments were compared with BES-2 results. A total of 190 teachers rated students from regular ($N = 82$) and special-education ($N = 108$) classrooms (K–12) on the BES-2 after having answered the question, "Relative to other students of this age, how would you generally rate this student's classroom behavior?" A 9-point scale was used by the teachers to rate students. Behavioral descriptions were provided for 1, "Student has significant behavior problems in comparison to others"; 5, "Student's behavior is about the same as that of others"; and 9, "Student has excellent classroom behavior in comparison with others." No additional guidelines on how to rate students on the 9-point scale were provided to teachers. The five BES-2 subscales and total score produced significant correlation coefficients at the .01 level of confidence except for emotionally/behaviorally disordered students rated on Physical Symptoms/Fears. Correlations ranged from .45 to .75 for regular-education students and from .15 to .59 for behaviorally disordered students.

Evidence for construct validity is based on studies showing that students identified as behaviorally disordered exhibited significantly more psychopathology across all five subscales.

Summary

The BES-2 is a 76-item rating scale for children enrolled in kindergarten through grade 12. Three subscales produce raw scores that are converted to standard scores (mean = 10, standard deviation = 3). The total score is the only score that can be represented as a percentile rank. The standardization procedures appear to be appropriate (norm tables are provided by age–gender groups), although reliability measures were not reported in this manner. Validity studies support the criterion-related and construct validity of the BES-2 as a device that is adequate for screening purposes.

Behavior Evaluation Scale–2, Home Version (BES-2HV)

The Behavior Evaluation Scale–2, Home Version (BES-2HV; J. McCarney, 1994) is a norm-referenced rating scale intended to provide a measurement of behavior in the home environment; to identify the characteristics of emotionally disturbed (or behaviorally disordered) students, as defined in federal legislation; to measure changes in behavior over time, and to ascertain areas needing behavioral intervention. The BES-2HV consists of 73 items arranged into five subscales:

1. Learning/Self-Control (8 items)

2. Interpersonal/Social (14 items)

3. Inappropriate Behavior Under Normal Circumstances (35 items)

4. Unhappiness/Depression (7 items)

5. Physical Symptoms/Fears (9 items)

Each item is rated on a 7-point scale:

1 Not in the rater's presence

2 One time

3 Several times

4 More than one time a month, up to one time a week

5 More than one time a week, up to once a day

6 More than once a day, up to once an hour

7 Once an hour (or more)

Scores

Raw scores on each subscale are converted to standard scores with a mean of 10 and a standard deviation of 3. Subscale standard scores are summed to convert to quotients (presumably a standard score with a mean of 100 and a standard deviation of 15) and percentiles.

Norms

The BES-2HV was standardized on 1,769 individuals ranging in age from 4.5 years to 21 years. However, separate norms are provided for males and females in four age ranges (5 through 7 years, 8 through 10 years, 11 through 14 years, and 15 through 18 years); no norms are provided for individuals younger than 5 or older than 18. An unreported number of these students had been identified as behaviorally disordered. The students resided in 18 states. The author compares the total standardization sample to the U.S. population (presumably the 1990 census). However, the information of interest (that is, the representativeness of each age–sex normative sample) is missing. As a whole, the normative sample greatly overrepresents European Americans, blue-collar workers, individuals from rural areas, and individuals from the North Central region of the United States.

Reliability

Stability was estimated using 201 individuals from the normative sample who were rerated within 30 days of their initial rating. Correlations, across all ages, between the first and second ratings ranged from .88 to .93 for the five subscales and was .90 for the total score.[4]

Interrater agreement for the total score was estimated using 147 pairs of parents and 200 students. Correlations between raters were calculated at 13 age groups (including individuals who were older or younger than those used for the normative conversion tables).[5] Interrater agreement ranged from .83 to .91; in 3 of the 13 age groups, the agreement equaled or exceeded .90.

Using the total normative sample, internal consistency was estimated by KR-20 for each subscale.[6] Estimates ranged from .74 to .93; only one subscale had an estimated reliability greater than .90.

Validity

The technical manual is poorly organized, and validity information is incompletely reported. Some evidence for content validity comes from the way in which the scale was developed. Items for the BES-2HV were derived from the literature and from input from education professionals and parents and guardians. In addition, item-total correlations and the distributions of responses to each item were examined. Moderate correlations between the BES-2HV and the BRP for 49 children provide some evidence for criterion-related validity.

Construct validity of the BES-2HV was addressed in several ways. First, a series of factor analyses suggests that the scale is factorially complex. However, these analyses do not suggest that the subscales of the BES-2HV correspond to the instrument's factor structure.[7] Second, the ratings for a group of 104 students previously identified as behaviorally disordered were compared to those for a randomly selected subsample of 104 individuals from the normative sample. The behaviorally disordered students received ratings that were about 1 to 1.3 standard deviations below the mean, while the randomly selected students had ratings at the mean. However, variances are not reported, and so it is impossible to ascertain the degree of overlap between the groups.

Summary

The BES-2HV is a behavior rating scale for use with individuals from 5 through 18 years of age. The 73 items are clustered into five subscales that parallel the criteria for identification of seriously emotionally disturbed students provided in federal regulations. Although reliability estimates are usually sufficient for screening purposes, the BES-2HV's norms do not appear representative of the U.S. population. Information about the scale's validity is presented incompletely and is, therefore, limited.

4. The author does not report whether the correlations are based on raw or standard scores. Correlations based on raw scores would be inflated to the extent that raw scores and age are correlated.

5. The number of students in each age group is not reported. However, if the students were distributed equally among age groups, there would be about 15 students in each age group.

6. As you will recall, KR-20 (a special case of coefficient alpha) is used with dichotomously scored items. The items on this scale are scored on a 7-point scale. Thus, how KR-20 could be used is unclear. Moreover, because internal consistency was estimated across ages, these reliabilities would be inflated to the extent that raw scores and age are correlated.

7. The author reports 17 factors with Eigenvalues greater than 1 but fails to report the percentage of variance accounted for by each factor. A skree plot of factors suggests, to us, a single-factor solution. When individual subscales are factor-analyzed, some have several factors.

Early Childhood Behavior Scale (ECBS)

The Early Childhood Behavior Scale (ECBS; S. B. McCarney, 1992a) was developed to assess children 36 to 72 months of age. The ECBS consists of 53 items divided into three subscales: Academic Progress (10 items), Social Relationships (12 items), and Personal Adjustment (31 items). Estimated time to complete the ECBS is approximately 15 minutes. The primary purpose of the ECBS is to facilitate the identification of children with emotional and behavioral disturbances in preschool environments. In addition, the author claims that the information gathered from this rating scale can be translated directly into goal statements and behavioral objectives for a child's educational programming.

Each scale consists of a series of behavioral items that are rated by educators familiar with the child of concern. For example, items from the Academic Progress scale include "Is unable to perform tasks independently" and "Requires repeated drill and practice to learn what other children master easily." Examples from the Social Relationships scale include "Fights with others" and "Will not share possessions or materials." Finally, examples of items from the Personal Adjustment scale include "Exhibits extreme mood changes" and "Does not accept changes in established routines."

Educators rate each item according to a 6-point scale of perceived frequency to quantify their concerns: 0, Not in my presence; 1, One time; 2, Several times; 3, More than one time a month, up to one time a week; 4, More than one time a week, up to once a day; 5, More than once a day, up to once an hour; 6, More than once an hour. A sound rationale for and further description of the six-point scale can be found in the technical manual.

Scores

Scores on three individual scales are computed by tabulating teacher ratings for each item within a specific subscale. Raw scores are converted to standard scores using conversion tables provided in the appendix. Standard scores have a mean of 10 and a standard deviation of 3. In addition, a total score is calculated by adding standard scores across all three subscales. The total score is then converted to a percentile rank. Because of the different outcomes evidenced by the standardization sample, three separate norm tables are provided for males by age: 36–47 months, 48–59 months, and 60–71 months. Females required only two age clusters: 36–47 months and 44–71 months. A summary table on the front of the scoring protocol provides an area for scores and the percentile rank to be plotted.

Norms

The standardization sample consisted of 1,314 children, ages 3 to 6 years. The author provides additional data on the number of children by age in three-month increments. The standardization sample is distributed across these age groups, with each age group having 100 children or more, with the exception of ages 45–47 months ($N = 91$), 48–50 months ($N = 98$), and 51–53 months ($N = 82$). For all age groups, N ranged from 82 to 127. Participants were enrolled in classrooms for both regular and behavior-disordered students. Rating scales were completed by 289 teachers from 68 public schools across 17 states. Characteristics of the standardization sample were compared with actual percentages of the U.S. census. In general, it appears that the author has provided a sample representative of the U.S. population with regard to race/ethnicity, region, and SES. However, the sample does appear to overrepresent the Northeast and underrepresent the South by 8 percent and 11 percent, respectively.

Reliability

Three types of reliability data are provided: test–retest, internal consistency, and interrater agreement. All reliability studies involve random samples drawn from the standardization sample. Test–retest reliability results are provided by subscale but not by sex or age. This is a concern because of the author's own claims of differential effects found for the different gender–age groupings. Reliability coefficients for the different scales were .88 for Academic Progress, .81 for Social Relationships, and .91 for Personal Adjustment.

Internal-consistency coefficients exceed .90, but the sample on which these results are based is not clearly described. Item–total and item–subscale correlations are presented in the technical manual, with correlations ranging from .28 to .85.

Interrater agreement was based on the ratings of two educators with equal knowledge of each child rated. A total of 101 pairs of teachers rated 237 children on the ECBS. The author presents extensive results of Pearson product–moment correlations across three-month age intervals; however, once again, results are not presented separately by gender. Coefficients ranged from .81 to .88, with a mean of .85.

Validity

Content validity of the ECBS is based on a comprehensive review of the literature, as well as input from experienced practitioners who helped produce an initial pool of scale items. The author reports that the literature review supports the five-category definition of emotionally disturbed/behaviorally disordered children on which the ECBS is based. However, the ECBS collapses these five categories into a three-scale format (academic, social, and personal) to address the National Mental Health and Special Education definitions of the emotionally disturbed/behaviorally disordered. Finally, an item analysis was conducted to assess whether adequate differentiation occurs across items. The 53-item rating scale is the result of this process.

Criterion-related validity data are reported from a single study on 57 students previously identified as behaviorally disordered and receiving special-education services. Teachers with the most knowledge of the child's behavior rated each of the 57 children on the ECBS and the corresponding form of the CBCL for ages 2–3 and ages 4–18 (Achenbach, 1991b, 1992). All correlations were significant at the .001 confidence level. Once again, results were not differentiated by age or gender.

A principal-components analysis and a factor-analytic procedure were used to verify whether the three theoretically separate subscales could be empirically confirmed. The ECBS appears to measure the overall construct of behavior disorders, but the results from the factor analysis do not support the definition of three subscales. Further evidence of a unitary construct is found in the high intercorrelations of the subscales.

A sample of 196 students randomly selected from the standardization sample was compared with a corresponding group of identified behaviorally disordered students from 11 school districts who were receiving program services. Mean total subscale scores and percentile scores were significantly different at the .001 confidence level. However, it should be noted that the previously identified subsample scored within one standard deviation on all subscales except for Personal Adjustment. Children ages 36–47 months were the only subgroup that consistently scored one standard deviation below the mean on all three subscales.

Summary

The ECBS is a 53-item rating scale for children ages 36–72 months. Three subscales produce raw scores that are converted to standard scores (mean = 10, standard deviation = 3). The total score is the only score that can be represented as a percentile rank. The standardization procedures appear to be well controlled; demographic characteristics and distribution of age groups are well documented. Although norm tables were provided by gender–age groups, reliability measures were not reported in this manner. Initial data indicate that the test is adequate for screening purposes. Questions still remain about the usefulness of the ECBS for diagnostic purposes. Specifically, the inability of the three subscales of the ECBS to differentiate previously identified emotionally disturbed/behaviorally disordered students from regular-education students may call into question the relevance of the three subscales for diagnostic purposes. Ultimately, the true test of the effectiveness of the ECBS will be the extent to which it leads to better diagnostic and educational program planning for emotionally disturbed/behaviorally disordered students. Although support may accrue over time, additional evidence of technical adequacy and diagnostic precision is needed.

Behavior Rating Profile, Second Edition (BRP-2)

The Behavior Rating Profile, second edition (BRP-2; L. Brown & Hammill, 1990) is a multirater, multi-context instrument designed for use with students ages 6-6 to 18-6 years. The BRP-2 consists of three Student Rating Scales (Home, SRS:H; School, SRS:S; and Peers, SRS:P), a Teacher Rating Scale (TRS), a Parent Rating Scale (PRS), and a Sociogram. The three student scales are printed in a single booklet and are administered simultaneously. The authors propose that the BRP-2 be used to help identify students with emotional, behavioral, personal, or social adjustment problems in home, school, or social–interpersonal settings. The ecological framework is depicted in Table 25.2.

Each Student Rating Scale has 20 items that are answered as either true or false. Representative SRS:H items include "I don't listen to my parents when they are talking to me" and "I have lots of nightmares and bad dreams." SRS:S items include "My teachers give me work that I cannot do" and "I can't seem to stay in my desk at school." SRS:P items include "Other children are always picking on me" and "I seem to get into a lot of fights."

The Teacher Rating Scale has 30 items that include statements about the student's school behavior. These statements are negatively oriented and are rated on a 4-point scale (1, Very much like the student; 2, Like the student; 3, Not much like the student; 4, Not at all like the student). Examples of items from the TRS include "Swears in class" and "Tattles on classmates."

The PRS contains 30 negatively worded items describing behaviors that may be observed at home. These are rated on the same 4-point scale as the TRS. Examples of the PRS items include "Is verbally aggressive to parents" and "Violates curfew."

The Sociogram uses a peer-nomination technique to get peer perceptions of the target student. Pairs of stimulus questions selected from the manual or devised by the examiner are given to the students—for example, "Which students in your class would you like most to have as a class officer?" and "Which students would you least like to have as a class officer?" Students then nominate three of their peers whom they would "like most" and "like least." The examiner then rank-orders students based on their acceptance and rejection rates.

Scores

All five scales of the BRP-2 yield raw scores, standard scores, and percentile ranks. Scoring of the rating scales is straightforward; however, scoring the Sociogram involves a more complex six-step computation and ranking procedure. Standard error of measurement (SEM) data are complicated.

TABLE 25.2 ● Ecological Orientation of the BRP-2

BRP-2 Scale	Respondent				Ecology		
	Student	*Teacher*	*Parent*	*Peer*	*Home*	*School*	*Social*
Student Rating Scale: Home	X				X		
Student Rating Scale: School	X					X	
Student Rating Scale: Peer	X					X	X
Teaching Rating Scale		X				X	
Parent Rating Scale			X		X		
Sociogram				X			X

SOURCE: From L. Brown and D.D. Hammill, *Behavior Rating Profile*, 2nd Edition. Copyright © 1990 by Pro-Ed. Reprinted by permission of the publisher.

An SEM of 1 is printed on the BRP-2 profile form for all scales. However, SEMs actually vary by subtest and grade level from 0.4 to 1.6. Thus, the example of how to use the SEM provided in the manual is not easy to follow.

Norms

Three norm samples (L. Brown & Hammill, 1978, 1983, 1989) have been integrated for the BRP-2. A total of 2,682 students ages 6-6 to 18-6 from 26 states are included in the complete group. Data to support the representativeness of the norm sample are provided. Students at the anchor points (ages 6 and 18 years) are underrepresented, and the educational attainment of students' parents is biased toward the high end. A notable exclusionary practice of the BRP-2 is the authors' decision not to assess students with social–emotional disturbances (SEDs) in the normative process. Salvia and Ysseldyke (this edition) consider it inappropriate to exclude students with particular characteristics from the norm group of a test designed to help identify them. Readers are cautioned that in using the BRP-2, they will be making normative comparisons to a sample presumably less prone to behavior problems.

Norm data for the PRS were gathered from 1,948 parents in 19 states. Procedures for gathering parent data included sending BRP-2 scales home, asking those attending PTA (Parent Teacher Association) meetings to fill out the scales, and asking parents at school conferences to complete the instrument. Again, no students with SED were rated in these processes.

For the TRS, data are available from 1,452 teachers from 26 states. Teachers were asked to rate every fifth student on their class rosters, except students with SED. Overall demographics for the PRS and TRS appear to closely match national averages.

No norm sample data on the Sociogram are presented because the target student's own classmates serve as the normative comparison. Normative scoring information for the Sociogram was prepared by examining normalized distributions of student ranks for different class sizes.

Reliability

Two types of reliability data are offered to support the BRP-2: internal consistency using coefficient alpha and test–retest stability. Reliability coefficients are reported for five grade levels for the five rating scales. Each scale's internal consistency was calculated for a sample size of about 200 across these grade levels. Coefficients ranged from .77 to .98 and are adequate for the test's intended purpose as a screening device. Internal-consistency estimates with special populations (emotionally disturbed elementary and learning-disabled secondary students) ranged from .76 to .97. Overall, these also are of adequate magnitude for the BRP-2's intended use.

Test–retest reliability is presented from several studies. For a group of 36 high-school students, their teachers, and their parents, reliability coefficients ranged from .78 to .91 across a two-week interval. The TRS was the most stable scale. Another study of 198 students in grades 1 through 12, including 212 parents and 176 teachers, yielded test–retest reliability ranging from .43 to .96. Coefficients for grades 1 and 2 were lowest (SRS:H = .43, SRS:S = .58, SRS:P = .52, PRS = .69, TRS = .94). No explanation for or speculation about these coefficients is provided; however, the capriciousness of self-reports by young children and their reading difficulties may be partial explanations. Ninety-seven secondary students with emotional disturbances, their parents, and their teachers provided test–retest data on the BRP-2 scales. Coefficients for these subjects ranged from .76 to .82.

Information on an important type of reliability data for rating scales, interrater reliability, is missing from the BRP-2 technical manual. The authors' discussion of interpretation of scores from an ecological perspective includes issues of multiple raters and possible discrepancies among their scores. Still, some indication of interrater agreement can be gleaned from their discussion of patterns across student, teacher, and parent ratings. Students tend to give themselves the highest scores, whereas parents usually assign the lowest scores. Omission of direct interrater reliability data, however, weakens the overall data support for the instrument.

Validity

The authors believe validity is not easily discussed along traditional lines of content, criterion-related, and construct validity data. Evidence of overall validity is provided for "more punctilious readers" (L. Brown & Hammill, 1990, p. 48) in sections devoted to relationships among BRP-2 items or scales and other variables or criteria.

Content validation was approached through the authors' examination of the professional literature, existing checklists, rating scales (such as Walker Problem Behavior Identification Checklist, Quay–Peterson Behavior Problem Checklist), and other assessments. Parents of students with emotional and learning problems provided written input about behavior concerns. Longer, experimental versions of the BRP scales were reduced to a more manageable length through empirical item analyses.

Criterion-related, concurrent, and construct validity data are supplied in several sections describing the relationship of BRP-2 scales to measures of achievement, aptitude, and affect. Correlations with tests of achievement and aptitude produce low (near-zero) coefficients, as was expected by the authors. Stronger correlations between the BRP-2 and measures of affect were expected as evidence that these criterion variables were measuring the same construct.

The strongest evidence for validity rests on data from a study conducted on 108 students in Kansas (27 in each of four groups: normal, learning disabled, public school socially/emotionally disturbed, and institutionalized socially/emotionally disturbed). All BRP-2 scales except the Sociogram were correlated with the Walker Problem Behavior Identification Checklist, the Quay–Peterson Behavior Problem Checklist, and the Vineland Social Maturity Scale. Inspection of the data shows that 64 of 72 resulting correlations were significant and exceeded their target magnitude of .35. The results were weakest for the students with SED who received services in the public schools. There is some confusion, however, in the reporting of these data. The authors' explanations of the data account for only 60 of the 72 reported correlations, and this research is not discussed in sufficient detail.

Other studies correlate BRP-2 scales with the Test of Early Socioemotional Development, the Behavior Evaluation Scale, the Devereaux Elementary School Behavior Rating Scale II, the Children's Manifest Anxiety Scale, and the Index of Children's Personality Characteristics. These data support the concurrent and construct validity of the BRP-2 as a measure of overall behavior and social adjustment.

Support for the discriminative validity of the BRP-2 scales (except the Sociogram) is provided in a section listing 15 studies reporting BRP-2 scores for different student groups. (Some of the studies were conducted by the authors.) As a whole, these studies reveal the expected differences in group means. Students with social/emotional disturbance and mental retardation score lower than learning disabled and nondisabled students, who tend to receive average scores. Gifted students tend to score higher than all other groups. Several of the studies are described in some detail. The statistical significance of the findings in these studies, however, is not detailed.

Summary

The BRP-2 is designed to assess students' behavior in different ecologies and is intended to identify students with emotional, behavioral, and social adjustment problems. The device is made up of five rating scales and a Sociogram. The rating scales require true–false responses of the students and Likert-type ratings from teachers and parents. Norms for the BRP-2 exclude students with SED but otherwise appear well defined. Users of the BRP-2 must recognize this design characteristic and adjust their interpretations accordingly. Reliability for the scales is supported by adequate internal-consistency and test–retest data. No interrater reliability data are provided. Content validity of the BRP-2 scales was ensured by a well-planned development process. The tests appear to have high criterion-related, concurrent, and construct validity. There is some question of the instrument's ability to discriminate between students with learning problems and students with behavior problems. The BRP-2 should be used with confidence as a screening tool but should not be used as the primary data source for classification or diagnostic decisions.

Walker–McConnell Scale of Social Competence and School Adjustment (W-M)

The Walker–McConnell Scale of Social Competence and School Adjustment (W-M; H. M. Walker & McConnell, 1988) is a norm-referenced rating scale of social skills for use with elementary-age children. The instrument consists of three subscales (Teacher-Preferred Social Behavior, Peer-Preferred Social Behavior, and School Adjustment Behavior) intended to be used for "screening and identification of social skills deficits" (H. M. Walker & McConnell, 1988, p. 1). The W-M was "not designed as either a diagnostic or classification instrument" (p. 3). Information on students' social competence and school adjustment that can be used as part of referral or child-study team processes, as well as for program planning, is obtained from item subscale and total scores and through normative comparisons. The authors suggest that in addition to the national norms provided in the manual, a classroom normative reference can be gained by assessing typical peers of the target student on the W-M. This procedure also helps validate the ratings of the target student.

The W-M consists of 43 positively worded descriptions of social skills. Subscale 1 (Teacher-Preferred Behavior) consists of 16 items that assess sensitivity, empathy, cooperation, self-control, and maturity. Examples of items include "Shows empathy" and "Cooperates with peers." Subscale 2 (Peer-Preferred Behavior) has 17 items that address peer values and relations in social situations. Items include "Invites peers to play or share activities" and "Compromises when the situation calls for it." Subscale 3 (School Adjustment Behavior) has 10 items that assess competencies in academic settings. Sample items include "Displays independent study skills" and "Listens carefully to teacher directions." All items are rated on a 5-point Likert scale from "Never occurs" to "Frequently occurs." The upper anchor point is defined in somewhat vague terminology ("Frequently occurs" is defined as "a high rate"), and a rationale for the scaling choice is not provided. More explicit definitions may help raters make more objective evaluations of student behavior.

Scores

The W-M yields raw scores (subscale and total) by adding the numerical Likert ratings. Raw scores are converted to standard scores for the subscales (mean = 10, standard deviation = 3) and for the total scale (mean = 100, standard deviation = 15). Standard scores are converted to percentile rankings.

Norms

Normative data for the W-M are based on a sample of 1,812 students from grades K–6. Sixty percent of these students were in grades 1, 2, and 4, but there were at least 125 students per grade. Data were collected over a two-year period from 1985 to 1987. Students were from 15 states, with 3 states (Alabama, Montana, and Oregon) supplying 48 percent of the sample. The authors provide data to show that the mean scores of subjects from the four geographic regions were all within one SEM. Other demographics (such as urban/suburban and ethnicity) appear representative of the nation.

Reliability

The authors supply three types of reliability data: test–retest, interrater, and internal consistency. In addition, item-total correlations (considered by Salvia and Ysseldyke to be reliability data) are found in the manual's section on item validity.

Test–retest reliability is supported by data from several studies, some of which were conducted by other investigators. Coefficients range from .67 to .97 for studies with test–retest intervals of two to four weeks. A study of test–retest stability with an-

tisocial and normal boys over a six-month period produced slightly lower correlations.

Interrater reliability studies produced what the authors call "modest agreement levels" (p. 33). What is missing is an estimate of interrater reliability using two same-type raters (e.g., two teachers or two teacher's aides). Such data provide an estimate of the consistency of assessments of student functioning from a common frame of reference.

Internal-consistency data are presented in the form of alpha coefficients for the total norm sample. All subscales were above .95, and all coefficients by grade level were above .94. Collectively, these data support the claim that the W-M has adequate reliability for its intended purposes.

Validity

Twenty-four pages of the 50-page manual for the W-M are devoted to text, tables, and figures on validity data (including the item–total correlations discussed previously). The authors report their own studies and those of other investigators using the W-M in research.

Content Validity The authors of the W-M examined the professional literature, existing teacher-rating instruments, and materials from other national projects to develop an initial item pool of 100 descriptors of school-related social skills. Then 83 items were selected for testing, and the final 43 items were chosen based on (a) item means, (b) item variances, (c) item–total correlations, and (d) item loadings from first- and second-order factor analyses. Clearly, the authors have employed empirical processes for the identification of the items included in the W-M.

Criterion-Related and Discriminative Validity Several studies are presented to support the criterion-related validity of the W-M. These are mostly supportive of concurrent validity. In a study using the Walker Problem Behavior Identification Checklist (WPBIC) as the criterion, 13 elementary students who had been referred for resource-room services and 17 nondisabled students who had been referred for counseling were rated by teachers and by their parents. The WPBIC and W-M are scaled in opposite ways; thus the resulting validity coefficients were negative and significant (range = −.69 to −.89).

In another study using teacher ratings of social adjustment, peer sociometrics, and academic achievement variables as criteria, 65 elementary students were also rated on the W-M. Moderate to high correlations were found between the teacher ratings and the W-M subscale and total scores. Low to moderate correlations were found for peer sociometrics and achievement data. The W-M does not appear to correlate with measures of academic engagement.

Correlations with the Social Skills Rating System for Teachers (SSRS-T) provide potentially strong evidence of concurrent validity. The SSRS-T is an earlier version of the teacher scale of the Social Skills Rating System (Gresham & Elliott, 1990). Unfortunately, the authors do not report the number of subjects or population(s) involved in the validity study. The total scores of the W-M and the SSRS-T correlated. The subscales of the W-M and factors of the SSRS-T correlated in the expected directions.

Discriminative validity of the W-M is supported by studies designed to document the sensitivity of the instrument in discriminating groups defined by researchers or based on school-district classifications. Other discriminative-validity studies involved research-defined groups of antisocial and normal students, students categorized under a two-dimensional model of behavior (disciplinary problems and peer acceptance), sociometrically defined groups (for example, popular and rejected), and school-identified groups of at-risk and disabled students. In most cases, the W-M appears sensitive to group differences and predicts membership or performance in expected directions. Scores on Subscales 1 and 2 and total score on the W-M appear to discriminate better than Subscale 3 scores.

Standard scores between 7 and 13 on the W-M are within "normal" limits. In plotting the "characteristic profiles" of five student groups (normal, learning disabled, residential severely emotionally disturbed, resource room, antisocial), the normal group scored highest, and the scores of the other four groups were lower. However, there is very little differentiation among these four groups, and, although the authors say these students show moderate to severe deficits on the W-M, nearly all subscale standard scores of these groups are within one standard deviation of the mean. The W-M, as the authors state, is not to be used for differential diagnoses among disability groups.

Construct Validity   The authors report evidence of construct validity and factorial validity. Subscale 2 is specifically supported by longitudinal research on 100 boys at risk for antisocial behavior. The construct validity of the W-M is also argued on the basis of data showing near-zero correlations with student age and very low correlations with student gender, although gender differences favoring females might be expected.

Summary

The Walker–McConnell Scale of Social Competence and School Adjustment is a 43-item rating scale for screening and identification of social-skills deficits in elementary school students. The W-M is easy to administer and score; it yields raw scores, standard scores, and percentiles. The norms for the W-M are adequate, although there is some overrepresentation of Western states. Reliability data to support its use include test–retest, interrater, and internal-consistency coefficients. Coefficients are generally above .80. Content, criterion-related, and construct validity data are convincing for the intended purposes of the device. Though three subscales are identified, the W-M is best used for normative comparisons as a global measure of social competence. Subscales and items within subscales may provide teachers with indications of specific areas of skills deficits for individual students. Educators must remember, however, that item-reliability data are not provided, and the authors' suggestions of remediation based on individual item data need further research support.

Behavior Assessment System for Children (BASC)

The Behavior Assessment System for Children (BASC; Reynolds & Kamphaus, 1992) is "a multimethod, multidimensional approach to evaluate the behavior and self-perception of children 4 to 18 years of age" (p. 1). This comprehensive assessment system is designed to assess the numerous aspects of behavior and personality, including both adaptive and maladaptive behavior. The BASC is composed of five main measures of behavior: (1) Teacher Rating Scale, (2) Parent Rating Scale, (3) Self-Report of Personality, (4) Structured Developmental History Inventory, and (5) Student Observation System.

Behaviors Sampled

The Teacher Rating Scale (TRS) is a comprehensive measure of both adaptive (such as "Adjusts well to new teachers") and problem (such as "Refuses to talk") behaviors that children exhibit in school settings. Three different forms are available—preschool (4–5 years), child (6–11 years), and adolescent (12–18 years)—with the behavior items specifically tailored for each age range. Teachers or school personnel rate students on a list of behavioral descriptions using a 4-point scale of frequency (N, Never; S, Sometimes; O, Often; A, Almost always). Estimated time to complete the TRS is 10 to 20 minutes. The TRS for preschool is composed of 109 items, the TRS for children, of 148 items, and the TRS for adolescents, of 138 items; items are tailored to the specific age groups. Examples of general items in the TRS include "Bullies others," "Stares blankly," "Changes moods quickly," "Uses illegal drugs," "Uses foul language," and "Is good at getting people to work together."

The Parent Rating Scale (PRS) is a comprehensive measure of a child's adaptive and problem behavior exhibited in community and home settings. The PRS uses the same 4-point rating scale as the TRS. In addition, three forms are provided by age groups, as defined previously. Estimated time to complete this measure is 10 to 20 minutes.

The Self-Report of Personality (SRP) contains short statements that a student is expected to endorse or reject by marking true or false on the rating form. Because of the nature of the task, only two forms are available by age level: child (8–11 years) and adolescent (12–18 years). Estimated time per administration is 30 minutes.

The Structured Developmental History Inventory (SDH) is a broad-based developmental history instrument developed to obtain information on the following areas: social, psychological, developmental, educational, and medical history. The SDH may be used either as an interview format or as a questionnaire. The organization of the SDH may help in conducting interviews and obtaining important historical information that may be beneficial to the diagnostic and treatment processes.

The Student Observation System (SOS) is an observation tool developed to facilitate diagnosis, treatment planning, and monitoring of intervention programs. Both adaptive and maladaptive behaviors are coded during a 15-minute classroom observation. It is important to note, however, that the SOS is a nonnormed instrument, and therefore, as the authors suggest, it may not be best used for making diagnostic decisions.

The SOS is divided into three parts. The first section, behavior key and checklist, is a list of 65 specific behaviors organized into 13 categories (4 categories of positive behavior and 9 categories of problem behavior). Following a 15-minute observation, the coder rates the child on the 65 items, according to a 3-point frequency gradation (NO, Never Observed; SO, Sometimes Observed; and FO, Frequently Observed).

The second part, time sampling, requires the informant to decide whether a behavior is present during a 3-second period following a 30-second interval of observation. Observers place a checkmark in separate time columns next to any of the 13 categories of behavior that occur during any one interval. The third section, teacher's interaction, is completed following the 15-minute observation. The observer scores the teacher's interactions with the students on three aspects of classroom interactions: (1) teacher position during the observation, (2) teacher techniques to change student behavior, and (3) additional observations that are relevant to the assessment process.

Scores

A hand-scored response form is used for the first three instruments (TRS, PRS, and SRP). The protocols are constructed in a unique format, using pressure-sensitive paper, that provides the examiner with an immediate translation of ratings to score. After administration of the different rating forms, the administrator removes the outer page to reveal a scoring key. Scale and composite scores are totaled easily, and a behavior profile is available to represent the data graphically. Validity scores are tabulated to evaluate the quality of completed forms and to guard against response patterns that may skew the data profiles positively or negatively. Detailed scoring procedures that use a ten-step procedure for each of these scales are described in the administration manual.

Raw scores for each scale are transferred to a summary table for each individual measure. T-scores (mean = 50, standard deviation = 10) and percentiles are obtained after selecting appropriate norm tables for comparisons. In addition, a high/low column is provided to allow the assessor a quick and efficient method for evaluating whether differences among composite scores on one individual are statistically significant.

The TRS produces three composite scores of clinical problems: externalizing problems, internalizing problems, and school problems. Externalizing problems include aggression, hyperactivity, and conduct problems. Internalizing problems include anxiety, depression, and somatization. School problems are broken down into attentional and learning deficits. A broad composite score of overall problem behaviors is provided on the behavioral symptoms index (BSI). In addition, positive behaviors are presented on an adaptive skills profile scale; these include leadership, social skills, and study skills. The PRS provides the same scoring categories and subscales, with the exception that the school problems composite scores, composed of subscales for learning problems and study skills, are omitted.

The Self-Report of Personality (SRP) produces four composite scores: clinical maladjustment, school maladjustment, personal adjustment, and an overall composite score referred to as an emotional symptoms index (ESI). The composite ESI score includes both negative and adaptive scales. Clinical maladjustment includes anxiety, atypicality, (inappropriate) locus of control, social stress, and somatization groupings. School maladjustment subscales are attitude toward school, attitude toward teachers, and sensation seeking. Personal adjustment groupings include relations with parents, interpersonal relations, self-esteem, and self-reliance. There is also a category of "other problems," which includes depression and sense of inadequacy.

Three validity scores are provided. To detect either consistently negative bias or consistently positive bias in the responses provided by the student, there is an F index (fakes bad) and an L index (fakes good). The V index incorporates nonsensical items (such as, "Superman is a real person") such that a child who consistently marks these items true may be exhibiting poor reading skills, may be uncooperative, or may have poor contact with reality.

The Structured Developmental History Inventory (SDH) and Student Observation System (SOS) are not norm-referenced measures and do not provide individual scores of comparisons. Rather, these instruments provide additional information about a child, which may be used to describe his or her strengths and weaknesses.

Norms

Standardization and norm development for the general and clinical norms on the TRS, PRS, and SRP took place between the fall of 1988 and the spring of 1991. A total of 116 testing sites were used to obtain general standardization data. The number of children who received behavioral ratings across the different measures were, for the TRS, $N = 2,401$; for the PRS, $N = 3,483$; and for the SRP, $N = 9,861$. Efforts were made to ensure that the standardization sample was representative of the U.S. population of children ages 4–18, including exceptional children. The standardization sample was compared with census data for geographic region, SES, culture, and ethnicity. The authors present data to support mostly balanced norms; however, the Northwest appears to be underrepresented for scales used with preschool-age children, and the Midwest is overrepresented for the PRS. The authors claim that children with behavioral–emotional disturbances are represented appropriately at each grade level of each instrument, and the data provided in the manual support this claim. Finally, children with mild mental retardation are underrepresented on the SRP, given the nature of the task (that is, their difficulty in completing a self-report questionnaire).

Clinical population sample norms consist of data collected on children receiving school or clinical services for emotional or behavioral problems. Special-education students (such as those with learning disabilities) were not included unless coexisting emotional or behavioral problems were identified. Thirty-six sites in the United States and Canada were used as settings for gathering data. Sample sizes were, for the TRS, $N = 693$; for the PRS, $N = 401$; and for the SRP, $N = 411$. The authors state that the clinical sample was not controlled demographically because this subgroup is not a random set of children. For example, significantly more males were included than females.

Reliability

The manual has a chapter devoted to the technical information supporting reliability and validity for each normed scale (TRS, PRS, and SRP). Three types of reliability are provided within the technical manual: internal consistency, test–retest, and interrater agreement. Results are generally reported for three age levels: preschool (4–5 years), child (6–11 years), and adolescent (12–18 years).

Internal Consistency For the TRS, median internal-consistency coefficients for all scales were above .80 across all three age groups of the general population (preschool, child, and adolescent). In general, externalizing dimensions produced higher reliability, compared with internalizing dimensions. For the PRS, internal consistency at all three age levels for both genders ranged from .56 to .94. A majority of the coefficients are in the .70 to .80 range. The BSI coefficients ranged from .88 to .94. On average, the clinical sample produced higher PRS internal-consistency coefficients. Reported reliability scores by age ranged from .72 to .94. For the SRP, internal-consistency coefficients computed for each SRP by age and gender averaged about .80 (range = .54–.97). The clinical norm sample demonstrated similar internal consistency (range = .64–.96). Composite reliability coefficients are very high, ranging from .85 to .97.

Test–Retest Reliability TRS test–retest reliability was computed by having teachers rate the same child after a period of between two and eight weeks. A total of 246 students were selected from across the three age levels. Median test–retest correlations of .89, .91, and .82 were found for the preschool, child, and adolescent age levels, respectively. Long-term stability (seven months) was computed on ratings produced for 55 children classified as emotionally/behaviorally disordered. A median correlation of .69 was obtained. Test–retest reliability of the PRS was examined by looking at correspondence between same-parent ratings with an interval of two to eight weeks between ratings. Median correlation values were .85, .88, and .70 for preschool, child, and adolescent levels, respectively. SRP test–retest reliability was evaluated by readministering this instrument one month after the initial presentation. Median correlations were .76 at each age level (child and adolescent). Test–retest correlations for composite scores ranged from .78 to .86. This suggests that children and adolescents are relatively consistent in their interpretation of items.

Interrater Reliability Two types of interrater data are presented for the TRS—preschool and TRS—child. First, a total of 48 preschool children were scored by four pairs of teachers. Interrater correlations represent the similarity of rankings by a few teachers on many children across the various scales. Correlation values of the scales and composites ranged from .60 to .91. Second, 87 children (preschool and child forms) were rated across different teacher informants. Correlations suggest moderate to high agreement with a median scale value of .83 (range = .29–.93). Interrater reliability is not reported for the TRS—adolescent form. PRS interrater reliability was computed by examining both parents' ratings of their child at about the same time. The most notable difference produced is that mothers tend to rate children higher on the social-skills scale than fathers do. Median interparent correlation values were .46, .57, and .67 at the preschool, child, and adolescent age levels, respectively. Overall, parents demonstrated higher concordance on externalizing dimensions of behavior than on internalizing factors. No interrater reliability correlations are provided on the SRP, as it is a self-report instrument.

In an attempt to examine reliability across measures of the BASC, correlations between the TRS and the PRS were computed on a subsample of 1,423 children selected from the standardization sample. Correlations are low to moderate and increase with age. Across all three age levels, like-named scales correlated highest across instruments. Furthermore, correlations were found to be highest among externalizing dimensions and lowest among internalizing dimensions.

Validity

Content Validity For the TRS, PRS, and SRP development process, the authors reviewed behavior ratings, self-report measures, and literature on social/emotional assessment, and they drew on their clinical and consultation work in an effort to identify the most important content and constructs for the BASC. In item development and tryouts, the authors relied on data-based decision making to revise, delete, or add items and alter formats. The BASC went through three item-selection/tryout phases, and the final sets of items per form appear to include appropriate content and to be of high validity. Composite scales were developed through factor-analytic studies and inspection of scale intercorrelations. Data appear to support the three-factor preschool and four-factor child and adolescent composite scores.

The authors also describe their efforts to test BASC items for bias against different subject groups on the basis of factors such as gender and ethnicity. Several items were found to be unsatisfactory in this regard and were dropped. The development of the validity scales (F, L, and V) is also described. Overall, users of the BASC system can be confident of the content and representativeness of the instrument and its scales.

Criterion-Related and Construct Validity The authors of the BASC do not describe validity along traditional criterion-related and construct breakdowns. Factor-analytic studies to support the structure of composite scales are provided, as are a series of studies of correlations among BASC scales and other measures. Construct validity of the BASC is supported by the extensive factor modeling used to define the scales and subscales. Intercorrelations among components and scales support the overall test as a measure of social/emotional status. Diagnostic validity data are also presented.

Criterion-related validity was evaluated by examining correlations of the TRS with five separate standardized measures. Correlations between externalizing dimensions approach .90 for both children and adolescents. Correlations between internalizing dimensions produced lower coefficients of .53 and .81 for children and adolescents, respectively.

A third study compared the Conners Teacher Rating Scale (CTRS-39; Conners, 1989) with the

TRS for children ages 4 and 5 years ($N = 91$). Correlations were low to moderate, suggesting that the two measures do not have a close match. The highest correlation ($r = .69$) was found between the TRS depression scale and the CTRS-39 emotional indulgent scale. Correlations between the TRS hyperactivity scale and the Conners hyperactivity scale and hyperactivity index were more modest ($r = .57$ and $.54$, respectively).

Finally, a validity study comparing scores produced on the Teacher Rating Scale of the Behavior Rating Profile (BRP; L. Brown & Hammill, 1983) and the BASC TRS for children enrolled in regular-education classrooms ($N = 37$) is reported. The BRP provides a profile of problem-behavior excesses; therefore, positive correlations were expected on the TRS adaptive grouping and negative correlations on problem behavior. Overall, correlations were low to moderate in strength. The correlations were highest on measures of school problems and, given the characteristics of the sample, provided only limited correlation support for overall validity.

Criterion-related validity for the PRS was evaluated by examining correlations of the PRS with four separate standardized measures. Correlations for externalizing composites were higher than for internalizing composites.

A second study of the PRS compared scores of 39 children ages 4–5 years on the PRS and on the Personality Inventory for Children–Revised (PIC-R; Lachar, 1982). Correlation levels are moderate at best, with the highest correlation between PRS withdrawal and PIC-R withdrawal scores at .57. Also, scores were obtained on the PRS and the CPRS-39 (Conners, 1989) for a total of 46 children ages 6–11 years who were rated by their parents on both scales. Children who scored high on the PRS externalizing composite produced high scores on the CPRS-39 scales of Conduct Disorder, Antisocial, and Learning Problems ($r = .78$, $.71$, and $.67$, respectively). Internalizing scales produced lower overall correlations with internalizing PRS; correlations were $r = .51$ on the anxious/shy profile and $r = .45$ on the psychosomatic.

The final comparison examined correspondence between the PRS and the Behavior Rating Profile (BRP; Brown & Hammill, 1983). A total of 35 children between the ages of 6 and 11 years were rated by parents on both scales. The BRP scores correlate at a low to moderate level with all three PRS composite scores and the BSI composite.

Criterion-related validity of the SRP was evaluated across a series of correlation studies with other self-report measures of personality. The first study examined a comparison of scores produced on both the SRP and the Minnesota Multiphasic Personality Inventory (MMPI; Hathaway & McKinley, 1970). Also examined was a concordance of scores produced on the SRP and the Children's Personality Questionnaire, form A (CPQ; Porter & Cattell, 1975). The CPQ scales reflect normal dimensions of personality. Correlations with the MMPI were high, but the CPQ appears to function differently as a measure of personality, although a few strong relationships exist among scales.

Diagnostic Validity   Diagnostic validity in the form of differential group profiles for clinical groups is provided for the TRS, PRS, and SRP. The purpose is to help in interpretation of scale scores and to provide empirical support for BASC scales and composites. The following clinical classifications were used to select a clinical sample: conduct disorder, behavior disorder, depression, emotion disturbance, attention deficit/hyperactivity disorder, learning disorder, mild mental retardation, and autism. Overall, the three BASC measures were able to provide moderate evidence of diagnostic/discriminant validity; however, because of small sample sizes for many of the clinical classifications, these results should be considered with care.

Summary

The BASC is a comprehensive instrument that may be used to evaluate the behavior and self-perception of children 4 to 18 years of age. This integrated system comprises five separate measures of behavior: (1) Teacher Rating Scale, (2) Parent Rating Scale, (3) Self-Report of Personality, (4) Structured Developmental History Inventory, and (5) Student Observation Scale. Although the multimethod and multidimensional approach should be commended, the TRS, PRS, and SRP are the only scales for which normative data are provided on which any classification or interpretive statements can be made. Norms for the BASC are more than adequate, with general and clinical norm data provided. Reliability of the instruments' scales and composites is very good, although the conduct problems composite yields somewhat lower reliability coefficients. As with other rating scales, the

BASC appears better able to differentiate externalizing dimensions than internalizing dimensions of emotional disturbance. Moreover, in evaluation of previously identified clinical samples, the BASC did not appear to adequately differentiate various diagnostic categories between referred and nonreferred samples. In conclusion, the BASC, like the CBCL (Achenbach, 1991a), provides one of the most comprehensive assessment tools on the market today. Support is presented for content, criterion-related, and construct validity. Although the BASC is a relatively new instrument, it already has an impressive foundation of support.

Systematic Screening for Behavior Disorders (SSBD)

The Systematic Screening for Behavior Disorders (SSBD; H. M. Walker & Severson, 1992) is a series of three interrelated measures of behavior for children in grades 1 to 6. This three-stage sequential screening system incorporates a procedure known as gating. Gating refers to the progressively more detailed and precise assessment procedures that identify students who may be at risk, in this case for behavioral problems. Assessment in Stages 1 and 2 of the SSBD relies solely on teacher judgments of child behavior across externalizing and internalizing dimensions. The final assessment step, Stage 3, consists of repeated observations conducted by a trained observer (someone other than the teacher) to validate teacher concerns about students who have passed through the previous two gating procedures.

The authors state that "the SSBD provides for mass screening of all students enrolled in a regular classroom. The system also gives each child an equal chance to be screened and identified for either externalizing or internalizing behavior disorders and problems" (p. 3). Referral for further assessment is contingent on a child's passing

through the entire multiple-gating process. A description of the three-stage process follows.

Stage 1: Rank-Ordering of All Students Enrolled in Regular Classrooms

Teachers rate (for a minimum of 30 days) all students enrolled in their classroom on both externalizing and internalizing dimensions of problem behavior. Clear operational definitions are provided to facilitate teacher ratings of children's behavior. Initially, teachers nominate ten children according to the externalizing and internalizing descriptions provided. Next, teachers rank-order the ten students from one to ten for each dimension. The three top-ranked students who best match the behavioral profile for either the internalizing or the externalizing dimension may be passed through to Stage 2.

Stage 2: Teacher Rating Scales

The teacher rating scales include a 33-item critical events index (CEI) to rate low-frequency, high-intensity events. For example, items include

"Steals," "Sets fires," or "Damages property." Two open items are provided on the CEI scale so that teachers can provide information on critical events that may not appear on the prepared list. Although these teacher-provided critical events are included in the total score, no criteria or guidelines on acceptable or unacceptable items are provided to teachers. This may invite an unnecessary degree of subjectivity that could skew results or decisions.

The second part of the Stage 2 procedure produces a combined frequency index (CFI), which is calculated by summing scores on Adaptive Behavior and Maladaptive Behavior scales. The Adaptive Behavior section is a 12-item scale with specific behaviors that are rated by a teacher to describe a child's current functioning. Items include statements such as "Follows established classroom rules" and "Initiates positive social interactions with peers." The Maladaptive Behavior scale is composed of 11 items. Examples from this scale include statements such as "Refuses to participate in games and activities with other children at recess" and "Creates a disturbance during class activities."

Stage 3: Observations of Academic and Social Behavior

All students who pass through Stages 1 and 2 are further observed using two different observational measures. The purposes of these observations are to (a) verify teachers' rankings of student behavior, (b) provide a direct measure of children's required behavioral adjustments to teachers and peers, and (c) evaluate students' normative levels of performance regarding their adjustment to teachers and peers.

The first measure is a record of a child's Academic Engaged Time (AET). An observer using a stopwatch records the total amount of time a child is engaged on an instructional task. The second measure is a rating of Peer Social Behavior (PSB) during playground interaction, using a 10-second-interval recording system. Coders are asked to record children's social behavior according to five categories: social engagement, participation, par-

allel play, alone, and no code. Each observation is scheduled for a total of 15 minutes and the recording of behavior on the two measures occurs across two days. A significant amount of training is required for observers of Stage 3 measures. Quizzes and videotaped practice observations are used to train observers to reach what is called an "expert" criterion.

Scale Development

The development of the SSBD and the collection of data to support its technical adequacy involved five years of research. Instrument development and preliminary testing were conducted during an initial phase. Extensive research on the reliability and validity of the measures was done in a secondary phase. Normative studies were conducted in the latter phase. A technical development section of more than 50 pages is included in the manual. Interested readers should consult this source for the complete report on all research and development activities.

Scores Produced

Stage 1 produces no scores, as teachers rank-order children on internalizing and externalizing dimensions of problem behavior. Stage 2 comprises two indexes of behavior, the CEI and the CFI. The CEI is scored by adding the number of items endorsed. The range of scores on the CEI is from 0 to 35. The CFI comprises two scales: Adaptive Behavior and Maladaptive Behavior. These two scales use a 1-to-5 continuous rating scale (1, Never; 3, Sometimes; 5, Frequently). Although these anchor points are not defined further, teachers are encouraged to choose any number between 1 and 5 that best describes the frequency of a child's behavior during the preceding six months. In addition, teachers are instructed to endorse items that they may not have witnessed but that can be confirmed by a reliable source. Total subscale scores are computed by summing the points assigned to all items within the subscale. The ranges of scores are from 12 to 60 for the Adaptive scale and from 11 to 55 for the Maladaptive scale.

In Stage 3, the score for the AET measure is calculated by recording the total seconds a child is engaged in instructional tasks. An average of the two observations is computed and compared, to separate norm scores by group (normal, externalizers, internalizers, and combined) and by grade (1–3, 4–6).

Scores for the five social behavior categories on the PSB measure are transferred to an observation summary sheet. Summary scores are reported as a percentage of intervals observed. Both individual code categories and summary scores (composed of code-category combinations) are reported on this summary form.

Decision Rules

Decision rules for determining whether a child continues to progress through Stages 1, 2, and 3 are described thoroughly in the administration manual for each level. Straightforward criteria are presented separately for children rated on the externalizing and internalizing dimensions of problem behavior. Flowcharts are presented in the manual, with separate cutoff scores for all scales (by behavioral dimension). Stage 3 decision rules for the PSB scale are provided by grade level. The authors suggest that an additional level of evaluation can be conducted at Stage 3 by collecting comparable observation data on a same-sex, nonreferred peer. In this manner, peer-referenced norms can be created for specific classrooms.

Additional Score Comparisons

Means, standard deviations, and standard errors for Stage 2 and Stage 3 are presented in the administration manual. Additional conversions of raw scores to T-scores and percentile ranks are also available for these measures. All norm tables are provided separately for children initially ranked by teachers on externalizing and internalizing dimensions. Norms are presented separately for males and females for AET and PSB measures. Finally, norm tables are provided for nonranked students from the standardization sample for Stage 3 measures.

Norms

The SSBD was normed on a national sample of children enrolled in regular-education classrooms from 18 school districts across eight states. Stage 2 included 4,463 students, with 72 percent of the sample coming from three states (Kentucky, Oregon, and Utah). Stage 3 observations were conducted on 1,275 students, with 70 percent of the sample drawn from the same three states. No additional information is provided on the gender, age, grade distribution, or educational classifications of subjects participating in the national sample. Demographic data are included for only 66 percent of the standardization sample. In addition, demographic data are reported only by the total enrollment of participating school districts, not by the actual students included in the standardization sample.

Reliability

Test–retest, internal-consistency, and interrater reliability data were collected during both phases of development of the SSBD. Data on these reliabilities are summarized here.

Test–Retest Reliability For Stage 1 measures (teacher rankings), stability of behavioral classifications (internalizing, externalizing) was calculated during early tests of the SSBD. In a study involving 168 students, 78 percent of the students were classified in the same category on two occasions.

For Stage 2 measures (ratings on the CEI and CFI), short-term stability coefficients are provided. Reported correlations are in the .80s; however, the authors warn about possible inflation of these values because categories of students were collapsed for data analysis. No test–retest data for the Stage 3 (observational) measures are provided in the technical manual.

Internal-Consistency Reliability Data related to the internal consistency of Stage 2 measures are reported. Reliability coefficients for the CFI Adaptive Behavior scale range from .85 to .94 and for the Maladaptive scale, from .82 to .92. Item–total correlations are provided for the scales of the CFI. Coefficients obtained in early testing of the measures were lower than those obtained during the standardization/validation studies.

Interrater Agreement   The authors made extensive use of interrater agreement data in the development of the Stage 1 measures. Rankings of students by two teachers, or by a teacher and a teacher's aide, on early versions of the SSBD yielded coefficients ranging from .60 to .94 for externalizing students and from .35 to .72 for internalizing students. For the final version (after group membership definitions were clarified), coefficients obtained by eight pairs of raters were .89 to .94 for externalizers and .82 to .90 for internalizers.

Stage 3 measures by trained observers have repeatedly resulted in high interrater agreement. The authors state that "interrater agreement levels have not been as yet established for Stage 2 measures" (Walker & Severson, 1992, p. 34).

Overall, the reliabilities of the SSBD measures are adequately supported by appropriate data from multiple-trial testing and validation studies. Some gaps in evidence are noticeable, and the potential user of the SSBD is not provided with comprehensive reliability data for all measures and for the full range of ages for which the SSBD is intended (grades 1–6). Because some portions of the device are age-sensitive (such as Stage 3), reliability of these measures for these ages would be better substantiated if supporting data were made available.

Validity

Content Validity   Publication of the SSBD was preceded by extensive development and research procedures. The selected behavioral items and the internalizing and externalizing dimensions have undergone a thorough testing, refinement, and validation process that has included both regular- and special-education teachers. For the Stage 3 observation codes, a previous observation code developed by Walker, Hops, and Greenwood (1984) served as a model. The authors provide adequate data to support their claim that these observation

codes have been used and validated across numerous school settings.

Criterion-Related Validity   Two types of criterion-related validity (concurrent and predictive) are referred to in the technical manual. Support for concurrent validity is provided by a series of correlational studies conducted during the instrument-development phase and during the research phase of the development process. In one such study, correlation coefficients between the SSBD—CFI scales and the CBCL were calculated. On two occasions, correlations between the CBCL externalizing and the SSBD Adaptive Behavior scale were −.63 and −.68, and for the Maladaptive Behavior scale, .81 and .77 (compared at two different times). All correlations were significant at the .001 confidence level.

In addition, Stage 2 measures were correlated with the Walker–McConnell Scale of Social Competence and School Adjustment (W-M; H. M. Walker & McConnell, 1988) and the Classroom Adjustment Code (CAC; H. M. Walker, Block-Pedego, McConnell, & Clark, 1998). Total score correlations were computed between the W-M and the CEI, the Adaptive Behavior and the Maladaptive Behavior scales. All three comparisons were found to be statistically significant at the .001 confidence level (correlations were −.57, .79, and −.44, respectively). Correlations obtained between the CAC scales of on-task and unacceptable behavior with the CEI were −.45 and .15, respectively. The Adaptive Behavior and Maladaptive Behavior scales correlated in the low to moderate range in expected directions with the CAC measures.

To assess the predictive validity of the SSBD, a total of 155 students (grades 1–5) were assessed on all measures and reassessed one year later by different raters and observers. Students initially rated as externalizers were found to be rated in the top three externalizers one year later, 69 percent of the time. Internalizers were rated among the top three at a lower level one year later, 52 percent of the time. Correlations between first-year and second-year scores on Stage 2 measures for combined internalizing and externalizing groups ranged from .32 (CEI) to .70 (Maladaptive Behavior scale). Overall, correlations between Time 1 and Time 2 were in the low to moderate range. In addition, the criterion of teacher ratings at different times, which was used to suggest predictive validity, seems more appropriate for evidence of long-term stability. It might have served consumers better if an independent standard of comparison had been included.

Construct Validity   To establish construct validity, the authors present data explaining factor-analytic and discriminant function analyses conducted on the SSBD. Evidence of construct validity in the form of convergent and divergent correlational studies is also presented. Correlations between the CBCL internalizing and externalizing dimensions and Stage 3 (AET and PSB scales) were calculated. Stage 3 AET correlated –.42 with the CBCL at a .01 confidence level, and the PSB produced two significant correlations with the CBCL: negative social interaction and positive social interaction, with correlations of .29 and –.35, respectively. No SSBD observation measures were found to be significantly correlated with the CBCL internalizing scales.

In another study, a total of 66 students from Washington enrolled in grades 1, 3, and 5 were assessed on the SSBD Stage 2 measures. Additional instruments were used to collect information regarding the children's status on sociometrics, direct observation, school records, and social-skills ratings. The authors created a "deviance index" (p. 59) by combining selected variables from within the SSBD and from other measures judged to be best-evidence variables for each group. Then, Stage 1 rankings of the students were compared with the deviance index. Correlations between Stage 1 rankings and these multiple instruments for internalizers and externalizers were .71 and .76 (p < .001); these students were correctly identified most of the time (82 percent and 73 percent, respectively).

The authors also describe a study in which a total of 40 regular-education teachers, who had been assigned 54 children identified previously as severely behaviorally disordered (45 externalizers and 9 internalizers), completed the SSBD. The teachers, having no prior knowledge of the students' educational history, were able to identify all 54 students by using the SSBD gating procedures. Overall, these correlations and classifications appear to be in the moderate to high range and to provide support for the SSBD as a measure of school-adjustment problems.

Discriminant Validity   Discriminant validity of the SSBD system and its component measures is very important to the authors, given that one of the main constructs of the SSBD is the notion of differentiating children on a bipolar continuum of externalizing and internalizing problem behaviors. In prevalidation studies of the SSBD, almost 90 percent of students were correctly classified as internalizers or externalizers using Stage 2 and Stage 3 measures.

In one validation study, 170 teachers (for grades 1 to 5) completed Stage 1 and Stage 2 measures for students enrolled in classrooms in Oregon. Analysis of variance (ANOVA) on group differences for Stage 2 measures were highly significant. Post hoc *T*-tests indicated that all possible combinations of comparisons among three groups (internalizers, externalizers, and controls) were significant at the .01 confidence level.

In a second study conducted to replicate the first, a total of 40 regular-education teachers from the state of Washington completed Stage 1 and Stage 2 measures for 270 students. All post hoc *T*-tests identified mean differences among all comparisons of these groups, which were significant at the .05 level of confidence. These two studies suggest that the SSBD has sufficient discriminant power to differentiate among these three groups.

An additional study examined a more clinical sample of 106 students who were assigned to a residential facility serving severely disturbed or abused children in kindergarten through grade 12. Students were enrolled in four different programs that included two residential and two day-treatment programs: secure unit ($N = 17$), residential ($N = 52$), day treatment ($N = 20$), and community based ($N = 17$). Separate one-way ANOVAs were

Coping with Dilemmas in Current Practice

The subjectivity inherent in ratings or self-reports of problem behavior causes two problems. First, raters must know the person being rated in order to make judgments about problem behaviors. Yet, familiarity can cloud judgments. Raters may take into account unrelated attributes. For example, a teacher might rate Billy more leniently because he is a bright child, really tries hard to behave, and has parents who seem concerned. Second, raters sometimes have a stake in the decision. Self-ratings or ratings of others may exaggerate or downplay the frequency or severity of problem behavior. For example, parents or teachers who feel that problem behavior reflects badly on themselves may unintentionally downplay the frequency or severity of behavior; on the other hand, parents or teachers who cannot cope with the behavior any longer may unintentionally overestimate the frequency or severity of problem behavior.

Diagnosticians can do two things to reduce some of the subjectivity inherent in evaluating problem behavior. First, they can select instruments that are likely to minimize subjectivity. For example, scales that attempt to objectively quantify behavior should be less prone to bias than scales that do not. Scales that ask about observable behavior (such as hitting) should be less prone to bias than scales that require inferences (such as aggressiveness). Second, diagnosticians can obtain information from several people who have had the opportunity to observe in the same contexts.

Scores from rating scales or checklists do not correlate highly with external criteria or measures of behavior. In particular, rating scales that have internalizing dimensions are not very good at identifying students with depressive disorders and do not agree with clinical or interview data. (B. Egeland, personal communication, March 30, 1994). Therefore, students suspected of being at risk for internalizing disorders such as childhood depression are best served via a comprehensive clinical evaluation.

Finally, all social–emotional assessment is linked to the idea that effective interventions and treatments will be available for the students whom we identify as being in need of service. Some of the instruments reviewed in this chapter have companion manuals that describe interventions based on specific items or groups of items assessed by the rating scales or checklists. Some of these ideas are tried-and-true methods that fit into most useful social-skills training programs. Others are less well documented and lack effective instructional or intervention strategies. Social–emotional and behavioral assessment practices are neatly summed up by Brown and Hammill (1990) with the phrase "caveat utilitor." Interventions with students must be based on sound assessment data, and it is up to the users of these devices to evaluate the instruments and to plan for instruction. Assessments and rating scales are only as good as the practitioners who use them. It is essential that any sort of treatment based on information gleaned from rating scales or other social–emotional assessment be evaluated in terms of its positive and negative impact on student behavior and social–emotional progress.

conducted for the CEI, the Maladaptive Behavior scale, and the Adaptive Behavior scale. Results indicated significant differences among the four categories of students on the CEI. No statistical differences were observed on the Maladaptive Behavior or Adaptive Behavior rating scale. Post hoc *T*-tests identified differences between the secure unit and the residential students. No other mean differences were found to be significant. This may suggest that although the SSBD has sufficient discriminant power to differentiate classification between clinical and general population samples, further specificity within clinical populations is not as well established.

Taken together, discriminant-validity studies demonstrate that the SSBD is effective at distinguishing internalizing and externalizing students from the larger population of students without behavioral and adjustment problems. Students classified as externalizers on the SSBD were found to engage in less adaptive behavior and more maladaptive behavior than controls and internalizers. In addition, this group spent less time academically engaged and more time in negative interactions than did internalizers and control children. Children rated as internalizers on the SSBD were found to engage in less adaptive behavior and more maladaptive behavior and to spend more time alone than control students.

Summary

The SSBD is a well-conceived and well-researched instrument for screening and identifying children in need of further assessment for behavioral disorders. In fact, the SSBD has been nominated as an example of an effective instrument by the Program Effectiveness Panel of the U.S. Department of Education. However, to date, the SSBD has been used largely in a research capacity that has consistently produced discrete evidence of reliability and validity. Normative and demographic data and defining characteristics of the students who participated in the standardization sample are difficult to discern. The authors provide substantial evidence of the SSBD scales' ability to differentiate between students exhibiting internalizing or externalizing problem behavior and well-adjusted students. Although reported reliability and validity studies appear adequate, there are gaps in some areas (such as interrater reliability and grade-specific reliabilities). These gaps may ultimately restrict the types of interpretations that can be made from the results of the SSBD instrument. The essential strength of the SSBD is the conceptual framework of multiple-gating procedures, which serves to organize and standardize what teachers and practitioners have been doing informally for years.

. . . .

Summary

In recent years, the assessment of internalizing and externalizing problem behavior has become more frequent. Most often, assessment is considered for children at risk for emotional/behavioral disorders; however, children with academically based deficits may also be referred for social skills or behavioral evaluations. Common methods of measurement include rating scales, teacher questionnaires, and direct observation. Assessment of social–emotional behavior, like most academic assessment, should be conducted

with the intention of providing assessment-based interventions to ameliorate identified problems.

Questions for Chapter Review and Thought

1. What are the major concerns of using rating scales to describe student social–emotional behavior?

2. Design an assessment session that incorporates the concept of multifactor evaluation. Why might some portions of the session be more relevant

than others to particular concerns? Which type (or types) of measurement do you believe results in the best assessment data?

3. Ms. Jansen, a seventh-grade teacher, wants you to assess Marie because Marie seems to be depressed all the time. Ms. Jansen specifically requests that you use the Systematic Screening for Behavior Disorders because she has heard that it uses a multiple-gating procedure to move the diagnosis from broad emotional difficulties to specific types of depression. How would you respond to this request?

4. Assume that you had to assess a student's social-emotional behavior. How would you go about doing so in a way that would be appropriate?

Resources for Further Investigation

Project

Compare the results obtained from two of the assessments described in the chapter. Note where differences appear, and explain the reasons for the differences.

Print Resources

Knoff, H. M. (1986). *The assessment of child and adolescent personality* (Chapter 3, A conceptual model and pragmatic approach toward personality assessment referrals). New York: Guilford Press.

Martin, R. P. (1988). *Assessment of personality and behavior problems: Infancy through adolescence.* New York: Guilford Press.

McCarney, J. (1994). *The Behavior Evaluation Scale–2, Home Version: Technical Manual.* Columbia, MO: Hawthorne Educational Services.

McCarney, J. (1995a). *Attention-Deficit Disorders Evaluation Scale, Home Version–Second Edition: Technical Manual.* Columbia, MO: Hawthorne Educational Services.

McCarney, J. (1995b). *Attention-Deficit Disorders Evaluation Scale, School Version–Second Edition:*

Technical Manual. Columbia, MO: Hawthorne Educational Services.

Merrell, K. W. (1994). *Assessment of behavioral, social, and emotional problems.* New York: Longman.

Technology Resources

Welcome to AGS On-Line Products and Services

http://www.agsnet.com/

Look for product and ordering information about the instruments available from American Guidance Service. Here you can find out information about the *Behavior Assessment System for Children.*

Pro-ed Catalog Information for Products

http://www.proedinc.com

Find product and ordering information about the *Autism Screening Instrument for Educational Planning–2,* and the *Behavior Rating Profile,* second edition.

Autism Resources

http://web.syr.edu/~jmwobus/autism/

Look here to find an index of materials, information, and resources about autism and about Asperger's syndrome.

The Child Behavior Checklist Homepage

http://www.uvm.edu/~cbcl/

Find product and ordering information about the *Child Behavior Checklist.*

Attention Deficit Disorder

http://www.adhd.com

This web site has a list of information about attention deficit disorder and provides many links to related sites.

Functional Behavior Assessment and Behavior Intervention Plans

http://www.cec.sped.org/digests/e571.htm

This document discusses the need to appropriately assess problem behavior of students with disabilities so that the constructed individualized education program is as effective as possible.

chapter
26

Assessment of Adaptive Behavior

*A*daptive behavior is the way individuals adapt themselves to the requirements of their physical and social environment (Schmidt & Salvia, 1984). In part, adaptation means survival: Adaptive behaviors are those that allow individuals to continue to live by avoiding dangers and by taking reasonable precautions to ensure their safety. Yet, adaptivity refers to more than mere survival; it implies the ability to thrive in both good and adverse times.

Adaptive behavior also requires more than an appropriate response to the demands of the immediate environment; it also requires preparation for responses to probable future environments. Certain current behaviors (for example, smoking or high-risk sexual activity) can have life-threatening future consequences. Similarly, acquiring more education or job training and saving money increase the likelihood of thriving in later years. Adaptive behavior, in the present and for the future, must also take into account the demands of a person's physical surroundings and the expectations of that person's culture.

● ● ● ● ● ● ● ● ● ● ● ● ● ● ● ● ● ● ● ●

Defining Adaptive Behavior

Physical Environment

The knowledge and skill required to avoid danger (or to react appropriately when in danger) vary considerably from environment to environment. For example, different environments require different protective clothing and different precautions against climatic conditions. Living in the desert Southwest in summer requires guarding against dehydration and heat stroke, whereas living in New England in the winter requires guarding against hypothermia and frostbite. Different environments have different dangerous wildlife: alligators in southeastern swamps, scorpions and Gila monsters in the Southwest, rats in many urban areas, and so forth. In addition to natural hazards, different environments present human-made hazards: automobiles, electrical appliances, cutting tools, chemicals, and so forth.

Social and Cultural Expectations

Social expectations vary considerably from culture to culture, and the ability to thrive in a culture requires some degree of conformity to that society's cultural norms. Societal expectations manifest themselves in language usage (for example, polite or respectful language, speaking distance, and speaking volume), role performance, personal responsibility, and independence.

Age and Adaptation

Sociocultural expectations are also a function of the person's age. In the United States, we have different expectations of infants, children, adolescents, and adults. For infants and young children, expectations center on maturational processes; at some points in these processes, reflexive behavior (for example, sucking) is a necessary component of survival. After infancy, maturational processes merely enable behavior. "Thus, goodness of vision and hearing, intactness of motor skills, neuromotor integrity, and similar characteristics are not adaptive behaviors of the individual; they are biological characteristics of the human species and provide the basis for behavior" (Salvia, Neisworth, & Schmidt, 1990, p. 57). Thus, for older individuals, adaptive behavior is learned behavior.

We expect youngsters to use language socially, to play appropriately, to assume limited responsibilities (for example, picking up toys), and to function in increasingly independent ways (for example, self-feeding, self-dressing, and moving around in their homes and neighborhoods). As children get older, the expectations for independence and responsibility increase, both at home and in school. With adolescence come demands for making the transition to adulthood (for example, preparing for employment and accepting more complete personal responsibility).

Performance Versus Ability

The *ability* to behave in expected ways is not synonymous with the performance of adaptive behavior. Knowing how to survive and thrive does not ensure that people will behave accordingly. For example, children may know that they should look both ways before crossing streets, and they may know how to do so; however, the important consideration is whether they *do* look both ways. Not only must a behavior be performed regularly (habitually and customarily), but it must also be performed without prompting or assistance.

Maladaption

In their definitions of adaptive behavior, some theorists include an absence of marked maladaption. Although such a position may have intuitive appeal, there are at least two conceptual problems with including maladaptive behavior on formal tests. First, the absence of maladaptive behavior does not imply the presence of adaptive behavior. Second, except for suicidal behavior and a very few universally taboo behaviors (for example, adolescents or adults smearing human excrement on themselves), maladaptive behavior is determined by context, as well as frequency and amplitude.

Context

The *context of behavior* refers to both social tolerance and the specific situation in which a behavior occurs. Social tolerance is an important qualifier because very few behaviors are universally taboo. For example, certain types of hallucinations may be prized as religious experiences in some societies but seen as psychotic in others; homosexuality is accepted in some societies but punished in others. The list of potential examples is very long. Within a society, taboo behavior is codified by custom, religion, and law.

Some behaviors are evaluated solely on the basis of context. For example, disrobing is usually considered deviant in a classroom full of students but normal before bathing; failure to disrobe is normal in classrooms but abnormal before bathing. Even when certain behaviors are proscribed, the circumstances in which those behaviors are demonstrated is important. For example, in the United States, killing another person is not necessarily murder. The context in which the death occurred determines whether it is a crime (murder or voluntary manslaughter) or not (self-defense or accidental death).

Finally, for a behavior to be considered deviant, either the behavior or its consequence must be observed. If no one witnesses the act or its consequence, it will not be considered maladaptive. Moreover, the person observing the behavior (or consequence) must be willing and must have the authority to label the behavior as deviant.

Frequency and Amplitude

The frequency and amplitude of behavior are also important in labeling a behavior as maladaptive. Some behavior will be tolerated or condoned if it occurs infrequently. For example, occasional drunkenness may be ignored, but chronic drunkenness is considered alcoholism. The boundaries separating tolerated occasional misbehavior from deviance vary with context, status of the person, and consequences of the behavior. The amplitude of behavior also affects social and cultural tolerance. For example, fingernail biting is seldom, in and of itself, considered significant. However, when fingernail biting produces bleeding, scarring, and deformity, the behavior has crossed a line into self-mutilation.

Assessing Adaptive Behavior

Historically, the assessment of adaptive behavior has relied on the report of a third person (typically designated as a *respondent*). Thus, we do not assess an individual's adaptive behavior directly; an examiner does not test or observe the individual being assessed. Instead, the examiner relies on the cumulative observations of a respondent who is both truthful and sufficiently familiar with the subject of the assessment to make a judgment about that subject's behavior.

This method of administration is susceptible to a variety of errors and biases. The student being evaluated may generally conceal behavior that is culturally taboo, or the student may conceal behavior from the respondent if the student knows that the respondent disapproves of the behavior. The student being evaluated may selectively demonstrate the behavior. For example, when the respondent (a parent or teacher) is present, the student may behave appropriately; when the respondent is absent, the student may not. Finally, when respondents have a stake in the outcome, they may be less than truthful or objective. For example, if a parent respondent does not want a student classified as mentally retarded, that parent may give the child the benefit of the doubt in every response.

Why Do We Assess Adaptive Behavior?

There are two major reasons for assessing adaptive behavior: (1) identification of mental retardation, and (2) program planning. First, mental retardation is generally defined, in part, as a failure of adaptive behavior. In theory, in order to classify a pupil as mentally retarded, for example, an evaluator needs to assess adaptive behavior. More important, however, are the federal regulations and state school codes requiring that adaptive behavior be assessed before a pupil can be considered mentally retarded.

Second, for program planning, educational objectives in the domain of adaptive behavior are frequently developed for moderately and severely retarded individuals, as well as for students with other disabilities. Adaptive behavior is often important in planning habilitative and transition services for various students. Thus, scales of adaptive behavior are often the source of educational goals.

Specific Tests of Adaptive Behavior

The seven devices reviewed in the pages that follow are used most often in assessment of handicapped individuals: Vineland Adaptive Behavior Scale; American Association on Mental Deficiency (AAMD) Adaptive Behavior Scale: Residential and Community Scale, Second Edition; AAMR Adaptive Behavior Scale–School 2; Adaptive Behavior Evaluation Scale: Home Version, Revised; Adaptive Behavior Inventory; Scales of Independent Behavior–Revised; and Responsibility and Independence Scale for Adolescents (RISA).

Vineland Adaptive Behavior Scale (VABS)

The Vineland Adaptive Behavior Scale (VABS) is an individually administered scale given to someone—such as a parent, caregiver, or teacher—who is familiar with the person who is the subject of the assessment. The VABS has been termed the 1984 revision of the Vineland Social Maturity Scale (VSMS). As would be expected, the revision entailed conversion of the old VSMS from an age scale to a much more modern point scale and complete restandardization. The revision is far more sweeping, however; thus, the new VABS might better be considered a new device. The VABS is available in three forms that have three separate technical manuals. Two forms are termed interview editions: the expanded form (Sparrow, Balla, & Cicchetti, 1984a) and the survey form (Sparrow, Balla, & Cicchetti, 1984b). The third form is the classroom edition (Harrison, 1985). The three forms vary in the number and types of items included, as well as in the respondent who completes the form. The survey form contains 297 items and is intended to provide a general appraisal of the individual; it requires about 20 to 60 minutes to administer to a parent or caregiver. The expanded form contains 577 items and is intended to provide a comprehensive appraisal suitable for planning educational programs; it requires 60 to 90 minutes to administer to a parent or caregiver. The classroom edition contains 244 items and requires about 20 minutes for a teacher to complete. Various individual items form subdomains, and multiple subdomains form domains. All three editions assess Communication, Daily Living Skills, Socialization, and Motor Skills domains. The two interview editions also assess the Maladaptive Behavior domain.

Domains

Communication This domain consists of three subdomains: receptive (for example, listens to a story for at least 20 minutes), expressive (for example, uses *around* as a preposition in a phrase), and written (for example, addresses letters correctly).

Daily Living Skills This domain consists of three subdomains: personal (for example, dresses self completely, except for tying shoelaces), domestic (for example, puts clean clothes away without assistance), and community (for example, states current date when asked).

Socialization This domain consists of three subdomains: interpersonal (for example, shows desire to please caregiver), play and leisure time (for example, shares toys or possessions without being told to do so), and coping skills (for example, does not talk with food in mouth).

Motor Skills   This domain consists of two subdomains: gross (for example, can jump over small objects) and fine (for example, can unlock key locks).

Maladaptive Behavior   This domain consists of 36 behaviors. Part 1 contains 27 maladaptive behaviors that are described as *minor* (for example, sucks thumb or finger, bites fingernails, is stubborn or sullen, and so forth); Part 2 contains 9 behaviors that are considered more serious (for example, displays inappropriate sexual behavior, uses bizarre speech, rocks back and forth when sitting or standing).

The subdomains are not evenly distributed throughout the domains. For example, in Communication, the receptive subdomain is assessed, with one exception, totally in the first half of the domain, and the written subdomain is assessed exclusively in the second half of the domain.

Scores

Within the Communication, Daily Living Skills, Socialization, and Motor Skills domains, items between basal and ceiling are scored 2 (yes or usually), 1 (sometimes or partially), or 0 (no or never). Items may also be scored "DK" (respondent does not know) or "N" (no opportunity). In Part 1 of the Maladaptive Behavior domain (minor maladaptive behaviors), items are scored 2 (usually), 1 (sometimes), or 0 (never or very seldom). In Part 2, items are scored for their intensity (severe, moderate, or absent). Subdomain scores are combined into domain scores, and the Communication, Daily Living Skills, Socialization, and Motor Skills domains can be combined into an adaptive behavior composite.

Domain and composite scores can be transformed to standard scores (mean = 100, standard deviation = 15), percentile ranks, age equivalents, and adaptive levels. The adaptive levels are high (more than two standard deviations above the mean), moderately high (between one and two standard deviations above the mean), adequate (between one standard deviation above and one below the mean), moderately low (between one and two standard deviations below the mean), and low (more than two standard deviations below the mean).

Norms

Several sets of norm groups are available. For the two interview editions, a national sample of 3,000 individuals ranging in age from newborn to 18 years, 11 months was tested. The sample is quite similar to the population at the time of the 1980 U.S. census in terms of geographic region, racial/ethnic group, parental education, and community size. For the classroom edition, 1,984 children between the ages of 3 and 12 years, 11 months were tested. The sample resembles the population at the time of the 1980 census with respect to racial/ethnic group. It appears unrepresentative with respect to geographic region (overrepresenting the North Central region and underrepresenting the others), parental education (overrepresenting the college-educated and underrepresenting those with only a high-school education or less), and community size (overrepresenting central cities and underrepresenting rural areas). Supplementary samples are also available: institutionalized and noninstitutionalized mentally retarded adults and institutionalized children who were either emotionally disturbed, visually handicapped, or hearing-impaired. The supplementary norms are not carefully described but must be used for Part 2 of the Maladaptive Behavior domain.

Reliability

Interview Editions   Internal consistency of the survey form was estimated by odd–even correlations corrected by the Spearman–Brown formula. For Communication, coefficients for the different age groups range from .73 to .94; only 6 of the 15 coefficients equal or exceed .90. For Daily Living Skills, coefficients for the 15 age groups range from .83 to .92; 8 of the 15 coefficients equal or exceed .90. For Socialization, the 15 coefficients range from .78 to .94; only 2 of the 15 coefficients equal or exceed .90. For Motor Skills, the 6 coefficients range from .70 to .95; only for the 0-0 to 0-11 age group is the reliability greater than .89. The estimated reliabilities for the adaptive behavior composite are generally higher; the lowest coefficient is .89 for the 14-0 to 15-11 age group. Finally, the 10 coefficients for Maladaptive Behavior (Part 1) ranged from .77 to .88. As could be anticipated, the estimated reliabilities for the subdomains are considerably lower.

The split-half correlations from the survey form were used "to estimate split-half reliability coefficients for the Expanded Form" (Sparrow, Balla, & Cicchetti, 1984a, p. 30).[1] For Communication, the reported coefficients for the 15 age groups range from .84 to .97; only 5 of the 15 coefficients are less than .90. For Daily Living Skills, coefficients for the 15 age groups all exceed .90. For Socialization, the 15 coefficients range from .88 to .97; only 2 of the 15 coefficients are less than .90. For Motor Skills, the 6 coefficients range from .83 to .97; half of the coefficients are .90 or larger. The estimated reliabilities for the adaptive behavior composite all exceed .93. The 10 coefficients for Maladaptive Behavior (Part 1) range from .77 to .88. As we would anticipate, the estimated reliabilities for the subdomains are considerably lower.

Stability is estimated by correlating raw scores for age groups. The 15 age groups were combined into just 6, however. Consequently, stability coefficients are inflated by the degree to which chronological age correlates with the raw scores. For Communication, the estimated stabilities for the age groups ranged from .80 to .98; two coefficients were less than .90. For Daily Living Skills, the estimated stabilities ranged from .87 to .96;

half of the coefficients were less than .90. For Socialization, they ranged from .77 to .92; only one exceeded .89. For the three combined age groups for Motor Skills, two stability coefficients were below .90. Stability for the domain of Maladaptive Behavior ranged from .84 to .89 for the four age groups for which this domain is appropriate. The stability of composite scores is not reported.

Interrater agreement was assessed for 160 individuals who varied in age from 0-6 to 18-11. In these computations, the effect of chronological age on the correlations between rates was removed statistically.[2] For Communication and Daily Living Skills, interrater agreement exceeded .90; for Socialization and Motor Skills, it was less than .87.

Classroom Edition Coefficient alpha was used to estimate internal consistency for subdomains and domains for ten age groups (a combined 3-0 to 4-11 group and 1-year groups between 5-0 and 12-11). For Communication, alphas ranged from .88 to .95, with only one coefficient less than .89. For Daily Living Skills and Socialization, alphas ranged from .91 to .96. For Motor Skills, the two coefficients were .84 and .77. The adaptive behavior composite exceeded .95 at each age.

Validity

Evidence of the validity of the classroom edition and the survey form comes from several sources. Content validity is difficult to assess because a precise definition of the domain to be assessed is never offered. The authors state that they conducted an intensive review of the child-development literature and drew on their own clinical and research experiences to determine the four behavioral domains (Communication, Daily Living Skills, Socialization, and Motor Skills). How daily activities are related to adaptive behavior is unclear.

---

1. The procedure used rests on several assumptions: One is that the "items in the Expanded Form constituted the complete universe from which a representative sample of about 48% was used to develop the Survey Form" (Sparrow, Balla, & Cicchetti, 1984a, p. 30). Of course, if this assumption were met, then there would be no need to estimate the reliability of the expanded form because, by most definitions, the obtained scores would have to equal true scores.

2. First-order partial correlations were computed. Because this procedure was used for interrater agreement, it seems inconsistent not to have used it with stability estimates.

Evidence of construct validity comes from the correlation of VABS scores and chronological age. Results of factor analyses only partially confirm the subdomains, however. The differential performances of supplementary norm groups are also used to support the construct validity of the scale. In addition, correlations between VABS and intelligence-test scores are reported. Evidence for criterion-related validity comes from the correlation of the VABS with the original Vineland Social Maturity Scale, the Adaptive Behavior Inventory for Children, and the American Association on Mental Deficiency (AAMD) Adaptive Behavior Scale. No independent evidence of criterion-related validity is offered for the expanded form. Rather, validity is estimated from correlations between the VABS survey form and the criterion measures discussed in the preceding paragraph.

Summary

The VABS is an individually administered, norm-referenced device intended to assess the adaptive and maladaptive behaviors of individuals under 19 years of age. Norming appears quite good. Reliability of the scale varies considerably, however, and only sometimes are the domains and subdomains suitable for use in making important individual decisions. Validity data are adequate.

AAMD Adaptive Behavior Scale: Residential and Community Scale, Second Edition (ABS-RC2)

The AAMD Adaptive Behavior Scale: Residential and Community Scale, Second Edition (ABS-RC2; Nihira, Leland, Lambert, 1993b) is an individually administered, norm-referenced scale designed for use with individuals between 18 and 79 years of age. Since its introduction in 1969, this scale has undergone numerous modifications. For this latest version, items from previous editions were selected because of their interrater reliability and effectiveness in discrimination among various levels of adaptation.

The scale is divided into two parts. Part I focuses on ten domains related to independent and responsible functioning, physical development, language development, and socialization. Three factors underlie these domains: personal self-sufficiency, community self-sufficiency, and personal–social responsibility.

Two administration formats are used in this part. In the first format, responses to items consist of a series of statements denoting increasingly higher levels of adaptation. These items are scored by circling the highest level of functioning demonstrated by the client. For example, in the domain of physical development, the response to Item 25 (vision) has four levels: Has no difficulty seeing, Has some difficulty seeing, Has great difficulty seeing, and Has no vision at all.

In the second format, each item consists of a series of statements that are answered either yes or no. A socially desirable response is awarded 1 point. For example, Item 62 (persistence) in the self-direction domain consists of five statements: Cannot organize task, Becomes easily discouraged, Fails to carry out tasks, Jumps from one activity to another, and Needs constant encouragement to complete task. For this item, "No" is the socially desirable response; each time a statement does not apply to the subject, the subject is awarded 1 point. Thus, a subject may receive between 0 and 5 points on this item. Students can earn from 3 to 9 points on each item scored in this format.

The items in Part II of the scale are concerned with maladaptive behaviors that are manifestations of personality and behavior disorders. These items are grouped into eight domains, and only one administration format is used. Two factors underlie these eight domains: social adjustment and personal adjustment. Each item consists of multiple statements and is scored on a 3-point scale (never, 0; occasionally, 1; or frequently, 2). (See Table 26.1 for a list of domains and factors.)

Scores

All raw scores from the ABS-RC2 can be converted to percentiles, standard scores for domains (mean = 10, standard deviation = 37), and quotients for factors (mean = 100, standard deviation = 15). Age equivalents are also available for scores from Part I; Part II scores are not related to age, so no age equivalents are available. Derived scores

for an adaptive behavior total or composite are not available.

Domain scores provide measures of relative standing in each topical domain. In addition, five factor scores (based on previous research and a confirmatory factor analysis) can be obtained for the three factors in Part I (personal self-sufficiency, community self-sufficiency, and personal–social responsibility) and two factors in Part II (social adjustment and personal adjustment). The factor scores are obtained by summing item raw scores and converting the totals to derived scores.

Norms

The ABS-RC2 was standardized on 4,103 individuals with developmental disabilities. Participants in the standardization were stratified on living arrangements: those living in the community (for example, living at home or in small community-based residences) and those living in institutions. Some subjects were selected by site coordinators in

TABLE 26.1 • Domains and Factors in Parts I and II of the ABS-RC2

	Domains (number of items in each)	Factors
Part I	1. Independent Functioning (24)	Personal Self-Sufficiency
	2. Physical Development (6)	Community Self-Sufficiency
	3. Economic Activity (6)	Personal–Social Responsibility
	4. Language Development (10)	
	5. Numbers and Time (3)	
	6. Domestic Activity (6)	
	7. Prevocational/Vocational Activity (3)	
	8. Self-Direction (5)	
	9. Responsibility (3)	
	10. Socialization (7)	
Part II	11. Social Behavior (7)	Social Adjustment
	12. Conformity (6)	Personal Adjustment
	13. Trustworthiness (6)	
	14. Stereotyped and Hyperactive Behavior (5)	
	15. Sexual Behavior (4)	
	16. Self-Abusive Behavior (3)	
	17. Social Engagement (4)	
	18. Disturbing Interpersonal Behavior (6)	

Connecticut, Florida, Ohio, and California; other subjects were located through a mailing to members of the American Association on Mental Deficiency who were asked to participate in the standardization.

These techniques for finding subjects resulted in a sample drawn from 46 states and the District of Columbia. Subjects in the normative sample were predominantly between the ages of 18 and 39; there were 1,339 individuals between 18 and 29, 1,254 individuals between 30 and 39, 759 individuals between 40 and 49, 418 individuals between 50 and 59, and 333 individuals 60 or older. The sample is generally representative of the nation in terms of geographical region, race, and ethnicity; however, it overrepresents males and individuals living in urban areas. The extent to which this sample represents the population of individuals with mental retardation is unclear: 18 percent of the sample had IQs less than 20, 43.2 percent had IQs between 20 and 49, and 38.8 percent had IQs between 50 and 70. Professionals who conduct assessments with the ABS-RC2 must be very aware that the percentiles and standard scores are based on the performances of individuals with mental retardation. Thus, the usual score interpretations are not correct. A person earning a percentile of 50 on this test has performed equal to or greater than 50 percent of the retarded individuals in the normative sample.

Reliability

Reliability of the ABS-RC2 was estimated for items (using coefficient alpha), for times (stability), and for raters.[3] In Part I, alphas for domains ranged from a low of .80 (for ages 18–29 on prevocational/vocational activity) to a high of .98 (independent functioning for ages 18–29 and 30–39); of the 50 domain alphas, 41 equaled or exceeded .90. Alphas for Part I factors were all quite high,

3. The authors provide information about what they call "interscorer reliability." In the study they cite, two graduate students tabulated completed protocols. Because the tabulation of scores is not particularly complicated on this scale, the high correlations are not surprising.

ranging from .96 to .99. In Part II, alphas for domains ranged from a low of .80 (sexual behavior of ages 60 and older and self-abusive behavior for ages 35–39 and 40–49) to a high of .95 (social behavior for ages 18–29 and 50–59). Of the 40 alphas for Part II domains, only 13 equaled or exceeded .90. Alphas for Part II factors all exceeded .90. The reason alphas were higher for factor scores than for domain scores is probably because there are more items in factor scores and the factor scores are more homogeneous than domain scores.

Two-week stability was estimated based on scores of 45 individuals working in a sheltered workshop. The individuals ranged in age from 24 to 61 years, but it is unclear whether standard scores or other methods of controlling for age range were used. Uncorrected correlations between test and retest for Part I domains ranged from .86 to .98; seven of the ten coefficients equaled or exceeded .90. Uncorrected correlations for factors ranged from .93 to .98. For Part II, uncorrected correlations ranged from .81 to .97 for domain scores; four of the eight coefficients equaled or exceeded .90. Part II factor scores were .94 and .82.

The authors also provide information about interrater agreement (which they term *ecological validity*) for 45 employees of a sheltered workshop. Supervisors and the parents of the employees were independently rated. For Part I domain scores, agreement ranged from .31 (prevocational/vocational) to .87 (physical development); the agreement for Part I factor scores ranged from .47 (personal–social responsibility) to .88 (personal self-sufficiency). For Part II domain scores, agreement ranged from .07 (social behavior) to .85 (sexual behavior); for Part II factors, agreement was .31 (social adjustment) and .39 (personal adjustment).

Validity

Content Validity   The content of the revised scale remains quite similar to the content of previous versions of this device. In previous editions of this text, we questioned the content validity of the scale because the authors presented no conceptualization of the domain used to guide inclusion and exclusion of items. We were also troubled because many of the items assess physical and emotional states (not behavior) and because many items that appeared in Part II probably should not be considered maladaptive (for example, "Gossips about others," "Is always in the way," "Bites fingernails"). We still find the rationale for item selection and the scale's content to be troubling.

Criterion-Related Validity   Two criterion-related validity studies are reported. In the first, 63 individuals were tested using the ABS-RC2 and the Vineland Adaptive Behavior Scales. In the second study, 30 individuals were tested using the ABS-RC2 and the Adaptive Behavior Inventory.[4] In both studies, the correlations between the Part I ABS-RC2 scores and the other measures were generally moderate to high; the correlations between Part II ABS-RC2 scores and the other measures were generally not significantly different from zero. These findings strongly suggest that Part II is not measuring what is typically measured on other measures of adaptive behavior. The findings also provide some support for the criterion-related validity of Part I scores.

Construct Validity   Although several indexes of construct validity are provided in the ABS-RC2 manual, three seem most pertinent to our discussion. The first evidence comes from the relationship between age and both Part I and Part II of the scale. As expected for a valid measure of adaptive behavior, Part I scores show some relationship to

age for normally developing children and youths, but no relationship to age for adults with mental retardation. Part II scores are unrelated to age—also as would be expected of a valid measure.

Second, the empirical factor structure of the ABS-RC2 supports the hypothesis of three factors for Part I (as is typically found in factor-analytic studies of adaptive behavior) and two factors for Part II. Thus, not only do Parts I and II measure different things, but Part I appears to be measuring constructs similar to those assessed by other measures of adaptive behavior. The meaning of Part II is not clarified by these results.

Third, scores on the ABS-RC2 differentiate youngsters with and without disabilities, and both these groups of youngsters perform differently from adults with mental retardation. Although these results are suggestive of the construct validity of the scale, we note that the ABS-RC2 is not intended for use with children and youths. As expected, scores frequently discriminated individuals living in community placements from those living in residential settings.

Summary

The ABS-RC2 is an individually administered, norm-referenced scale designed for use with individuals between 18 and 79 years of age. The scale is divided into two parts. Part I focuses on ten domains that assess three factors: personal self-sufficiency, community self-sufficiency, and personal–social responsibility. Part II focuses on eight domains that assess (the lack of) social adjustment and personal adjustment. The ABS-RC2 represents a substantial improvement over previous editions of the ABS. The norming is far more comprehensive and appears much more representative. However, given the elusive nature of mild retardation, the identification of which is affected by economic and social circumstances, conclusions about the population of reference must be tentative.

The information about the scale's reliability is far more extensive than in previous editions. The internal consistency of factor scores on both parts

---

4. The same study appears to have been reported in the examiner's manual for the school version of the ABS. (Identical correlations are reported, and the subject description is similar.) In that manual, the subjects are described as attending school. At worst, these individuals fall outside of the age range with which the ABS-RC2 is intended to be used; at best, these individuals represent only one extreme of the age range with which the ABS-RC2 is intended to be used.

of the scale is excellent; the domain alphas are not nearly as high. The factor scores also appear to be quite stable. Interrater agreement (called "ecological validity" by the authors) is weak, however. Thus, examiners should expect the ABS-RC2 to produce internally consistent scores that are stable over time but that vary according to who provides the information. Evidence of the scales' validity is emerging. The content of specific items is troubling, but there is no indication that the scale lacks criterion-related or construct validity.

AAMD Adaptive Behavior Scale–School 2 (ABS-S2)[5]

The revised school version of the AAMD Adaptive Behavior Scale (ABS-S2; Nihira, Leland, & Lambert, 1993a) is an individually administered, norm-referenced scale designed for use with children and youths ages 3 to 21 years. The 1993 revision is the latest version of the 1969 and 1974 AAMD Adaptive Behavior Scales. Like the Residential and Community version of this scale, the ABS-S2 has undergone numerous modifications since its introduction in 1969. In this edition, items from previous editions were selected because of their interrater reliability and effectiveness in discrimination among various levels of adaptation.

The items and scoring procedures of the school version of the ABS are identical to those used with the residential and community edition, with two exceptions. On the school version, one domain has been deleted from each part of the scale, domestic activity from Part I and sexual behavior from Part II. Otherwise, the two scales appear to be identical. (Readers familiar with the community and residential version of the ABS should skip to the sections dealing with technical characteristics of this version.)

Thus, the scale is divided into two parts. Part I focuses on nine domains related to independent and responsible functioning, physical develop-

ment, language development, and socialization. Three factors underlie these domains: personal self-sufficiency, community self-sufficiency, and personal–social responsibility. In this part, two administration formats are used. In the first format, items consist of a series of statements denoting increasingly higher levels of adaptation. These items are scored by circling the highest level of functioning demonstrated by the client. For example, in the domain of physical development, Item 25 (vision) has four levels of functioning: Has no difficulty seeing, Has some difficulty seeing, Has great difficulty seeing, and Has no vision at all. In the second format, each item consists of a series of statements that are answered either yes or no. A socially desirable response is awarded 1 point. For example, Item 62 (persistence) in the self-direction domain consists of five statements: Cannot organize task, Becomes easily discouraged, Fails to carry out tasks, Jumps from one activity to another, and Needs constant encouragement to complete task. For this item, "No" is the socially desirable response; each time a statement does not apply to the subject, the subject is awarded 1 point. Thus, a subject may receive between 0 and 5 points on this item. Students can earn from 3 to 9 points on each item scored in this format.

The items in Part II of the scale are concerned with maladaptive behaviors that are manifestations of personality and behavior disorders. These items are grouped into seven domains that form two factors: social adjustment and personal ad-

---

5. The ABS-RC2 and the ABS-S2 are highly similar devices. Even though much of the material is redundant, we have treated them as separate scales to facilitate the use of this text as a reference work.

justment. Only one administration format is used in Part II. Each item consists of multiple statements and is scored on a 3-point scale (never = 0, occasionally = 1, and frequently = 2). (See Table 26.2 for a list of domains and factors.)

Scores

Raw scores from the ABS-S2 can be converted to standard scores and percentiles for domains (mean = 10, standard deviation = 3), or to quotients for factors (mean = 100, standard deviation = 15), and factor standard scores can be converted to percentiles on the basis of the normal curve. Age equivalents are also available for scores from Part I; Part II scores are not related to age, so no age equivalents are available. Derived scores for an adaptive behavior total or composite are not available.

Norms

As with the ABS-RC2, two different sampling procedures were used to develop norms for the ABS-S2. First, standardization sites were established in Connecticut, Florida, Ohio, and California. A site coordinator with experience in collecting standardization data was selected for each location and trained with the ABS-S2. Second, individual educators were contacted and asked to complete 10–20 evaluations. Individuals selected under either procedure were pooled into two normative samples. One sample consisted of 2,074 individuals with mental retardation; these individuals ranged in age from 3 to 21 and resided in 40 different states. The second sample consisted of 1,254 individuals without mental retardation, who ranged in age from 3 to 18 and resided in 44 states and the District of Columbia.

Both samples adequately approximate the demographic makeup of the United States in terms of race, ethnicity, sex, and geographic region. Both normative samples are more urban than the nation is. Table 26.3 indicates the number of individuals from each group at each age. About two thirds of the time, the number of people in the age groups is less than 100. Thus, some care must be exercised when interpreting derived scores based on these

TABLE 26.2 ● Domains and Factors in Parts I and II of the ABS-S2

	Domains (number of items in each)	Factors
Part I	1. Independent Functioning (24)	Personal Self-Sufficiency
	2. Physical Development (6)	Community Self-Sufficiency
	3. Economic Activity (6)	Personal–Social Responsibility
	4. Language Development (10)	
	5. Numbers and Time (3)	
	6. Prevocational/Vocational Activity (3)	
	7. Self-Direction (5)	
	8. Responsibility (3)	
	9. Socialization (7)	
Part II	10. Social Behavior (7)	Social Adjustment
	11. Conformity (6)	Personal Adjustment
	12. Trustworthiness (6)	
	13. Stereotyped and Hyperactive Behavior (5)	
	14. Self-Abusive Behavior (3)	
	15. Social Engagement (4)	
	16. Disturbing Interpersonal Behavior (6)	

TABLE 26.3 ● Norm Samples Used for the ABS-S2

Age	Individuals Without Retardation	Individuals With Retardation
3	72	74
4	65	74
5	96	91
6	79	90
7	83	83
8	110	98
9	85	143
10	108	134
11	85	133
12	93	132
13	81	123
14	69	146
15	69	123
16	66	126
17	48	94
18	45	114
19		101
20		105
21		90

samples. They are too small to allow a full range of scores.

The authors offer no guidance on when an examiner should use one set of norms or the other. However, it seems logical to use the norms based on individuals without retardation when the purpose of assessment is to establish entitlement to services. Interpretations based on the norm group of individuals with retardation should be made most carefully because these individuals have very limited intellectual ability (that is, 60% have IQs below 50).

Reliability

Reliability of the ABS-S2 was estimated separately for each normative group. The authors present reliability estimates for items (coefficient alpha), for times (stability), and for raters.[6] For the sample

6. See Footnote 3 on page 584.

with mental retardation, alphas for the 171 domain–age reliabilities in Part I ranged from a low of .81 to a high of .98; 42 of the 171 coefficients (primarily associated with the prevocational/vocational and responsibility domains) were below .90. The reliability of factor scores at all ages equaled or exceeded .95. In Part II, alphas for the 133 domain–age reliabilities ranged from a low of .80 to a high of .96; 49 of the 133 coefficients were below .90. With one exception, the reliability of factor scores at all ages equaled or exceeded .90. For the sample without mental retardation, in Part I, alphas for the 144 domain–age reliabilities ranged from a low of .79 to a high of .97; 100 of the 144 coefficients were below .90. The reliability of the factor scores at the 16 ages ranged from .80 to .97, and 14 of the 32 coefficients were below .90. In Part II, alphas for the 112 domain–age reliabilities ranged from a low of .80 to a high of .98; 69 of the 112 coefficients were below .90. Reliability of the factor scores was higher. Only 7 of the 32 factor–age alphas were below .90.

In summary, for both samples, domain scores should be used with some caution because their reliabilities frequently are below .90, especially for the normative sample without mental retardation. Factor scores had more consistently acceptable reliability. The reason alphas were higher for factor scores than for domain scores is probably because there are more items in factor scores, and the factor scores are more homogeneous than the domain scores.

Two-week stability was estimated based on scores of 45 students with emotional disturbance in ninth through eleventh grades. Uncorrected correlations between test and retest for Part I domains ranged from .42 to .79; none of the nine coefficients equaled or exceeded .90. Uncorrected stability estimates for factors ranged from .61 to .72. For Part II, uncorrected test–retest correlations ranged from .72 to .89 for domain scores; Part II factor scores were .84 and .81. Thus, none of the stabilities reach .90.

The authors also provide information about interrater agreement ("ecological validity") for 50 students with emotional disabilities. The students' teacher and the teacher's aide each completed an ABS-S2. For Part I domain scores, agreement ranged from .51 (physical development) to .92 (numbers and time); the reliability of only one domain score reached or exceeded .90. For Part I factor scores, the reliabilities were .80, .66, and .76. For Part II domain scores, agreement ranged from .55 (social engagement) to .88 (conformity); for Part II factors, agreement was .61 (social adjustment) and .53 (personal adjustment).

Validity

Content Validity   The content of the revised scale remains quite similar to the content of previous versions of this device. In previous editions of this textbook, we questioned the content validity of the scale because the authors presented no conceptualization of the domain used to guide inclusion and exclusion of items. We were also troubled because many of the items assess physical and emotional states (not behavior) and because many items that appeared in Part II probably should not be considered maladaptive (for example, "Gossips about others," "Is always in the way," "Bites fingernails"). We still find the rationale for item selection as well as the scale's content itself to be troubling.

Criterion-Related Validity   One criterion-related validity study dealing specifically with the ABS-S2 is reported. In this study, 30 students with mental retardation were tested using the ABS-S2 and the Adaptive Behavior Inventory (ABI). The correlations between the Part I ABS-S2 scores and the ABI were generally moderate to high; the correlations between Part II ABS-S2 scores and the ABI were generally not significantly different from zero. These findings strongly suggest that Part II is not measuring what is typically measured on other measures of adaptive behavior. They also provide some support for the criterion-related validity of Part I scores.

Construct Validity   Although several indexes of construct validity are provided in the ABS-S2 manual, three seem most pertinent to our discussion.

The first evidence comes from the relationship between age and Parts I and II of the scale. As expected for a valid measure of adaptive behavior, most scores from Part I show some relationship to age for normally developing children and youths; however, they do tend to flatten out around age 15 or 16 years, depending on the particular score. Part II scores show a much weaker developmental trend to about age 15 or 16 but then tend to decline. This observation suggests that students with maladaptive behavior were lost, possibly because they dropped out of school. These data generally appear consistent with the developmental domains being assessed.

Second, the factor structure of the ABS-S2 supports the notion of three factors for Part I (as is typically found in factor-analytic studies of adaptive behavior) and two factors for Part II. Thus, not only do Parts I and II measure different things, but Part I appears to be measuring constructs similar to those assessed by other measures of adaptive behavior. The meaning of Part II is not clarified by these results.

Third, scores on the ABS-S2 differentiate children and youths with and without mental retardation. Thus, individuals with mental retardation earn lower scores than individuals without mental retardation.

Summary

The ABS-S2 is an individually administered, norm-referenced scale designed for use with individuals between 3 and 18 years of age. The scale is divided into two parts. Part I focuses on nine domains that assess three factors: personal self-sufficiency, community self-sufficiency, and personal–social responsibility. Part II focuses on seven domains that assess (the lack of) social adjustment and personal adjustment. The ABS-S2 represents a substantial improvement over previous editions. The norming is far more comprehensive and appears much more representative.

The information about the scale's reliability is far more extensive than in previous editions. The internal-consistency estimates vary by norm group, score, and age. Surprisingly, the scale is more reliable with the sample of individuals who have mental retardation; generally, reliability estimates based on the performance of extreme populations are lower, for reasons we can only speculate about. For all subjects, factor scores are generally more reliable than domain scores. However, examiners are cautioned that specific age–score combinations frequently fail to meet minimum standards (.90)

recommended when making important educational decisions. Similarly, neither the domain nor the factor scores appear to be sufficiently stable to be used as the basis for important educational decisions. Interrater agreement ("ecological validity") is weak. Evidence of the scales' validity is emerging. Specific content items are troubling, but there is no indication that the scale lacks criterion-related or construct validity.

Adaptive Behavior Evaluation Scale: Home Version, Revised (ABE, H-R)[7]

The Adaptive Behavior Evaluation Scale, Home Version, Revised (ABE, H-R; J. McCarney, 1995a) is a norm-referenced scale designed to assess the adaptive behavior of individuals between the ages of 5 and 18 years. The 104 items on the ABE, H-R are arranged in ten subtests, intended to assess skill in (1) communication, (2) self-care, (3) home living, (4) social interactions, (5) community use, (6) self-direction, (7) health and safety, (8) functional academics, (9) leisure, and (10) work. Each item is scored on a 6-point scale: 0 (not developmentally appropriate), 1 (does not demonstrate behavior), 2 (is developing the behavior), 3 (demonstrates the behavior inconsistently), 4 (demonstrates the behavior most of the time), and 5 (demonstrates the behavior consistently).

Scores

Because the same item may be used in several different subtests, scores are based on 173 responses.

7. McCarney is also the author of the *Adaptive Behavior Evaluation Scale: School Version, Revised* (ABE, S-R; J. McCarney, 1995b). With a few very minor rewordings, items on the ABE, S-R are identical to the ones on the home version. However, the respondents on the school version are teachers rather than parents. The technical characteristics of the school version are essentially the same as those of the home version.

Raw scores are converted separately for males and females. Given the significant mean differences between males and females, and given the highly skewed male distributions, separate conversions are most appropriate.

Subtest totals may be converted to standard scores with a mean of 10 and a standard deviation of 3. Subtest standard scores can be summed and converted to an adaptive skills quotient with a mean of 100 and a standard deviation of 15. Total scores can also be converted to percentiles, which appear to have been independently calculated, rather than simply inferred by using normal-curve equivalents. Because the total score distributions depart so greatly from a normal curve, percentiles are more interpretable than standard scores.

Norms

About 9,500 school districts (both public and private) were requested to participate in the development of norms. An unknown number of participating districts selected parents "at random" from each grade and from several disability categories. Overall, 4,740 usable protocols were returned from individuals in 26 states.

The resulting norms are poorly described. Although there are 24 age-by-sex comparison groups,[8] the author compares only the total standardization sample against data from the 1990 census. Thus, the information of interest (that is, the representativeness of each age–sex normative sample) is missing. As a whole, the norms overrepresent European-American individuals from rural areas and from the North Central region of the United States; African Americans, Hispanics, and individuals from urban/suburban areas and from the Northeastern and Western regions of the United States are quite underrepresented in the norms. Given the information in the technical manual, there is little reason to conclude that individual age groups are representative.

Reliability

The author provides information about the ABE, H-R's stability, internal consistency, and interscorer agreement. Stability (30-day retest interval) was estimated from the performance of 83 individuals selected at random from the normative sample. Males and females were separately grouped in five age ranges. (While the number of students in an age-by-sex group is not reported, if the 83 individuals were distributed equally among the groups, there would be about 8 persons per group.) The stability of each subtest (but not the total score) is reported for each of the ten age-by-sex groups. Of these 100 coefficients, 15 equaled or exceeded .90, and 15 were less than .80.

The author reports a coefficient alpha for each subtest and for the total score. The alphas for five subtests equal or exceed .90; the remaining five alphas are in the .80s. The alpha for the total test is reported to be .95. However, the author provides no information about the individuals whose scores were used in the computations. If the scores are from the entire range of ages, these alphas are likely to be inflated. Moreover, these are not the alphas about which test users will typically be con-

cerned. No estimates of internal consistency are presented for subtests at each age.[9] The author does present the standard errors of measurement (SEMs) of each subtest for males and females at each age. However, insufficient data are presented in the test manual to interpret these SEMs.

To estimate interrater agreement, 60 pairs of parents each rated their child. Correlations between the raters are presented for 14 age groups. While the number of participants in each group is not specified, if they were divided equally among the groups, the resulting correlations would be based on about 4 pairs per group. The obtained correlation coefficients range from .75 to .82.

Validity

The ABE, H-R is intended to represent the ten areas of adaptive behavior proposed by the American Association on Mental Retardation (AAMR, 1992). To establish the content validity of the specific items, a panel of 43 "diagnosticians and special education personnel" (J. McCarney, 1995a) supplied a list of skills believed necessary for success in each area assessed by the ABE, H-R. These skills were collapsed into a pool of 128 skills and returned to panel members, 39 of whom reviewed and revised the items. The 110 remaining items were arranged in the ten content areas and then field tested in 14 Missouri school districts. Item–total correlations were also examined.

Construct validity was investigated through factor-analytic techniques. First, individual items were factor analyzed. The author identified three

---

8. The separate norms provided for males and females are appropriate, given the reported differences in male–female distributions (such as means and skew).

9. The author does present the SEMs of each subtest for males and females at each age. However, insufficient data are presented in the test manual to allow calculation of alpha from these SEMs. Clearly, the SEMs cannot refer to standard scores with a standard deviation of 3 unless the SEMs are incorrectly calculated. (Many SEMs are larger than 3, a mathematical impossibility if the standard deviation is 3.) We can only assume that raw-score standard deviations were used in the calculation of SEMs. However because raw-score standard deviations are not reported for males and females at each age for each subtest, we cannot either be sure of our hypothesis or calculate alphas from the SEMs.

common factors.[10] Next, the items in each of the individual subtests were factor analyzed. The number of factors identified for each subtest ranged from one to four and do not appear to correspond to the factors identified when all items are simultaneously factor analyzed. Frankly, we are confused by the presentation of factor-analytic results. It does not appear to us that the subtests correspond to factor structure. Moreover, we are also unsure how the factor-analytic results, as presented, provide evidence of construct validity.

Construct validity was also investigated by examining the protocols of previously identified moderately or severely retarded individuals who participated in the standardization. As expected, these individuals earned standard scores on the subtests that were at least one standard deviation below the mean.

Two studies examined the criterion-related validity of the ABE, H-R. In the first study, ratings from the Adaptive Behavior Inventory for Children and ABE, H-R were obtained for 47 children who ranged in age from 5 to 12 years. The correlations between subtests on each measure were substantial, ranging from .59 to .91. In the second study, ratings from the Vineland Adaptive Behavior Scales (classroom edition) and the ABE, H-R were obtained for 31 children who ranged in age from 5 to 11. The correlations between subtests on each measure were variable, ranging from .21 to .88. In each study, the pattern of correlations was as would be expected: Subtests measuring similar behavior correlated more highly than subtests measuring dissimilar behavior.

Summary

The ABE, H-R is a norm-referenced scale designed to assess the adaptive behavior of individuals between the ages of 5 and 18 years. Although poorly described, the norms appear unrepresentative of the United States as a whole. The number of students used to estimate stability and interrater agreement is too small for confidence that scores earned by males or females at any age are stable or consistently evaluated. Evidence for ABE, H-R's internal consistency is incompletely reported. The ABE, H-R does correlate with other measures of adaptive behavior and does discriminate between individuals selected at random from the population and individuals with moderate to severe levels of mental retardation.

Adaptive Behavior Inventory (ABI)

The Adaptive Behavior Inventory (ABI; L. Brown & Leigh, 1986a) is a norm-referenced scale appropriate for use with students who range in age from 6-0 to 18-11. The ABI is intended to be used to provide information about adaptive behavior during the diagnosis of mental retardation, to compare various components of adaptive behavior exhibited by one individual, and to evaluate instructional programs designed to affect a student's adaptation. Like other adaptive-behavior measures, it is administered by having a respondent answer questions about the subject being assessed. The preferred respondent for the ABI is "the classroom teacher or other professional who has relevant contact with the student being assessed" (L. Brown & Leigh, 1986b, p. 4). It is particularly praiseworthy that ABI users are urged to postpone administration of the device if a rater cannot be

10. The author used a skree plot to determine the number of factors. Eleven factors had eigenvalues greater than one, but no information about the percentage of variance accounted for by each factor is presented. From the skree plot, it appears to us that the results yielded one very strong factor, one factor of moderate strength, and nine weak factors.

found who has had sufficient contact with the student to provide complete and reliable information.

Subtests

The ABI consists of five subtests that can be given independently in about five minutes each.

Self-Care Skills   This subtest contains 30 items that range from asking about how students get from one school area to another to questions about grooming and about students' awareness of social-service agencies.

Communication Skills   This subtest contains 30 items that range from asking about how students orally communicate their needs to questions about how students describe abstract ideas in writing.

Social Skills   This subtest contains 32 items that ask about behaviors ranging from referring to others by name through sharing things with others to organizing and leading groups.

Academic Skills   This subtest contains 30 items that range from asking whether students can identify alphabet letters and their own names to questions about whether they take adequate notes to wondering whether they can perform advanced mathematical tasks.

Occupational Skills   This subtest contains 28 items that ask about behaviors ranging from being punctual to supervising the work of others.

A short form of the ABI is also available. It contains selected items from each subtest.

Scores

Individual items are scored using a 4-point scale, with which the respondent indicates that the subject does not perform the behavior (0 points), is beginning to perform the behavior (1 point), performs the behavior most of the time (2 points), or has mastered the behavior (3 points). Raw scores on each subtest can be converted into percentiles and standard scores (mean = 100, standard deviation = 15). If four or five subtests are administered,

a weighted composite deviation score can also be obtained.

Norms

Two sets of norms are available. One set, the normal intelligence sample, is intended to be representative of students in the general U.S. population; the other set is intended to be representative of mentally retarded pupils in special-education programs and residential facilities. Sampling plans are not provided for either normative sample, and the samples are poorly described.

The normal-intelligence sample was composed of about 1,300 individuals who ranged in age from 5-0 to 18-11 and resided in 24 states. This sample, as a whole, corresponds to the U.S. population at the time of the 1980 census in terms of sex, race, ethnicity, geographic area, and socioeconomic status (SES). However, the correspondence of each age group with these characteristics is not described.

The mentally retarded sample was composed of about 1,100 individuals from the same age range drawn from the same 24 states. This sample, as a whole, corresponds to the population at the time of the 1980 census in terms of sex and measured IQ. The sample underrepresents students in special day schools.

Reliability

Internal consistency was estimated by coefficient alpha. Adjacent age groups were combined (5- and 6-year-olds, 7- and 8-year-olds, and so forth), and the responses for 50 individuals at each age level in the two standardization groups were randomly selected. For the normal-intelligence groups, 42 coefficients were computed (five subtests and total score for the seven ages). The 35 subtest-by-age coefficients ranged from .86 (for the 5- and 6-year-old group) to .97; 25 of the 35 coefficients equaled or exceeded .90. All of the coefficients for the total ABI score exceeded .90. The internal consistency of the ABI short form also exceeded .90 for each of the age groups. Stability was estimated by test–retest reliability using 39 students of normal intelligence who ranged in age from 5 to 18 years and 56 mentally retarded students who ranged in age from 6 to 18 years. The effects of age were held constant statistically. Estimated stabilities for the subtests, the composite, and the short-form composite all exceeded .90.

Validity

Reports on validity data are superficial. Thus, most of the evidence provided is difficult to evaluate. Inspection of the items included in the ABI may provide some evidence of content validity. Some items are too subjective, however, and criteria for scoring/marking each item may not be clear to the person completing the form. For example, teachers are asked to rate a student's performance on intermediate reading tasks, understanding of basic measurement concepts, knowledge of the approximate cost of common items, and so forth.

As evidence of criterion-related validity, the authors provide correlations with teacher judgments of adaptive behavior and modest to high correlations with the AAMD Adaptive Behavior Scale and the Vineland Adaptive Behavior Scale. These studies are incompletely described, however, so it is difficult to evaluate the ABI's criterion-related validity.

As evidence of construct validity, the authors offer the correlations of the ABI with achievement tests, intelligence tests, and age, as well as the intercorrelations of the ABI's subtests. Finally, to show construct validity, the performances of retarded and normal students in the standardization samples were compared. "In every instance, there were significant differences between each of the pairwise comparisons of the groups, with higher ABI means attributed to students in less restrictive classroom environments" (Brown & Leigh, 1986b, p. 40).

Summary

The ABI is a norm-referenced scale that assesses five aspects of adaptive behavior through ratings by a student's teacher. The norms appear adequate, and the device appears to have adequate reliability and validity.

Scales of Independent Behavior–Revised (SIB–R)

The Scales of Independent Behavior–Revised (SIB-R; Bruininks, Woodcock, Weatherman, & Hill, 1996) is an individually administered, norm-referenced device suitable for use with infants to individuals 90 years old. SIB-R is intended to be used to identify individuals who lack independence in various settings (home, school, community, work, and so forth), provide instructional and training goals, contribute to placement decisions, and provide evidence for program evaluation, as well as to be used in research and training. SIB-R can be administered to a respondent who is thoroughly familiar with the subject being as-

sessed. SIB-R may be completed as an interview or checklist.

The 259 adaptive-behavior items are arranged into 14 subscales; subscales are grouped into four clusters. The motor skills cluster consists of two subscales: Gross Motor Skills and Fine Motor Skills. The social interaction and communication skills cluster consists of three subscales: Social Interaction, Language Comprehension, and Language Expression. The personal living skills cluster consists of five subscales: Eating and Meal Preparation, Toileting, Dressing, Personal Self-Care, and Domestic Skills. The community living skills cluster consists of four subscales: Time and Punctuality, Money and Value, Work Skills, and Home and Community Orientation. Cluster scores are combined into a total score (broad independence). Each item is evaluated on the same scale:

0 The person never or rarely performs the skill even if asked

1 The person performs the skill. However, the person does not perform the task well or performs the task about a quarter of the time. The person may need to be asked to perform.

2 The person performs the skill fairly well or about three quarters of the time. The person may need to be asked to perform the skill.

3 The person performs the skill very well (always or almost always) without being asked.

Three forms are available to assess adaptive behavior: the full-scale form, the short form, and the early development form. The full-scale form uses all 14 adaptive subscales. The short form, intended as a screening device, consists of 40 items culled from the 259 adaptive items. The early development form also consists of 40 items that are "particularly suitable for assessing the development of preschoolers and the adaptive skills of youths or adults with serious disabilities" (Bruininks et al., 1996, p. 16).

Maladaptive behavior is assessed by interviewing the respondent about *areas* of problem behavior, rather than asking about specific behaviors.[11] There are three broad clusters of maladaptive behavior. The internalized maladaptive cluster consists of three areas: behavior that is hurtful to self, unusual or repetitive habits, and withdrawn or inattentive behavior. The externalized maladaptive cluster also consists of three areas: behavior that is

hurtful to others, destruction of property, and disruptive behavior. The asocial maladaptive cluster consists of two areas: socially offensive behavior and uncooperative behavior. Each area is assessed on two dimensions: a frequency scale and a severity scale. The frequency scale is a 5-point scale.

1 Less than once a month

2 1 to 3 times a month

3 1 to 6 times a week

4 1 to 10 times a day

5 1 or more times an hour

The severity scale is also a 5-point scale (beginning at zero):

0 Not serious (not a problem)

1 Slightly serious (a mild problem)

2 Moderately serious (a moderate problem)

3 Very serious (a severe problem)

4 Extremely serious (a critical problem)

Scores

Except for age equivalents for adaptive-behavior subscales, obtaining commonly used scores on the SIB-R is unnecessarily complicated. Seven steps are required to find standard scores or percentiles for each adaptive-behavior cluster. (Computer scoring disks are available.) Other norm-referenced scores are arcane.

Norms

SIB-R norms are a composite of the first edition norms ($N = 1,764$) and an additional 418 individuals added from a separate standardization conducted for the second edition. Considering both norming groups, SIB-R norms are based on the performances of 2,182 individuals ranging in age from 3 months to 90 years. These individuals came from more than 60 cities and 15 states. The total sample approximates the 1990 U.S. census in terms of gender, race, and community size. More

---

11. We believe this format is a distinct improvement over other formats used to assess problem behavior. (Typical respondents are asked to rate the subject on a long list of problem behaviors that may or may not contain the specific behavior that is causing problems.) The SIB-R format also avoids the dilemma of differing importance of maladaptive behavior (for instance, is nail biting as important or significant as eye gouging?).

than half of the sample comes from the Midwest, although less than 25 percent of the U.S. population lives in that region. However, the comparisons of interest (that is, the degree to which each normative group approximates the U.S. census) are absent. Nonetheless, the statistical values obtained for the combined sample were then adjusted. Three-hundred-twenty-five individuals who participated in the 1995 standardization of the SIB-R also participated in the standardization of the Woodcock–Johnson Psychoeducational Battery–Revised (WJ-R). Based on the performances of these 325 individuals in comparison with the entire standardization sample of the WJ-R, the SIB-R norms were altered.

Reliability

Internal consistencies of the adaptive behavior subscales and clusters were estimated using corrected split-half correlations. Estimates of the internal consistency of each subscale are provided for ten age ranges: 3 to 11 months, 1 year, 2 years, 3 years, 4 years, 5 to 7 years, 8 to 9 years, 10 to 12 years, 13 to 19 years, and 20 to 90 years. Reliability coefficients for subscales range from .40 to .96; about 15 percent of the coefficients equal or exceed .90. As is typically the case, cluster reliabilities are substantially higher, ranging from .67 to .97; 25 of the 40 cluster-by-age coefficients equal or exceed .90. Broad independence (the total score) equals or exceeds .90 for each age group. The internal consistency of the short form equals or exceeds .90 in only one age group (3 to 11 months). The internal consistency of the early development form is less than .90 from ages 2 through 7.

The stabilities of adaptive behavior subscales and clusters, as well as maladaptive behavior clusters and broad independence, were also examined in several studies. In one study, 31 individuals between the ages of 6 and 13 years were retested within a four-week period. Subscale stabilities ranged from .83 to .94; 11 of the 14 coefficients equaled or exceed .90. Cluster and broad independence stabilities all exceeded .90. The stabilities of the three maladaptive indexes and the general maladaptive score were in the low .80s. The stability of the short form was .97. The authors report additional studies examining the stability of the maladaptive indexes. The results of these studies are consistent with the previously reported study.

The authors report four studies examining interrater agreement. In the first study, mothers and fathers of 26 individuals (between the ages of 6 and 13 years) without disabilities were interviewed separately. For adaptive subscales, the correlations between mother's report and father's report ranged from .58 (Toileting) to .94 (Language Expression). Three of the four coefficients of agreement for the clusters were in the .80s; one was .93. The agreement for broad independence was .95, and the agreement for the short form was .93. Agreements for the maladaptive indexes were somewhat lower: One coefficient was in the .70s while the rest were in the .80s.

In the second study, teachers and teacher aides rated 30 students with moderate mental retardation between the ages of 6 and 13 years. For adaptive subscales, the correlations between teacher report and teacher-aide report ranged from .71 (Domestic Skills) to .96 (Gross Motor Skills and Language Expression). Three of the four coefficients of agreement for the clusters were in the .90s; one was .88. The agreement in broad independence score was .96, and the agreement for the short form was .95. Agreements for the maladaptive indexes were substantially lower: .57, .87, and .78; the consistency for the general maladaptive index was .84.

In the third study, teachers and teacher aides rated moderately to severely retarded students between the ages of 12 and 21. Agreement on each cluster ranged from .74 to .86, and agreement for broad independence was .80. The consistency of ratings of the maladaptive indexes ranged from .69 to .81; the consistency for the general maladaptive index was .80.

In the last study, teachers and teacher aides rated 63 children between the ages of 2 and 5 years. The consistency of broad independence (early development form) was .91. The agreement for maladaptive indexes ranged from .68 to .83, while the agreement for general maladaptive index was .79.

Validity

The validity of the SIB-R rests largely on the validity of the first edition, although the items on the two editions differ somewhat. Some new items were prepared for SIB-R, and some old items from SIB were dropped. Nonetheless, scores from the two forms are reported to be highly correlated. Content validity for SIB was established through delineation of the domain and through careful item selection.

Construct validity was established in several ways. On SIB-R, adaptive behavior scores increase with age (although maladaptive behavior is essentially unrelated to age). SIB-R scores are also moderately correlated with intelligence (as measured by the cognitive portion of the Woodcock–Johnson Psychoeducational Battery). Several studies are reported in which the adaptive (or maladaptive) behavior of individuals with disabilities is compared with the behavior of individuals without disabilities. In one such study, the SIB-R early development form was used with 30 children with disabilities or delays and 30 children of the same age but without disabilities. The children with disabilities earned substantially lower scores on the adaptive items and on two of the four maladaptive scores. The remaining comparison studies were conducted with the SIB. In these studies, the scores earned by individuals from special populations (for example, trainable mentally retarded individuals) were compared with the scores earned by nonhandicapped persons drawn at random from the normative sample. The comparisons showed that individuals with disabilities earned consistently lower SIB scores when compared with persons without disabilities. Moreover, differences in adaptive behavior were on expected dimensions. For example, hearing-impaired individuals earned significantly lower scores on the Social Interaction and Language Comprehension subscales.

Criterion-related validity of the SIB was previously investigated in two studies in which SIB scores were correlated with scores from the AAMD Adaptive Behavior Scale (School Edition). Correlations between SIB-R cluster scores and ABS-S2 factor scores ranged from .33 to .86. Maladaptive indexes of the SIB were correlated with results of the Revised Problem Behavior Checklist (RPBC; Quay & Peterson, 1987); the pattern of correlations supports the validity of the SIB-R (for example, the asocial maladaptive behavior index of the SIB-R correlates better with scores on the Socialized Aggression, Attention Problems, and Motor Excess scales of the RPBC than with scores on the other subscales of the RPBC). A study comparing the SIB-R early development form with the Early Screen Profiles was also conducted. The two measures were highly correlated.

Summary

The SIB-R is an individually administered, norm-referenced adaptive behavior scale that is useful with individuals ranging in age from infancy through adulthood. The SIB-R includes four clusters of adaptive behavior (motor skills, social interaction and communication skills, personal living skills, and community living skills) and four maladaptive behavior indexes (general maladaptive behavior, internalized maladaptive behavior, asocial maladaptive behavior, and externalized maladaptive behavior). SIB-R's norms are difficult to evaluate. They are a mixture of old and new norms that have been adjusted, and they do not appear representative of the United States as a whole. Reliability estimates for each age are not presented. Internal consistencies of the adaptive behavior subscales, early development form, and short form are generally too low to use in making important educational decisions about students. The internal consistencies of cluster scores are variable, but the internal consistency of the total score (that is, broad independence) exceeds .90 for all ages reported. No stability data are presented for individuals older than 13 years. For individuals 13 years or younger, stabilities are moderate.

However, no data are presented for individual ages. Interrater agreement for students between the ages of 6 and 13 years was quite variable. Given the data reported in the technical manual, the broad independence score is probably reliable at any age; other scores should be interpreted cautiously. Evidence for SIB-R's validity suggests that the scale indeed measures adaptive behavior.

Responsibility and Independence Scale for Adolescents (RISA)

The Responsibility and Independence Scale for Adolescents (RISA; Salvia, Neisworth, & Schmidt, 1990) is an individually administered, norm-referenced device intended to assess the adaptive behavior of adolescents between the ages of 12 and 19 years. The scale contains 136 items, in question format. A respondent (for example, a parent or, in the case of older adolescents, a spouse), answers each question with *yes* or *no,* to indicate whether the adolescent performs various actions. To facilitate comprehension of the questions, each item is illustrated by a line drawing that is shown to the respondent as the question is asked. These drawings (with the question written at the bottom) are spiral-bound into a book. Although no specialized training is required to administer RISA, the authors provide practice exercises for individuals who are not experienced in the use of this type of instrument.

The 136 items are arranged in two subtests named Responsibility and Independence. Items assessing maladaptive behavior are not included. Responsibility consists of 52 items that assess "a broad class of adaptive behaviors that meet social expectations and standards of reciprocity, accountability, and fairness that enable personal development" (p. 2). The items are clustered in three areas. Self-management contains 17 items that deal with topics such as resisting peer pressure, using constructive criticism, and following household rules (for example, regarding phone use). Social maturity contains 21 items dealing with topics such as friendships and appropriate public behavior. Social communication contains 14 items dealing with polite listening and speaking, asking permission to borrow things, and using the telephone to obtain information.

Independence consists of 84 items that assess "behaviors that allow individuals to live separately and free from the control or determination of others, and to conduct themselves effectively" (p. 2). The items are clustered in five areas: The domestic skills area contains 9 items dealing with such topics as following laundry-care labels, maintaining a supply of frequently used foods, and using safety equipment and clothing when necessary. Money management contains 23 items dealing with such topics as realistically estimating the cost of common household items, saving money for the future, using coupons, and using unit pricing. Citizenship contains 5 items related to voting, political awareness, and civic responsibility. Personal organization contains 15 items dealing with topics such as using lists, making preparations for the future, and taking actions to improve personal health. The transportation skills area contains 18 items dealing with behavior related to safe driving, asking for directions when lost, and using public transportation. The career skills area contains 14 items dealing with job training, securing employment, and career advancement.

Scores

Responsibility, Independence, and total scores can be converted to percentiles and standard scores (mean = 100, standard deviation = 15). A table is also available to convert differences between Responsibility and Independence standard scores.

Norms

A two-stage cluster sampling technique was used to select the normative sample. First, the United States was divided into four regions (Northeast, North Central, West, and South), and clusters of communities within regions were identified. Several community characteristics guided selection: degree of urbanization (central cities, urban fringe, cities with populations between 2,500 and 49,999 located at least 50 miles from the central city, and rural communities with populations less than 2,500); community educational attainment; community income; community employment status; and community occupational type. Seventy target communities that were broadly representative of the United States at the 1980 census were selected. Adolescents were selected at random from public and private schools and agencies that served high, middle, and low socioeconomic sections of their communities. The norms are based on the ratings of 1,900 adolescents from nine age groups. The largest sample ($N = 291$) consisted of 15-year-olds, and the smallest sample ($N = 124$) consisted of 19-year-olds. Each age group was weighted (using sex, community size, educational attainment of parents, and geographic region) so that the standardization sample closely approximated the most recent census data available at the time. Students with disabilities were included in the norms for each age group, although their proportions are not reported.

Reliability

Three types of reliability data are presented. Corrected split-half estimates of reliability are presented for each age and are based on the ratings of the adolescents who were the normative sample. All subtest reliabilities equaled or exceeded .90 at every age except for Responsibility at age 14, where r_{xx} equaled .83. Corrected split-half estimates for the total exceeded .90 at every age. Test–retest correlations were computed to estimate stability for three age groups: ages 12 and 13 ($N = 40$), ages 15 and 16 ($N = 45$), and ages 18 and 19

($N = 34$). All subtest and total-score coefficients exceeded .90. The reliability of the difference between Independence and Responsibility scores was also estimated. These estimates ranged from a low of .76 (at age 19) to a high of .89 (at both 12 and 13). Thus, differences between subscales are not sufficiently reliable to allow use of the subscales in making important educational decisions.

Validity

Evidence for content, criterion-related, and construct validity is presented in RISA's technical manual. The authors can lay some claim to content validity based on their careful generation and selection of items. Moreover, most of the test's items assess behavior that would be appropriate for high-school students or young adults. Correlations with two other measures of adaptive behavior (the Vineland Adaptive Behavior Scale and the Scales of Independent Behavior) are presented as evidence for RISA's concurrent validity. Total scores on these other two measures correlate as well with RISA total scores as they do with each other (that is, about .50).

Finally, several studies support RISA's construct validity. First, RISA scores increase with age. Second, the factor analysis supports the use of the two subtests, and the factors identified are consistent with those identified in studies of other adaptive behavior measures. Third, there is a relative absence of differences in the performances of different racial and ethnic groups. Last, adolescents previously and independently identified as mentally retarded earned substantially lower scores than nonhandicapped peers.

Summary

RISA, a scale intended for use only with adolescents, assesses two major components of adaptive behavior: Responsibility and Independence. The technical manual provides clear evidence of a representative norm group and reliability. Some evidence of the scale's validity is also presented.

Coping with Dilemmas in Current Practice

There are three severe problems in the use of currently available instruments to assess adaptive behavior: (1) lack of internal consistency, (2) poor norms, and (3) lack of interrater agreement. First, there is no theoretical reason why adaptive behavior scales should not be internally consistent. That some scales are not homogeneous can reasonably be attributed to the lack of a clear definition of adaptive behavior, a problem to which we alluded earlier in this chapter. There is no professional consensus about the types of behavior that are indicative of adaptation. Indeed, inspection of the behaviors sampled by the various devices suggests a lack of agreement about what adaptive behavior is—there is a broad range of behaviors sampled and of orientations toward measurement. Without a more precise concept of adaptive behavior, we should probably expect heterogeneous operationalizations of the definition (that is, heterogeneous scales of adaptive behavior) to continue. One solution to this problem is for test authors to rely more heavily on factor-analytic studies of adaptive behavior. If scores on adaptive behavior scales represent underlying factors, the scores will be more homogeneous and, therefore, more reliable. This point is clearly illustrated by the ABS-RC2, for which domain scores are less reliable than factor scores. Therefore, whenever possible, test users should rely on scores that represent the underlying factors that make up adaptive behavior, rather than using scores that describe interrelated surface performances (for example, eating or dressing).

The second problem is that scales of adaptive behavior frequently are poorly normed (sometimes normed only on individuals with disabilities). If its norm samples are unrepresentative, a scale should not be used. An alternative to using unrepresentative norms is simply to identify one or two students to use for social comparison. Teachers or parents can be asked to nominate individuals of the same age and sex as those in the norm group, whom they believe have "adapted" successfully. The behavior of these adaptive peers can then be used to make rather simple comparisons. Although one or two children certainly are no substitute for a normative sample, they may prove adequate for some comparisons.

The third and most vexing problem, both theoretically and practically, is the lack of agreement among raters. When reported at all for adaptive behavior scales, interrater agreement is often poor. The interpretation of such findings can proceed along two lines. First, poor agreement can suggest lack of reliability. Thus, we would suspect at least three potential problems: (1) The specific items are difficult to understand or interpret; (2) the criteria used to rate the behavior are subjective; or (3) one or both of the raters are insufficiently familiar with the student.

Lack of interrater agreement can also suggest lack of validity, in addition to lack of reliability. Thus, we would suspect at least two potential problems: (1) One of the raters may have distorted perceptions or may not be entirely truthful; or (2) the student's behavior may vary in different contexts. In practice, examiners have few options for dealing with rater disagreement. Assessors should select as the respondent the person who is most familiar with the student, who has seen the student in the most contexts, and who will provide the most truthful and objective responses. Examiners should also guard against conveying their own expectations to the respondent. Finally, when behavior clearly varies across contexts, examiners should consider elements in those contexts that may set the occasion for behavior because such elements may have importance in educational interventions.

Summary

In the assessment of adaptive behavior, we are interested in what an individual regularly does, not what the individual is capable of doing. Ultimately, the behaviors of interest in adults are those that allow individuals to manage their affairs sufficiently well that they do not require societal intervention to protect them or others. The behaviors that are believed to be important vary from time to time and from theory to theory. In general, in the United States, adults are expected to take reasonable care of themselves (by managing their own health, dressing, eating, and so on), to work, and to engage in socially acceptable recreational or leisure activities. In children and adolescents, the behaviors of interest are those that are believed to enable the development or acquisition of desired adult behaviors and skills.

The assessment of adaptive behavior usually takes the form of a structured interview with a person (for example, a parent or teacher) who is very familiar with the person being assessed (the subject of the interview). The assessment of adaptive behavior has been plagued by inadequate instruments—scales that lack reliability and are poorly normed. Assessors must select scales (or parts of scales) with great care.

Questions for Chapter Review and Thought

1. How does the assessment of adaptive behavior differ from most other types of assessment discussed in this textbook?

2. Describe some of the factors that help determine whether a behavior is considered adaptive.

3. The current state of the art in adaptive-behavior instruments presents a number of problems for examiners. Briefly discuss two of them.

4. How might a teacher or psychologist overcome the problems associated with the inadequate norms of adaptive behavior scales when assessing a child?

5. With the increasing use of computers and robots in American industry, what do you think will happen to current definitions of adaptive behavior?

Resources for Further Investigation

Project

Using information found in the text, write a summary for two tests used in the assessment of adaptive behavior. Upon completion, compare your summary with the text summary. Then go to *The Twelfth Mental Measurements Yearbook* (see Chapter 24, "Print Resources"), and compare and contrast your summaries with the reviews of the tests you selected. If your summary differs from the review, did the reviewer use information and standards different from those that you used?

Print Resources

American Association on Mental Retardation. (1997). *Mental retardation: Definition, classifica-*

tion, and systems of support (9th ed.). Washington, DC: Author.

Bruininks, R., Woodcock, R., Weatherman, R., & Hill, B. (1996). *Scales of independent behavior, revised, comprehensive manual*. Chicago: Riverside.

Kamphaus, R. W. (1987). Conceptual and psychometric issues in the assessment of adaptive behavior. *Journal of Special Education, 21,* 27–35.

McCarney, S. (1995). *Adaptive behavior evaluation scale, home version, revised*. Columbia, MO: Hawthorne Educational Services.

Sattler, J. M. (1992). *Assessment of children* (Chapter 15, Assessing adaptive behavior). San Diego: Jerome Sattler.

Schmidt, M., & Salvia, J. (1984). Adaptive behavior: A conceptual analysis. *Diagnostique, 9*(2), 117–125.

Technology Resources

Welcome to AGS On-line Products and Services

http://www.agsnet.com/

Look for product and ordering information about the instruments available from American Guidance Service. Search by product title to find information about the *Vineland Adaptive Behavior Scales*.

Psychological Assessment Resources

http://www.parinc.com/home.html

Look for product and ordering information about the instruments available from Psychological Assessment Resources, including the *Adaptive Behavior Scales*.

chapter

27

Diagnostic Systems

*E*arlier in this text, we noted that tests are samples of behavior. Most tests sample behaviors from a single domain (for example, intelligence, achievement, or adaptive behavior). Two tests that sample behaviors from the same domain may actually differ significantly because they sample different behaviors from that domain.

In the late 1970s, test publishers began to develop measures that sample behaviors from several domains. Whereas other chapters in Parts 3 and 4 of this text are restricted to specific domains (although achievement covers multiple domains), the measures reviewed in this chapter are entire diagnostic systems.

●　●　●　●　●　●　●　●　●　●　●　●　●　●　●　●　●　●　●

Why Do We Use Diagnostic Systems?

Diagnostic systems were designed to provide a comprehensive testing instrument to link students' learning abilities to their school achievement in one continuous system of measurement. Teachers can use these interrelated findings as the basis for instructional planning. Diagnostic systems offer two major advantages: accurate comparison of scores and convenience. The first advantage is technical. The same normative sample provides derived scores for all measures in the various domains assessed in the diagnostic system. As you recall from Chapter 6, differences between test scores may be a function of differences in normative samples. Thus, if an intelligence test shows that Sam's IQ is 115 and his standard score on an achievement test is 106 (mean = 100, standard deviation = 15), part of the difference between 115 and 106 may be attributable to differences in the norms of the two tests. Diagnostic systems provide more accurate comparisons of a person's performances in different domains because the derived scores in the different domains are based on the same norm group.

The second advantage of diagnostic systems is that they may be more convenient for the assessor to use than several tests of single domains. For example, the time it takes to administer tests may be reduced because redundancies in several domains may be lessened. In addition, it may take assessors less time to put together the necessary materials for testing.

Specific Diagnostic Systems

Kaufman Assessment Battery for Children (K-ABC)

The Kaufman Assessment Battery for Children (K-ABC; Kaufman & Kaufman, 1983) is an individually administered, norm-referenced battery intended to provide a comprehensive assessment of intelligence (learning potential and preferred learning style) and achievement for children between the ages of 2-5 and 12-5. Kaufman and Kaufman claim that the test is useful for the following purposes: (1) psychological and clinical assessment (including projective interpretation of personality and inferences about impulsivity–reflectivity, perseverative behavior, rigidity–flexibility, and tolerance for frustration); (2) psychoeducational evaluation of exceptional children, particularly the learning disabled; (3) educational placement and planning; (4) assessment of minorities (especially African Americans, Hispanics, and bilingual children); (5) preschool assessment; and (6) neuropsychological assessment.

Sixteen subtests are combined into three regularly administered scales and one supplementary scale. Intelligence is assessed on three scales: the Simultaneous Processing Scale, the Sequential Processing Scale, and the optional Nonverbal Scale. Simultaneous and Sequential Processing scales are combined to form the Mental Processing Scale. Achievement is assessed with the Achievement Scale.

The K-ABC draws heavily on the information-processing theories of Das (for example, Das, Kirby, & Jarman, 1975) and Luria (1966), as well as the neuropsychological research of Cohen (1972). In these theories, the processing of information is viewed dichotomously. Test takers may act upon information sequentially or simultaneously. Many examples of tasks that are essentially sequential in nature are provided in the K-ABC manuals, such as memorization of number facts,

spelling, application of stepwise procedures in arithmetic (for example, the division algorithm), word-attack skills, and so on. The other method of acting on information is simultaneous processing. In many tasks, separate elements are not handled sequentially; rather, the elements are handled (processed) at once, as a whole. For example, skilled readers seldom ponder individual letters in a word; they grasp the word as a whole.

Kaufman and Kaufman are also concerned with the assessment of culturally atypical children. The optional Nonverbal Scale combines subtests that can be administered gesturally and to which students can respond nonverbally. The Nonverbal Scale is believed to be "a good estimate of intellectual potential for . . . deaf, hearing-impaired, speech- or language-disordered, autistic, and non–English-speaking children" (Kaufman & Kaufman, 1983, p. 35).

Achievement is conceptualized as "the ability to integrate the two types of mental processing and apply them to real-life situations" (p. 33). The "Achievement Scale is intended to assess factual knowledge and skills usually acquired in a school setting or through alertness to the environment" (p. 33).

Brief descriptions of each subtest follow and are based on the descriptions provided by Kaufman and Kaufman in the Interpretative Manual. Unless otherwise indicated, each subtest can be administered to children between ages 2–5 and 12–5.

Sequential Processing Scale

- *Hand movements* requires a child to copy a sequence of taps made by the tester with the fist, palm, or side of the hand
- *Number recall* requires a child to repeat a series of digits read by the tester

- *Word order* (ages 4-0 to 12-5) requires a child to point to silhouettes of common objects in the order named by the tester

Simultaneous Processing Scale

- *Magic window* (ages 2-6 to 4-11) requires a child to identify a picture that the tester rotates behind a narrow slit, exposing only a part of the picture at any one time
- *Face recognition* (ages 2-6 to 4-11) requires a child to recall one or two faces that have been presented briefly by selecting the correct face(s), in a different pose, from a group photograph
- *Gestalt closure* requires a child to complete an inkblot drawing and to name or describe it
- *Triangles* (ages 4-0 to 12-5) requires a child to assemble triangles (one side blue, one side yellow) to match an abstract design
- *Matrix analogies* (ages 5-0 to 12-5) requires a child to select the picture or design that completes a two-by-two visual analogy
- *Spatial memory* (ages 5-0 to 12-5) requires a child to remember where pictures were arranged on a page
- *Photo series* (ages 6-0 to 12-5) requires a child to organize photographs that illustrate an event and to place them in proper chronology

Achievement Scale

- *Expressive vocabulary* (ages 2-6 to 4-11) requires a child to name objects from photographs
- *Faces and places* requires a child to name famous persons, fictional characters, or places shown in pictures
- *Arithmetic* (ages 3-0 to 12-5) requires a child to name numbers, to count, to compute, and to understand mathematical concepts
- *Riddles* (ages 3-0 to 12-5) requires a child to name a concrete or abstract concept when given several of its characteristics

- *Reading/decoding* (ages 5-0 to 12-5) requires a child to name letters and to read words orally
- *Reading/understanding* (ages 7-0 to 12-5) requires children to act out commands given in sentences that they read

Nonverbal Scale

The composition of the Nonverbal Scale varies with a child's age. For 4-year-olds, the scale consists of face recognition, hand movements, and triangles. For 5-year-olds, the scale consists of hand movements, triangles, matrix analogies, and spatial memory. For children 6 years old and older, the scale consists of hand movements, triangles, matrix analogies, spatial memory, and photo series.

Scores

A variety of transformed scores are used. Scaled scores (mean = 10, standard deviation = 3) are available by chronological age for the Mental Processing subtests. Mental Processing subtests are combined into Sequential Processing, Simultaneous Processing, mental processing composite, and Nonverbal scales (mean = 100, standard deviation = 15). Raw scores on the Achievement Scale yield standard scores (mean = 100, standard deviation = 15). Percentile ranks are available for each subtest and scale. Age equivalents are available for each subtest of the Mental Processing Scale, and grade equivalents are available for each of the Achievement subtests.

Norms

National norms and sociocultural norms are available for comparisons. The national norms consist of 100 students at each half-year of age from 2-6 to 12-5. A representative sample was obtained by stratifying on sex, education of the parent, ethnic background (European American, African American, Hispanic, and other), geographic considerations, and school placement. In addition, sociocultural norms are provided to compare a child with others of similar racial and ethnic background and socioeconomic status on the Mental Processing Scale and Achievement subtests (except expressive vocabulary). The standardization procedures were excellent.

Reliability

Both split-half and test–retest reliability coefficients, based on the standardization sample, are provided. Split-half coefficients, corrected with the Spearman–Brown formula, range from a high of .92 (triangles at age 5) to a low of .62 (gestalt closure at age 7) on the Mental Processing subtests. Of the 80 coefficients reported, only one equaled or exceeded .90. Corrected split-half coefficients on the Mental Processing Scale (including the Nonverbal Scale) range from a high of .95 (for several ages on the composite Mental Processing Scale) to a low of .84 (for ages 2 and 3 years on the Simultaneous Processing Scale). As would be expected, the composites are more reliable than the subtests; of the 42 coefficients, 30 equal or exceed .90. On the achievement subtests, corrected split-half reliabilities range from .97 (reading/decoding at age 6) to .70 (faces and places at age 3). Of the 48 age–subtest coefficients, 12 equal or exceed .90. The reliability of the composite Achievement Scale exceeds .90 at all ages.

Test–retest reliabilities (two- to four-week interval between tests) were obtained by retesting 246 children from the standardization sample. The correlations were, however, based on several combined ages. Stabilities for the Mental Processing subtests range from .86 (gestalt closure for age range 9-0 through 12-5) to .59 (hand movements for age range 9-0 through 12-5). Of the 23 stability coefficients, none equals or exceeds .90. Stabilities for the Mental Processing Scale range from .93 (composite for age range 9-0 through 12-5) to .77 (Sequential Processing and Simultaneous Processing for age range 2-6 through 4-11). Of the 12 coefficients, 2 equal or exceed .90. Stabilities on the Achievement subtests range from .98 (reading/decoding for age range 5-0 through 8-11) to .72 (riddles for age range 2-6 through 4-11). Of the 14 age-range-subtest coefficients, 8 equal or

exceed .90; the composite Achievement Scale exceeds .90 at the three age ranges.

Validity

Forty pages of the Interpretative Manual, describing numerous unpublished studies, are devoted to the validity of the the K-ABC. Several types of evidence are presented to demonstrate construct validity. Scores on each subtest of the K-ABC increase with age. The subtests are internally consistent (although this type of information is better considered as evidence of reliability). The results of several factor analyses that partially support the theorized factor structure of the K-ABC are also discussed. Convergent/discriminant validity is reported.

Criterion-related validity is also examined by correlating the K-ABC with several other tests. To support the contention that the K-ABC measures intelligence, correlations between the K-ABC scales and various intelligence scales were examined. Correlation with the WISC-R Full-Scale IQ and the mental processing composite was .70. The WISC-R Full-Scale IQ and the individual scales making up the Mental Processing Scale were moderately correlated: correlations with the Simultaneous Processing and Nonverbal Scales, were in the .60s; correlation with Sequential Processing was .47. Correlations with the 1970 Stanford–Binet using various samples of children ranged from .36 to .72 for the mental processing composite, from .15 to .65 for the Simultaneous Processing Scale, from .27 to .63 for the Sequential Processing Scale, and from .31 to .70 for the Nonverbal Scale. Other tests of intelligence that were used as criteria include the McCarthy Scales, the Cognitive Abilities Test, the Woodcock–Johnson Cognitive Ability subtests, the Columbia Mental Maturity Scale, and the Slosson Intelligence Test. Finally, several studies examined the relationship of the K-ABC with the Peabody Picture Vocabulary Test. The 60 coefficients ranged from .21 (for Sequential Processing) to .75 (for the mental processing composite).

K-ABC scores were also used to predict achievement. Generally the correlations were unimpressive. For example, correlations between the PIAT-R subtests and the Sequential Processing Scale ranged from .12 (spelling) to .64 (math); with the Simultaneous Processing Scale, from .02 (reading recognition) to .62 (math); with the Nonverbal Scale, from .12 (reading recognition) to .51 (math). Correlations with various subtests from the Iowa Tests of Basic Skills, the California Achievement Tests, and the SRA Achievement Series are comparable to the PIAT-R correlations.

Validation of the Achievement Scale is less persuasive, largely because of the definition of achievement employed: "factual knowledge and skills usually acquired in a school setting or through alertness to the environment" (Kaufman & Kaufman, 1983, p. 33). (Achievement is usually defined as the consequence of direct instruction.) The issue is further complicated by the way the achievement subtests are described. For example, "Expressive Vocabulary is a direct adaptation of the Stanford–Binet Picture Vocabulary task" (p. 51) or "Riddles probably comes closest to a Wechsler or Stanford–Binet Vocabulary subtest in terms of what it measures" (p. 54). The problem is that the Wechsler scales and the Stanford–Binet are used by the Kaufmans to validate the achievement components of their scale. This is not the same as proving that the scale measures achievement. In addition,

the K-ABC provides no linkages to curricula; there is no table of specifications. Numerous correlations between the Achievement Scale and various achievement tests are presented. However, the composite achievement score is not meaningful because it mixes such disparate contents.

Although the manuals present considerable evidence to indicate that the K-ABC assesses two different types of mental processing, there is little convincing evidence that the K-ABC can be substituted for more traditional measures of intelligence or achievement. No data are presented to validate the K-ABC as a measure of learning potential, for use in educational placement and planning, for clinical assessment, or for neurological assessment.

Summary

The K-ABC is designed to assess the way children process information and the amount of information they have obtained, compared with others of similar age and background. The battery was adequately standardized. The composite scales are generally reliable; the subtests are not. Although there is considerable indication that the battery measures different mental processes, the validity of the battery for the purposes for which it is intended is not established.

Woodcock–Johnson Psychoeducation Battery–III (WJ-III): Tests of Cognitive Abilities and Tests of Achievement

The Woodcock–Johnson Psychoeducational Battery–III (WJ-III; Woodcock, McGrew, & Mather, 2001) is an individually administered, norm-referenced assessment system for the measurement of general intellectual ability, specific cognitive abilities, scholastic aptitudes, oral language, and achievement. The battery is intended for use from the preschool to geriatric ages. The complete set of WJ-III test materials includes four easels for presenting the stimulus items: one for the standard battery cognitive tests, one for the extended battery cognitive tests, one for the standard achievement battery, and one for the extended achievement battery. Other materials include examiner's manuals for the cognitive and achievement tests, one technical manual, test records, and subject response booklets.

The WJ-III contains several modifications. The Tests of Cognitive Abilities (WJ-III-COG) were revised to reflect more current theory and research on intelligence, and several clusters have been added to the battery. New clusters were added to the Tests of Achievement (WJ-III-ACH) to assess several specific types of learning disabilities. Finally, a new procedure was added to ascertain intra-individual differences. The procedure allows professionals to compute discrepancies between cognitive and achievement scores within any specific domain.

WJ-III Tests of Cognitive Abilities

The 20 subtests of WJ-III-COG are based on the Cattell-Horn-Carroll theory of cognitive abilities (CHC theory). General Intellectual Ability (GIA) is intended to represent the common ability underlying all intellectual performance. A Brief Intellectual Ability score is also available for screening purposes.

The primary interpretive scores on the WJ-III-COG are based on the broad cognitive clusters. Examiners are urged to note significant score differences among the tests comprising each broad ability to learn how the narrow abilities contribute. The broad and narrow abilities measured by the WJ-III-COG are presented in Table 27.1.

The standard WJ-III-COG subtests shown in Table 27.1 can be combined to create additional clusters: Verbal Ability, Thinking Ability, Cognitive Efficiency, Phonemic Awareness, and Working Memory. If the supplemental subtests are also administered, additional clusters can be created: Broad Attention, Cognitive Fluency, and Executive Processes.

Comprehension–Knowledge (Gc) assesses a person's acquired knowledge, the ability to communicate one's knowledge (especially ver-

bally), and the ability to reason using two subtests: *Verbal Comprehension* (measuring lexical knowledge and language development) and *General Information*.

Long-Term Retrieval (Glr) assesses a person's ability to retrieve information from memory fluently. Two subtests are included: *Visual-Auditory Learning* (measuring associative memory) and *Retrieval Fluency* (measuring ideational fluency).

Visual-Spatial Thinking (Gv) assesses a person's ability think with visual patterns with two subtests: *Spatial Relations* (measuring visualization) and *Picture Recognition* (a visual memory task).

Auditory Processing (Ga) assesses a person's ability to analyze, synthesize, and discriminate speech and other auditory stimuli with two subtests: *Sound Blending* and *Auditory Attention* (measuring one's understanding distorted or masked speech).

Fluid Reasoning (Gf) assesses a person's ability to reason and solve problems using unfamiliar information or novel procedures. The Gf cluster includes two subtests: *Concept Formation* (assessing induction) and *Analysis-Synthesis* (assessing sequential reasoning).

Processing Speed (Gs) assesses a person's ability to perform automatic cognitive tasks. Two subtests; are included: *Visual Matching* (a measure of perceptual speed) and *Decision Speed* (a measure of semantic processing speed).

Short-Term Memory (Gsm) is assessed by two subtests: *Numbers Reversed* and *Memory for Words*.

WJ-III Tests of Achievement

Several new subtests have been added to the WJ-III-ACH. As shown in Table 27.2, the WJ-III-ACH now contains 22 tests that can be combined to form several clusters. The subtests and clusters from the standard battery can be combined to

Table 27.1 ● Broad and Narrow Abilities Measured by the WJ-III Tests of Cognitive Abilities

Broad CHC Factor	WJ-III Tests of Cognitive Abilities	
	Standard Battery Test *Primary Narrow Abilities Measured*	**Extended Battery Test** *Primary Narrow Abilities Measured*
Comprehension– KnowLedge (*Gc*)	Test 1: Verbal Comprehension *Lexical knowledge* *Langauge development*	Test 11: General Information *General (verbal) information*
Long-Term Retrieval (*Glr*)	Test 2: Visual-Auditory Learning *Associative memory* Test 10: Visual-Auditory Learning— Delayed *Associative memory*	Test 12: Retrieval Fluency *Ideational fluency*
Visual-Spatial Thinking (*Gv*)	Test 3: Spatial Relations *Visualization* *Spatial relations*	Test 13: Picture Recognition *Visual memory* Test 19: Planning *Deductive reasoning* *Spatial scanning*
Auditory Processing (*Ga*)	Test 4: Sound Blending *Phonetic coding: Synthesis* Test 8: Incomplete Words *Phonetic coding: Analysis*	Test 14: Auditory Attention *Speech-sound discrimination* *Resistance to auditory stimulus distortion*
Fluid Reasoning (*Gf*)	Test 5: Concept Formation *Induction*	Test 15: Analysis-Synthesis *Sequential reasoning* Test 19: Planning *Deductive reasoning* *Spatial scanning*
Processing Speed (*Gs*)	Test 6: Visual Matching *Perceptual speed*	Test 16: Decision Speed *Semantic processing speed* Test 18: Rapid Picture Naming *Naming facility* Test 20: Pair Cancellation *Attention & concentration*
Short-Term Memory (*Gsm*)	Test 7: Numbers Reversed *Working memory* Test 9: Auditory Working Memory *Working memory*	Test 17: Memory for Words *Memory span*

SOURCE: Copyright © by the Riverside Publishing Company. Reproduced from the *WJ III Technical Manual* by Kevin S. McGrew and Richard W. Woodcock with permission of the publisher.

Table 27.2 ● Broad and Narrow Abilities Measured by the WJ-III Tests of Achievement

	WJ-III Tests of Achievement	
Broad CHC Factor	**Standard Battery Test** *Primary Narrow Abilities Measured*	**Extended Battery Test** *Primary Narrow Abilities Measured*
Reading–Writing (*Grw*)	Test 1: Letter–Word Identification *Reading decoding* Test 2: Reading Fluency *Reading speed* Test 9: Passage Comprehension *Reading comprehension* *Lexical knowledge* Test 7: Spelling *Spelling* Test 8: Writing Fluency *Writing ability* Test 11: Writing Samples *Writing ability*	Test 13: Word Attack *Reading decoding* *Phonetic coding: Analysis &* *synthesis* Test 17: Reading Vocabulary *Language development/* *comprehension* Test 16: Editing *Language development* *English usage* Test 22: Punctuation & Capitalization *English usage*
Mathematics (*Gq*)	Test 5: Calculation *Mathematics achievement* Test 6: Math Fluency *Mathematics achievement* *Numerical facility* Test 10: Applied Problems *Quantitative reasoning* *Mathematics achievement* *Knowledge of mathematics*	Test 18: Quantitative Concepts *Knowledge of mathematics* *Quantitative reasoning*
Comprehension– Knowledge (*Gc*)	Test 3: Story Recall *Language development* *Listening ability* Test 4: Understanding Directions *Listening ability* *Language development*	Test 14: Picture Vocabulary *Language development* *Lexical knowledge* Test 15: Oral Comprehension *Listening ability* Test 19: Academic Knowledge *General information* *Science information* *Cultural information* *Geography achievement*

(continued)

form scores for broad areas in reading, mathematics, and writing.

The *Oral Expression* cluster assesses linguistic competency and semantic expression with two subtests: *Story Recall* (measuring listening skills) and *Picture Vocabulary.*

The *Listening Comprehension* cluster assesses listening comprehension with two subtests: *Understanding Directions* and *Oral Comprehension.*

The *Basic Reading Skills* cluster assesses sight vocabulary and phonological awareness with

Table 27.2   ⬤   Broad and Narrow Abilities Measured by the WJ-III Tests of Achievement (continued)

	WJ-III Tests of Achievement	
Broad CHC Factor	**Standard Battery Test** *Primary Narrow Abilities Measured*	**Extended Battery Test** *Primary Narrow Abilities Measured*
Auditory Processing (***Ga***)		Test 13: Word Attack *Reading decoding* *Phonetic coding: Analysis & synthesis* Test 20: Spelling of Sounds *Spelling* *Phonetic coding: Analysis* Test 21: Sound Awareness *Phonetic coding: Analysis* *Phonetic coding: Synthesis*
Long-Term Retrieval (***Glr***)	Test 12: Story Recall—Delayed *Meaningful memory*	

SOURCE: Copyright © by the Riverside Publishing Company. Reproduced from the *WJ III Technical Manual* by Kevin S. McGrew and Richard W. Woodcock with permission of the publisher.

two subtests: *Letter–Word Identification* and *Word Attack* (measuring one's skill in applying phonic and structural analysis skills to nonwords).

The *Reading Comprehension* cluster assesses reading comprehension and reasoning with two subtests: *Passage Comprehension* and *Reading Vocabulary.*

The *Phoneme/Grapheme Knowledge* cluster assesses knowledge of sound/symbol relationships.

The *Math Calculation Skills* cluster assesses computational skills and automaticity with basic math facts with two subtests: *Calculation* and *Math Fluency.*

The *Math Reasoning* cluster assesses mathematical problem solving and vocabulary with two subtests: *Applied Problems* (measuring skill in solving word problems) and *Quantitative Concepts* (measuring mathematical knowledge and reasoning).

The *Written Expression* cluster assesses writing skills and fluency with two subtests: *Writing Samples* and *Writing Fluency.*

Scores

The WJ-III must be scored by a computer program, a change that eliminates complex hand-scoring procedures. Age norms (age 2 to 90+) and grade norms (from kindergarten to first year graduate school) are included. Although WJ-III age- and grade-equivalents are not extrapolated, they still imply a false standard and promote typological thinking. (See Chapter 5 for a discussion of these issues.) A variety of other derived scores are also available: percentile ranks, standard scores, and Relative Proficiency Indexes (RPIs). Scores can also be reported in 68 percent, 90 percent, or 95 percent confidence bands around the standard score. Discrepancy scores (predicted differences) are also available. Finally, each Test Record contains a seven-category Test Session Observation Checklist to rate a student's conversational proficiency, cooperation, activity, attention and concentration, self-confidence, care in responding, and response to difficult tasks.

Norms

WJ-III norms are based on the performances of 8,818 individuals living in more than 100 geographically and economically diverse communities in the United States. Individuals were randomly selected within a stratified sampling design that controlled for ten specific community and individual variables. The preschool sample includes 1,143 children from 2 to 5 years of age (not enrolled in kindergarten). The kindergarten to 12th grade sample was composed of 4,784 students. The college/university sample is based on 1,165 students. The adult sample includes 1,843 individuals. An oversampling plan was employed to assure that the resultant norms would match, as closely as possible, the most recent (1995) statistics from the U.S. Department of Commerce Bureau of the Census.

Reliability

The *WJ-III Technical Manual* (McGrew & Woodcock, 2001) contains extensive information on the reliability of the WJ-III. The precision of each test and cluster score is reported in terms of the Standard Error of Measurement (SEM). SEMS are provided for the W and standard score at each age level. The precision with which relative standing in a group can be indicated (rather than the precision of the underlying scores) is reported for each test and cluster by the reliability coefficient. The reliability of the various WJ-III aptitude-achievement discrepancy scores, as well as the intracognitive, intra-achievement, and intra-individual discrepancy scores are also reported. Odd–even correlations, corrected by the Spearman–Brown formulas, were used to estimate reliability for each untimed test.

Some human traits are more stable than others are; consequently, some WJ-III tests that precisely measure important, but less stable, human traits show reliabilities in the .80s. However, in the WJ-III, individual tests are combined to provide clusters for educational decision making. All reliabilities for the broad cognitive and achievement clusters exceed .90.

Validity

Careful item selection is consistent with claims for the content validity of both the Tests of Cognitive Ability and the Tests of Achievement. All items retained had to fit the Rasch measurement model as well as other criteria, including bias and sensitivity.

The evidence of concurrent validity comes from studies using a broad age range of individuals. For the Tests of Cognitive Ability, scores were compared with performances on other intellectual measures appropriate for individuals at the ages tested. The criterion measures included the Wechsler Intelligence Scale for Children–III, the Differential Ability Scale (DAS), the Universal Nonverbal Intelligence Test (UNIT), and the Leiter–R. The correlations between the WJ-III General Intellectual Ability score and the WISC-III Full Scale IQ range from .69 to .73.

For the Tests of Achievement, scores were compared with other appropriate achievement measures (for example, the Wechsler Individual Achievement Tests, Kaufman Tests of Educational Achievement, and Wide Range Achievement Test–III). The pattern and magnitude of correlations suggests that the WJ-III-ACH is measuring skills similar to those measured by other achievement tests.

Factor analytic studies support the presence of seven CHC factors of cognitive ability, and several domains of academic achievement. To augment evidence of construct validity, the authors examined the intercorrelations among tests with each battery. As expected, tests assessing the same broad cognitive ability or achievement area usually correlated more highly with each other than with tests assessing different cognitive abilities or areas of achievement.

Summary

The WJ-III consists of two batteries: The WJ-III Tests of Cognitive Abilities and the WJ-III Tests of Achievement. These batteries provide a comprehensive system for measuring general intellectual ability, specific cognitive abilities, scholastic aptitude, oral language, and achievement over a broad age range. There are 20 cognitive tests and 22 achievement tests. A variety of scores are available for the tests and are combined to form clus-

ters for interpretive purposes. A wide variety of derived scores are available. The WJ-III's norms, reliability, and validity appear adequate.

Summary

Two *diagnostic systems*—assessment devices sampling behaviors in multiple domains—were reviewed in this chapter: the K-ABC and the WJ-III. Each system offers the advantage of being standardized on one sample for all its domains. Therefore, differences between domains within a particular diagnostic system do not result from differences in standardization samples, and the tester is freed from a previously uncontrolled source of error in the examination of intra-individual differences. Other than sharing this common advantage, the diagnostic systems considered in this chapter differ sharply from each other.

The Kaufman Assessment Battery for Children has four components: a Sequential Processing Scale, a Simultaneous Processing Scale, an Achievement Scale, and an optional Nonverbal Scale. The first two scales are derived from a model of intellectual function that stresses how people process information; this model is different from the models on which many other measures of intelligence are based (a general intellectual factor, *g*).

The Woodcock–Johnson Psychoeducational Battery–III (WJ-III) is a comprehensive system designed to assess cognitive functioning and achievement. The cognitive battery is based on the Horn–Cattell theory of fluid and crystallized intelligence. Although the domains assessed and their interpretations are well within the mainstream of modern testing, the methodology used to develop the test is quite different from that used to develop most other tests. The WJ-III uses *Rasch's model of item-response theory*. In this model, selection of test items and the development of norms are based on a set of assumptions and

Coping with Dilemmas in Current Practice

The general problems raised by diagnostic systems are often the same as those raised in the measurement of the domains that are included in the systems. Methods for coping with the problems are also the same. For example, when a diagnostic system examines achievement, the question of curriculum match must be addressed.

One problem is particularly noteworthy. The theoretical constructs on which diagnostic systems are based often force the assessor to interpret behavior samples in novel and unusual ways. The K-ABC provides an example. Simultaneous and sequential processing are proposed as measures of intelligence. However, such an orientation to intellectual assessment is quite revolutionary. For many diagnosticians, a considerably larger base of research support is necessary before they can accept the K-ABC's orientation. We believe it is preferable to defer acceptance of novel theoretical orientations until a firm base of research indicates their validity. Until such research is available, patience and skepticism may serve the tester well.

procedures that are quite different from the assumptions and methods used in the more traditional models discussed earlier in this book. Thus, much of the technical discussion of test development and some of the derived scores that are available may be unfamiliar to traditionally trained readers.

Each diagnostic system is intended by its authors to be used in its entirety, but some practicing psychologists use only parts of a system. For example, it is not uncommon for a psychologist to use the Wechsler Intelligence Scale for Children–Revised in conjunction with the achievement battery from the Woodcock–Johnson Psychoeducational Battery–III or the achievement scale from the Kaufman Assessment Battery for Children. Although such practices do not give a diagnostician the advantage of a shared normative sample, they do make sense; relevant domains are assessed in a way that provides the tester with technically adequate and meaningful information. In the final analysis, diagnostic systems provide additional ways and domains for assessment.

Questions for Chapter Review and Thought

1. Discuss the advantages and disadvantages of using diagnostic assessment systems.

2. Contrast suggestions for instruction that a teacher might derive from a student's performance on the Faces and Places, Riddles, and Reading/Decoding subtests of the K-ABC.

3. What is there about the scoring of the Woodcock–Johnson Psychoeducational Battery–III that might lead educators to suggest the need for information about interscorer agreement?

Resources for Further Investigation

Project

Assume that you wish to use one of the systems reviewed in this text. Which system would be your first choice? Why? Compare your answer with a classmate's answer. Reconcile any differences.

Print Resources

Journal of Special Education, Fall 1984 issue. (The entire issue is a symposium on the Kaufman Assessment Battery.)

McGrew, K. S. (1994). *Clinical interpretation of the Woodcock–Johnson Test of Cognitive Ability–Revised.* Boston: Allyn and Bacon.

Woodcock, R. (1990). Theoretical foundations of the WJ-R measures of cognitive ability. *Journal of Psychoeducational Assessment, 8,* 231–258.

Technology Resources

Welcome to AGS On-Line Products and Services
http://www.agsnet.com/

Look for product and ordering information about the instruments available from American Guidance Service. Search by product title to find information about the *Kaufman Assessment Battery for Children.*

Assessment & Guidance
http://assess.nelson.com/nelson/assess/a-ind.html

Here is a list of several tests of assessment, including the *Woodcock–Johnson Psychoeducational Battery–Revised,* with links to detailed product information.

Developmental Appraisal

P rior to the 1960s, the concept of school readiness was frequently used to delay or deny school admission to students who were judged developmentally unready to attend or profit from school. In the 1960s, the importance of early educational experience became more widely understood and accepted. Considerable attention was focused on the early identification of children who are handicapped or at risk of handicap, in order to provide developmental and remedial services. In 1968, the Handicapped Children's Early Education Model Program was established; this led to the establishment of Child Service Demonstration Centers. By 1975, Public Law 94-142 required schools to serve children as young as 5 years of age. In 1986 Public Law 94-142 was extended by Public Law 99-457, which required states to serve children between 3 and 5 years of age who met the conditions specified in Public Law 94-142. Public Law 99-457 also extended services to children from birth to age 3, provided that the children (1) have physical or mental conditions with a high probability of producing developmental delays (for example, cerebral palsy or trisomy), (2) are at risk medically or environmentally for developmental delay, or (3) have developmental delays in cognition, physical development, speech and language, or psychosocial behavior. Since then, it has no longer been legally acceptable to delay or deny school admission to children who are developmentally delayed or otherwise disabled.

Today, substantially less emphasis is placed on school readiness and much more on comprehensive assessment of infants, toddlers, and young children. In many important ways, assessment of these children is quite different from the assessment of older individuals. The types of behavior assessed differ from the behaviors examined in older individuals. Infants and young children are not miniature adults possessed of adult abilities and behavior. Infant behavior is undifferentiated, molar, and limited; for example, infants fuss with their bodies and their voices. Infant assessment frequently involves *neurobiological* appraisal in four areas: neurological integrity (for example, reflexes and postural responses), behavioral organization (for example, attention and response to social stimuli), temperament (for example, consolability and responsivity), and state of consciousness (for example, sleep patterns and attention). As infants develop into toddlers and preschoolers, their behavior differentiates, and broad domains of behavior emerge. Assessment of toddlers and preschoolers frequently involves appraisal of communication, cognition, personal–social behavior, and motor behavior.

The evaluation of toddlers and preschoolers generally relies on their attainment of developmental milestones (significant developmental accomplishments), such as using words, walking, and so on. Although children's development is quite variable, children are usually considered to be at risk for later problems when their attainment of developmental milestones is delayed. Thus, examiners must have a thorough understanding of normal development. Moreover, examiners must understand family systems and the role of culture in child-rearing practices so that they can understand the environments in which infants, toddlers, and preschoolers are developing.

Finally, the procedures used to assess infants, toddlers, and preschoolers differ from those used to evaluate older children and adults. Bailey and Rouse (1989) have reported a number of reasons why infants and young children are difficult to test. Infants between 6 and 18 months are distressed by unfamiliar adults. Although they may have better responses to strangers when held by their caregivers, they may still refuse to respond to an unfamiliar adult. Infants and preschoolers may be very active, inattentive, and distractible; they frequently perform inconsistently in strange situations. Because the language of children is, by definition, undeveloped, they may not completely understand even simple questions and oral requests. Thus, traditional assessment formats in which students respond to examiner questions can be problematic. Not surprisingly, many toddlers and preschoolers are described as untestable.

● ●

Why Do We Assess Infants, Toddlers, and Preschoolers?

There are two major reasons to assess young children. First, we use developmental tests with young children much as we use achievement and intelligence tests with students who have enrolled in schools. We use tests to facilitate eligibility decisions. Eligibility for special services and programs is based on criteria, and these criteria are operationalized by tests and rating scales. We also use tests to facilitate programming decisions. Assessments play an integral role in the development of individualized family service plans for eligible students; delayed developmental areas are targeted for intervention. Finally, tests and rating scales are used to facilitate decisions about the effectiveness of intervention programs for children with and without disabilities. Indeed, many measures currently available for use with very young children were developed exclusively for measuring attainment of goals in Head Start programs. Kelley and Surbeck (1985) report that well over 200 assessment instruments were constructed and published between 1960 and 1980, in part as a response to the 1960 congressional mandate to evaluate the programs authorized as the Handicapped Children's Early Education Program.

The second major reason to assess young children is to ascertain the readiness of nondisabled children to enter school. Information from readiness tests may lead educators to recommend delaying school entrance for unready students or to track pupils into various programs. Readiness for kindergarten or first grade refers to both academic and social readiness. *Academic readiness* is most often thought of in terms of reading readiness but properly includes readiness for all academic instruction. We must also consider children's *readiness* for the *social* milieu of school. In school, children must follow the directions of adults other than their parent or caretaker, must enter into cooperative ventures with their peers, must not present a physical threat to themselves or others, must have mastered many self-help skills (such as toileting and feeding), and so forth.

Tests Used with Infants, Toddlers, and Preschoolers

Bayley Scales of Infant Development, Second Edition (BSID-II)

The second edition of the Bayley Scales of Infant Development (BSID-II; Bayley, 1993) shares the format and rationale of the earlier edition. The BSID-II remains a norm-referenced, individually administered test intended to assess the developmental functioning of children. However, the norms have been updated, and the age range has been extended through 42 months. In addition, 63 new items were added to the Mental Scale, and 29 old items were deleted; 44 new items were added to the Motor Scale, and 8 old items were deleted. The Behavior Rating Scale was completely revised.

The BSID-II has three subscales. The Mental Scale assesses memory, problem solving, conceptualization, language, and social skills. The Motor Scale assesses fine and gross motor skills. Items assessing mental and motor ability are mixed together; this format requires examiners to identify which items go on each scale and to tally them separately. General basal and ceiling rules apply to all items together, not individually to the Mental or Motor Scale. The Behavior Rating Scale is separate; it assesses "qualitative aspects of the child's test-taking behavior" (p. 1) and allows an examiner to rate arousal/attention, orientation/engagement, emotional regulation, and quality of movement. This scale is completed after the Mental and Motor Scales have been administered.

Scores

Each item on the Mental and Motor Scales is scored as C (credit), NC (no credit, incorrect), RF (refused, no credit awarded), O (omit, no credit awarded), RPT (child is reported to have the skill, no credit awarded). Raw score totals for the Mental Scale and the Motor Scale are obtained by adding the credited items between the basal and the ceiling items to the basal score. Each of these totals can be converted to a normalized standard score with a mean of 100 and a standard deviation of 15. The Mental Scale standard scores are called the mental development index, and the Motor Scale standard scores are called the psychomotor development index. The authors also provide confidence intervals (90% and 95%) in the conversion tables for these indexes. Items can also be combined into facets (subareas) of cognitive, language, social, and motor functioning. These scores may be of some clinical value to highly experienced examiners.

Items on the Behavior Rating Scale are scored on a 5-point scale. Composites can be converted to percentile ranks for motor quality, attention/arousal, orientation/engagement, emotional regulation, and the total score. Classifications of behavior (within normal limits, questionable, and nonoptimal) are also available from the conversion tables.

Norms

The BSID-II was standardized on 1,700 children, 50 boys and 50 girls in each of 17 age groups. Children between 1 and 6 months of age are grouped in one-month intervals; children between 6 and 12 months of age are grouped into 3 two-month intervals; children between the ages of 12 and 30 months are grouped into 6 three-month intervals; and children between 30 and 42 months are grouped into 2 six-month intervals. Each age group closely approximates the U.S. 1988 census update in terms of race/ethnicity, geographic region, parental education, and sex.

Reliability

Alphas were used to estimate the internal consistency of the Mental Scale and the Motor Scale at each age.

For the Mental Scale, alpha ranged from .78 to .93; 9 of the 17 coefficients equaled or exceeded .90. For the Motor Scale, alpha ranged from .75 to .91; 1 coefficient exceeded .90. Alphas associated with the total score from the Behavior Rating Scale ranged from .82 to .92; 6 of the 17 coefficients equaled or exceeded .90. Alphas for subscales of the Behavior Rating Scale ran as low as .64, with only 2 coefficients reaching .90. Information about the BSID-II's stability is presented for three age ranges. Thus, the reliability of the Mental Scale and Behavior Rating Scale (total) is sufficient for making important decisions about children in about a third to half of the age ranges; the reliability of the Motor Scale is usually inadequate for making important decisions.

Test–retest correlations for the Mental Scale were .83, .91, and .87; correlations for the Motor Scale were .77, .79, and .78; correlations for the total Behavior Rating Scale were .55, .90, and .60. The evidence presented in the BSID-II manual indicates limited stability. However, given the rapid development of young children, this finding should be expected.

Interscorer agreement (between the examiner and an observer of the examination) for 51 children varied. For the Mental Scale, the correlation between scorers was .96; for the Motor Scale, .75. For the total Behavior Rating Scale, correlations (for two age groups) were .70 and .88. Thus, interscorer agreement appears adequate only for the Mental Scale.

Validity

Several pages of the BSID-II manual review research conducted on the previous edition. However, to the extent that items have been changed, these studies do not establish the BSID-II's validity, but rather set the stage for new research. Project staff and subject-matter experts, as well as users of the scale, reviewed the content of the BSID in preparing new items. Particular attention was paid to assessing potential racial or sex bias.

Empirical evidence of the validity of the BSID-II is very limited. Some evidence that the Mental and Motor Scales measure different abilities comes from the procedure for placing the items on each scale. Initially, items were placed on the basis of experts' judgments; during field testing, item–total correlations were examined to ascertain whether a particular item did indeed relate more closely to the Mental or the Motor Scale. The same procedures were followed for the facets. However, factor-analytic techniques were not used to establish the independence of the two scales or the facets.

More empirical evidence was gathered for the Behavior Rating Scale (BRS). Factor analyses established that there were two factors (that is, attention/arousal and motor quality) for children from 1 to 5 months old and three factors (that is, orientation/engagement, motor quality, and emotional regulation) for older children. The authors also compared the performance of children on the Mental and Motor Scales of the BSID-II with their ratings on the BRS. The pattern of correlations was as would be expected: Items requiring orientation or engagement correlated more highly with the BRS orientation/engagement factor than with other factors; items requiring motor responses correlated more highly with the BRS motor quality factor than with other factors; and items that have an emotional component correlated more highly with the BRS emotional regulation factor than with the other factors. Finally, BRS ratings were modestly correlated with classifications based on the Mental and Motor Scales (hardly surprising, since the items from the scales correlate with the BRS factors).

Summary

The BSID-II is a norm-referenced, individually administered test intended to assess developmental functioning of children between 1 and 42 months of age. The BSID-II has three subscales: the Mental Scale, the Motor Scale, and the Behavior Rating Scale. The scales' norms appear representative in terms of race/ethnicity, geographic region, parental education, and sex. Raw scores for the Mental and Motor Scales are converted to a normalized standard score with a mean of 100 and a standard deviation of 15. Scores from the Behavior Rating Scale can be converted to percentile ranks for motor quality, attention/arousal, orientation/engagement, emotional regulation, and the total score. Internal consistency of the Mental Scale is adequate for making important decisions for children at about half the ages; the consistencies of the Motor Scale and the total Behavior Rating Scale are adequate for about one third of the ages. As should be expected for scales intended for use with this population, scores are moderately stable. Interscorer agreement is adequate only for the Mental Scale. Although the content of the BSID-II appears comprehensive and appropriate, only limited evidence for criterion-related and construct validity is reported.

Infant Mullen Scales of Early Learning (IMSEL)

The Infant Mullen Scales of Early Learning (IMSEL; Mullen, 1989) is an individually administered, norm-referenced test intended to assess mental and motor ability in infants from birth to 36 months of age. Basal and ceiling rules are used. The 37 items in the IMSEL are arranged in the following five scales.

Subtests

Gross Motor Base (GMB) Scale   Items in this test require muscle control, balance, and coordination of large muscle activities. Examples of items (at the oldest age in the level where the item is placed) include lifting and rotating head (4 months), standing unassisted (14 months), and hopping on either foot (39 months).

Visual Receptive Organization (VRO) Abilities Scale   Items in this test require visual localization, tracking, and scanning. Examples of items include inspecting own hand (7 months), finding a partially hidden ring (11 months), and nesting cups (27 months).

Visual Expressive Organization (VEO) Abilities Scale   Items in this test require fine-motor skill (primarily manipulation), hand patterns, and prewriting readiness. Examples of items include reaching and holding with palmar grasp (7 months), taking a Cheerio with a refined pincer grasp (15 months), and stringing three or more beads (39 months).

Language Receptive Organization (LRO) Abilities Scale   Items in this test require auditory discrimination and auditory/oculomotor ability. Examples of items include looking at a person who is speaking (4 months), following simple commands (20 months), and comprehending action words (39 months).

Language Expressive Organization (LEO) Abilities Scale   Items in this test assess overall verbal expressive abilities. Some examples are smiling and making happy sounds (4 months), using one word (15 months), and orally repeating spoken numbers (33 months).

Scores

Clear and specific scoring criteria are provided for each of the 37 items. Suggested starting points are also given in the manual. Because rules for establishing ceilings and basals are used, children are not required to complete all items. Each scale receives a score (age scores, developmental stages, and normalized T-scores). Test ages are calculated by adding the number of passed items above the basal to the number of items below the basal and finding, on the test protocol, the number of months that correspond to this sum.[1] Develop-

---

1. No data are presented in the test manual to indicate how ages were assigned to specific items. Working backward from T-scores to test ages indicates that ages are only approximately correct.

mental stages are determined by locating the developmental stage (one through eight) in which the test age is located.[2] The number correct can also be converted to *T*-scores by using tables based on the child's age. *T*-scores of 35 or less, in the author's judgment, indicate significant delay and warrant early intervention.

Norms

No sampling plan was described in the IMSEL manual. The norms, which required eight years to develop, consist of 1,231 children from 100 different sites. Norm tables are available for the following 16 age groups:

1. 1 month
2. 2 months
3. 3 months (children 3 and 4 months old)
4. 4 months (children 4 and 5 months old)
5. 6 months (children 6 and 7 months old)
6. 8 months (children 8 and 9 months old)
7. 10 months (children 10 and 11 months old)
8. 12 months (children 12 and 13 months old)
9. 14 months (children 14 and 15 months old)
10. 16 months (children 16 to 18 months old)
11. 19 months (children 19 to 21 months old)
12. 22 months (children 22 to 24 months old)
13. 25 months (children 25 to 27 months old)
14. 28 months (children 28 to 30 months old)
15. 31 months (children 31 to 33 months old)
16. 36 months (children 34 to 39 months old)

However, sampling was based on only 11 age groups. Because only the number of children in each sampling group is reported, it is not possible to de-termine the number of children in several norm groups. However, it appears that as many as 9 of the 11 norm groups are based on fewer than 100 children, an inadequate number. For geographic region, the representativeness of the normative samples varies by age; at some ages, the norms closely approximate the U.S. population; at other ages, they do not. The norms appear representative for sex, race (European American, African American, and Asian American), and parent occupation.

Reliability

Three types of reliability information are presented in the IMSEL manual: internal consistency, test–retest, and interscorer. Internal consistency of each subtest was estimated by coefficient alpha for three age groups: At 1–12 months, alpha ranged from .90 to .91; at 14–25 months, alpha ranged from .89 to .91; and at 28–36 months, alpha ranged from .83 to .89. Because alphas are calculated over a large range of ages, they are probably inflated by the correlation of age and item and are likely to overestimate the reliability of the subscales. Thus, the internal consistency of the subtests is sufficiently high to use the IMSEL for screening purposes but insufficient for making important educational decisions about children.

Stability was assessed by retesting 68 children; the average test–retest interval was two weeks. Stabilities are reported for most subtests at four age ranges: 10 to 12 months ($N = 24$, $r_{xx} = .70–.99$); 14 months ($N = .15$, $r_{xx} = .93–.98$); 16–25 months ($N = 16$, $r_{xx} = .77–.94$); and 28–36 months ($N = 13$, $r_{xx} = .80–.98$). Thus, the stability of the IMSEL varies considerably. Before making important decisions about children, examiners should make sure that the IMSEL is stable for the ages of the children being assessed.

Interscorer reliability was estimated for each subtest for ten age groups. Except for GMB at 1–2 months (where $r_{xx} = .78$), all subtests had interscorer agreement exceeding .90. Thus, the IMSEL appears to have excellent interscorer reliability.

2. The basis and meaning of *developmental stage* is unclear, and no references are provided in the manual to suggest the theory underlying those stages.

Validity

Although test items seem to represent the target domains, the author presents no specific information about how specific test items were selected. Therefore, test users must judge the IMSEL's content for themselves. Information about the criterion-related validity of the IMSEL is incompletely reported. The VRO, VEO, LRO, and LEO subscales correlate moderately ($r_{xy} = .5–.6$) with the total score on the Bayley Scales of Infant Development, and the GMB correlates almost perfectly ($r_{xy} = .95$) with the Bayley Motor Scale. Some evidence is also presented to suggest that the IMSEL is useful in discriminating children with normal development from children with developmental delays and in discriminating subgroups of children with developmental delays.

Because the IMSEL consists of five independent subtests and because no total score is used, we would expect some evidence of factor independence of the subtests. No factor analyses were conducted; rather, subtest intercorrelations were examined. However, in our opinion, the correlations do not suggest subtest independence.

Summary

The IMSEL is an individually administered, norm-referenced test intended for use with children from birth to 36 months of age. The test has five subtests: Gross Motor Base, Visual Receptive Organization, Visual Expressive Organization, Language Receptive Organization, and Language Expressive Organization. The IMSEL is constructed as an age test, but test ages can be converted to normalized T-scores. The technical information that appears in the test manual is very incomplete. With that caveat, the IMSEL's norms appear to be generally representative. Interscorer reliability is excellent, but stability varies by age. Internal consistency is generally suitable only for screening purposes. The information about content validity presented in the IMSEL manual is inadequate, although our inspection of the items suggests content very similar to that of other developmental measures. The IMSEL appears to discriminate youngsters who are developmentally delayed from those who are not.

Mullen Scales of Early Learning (MSEL)

The Mullen Scales of Early Learning (MSEL; Mullen, 1992) is an individually administered, norm-referenced test intended to assess modality performance and to identify learning ability, learning disability, and mental retardation in children between 21 and 63 months of age. The MSEL differs from the IMSEL in that MSEL does not have a scale for gross motor ability.

Subtests

The 144 items in the MSEL are equally distributed among the test's four subtests. Each subtest is subdivided into 9 half-year age intervals, and basal and ceiling rules are used in each subtest. The subtests are as follows:

Visual Receptive Organization (VRO) Scale
Items in this test require visual localization, tracking, and scanning. Examples of items (at specific age levels) include discriminating forms (24 months), matching letters (48 months), and demonstrating memory for form (66 months).

Visual Expressive Organization (VEO) Scale
Items in this test require fine-motor skill, eye–hand coordination, and motor planning and control. Examples of items (at specific age levels) include

copying a vertical line (24 months), stringing beads (36 months), and copying a square (60 months).

Language Receptive Organization (LRO) Scale
Items in this test require auditory discrimination and auditory/motor ability. Examples of items include comprehending action words (30 months), following three unrelated commands (54 months), and knowing left from right (60 months).

Language Expressive Organization (LEO) Scale
Items in this test assess overall verbal expressive abilities. Some examples are using two-word phrases (24 months), comprehending spoken questions (36 months), and orally repeating spoken sentences (60 months).

Scores

Clear and specific scoring criteria are provided for each of the 144 items. Suggested starting points are also given in the manual. Because rules for establishing ceilings and basals are used, children are not required to complete all items. Test ages are computed for each subtest by adding 1.5 months for each item passed above the basal age.[3] Test ages can be converted to normalized *T*-scores by using tables based on the child's age. Thus, test ages correspond to different *T*-scores at different ages, and *T*-scores have the same meaning regardless of a child's age.

Norms

No sampling plan is described in the MSEL manual. The norms, which required eight years to develop, consist of 1,016 children from 100 different sites. Norm tables are available for the following ten age groups:

1. 22 months (children 22 through 23 months old)
2. 25 months (children 24 through 26 months old)
3. 28 months (children 27 through 29 months old)
4. 31 months (children 30 through 32 months old)
5. 36 months (children 33 through 38 months old)
6. 42 months (children 39 through 44 months old)
7. 48 months (children 45 through 50 months old)
8. 54 months (children 51 through 56 months old)
9. 60 months (children 57 through 62 months old)
10. 66 months (children 63 through 68 months old)

However, sampling was based on eight age groups. (The 21- to 23-month and 24- to 26-month groups were collapsed into one group, and the 27- to 29-month and 30- to 32-month groups were collapsed into one group.)[4] Except for the collapsed age groups, the number of children in each age group is adequate (that is, between 108 and 140). For geographic region, the representativeness of the normative samples varies by age; at some ages, the norms closely approximate the U.S. population, while at other ages, they do not. The norms appear representative for sex, race (European American, African American, and Asian American), and parent occupation.

Reliability

Three types of reliability information are presented in the MSEL manual: internal consistency, test–retest, and interscorer. Internal consistency of each subtest was estimated by coefficient alpha for four age groups: At 24–30 months, alpha ranged from .82 to .88; at 36–42 months, alpha ranged from .87 to .90; at 48–54 months, alpha ranged from .84 to .89; and at 60–66 months, alpha ranged from .74 to .83. Thus, the internal consistency of the subtests is generally insufficient for making important educational decisions about children.

Stability was assessed by retesting 59 children; the average test–retest interval was two weeks. Stabilities are reported for each subtest at three

---

3. No data are presented in the test manual to indicate how ages were assigned to specific items. Working backward from *T*-scores to test ages suggests that ages are overestimates of the age group's mean.

4. Thus, the number of children sampled does not correspond to the number of children at four ages (21–23 months, 24–26 months, 27–29 months, and 30-32 months) on whom norm conversions are based.

age groups: 24 months ($N = 12$, $r_{xx} = .98–.99$); 30–42 months ($N = 16$, $r_{xx} = .86–.98$); and 48–66 months ($N = 31$, $r_{xx} = .83–.94$). Thus, the MSEL is generally stable enough to use in making important educational decisions about children.

Interscorer reliability was estimated for each subtest for three age groups: 24 months ($N = 12$), 30 months ($N = 14$), and 36–48 months ($N = 18$). All coefficients equaled or exceeded .98. Thus, MSEL appears to have excellent interscorer reliability.

Validity

Although test items seem to represent the target domains, the author presents no specific information about how specific test items were selected. Therefore, test users must judge the MSEL's content for themselves. Information about the criterion-related validity of the MSEL is incomplete. However, it appears that the LRO and LEO subtests correlated highly with the Auditory Comprehension and Verbal Ability subtests of the Preschool Language Assessment (r_{xx} from .78 to .95 for two age groups of children). The VEO subtest correlates highly ($r_{xy} = .94$) with the Fine Motor subtest of the Brigance Inventory of Early Development with one group of children and with the Developmental Test of Visual–Motor Integration ($r_{xy} = .81$) with a different group of children. Finally, there is some evidence that the MSEL predicts subsequent performance on the Metropolitan Readiness Tests after a one-year interval.

Because the MSEL consists of four independent subtests and because no total score is used, we would expect some evidence of factor independence of the subtests. No factor analyses were conducted; rather, subtest intercorrelations were examined. However, in our opinion, the correlations do not suggest subtest independence. Strikingly absent from the manual is any indication that the MSEL is capable of identifying learning disability and mental retardation in children between 21 and 63 months of age.

Summary

The MSEL is an individually administered, norm-referenced test intended for use with children between 21 and 63 months of age. The test has four subtests: Visual Receptive Organization, Visual Expressive Organization, Language Receptive Organization, and Language Expressive Organization. The MSEL is constructed as an age test, but test ages can be converted to normalized T-scores. The technical information that appears in the test manual is very incomplete. With that caveat, the MSEL's norms appear to be generally representative. Interscorer reliability is excellent, and stability is generally good. However, internal consistency is generally suitable only for screening purposes. The information related to content validity presented in the MSEL manual is inadequate, although our inspection of the items suggests content very similar to that of other developmental measures. This similarity is borne out by extremely high concurrent validity coefficients with measures such as the Preschool Language Assessment and the Brigance Inventory of Early Development. Other validity coefficients are more modest. No evidence of MSEL's ability to identify children with learning disabilities or mental retardation is presented in the test manual.

Boehm Test of Basic Concepts–Revised (BTBC-R)

The Boehm Test of Basic Concepts–Revised (BTBC-R; Boehm, 1986) differs somewhat in content from the original version. There are seven new items, one item was divided into two items, two items were deleted, and four items were moved to a downward extension of the test. Like the earlier edition, the BTBC-R is a group-administered, norm-referenced device that assesses knowledge of 50 abstract, relational concepts that occur frequently in preschool and primary curricula. The concepts are "both fundamental to understanding verbal instruction and essential for early school achievement" (Boehm, 1986, p. 1). The BTBC-R is intended primarily for use in identifying children who have not mastered the concepts and in identifying those concepts that a teacher should systematically teach. In addition, Boehm states that the test may be used as part of a battery to identify children who are at risk for learning problems and to evaluate the effectiveness of instruction in the concepts assessed. The test is available in two forms, C and D.

The 50 concepts are arranged in order of increasing difficulty in two booklets. Each booklet takes about 15 to 20 minutes to administer and includes three practice items. The testing format requires children to mark the picture that best answers the question read by the teacher (for example, "Mark the one where the boy is next to the horse"). The items can be categorized as *spatial* (requiring understanding of the concept of *next to,* for example), *quantitative* (for example, *few*), *temporal* (for example, *after*), and *miscellaneous* (for example, *other*).

Scores

Two types of scores are provided: pass or fail on each item and a percentile rank for the total score. In addition, tables give the percentage of children passing each item. The interpretive materials for the two types of scores are similar in several respects: Both provide normative data for kindergarten, grade 1, and grade 2; both provide separate norms for the beginning of the year and the end of the year; and both provide a means of comparing a student's performance with that of the total sample and that of other students at the same socioeconomic level.

Forms C and D have separate sets of norms for the percentage of students passing each item. The percentile norms, however, are for forms C and D combined. This is troublesome because forms C

and D were standardized separately and were not equated for variations in the samples. Although Boehm claims that the two samples were selected to be comparable in ability, no specifics are given.

Norms

The standardization sample was intended to be broadly representative of the U.S. population, although it appears that only children from public school who attended regular classes were included. School-district size and geographic area were the bases of stratification. The obtained data were statistically weighted to make the sample conform to the national population with respect to the stratification variables.

Boehm claims that her sample is also representative of the socioeconomic levels of schools in the United States. "Participating districts were asked to select groups of school buildings that, together, would provide a sample representative of the range of schools within the districts" (p. 45). Her data are not convincing, however.[5]

Reliability

Although not presented as reliability data in the test manual, information about alternate-forms reliability, based on the performances of 625 children, indicates poor reliability: .82 at kindergarten, .77 at first grade, and .65 at second grade. Twenty-four split-half reliability estimates (one for each form, grade/socioeconomic class, and total sample) are also presented. These range from .55 to .87; only ten coefficients exceed .80. Stability estimates (with an interval of one school year) are also given for each form at each grade. The six coefficients range from .55 to .88, with only two of the six exceeding .80.

---

5. To estimate the SES of her sample, Boehm used the percentage of children in each school who received subsidized lunches. Schools were classified as high SES if no more than 10 percent of the students were eligible for subsidized lunches and as middle SES if 11–50 percent of the students were eligible.

Validity

Because the BTBC-R is essentially a specialized achievement test, its content validity is of primary concern. Substantial evidence is presented that the words in the test are commonly used, and some evidence is presented that they are important. Some evidence of predictive validity is also presented. The BTBC-R correlates modestly with achievement, assessed after one year. Boehm presents 17 coefficients of correlation with achievement tests that range from .38 to .64 (median .4). No evidence is presented, however, to show that the BTBC-R can identify children who are at risk for learning problems.

Seven pages of the BTBC-R manual are devoted to a review of validity studies conducted with the BTBC. Because the content of the two devices is so similar—there is about 80 percent overlap between the two devices—many of these studies are applicable to the BTBC-R. Reported studies indicate that the BTBC had some criterion-related validity for achievement, readiness, and language and was sensitive to instruction in the concepts tested; the same studies found no sex differences but did find differences among SES and ethnic groups.

Summary

The BTBC-R is a group-administered test that assesses knowledge of 50 relational words. Although there is some evidence for the importance of the words (and hence for use of the test as a criterion-referenced device), the device has inadequate reliability and norms for purposes other than screening.

Developmental Indicators for the Assessment of Learning–Third Edition (DIAL-3)

The Developmental Indicators for the Assessment of Learning–third edition (DIAL-3; Mardell-Czudnowski & Goldenberg, 1998) is an individually administered, 30-minute screening test to assess the development of children between the ages of 3-0 and 6-11. Several new items were developed for this edition of the scale, and a Parental Questionnaire was added to assess self-help, social development, family background, and general developmental information. Finally, a short form (called the Speed Dial) is now available. Both the DIAL-3 and the Speed Dial can be administered in English or Spanish. Although individual children are screened, the testing procedures are designed to handle large numbers of children; different examiners (called operators) administer the Motor, Concepts, and Language subtests to a child, who moves from one testing area (and one tester) to another. There are no special qualifications for operators.

Subtests

Three subtests (called *Areas* on the DIAL-3) require direct observation of a child's performance on various *items* that may require multiple responses. The Speed Dial includes eight of the DIAL-3 subtests. Here we describe the subtests, and name and describe the items.

Motor   This subtest includes Catching a beanbag with one and two hands, Jump–Hop–Skip, Building[6] with blocks, touching Thumbs and Fingers of the same hand in various sequences, Cutting with scissors, Copying[6] four geometric shapes and four letters, and Writing (own) Name.

Concepts   This subtest includes pointing to Body Parts,[6] identification of Colors,[6] Rapid Color Naming,[6] rote Counting, using blocks to demon-

---

6. This item is also used in Speed Dial.

strate relative Positions (front, down, and so forth), Concepts[6] (for example, *big*), and sorting by Shapes.

Language   This subtest includes providing Personal Data (name, age, and so forth), Articulation (repeating the names of objects), naming Objects and Actions,[7] Letters and Sounds[6] (saying the alphabet, naming letters presented in random order, and producing the sound of a letter), Rhyming and I Spy (rhyming and alliteration), oral Problem Solving[6] about social situations, and Intelligibility rating by the examiner).

Self-Help Rating   Parents rate their children's development of eating, toileting, dressing, and other daily-living skills. Parents indicate whether the child performs the skill most of the time with no help, sometimes or with help, not yet, or not allowed.

Social Development Rating   Parents rate the frequency with which their children exhibit feelings and behaviors that are related to successful relationships with family and peers.

Scores

Raw scores for each item are converted to an intermediate score called a Scaled Score for the areas/subtests of Motor, Concepts, and Language and the Speed Dial.[8] The Scaled Scores for each subtest can also be summed into the DIAL-3 Total Score. Testers can look up children's ages (in two-

6. This item is also used in Speed Dial.
7. Only the *Actions* portion of this subtest is used in the Speed Dial.
8. As explained in Chapter 5, the term *scaled score* usually refers to a standard score with a predetermined mean and standard deviation. However, the DIAL-3 manual defines a Scaled Score as the median of an age distribution, and so it is a developmental score. (A Scaled Score of 0 is the median for children younger than 3 years old; 1 is the median for 3-year-olds; 2, for 4-year-olds; 3, for 5-year-olds; and 4, for 6-year-olds.) The manual provides no explanation for the ranges associated with each Scaled Score. For example, in Rapid Color Naming, a Scaled Score of 0 corresponds to raw scores of 0 to 4, a Scaled Score of 1 corresponds to raw scores of 5 to 9, a Scaled Score of 2 corresponds to raw scores of 10 to 19, and so forth. It appears that the Scaled Scores on the DIAL-3 are at best ordinal and cannot provide for equal weighting of items as claimed on page 70 of the manual.

month intervals) in tables to convert Scaled Score sums to percentiles and cutoff levels for potential delay. Raw-score sums for Self-Help and Social Development ratings can also be converted to percentiles and cutoff levels for potential delay.

The authors provide multiple ways to use the DIAL-3 scores to reach a decision and identify a child as needing further assessment. However, they offer users little guidance beyond the fact that more children can be identified with less stringent criteria and fewer children with criteria that are more rigorous.

Norms

The DIAL-3 was standardized on 1,560 children between the ages of 3-0 and 6-11 who were tested between November 1995 and June 1997. The children resided in 36 states, the District of Columbia, Puerto Rico, and Panama. The proportions of individuals in the DIAL-3 norms are comparable to the 1994 census in terms of sex, race/ethnicity, geographic region, and parental educational level.

Reliability

Internal consistency was estimated using coefficient alpha for 8 six-month age groups (3-0 to 3-5, 3-6 to 3-11, and so forth). We consider .80 to be the minimum reliability for a screening device. The Motor, Language, and Self-Help subtests are usually not sufficiently reliable to use for screening decisions: For Motor, none of the alphas for the eight age groups equals or exceeds .80; For Language and Self-Help, two of the eight alphas equal or exceed .80. The remaining two subtests have more age groups for which alphas equal or exceed .80: six age groups for Concepts and all eight for Social. The reliability of the Speed Dial equals or exceeds .80 in half of the age groups, and the reliability of the DIAL-3 total exceeds .80 except for the oldest group of children.

To estimate stability, 158 children were divided into two groups: A younger group contained 80 children between 3-6 and 4-5, and an older group contained 78 children between 4-6 and 5-10). The children were retested on average after about 28 days. For the younger group, two subtests had stability estimates that equaled or exceeded .80; stabilities for the DIAL-3 total and the Speed Dial both exceeded .80. For the older group, Social was the only subtest that exceeded .80; stabilities for the DIAL-3 total and the Speed Dial both exceeded .80.

Thus, only the DIAL-3 total appears to have sufficient reliability for use in making screening decisions. It should also be noted that the age groups used to estimate reliability are not the same as the age groups used to convert raw scores to percentiles and delay ratings.

Validity

Some claim can be made for the content validity of the DIAL-3 because of the careful selection and field testing of the items. Some evidence for criterion-related validity comes from modest (that is, .25 to .45) correlations with similar subtests on the Early Screening Profile, moderate (that is, .30 to .55) correlations with similar subtests on the Battelle Screening Test, and fairly strong correlations of the total score on the Brigance Preschool Screen with Concepts Language, and the DIAL-3 total (that is, .53 to .79), and of Language with the Peabody Picture Vocabulary Test. The Self-Help and Social ratings were also correlated with parent ratings of social skills on the Social Skills Rating System. Finally, children with disabilities who were identified by means other than the DIAL-3 earned lower normalized standard scores. However, as interesting as this finding is, it is difficult to interpret because no standard scores are available for the DIAL-3.

The validity of Speed Dial rests on the validity of the DIAL-3. There is a strong correlation (.94) between the two when scores are converted to normalized standard scores. However, no data are presented about frequency of false-negatives and false-positives.

Summary

The DIAL-3 is an individually administered screening device assessing development in motor, conceptual, language, self-help, and social domains. The norms are generally representative, the reliability for the total score is generally adequate (although the reliabilities of the subtests usually are not), and the validity appears clearly established. Users are urged to make screening decisions based on the total score.

Metropolitan Readiness Tests, Sixth Edition (MRT6)

The sixth edition of the Metropolitan Readiness Tests (MRT6; Nurss & McGauvran, 1995) is intended to assess beginning reading, story comprehension, and quantitative concepts, three skill areas believed to be "essential for prereading and premathematics learning in the early school years" (p. 11). There are two levels of the test. Level I is individually administered and intended to assess skills needed before and during kindergarten. Level 2 is group-administered and intended to assess skills needed from mid-kindergarten through beginning first grade.

Three subtests form the Beginning Reading composite. Story Comprehension and Quantitative Concepts and Reasoning are each assessed by one subtest named for the area. The subtests are briefly described below.

Visual Discrimination   (Level I) This is a Beginning Reading subtest that assesses skill in matching individual letters, letter sequences, and words.

Beginning Consonants   (Levels I and II) This is a Beginning Reading subtest that assesses skill in discriminating initial phonemes.

Sound–Letter Correspondence (Levels I and II) This is a Beginning Reading subtest that assesses skill in identifying letters that correspond to sounds.

Aural Cloze (Level II) This is a Beginning Reading subtest that assesses skill in matching the initial sound of a picture that is contextually appropriate for a sentence read by the examiner.

Story Comprehension (Levels I and II) This subtest assesses understanding of the vocabulary and concepts of a story to which subjects listen.

Quantitative Concepts and Reasoning (Levels I and II) This subtest assesses basic mathematical concepts (such as number–numeral and part–whole relationships) and operations (for example, addition).

Scores and Norms

Raw scores for Visual Discrimination, Beginning Consonants, and Sound–Letter Correspondence are summed to form the Beginning Reading composite. Story Comprehension and Beginning Reading composite are summed to form the Prereading Composite Score. All raw scores can be summed to form a Total Test Composite, although there is no provision on the record forms for this score.

Raw scores and composites can be converted to several norm-referenced scores: percentiles, stanines, scaled scores that are indecipherable,[9] and normal-curve equivalents that appear to be based on percentile ranks in a normal curve. In addition, there are two kinds of "content-referenced" scores. The first content-referenced score is the raw score. No rationale is provided for considering these scores content-referenced. The second type of content-referenced score, a performance rating, is a three-point scale that indicates that a student currently has "learned enough of the

skills . . . to be judged proficient" (a + rating), "is in the process of learning the skills" (a ✓ rating), or "needs instruction in the skills" (a − rating).

Apparently school districts were stratified and sampled to represent the U.S. population in terms of geographic region, socioeconomic status, urban/suburban/rural residence, ethnicity, and public–private school attendance. No further explanation of the sampling plan is provided, and no data are provided to demonstrate that the selected districts are indeed representative. Rather, the authors present tables to show that the children are generally representative of children in the United States; the actual norms are based on weighted samples.

Reliability

Internal consistencies (KR-20) for subtests and the Total Test Composite for Level 1 were calculated for two prekindergarten samples (tested at midyear or spring) and three kindergarten samples (tested at fall, midyear, or spring); for Level 2, they were calculated for two kindergarten samples (midyear and spring) and for first-graders in the fall. Five of the eight internal-consistency estimates for the Total Test Composite equaled or exceeded .90; 2 of the 40 internal consistencies of subtests equaled or exceeded .90, and 25 were less than .80. Test–retest reliability was estimated using 124 undescribed students who were retested with Level 2 after an unspecified period. Only the stability of the Total Test Composite was greater than .90; two subtests had stabilities less than .80. Thus, only the reliability of the composite is occasionally high enough for making important decisions for individual students.

Validity

Evidence for the validity of the MRT6 is inadequate. No evidence of content validity is presented; no evidence of construct validity is presented. No evidence of predictive validity is presented for Level I. The only validity evidence presented is for Level II and indicates that the MRT6 correlates moderately with the Metropolitan Achievement Tests, seventh edition, and the Stanford Achievement Test, ninth

---

9. The authors explain that the "scaled score system links together common Skill Areas and the Prereading Composite across the two levels" (p. 15). As they have failed to do in earlier editions, the authors continue to fail to provide means and standard deviations for the scaled scores and do not indicate *how* the two levels are linked.

edition. Most troubling is the authors' failure to present any data whatsoever to support their interpretations of "content-referenced" scores.

Summary

The sixth edition of the MRT is the latest version of a test originally published in 1933. The technical qualities of the test are marginal. The reliability of the total composite is usually sufficient for making important decisions for individual students; the other scores are usually not reliable enough for that purpose. The norming procedures are poorly described. Validity evidence is largely absent.

Work Sampling System (WSS)

The Work Sampling System (WSS; Meisels, Jablon, Marsden, Dichtelmiller, & Dorfman, 1994) is a comprehensive performance assessment for use with children in preschool through grade 5. The system is used to document and assess children's knowledge, behavior, and accomplishments. A curriculum-embedded system that records how children respond to real classroom tasks and actual life situations, it is used to monitor physical, social, emotional, and academic progress.

The Work Sampling System consists of three parts: (1) Developmental Guidelines and Checklists, (2) Portfolios, and (3) Summary Reports. Classroom teachers observe student behavior and performance using the structured framework provided by the Developmental Guidelines. They record their observations on Checklists and gather student products in Portfolios as backup support for their observations. Three times each year, they summarize their observations of student performance and progress using the Summary Reports. These three components are described below in more detail.

Developmental Guidelines give teachers a framework for observation. They are a set of observational criteria based on national standards and current knowledge of child development, expectations used to evaluate student performance at different ages.

Developmental Checklists are lists of grade-specific performance indicators. Teachers check off those behaviors, skills, and knowledge that children exhibit.

Portfolios are purposeful collections of children's work and progress over time. Portfolios comprise two kinds of items: core items and individualized items. Core items describe growth in student performance over time in one area. Individualized items describe the growth of an individual student across several domains.

The authors of the Work Sampling System have identified seven categories of student behavior and performance in which data are collected. These are listed and described as follows:

Personal and Social Adjustment: Teachers record information both about social development and about how children feel about themselves. They gather it by observing and questioning individual students.

Language and Literacy: Teachers record data on acquisition of language skills.

Mathematical Thinking: Teachers observe and record development of mathematical problem-solving skills.

Scientific Thinking: Teachers observe and record development of the ways in which students think about and ask about the natural and physical world. They note how children actively investigate through observing, recording, describing, questioning, forming explanations, and reaching conclusions.

Social Studies: Teachers gather data on acquisition of social and cultural understanding.

Arts: Data are collected on children's engagement with dance, drama, music, and art.

Physical Development: Teachers note changes in students' gross motor skills, fine motor skills, and personal health and safety.

There are specific factors that teachers must observe as they record and make judgments about student development. For each domain, the authors specify functional components and performance indicators. Teachers make judgments using a simple rubric. They record on the summary record whether the student is performing as expected or needs improvement.

Reliability

The most critical kind of reliability for a measure of this type is interrater agreement. The authors do not include data on the extent to which there is agreement across teachers in ratings of student performance and behavior.

Validity

There is no evidence for validity included in the manuals for the Work Sampling System. Meisels,

Bickel, Nicholson, Xue, and Atkins-Burnett (1998) have published a technical report that accompanies the manuals and addresses the validity of the Work Sampling System. Correlations of scores on the WSS Checklist and Summary Report ratings with scores on the Woodcock–Johnson Psychoeducational Battery–Revised were within the range of .50 to .75 across four grade levels. Scores on the WSS were better predictors of future WSS scores than were any other demographic factors.

Summary

The Work Sampling System is a curriculum-embedded performance assessment that provides a profile of individual students' strengths and weaknesses across seven curriculum domains. Teachers are provided with a conceptual framework of performance indicators in the seven domains and use observation and collection of student work to make judgments about student performance and progress. The WSS is a rating system, and there are no data on the extent to which teachers agree in their ratings of student performance. Evidence for validity of the system is based on correlations with performance on the Woodcock–Johnson Psychoeducational Battery–Revised.

Early Screening Inventory–Revised (ESI-R)

The Early Screening Inventory–Revised (ESI-R; Meisels, Marsden, Wiske, & Henderson, 1997) is a developmental screening test that provides a quick assessment of a child's development of visual–motor/adaptive, language and cognition, and gross motor skills and abilities. It is not an intelligence test, nor is it intended for use in making decisions about school readiness. The test is the sixth revision of a measure first introduced in 1975 as the Eliot–Pearson Screening Inventory (Meisels &

Wiske, 1975). In 1983 the test was renamed the Early Screening Inventory; it has undergone five major revisions prior to this edition.

The ESI-R is available in two forms. The preschool version (ESI-P) is intended for use with children from their third birthday until they become four and one-half years old. The kindergarten version (ESI-K) is designed to screen children 4 years, 5 months, 16 days to 6 years of age. The authors indicate that the purpose of the test is to identify children who may need special-education services in order to perform successfully in school. The test is available in both English and Spanish versions.

Scores and Norms

The ESI-R does not provide scores per se. Rather, it provides three classifications: OK, Rescreen, and Refer. A score in the Refer range is said to suggest the possibility of a delay or disorder in the child's potential for acquiring knowledge.

The ESI-K and ESI-P were normed separately. In norming the ESI-K, data were collected on 5,034 children enrolled in 60 classrooms in 10 states. Twenty of these classrooms were Head Start programs, 26 were public-school programs, and the remainder were other kinds of programs. A stratified sample was not used. Although demographic characteristics of the students were recorded and are reported in the manual, these data are not compared to national population characteristics. Because sufficient information is not provided, it is impossible to judge the extent to which the sample is representative of the population. The ESI-P was standardized on 974 children selected from 16 sites, of which 10 were Head Start programs. Again, the demographic characteristics of the sample are reported in the manual, but no comparison to national norms is provided.

Reliability

Interrater reliability for the ESI-K is reported to be .97, indicating excellent agreement among raters in their evaluations of student performance. Test–retest reliability coefficients for 174 children ranged from .79 to .84. Reliabilities are sufficient for screening, the intended use of this measure. Reliability data on the ESI-P are on so few children ($N = 5$) that the coefficients must be disregarded.

Validity

The authors assessed the predictive validity of the ESI-K on a sample of 251 children who were given the McCarthy Scales of Children's Abilities seven months after being given the ESI-K. A correlation of .73 was obtained. The same coefficient was obtained for 130 children who were given the ESI-P and the McCarthy. The authors also examined the extent to which the same diagnostic decision (at risk/ refer) was reached using the two scales. It was demonstrated that both scales identify students who are at risk, although the ESI-P and ESI-K overrefer 18 to 20 percent of the sample.

Summary

The ESI-R is a brief developmental screening instrument that is administered in 15 to 20 minutes to children 3 to 6 years of age. The test provides information about a child's development of visual–motor/adaptive, language and cognition, and gross motor skills. We were unable to ascertain the extent to which the normative sample is representative of the U.S. population, and evidence for reliability and validity is limited.

Preschool Evaluation Scale (PES)

The Preschool Evaluation Scale (PES; S. B. McCarney, 1992) is an individually administered, norm-referenced rating scale intended "to contribute to the early identification of students with developmental delays" (S. B. McCarney, 1992, p. 4). Different forms are used for children from birth through 35 months and for children between 36 and 72 months of age.

Domains

Designed to assess the domains enumerated in Public Law 99-457, PES assesses performance in the six domains that are briefly described here.

Large Muscle   This subscale assesses large-muscle movements, as well as reflexes, muscle tone, positioning, and use of adaptive equipment. Examples of required movements include waving arms and sitting down.

Small Muscle   This subscale assesses small-muscle movements, as well as reflexes, muscle tone, positioning, and use of adaptive equipment. Examples of required movements include building a tower of three to four blocks or holding a pencil with three- to four-finger grasp.

Cognitive Thinking   This subscale assesses mental concepts such as object permanence, causality, means–end behavior, and spatial relationships, as well as preacademic skills, including concept-development prereading skills and premath skills. Examples of items include recognizing parent visually, enjoying repetitive sound-producing actions, and matching colors.

Expressive Language   This subscale measures aspects of communication through verbal expression. Examples of items on this subscale include calling parents "mama" and "dada," naming objects and pictures, and rhyming words.

Social/Emotional   This subscale contains test items that sample knowledge of social rules, appropriate play behavior, and demonstration and awareness of feelings and emotions. Examples include smiling in response to adult attention, choosing friends, and initiating play.

Self-help Skills   This subscale assesses the child's ability to care for herself or himself. Items assess dressing, toileting, feeding, and self-help.

Although the subtest names are the same, the specific items and the number of items differ on

TABLE 28.1 ● Subtests and Number of Items on the PES

| | Number of Items | |
Subtest	*Birth–35 Months*	*36–72 Months*
Large Muscle	18	11
Small Muscle	16	13
Cognitive Thinking	17	13
Expressive Language	15	15
Social/Emotional	13	17
Self-help Skills	15	16
Total	94 items	85 items

each form. Table 28.1 contains the number of items for each subtest on each form.

Scores

For each item, the child is rated (usually by the child's teacher or aide) on a 3-point scale: 0 (cannot perform the behavior), 1 (performs successfully but inconsistently), and 2 (performs successfully and independently). Raw scores on subscales are converted to scaled scores (mean = 10, standard deviation = 3). Subscales are summed to provide percentiles for total scores.

Norms

No sampling plan is described in the manual, but the norms are based on the ratings of 472 educators from 24 states who rated 2,893 children. The author provides separate norms (combining boys and girls) for different age groups in four-month intervals from birth through 28 months; the number of children in each norm group is clearly presented and adequate. After 28 months, however, the norms become less clear. For example, norm tables are available for boys from 36 to 47 months, boys from 48 to 59 months, boys from 60 to 72 months, and girls from 36 to 72 months. No rationale is given for the asymmetry of the norms, nor is it possible to ascertain the actual number of children in norm groups after 28 months.

Overall, the norms appear representative of the U.S. census in 1980 in terms of sex, race, urban/rural residence, and geographic area for children between birth and 35 months of age. For children between 36 and 72 months, the norms appear representative in terms of sex and race; urban children and children from the North Central region are overrepresented. Although the author notes that children with disabilities were included in the normative sample, no data on them are provided.

Reliability

The author presents data on the PES's internal consistency, stability, and interrater agreement. The data, however, are incompletely reported. Alphas are reported for each subscale for two age groups, birth through 35 months and 36 months through 72 months; alphas are not reported for total score. With the exception of the Large Muscle subscale for the older group, all alphas exceeded .90. However, because alphas were calculated across age groups, they are likely to be inflated.

Stability (test–retest reliability) over a 30-day interval was estimated for each subscale and for the total score on the performance of 391 children of unknown characteristics. Three of the six coefficients equaled or exceeded .90. Based on the author's discussion of the procedures used to estimate stability, it is unclear whether the resulting coefficients are contaminated by the effects of age or the results apply to children of all ages.

To estimate interrater reliability, 142 pairs of educators rated 428 children. A total of ten correlations are presented that correspond to age ranges of the children. Thus, it appears that only total score agreement was estimated. The obtained coefficients ranged from .80 to .89. Agreement for subscale scores is not reported.

Validity

Content Validity   Some claim for content validity can be made by the way items were developed.

Appropriate literature was reviewed, items were developed, and early childhood professionals reviewed the items. However, there are certain notable omissions. For example, PES ignores receptive language.

Criterion-Related Validity   Criterion-related validity was evaluated in two incompletely reported studies. In the first study, 60 children between birth and 35 months of age were assessed with the PES and the Early Learning Accomplishment Profile (ELAP). Correlations between PES subtests and ELAP ranged from .58 (Cognitive Thinking) to .71 (Large Muscle). However, it is unclear what PES scores (that is, raw scores or standard scores) and what ELAP scores were correlated. In the second study, 58 children between 36 and 72 months of age were assessed with the PES and the Learning Accomplishment Profile (LAP). Correlations between the PES subtests and the LAP ranged from .61 (Cognitive Thinking) to .80 (Large Muscle). Again, it is unclear what PES scores (that is, raw scores or standard scores) and what LAP scores were correlated. Nonetheless, correlations of the magnitude obtained in the two studies strongly suggest that the PES is measuring constructs similar to those measured by ELAP and LAP.

Construct Validity   The author presents three types of information about construct validity: diagnostic, subscale interrelationships, and item validity. Diagnostic validity was investigated by examining 121 children between the ages of 24 and 60 months with the PES. The profiles of these children were compared with the PES profiles of "a corresponding group" of children who were identified as having developmental delays. The developmentally delayed children obtained significantly lower scores than the randomly selected children.

The author also presents subscale intercorrelations to establish that all subscales assess development. Indeed, the subscales are highly intercorrelated for children between birth and 35 months; correlations range from .83 to .92. For older students (between the ages of 36 and 72 months), the correlations are substantially lower, ranging from .60 to .83. These correlations suggest that a single factor underlies the scale, and this finding casts doubt on the differential meaning of the subscales. The author also presents data on item–total correlations. We believe these data are redundant, given the reliability information provided.

Summary

PES is an individually administered, norm-referenced rating scale intended to facilitate the identification of young children with developmental disabilities. Different forms are available for two different age groups: birth through 35 months and 36 through 72 months. Both forms assess children on six subscales (Large Muscle, Small Muscle, Cognitive Thinking, Expressive Language, Social/Emotional, and Self-help Skills). Subscale raw scores are converted to scaled scores, and subscale totals are converted to percentiles. PES norms are generally representative. Reliability information is incompletely reported for internal consistency and stability, although the information that is presented suggests adequate reliability. Nonetheless, users should interpret PES results cautiously. Interrater agreement for total score is marginal (that is, .80 to .89, depending on the age of the children); no interrater agreement is presented for subscales. Content validity is generally adequate, but users should be cautious about generalizing the Expressive Language subscale to receptive-language functioning. Criterion-related validity, although incompletely reported, appears adequate. Construct validity is limited, but the PES does appear to discriminate between children with and children without developmental disabilities.

Test of Early Reading Ability, Revised (TERA-2)

The Test of Early Reading Ability, Revised, (TERA-2; Reid, Hresko, & Hammill, 1989) is an individually administered, norm-referenced test designed to evaluate the emerging literacy skills in children between the ages of 3-0 and 9-0. Basal and ceiling rules usually allow TERA-2 to be administered in 30 minutes or less.

Subtests

Drawing on a whole-language perspective of reading, 46 items (for each of two forms) were developed to assess three types of skills associated with reading.

Construction of Meaning Items of this type include logo reading, print in the environment (such as traffic signs), and print in connected discourse.

Knowledge of the Alphabet and Its Functions Items of this type include reading letters and numbers in isolation, reading words, and reading comprehension.

Conventions of Written Language Items of this type include book handling (for example, recognizing the top and bottom of a book), knowing conventions of print (for instance, that the symbol *?* is used in a sentence that asks a question), and proofreading.

Scores

Raw scores can be converted to percentiles, normal-curve equivalents, and reading quotients (RQs) (that is, a standard score with a mean of 100 and a standard deviation of 15).

Norms

TERA-2 norms are based on the performances of 1,454 children from 15 states. No description of how these students came to be included in the norms is provided in the technical manual. Overall, the total sample appears representative in terms of sex, race, geographic region, and ethnicity. Urban children are overrepresented. However, no data are provided for the representativeness of each age sample—the information that allows a test user to assess the representativeness of the norms for the particular child being assessed. The number of students in each age group varies from 107 (at age 3) to 350 (at age 7).

Reliability

Estimates of internal consistency (coefficient alpha) are presented for each age for each form. On both forms, only two of the seven coefficients are less than .90 (that is, .89 at age 5 years and .78 at age 9 on form A and .80 at ages 8 and 9 on form B).[10] Alternate-forms reliability and stability (retesting occurred within a two-week period) were studied with a group of 49 children between 7 and 9 years of age. The resulting correlation coefficient (.79) included error associated with both items and time. When the error attributable to a lack of internal consistency is removed, the estimated stability is .89 for this age group. The stability of TERA-2 scores at other ages is not reported.

Validity

The major purpose of TERA-2 is to identify children who are ahead of or behind their age peers in the development of emerging literacy skills. Evidence that TERA-2 is valid for this purpose comes from several sources. First, some claim can be laid to content validity.[11] A panel of experts reviewed items prepared by the authors, and the items that could be consistently placed in one of the three

categories of reading skills (that is, Construction of Meaning, Knowledge of the Alphabet and Its Functions, and Conventions of Written Language) were subsequently field-tested. Analysis of the point-biserial correlations and *p*-values suggested a need for additional items. The authors generated more items, and the process was repeated. Second, the authors present the results of two criterion-related validity studies showing that TERA-2 correlates modestly (that is, .34 to .61) with other tests of reading. Finally, some evidence of construct validity is presented: TERA-2 is highly correlated with age; students with learning disabilities earned between 0.75 and 1.0 standard deviations below TERA-2's mean; and scores on TERA-2 correlate with the writing and total scores from the BSSI-D.

Summary

TERA-2 is an individually administered, norm-referenced test designed to evaluate emergent literacy skills between the ages of 3-0 and 9-11. It assesses these skills in three areas: Construction of Meaning, Knowledge of the Alphabet and Its Functions, and Conventions of Written Language. The process for locating children for TERA-2's norms is not described, and insufficient information is presented about the resulting norms to be confident that they are representative for each age group. The test has excellent internal consistency at most ages, and the evidence for stability, while limited, suggests that TERA-2 has adequate consistency over time. Evidence for content validity may be problematic, depending on the educator's orientation to reading. Clearly, there is some controversy about what are important elements to consider, and TERA-2's content may not be well received by professionals preferring a skills approach to teaching reading. Evidence for criterion-related and construct validity is limited.

---

10. The authors also used the one-parameter Rasch model (from item-response theory) to estimate reliability. However, because it is possible for children to guess on some of the items, this model seems inappropriate to us.

11. Test users who have a different orientation to reading are unlikely to find the number of items testing oral reading and comprehension sufficient for their purposes.

Test of Early Mathematics Ability, Second Edition (TEMA-2)

The Test of Early Mathematics Ability, second edition (TEMA-2; Ginsburg & Baroody, 1990) is an individually administered, norm-referenced test designed to evaluate the informal and formal mathematical thinking of children between the ages of 3-0 and 8-11. The 35 items assessing informal mathematical thinking tap children's understanding of relative magnitude (such as larger and smaller, closer and farther), counting, and calculation (that is, adding concrete objects). The 30 items assessing formal mathematical thinking evaluate children's knowledge of conventions (that is, reading and writing numbers), number facts, calculation (that is, use of formal addition and subtraction algorithms), and base-ten concepts. Basal and ceiling rules allow TEMA-2 to be administered in about 20 minutes.

Scores

Raw scores can be converted to percentiles and math quotients (MQs; standard scores with a mean of 100 and a standard deviation of 15). In addition, the authors claim that differences between formal and informal items can provide additional insight into the mathematical thinking of children. However, great care should be exercised in making such comparisons. Formal and informal items are not treated as separate subtests with independently calculated percentiles or standard scores; the reliability of the difference between formal and informal items is not provided.

Norms

TEMA-2 norms are a composite of 426 of the 617 children from the original TEMA normative sample and 470 additional students specifically tested for TEMA-2. The criteria and procedures for retaining children from the original normative sample are not discussed. The new sample was constructed using three techniques. First, Pro-Ed customers were asked to test 20 to 30 children. Second, professionals who had assisted in the norming of other tests published by Pro-Ed were also asked to test 20 to 30 students. Finally, examiners tested children in four "major census districts." The total sample closely approximates the U.S. (1985) demographics for sex, race, geographic region, urban/rural residence, and occupation of parents. However, no data are provided for the representativeness of each age sample—the information that allows a test user to assess the representativeness of the norms for the particular child being assessed. Each norm group consisted of more than 100 children, except for the 3-year-old group, which had 75 children.

Reliability

Estimates of internal consistency (coefficient alpha) are presented for each age; all coefficients exceed .90. Stability was estimated by retesting seventy-one 4- and 5-year-old children from Austin, Texas, after one week. The resulting coefficient was .94. No data are represented for other ages.

Validity

The major purpose of TEMA-2 is to identify children who are ahead of or behind their age peers. Evidence that TEMA-2 is valid for this purpose comes from the careful conceptualization of the domain (such as formal and informal thinking and their components) and from the statistical procedures used to retain items. Additional evidence comes from criterion-related validity studies. Although quite limited, there is some evidence to suggest that TEMA-2 relates to other measures of mathematics. Finally, we believe evidence for TEMA-2's construct validity comes from three sources: TEMA-2 scores are (1) highly correlated with chronological age, (2) moderately correlated with intelligence, and (3) substantially lower for "high-risk" children than for "normal" children. No evidence is presented that bears on three of TEMA-2's purposes: identifying strengths and weakness in mathematical thinking, suggesting instructional practices, or documenting achievement growth.

Summary

TEMA-2 is an individually administered, norm-referenced test designed to evaluate the informal and formal mathematical thinking of children from ages 3-0 to 8-11. Raw scores can be converted to percentiles and MQs. TEMA-2's norms are a mixture of old and new norms. Although the total sample appears representative, no information is provided about the representativeness of individual norm groups. Thus, some caution is warranted in interpreting scores. The total score has excellent internal consistency at all ages. Stability at ages 4 and 5 years (the only ages for which data are reported) is also excellent. Evidence for validity is limited to TEMA-2's ability to discriminate between high and low levels of mathematical thinking ability.

Coping with Dilemmas in Current Practice

There are three major dilemmas in assessing infants, toddlers, and preschoolers. The first is that the performances of children who are very young are so variable that long-term prediction (for example, one year) is not feasible. This inability to predict precisely is particularly pronounced with shorter, quickly administered (and less reliable) measures. Because there is relatively poor predictive validity, most inferences must be drawn with great care. If individuals wish to use these measures to predict school success, they should recognize that the closer the predicted measure (that is, the criterion) is to the predictor measure (that is, the test), the greater is the accuracy of the prediction. For example, language tests predict later language skills better than perceptual–motor tests do.

The second occurs when using tests of readiness and development as measures of current functioning and current attainment. If tests are to be used in this way, they must be scrutinized. This is especially true when using developmental measures to document pupil progress at the preschool level. To use developmental measures in this way, educators must make sure that there is appropriate linkage between the curriculum and the content of the test.

The third is the fact that students must be labeled to be eligible for preschool programs, but the act of labeling may set up expectations for limited pupil performance. Those who assess infants, toddlers, and preschool children need to assess within a context of situational specificity. There is much situational variability in performance, and this must be taken into account when making predictions or planning interventions.

Summary

Tests are used with preschoolers, infants, and toddlers for the purpose of screening. Focus generally is on identification of those children who would profit from early intervention. Assessment is based on the notions of prevention and developmental plasticity. It is assumed that it is a good idea to identify students early, intervene, change them, and prevent later problems. The impetus for preschool assessment is largely a legal one. The most recent major federal legislation to affect early assessment is Public Law 99-457.

There have been major advances in early assessment since the law was enacted in 1986. Educators now assess newborn infants, and that assessment typically involves neurobiological appraisal, consisting of assessment of neurological integrity, behavioral organization and needs, temperament, and state of consciousness. Increasingly, early childhood educators are engaged in planning interventions for medically high-risk infants and special-needs infants and toddlers, and they develop IFSPs.

Readiness measures are a special form of preschool assessment. They are administered for the purposes of predicting who is not ready for formal school entry and who will profit from remedial or compensatory intervention. Specific measures of school readiness were reviewed in the chapter.

There are three major dilemmas in early assessment. First, tests are administered for the purpose of predicting later performance, but at these young ages, performance is so highly variable that prediction is very difficult. Second, it is dangerous to use preschool measures as indexes of current standing. Third, provision of services is dependent on labeling children, but labeling may set up expectations for limited pupil performance.

Questions for Chapter Review and Thought

1. What two primary factors have contributed to the push for early intervention and associated assessment activities?

2. Describe the assessment-related parts of Public Law 99-457 and the basic components of the IFSP required by the law.

3. Discuss the four major areas of neurobiological assessment.

4. Identify and briefly discuss two features that distinguish readiness assessments from other forms of assessment instruments.

5. Delineate the three major dilemmas in assessing infants, toddlers, and preschoolers.

Resources for Further Investigation

Project

Using information found in the text, write a summary of three tests used to assess school readiness. Upon completion, compare your summary with the text summary. Then go to the *Mental Measurements Yearbook* (see "Print Resources"), and compare and contrast your summaries with the reviews of the tests you selected. If your summary differs from the review, did the reviewer use information and standards different from those that you used?

Print Resources

Als, H. (1984). *Manual for the Naturalistic Observation of Newborn Behavior (Preterm and Full-term Infants).*

Als, H., Lester, B., Tronick, E., & Brazelton, T. (1982). Toward a research instrument for the Assessment of Preterm Infants' Behavior (APIB). In H. E. Fitzgerald, B. M. Lester, & M. W. Yogman (Eds.), Theory and research in behavioral pediatrics (Vol. 1). New York: Plenum.

Bracken, B. A. (1988). Limitations of preschool instruments and standards for minimal levels of technical adequacy. *Journal of Psychoeducational Assessment, 5,* 313–326.

Brazelton, T. (1984). *Neonatal Behavioral Assessment Scale.* Philadelphia: J. B. Lippencott.

Buros, O. K. (1978). *The eighth mental measurements yearbook* (TOBE, p. 34). Highland Park, NJ: Gryphon.

Conoley, J. C., & Impara, J. C. (1995). *The twelfth mental measurements yearbook* (DIAL-R, pp. 283–286). Lincoln, NE: University of Nebraska Press.

Conoley, J. C., & Kramer, J. J. (1989). *The tenth mental measurements yearbook* (Bayley, pp. 72–84; BTBC-R, pp. 98–102).

Dubowitz, L. & Dubowitz, V. (1981). *The neurological assessment of the preterm and fullterm newborn infant.* [Clinics in developmental medicine, Spastics International Medical Publications, No. 79.] Philadelphia: J. B. Lippencott.

Ginsburg, H. & Baroody, A. (1990). *Test of Early Mathematics Ability, second edition.* Austin, TX: Pro-Ed.

Kramer, J. J., & Conoley, J. C. (1992). *The eleventh mental measurements yearbook* (IMSEL, pp. 407–408). Lincoln, NE: University of Nebraska Press.

Mitchell, J. V. (1985). *The ninth mental measurements yearbook* (MRT, pp. 968–970). Lincoln, NE: University of Nebraska Press.

Paget, K. D., & Nagle, R. J. (1986). A conceptual model of preschool assessment. *School Psychology Review, 15,* 154–165.

Reid, D., Hresko, W., & Hammill, D. (1989). *Test of Early Reading Ability, second edition.* Austin, TX: Pro-Ed.

Rosenblith, J. (1961). The modified Graham behavior Test for Neonates: Test–retest reliability, normative data, and hypotheses for future work. *Biologia Neonatorum, 3,* 174–192.

Technology Resources

Welcome to AGS On-Line Products and Services

http://www.agsnet.com/

Look for product and ordering information about the instruments available from American Guidance Service. Here you can find out information about the *Mullen Scales of Early Learning: AGS Edition; Developmental Indicators for the Assessment of Learning–Revised; System to Plan Early Childhood Services;* and the *Kaufman Survey of Early Academic and Language Skills.* Just search by product title.

Pro-Ed Catalog Information for Products

http://www.proedinc.com

Find product and ordering information about the *Developmental Observation Checklists.*

Assessment of Preschool Children

http://www.ed.gov/databases/ERIC_Digests/ed3899 64.html

The authors of this article describe why young children are difficult to assess and make suggestions about good assessment practices with preschool children.

Work Sampling System

http://www.hbem.com/trophy/perfermn/workss.htm

This page contains detailed informatoin concerning *Work Sampling System.*

chapter 29

Outcomes-Based Accountability Assessment

Are our schools producing the results we want? Until very recently, the focus in special education was on counting numbers of students served and on provision of services. Administrators could tell you how many students of what types had been tested and were being served in what kinds of settings by whom. What few administrators could do was provide evidence for the results or outcomes of the services being provided. The new Individuals with Disabilities Education Act (1997) requires state departments of education to account for educational outcomes for all students with disabilities. Since the early 1990s, there has been a dramatic shift in focus from serving students with disabilities to measuring the outcomes or results of the services provided.

Much of the impetus for this shift was the publication of *A Nation at Risk: The Imperative for Educational Reform* (U.S. Department of Education, 1983). In this document, the then-Secretary of Education revealed the low status of U.S. schoolchildren relative to their counterparts in other nations and reported that "the educational foundations of our society are presently being eroded by a rising tide of mediocrity that threatens our very future as a nation and a people" (p. 5). In this report, the secretary argued that the nation was at risk because mediocrity, not excellence, was the norm in education. Recommendations included more time for learning, better textbooks and other materials, more homework, higher expectations, stricter attendance policies, and improved standards, salaries, rewards, and incentives for teachers. The entire nation began to focus on raising educational standards, measuring performance, and achieving results. Policymakers and bureaucrats, who had been spending a great deal of money to fund special education, began demanding evidence of its effectiveness. In essence, they employed the old saw, "The proof of the pudding is in the eating"—arguing that it matters little what you do if it does not produce what you want.

Questions about how educational services are provided to students with disabilities echo the importance of looking at outcomes. For example, a special-education study group formed by the National Association of State Boards of Education recommended the integration of students with disabilities into general-education programs, based on the belief that all children can learn—not in an attempt to save money (National Association of State Boards of Education, 1992). The group also pointed out the need for (a) accountability systems that include students with disabilities and (b) local efforts to restructure schools to make special education an integral part of schools. The bottom line in educational reform is that it needs to focus on assessment of educational outcomes for students in general and for students in special-education programs in particular.

There is little disagreement about the need to focus our attention on the results of providing educational services to students with disabilities. Yet, until the 1990s, there was no agreement on the kinds of data that ought to be collected and used to assess the results of educational services and no agreement on a conceptual model to guide the practice of assessing outcomes. A major activity of the National Center on Educational Outcomes (NCEO), located at the University of Minnesota, is to develop a conceptual model of outcomes and indicators for guiding the outcomes-assessment process. NCEO developed a self-study guide for states and school districts to use in the development of systems of outcomes and indicators (Ysseldyke & Thurlow, 1993). In this chapter, we rely on the content of the self-study guide and describe the process that a school or school district would go through in developing a system to assess the extent to which it is achieving desired results. We use the model of outcomes and indicators as an example of an outcomes-and-indicators system, but not as the only example. We talk about how local communities can adopt or adapt the model to meet their needs. We describe ways to accomplish the following:

- Establish a solid foundation for educators' assessment efforts
- Develop, adopt, or adapt a conceptual model of outcomes and indicators
- Establish a data-collection and -reporting system
- Install an outcomes-based accountability system

Establish a Solid Foundation for Assessment Efforts

Accountability systems must be carefully thought out. It is important that stakeholders be involved up front and that they give considerable thought to why they want to measure outcomes. Considerable confusion exists in this field, so it is very important to define terms and consider the assumptions that underlie efforts to account for educational outcomes. Finally, it is critical to resolve some fundamental issues before beginning.

Involve Stakeholders Up Front

Stakeholders are those individuals in a community who have a personal interest in the measurement of educational outcomes: teachers, supervisors, providers of related services, parents, representatives of community agencies, and students. Involving stakeholders up front in the process of developing educational outcomes enhances their feeling of investment in the assessment process and their desire to participate in it. Involvement up front empowers those individuals or groups to chart their own activities and futures.

Decide Why We Measure Outcomes

There are four major reasons why stakeholders want to measure educational outcomes: instructional improvement, public accountability, public information, and policy formulation. First, data on the results of service provision can be useful in improving instructional programs for students. In fact, to improve instructional practices, it is imperative that school personnel have data illustrating the extent to which what they are doing is achieving the desired results. For example, school personnel might want to know the extent to which the math curriculum they are using is resulting in students earning high scores on math tests. Knowledge of results enables professionals to consider making changes in instructional programs. For instructional improvement, it is important that stakeholders reach agreement on assessment goals.

Second, data on outcomes are important for accountability: to document for people in authority that desired goals are being met. Tests are regularly given to students in most states, and data indicating how pupils are doing are provided to state agencies and school districts within states. The test scores can be used by legislators and policymakers to decide whether they are getting their money's worth from funds invested in education.

Third, data on educational outcomes are also useful in providing public information on the outcomes of schooling. You may have seen reports in newspapers indicating how the nation's youths are doing in math, reading, science, or other forms of literacy.

Fourth, data on outcomes are useful in policy formulation. Those who formulate educational policy repeatedly indicate the need to have information about outcomes of schooling in order to allocate resources and establish instructional processes.

Define Terms

The terms *outcomes* and *indicators* are used in many ways in the professional and popular literature. In fact, the multiple uses of the terms cause confusion. For example, some educators talk of assessing educational outcomes, whereas others talk about outcomes-based education. In this chapter, we talk about outcomes-based accountability. *Outcomes-based education* and *outcomes-based accountability* are not the same thing. The NCEO defines *outcomes* as "the results of interactions between individuals and schooling experiences" (Ysseldyke & Thurlow, 1993). Outcomes may be direct or indirect, positive or negative, and intended or unintended. Knowledge of the procedures necessary to register and vote may be a direct outcome of schooling. Whether a student votes later in life is an indirect outcome; it is determined by many more factors than what is learned in school. Employment is an indirect outcome of schooling. Schooling enables individuals to be employed, but actual employment is the result of many factors in addition to schooling. Those who measure the outcomes of schooling are concerned about both positive outcomes (such as learning to read) and negative outcomes (such as dropping out of school). They are also concerned about intended outcomes (for instance, the student's becoming a productive citizen) and unintended outcomes (for example, the student's getting arrested).

Indicators are defined as symbolic representations of one or more outcomes that can be used in making comparisons. They provide ways of knowing what could or should be considered to find out whether desired results are being reached. They can be numbers or other representations, such as test scores, levels of participation in activities, or perceptions of student accomplishments by parents or others. In the NCEO model of outcomes and indicators illustrated later in this chapter, we note that stakeholders have decided that an important outcome of schooling is that students "comply with school and community rules." Indicators of this outcome follow:

- Percentage of students who have been suspended or subjected to other disciplinary action
- Vandalism rate and magnitude
- Crime rate and magnitude

Consider the Assumptions That Underlie a Conceptual Model of Outcomes and Indicators

Any system of outcomes and indicators is based on a number of assumptions. Those who want to assess educational outcomes will have to consider carefully the assumptions that underlie the system they develop. The NCEO and educational stakeholders engaged in much discussion and debate on the assessment of educational outcomes and came to agreement on the following:

- A model of outcomes is needed for all students and, at the broadest level, should apply to all students, regardless of the characteristics of individuals.
- A model of outcomes should primarily focus on intended outcomes but be sensitive to unintended outcomes of schooling.
- A model of outcomes should include both direct and indirect outcomes.
- Indicators of outcomes for students receiving special-education services should be related, conceptually and statistically, to those identified for students without disabilities.
- Indicators should reflect the diversity of gender, culture, race, and other characteristics of the students in today's school population.
- Whereas indicators should meet research standards, those that do not meet such standards may still be used in assessing educational outcomes.

- A comprehensive system of indicators should provide the data needed to make policy decisions at the national, state, and local levels.
- A comprehensive system of indicators should be based on demonstrated functional relationships between outcome indicators and indicators of educational inputs, as well as contextual characteristics and processes; however, valued indicators may be included even if functional relationships have not been established.
- A comprehensive system of indicators should be flexible, dynamic, and responsive to review and criticism. It should also change to meet identified needs and future developments in the measurement of educational inputs, contexts, processes, and outcomes.

Resolve Fundamental Issues in Outcome Assessment

It is important to resolve a number of fundamental issues before trying to put in place an outcomes-based accountability system. In our experience trying to implement such systems, we have found that school-district personnel first need to decide whether they are going to support a single accountability system for all students or one that is different for students with and without disabilities. They must also decide whether to assess and account for the same or different outcomes for students of differing ages and grade levels. Also, for students with disabilities, district personnel must decide whether to have different accountability systems for differing categories of students. Finally, they must decide whether they are going to collect data on the performance of individuals, school systems, or both. Unless these issues are resolved up front, there will be much confusion and debate in the development of a system.

Develop, Adopt, or Adapt a Model of Outcomes

It is critical that consensus be reached on the approach that will be used to measure outcomes of schooling. This involves selecting an approach, defining outcome domains, and defining outcomes and indicators.

Select an Approach

The outcome-assessment process should be driven by a conceptual model that shows how the educational system should work. The NCEO developed a conceptual framework for educational accountability by convening groups of stakeholders to identify what they wanted out of the educational system. These stakeholders did not identify a narrow set of desired outcomes; rather, they indicated that they expect students to complete the educational process with a broad set of skills and behaviors that go beyond literacy and academic content knowledge. Stakeholders identified six outcome domains: physical health, responsibility and independence,

● ● ● ● **FIGURE 29.1**   *NCEO Conceptual Model of Outcomes*

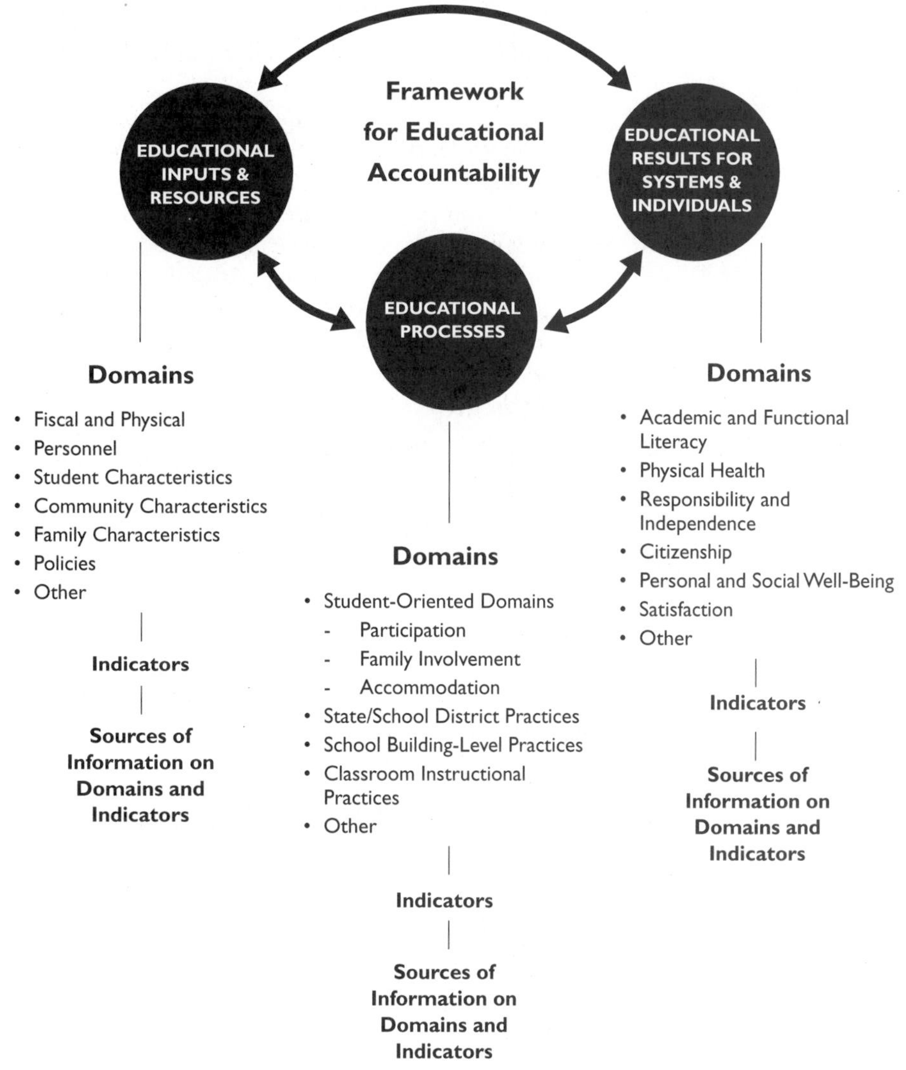

Framework for Educational Accountability

EDUCATIONAL INPUTS & RESOURCES

EDUCATIONAL RESULTS FOR SYSTEMS & INDIVIDUALS

EDUCATIONAL PROCESSES

Domains

- Fiscal and Physical
- Personnel
- Student Characteristics
- Community Characteristics
- Family Characteristics
- Policies
- Other

Indicators

Sources of Information on Domains and Indicators

Domains

- Student-Oriented Domains
  - Participation
  - Family Involvement
  - Accommodation
- State/School District Practices
- School Building-Level Practices
- Classroom Instructional Practices
- Other

Indicators

Sources of Information on Domains and Indicators

Domains

- Academic and Functional Literacy
- Physical Health
- Responsibility and Independence
- Citizenship
- Personal and Social Well-Being
- Satisfaction
- Other

Indicators

Sources of Information on Domains and Indicators

citizenship, academic and functional literacy, personal and social well-being, and satisfaction. The conceptual framework is shown in Figure 29.1.

Underlying the model is the assumption that schools, districts, and states differ in the inputs and resources available to educate students and that they both provide educational opportunities and put students through an educational process. Figure 29.1 illustrates the reciprocal relationship between inputs, processes, and results. The framework illustrated in the figure is now being used in states and local districts to guide the process of assessing outcomes.

Define Outcome Domains

The outcome domains shown in Figure 29.1 are defined as follows:

- *Physical health*—healthy behaviors, attitudes, and knowledge related to physical health
- *Responsibility and independence*—behavior that reflects the ability to function independently and to assume responsibility for self
- *Citizenship*—participation as a good citizen in society
- *Academic and functional literacy*—use of information obtained in school to function in society, to achieve goals, and to develop knowledge
- *Personal and social well-being*—socially acceptable and healthy behaviors, attitudes, and knowledge regarding mental adjustment
- *Satisfaction*—favorable attitude toward education

Specify Indicators

Before we attempt to develop measures of educational outcomes, we must, of course, identify indicators. The NCEO framework includes a specification of indicators at five developmental levels: age 3 years, age 6 years, grade 4, grade 8, and school completion. The important indicators were identified through a consensus-building process involving many stakeholder groups. Figure 29.2 lists

⬤ ⬤ ⬤ **FIGURE 29.2**   Indicators for Responsibility and Independence Domain

Students Demonstrate Age-Appropriate Independence

- Separate easily from parents/guardians in familiar and comfortable situations
- Initiate and follow through on activities
- Occupy self without continuous adult involvement
- Show concern for others, including family members
- Able to decide when help is needed and obtain it in an emergency
- Act responsibly in a family, group, or individual situation

Students are Responsible for Self

- Feed self with limited assistance
- Feed self and participate appropriately in mealtime routines
- Use the toilet with limited assistance
- Dress self with limited assistance
- Dress self
- Attend to own hygiene needs
- Follow basic safety rules
- Take care of own belongings
- Look to others for support
- Access a support network that effectively advocates for student
- Effectively advocate for self
- Prioritize and set goals, and persevere toward them

Students Get About in Environment

- Get to and from destinations within school (i.e., familiar locations)
- Get to and from a variety of destinations (e.g., walk, bicycle, use public transportation)
- Have an awareness of the larger community
- Complete transactions in the community (e.g., shop, to the library, bank, etc.)
- Know how to access community services (e.g., rehabilitation, counseling, employment, health, etc.)
- Have a driver's permit or license

the school-completion indicators identified for the responsibility and independence domain. School personnel will have to engage in a consensus-building process in their own districts to reach agreement about those indicators that are most important in each of the outcome domains.

Establish a Data-Collection and Reporting System

Stakeholders should give considerable thought to sources of information or data that can be used to illustrate educational results. Decisions need to be made about where data will come from, how they will be collected, and how results will be reported to and used by the general community.

Identify Data Sources

Those who engage in outcomes-based accountability will necessarily have to identify sources from which they can get data or the extent to which results are being met. In the development of such a system, consider the sources of data shown in Table 29.1 as possible places to get information. A fundamental premise to guide the data-collection process is that it should rely as much as possible on use of existing information. Developing new data-collection instruments and procedures requires a carefully considered process of design, development, field testing, revision, sampling, training, data collection, data entry, error checking, and analysis.

TABLE 29.1 ● *Possible Sources of Data on Responsibility and Independence*

Responsibility and Independence

- Teacher observations in free-time situations (e.g., recess, lunch, before and after school)
- Records of parent/guardian–teacher conferences
- Parent/guardian survey or interview
- Teacher survey or interview
- Student records regarding on-time assignments and finished assignments
- Student survey or interview
- School or district records
- Data on use of personal care assistant services
- Lost and found reports in building or district
- School counselor records
- Teacher observation of cooperative learning groups
- Teacher observation of personal appearance
- Results of teacher assessments, e.g., the *Vineland Adaptive Behavior Scales* or the *Performance Assessment for Self-Sufficiency (PASS), Responsibility and Independence Scale for Adolescents, Scales of Independent Behavior*
- Open-ended test
- Administrative records from postsecondary institutions

Outcomes-based accountability systems that require development of new measures or methods of data collection probably will not fare well.

Develop or Adapt Data-Collection and -Analysis Mechanisms

You will probably have to create new data-collection mechanisms to address new indicators or to include new populations that you have not included before. Data-collection systems must be designed in such a way that they are sensitive to cultural differences during sampling, instrument development, data collection, and data analysis.

Decide How Information Will Be Reported and Used

Information on educational outcomes (accountability systems) needs to be reported in ways that are meaningful to the intended audience. It is important to ask members of the audience (for instance, administrators, school board members) what would help them make decisions consistent with the stated purpose of the accountability system (such as program improvement, public information, or policy formulation). Probably the most important decision to be made is how the data will be used. Will rewards and consequences be given as a result of educational outcomes? Other reporting decisions to be made include levels of reporting (system versus individual), formats and types of reports, types of comparisons to be reported, ways of presenting and grouping data, and vehicles for dissemination of information.

● ● ● ● ● ● ● ● ● ● ● ● ● ● ● ● ● ● ● ●

Install an Outcomes-Based Accountability System

A system of outcomes and indicators cannot be installed overnight. Those who use the information on outcomes will need to see personal and programmatic benefits before the system can be considered fully in place. There must be incentives for teachers, parents, and administrators who will ultimately ensure the success of the system.

Two commonly used incentives are public comparisons and sanctions for failure to meet standards or goals. *Public comparisons* formally display schools, districts, or states side by side. *Sanctioning* involves negative techniques such as withdrawal of accreditation, takeovers of schools, and reduction of funding based on identification of inadequate outcomes. Both comparisons and sanctions are high-stakes uses of any accountability system. They can lead to overemphasis on appearances, without substantive changes.

Change in measurement and accountability systems occurs in the same way as it occurs in any system. State or governmental agencies fund research and demonstration projects, establish networking and recognition systems, and provide resources for use of outcomes-based accountability systems. Personnel in state departments of education provide technical assistance to local school districts that are trying to implement accountability systems.

Once an outcomes-based accountability system is in place and being used, we may be able to identify the extent to which the interventions used with individuals who have disabilities are working as we would like them to work. Systemwide accountability assessment should enable us to make judgments about the extent of the system's success.

Current State Practices in Assessment of Educational Outcomes

Since 1991, the NCEO has surveyed state assessment personnel to identify state practices and activities in the assessment of educational outcomes for students with disabilities. Some of the major findings of its surveys follow:

- States gather very few data on students with disabilities. They usually gather data only on attendance, participation in programs, and the way in which the students exit the system (for instance, as graduates or as dropouts).
- Few state-level special data-collection efforts, other than postschool status studies, yield outcome data on students with disabilities.
- We cannot say much about the performance of students with disabilities because they are excluded from most assessment and accountability systems. The students often are excluded from testing, or their scores are excluded from reports of the results of testing.
- Several states are exploring ways to collect outcomes data.

In the sections that follow, we describe outcomes-based accountability practices in two states: Texas and North Carolina. You can obtain similar information about the accountability system used in your own state by going to the web site for the Council of Chief State School Offices (**www.ccsso.org**).

North Carolina

Standards and Assessment System

North Carolina has a fully implemented statewide accountability reform program called the "ABCs of Public Education" that is entering its third year of implementation as we go to press. As part of the accountability system, the state set achievement (growth/gain) goals and performance standards in reading, writing, and mathematics at the elementary/middle school years, and in reading, mathematics, science, and social studies at the high school level. In addition to these achievement standards, the state has also set performance standards. At least 50 percent of students in each school are expected to be at or above grade level. The state has also mandated a level of competency for each of its content standards in reading, writing, history, mathematics, and science.

North Carolina Testing Program, Grades 3–8   As part of the assessment system, students are administered the North Carolina End-of-Grade (EOG) tests. These are multiple-choice, criterion-referenced tests that measure the achievement of the curricular objectives described in the math and reading comprehension statewide content standards. Most recently, North Carolina passed new Student Accountability Standards that require students in the third, fifth, and eighth grades to demonstrate that they are performing at grade level in reading, writing, and math in order to be promoted to the next grade.

North Carolina Testing Program, Grades 9–12   High school students are administered the North Carolina End-of-Course (EOC) tests in order to evaluate the competencies they have gained in a number of subject areas (Algebra I and II, Biology, Chemistry, English I and II, Geometry, U.S. History, Physical Science, and Physics). Again, these are criterion-referenced, multiple-choice tests, except for the English II writing test, which requires students to produce an essay. In addition to the EOCs, there are competency tests in math and reading that all students must pass in order to receive a high school diploma. In grade 10, students take a multiple-choice test designed test to measure competencies in language arts and math by the end of grade 10. New legislation has recently added a new exit exam of essential skills, to be taken in eleventh grade. Students must pass the exam to graduate.

Exemptions

A limited-English-proficient (LEP) student (English-language learner) may be exempted for up to two years if the student's English-language proficiency has been assessed as novice/low to intermediate/low in listening, reading, and writing. A student whose English-language proficiency has been assessed as intermediate/high or advanced may also be exempted from tests that require written responses for two years. Local committees are responsible for making the appropriate decisions about participation and accommodations. Testing accommodations available to LEP students include repeating of directions, oral reading of questions in English, a familiar test giver, and translated directions.

Students with disabilities may be exempted from the competency tests if the exemption is stated in the student's IEP and if the student is not following the standard course of study. IEP committees are responsible for determining participation eligibility and accommodation use. Criteria for determining eligibility include type or severity of disability, time spent in special-education settings, alignment of instructional goals and test content, and coursework completed in regular educational settings. Parents must sign a statement indicating that they fully understand the consequences of exemption, and this statement becomes a part of the student's permanent record. Testing accommodations available for students with disabilities include oral reading of directions, signing of directions, repeating of directions, Braille editions, use of magnifying equipment, large-print editions, and oral reading of questions for tests other than reading tests.

Recently, a new accountability measure required that every K–8 school test at least 98 percent of its eligible students. If a school fails to test 98 percent of its students, the State Board of Education may designate the school as low-performing.

Rating of Schools

Schools are classified into several categories in order to determine whether they are in need of improvement or eligible to receive awards. The award or recognition a school receives is determined in most cases by the school's attainment as reflected in the growth composites (expected and exemplary) by the performance composite. The categories include Schools of Excellence, Schools of Distinction, Top 25 Schools in Academic Growth and Top 10 High Schools in Gain, Schools with Exemplary Growth, Schools with Expected Growth, Schools Receiving No Recognition, and Low-Performing Schools. For example, Schools of Excellence are those that meet expected growth or expected gain standards and in which at least 90 percent of students are performing at or above Level III and Level IV (on a four-level scale). Low-Performing Schools fail to meet their expected growth/ gain standard and see fewer than 50 percent of the students performing at or above grade level.

Public Reporting

North Carolina produces *A Report Card for the ABCs of Public Education* in two annual volumes to provide the results of the statewide accountability program and to report subgroup statistics. The *Report Card* contains statewide and school system–level data on those at or above grade level by grade, race, gender, and disability status. It is also disseminated electronically via the Internet.

Rewards

School incentive rewards recognize those schools that achieve or exceed expected annual gain/growth. Schools with expected growth can receive up to $750 for each certified staff member and up to $375 for each teacher assistant. Schools with exemplary growth can receive up to $1,500 for each certified staff member and up to $500 for each teacher assistant. School improvement grants are also available on a competitive basis.

Sanctions

North Carolina has a statewide system of school support with many components: assistance teams for the lowest-performing schools, NC HELPS (which provides financial resources, professional development, and services such as Curriculum alignment), and school improvement grants. If sanctions are still needed after an assistance team intervention, a second assistance team intervention will be provided. This team may recommend that a teacher, principal, director, or supervisor be dismissed or demoted. It will also notify parents of students attending the school that the school has failed to meet the minimum growth standards. These schools may also be subject to loss of accreditation.

(Data adapted from the CCSSO web site of *State Education Accountability Systems*)

Texas

Standards and Assessment System

Texas is a state that is further along in the development of its educational accountability system; it was attempting to be inclusive of all student needs even before IDEA 97. It has statewide content and student performance standards in reading, writing, mathematics, science, and social studies, known as Texas Essential Knowledge and Skills (TEKS). These were first implemented in 1985, with 1997 revisions to clarify instructional objectives for each grade and subject. A core component of evaluating students' achievement is a statewide student assessment (Texas Assessment of Academic Skills, or TAAS) that is administered in grades 3–8 and 10 in reading and math; in grades 4, 8, and 10 in writing; and in grade 8 in social studies and science. The grade 10 TAAS is an exit-level assessment required for high school graduation. Students have seven more opportunities to take the TAAS exit exam. Year-to-year progress is measured and tracked for individual, school, district, and state growth via the Texas Learning Index.

Not only are students tested on the TAAS, but students completing specific coursework are required to take end-of-course examinations in Algebra I, Biology I, English II, and U.S. History. These tests are considered part of the state assessment system but are not part of TAAS (CCSSO Accountability System Survey, 1999). Students planning to continue in higher education in a Texas public college or university must take the Texas Academic Skills Program test (TASP).

Exemption Policies

There are exemption policies for students with disabilities and English-language learners (ELLs). The local Admission, Review, and Dismissal committee (ARD) recommends the appropriate state assessment option for students in special education. If exempted from the TAAS, the student with disabilities must take an alternative assessment. Decisions are made for each tested subject area. The ARD committee also specifies the accommodations and modifications available to the student with disabilities during testing. This same committee determines whether the student must pass the exit-level TAAS in order to graduate; regular-education students must pass all sections of the test in order to receive a high school diploma. Local Language Proficiency Assessment committees recommend the appropriate state assessment option for each ELL student. An ELL student in grades 3 through 8 may take an alternative assessment (such as a Spanish TAAS or a test from the state-approved list of alternative assessments) only three separate times. After that, the student must take the English version of the test. In Texas, approximately 90 percent of the ELL students are Spanish-speaking.

Rating of Schools and Accreditation

Schools in Texas must achieve adequate yearly progress on three indicators: pass rates on the reading, math, and writing sections of the TAAS at grades 3–8 and 10; annual dropout rate, grades 7–12; and annual attendance rate, grades 1–12. Schools are rated as exemplary, recognized, acceptable, or low-performing. Performance standards are raised annually: the TAAS pass-rate standard for academically acceptable schools was 25 percent in 1994. This rate has risen 5 percent per year, and districts will have to meet a 50 percent passing rate for all students and all student groups by 2000. To be ranked as recognized, the school must meet a pass-rate standard of 80 percent, and for exemplary status, the pass rates have remained at 90 percent. From 1994 to 1998, TAAS pass rates excluded the results of students with disabilities who met district mobility criteria; in 1999, pass rates will reflect the results of students with disabilities and students tested on the Spanish TAAS who meet mobility criteria.

Public Reporting

Texas has an information management system, the Academic Excellence Indicator System (AEIS), which provides reports at the district and school levels on all performance indicators as well as profile data items (student, staff, and financial information). Student data are disaggregated by ethnicity, sex, and socioeconomic status, and for students in special education.

Rewards

The Texas Successful Schools Award System (TSSAS) provides monetary awards to schools that are rated exemplary or recognized. A portion is also reserved for schools that are rated acceptable, but that have made significant gains in student performance as measured by comparable improvement in the preceding year. Comparable improvement is determined by comparing a school's annual Texas Learning Index (TLI) growth for matched students in math and reading to the growth of 40 other schools with similar demographic characteristics. Five million dollars has been appropriated for this program in the 1998–99 school year. The highest-performing districts and schools are also exempted from specific regulations and requirements. Minimum awards range from $500 to $5,000 per school. These monies must be used first for academic enhancement purposes. The state also provides assistance to the local education agency or school through the Texas School Improvement Initiative. These on-site reviews are completed by peer review teams who volunteer their time (travel is covered by the district).

Sanctions

If a district does not meet accreditation criteria, the commissioner may take any number of actions, including issue of public notice, a public hearing by the district board of trustees, submission of an improvement plan for state review, and an on-site peer review. If the school and/or district fails to meet acceptable standards, the commissioner may assign a monitor or management team. State takeover of a district is a possibility, but has occurred only once in previous history.

(Data adapted from the CCSSO web site on State Education Accountability Systems, 1999)

Summary

Today, much activity is directed toward demonstrating the extent to which education is working for students with disabilities. This has been part of a larger focus on the results of education. One way to demonstrate results is to systematically evaluate the extent to which desired results or outcomes are being achieved. This, of course, involves specifying the desired outcomes and then measuring or assessing the extent to which they are being met.

As school districts and states establish outcomes-based accountability systems. it is important that they go through a number of steps. Stakeholders must be involved in all phases of the accountability assessment process—especially in the beginning phase. Those who assess the outcomes of schooling must decide specifically why they want to measure results and then carefully define their terms. The process of deciding what outcomes and indicators are to be measured should be a shared process involving representatives of all relevant stakeholder groups.

Questions for Chapter Review and Thought

1. What fundamental assumptions underlie the process of collecting outcome-assessment information?

2. What do we know about current state practices in the assessment of educational outcomes?

3. What steps should state and school-district personnel go through as they develop outcomes-based accountability systems?

Resources for Further Investigation

Project

Go to the CCSSO web site (**www.ccsso.org**) and look under State Education Accountability Systems. Look up the system for your state, and describe the ways in which assessment data are collected.

Print Resources

Shriner, J. G., Gilman, C. J., Thurlow, M. L., & Ysseldyke, J. E. (1995). Trends in state assessment of educational outcomes. *Diagnostique, 20,* 101–119.

Thurlow, M. L., Ysseldyke, J., Vanderwood, M. L., & Spande, G. (1994). A guide to developing and implementing a system of outcomes and indicators. *Special Services in the Schools, 9,* 115–126.

Ysseldyke, J. E., Krentz, J., Elliott, J., Thurlow, M. L., Erickson, R., & Moore, M. (1998). *NCEO framework for educational accountability.* Minneapolis: National Center on Educational Outcomes, University of Minnesota.

Technology Resources

National Education Goals Panel

http://www.negp.gov/

This is the web site that reports progress toward the eight National Education Goals focusing on academic standards and student assessment.

National Institute on Student Achievement, Curriculum and Assessment

http://www.ed.gov/offices/OERI/SAI

This home page reports on the coordinated and comprehensive program of research and development of the National Institute on Student Achievement, Curriculum and Assessment.

National Assessment Governing Board

http://www.nagb.org/

Learn about the National Assessment of Educational Progress, the only ongoing, national test of academic progress. Included is a self-critical plan for redesigning the testing program.

National Center on Educational Outcomes

http:/www.coled.umn.edu/NCEO/

This home page describes the focus of NCEO activities on educational outcomes for all students, including students with disabilities. Also offered are summaries of the center's publications and links to related web sites.

PDE—Gifted Outcomes-Based Education

http://www.bbpages.psu.edu/reference/40006/400065.html

This document explains the basis of outcome-based education including strategies for success with gifted students.

Assessment of Student Learning Outcomes

http://www.sbctc.ctc.edu/Board/Educ/outcomes/DEassessment.html

This web page lists references with links to other web pages concerning a broad selection of topics, including learning outcomes and their assessments.

Appendixes

Appendix 1

AREAS OF THE NORMAL CURVE

Area equals the proportion of cases between the z-score and the mean; extreme area equals .5000 less the proportion of cases between the z-score and the mean.

z	.00	.01	.02	.03	.04	.05	.06	.07	.08	.09
0.0	.0000	.0040	.0080	.0120	.0160	.0199	.0239	.0279	.0319	.0359
0.1	.0398	.0438	.0478	.0517	.0557	.0596	.0636	.0675	.0714	.0753
0.2	.0793	.0832	.0871	.0910	.0948	.0987	.1026	.1064	.1103	.1141
0.3	.1179	.1217	.1255	.1293	.1331	.1368	.1406	.1443	.1480	.1517
0.4	.1554	.1591	.1628	.1664	.1700	.1736	.1772	.1808	.1844	.1879
0.5	.1915	.1950	.1985	.2019	.2054	.2088	.2123	.2157	.2190	.2224
0.6	.2257	.2291	.2324	.2357	.2389	.2422	.2454	.2486	.2517	.2549
0.7	.2580	.2611	.2642	.2673	.2704	.2734	.2764	.2794	.2823	.2852
0.8	.2881	.2910	.2939	.2967	.2995	.3023	.3051	.3078	.3106	.3133
0.9	.3159	.3186	.3212	.3238	.3264	.3289	.3315	.3340	.3365	.3389
1.0	.3413	.3438	.3461	.3485	.3508	.3531	.3554	.3577	.3599	.3621
1.1	.3643	.3665	.3686	.3708	.3729	.3749	.3770	.3790	.3810	.3830
1.2	.3849	.3869	.3888	.3907	.3925	.3944	.3962	.3980	.3997	.4015
1.3	.4032	.4049	.4066	.4082	.4099	.4115	.4131	.4147	.4162	.4177
1.4	.4192	.4207	.4222	.4236	.4251	.4265	.4279	.4292	.4306	.4319
1.5	.4332	.4345	.4357	.4370	.4382	.4394	.4406	.4418	.4429	.4441
1.6	.4452	.4463	.4474	.4484	.4495	.4505	.4515	.4525	.4535	.4545
1.7	.4554	.4564	.4573	.4582	.4591	.4599	.4608	.4616	.4625	.4633
1.8	.4641	.4649	.4656	.4664	.4671	.4678	.4686	.4693	.4699	.4706
1.9	.4713	.4719	.4726	.4732	.4738	.4744	.4750	.4756	.4761	.4767
2.0	.4772	.4778	.4783	.4788	.4793	.4798	.4803	.4808	.4812	.4817
2.1	.4821	.4826	.4830	.4834	.4838	.4842	.4846	.4850	.4854	.4857
2.2	.4861	.4864	.4868	.4871	.4875	.4878	.4881	.4884	.4887	.4890
2.3	.4893	.4896	.4898	.4901	.4904	.4906	.4909	.4911	.4913	.4916
2.4	.4918	.4920	.4922	.4925	.4927	.4929	.4931	.4932	.4934	.4936
2.5	.4938	.4940	.4941	.4943	.4945	.4946	.4948	.4949	.4951	.4952
2.6	.4953	.4955	.4956	.4957	.4959	.4960	.4961	.4962	.4963	.4964
2.7	.4965	.4966	.4967	.4968	.4969	.4970	.4971	.4972	.4973	.4974
2.8	.4974	.4975	.4976	.4977	.4977	.4978	.4979	.4979	.4980	.4981
2.9	.4981	.4982	.4982	.4983	.4984	.4984	.4985	.4985	.4986	.4986
3.0	.4987	.4987	.4987	.4988	.4988	.4989	.4989	.4989	.4990	.4990

SOURCE: From *Statistics: An Intuitive Approach,* by G. H. Weinberg and J. A. Schumaker. Copyright © 1981, 1974, 1969, 1962 Brooks/Cole Publishing Company, Pacific Grove, California 93950. A division of International Thompson Publishing, Inc. By permission of the publisher.

Appendix 2

LIST OF EQUATIONS USED IN THE TEXT

Location in Text	Term Defined	Equation
Ch. 4, p. 77	Mean	$\overline{X} = \dfrac{\Sigma X}{N}$ (Equation 4.1)
Ch. 4, p. 78	Variance	$S^2 = \dfrac{\Sigma(X - \overline{X})^2}{N}$ (Equation 4.2)
		or
		$S^2 = \dfrac{\Sigma X^2}{N} = \left(\dfrac{\Sigma X}{N}\right)^2$
Ch. 4, p. 85	Pearson product–moment correlation coefficient, where X and Y are scores on two tests	$r = \dfrac{N\Sigma XY - (\Sigma X)(\Sigma Y)}{\sqrt{N\Sigma X^2 - (\Sigma X)^2}\ \ \sqrt{N\Sigma Y^2 - (\Sigma Y)^2}}$
		or
		$r = \dfrac{\Sigma Z_x Z_y}{n}$
Ch. 5, p. 95	Percentile rank for a particular score	%ile = Percentage of people scoring below the score plus one half the percentage of people obtaining the score
Ch. 5, p. 97	z-score	$z = \dfrac{(X - \overline{X})}{S}$ (Equation 5.1)
Ch. 5, p. 97	Any standard score	$SS = \overline{X}_{ss} + (S_{ss})(z)$ (Equation 5.2)
Ch. 7, p. 126	Coefficient alpha	$r_{aa} = \dfrac{k}{k-1}\left(1 - \dfrac{\Sigma S^2_{items}}{S^2_{test}}\right)$ (Equation 7.2)
Ch. 7, p. 128	Point-to-point agreement	$\dfrac{(100)\text{number of agreements on occurrence and nonoccurrence}}{\text{number of observations}}$ (Equation 7.3)
Ch. 7, p. 128	Percent agreement on occurrence	$\dfrac{100(\text{number of agreements on occurrence})}{\text{number of observations} - \text{number of agreements on nonoccurrence}}$ (Equation 7.4)

Location in Text	Term Defined	Equation
Ch. 7, p. 129	Cohen's coefficient of agreement	$\text{Kappa} = \dfrac{P_{\text{occurence}} - P_{\text{expected}}}{1 - P_{\text{expected}}}$ (Equation 7.5)
Ch. 7, p. 130	Spearman–Brown formula to correct for test length	$r_{xx} = \dfrac{2r_{(\frac{1}{2})(\frac{1}{2})}}{1 + r_{(\frac{1}{2})(\frac{1}{2})}}$ (Equation 7.6)
Ch. 7, p. 134	Standard error of measurement	$\text{SEM} = S\sqrt{1 - r_{xx}}$ (Equation 7.7)
Ch. 7, p. 136	Estimated true score	$X' = \overline{X} + (r_{xx})(X - \overline{X})$ (Equation 7.8)
Ch. 7, p. 139	Lower and upper limits of a confidence interval, where z-score determines level of confidence	Lower limit $= X' - (z)(\text{SEM})$ Upper limit $= X' + (z)(\text{SEM})$ (Equation 7.9)
Ch. 7, p. 141	Reliability of a predicted difference	$\hat{D} = \dfrac{r_{bb} + (r_{aa})(r^2_{ab}) - 2r^2_{ab}}{1 - r^2_{ab}}$ (Equation 7.10)
Ch. 7, p. 141	Standard deviation of a predicted difference	$S_{\hat{D}} = S_b\sqrt{1 - r^2_{ab}}$ (Equation 7.11)
Ch. 7, p. 141	Reliability of a difference of obtained scores	$r_{\text{dif}} = \dfrac{\frac{1}{2}(r_{aa} + r_{bb}) - r_{ab}}{1 - r_{ab}}$ (Equation 7.12)
Ch. 7, p. 142	Standard deviation of obtained difference	$S_{\text{dif}} = \sqrt{S^2_a + S^2_b - 2r_{ab}S_aS_b}$ (Equation 7.13)
Ch. 7, p. 142	Standard error of measurement of a difference	$\text{SEM}_{\text{dif}} = \sqrt{S^2_a + S^2_b - 2r_{ab}S_aS_b} \times$ $\sqrt{1 - \dfrac{\frac{1}{2}(r_{aa} + r_{bb}) - r_{ab}}{1 - r_{ab}}}$ (Equation 7.14)
Ch. 7, p. 142	Estimated true difference	$d' = (\text{obtained difference})(r_{xx\,(\text{dif})})$ (Equation 7.15)

Appendix 3

HOW TO REVIEW A TEST

We have often been asked how we go about analyzing and reviewing tests—both for this book and in general. So we have decided to include a how-to section. Before starting an analysis of a test, you must first assemble the materials. We find that it is best to order a specimen kit and any supplementary manuals available. Be prepared to experience difficulty obtaining material from some test publishers. When you request a specimen kit and supplementary materials, you will occasionally receive all materials. More often, when you review specimen sets, you'll learn that additional materials must be ordered separately. Sometimes, it takes a very long time to figure out just what is published where. It may take up to six months to acquire all the material on a test. Sometimes, you just never obtain materials. Patience and perseverance are almost always required.

When materials arrive, prepare yourself properly to begin your review. The right setting is very important. A well-ventilated, well-lit room (preferably a bit on the chilly side) and a hard, straight-backed chair are essential.

Next, and more important, adopt a show-me attitude. Do not expect test authors to admit in the manuals that the test was poorly normed because there was no money to pay testers or that the test has inadequate reliability because they didn't develop enough test items. Test authors put the best possible face on their tests, as might be expected. You simply cannot accept the claims made by test authors and their colleagues who write the technical manuals. If you accepted them at their word, they would only have to say that they had a "good, reliable, valid, and well-normed test." Test authors must *demonstrate* that their tests are reliable, valid, and well normed.

After assembling the relevant materials and finding a suitable place in which to ask, "Where's the proof?" we usually follow these procedures. First, we skim through the material to get a general idea of what the test is intended to do and what is included in each document that accompanies it. We generally keep notes on several separate sheets of paper—one for each topic that we consider: background and purposes, behavior sampled, scores, norms, reliability, and validity.

Then we reread the manuals. You might expect that test authors would organize test manuals neatly so that you could turn to the table of contents, find the section on, for example, reliability, and turn to the pages indicated. Sometimes, yes—but more often, no. If a manual does not have section headings or chapters, we just begin reading and making notes under our headings. If a manual is divided into sections, we start by reading about the behaviors sampled by the test. (It doesn't matter too much where you start, except that validity is best left until last.) Test manuals frequently contain a useful description of the behaviors sampled, but more often they merely name the domains sampled. For example, the authors of a test may say that it assesses reading, but that does not tell you whether it assesses reading recognition, reading comprehension, or oral reading. Look at the test directions (especially directions on how to score student responses) and the protocol (the answer form). These materials generally give you a pretty good idea of what behaviors are actually measured. Then, try to describe the behaviors in straightforward terms—avoid psychological and educational jargon.

Next, we look at the section on norms. When evaluating a test's norms, first note the ages (or grades, in the case of achievement tests) of the students on whom the test was normed. Then look for statements describing the students. Also, anticipate quantification of the norm groups. For example, you should anticipate that the test author will tell you how many boys and how many girls and how many persons from various ethnic or racial groups were tested at each age or grade. You should also look for geographic information. For example, what percentage of the sample lived in big cities or in the Northwest? Finally, expect socioeconomic information about the students: parents' occupations, parents' educational attainment, or income of the household. Look for an explicit comparison of the characteristics of the norm group with the national population, as described in the most recent census. (Sometimes, test authors include all the data and all the comparisons in neat tabular form.) You may find substantial discrepancies between the norm sample and the population. Generally, we look for correspondence between the sample and the population within about 5 percent. Thus, if 31 percent of the sample lived in the Southwest and only 26 percent of the U.S. population live in the Southwest, we would not be overly concerned about the discrepancy. We realize that this is an arbitrary margin of error. If you prefer a different one, that's fine.

Information on scores is apt to be located in many places: in the section on scoring the test, in the description of the norms, in a separate section on scores, in the section dealing with the interpretation of scores, or in the norm tables themselves. Generally, the best place to find information on the types of scores available is in the norm tables. These tables allow the conversion of raw scores to derived scores and subtest scores to total scores. The next best place to look is in the section on scoring the test. There you find the directions for crediting responses and combining raw scores into derived scores. In the norms section, you may find phrases such as "percentile norms" or "grade-equivalent norms," sure tip-offs that percentiles and grade equivalents will be available. In the sections on interpretation, you may find information on the proper interpretation of derived scores. For example, many test authors will tell you the mean and standard deviation of standard scores and how they are to be interpreted. However, it pays to double-check against the norm tables themselves because test authors occasionally err in their descriptions.

Finding reliability data may be more difficult. If there is a section on reliability, the task is fairly simple. You want to see whether there is evidence of each appropriate type of reliability. Demand numbers—do not settle for statements about the test's reliability. The authors should show statistical proof of reliability. Read the tables. You can anticipate finding estimates of generalization across items (split-half, KR-20, coefficient alpha, alternate-form, and so on) and across time (test–retest reliability). If the scoring is difficult, you should also find a section on interscorer agreement. (Data on the extent to which you can generalize across scores can often be found in the section on scoring.) You should find reliability estimates for each subtest at each grade or age. In addition, tables giving the standard error of measurement for each subtest at each grade or age are occasionally provided.

The next step is very important: You must determine what scores are to be interpreted, because those are the ones you must judge for adequacy. In the sections dealing with score interpretation, you will often find the scores that the test authors think are most important. Many tests have subtests that are combined into a total score. Sometimes, the subtest scores are stressed over the total score (for example, in the Illinois Test of Psycholinguistic Abilities), whereas in other tests, the total score or part scores are stressed more than subtest scores (for example, in the Wechsler Intelligence Scale for Children–Revised. The scores that are identified as important and that are to be interpreted must meet the minimum desirable standards of reliability. Consequently, different tests are held to different standards. For example, the subtests on the ITPA must meet a higher standard of reliability than the subtests on the WISC-R because we are urged by the authors to interpret the ITPA subtests but not the WISC-R subtests.

If there is no section on reliability, check the table of contents to see whether there are tables for standard errors of measurement or reliability coefficients. You can usually find all the information that you need in the tables without reading the test. If there are no tables and no section on reliability, there may be no data on reliability in the manuals; this happens frequently. However, reliability information may be hidden in the section on validity, in the section on scores, or in the section on interpretation. Keep a lookout for it as you skim and read.

The evaluation of a test's validity is the most difficult aspect of reviewing a test. If the norms and the reliability are inadequate, there will be severe problems with validity. Even if they are adequate, the authors must still prove that the test is valid for each recommended use. This means that you must learn how the authors recommended using the test. Do not expect to find this information in a section labeled "validity." More often, you will find such statements in the beginning of the test manuals or in the promotional materials.

You will always find a statement to the effect that the test measures some domain. How do the test authors prove this? Data on content validity is often included in a section called "the development of the test" or "selection of items." In these sections, the authors explain how they chose the items in the test. For other tests, the information will be buried elsewhere in the manual. For still others, there will be no mention of how items were chosen—no proof of content validity.

Depending on the particular type of test, you may also find information on concurrent, predictive, and construct validity. Again, you must remember that the purpose of presenting these data is to demonstrate that the test measures the domain its authors claim it measures. The data should logically bear on the issue of validity.

Beyond claims that the test assesses a particular domain, you may find assertions that the test can be used in particular ways. This is especially true of tests of achievement, which authors often assert can be used in program planning. When we see such assertions, we expect to find a large number of test items appropriate for each grade. We look at the test items and at the norm tables to get an idea of the difference in the number of test items at each grade. All you have to do is find the raw score at the fiftieth percentile at two adjacent grades. For example, suppose that 17 points correct was the fiftieth percentile at the second grade and 21 points correct was the fiftieth percentile at the third grade. Then, only 4 raw-score points would separate second- and third-grade work. This is probably too few items on which to base an educational plan, although the test may well discriminate among test takers.

Sometimes, we are told that scores can be used in particular ways. Such assertions are often found in the interpretation sections of the manuals. For example, you may find information on critical levels of performance; the authors may tell you that scores below a particular value are indicative of potential problems or that students earning such scores require special instructional interventions. Check out each assertion for the use of the test, and look for proof.

Finally, we tend to be suspicious of strange formulations of reliability, validity, or scores. You should be, too. Remember, the test author should provide all the necessary data in clear and usable form. If it isn't there, it isn't your fault, and you should use the test cautiously—or not at all.

Appendix 4

A BRIEF EXPLANATION OF ITEM-RESPONSE THEORY[1]

Conceptual Background

Item-response theory (IRT) offers a different way to construct tests. As its name implies, the characteristics of individual test items are at the heart of the theory. Individual test items are important in both IRT and classical psychometric theory, but IRT and classical theory differ in the way test items are viewed and used. We expect the proportion of individuals passing an item (that is, the p-value) to vary as a function of the individuals' ability, although this assumption is seldom explicated in classical psychometric theory. Thus, the proportion of individuals getting a valid item correct is correlated with ability.[2]

p-Values in Classical Psychometric Theory

In classical theory, we think of test items and their aggregates as dependent on the characteristics of the individuals who respond to them. Thus, easy tests are tests on which most people answer most items correctly; more difficult tests are tests on which few people answer most items correctly. Test items do not possess characteristics independent of test takers. Thus, the various statistics used to describe tests are sample-specific, and we depend on the performance of a representative sample of individuals to estimate these statistics (for example, p-values, indexes of reliability) and for score interpretation. As we stressed in Chapter 6 (on norms), a relatively large representative normative sample is necessary to provide test users with accurate information about individual items and total scores. Clearly, descriptive statistics about a test (mean, standard deviation), transformed scores (IQs, T-scores, and so on), estimates of reliability, and estimates of validity are closely tied to the normative sample. For example, if a test were normed on relatively homogeneous groups of students with limited ability, we should expect the following consequences:

1. Our discussion of item-response theory is derived from *Principles of Test Theories* (1990) by Hoi K. Suen, to whom we are indebted for providing useful suggestions after reading drafts of this appendix.
2. When individual test items are negatively correlated or uncorrelated with the ability assessed by the test (usually estimated by the total score on the test), the items ought to be deleted. Deletion of such items ensures the development of a homogeneous test.

668

1. The raw-score mean would be lower than the mean of a representative sample.

2. The raw-score standard deviation would be less than the standard deviation of a representative sample (because the sample is homogeneous, and the range of scores is restricted).

3. Derived scores based on the unrepresentative sample would yield inflated scores for the general population (because the students being assessed are compared with students of limited ability).

4. Internal consistency and stability would be underestimated for a representative sample (because of the constricted range of the sample).

5. Empirical estimates of validity would be attenuated for a representative sample (because of the constricted range of the sample).

It follows from the preceding example that various statistics describing the technical characteristics of a test actually describe the test used with a particular group of test takers. Nowhere is this conclusion clearer than with regard to a test item's p-value. Suppose the p-value for a group of 5-year-olds is .25. Twenty-five percent of the 5-year-olds answer the item correctly; 75 percent do not. Yet, the same item may have a p-value of .50 for 6-year-olds. The p-value of an item is not a function of the item but a function of the item *used with a specific sample*.

Classic psychometric theory assumes that good test items discriminate through a wide range of abilities. In addition, a greater proportion of individuals with high total scores should answer the question correctly when compared with individuals with lower total test scores. Because p-values and point-biserial correlations are average statistics, educators cannot tell from these values alone whether an item acts in this way. Therefore, more sophisticated test developers plot item-characteristic curves by graphing the p-values of an item for individuals with different total test scores (under the assumption that the total score is a good approximation of the underlying ability).

To illustrate, suppose we were developing a test of intelligence. We could calculate and plot p-values for a test item for students who had total scores that were extremely low ($p = .10$), very low ($p = .15$), somewhat below average ($p = .25$), average ($p = .50$), somewhat above average ($p = .75$), very high ($p = .90$), and extremely high ($p = .95$). It is implicit in this example that even some students with extremely low scores pass a given item and even some students with extremely high scores fail the item. Thus, although an item may demonstrate good discrimination throughout the range of ability, it is not perfect. In part a of Figure A4.1, these hypothetical p-values are plotted against hypothetical total scores. In this example, the curve (or ogive) is relatively steep. A test author would prefer an item to have this type of curve, rather than a relatively flat curve or one that zigzagged across the range of total scores. An item that discriminates perfectly is shown in part b of Figure A4.1. For this perfect item, all students with low ability fail the item and all students with high ability pass the item; how low (or high) student ability is will depend, of course, on the difficulty of the specific item.

● ● ● **FIGURE A4.1**   Item Characteristic Curves for Items with Imperfect Discrimination (a) and Perfect Discrimination (b)

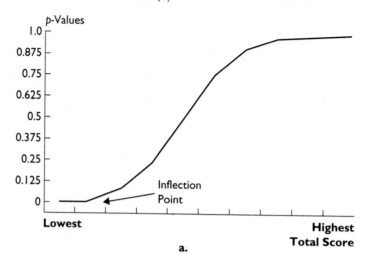

a.

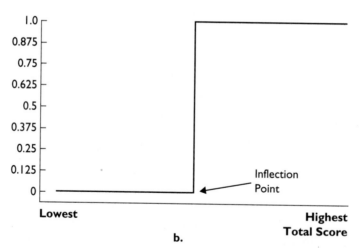

b.

Comparing the two curves, you can see that both curves (parts a and b) have three segments, although these segments can be seen more easily in the graph of the perfect item. There are two tails. For the perfect item, the tails are horizontal; for the imperfect item, the tails flatten as each curve reaches its limits (that is, asymptotes). Both curves have a segment where the curve accelerates (the vertical part of the perfect curve in part b). It is in the accelerating segment of the curve that the test item discriminates most among examinees. The point where the curve begins to accelerate is termed the *inflection point*. The left–right placement of the item on the graph is a function of the item mean (*p*-value). Easier items begin to accelerate at the left part of the graph; more difficult items accelerate further to the right.

p-Values in IRT

In IRT, item-characteristic curves are generated for the relationship between a person's latent (hidden) ability and the probability of answering an individual item correctly. The mathematics required to estimate these ogives is quite complex, and the actual solution is intractable; however, these ogives can be estimated using logistic models and computers. The relationship between ability and the probability of correctly responding to a test item is a function of three parameters. The *discrimination parameter* (*a*) is the slope at the inflection point. The *difficulty parameter* (*b*) is the ability level Θ that corresponds to the inflection point of the ogive. The *guessing parameter* (*c*) is the lower asymptote of the curve—the point where an examinee has minimal probability of responding correctly.

Because the relationship between the probability of a correct response and ability is effectively represented by a logistic ogival function, this relationship can be determined with the following equations. When all three parameters are used to estimate the relationship between the probability of a correct response to any item (P_i) and ability Θ, the model is called the "three-parameter model"; this function for the logistic ogive is given in Equation A4.1. However, if we assumed that no guessing occurred, parameter *c* could be eliminated, and the model could be simplified to a two-parameter model; this function for the logistic ogive is given in Equation A4.2. Similarly, if we assumed that all items have the same discrimination power, *a* could be eliminated, and the model could be simplified to a one-parameter model, often called the "Rasch model." This logistic ogive function is given in Equation A4.3. (In all three equations, D is a constant equal to 1.7, and *e* is the base for the natural logarithm.)

$$P_i(0) = c_i + (1 - c_i)\ \frac{1}{1 + e^{-Da_i(\Theta - b_i)}} \tag{A4.1}$$

$$P_i(0) = \frac{1}{1 + e^{-Da_i(\Theta - b_i)}} \tag{A4.2}$$

$$P_i(0) = \frac{1}{1 + e^{-D(\Theta - b_i)}} \tag{A4.3}$$

In practice, it is necessary to estimate the difficulty parameter (*b*), the discrimination parameter (*a*), and the guessing parameter (*c*) on the basis of the performances of a sample of examinees. Because they are characteristics of the item and not of test takers, these parameters can be estimated (that is, calibrated) independently of the characteristics of any sample of test takers. Thus, samples used to estimate parameters need not be representative of the population of test takers at large.

Item parameters are jointly estimated, usually through a logarithmic likelihood function. Basically, we use a mathematical equation to ascertain the probability that a particular pattern of correct and incorrect responses for a group of examinees is associated with specific levels of ability. Accurate estimation of parameters requires us to assume that an examinee's response to one question is not related to the same person's response to another question. This assumption, frequently referred to as "local independence," in essence presumes that an item measures only one trait or ability (that is, the term is unidimensional). Once the relationship between each item and the latent trait is estimated, the ability of any other examinee can be estimated from the parameters.

To use item-response theory, test authors must first select the model to be used (three parameters, two parameters, or one parameter) and then estimate the parameters. However, an author may not be able to estimate parameters because of the specific characteristics of the sample. Moreover, the obtained data may not fit the model selected.[3] Because the amount of estimation required increases greatly as the number of parameters increases from one to three, the one-parameter Rasch model is more commonly used when constructing tests that are used in applied settings. Estimation is a straightforward operation in the Rasch model because ability and the probability of answering a question correctly are monotonic transformations of the total score and p-values used in classical psychometrics. However, this model is clearly acceptable only in circumstances in which the c parameter (guessing) can be assumed to be zero and the a and the b parameters (difficulty and discrimination) are the same and presumed normal.

Interpreting Tests Developed Using IRT

In practice, interpreting the results of a test developed using an IRT model is quite similar to interpreting the results of a test developed using classical psychometric theory. There are subtle differences, however, in considering the technical characteristics.

Scores

As is true of those for tests developed using classical psychometric theory, raw scores from tests developed using IRT have no intrinsic meaning. Indeed, although it is an equal-interval scale, the ability scale is indeterminant. Therefore, ability scores are usually transformed to z-scores. After z-scores have been derived for total scores, they can be transformed to any other metric. Under the assumption that ability is normally distributed within age or grade, ability scores can be transformed to derived scores once the means and standard deviations of ages and grades are determined empirically. This determination does require representative norms.

3. Several statistical procedures are available to test the goodness of fit of the observed data and the IRT model.

Norms

Because of the assumptions underlying item-response theory, norms play a much smaller role in item selection and estimation of a test's reliability. Norms must be sufficiently large to calibrate the scale (that is, to estimate parameters empirically). The more parameters that must be estimated, the larger the number of test items and test takers that must be employed. Based on the research of several authors, Suen (1990) offered the following recommendations: (1) For the one-parameter model, 20 test items and 200 examinees are required; (2) for the two-parameter model, 30 items and 500 examinees are required; and (3) for the three-parameter model, 60 items and 1,000 examinees are required. As previously mentioned, norms must be representative to estimate derived scores for particular groups (for example, for 12-year-olds).

Reliability

Because each ability level has its own unique error variance, no generalized estimates of reliability are provided in IRT. Rather, standard errors of estimation are used for each ability score. This statistic is conceptually equivalent to specific standard errors of measurement for each ability score and will have different values for different ability scores. The actual calculation of this error is determined by the number of parameters used in the IRT model. Therefore, test authors select the appropriate computational formulas from the following ones, to calculate the information function of an item (I). $P'_1\Theta$ is the slope of the curve at Θ. P is the probability of a correct response, and Q is the probability of an incorrect response in Equations A4.4 (three-parameter model), A4.5 (two-parameter model), and A4.6 (one-parameter model). The information function for the total test is the sum of the information functions of all items, as shown in Equation A4.7. From the total test information function, the standard error of Θ can be calculated using Equation A4.8.

To the extent that the stability of the ability being measured is important, traditional methods (that is, test–retest) are used to estimate this type of reliability. Similarly, to the extent that scoring is a problem, traditional methods of estimating interscorer agreement are used.

$$I(0, \mu_i) = \frac{D^2 a_i^2\, Q(\Theta)\, [P_i(\Theta) - c_i]^2}{(1 - c_i)^2} \qquad (A4.4)$$

$$I(0, \mu_i) = D^2 a_i^2\, P_i(\Theta)\, Q_i(\Theta) \qquad (A4.5)$$

$$I(0, \mu_i) = D^2\, P_i(\Theta)\, Q_i(\Theta) \qquad (A4.6)$$

$$I(0) = \sum_{i=1}^{k} \frac{P'_i(\Theta)^2}{P_i(\Theta)\, Q(\Theta)} \qquad (A4.7)$$

$$SE(0) = \frac{1}{\sqrt{I}\,(\Theta)} \qquad\qquad (A4.8)$$

Validity

The methods used to validate classically developed tests are also used to validate tests developed using IRT. However, tests developed using IRT raise additional validation issues. Test users should expect to see the results of research demonstrating that the items are unidimensional and locally independent; these results frequently come from factor-analytic studies. In addition, when a one-parameter (Rasch) model is employed, test users should expect to see evidence that item ogives are normal, such as a likelihood ratio test, a Q_1 statistic, or the like.

Glossary

abscissa The horizontal axis of a graph, representing the continuum on which individuals are measured

accommodative ability The automatic adjustment of the eyes for seeing at different distances

acculturation A child's particular set of background experiences and opportunities to learn in both formal and informal educational settings

achievement What has been learned as a result of instruction

adaptive behavior Behavior that allows individuals to adapt themselves to the expectations of nature and society

age equivalent A derived score that expresses a person's performance as the average (the median or mean) performance for that age group. Age equivalents are expressed in years and months; a hyphen is used in age scores (for example, 7-1 is 7 years, 1 month); an age-equivalent score is interpreted to mean that the test taker's performance is equal to the average performance of an X-year old

aid An error in oral reading, recorded when a student hesitates for more than 10 seconds and the word or words are supplied by the teacher

algorithms The steps, processes, or procedures used for solving a problem or reaching a goal

alternate forms Two tests that measure the same trait or skill to the same extent and that are standardized on the same population; alternate forms offer essentially equivalent tests; sometimes, in fact, they're called "equivalent forms"

amplitude The intensity of a behavior

assessment The process of collecting data for the purpose of (a) specifying and verifying problems and (b) making decisions about students

attainment What an individual has learned, regardless of where it has been learned

audiogram A graph of the results of the pure-tone threshold test

behavioral observation Observation of spontaneous behavior, which has not been elicited by a predetermined and standardized set of stimuli (that is, not test behavior)

bimodal distribution A distribution that has two modes

biserial correlation coefficient An index of association between two variables, one of which has been forced into an arbitrary dichotomy (for example, smart/dull) and one of which is equal interval (for example, grade-point average)

cash validity The notion that frequently used tests are valid tests

Category A data The basic, minimum information schools need in order to operate an educational program, including identifying information, as well as information about a student's educational progress

Category B data Test results and other verified information useful to the schools in planning a student's educational program or maintaining a student safely in school

Category C data Information that may be potentially useful to schools. This includes any unverified information, scores on personality tests, and so forth

classification A type of decision that concerns a pupil's eligibility for special services, special-education services, remedial education services, speech services, and so forth

coefficient alpha The average split-half correlation based on all possible divisions of a test into two parts, coefficient alpha can be computed directly from the variances of individual test items and the variance of the total test score

concurrent criterion-related validity A measure of how accurately a person's current test score can be used to estimate a score on a criterion measure

conductive hearing loss Abnormal hearing associated with poor air-conduction sensitivity but normal bone-conduction sensitivity

confidence interval The range of scores within which a person's true score will fall with a given probability

construct validity A measure of the extent to which a test measures a theoretical trait or characteristic

consultation A meeting between a resource teacher or other specialist and a classroom teacher to verify the existence of a problem, specify the nature of the problem, and develop strategies that might relieve the problem

content validity A measure of the extent to which a test is an adequate measure of the content it is designed to cover; content validity is established by examining three factors: the appropriateness of the types of items included, the comprehensiveness of the item sample, and the way in which the items assess the content

correlation   A measure of the degree of relationship between two or more variables; a correlation indicates the extent to which any two variables go together—that is, the extent to which changes in one variable are reflected by changes in the second variable

correlation coefficient   Numerical index of the relationship between two or more variables

criterion-referenced test   Test that measures a person's skills in terms of absolute levels of mastery

criterion-related validity   A measure of the extent to which a person's score on a criterion measure can be estimated from that person's score on a test of unknown validity

curriculum-based assessment   Use of assessment materials and procedures that mirror instruction in order to ascertain whether specific instructional objectives have been accomplished and to monitor progress directly in the curriculum being taught

deciles   Bands of percentiles that are ten percentile ranks in width; each decile contains 10 percent of the norm group

derived scores   A general term for raw scores that are transformed to developmental scores or to scores of relative standing

descriptive statistics   Numerical values, such as mean, standard deviation, or correlation, that describe a data set

developmental scores   Raw scores that have been transformed into age equivalents (AE) (mental ages, for example), grade equivalents, or developmental quotients using the following formula: $100 \cdot AE/CA$, where CA = chronological age

deviation IQs   Standard scores with a mean of 100 and a standard deviation of 15 or 16 (depending on the test)

deviation score   The distance between an individual's score and the average score for the group, such as z-scores, T-scores, and so on

discriminative stimuli   Stimuli that are consistently present when a behavior is reinforced and that elicit the behavior even in the absence of the original reinforcer

disregard of punctuation   An error in oral reading in which a student fails to give appropriate inflection in response to punctuation; for example, a student may not pause for a comma, stop for a period, or indicate voice inflection at a question mark or exclamation point

distractors   Incorrect options contained in a response set

distribution   The way in which scores in a set array themselves; a distribution may be graphed to demonstrate visually the relations among the scores in the group or set

duration   The length of time a behavior lasts

ecobehavioral observation   Observation targeting the interaction among student behavior, teacher behavior, time allocated to instruction, physical grouping structures, the types of tasks being used, and instructional content; ecobehavioral assessment enables educators to identify natural instructional conditions that are associated with academic success, behavioral competence, or problem behaviors

entitlement   In special education, the right to a free and appropriate education, related services, and due process

equal-interval scales   Scales on which the differences between adjacent values are equal, but on which there is no absolute or logical zero

error   Misrepresentation of a person's score, as a result of failure to obtain a representative sample of times, items, or scorers

ethnographic observation   Observation in which the observer does not participate in what is occurring

etiology   Cause of a disorder

expressive language   The production of language

free operant   A test situation that presents more problems than a student can answer in the given time period

frequency   The tabulation of the number of behaviors with discrete beginnings and endings that occur in a predetermined time frame; when the time periods in which the behavior is counted vary, frequencies are usually converted to rates

grade equivalent   A derived score that expresses a student's performance as the average (the median or mean) performance for a particular grade; grade equivalents are expressed in grades and tenths of grades; a decimal point is used in grade scores (for example, 7.1 is grade 7 and one tenth)

gross mispronunciation   An error in oral reading in which a student's pronunciation of a word is in no way similar to the word in the text

hesitation   An error in oral reading in which a student pauses for two or more seconds before pronouncing a word

historical information   Information that describes how a person has functioned in the past

individual consent   Consent by parent (or pupil) required for the collection of family information (religion, income, occupation, and so on), personality data, and other non-educational information

individualized education plan (IEP)   A document that specifies the long-term and short-term goals of an instructional program, where the program will be delivered, who will deliver the program, and how progress will be evaluated

informal assessment   Any assessment that involves collection of data by anything other than a norm-referenced (standardized) test

informed consent   Consent that a parent or a student gives for the collection or dissemination of information not directly relevant and essential to the child's education; the assumption underlying the notion of informed consent is that the parent (or pupil) is "reasonably competent to understand the nature and consequences of his [or her] decision" (Goslin, 1969, p. 17)

insertion   An error in oral reading in which a student inappropriately adds one or more words to the sentence being read

intelligence   An inferred ability; a term or construct used to explain differences in present behavior and to predict differences in future behavior

internal consistency   A measure of the extent to which items in a test correlate with one another

interscorer reliability   An estimate of the degree of agreement between two or more scores on the same test

inversion   An error in oral reading in which a student says the words in an order different from the order in which they are written

keyed response   Correct answer in a response set

kurtosis   The peakedness of a curve, or the rate at which a curve rises

language   A code for conveying ideas (see Bloom & Lahey, 1978; Fromkin & Rodman, 1978); although there is some variation, language theorists propose five basic components to describe the code: phonology, semantics, morphology, syntax, and pragmatics

leptokurtic curves   Fast-rising curves; tests that do not spread out (or discriminate among) those taking the test are typically leptokurtic

mean   The arithmetic average of scores in a distribution

median   A score that divides the top 50 percent of test takers from the bottom 50 percent; the point on a scale, above which 50 percent of the cases (not the scores) occur and below which 50 percent of the cases occur

metalinguistic   Relating to the direct examination of the structural aspects of language

mixed hearing loss   Abnormal hearing attributed to abnormal bone conduction and even more abnormal air conduction

mode   The most frequently obtained score in a distribution

momentary time sampling   A procedure used in systematic observation to determine when observations will occur; a behavior is scored as an occurrence if it is present at the last moment of an observation interval; if the behavior is not occurring at the last moment of the interval, a nonoccurrence is recorded

multiple-skill batteries   Tests that measure skill development in several achievement areas

negatively skewed distribution   An asymmetric distribution in which scores tail off to the low end; a distribution in which there are more scores above the mean than below it

nominal scales   A scale of measurement in which there is no inherent relationship among adjacent values

nonsystematic observation   Observations in which the observer notes behaviors, characteristics, and personal interactions that seem of significance

normal curve equivalents   Standard scores with a mean equal to 100 and a standard deviation equal to 21.06

normative sample, or norm group   A group of subjects of known demographic characteristics (age, sex, grade in school, and so on) to whom a person's performance may be compared

norm-referenced devices   Tests that compare an individual's performance to the performance of his or her peers

objective-referenced assessment   Tests referenced to specific instructional objectives rather than to the performance of a peer group or norm group

observation   The process of gaining information through one's senses—visual, auditory, and so forth; observation can be used to assess behavior, states, physical characteristics, and permanent products of behavior (such as a child's poem)

omission   An error in oral reading in which a student skips a word or a group of words

operationalize   To define a behavior or event in terms of the operations used to measure it; for example, an operational definition of intelligence would be a score on a specific intelligence test

ordinal scales   Scales on which values of measurement are ordered from best to worst or from worst to best; on ordinal scales, the differences between adjacent values are unknown

ordinate   The vertical axis of a graph of a distribution, showing the frequency (or the number) of individuals earning any given score

partial-interval recording   A procedure used in systematic observation in which an occurrence is scored if the behavior occurs during any part of the interval

partial mispronunciation   One of several kinds of errors in oral reading, including partial pronunciation, phonetic mispronunciation of part of the word, omission of part of the word, or insertion of elements of words

participant-observer approach Observation in which the observer joins the target social group and participates in its activities

Pearson product–moment correlation coefficient (r) An index of the straight-line (linear) relationship between two or more variables measured on an equal-interval scale

percentile ranks (percentiles) Derived scores that indicate the percentage of people whose scores are at or below a given raw score; percentiles are useful for both ordinal and equal-interval scales

phi coefficient An index of linear correlation between two sets of naturally dichotomous variables (for example, male/female, dead/alive)

phonology Speech sounds

platykurtic curves Curves that are flat and slow rising

point-biserial correlation An index of linear correlation between one naturally occurring dichotomous variable (such as sex) and a continuous, equal-interval variable (such as height measured in inches)

portfolio A collection of products that provide a basis for judging student accomplishment; in school settings, portfolios typically contain extended projects and may also contain drafts, teacher comments and evaluations, and self-evaluations

positively skewed distribution An asymmetrical distribution in which scores tail off to the higher end of the continuum; a distribution in which there are more scores below the mean than above it

power tests Untimed tests

pragmatics The social context in which language occurs

predictive validity A measure of the extent to which a person's current test scores can be used to estimate accurately what that person's criterion scores will be at a later time

prereferral assessment Activities that occur prior to formal referral, assessment, and consideration for placement; the goal of prereferral assessment and intervention is twofold: (1) verification and specification of the nature of a student's difficulties, and (2) provision of services in the least restrictive environment

probe A special testing format that is well suited to the assessment of direct performances; probes are brief (usually three minutes or less), timed, frequently administered assessments that can be used for any purpose

prognosis A prediction of future performance

qualitative data Information consisting of nonsystematic and unquantified observations

qualitative observation A description of behavior, its function, and its context; the observer begins without preconceived ideas about what will be observed and describes behavior that seems important

quantitative data Observations that have been tabulated or otherwise given numerical values

quartiles Bands of percentiles that are 25 percentile ranks in width; each quartile contains 25 percent of the norm group

random error In measurement, sources of variation in scores that make it impossible to generalize from an observation of a specific behavior observed at a specific time by a specific person to observations conducted on similar behavior, at different times, or by different observers

range The distance between the extremes in a set of scores, including those extremes; the highest score less the lowest score, plus one

ratio IQ A derived score based on mental age (MA), in relation to chronological age (CA), in which IQ equals

$$\frac{\text{MA (in months)}}{\text{CA (in months)}} \times 100$$

ratio scales Scales of measurement in which the difference between adjacent values is equal and in which there is a logical and absolute zero

readiness Extent of preparation to participate in an activity; the term most often refers to readiness to enter school but applies to all levels

receptive language The comprehension of language

referral A request for help from a specialist; for example, a teacher or parent may refer a student to a specialist who can provide the student with an appropriate educational program

reliability In measurement, the extent to which it is possible to generalize from an observation of a specific behavior observed at a specific time by a specific person to observations conducted on similar behavior, at different times, or by different observers

reliability coefficient An index of the extent to which observations can be generalized. The square of the correlation between obtained scores and true scores on a measure r^2_{xt}

repetition An error in oral reading in which a student repeats words or groups of words

representational consent Consent to collect data, given by appropriately elected officials, such as members of a state legislature

sample A representative subset of a population

scotoma A visionless spot in the eye

screening An initial stage of assessment in which those who *may* evidence a particular problem, disorder, disability, or disease are discriminated from the general population

selection formats   A method of presenting test questions in which students indicate their choice from an array of the possible test answers (usually called "response options"); true–false, multiple-choice, and matching are the three most common selection formats

semantics   The study of word meanings; although the scope of the term *semantics* can extend beyond individual words to include sentence meaning, the term generally applies to words

sensorineural hearing loss   Abnormal hearing associated with both poor bone-conduction sensitivity and poor air-conduction sensitivity

setting events   Environmental events that set the occasion for the performance of an action

single-skill tests   Tests that are designed to measure skill development in one specific content area (for example, reading)

skew   Asymmetry in a distribution; the distribution of scores below the mean is not a mirror image of the distribution above the mean

social comparison   Observing a peer whose behavior is considered to be appropriate and using the peer's rate of behavior as the standard against which to evaluate the target student's rate of behavior

social tolerance   The threshold above which behaviors are viewed as undesirable by others

social validity   A consumer's reaction to an intervention or assessment

Spearman rho   An index of correlation between two variables measured on an ordinal scale

speed tests   Timed tests

split-half reliability estimate   An estimate of internal-consistency reliability derived by correlating people's scores on two halves of a test

standard deviation   A measure of the degree of dispersion in a distribution; the square root of the variance

standard error of measurement (SEM)   The standard deviation of error around a person's true score

standard scores   The general name for derived scores that have been transformed to produce a distribution with a predetermined mean and standard deviation

stanines   Standard-score bands that divide a distribution into nine parts; the middle seven stanines are each 0.50 standard deviation wide, and the fifth stanine is centered on the mean

stem   In selection formats, the part of a problem that contains the question

substitution   An error in oral reading in which a student replaces one or more words in the passage with one or more meaningful words (synonyms)

supply format   A method of presenting test questions in which a student is required to produce a written or oral response; this response can be as restricted as a number or a word or can be as extensive as a sentence, a paragraph, or several pages of written response

syntax   Word order of sentences; syntax includes a description of the rules for arranging the words into a sentence

systematic error   Consistent error that can be predicted; bias

systematic observations   Observations in which an observer specifies or defines the behaviors to be observed and then counts or otherwise measures the frequency, duration, magnitude, or latency of the behaviors

test   A predetermined set of questions or tasks to which predetermined types of behavioral responses are sought

testing   Exposing a person to a particular set of questions in order to obtain a score

test–retest reliability   An index of stability over time

tetrachoric correlation coefficient   An index of correlation between two arbitrarily dichotomized variables (for example, tall/short, smart/dull)

true score   The score that a student would earn if the entire domain of items were assessed

T-score   A standard score with a mean of 50 and a standard deviation of 10

tunnel vision   Normal central visual acuity with a restricted peripheral field

validity   The extent to which a test measures what its authors or users claim it measures; specifically, test validity concerns the appropriateness of the inferences that can be made on the basis of test results

validity coefficient   A coefficient that measures the correlation between a test of unknown validity and an established criterion measure

variance   A numerical index describing the dispersion of a set of scores around the mean of the distribution; specifically, the variance is the average squared distance of the scores from the mean

visual acuity   The clarity or sharpness with which a person sees

whole-interval recording   A procedure used in systematic observation in which an occurrence is scored if the behavior is present throughout the entire observation interval

z-scores   Standard scores with a mean of 0 and a standard deviation of 1

References

Achenbach, T. M. (1986). *The Direct Observation Form (DOF)*. Burlington, VT: University of Vermont Department of Psychiatry.

Achenbach, T. M. (1991a). *Integrative guide to the 1991 CBCL, YSR, and TRF profiles*. Burlington, VT: University of Vermont Department of Psychiatry.

Achenbach, T. M. (1991b). *Manual for the Child Behavior Checklist/4–18*. Burlington, VT: University of Vermont Department of Psychiatry.

Achenbach, T. M. (1991c). *Teacher's Report Form (TRF)*. Burlington, VT: University of Vermont Department of Psychiatry.

Achenbach, T. M. (1991d). *Youth Self-Report (YSR)*. Burlington, VT: University of Vermont Department of Psychiatry.

Achenbach, T. M. (1992). *Child Behavior Checklist/2–3 Years (CBCL/2–3)*. Burlington, VT: University of Vermont Department of Psychiatry.

Achenbach, T. M., & Brown, J. S. (1991). *Bibliography of published studies using the Child Behavior Checklist and related materials* (1991 ed.). Burlington, VT: University of Vermont Department of Psychiatry.

Achenbach, T. M., & Edelbrock, C. (1983). *Manual for the Child Behavior Checklist and Revised Child Behavior Profile*. Burlington, VT: University of Vermont Department of Psychiatry.

Achenbach, T. M., & Edelbrock, C. (1987). *Manual for the Youth Self-Report and Profile*. Burlington, VT: University of Vermont Department of Psychiatry.

Adams, M. (1990). *Beginning to read: Thinking and learning about print*. Cambridge, MA: MIT Press.

Adams, D. (1991). Writing portfolios: A powerful assessment and conversation tool. *Writing Teacher, 12–15.*

Advantage Learning Systems, Inc. (1997). *Standardized Test for the Assessment of Reading*. Wisconsin Rapids, WI: Advantage Learning System, Inc.

Advantage Learning Systems, Inc. (1998). *STAR Math*. Wisconsin Rapids, WI: Advantage Learning System, Inc.

Alberto, P., & Troutman, A. (1990). *Applied behavior analysis for teachers* (3rd ed.). Columbus, OH: Merrill.

Algozzine, B., Christenson, S., & Ysseldyke, J. E. (1982). Probabilities associated with the referral to placement process. *Teacher Education and Special Education, 5,* 19–23.

Algozzine, B., & Ysseldyke, J. (1992). *Strategies and tactics for effective instruction*. Longmont, CO: Sopris West.

Algozzine, B., Ysseldyke, J., & Elliott, J. (1997). *Strategies and tactics for effective instruction* (2nd ed.). Longmont, CO: Sopris West.

American Association on Mental Retardation. (1992). *Mental Retardation: Definition, Classification, and Systems of Supports* (9th ed.). Washington, DC: Author.

American Educational Research Association (AERA), American Psychological Association, & National Council on Measurement in Education. (1985). *Standards for educational and psychological testing*. Washington, DC: American Psychological Association.

American Psychological Association (1992) *Ethical principles of psychologists and code of conduct*. Washington, DC: Author.

American Psychological Association, American Educational Research Association, & National Council on Measurement in Education. (1974). *Standards for educational and psychological tests*. Washington, DC: American Psychological Association.

American Speech–Language–Hearing Association. (1990). Guidelines for audiometric symbols. *ASHA, 32 (Suppl. 2),* 25–30.

Ames, W. (1965). A comparison of spelling textbooks. *Elementary English, 42,* 146–150, 214.

Anastasi, A. (1980). *Psychological testing* (4th ed.). New York: Macmillan.

Anastasi, A. (1988). *Psychological testing* (5th ed.). New York: Macmillan.

Archbald, D., & Newman, F. (1988). *Beyond standardized testing: Assessing authentic academic achievement in the secondary school*. Reston, VA: National Association of Secondary Principals.

Aronson, E., Blaney, N., Stephan, C., Sikes, J., & Snapp, M. (1978). *The jigsaw classroom*. Beverly Hills, CA: Sage.

Arter, J., & Spandel, V. (1992, May). Using portfolios of student work in instruction and assessment. *Instructional Topics in Educational Measurement,* 36–44.

Bachor, D. (1990). The importance of shifts in language level and extraneous information in determining word-problem difficulty: Steps toward individual assessment. *Diagnostique, 14*, 94–111.

Bachor, D., Stacy, N., & Freeze, D. (1986). *A conceptual framework for word problems: Some preliminary results.* Paper presented at the conference of the Canadian Society for Studies in Education, Winnipeg, Manitoba.

Bagnato, S., & Neisworth, J. (1990). *System to plan early childhood services.* Circle Pines, MN: American Guidance Service.

Bailey, D. B., & Rouse, T. L. (1989). Procedural considerations in assessing infants and preschoolers with handicaps. In D. B. Bailey & M. Wolery (Eds.), *Assessing infants and preschoolers with handicaps.* Columbus, OH: Merrill.

Baker, E., O'Neil, Jr., H., & Linn, R. (1993). Policy and validity prospects for performance-based assessment. *American Psychologist, 48*(12), 1210–1218.

Balow, I. H., Farr, R. C., & Hogan, T. P. (1992). *Metropolitan Achievement Test 7.* San Antonio, TX: Psychological Corporation.

Bankson, N. W. (1990). *Bankson Language Test* (2nd ed.). Austin, TX: Pro-Ed.

Barraga, N. (1976). *Visual handicaps and learning: A developmental approach.* Belmont, CA: Wadsworth.

Baumgardner, J. C. (1993). *An empirical analysis of school psychological assessments: Practice with students who are deaf and bilingual.* Unpublished doctoral dissertation, University of Minnesota, Minneapolis.

Baxter, G., Shavelson, R., Goldman, S., & Pine, J. (1992). Evaluation of procedure-based scoring for hands-on science assessment. *Journal of Educational Measurement, 29*(1), 1–17.

Bayley, N. (1993). *Manual: Bayley Scales of Infant Development* (2nd ed.). San Antonio, TX: Psychological Corporation.

Beery, K. E. (1982). *Revised Administration, Scoring, and Teaching Manual for the Developmental Test of Visual–Motor Integration.* Cleveland: Modern Curriculum Press.

Beery, K. E. (1989). *The Developmental Test of Visual–Motor Integration.* Cleveland: Modern Curriculum Press.

Beery, K. E. (1997). *Developmental Test of Visual-Motor Integration.* Cleveland, OH: Modern Curriculum Press.

Bender, L. (1938). *Bender Visual-Motor Gestalt Test.* New York: Grune & Stratton.

Bennett, R. (1993). On the meanings of constructed responses. In R. Bennett & W. Ward (Eds.), *Constructive versus choice in cognitive measurement: Issues in constructed response, performance testing, and portfolio assessment.* Hillsdale, NJ: Erlbaum.

Bleckman, E. (1985). *Solving child behavior problems at home and at school.* Champaign, IL: Research Press.

Bloom, B. (1956). *Taxonomy of educational objectives: The classification of educational goals: Handbook 1. Cognitive domain.* New York: McKay.

Bloom, B., Hastings, J., & Madaus, G. (1971). *Handbook of formative and summative evaluation of student learning.* New York: McGraw-Hill.

Boehm, A. E. (1986). *Boehm Test of Basic Concepts–Revised.* San Antonio: Psychological Corporation.

Boehm, A. E., & Weinberg, R. A. (1988). *The classroom observer: A guide for developing observation skills* (2nd ed.). New York: Teachers College Press.

Bond, G., & Dykstra, R. (1967). The cooperative research program in first-grade reading instruction (1967). *Reading Research Quarterly, 2*, 5–142.

Bower, E. M. (1981). *Early identification of emotionally handicapped children in school* (3rd ed.). Springfield, IL: Charles E. Thomas.

Bowers, P., & Wolf, M. (1993). Theoretical links between naming speed, precise timing mechanisms and orthographic skill in dyslexia. *Reading and Writing: An Interdisciplinary Journal, 5*, 69–85.

Bracken, B., & McCallum, R. S. (1998). *Universal Nonverbal Intelligence Test.* Itasca, IL: Riverside Publishing Company.

Bradbury, R. (1953). *Fahrenheit 451.* New York: Ballantine Books.

Breland, H. (1983). *The direct assessment of writing skill: A measurement review* (College Board Report No. 83-6). New York: College Entrance Examination Board.

Breland, H., Camp, R., Jones, R., Morris, & Rock, D. (1987). *Assessing writing skill.* New York: The College Board.

Briggs, A., & Underwood, G. (1984). Phonological coding in good and poor readers. *Reading Research Quarterly, 20*, 54–66.

Broderick, C. B. (1993). *Understanding family process: Basics of family systems theory.* Newbury Park, CA: Sage.

Bronfenbrenner, U. (1979). *The ecology of human development.* Cambridge, MA: Harvard University Press.

Brown, L., & Hammill, D. (1978). *Behavior Rating Profile.* Austin, TX: Pro-Ed.

Brown, L., & Hammill, D. (1983). *Behavior Rating Profile.* Austin, TX: Pro-Ed.

Brown, L., & Hammill, D. (1990). *Behavior Rating Profile* (2nd ed.). Austin, TX: Pro-Ed.

Brown, L., & Leigh, J. (1986a). *Adaptive Behavior Inventory.* Austin, TX: Pro-Ed.

Brown, L., & Leigh, J. (1986b). *The Adaptive Behavior Inventory manual.* Austin, TX: Pro-Ed.

Brown, L., Sherbenou, R., & Johnsen, S. (1997). *Test of Nonverbal Intelligence–3.* Austin, TX: Pro-Ed.

Brown, R., & Bellugi, U. (1964). Three processes in the child's acquisition of syntax. *Harvard Educational Review, 34*, 133–151.

Brown, V., Cronin, M., & McEntire, E. (1994). *Test of Mathematical Abilities–2*. Austin, TX: Pro-Ed.

Brown, V., Hammill, D., & Wiederholt, J. L. (1995). *Test of Reading Comprehension–3*. Austin, TX: Pro-Ed.

Bruer, J. (1993). *School for thought: A science of learning in the classroom*. Cambridge, MA: MIT Press.

Bruininks, R., Woodcock, R., Weatherman, R., & Hill, B. (1996). *Scales of Independent Behavior, Revised, Comprehensive Manual*. Chicago, IL: Riverside Publishing Company.

Caldwell, J., & Goldin, J. (1979). Variables affecting word problem difficulty in elementary school mathematics. *Journal of Research in Mathematics Education, 10*, 323–335.

Calfee, R., & Perfumo, P. (1993). Student portfolios: Opportunities for a revolution in assessment. *Journal of Reading, 36*(7), 532–537.

Camp, R. (1993). The place of portfolios in our changing views of writing assessment. In R. Bennett & W. Ward (Eds.), *Constructive versus choice in cognitive measurement: Issues in constructed response, performance testing, and portfolio assessment*. Hillsdale, NJ: Erlbaum.

Campbell, D., & Fiske, D. (1959). Convergent and discriminate validation by the multi-trait-multi-method matrix. *Psychological Bulletin, 56*, 81–105.

Cannell, J. J. (1988). Nationally normed elementary achievement testing in America's public schools: How all 50 states are above the national average. *Educational Measurement: Issues and Practice, 7*(2), 5–9.

Carroll, J. (1963). A model of school learning. *Teachers College Record, 64*, 723–733.

Carroll, J. B. (1985). The model of school learning: Progress of an idea. In L. W. Anderson (Ed.), *Perspectives on school learning: Selected writings of John B. Carroll* (pp. 82–102). Hillsdale, NJ: Erlbaum.

Carroll, J. G. (1993). *Human cognitive abilities: A survey of factor-analytic studies*. New York: Cambridge University Press.

Carrow-Woolfolk, E. (1985). *Test for Auditory Comprehension of Language, Examiner's manual* (rev. ed.). Allen, TX: Developmental Learning Materials.

Carrow-Woolfolk, E. (1995). *Manual for the Listening Comprehension and Oral Language Subtests of the Oral and Written Language Scales*. Circle Pines, MN: American Guidance Services.

Carrow-Woolfolk, E. (1996). *Manual for the Written Expression Subtest of the Oral and Written Language Scales*. Circle Pines, MN: American Guidance Services.

Chalfant, J., Pysh, M. V., & Moultrie, R. (1979). Teacher assistance teams: A model for within-building problem solving. *Learning Disability Quarterly, 2*, 85–96.

Chall, J. (1967). *Learning to read: The great debate*. New York: McGraw-Hill.

Cohen, G. (1972). Hemispheric differences in a letter classification task. *Perception and Psychophysics, 11*, 139–142.

Cohen, J. (1960). A coefficient of agreement for nominal scales. *Educational and Psychological Measurement, 20*, 37–46.

Collins, A. (1993). Alternative assessment in undergraduate science education, with emphasis on portfolios. *Proceedings of the National Science Foundation Workshop on the Role of Faculty from the Scientific Disciplines in the Undergraduate Education of Future Science and Mathematics Teachers*. Washington, DC: National Science Foundation.

Conners, C. K. (1989). *Conners Teacher Rating Scales*. North Tonawanda, NY: Multi-Health Systems.

Connolly, A. (1988). KeyMath–Revised: A Diagnostic Inventory of Essential Mathematics. Circle Pines, MN: American Guidance Service.

Connolly, A. (1998). *KeyMath: A diagnostic instrument of essential mathematics–Normative update*. Circle Pines, MN: American Guidance Services.

Cooper, C. (1977). Holistic evaluation of writing. In C. Cooper & L. Odell (Eds.), *Evaluating writing: Describing, measuring, judging*. Buffalo, NY: National Council of Teachers of English.

Corn, A. (1983). Visual function: A theoretical model for individuals with low vision. *Journal of Visual Impairment and Blindness, 77*, 373–377.

Crocker, L., & Algina, J. (1986a). *Introduction to classical and modern test theory* (Chapter 7: Procedures for estimating reliability). New York: Holt, Rinehart, and Winston.

Crocker, L., & Algina, J. (1986b). *Introduction to classical and modern test theory* (Chapter 10: Introduction to validity). New York: Holt, Rinehart, and Winston.

Cronbach, L. (1951). Coefficient alpha and the internal structure of tests. *Psychometrika, 16*, 297–334.

Cronbach, L., & Snow, R. (1977). *Aptitudes and instructional methods: A handbook for research on interactions*. New York: Irvington.

CTB/Macmillan/McGraw-Hill. (1992). *California Achievement Tests/5: Technical bulletin 1*. Monterey, CA: Author.

CTB/Macmillan/McGraw-Hill. (1993). *California Achievement Tests/5*. Monterey, CA: Author.

CTB/McGraw-Hill. (1997). *Terra Nova*. Monterey, CA: Author.

Das, J., Kirby, J., & Jarman, R. (1975). Simultaneous and successive syntheses: An alternative model for cognitive abilities. *Psychological Bulletin, 82*, 87–103.

Davilla, R. R. (1989). Letter to Mr. Robert Dawson, November 17, signed by Michael Vader, Acting Assistant Secretary of the U.S. Department of Education.

Davis, A., & Felknor, C. (1994). The demise of performance-based graduation in Littleton. *Educational Leadership, 51*(6), 64–65.

Deno, S. L. (1985). Curriculum-based assessment: The emerging alternative. *Exceptional Children, 52,* 219–232.

Deno, S., & Mirkin, P. (1977). *Data-based program modification: A manual.* Reston, VA: Council for Exceptional Children.

Dorans, N., & Schmitt, A. (1993). Constructed response and differential item functioning: A pragmatic approach. In R. Bennett & W. Ward (Eds.), *Constructive versus choice in cognitive measurement: Issues in constructed response, performance testing, and portfolio assessment.* Hillsdale, NJ: Erlbaum.

Down, A. L. (1969). Observations on an ethnic classification of idiots. In R. Vollman (Ed.), *Down's syndrome (mongolism), a reference bibliography.* Washington, DC: United States Department of Health, Education, and Welfare. (Original work published 1866)

Dunn, L. M., & Markwardt, F. C. (1970). *Peabody Individual Achievement Test.* Circle Pines: MN: American Guidance Service.

Dunn, L., & Dunn, M. (1997). *Peabody Picture Vocabulary Test-III.* Circle Pines, MN: American Guidance Services.

Dwyer, C. (1993). Innovation and reform: Examples from teacher assessment. In R. Bennett & W. Ward (Eds.), *Constructive versus choice in cognitive measurement: Issues in constructed response, performance testing, and portfolio assessment.* Hillsdale, NJ: Erlbaum.

Educational Testing Service. (1990). *Exploring new methods for collecting students' school-based writing: NAEP's 1990 portfolio study.* Washington, DC: U.S. Department of Education. ED 343154.

Elliott, J., Thurlow, M. L., & Ysseldyke, J. (1996). Assessment guidelines that maximize the participation of students with disabilities in large-scale assessments. Minneapolis, MN: University of Minnesota, National Center on Educational Outcomes.

Englemann, S., Granzin, A., & Severson, H. (1979). Diagnosing instruction. *Journal of Special Education, 13,* 355–365.

Englert, C., Cullata, B., & Horn, D. (1987). Influence of irrelevant information in addition word problems on problem solving. *Learning Disabilities Quarterly, 10,* 29–36.

Ervin, S. M. (1964). Imitation and structural change in children's language. In E. H. Lenneberg (Ed.), *New directions in the study of language.* Cambridge, MA: MIT Press.

Feagans, L., Sanyal, M., Henderson, F., Collier, A., & Appelbaum, M. I. (1986). The relationship of middle ear disease in early childhood to later narrative and attention skills. *Journal of Pediatric Psychology, 12,* 581–594.

Feldt, L. S., Forsyth, R. A., Ansley, T. N., & Alnot, S. D. (1996). *Iowa Tests of Educational Development.* Chicago: Riverside Publishing Company.

Flanagan, D. P., Genshaft, J. L., & Harrison, P. L. (1997). *Contemporary intellectual assessment: Theories, tests, and issues.* New York: Guilford Press.

Fleischer, K. (1997). *The effects of structured rating paradigms on the reliability of teacher ratings of written language samples over time.* Unpublished doctoral dissertation, The Pennsylvania State University.

Flesch, R. (1955). *Why Johnny can't read.* New York: Harper and Row.

Fodness, R. (1987). *Test–retest reliability of the Test of Language Development–Intermediate.* Unpublished master's thesis, Central Michigan University, Mt. Pleasant, MI.

Foorman, B., Francis, D., Fletcher, J., Schatschneider, C., & Mehta, P. (1998). The role of instruction in learning to read: Preventing reading failure in at-risk children. *Journal of Educational Psychology, 90,* 1–13.

Frazier, D., & Paulson, F. (1992). How portfolios motivate reluctant writers. *Educational Leadership, 62–65.*

Fredricksen, J., & Collins, A. (1989). A systems approach to educational testing. *Educational Researcher, 18,* 27–32.

Friel-Patti, S., & Finitzo, T. (1990). Language learning in a prospective study of otitis media with effusion in the first two years of life. *Journal of Speech and Hearing Research, 33,* 188–194.

Frostig, M., Maslow, P., Lefever, D. W., & Whittlesey, J. R. (1964). *The Marianne Frostig Developmental Test of Visual Perception: 1963 standardization.* Palo Alto, CA: Consulting Psychologists Press.

Fuchs, L., & Fuchs, D. (Eds.). (1986). Linking assessment to instructional intervention: An overview. *School Psychology Review, 15*(3).

Fuchs, L., Fuchs, D., & Maxwell, L. (1988). The validity of informal reading comprehension measures. *Remedial and Special Education,* 20–28.

Fudala, J. (1970). *Arizona Articulation Proficiency Scale.* Los Angeles: Western Psychological Services.

Gardner, M. (1990). *Expressive One-Word Picture Vocabulary Test.* Novato, CA: Academic Therapy Publications.

Gearhart, M., Herman, J., Baker, E., & Whittaker, A. (1992). *Writing portfolios at the elementary level: A study of methods for writing assessment* (CSE Technical Report No. 337). Los Angeles: Center for the Study of Evaluation (UCLA).

Gearhart, M., Herman, J., Baker, E., & Whittaker, A. (1993). *"Whose work is it?" A question for the validity of large-scale portfolio assessment* (CRESST/CSE Technical Report No. 363). Los Angeles: Center for the Study of Evaluation (UCLA).

Gelfer, J., & Perkins, P. (1998). Portfolios: Focus on young children. *Teaching Exceptional Children, 31*(2), 44–47.

Gillespie, C., Ford, K., Gillespie, R., & Leavell, A. (1996). Portfolio assessment: Some questions, some answers, some recommendations. *Journal of Adolescent & Adult Literacy, 39,* 480–491.

Ginsburg, H., & Baroody, A. (1990). *Test of Early Mathematics Ability* (2nd ed.). Austin, TX: Pro-Ed.

Gitomer, D. (1993). Performance assessment and educational measurement. In R. Bennett & W. Ward (Eds.), *Constructive versus choice in cognitive measurement: Issues in constructed response, performance testing, and portfolio assessment.* Hillsdale, NJ: Erlbaum.

Goldman, R., & Fristoe, M. (1986). *Goldman-Fristoe Test of Articulation.* Circle Pines, MN: American Guidance Service.

Good, R., & Salvia, J. (1989). Curriculum bias in published norm-referenced reading tests: Demonstrable effects. *School Psychology Review, 17*(1), 51–60.

Gordon, C. (1990). Students' and teachers' criteria for quality writing: Never the twain shall meet? *Reflections on Canadian Literacy, 8,* 74–81.

Goslin, D. A. (1969). *Guidelines for the collection, maintenance and dissemination of pupil records.* Troy, NY: Russell Sage Foundation.

Gottesman, I. (1968). Biogenics of race and class. In M. Deutsch, I. Katz, & A. Jensen (Eds.), *Social class, race, and psychological development.* New York: Holt, Rinehart and Winston.

Goyette, C. H., Conners, C. K., & Ulrich, R. F. (1978). Normative data on the revised Conners Parent and Teacher Rating Scales. *Journal of Abnormal Child Psychology, 6,* 221–236.

Grace, C., & Shores, E. (1992). *The portfolio and its use: Developmentally appropriate assessment of young children.* Little Rock, AR: Southern Association of Children Under Six.

Graden, J., Casey, A., & Bonstrom, O. (1983). *Prereferral interventions: Effects on referral rates and teacher attitudes* (Research Report No. 140). Minneapolis: Minnesota Institute for Research on Learning Disabilities.

Greenwood, C. R., Carta, J. J., & Atwater, J. (1991). Ecobehavioral analysis in the classroom: Review and implications. *Journal of Behavioral Education, 1, 59–77.*

Greenwood, C. R., Carta, J. J., Kamps, D., & Arreaga-Mayer, C. (1990). Ecobehavioral analysis of classroom instruction. In S. R. Schroeder (Ed.), *Ecobehavioral analysis and developmental disabilities: The twenty-first century* (pp. 33–63). New York: Springer-Verlag.

Greenwood, C., Carta, J., Kamps, D., & Delquadri, J. (1995). *Ecobehavioral Assessment System Software.* Kansas City, KS: Juniper Gardens Children's Center.

Greenwood, C. R., Delquadri, J., & Hall, V. (1978). *The code for instructional structure and student academic response.* Kansas City, KS: Juniper Gardens Children's Center.

Gresham, F., & Elliott, S. N. (1990). *Social Skills Rating System.* Circle Pines, MN: American Guidance Service.

Gronlund, N. E. (1976). *Measurement and evaluation in teaching* (3rd ed.). New York: Macmillan.

Gronlund, N. E. (1982). *Constructing achievement tests.* Englewood Cliffs, NJ: Prentice-Hall.

Gronlund, N. (1985). *Measurement and evaluation in teaching* (5th ed.; Part 2: Constructing classroom tests). New York: Macmillan.

Guilford, J. (1936). *Psychometric methods.* New York: McGraw-Hill.

Guilford, J. P. (1967). *The nature of human intelligence.* New York: McGraw-Hill.

Gustafson, J. E. (1984). A unifying model for the structure of intellectual abilities. *Intelligence, 8,* 179–203.

Hacker, J., & Hathaway, W. (1991, April). *Toward extended assessment: The big picture.* Paper presented at the annual conference of the American Educational Research Association, Chicago.

Hammill, D. D. (1991). *Detroit Tests of Learning Aptitude* (3rd ed.). Austin, TX: Pro-Ed.

Hammill, D. (1998). *Examiner's manual: Detroit tests of learning aptitude.* Austin, TX: Pro-Ed.

Hammill, D., Brown, L., & Bryant, B. (1992). *A consumer's guide to tests in print* (2nd ed.). Austin, TX: Pro-Ed.

Hammill, D., Brown, V., Larsen, S., & Wiederholt, J. (1994). *Test of Adolescent and Adult Language* (3rd ed.). Austin, TX: Pro-Ed.

Hammill, D., & Hresko, W. (1994). *Comprehensive Scales of Student Abilities.* Austin, TX: Pro-Ed.

Hammill, D., & Larsen, S. (1996). *Test of Written Language* (3rd ed.). Austin, TX: Pro-Ed.

Hammill, D., & Newcomer, P. (1999). *Test of Language Development-Intermediate* (3rd ed.). Austin, TX: Pro-Ed.

Hammill, D., Pearson, N., & Wiederholt, L. (1996). *Comprehensive Test of Nonverbal Intelligence.* Austin, TX: Pro-Ed.

Hammill, D., Pearson, N., & Voress, J. (1993). *Examiner's manual: Developmental Test of Visual Perception* (2nd ed.). Austin, TX: Pro-Ed.

Hammill, D., Pearson, N., & Voress, J. (1996). *Test of Visual-Motor Integration.* Austin, TX: Pro-Ed.

Hanna, P., Hanna, J., Hodges, R., & Rudoff, E. (1966). *Phoneme grapheme correspondence as cues to spelling improvement*. Washington, DC: Department of Health, Education, and Welfare.

Hansen, J. (1992). Literary portfolios emerge. *The Reading Teacher, 45*(8), 604–607.

Harcourt Brace Educational Measurement. (1996a). *Stanford Achievement Test* (9th ed.). San Antonio, TX: Psychological Corporation.

Harcourt Brace Educational Measurement. (1996b). *Stanford Diagnostic Mathematics Test 4*. San Antonio, TX: Psychological Corporation.

Harcourt Brace Educational Measurement. (1996c). *Stanford Early School Achievement Test*. San Antonio, TX: Psychological Corporation.

Harcourt Brace Educational Measurement. (1996d). *Test of Academic Skills*. San Antonio, TX: Psychological Corporation.

Harrison, P. (1985). *Vineland Adaptive Behavior Scales: Classroom edition manual*. Circle Pines, MN: American Guidance Service.

Hathaway, S., & McKinley, J. (1970). *Minnesota Multiphasic Personality Inventory*. Minneapolis: University of Minnesota Press.

Hebert, E. (1992, May). Portfolios invite reflection from students and staff. *Educational Leadership*, 58–61.

Herbert, E., & Schlutz, L. (1996). The power of portfolios. *Educational Leadership, 53*(7), 70–71.

Herrnstein, R., & Murray, C. (1994). *The Bell Curve: Intelligence and class structure in American life*. New York: The Free Press.

Hieronymus, A. N., Hoover, H. D., & Lindquist, E. F. (1986). *Iowa Tests of Basic Skills*. Chicago: Riverside Publishing Company.

Hoover, H. D., Hieronymus, A. N., Frisbie, D. A., & Dunbar, S. B. (1996). *Iowa Tests of Basic Skills*. Chicago: Riverside Publishing Company.

Horn, E. (1967). *What research says to the teacher: Teaching spelling*. Washington, DC: National Education Association.

Hurlin, R. G. (1962). Estimated prevalence of blindness in the U.S.–1960. *Sight Saving Review, 32*, 4–12.

Ireton, H., & Thwing, E. J. (1974). *Minnesota Child Development Inventory*. Minneapolis: Behavior Science Systems.

Isaacson, S. (1988). Assessing the writing product: Qualitative and quantitative measures. *Exceptional Children, 54*, 528–534.

Jenkins, J., & Pany, D. (1978). Standardized achievement tests: How useful for special education? *Exceptional Children, 44*, 448–453.

Jensen, A. (1974). Interaction of Level I and Level II abilities with race and socioeconomic status. *Journal of Educational Psychology, 66*, 99–111.

Jensen, A. R. (1980). *Bias in mental testing*. New York: Free Press.

Jose, R. T., Smith, A. J., & Shane, K. G. (1988). Evaluating and stimulating vision in multiply impaired children. In J. Erin (Ed.), *Dimensions: Selected Papers from the Journal of Visual Impairment and Blindness*.

Kappauf, W. E. (1973). Studying the relationship of task performance to the variables of chronological age, mental age, and IQ. In N. Ellis (Ed.), *International review of research in mental retardation* (Vol. 6). New York: Academic Press.

Karlsen, B., & Gardner, E. F. (1996). *Directions for Administering the Stanford Diagnostic Reading Test, Forms J/K*. San Antonio, TX: Harcourt Educational Measurement.

Katz, C., & Johnson-Kuby, S. (1996). Like portfolios for assessment. *Journal of Adolescent and Adult Literacy, 39*, 508–511.

Kaufman, A., & Kaufman, N. (1983). *Kaufman Assessment Battery for Children, interpretive manual*. Circle Pines, MN: American Guidance Service.

Kaufman, A., & Kaufman, N. (1985). *Kaufman Test of Educational Achievement, Comprehensive Form manual*. Circle Pines, MN: American Guidance Service.

Kaufman, A., & Kaufman, N. (1990). *Kaufman Brief Intelligence Test*. Circle Pines, MN: American Guidance Service.

Kaufman, A., & Kaufman, N. (1998a). *Kaufman Test of Educational Achievement–Normative update–Brief form manual*. Circle Pines: MN: American Guidance Services.

Kaufman, A., & Kaufman, N. (1998b). *Kaufman Test of Educational Achievement–Normative update–Comprehensive form manual*. Circle Pines: MN: American Guidance Services.

Kearns, J., Kleinert, H., Clayton, J., Burdge, M., & Williams, R. (1998). Principal supports for inclusive assessment: A Kentucky story. *Teaching Exceptional Children, 31*(2), 16–23.

Keefe, C. (1995). Portfolios: Mirrors of learning. *Teaching Exceptional Children, 27*(2), 66–67.

Kelley, M. F., & Surbeck, E. (1985). History of pre-school assessment. In K. D. Paget & B. Bracken (Eds.), *The psychoeducational assessment of pre-school children*. New York: Grune & Stratton.

Kirk, S., McCarthy, J., & Kirk, W. (1968). *Illinois Test of Psycholinguistic Abilities*. Champaign: University of Illinois Press.

Knowlton, M. (1988). *Minnesota Functional Vision Assessment*. Minneapolis: University of Minnesota. Mimeo.

Koening, A. J., & Holbrook, M. C. (1993). *Learning media assessment*. Austin, TX: Texas School for the Blind and Visually Impaired.

Koppitz, E. M. (1963). *The Bender Gestalt Test for Young Children*. New York: Grune & Stratton.

Koppitz, E. M. (1975). *The Bender Gestalt Test for Young Children: Volume II. Research and application, 1963–1973*. New York: Grune & Stratton.

Koretz, D. (1993). New report on Vermont Portfolio Project documents challenges. *National Council on Measurement in Education Quarterly Newsletter, 1*(4), 1–2.

Koretz, D., Klein, S., McCaffrey, D., & Stecher, B. (1993). *Interim report: The reliability of Vermont portfolio scores in the 1992–93 school year* (CRESST/CSE Technical Report No. 370). Los Angeles: Center for the Study of Evaluation (UCLA).

Koretz, D., Lewis, E., Skewes-Cox, T., & Burstein, L. (1992). *Omitted and not-reached items in mathematics in the 1990 National Assessment of Educational Progress (CSE Tech. Rep. 357)*. Los Angeles: University of California, National Center for Research on Evaluation, Standards, and Student Testing.

Krug, D. A., Arick, J. R., & Almond, P. A. (1993). *Autism Screening Instrument for Educational Planning* (2nd ed.). Austin, TX: Pro-Ed.

Kubiszyn, T., & Borich, G. (1984). *Educational testing and measurement: Classroom application and practice*. Glenview, IL: Scott, Foresman and Company.

Lachar, D. (1982). *Personality Inventory for Children–Revised*. Los Angeles: Western Psychological Services.

Langley, B., & DuBose, R. F. (1989). Functional vision screening for severely handicapped children. In J. Erin (Ed.), *Dimensions: Selected papers from the Journal of Visual Impairment and Blindness*.

Larsen, S., Hammill, D.D., & Moats, L. (1999). *Test of Written Spelling–4*. Austin, TX: Pro-Ed.

LeMahieu, P., Eresh, J., & Wallace, Jr., R. (1992). Using student portfolios for public accounting. *The School Administrator, 49*(11), 8–15.

Lidz, C. (1991). *Practitioner's guide to dynamic assessment*. New York: Guilford.

Lindsley, O. R. (1964). Direct measurement and prosthesis of retarded behavior. *Journal of Education, 147*, 68–81.

Linn, R., & Baker, E. (1993, Fall). Portfolios and accountability. *The CRESST Line: Newsletter of the National Center for Research on Evaluation, Standards, and Student Testing*. Los Angeles: NCRESST, 1, 8.

Linn, R., Graue, E., & Sanders, N. (1990, Fall). Comparing state and district test results to national norms: The validity of claims that "everyone is above average." *Educational Measurement: Issues and Practice*, 5–14.

Loeding, B. L., & Crittenden, J. B. (1993). Inclusion of children and youth who are hearing impaired and deaf in outcomes assessment. In J. Ysseldyke & M. L. Thurlow (Eds.), *Views on inclusion and testing accommodations for students with disabilities*. Minneapolis: National Center on Educational Outcomes, University of Minnesota.

Luria, A. (1966). *Higher cortical functions in man*. New York: Basic Books.

Madaus, G. (1993). A national testing system: Manna from above? A historical/technological perspective. *Educational Assessment, 1*, 9–26.

Maeroff, G. (1991, December). Assessing alternative assessment. *Phi Delta Kappan*, 272–281.

Mardell-Czudnowski, C., & Goldenberg, D. (1998). *Manual: Developmental indicators for the assessment of learning* (3rd ed.). Circle Pines, MN: American Guidance Service.

Markwardt, F. (1998). *Peabody Individual Achievement Test–Revised–Normative update*. Circle Pines, MN: American Guidance Services.

Marston, D., & Magnusson, D. (1985). Implementing curriculum-based measurement in special and regular education settings. *Exceptional Children, 52*, 266–276.

Martin, R. P. (1988). *Assessment of personality and behavior problems: Infancy through adolescence*. New York: Guilford Press.

Maynard, F., & Strickland, J. (1969). *A comparison of three methods of teaching selected mathematical content in eighth and ninth grade general mathematics courses*. Athens, GA: University of Georgia. ED 041763.

McCarney, J. (1994). *The Behavior Evaluation Scale-2, Home Version: Technical Manual*. Columbia, MO: Hawthorne Educational Services.

McCarney, J. (1995a). *Attention-Deficit Disorders Evaluation Scale, Home Version–Second Edition: Technical Manual*. Columbia, MO: Hawthorne Educational Services.

McCarney, J. (1995b). *Attention-Deficit Disorders Evaluation Scale, School Version–Second Edition: Technical Manual*. Columbia, MO: Hawthorne Educational Services.

McCarney, S. B. (1992a). *Early Childhood Behavior Scale: Technical manual*. Columbia, MO: Hawthorne Educational Services.

McCarney, S. (1992b). *Preschool Evaluation Scale*. Columbia, MO: Hawthorne Educational Services.

McCarney, S. B., & Leigh, J. E. (1990). *Behavior Evaluation Scale-2*. Columbia, MO: Educational Services.

McConaughy, S. H. (1993a). Advances in the empirically based assessment of children's behavioral and emotional problems. *School Psychology Review, 22*, 285–307.

McConaughy, S. H. (1993b). Evaluating behavioral and emotional disorders with the CBCL, TRF, and YSR cross-informant scales. *Journal of Emotional and Behavioral Disorders, 1*, 40–52.

McConaughy, S. H., Achenbach, T. M., & Gent, C. L., (1988). Multiaxial empirically based assessment: Parent, teacher, observational, cognitive, and personality correlates of Child Behavior Profiles for 6–11-year-old boys. *Journal of Abnormal Child Psychology, 16*, 485–509.

McGrew, K., Thurlow, M. L., Shriner, J., & Spiegel, A. N. (1992). *Inclusion of students with disabilities in national and state data collection programs* (Technical Report 2). Minneapolis: National Center on Educational Outcomes, University of Minnesota.

McGrew, K., Werder, J., & Woodcock, R. (1991). *Woodcock-Johnson Psychoeducational Battery-Revised: Technical Manual.* Chicago: Riverside Publishing Company.

McGrew, K. S., & Woodcock, R. W. (2001). *WJ III Technical Manual.* Itasca, IL: Riverside Publishing Company.

Meisels, S. J., Bickel, D. D., Nicholson, J., Xue, Y., & Atkins-Burnett, S. (1998). *Pittsburgh work sampling achievement validation study.* Ann Arbor, MI: School Restructuring Evaluation Project.

Meisels, S. J., Jablon, J., Marsden, D. B., Dichtelmiller, M. L., & Dorfman, A. (1994). *The work sampling system.* Ann Arbor: Rebus, Inc.

Meisels, S., Marsden, D. B., Wiske, M. S., & Henderson, L. W. (1997). *Early Screening Inventory–Revised.* Ann Arbor, MI: Rebus, Inc.

Meisels, S. J., & Wiske, M. S. (1975). *Eliot-Pearson Screening Inventory.* Medford, MA: Tufts University Department of Child Study.

Mercer, C., & Mercer, A. (1985). *Teaching students with learning problems* (2nd ed.). Columbus, OH: Merrill.

Merrell, K. W. (1994). *Assessment of behavioral, social, and emotional problems.* New York: Longman.

Meyer, C. (1992). What's the difference between *authentic* and *performance* assessment? *Educational Leadership, 49*(8), 39–40.

Miller, J. (1981). *Assessing language production in children.* Austin, TX: Pro-Ed.

Mills, R. (1989). Portfolios capture rich array of student performance. *The School Administrator, 46*(11), 8–11.

Mullen, E. (1989). *Infant Mullen Scales of Early Learning manual.* Circle Pines, MN: American Guidance Service.

Mullen, E. (1992). *Mullen Scales of Early Learning manual.* Circle Pines, MN: American Guidance Service.

Naglieri, J. A. (1985). *Matrix Analogies Test.* San Antonio, TX: Pyschological Corporation.

Naglieri, J. (1997). *Naglieri Nonverbal Ability Test.* San Antonio, TX: Harcourt Brace Educational Measurement.

Naglieri, J. (1999). *Essentials of CAS assessment.* New York: Wiley.

Naglieri, J., & Das, J. (1997). *Cognitive Assessment System.* Itasca, IL: Riverside Publishing Company.

National Association of School Psychologists. (1997). *Principles for professional ethics.* Bethesda, MD: Author.

National Association of State Boards of Education. (1992). *Winners all: A call for inclusive schools.* Washington, DC: Author.

National Council of Teachers of Mathematics. (1993). *Assessment standards for school mathematics, working draft.* Reston, VA: Author.

National Society for the Prevention of Blindness. (1961). *Vision screening in the schools.* New York: Author.

Newcomer, P. (1983). *Diagnostic Achievement Battery.* Austin, TX: Pro-Ed.

Newcomer, P. (1986). *Standardized Reading Inventory.* Austin, TX: Pro-Ed.

Newcomer, P. (1990). *Diagnostic Achievement Battery–2.* Austin, TX: Pro-Ed.

Newcomer, P., & Hammill, D. (1988). *Test of Language Development–Primary* (2nd ed.). Austin, TX: Pro-Ed.

Newcomer, P., & Hammill, D. (1999). *Test of Language Development–Primary* (3rd ed.). Austin, TX: Pro-Ed.

Nihira, K., Leland, H., & Lambert, N. (1993). *AAMR Adaptive Behavior Scale–School* (2nd ed.). Austin, TX: Pro-Ed.

Nihira, K., Leland, H., & Lambert, N. (1993). *Examiner's manual, AAMR Adaptive Behavior Scale–Residential and Community* (2nd ed.). Austin, TX: Pro-Ed.

Northern, J. L., & Downs, M. P. (1991). *Hearing in children* (4th ed). Baltimore, MD: Williams & Wilkens.

Nunnally, J. (1967). *Psychometric theory.* New York: McGraw-Hill.

Nunnally, J. (1978). *Psychometric theory.* New York: McGraw-Hill.

Nurss, J., & McGauvran, M. (1995). *The Metropolitan Readiness Tests: Norms book* (6th ed.). San Antonio, TX: Harcourt Brace & Co.

Nuttall, D. (1992). Performance assessment: The message from England. *Educational Leadership, 49*(8), 54–57.

O'Leary, K., & O'Leary, S. (1972). *Classroom management: The successful use of behavior modification.* New York: Pergamon.

Otis, A. S., & Lennon, R. T. (1989). *Otis–Lennon School Ability test.* San Antonio, TX: Psychological Corporation.

Otis, A., & Lennon, R. (1996). *Directions for Administering the Otis-Lennon School Ability Test.* San Antonio, TX: Harcourt Educational Measurement.

Pandey, T., & Smith, R. (Eds.). (1991). *A sampler of mathematics assessment.* ED 341553.

Paul, D., Nibbelink, W., & Hoover, H. (1986). The effects of adjusting readability on the difficulty of mathematics story problems. *Journal of Research in Mathematics Education, 17*, 163–171.

Paulson, F., Paulson, P., & Meyer, C. (1991). What makes a portfolio a portfolio? *Educational Leadership, 48*(5), 60–64.

Pflaum, S., Walberg, H., Karegianes, M., & Rasher, S. (1980). Reading instruction: A quantitative analysis. *Educational Researcher, 9,* 12–18.

Phillips, K. (1990). *Factors that affect the feasibility of interventions.* Workshop presented at Mounds View Schools, unpublished.

Phillips, S. (1992). *Testing condition accommodations for handicapped students.* Paper presented at the annual meeting of the American Educational Research Association, San Francisco, CA.

Polin, L. (1991, January/February). Writing technology, teacher education: K–12 and college portfolio assessment. *The Writing Notebook,* 25–28.

Porter, R. B., & Cattell, R. (1975). *Children's Personality Questionnaire.* Champaign, IL: Institute for Personality and Ability Testing.

Prutting, C., & Kirshner, D. (1987). A clinical appraisal of the pragmatic aspects of language. *Journal of Speech and Hearing Disorders, 52,* 105–119.

Psychological Corporation. (1992). *Wechsler Individual Achievement Test.* San Antonio, TX: Harcourt Brace Jovanovich.

Psychological Corporation. (1999). *Wechsler Abbreviated Scale of Intelligence.* San Antonio, TX: Author.

Quay, H., & Peterson, D. (1987). *Revised Behavior Problem Checklist.* Coral Gables, FL: University of Miami.

Reed, M. L., & Edelbrock, C. (1983). Reliability and validity of the Direct Observation Form of the Child Behavior Checklist. *Journal of Abnormal Child Psychology, 11,* 521–530.

Reid, D., Hresko, W., & Hammill, D. (1989). *Test of Early Reading Ability* (2nd ed.). Austin, TX: Pro-Ed.

Reschly, D. (1993). Consequences and incentives: Implications for inclusion/exclusion decisions regarding students with disabilities in state and national assessment programs. In J. Ysseldyke & M. L. Thurlow (Eds.), *Views on inclusion and testing accommodations for students with disabilities.* Minneapolis: National Center on Educational Outcomes, University of Minnesota.

Resnick, L. (1987). *Education and learning to think.* Washington, DC: National Academy Press.

Richman, N., Stevenson, J., & Graham, P. J. (1982). *Preschool-to-school: A behavioural study.* New York: Academic Press.

Roach, E. F., & Kephart, N. C. (1966). *The Purdue Perceptual-Motor Survey.* Columbus, OH: Merrill.

Roid, G., & Miller, N. (1997). *Leiter International Performance Scale-Revised.* Chicago: Stoelting.

Rubin, S. (1969). A re-evaluation of figure–ground pathology in brain-damaged children. *American Journal of Mental Deficiency, 74,* 111–115.

Sabers, D., Feldt, L., & Reschly, D. (1988). Appropriate and inappropriate use of estimated true scores for normative comparisons. *Journal of Special Education, 22*(3), 355–358.

Salend, S. (1998). Using portfolios to assess student performance. *Teaching exceptional children, 31*(2), 36–43.

Salvia, J., Algozzine, R., & Sheare, J. (1977). Attractiveness and school achievement. *Journal of School Psychology, 15*(1), 60–67.

Salvia, J., & Good, R. (1982). Significant discrepancies in the classification of pupils: Differentiating the concept. In J. T. Neisworth (Ed.), *Assessment in Special Education,* Rockville, MD: Aspen Systems.

Salvia, J., & Hughes, C. (1990). *Curriculum-based assessment: Testing what is taught.* New York: Macmillan.

Salvia, J., & Hunt, F. (1984). Measurement considerations in program evaluation. In B. Keogh (Ed.), *Advances in Special Education* (Vol. 4). New York: JAI Press.

Salvia, J., & Meisel, J. (1980). Observer bias: A methodological consideration in special education research. *Journal of Special Education, 14*(2), 261–270.

Salvia, J., Neisworth, J., & Schmidt, M. (1990). *Examiner's manual: Responsibility and Independence Scale for Adolescents.* Allen, TX: DLM.

Salvia, J., Sheare, J., & Algozzine, R. (1975). Facial attractiveness and personal–social development. *Journal of Abnormal Child Psychology, 3*(7), 171–178.

Scannell, D. P. (1996). *Tests of Achievement and Proficiency.* Chicago: Riverside Publishing Company.

Scannell, D. P., Haugh, O. M., Lloyd, B. H., & Risinger, C. F. (1993). *Tests of Achievements and Proficiency.* Chicago: Riverside Publishing Company.

Schmidt, M., & Salvia, J. (1984). Adaptive behavior: A conceptual analysis. *Diagnostique, 9*(2), 117–125.

Schrank, F. A., & Woodcock, R. W. (2001). WJ III Compuscore and Profiles Program. Itasca, IL: Riverside Publishing Company.

Shapiro, E. S. (1996). *Academic skills problems: Direct assessment and intervention* (2nd ed.). New York: Guilford Press.

Shapiro, E. S., & Derr, T. (1987). An examination of overlap between reading curricula and standardized reading tests. *The Journal of Special Education, 21*(2), 59ñ67.

Shapiro, E. S., & Kratochwill, T. R. (Eds.). (1988). *Behavioral assessment in schools: Conceptual foundations and practical applications.* New York: Guilford Press.

Share, D., & Stanovich, K. (1995). Cognitive processes in early reading development: A model of acquisition and individual differences. *Issues in Education: Contributions from Educational Psychology, 1,* 1–57.

Sharpe, M., McNear, D., McGrew, K. (1996). *Braille assessment inventory.* Columbia, MO: Hawthorne Educational Services.

Shavelson, R., Baxter, G., & Pine, J. (1991). Performance assessment in science. *Applied Measurement in Education, 4*(4), 347–362.

Shavelson, R., Gao, X., & Baxter, G. (1991). *Design theory and psychometrics for complex performance assessment: Transfer and generalizability* (Interim Report.) Los Angeles: University of California, Center for Research on Evaluation, Standards, and Student Testing.

Shinn, M., Tindall, G., & Stein, S. (1988). Curriculum-based measurement and the identification of mildly handicapped students: A review of research. *Professional School Psychology, 3,* 69–85.

Shriner, J., & Salvia, J. (1988). Content validity of two tests with two math curricula over three years: Another instance of chronic noncorrespondence. *Exceptional Children, 55,* 240–248.

Siegler, R. (1989). Strategy diversity and cognitive assessment. *Educational Researcher, 18*(9), 15–20.

Slobin, D. I., & Welsh, C. A. (1973). Elicited imitation as a research tool in developmental psycholinguistics. In C. Ferguson & D. Slobin (Eds.)., *Studies of child language development.* New York: Holt, Rinehart and Winston.

Snow, C., Burns, M., & Griffin, P. (1998). *Preventing reading difficulties in young children.* Washington, DC: National Academy Press.

Snow, R. (1993). Construct validity and constructed response tests. In R. Bennett & W. Ward (Eds.), *Constructive versus choice in cognitive measurement: Issues in constructed response, performance testing, and portfolio assessment.* Hillsdale, NJ: Erlbaum.

Sparrow, S., Balla, D., & Cicchetti, D. (1984a). *Interview edition, expanded form manual, Vineland Adaptive Behavior Scales.* Circle Pines, MN: American Guidance Service.

Sparrow, S., Balla, D., & Cicchetti, D. (1984b). *Interview edition, survey form manual, Vineland Adaptive Behavior Scales.* Circle Pines, MN: American Guidance Service.

Stake, R., & Wardrop, J. (1971). Gain score errors in performance contracting. *Research in the Teaching of English, 5,* 226–229.

Stanovich, K. (1986). Matthew effects in reading: Some consequences of individual differences in the acquisition of literacy. *Reading research quarterly, 21,* 360–406.

Stevens, R., & Rosenshine, B. (1981). Advances in research on teaching. *Exceptional Education Quarterly, 2*(1), 1–9.

Stevens, S. S. (1951). Mathematics, measurement, and psychophysics. In S. S. Stevens (Ed.), *Handbook of experimental psychology* (p. 23). New York: Wiley.

Stiggins, R. (1997). *Student-centered classroom assessment* (2nd ed.). Upper Saddle River, NJ: Prentice-Hall.

Stokes, S. (1982). *School-based staff support teams: A blueprint for action.* Reston, VA: Council for Exceptional Children.

Suen, H., & Ary, D. (1989). *Analyzing quantitative behavioral observation data.* Hillsdale, NJ: Erlbaum.

Sweetland, R., & Keyser, D. (1991). *Tests: A comprehensive reference for assessments in psychology, education, and business.* Austin, TX: Pro-Ed.

Taylor, B., Harris, L., Pearson, P. D., & Garcia, G. (1995). *Reading difficulties: Instruction and assessment* (2nd ed.). New York: McGraw-Hill.

Terman, L., & Merrill, M. (1916). *Stanford–Binet Intelligence Scale.* Boston: Houghton Mifflin.

Terman, L., & Merrill, M. (1937). *Stanford–Binet Intelligence Scale.* Boston: Houghton Mifflin.

Terman, L., & Merrill, M. (1973). *Stanford–Binet Intelligence Scale.* Chicago: Riverside Publishing Company.

Thorndike, R. (1963). *The concepts of over- and underachievement.* New York: Columbia University Press.

Thorndike, R. L. (1982). *Applied psychometrics.* Boston: Houghton Mifflin.

Thorndike, R., & Hagen, E. (1978). *Measurement and evaluation in psychology and education.* New York: Wiley.

Thorndike, R. L., & Hagen, E. (1994). *Cognitive Abilities Test* (2nd ed.). Chicago: Riverside Publishing Company.

Thorndike, R. L., Hagen, E., & Sattler, J. (1985). *Stanford–Binet Intelligence Scale.* Chicago: Riverside Publishing Company.

Thorndike, R. L., Hagen, E., & Sattler, J. (1986). *Technical manual: The Stanford–Binet Intelligence Scale* (4th ed.). Chicago: Riverside Publishing Co.

Thurlow, M. L., Elliott, J., & Ysseldyke, J. E. (1998). *Testing students with disabilities: Practical strategies for complying with district and state requirements.* Thousand Oaks, CA: Corwin Press.

Thurlow, M. L., Olsen, K., Elliott, J., Ysseldyke, J., Erickson, R., & Ahearn, E. (1997). *Alternate Assessment,* Policy Directions Paper, No. 9. Minneapolis, MN: University of Minnesota, National Center on Educational Outcomes.

Thurlow, M. L., Seyfarth, A., Scott, D., & Ysseldyke, J. (1997). State policies on participation and accommodations in state assessments for students with disabilities. *Synthesis Report No. 31.* Minneapolis, MN: University of Minnesota, National Center on Educational Outcomes.

Thurlow, M. L., Ysseldyke, J. E., & Silverstein, B. (1993). *Testing accommodations for students with disabilities: A review of the literature* (Synthesis Report 4). Minneapolis: National Center on Educational Outcomes, University of Minnesota.

Tierney, R., Carter, M., & Desai, L. (1991). *Portfolio assessment in the reading and writing classrooms.* New York: Christopher-Gorelon.

Torgesen, J., & Bryant, B. (1994). *Test of Phonological Awareness: Examineris Manual.* Austin, TX: Pro-Ed.

Torgesen, J., Morgan, S., & Davis, C. (1992). Effects of two types of phonological awareness training on word learning in kindergarten children. *Journal of Educational Psychology, 84,* 364–370.

Tucker, J. (1985). Curriculum-based assessment: An introduction. *Exceptional Children, 52,* 199–204.

Tunmer, W., Herriman, M., & Nesdale, A. (1988). Metalinguistic abilities and beginning reading. *Reading Research Quarterly, 23,* 134–158.

U.S. Department of Education. (1983). *A nation at risk: The imperative for school reform.* Washington, DC: Author.

U.S. Public Health Service. (1971). *Vision screening of children* (PHS Document No. 2042). Washington, DC: Author.

Wagner, R., Torgesen, J., & Rashotte, C. (1999). *Comprehensive Test of Phonological Processing.* Austin, TX: Pro-Ed.

Walberg, H. J. (1984). Families as partners in educational productivity. *Phi Delta Kappan, 65,* 397–400.

Walker, D. K. (1973). *Socioemotional measures for preschool and kindergarten children.* San Francisco: Jossey-Bass.

Walker, H. M. (1983). Assessment of behavior disorders in school settings: Issues, problems, and strategies. In M. Noel & N. Haring (Eds.), *Progress or change? Issues in educating the mildly emotionally disturbed.* Washington, DC: U.S. Department of Education, USOSE Monograph Series.

Walker, H. M., Hops, H., & Greenwood, C. R. (1984). The CORBEH research and development model: Programmatic issues and strategies. In S. Paine, G. Bellamy, & B. Wilcox (Eds.), *Human services that work* (pp. 57–78). Baltimore: Brookes.

Walker, H. M., & McConnell, S. R. (1988). *Walker–McConnell Scale of Social Competence.* Austin, TX: Pro-Ed.

Walker, H. M., & Severson, H. H. (1992). *Systematic Screening for Behavior Disorders* (2nd ed.). Longmont, CO: Sopris West.

Walker, H. M., Severson, H., Stiller, B., Williams, G., Haring, N., Shinn, M., & Todis, B. (1988). Systematic screening of pupils in the elementary age range for behavior

disorders: Development and trial testing of a multiple-gating model. *Remedial and Special Education, 9*(3), 8–14.

Wallace, G., & Hammill, D. (1994). *Comprehensive Receptive and Expressive Vocabulary Test.* Austin, TX: Pro-Ed.

Wechsler, D. (1939). *Wechsler–Bellevue Intelligence Scale.* New York: Psychological Corporation.

Wechsler, D. (1974). *Manual for the Wechsler Intelligence Scale for Children–Revised.* Cleveland, OH: Psychological Corporation.

Werner, H., & Strauss, A. A. (1941). Pathology of figure–background relation in the child. *Journal of Abnormal and Social Psychology, 36,* 236–248.

Wiederholt, L. (1986). *Formal Reading Inventory.* Austin, TX: Pro-Ed.

Wiederholt, L., & Bryant, B. (1992). *Examiner's manual: Gray Oral Reading Tests–3.* Austin, TX: Pro-Ed.

Wiley, J. (1971). A psychology of auditory impairment. In W. Cruickshank (Ed.), *Psychology of exceptional children and youth.* Englewood Cliffs, NJ: Prentice-Hall.

Wilkinson, G. (1993). *Wide Range Achievement Test–3.* Wilmington, DE: Jastak Associates.

Williams, C., & Wang, J. J. (1997). *Technical References to the Peabody Picture Vocabulary Test-III.* Circle Pines, MN: American Guidance Service.

Winograd, P., & Gaskins, R. (1992). Improving the assessment of literacy: The power of portfolios. *Pennsylvania Reporter, 23*(2), 1–6.

Wolf, D. (1989). Portfolio assessment: Sampling student work. *Educational Leadership, 46*(7), 35–39.

Wolf, M. (1991). Naming speed and reading: The contribution of the cognitive neurosciences. *Reading Research Quarterly, 26,* 123–141.

Woodcock, R. (1997). *Woodcock Diagnostic Reading Battery.* Allen, TX: DLM.

Woodcock, R. (1998). *Woodcock Reading Mastery Tests–Revised: Normative update.* Circle Pines, MN: American Guidance Services.

Woodcock, R. W., & Johnson, M. B. (1989). *Woodcock–Johnson Psychoeducational Battery–Revised.* Allen, TX: DLM.

Woodcock, R. W., McGrew, K. S., & Mather, N. (2001). *WJ III Tests of Cognitive Abilities and Tests of Achievement.* Itasca, IL: Riverside Publishing Company.

Woodcock, R., McGrew, K. & Werder, J. (1994). *Mini Battery of Achievement.* Chicago: Riverside Publishing Company.

Ysseldyke, J. E. (1973). Diagnostic–prescriptive teaching: The search for aptitude–treatment interactions. In L. Mann & D. A. Sabatino (Eds.), *The first review of special education.* New York: Grune & Stratton.

Ysseldyke, J. E., & Christenson, S. L. (1987a). Evaluating students' instructional environments. *Remedial and Special Education, 8,* 17–24.

Ysseldyke, J. E., & Christenson, S. L. (1987b). *The Instructional Environment Scale.* Austin, TX: Pro-Ed.

Ysseldyke, J. E., & Christenson, S. L. (1993). *The Instructional Environment System–II.* Longmont, CO: Sopris West.

Ysseldyke, J. E., Christenson, S. L., & Kovaleski, J. F. (1994). Identifying students' instructional needs in the context of classroom and home environments. *Teaching Exceptional Children, 26*(3), 37–41.

Ysseldyke, J. E., & Salvia, J. (1974). Diagnostic-prescriptive teaching: Two models. *Exceptional Children, 41,* 181–186.

Ysseldyke, J. E., & Thurlow, M. L. (1993). *Self-study guide to the development of educational outcomes and indicators.* Minneapolis: National Center on Educational Outcomes, University of Minnesota.

Ysseldyke, J. E., Thurlow, M. L., McGrew, K. S., & Shriner, J. G. (1994). *Recommendations for making decisions about the participation of students with disabilities in statewide assessment programs* (Synthesis Report 15). Minneapolis: National Center on Educational Outcomes, University of Minnesota.

Ysseldyke, J. E., Vanderwood, M., & Shriner, J. (1997). *Changes over the past decade in special education referral to placement probability: An incredibly reliable practice.* Minneapolis, MN: University of Minnesota.

Index

Note: Page numbers followed by n indicate footnotes.

New Chapter 23: Assessment of Oral and Written Language combines two chapters on oral and written language for a more comprehensive chapter on language.

Oral-Language Tests

Goldman–Fristoe Test of Articulation (GFTA)

(Side tab: Oral-Language Tests)

The Goldman–Fristoe Test of Articulation (GFTA; Goldman & Fristoe, 1986) is one of the more popular tools developed to assess phonology. It is an individually administered, norm-referenced device in which most consonant sounds and 11 common consonant blends (*st,* for example) are elicited in differing levels of complexity (word, sentence) and in a variety of word positions (beginning, middle, and end of word). Familiarity with the International Phonetic Alphabet (IPA) and experience in identifying and transcribing disordered speech are useful for administering and scoring the GFTA. Although the device does not specifically measure vowels, the examiner can observe the child's vowel production, because all vowels and diphthongs are used at least once within the stimulus words.

Subtests

The GFTA is divided into three sections.

Sounds-in-Words In this subtest, 35 pictures of familiar objects are presented to the child, who must either name the picture or answer questions pertaining to it. In all, 44 responses are elicited, including 11 common consonant blends and all single consonant sounds (except *zh*); medial position *h, w, wh,* and *y*; and final position voiced *th* (as in *bathe*).

Sounds-in-Sentences This subtest is designed to elicit a sample of a child's speech in a more complex, spontaneous context. The examiner reads two stories aloud to the child while presenting four or five pictures illustrating each story. After the story is read, the examiner again presents the pictures to the child, who recounts the story. The story is loaded with the sounds most commonly

misarticulated by children, and the examiner appraises the child's speech–sound production in the more complex context of sentences.

Stimulability After the first two subtests are completed, the examiner returns to the sounds the child has misarticulated and tries to st[...] rect production by means of a three[...] dure explained in the instructions. The[...] this subtest is to find out how stimul[...] is to intervention. This clinical infor[...] leads to a decision regarding progno[...] length of intervention.

Unlike some other articulation tests, t[...] sesses more than one speech sound in[...] test items. This places a greater load o[...] ing abilities of the examiner, although[...] viduals using this test seem to have [...] listening for more than one sound in a [...] The stimulus pictures are large and co[...] ing the test very motivating for your[...] However, older children might find th[...] juvenile, especially compared with th[...] white pictures of a test such as the Ari[...] lation Proficiency Scale (Fudala, 1970[...]

Scores

Percentile ranks are available for sch[...] dents for the Sounds-in-Words and S[...] subtests (ages 6-6 through 16-10). Perc[...] are also available for children betwe[...] years of age. These norms are from the[...] ple used to standardize the Khan–Lewi[...] ical Analysis. Pertinent characteris[...] children making up these norms are n[...]

Written-Language Tests

Test of Written Language–3 (TOWL-3)

(Side tab: Written-Language Tests)

The Test of Written Language–3 (TOWL-3; Hammill & Larsen, 1996) is a norm-referenced device designed to assess written-language competence of students between the ages of 7-0 and 17-11. Although the TOWL-3 was designed to be individually administered, the authors provide a series of modifications to al low group administration, with minimal follow-up testing of individual students to assure valid testing. The recommended uses of TOWL-3 include identifying students who have sufficient difficulty in writing to warrant special help, determining strengths and weaknesses of individual students, evaluating student progress, and conducting research. Two alternative forms (A and B) are available.

TOWL-3 uses two writing formats (contrived and spontaneous) to evaluate written language. In a contrived format, students' linguistic options are purposely constrained to force the students to use specific words or conventions. TOWL-3 uses these two formats to assess three components of written language (conventional, linguistic, and cognitive). The *conventional component* deals with using the rules of Standard American English in spelling, capitalization, and punctuation. The *linguistic component* deals with syntactic and semantic structures, and the *cognitive component* deals with producing "logical, coherent, and sequenced written products" (Hammill & Larsen, 1996, p. 3)

Subtests

The first five subtests, eliciting writing in contrived contexts, are briefly described here.

Vocabulary This area is assessed by having a student write correct sentences containing stimulus words.

Spelling The TOWL-3 assesses spelling by having a student write sentences from dictation.

Style Competence in this aspect of writing is assessed by evaluating the punctuation in sentences written from dictation.

Logical Sentences Competence in this area is assessed by having students rewrite illogical sentences so that they make sense.

Sentence Combining TOWL-3 requires students to write one grammatically correct sentence based on the information in several short sentences presented visually.

The last three subtests elicit more spontaneous, contextual writing by the student, in response to one of two pictures used as a story starter. After the story has been written (and the other five subtests administered), the story is scored on three dimensions. Each dimension is treated as a subtest. Following are brief descriptions of these subtests.

Contextual Conventions A student's ability to use mechanical conventions (such as punctuation and spelling) in context is assessed using the student's story.

Contextual Language A student's ability to construct grammatically correct sentences and appropriate vocabulary is assessed from the student's story.

Story Construction As described by Hammill and Larsen (1996, p. 6), this subtest evaluates the student's story on the basis of the "quality of its plot, prose, development of characters, interest to the reader, and other compositional aspects."